The Stuart Age

The Stuart Age

England, 1603–1714

FOURTH EDITION

Barry Coward

Longman
is an imprint of

Harlow, England • London • New York • Boston • San Francisco • Toronto • Sydney • Singapore • Hong Kong
Tokyo • Seoul • Taipei • New Delhi • Cape Town • Madrid • Mexico City • Amsterdam • Munich • Paris • Milan

PEARSON EDUCATION LIMITED

Edinburgh Gate
Harlow CM20 2JE
Tel: +44 (0)1279 623623
Fax: +44 (0)1279 431059
Website: www.pearson.com/uk

———————————

First published in Great Britain in 1980
Second edition published 1994
Third edition published 2003
Fourth edition published 2012

© Pearson Education Limited 1980, 1994, 2003, 2012

Pearson Education is not responsible for the content of third-party internet sites.

ISBN: 978-1-4058-5916-5

British Library Cataloguing-in-Publication Data
A catalogue record for this book is available from the British Library

Library of Congress Cataloging-in-Publication Data
Coward, Barry.
    The Stuart age : England, 1603--1714 / Barry Cowar. – 4th ed.
      p. cm.
    Includes bibliographical references and index.
    ISBN 978-1-4058-5916-5 (pbk.)
    1. Great Britain–History–Stuarts, 1603--1714. 2. England–Civilization–17th century.
    I. Title.
    DA375.C74 2011
    942.06–dc22
                              2011017336

10 9 8 7 6 5 4 3 2 1
15 14 13 12 11

Typeset in 10.5/13pt Baskerville MT by 35
Printed and bound in Malaysia (CTP-VP)

This book is lovingly dedicated to
the memory of Barry Coward (1941–2011)

Contents

List of maps, figures and genealogical tables

Maps

Figures

Genealogical tables

Acknowledgements

The publisher would like to thank the following for their kind permission to reproduce copyright material:

Figures

Figure 2.1 © GNU Free Documentation License: Wikipedia; Figures 2.2, 4.1, 6.1 and 7.4 © Mary Evans Picture Library; Figures 3.1, 7.3, 10.1, 13.1a and 13.1b © The Trustees of the British Museum. All rights reserved; Figure 6.2 © Topfoto/Fotomas; Figure 7.1 © British Library Board/Thomason Collection: E.833.14; Figure 7.2 © British Library Board/Thomason Collection: E.619.8; Figure 7.5a © Imagestate/The Print Collector/Heritage Images; Figure 7.5b © British Library Board: E.1052.2.

Tables

Table on page 11 from Outhwaite, R. B. (1982) *Inflation in Tudor and Early Stuart England* (Macmillan Studies in Economic History), 2nd edition, Macmillan. Reproduced with permission of Palgrave Macmillan and the Economic History Society; Table on page 327 from Chandaman, C. D. (1975) *English Public Revenue 1660–1688*, Oxford University Press, p. 332. By permission of Oxford University Press.

Every effort has been made to trace the copyright holders and we apologise in advance for any unintentional omissions. We would be pleased to insert the appropriate acknowledgement in any subsequent edition of this publication.

Preface to the fourth edition

Although the prefaces to earlier editions of this book have been deleted from this new edition, I would not like my thanks to all those who helped me write earlier editions to be consigned to the 'deleted items' of my personal computer. I received a great deal of encouragement from those who read various drafts of the first edition of the book, in particular Anthony Fletcher, Graham Gibbs, K. H. D. Haley, Ian Roy and Conrad Russell. They and the general editor of the series in which this book is published, W. N. Medlicott who read the typescript of the whole book, prevented me from making countless blunders. Since then, in response to later editions, I have received many unsolicited emails and messages from readers and from my students at Birkbeck pointing out (alongside, I am pleased to say, their complimentary comments on the book) factual and typographical errors, all of which I have corrected in this new edition. I am greatly indebted to all these people, but I need to make the customary qualification that I am responsible for any errors that remain. I am also extremely grateful to past and present history editors at Longman, who have given me the benefit of their professional knowledge, including Andrew McLennan, Heather Macallum, the present editor, Mari Shullaw, and Emma Devlin.

I had two major aims in preparing this fourth edition of my book. The first is, in response to reports from teachers who have used this book on their courses (and which presumably reflect the opinion of their students), to break up the text and make it more accessible to a generation of students who are used to a new style of presentation. This I have done by introducing four types of box. The first are 'summary boxes' that are introduced at the start of most chapters, setting out the major aims and scope of what follows. The second are 'biographical boxes' that give basic information about the lives and careers of some of the key characters of the Stuart age. The third are 'historiographical boxes' that sketch changes in historians' view about key characters or episodes. The fourth, and much the most numerous, are 'information boxes' that emphasize key features about major episodes and events that are dealt with in more detail in the text.

My second major aim has been to revise the text to take account of many of the new interpretations of the Stuart age that have appeared in the writings of historians on this period in recent years. In doing this, I have (as always) been amazed at the extent of the changes in historians' views about the history of Stuart Britain and the rapidity with which these changes are published. This makes the period an exciting one to teach (and, I hope, to study), but the changes can make it confusing for teachers and students alike as older interpretations come under the axe and new ones are put in their place. I have tried to make sense of these historiographical changes, while at the same time giving readers the information to enable them to make up their own minds about the validity of new interpretations. My view is that new ideas are not necessarily better than old ones and that there are no 'correct' views about any of them. I encourage readers of this book, having considered the views of past and present historians, to produce their own interpretations, with the essential qualification that they should be well argued and well supported by historical evidence.

The basic structure of the book remains the same, beginning with three chapters that set out the main themes of the economy, society, religion and constitution of England and Wales in the early Stuart period from 1603 to 1640, followed by ten chapters that follow the narrative history of the period from 1603 to 1714, ending with two concluding thematic chapters that estimate the extent of change and continuity over the whole period. Within this structure, however, I have introduced major changes in historians' views that I think are important and will endure.

Three major changes of emphasis in research and writing on the Stuart age stand out. All of them have been incorporated into the body of the text. The first recent trend is that 'revisionism', the label given to much work on the period published in the 1970s and 1980s that moved away from emphasizing deep-rooted causes for the conflicts of seventeenth-century Britain, is now on the back foot. The short-term causes for changes in this period, contingent and accentual factors that were given weight by revisionist historians, have been found by many historians to be unconvincing; instead 'post-revisionist' historians have turned to what they consider to be more fundamental, long-term causes to explain what happened.

One of these fundamental causes is said by post-revisionist historians (as it had been by revisionists) to be found by putting events in English history in a wider British and Irish context. So excited have some historians been by this second trend in new research that they have called it 'new British history' to distinguish it from the English-centred – Anglocentric – history of the Stuart period written in the past. Throughout this new edition of my book I have made every effort not to ignore what was happening in other parts of the British Isles apart from England, paying even more attention than in earlier editions to all three Stuart kingdoms of England and Wales, Scotland and Ireland, especially at times when interconnections between them became very important.

This second major recent trend that focuses on 'new British history' cannot be ignored, and indeed I have not done so. But it seems to me that it can be carried too far. Before 1707 'Britain' did not exist; nor is there much evidence in England and Wales, Scotland and Ireland that anyone felt themselves to be 'British'. All the Stuarts' multiple kingdoms had different political institutions, cultures and ideologies, as well as economic and social structures. Consequently, writing a history of the British Isles is fraught with major problems that would involve producing a massive multi-volume work. Moreover, a holistic history of the whole British Isles could easily lead historians to ignore the fact that many events that occurred in England had explanations that were rooted in England and that what happened elsewhere in the British Isles had only a relatively minor or complementary impact.

The third recent historiographical trend that has changed perceptions of the Stuart age is the increasing attention paid to the role of ideas and ideology in politics. It is now clearer than ever both that ideas and ideological divisions about religion and the constitution were at the centre of politics and society throughout the seventeenth century, and that public discussion of politics spread much more widely than had once been thought. There have been two main influences bringing about this new trend. The first is the influence of the 'new historicism', a critical movement amongst literary scholars, which places importance not in looking at ideas in isolation, but in putting ideas in their contemporary context. New historicists also attempt to construct contemporary political and religious ideas by looking at a wider range of sources than the writings of the great canonical figures of literary and intellectual history. They use ephemeral texts like sermons, satirical verses ('libels'), poems, ballads and also visual sources, including paintings and woodcuts, images, masques and festive processions, enabling them to show how discussion about political and religious ideas promoted divisions and debates.

Social historians have been equally important in showing how ideas were discussed widely in early modern England. One of the great discoveries of recent years by social historians has been how many more people held public offices and were aware of national political and religious issues than had even been thought, leading to exciting conclusions that England was a 'monarchical republic' in this period, that republican and classical humanist ideas were prevalent at the same time, and that there developed what Jürgen Habermas called a 'public sphere', the emergence of well-informed public opinion – conclusions that will reappear throughout this history of the Stuart age.

Abbreviations and short titles

The following abbreviations have been used in the notes:

Agric. H.R.	*Agricultural History Review*
American H.R.	*American Historical Review*
B.I.H.R.	*Bulletin of the Institute of Historical Research*
E.H.R.	*English Historical Review*
Econ. H.R.	*Economic History Review*
H.J.	*Historical Journal*
H.M.C.	*Historical Manuscripts Commission Reports*
H.R.	*Historical Research*
J.B.S.	*Journal of British Studies*
J. Eccl. H.	*Journal of Ecclesiastical History*
J.M.H.	*Journal of Modern History*
P. & P.	*Past and Present*
Scottish H.R.	*Scottish Historical Review*
T.R.H.S.	*Transactions of the Royal Historical Society*
Welsh H.R.	*Welsh Historical Review*

In each of the six parts, the first time reference is made to a book or an article, the title is given in full in the first chapter; thereafter a shortened title is used. For books which are frequently cited I have used the following abbreviated titles:

Clarendon, *History*

W. D. Macray, ed., *The History of the Rebellion and Civil Wars in England* (6 vols., 1888)

English Historical Documents 1603–60

B. Coward and P. Gaunt, eds., *English Historical Documents 1603–60* (2010)

Gardiner, *History*

S. R. Gardiner, *History of England from the Accession of James I to the Outbreak of the Civil War 1603–1642* (1883)

Kenyon, *Stuart Constitution*

J. P. Kenyon, ed., *The Stuart Constitution: Documents and Commentary* (2nd edn., 1986)

Tanner, *Constitutional Documents*

J. R. Tanner, ed., *Constitutional Documents of the Reign of James I 1603–1625* (1960)

Thirsk and Cooper

J. Thirsk and J. P. Cooper, eds., *Seventeenth-Century Economic Documents* (1972)

PART 1

Early Stuart England, 1603–1640

Introduction

This book is concerned with political-constitutional, religious-ecclesiastical and social-economic developments in Stuart England. Although these are often treated separately, I have been anxious throughout, wherever, possible, to see interconnections between them. In some respects this has become easier than it once was. As will be seen later, social historians have become more concerned than they once were with putting their subject into a wide political context, following Patrick Collinson's prescription to put 'politics back in' to social history. Making interconnections between the history of England and developments in the rest of the British Isles is also now more possible than it once was, given the vast explosion in interest in the 'new British history' in recent years, which grew out of the accession to the English throne of a king who was also the ruler of the multiple kingdoms of Scotland and Ireland.

However, research and writing on other areas of the Stuart age have not made making interconnections with other areas any easier. It is true that there are clear connections between economic and political developments in early Stuart England. The fortunes of England's major industry, the manufacture of woollen cloth, cannot be explained solely by the impact on it of political changes. However, the ending of the long war with Spain in 1604 contributed to the temporary boom in cloth exports in the early years of the reign of James I, while the Cockayne Project of 1614–17, which was essentially a product of the political world of the Jacobean court, was a severe blow to the cloth industry and trade. Economic developments generally in the early seventeenth century make little sense without a consideration of the impact of government intervention. The early Stuart state both indirectly, through its expenditure on armaments and dockyards, and directly, in its attempts to intervene in economic affairs, played a major role in influencing economic development, though not always in the direction it intended. Conversely, many aspects of early Stuart politics are inexplicable without a knowledge of economic developments. One major feature of economic life, the rise in prices, contributed both to the financial problems of James I and Charles I, which seriously weakened their political position, and to the creation of an expanding country electorate as inflation brought more people into the ranks of the 40 shilling freeholders. One of the best examples in the early seventeenth century of the way economic and political developments combined is the case of industrial and commercial patents of monopoly issued by both early Stuart kings, which became a major source of political contention in every parliament from 1597 to 1640. These connections will be examined throughout this book. However, economic historians have not proved as adept as social historians in bringing their subject into the mainstream history of the Stuart age and in this respect much work remains to be done.

Making connections between the history of England and the rest of the British Isles is also not without its problems. Throughout this book I have been anxious not to segregate England from the historical development of the rest of the British Isles. But, as has been made clear in the preface and in some of the later chapters of this book, I have also not ignored some of the dangers of taking the 'British' interconnections too far.

It is hoped that these and other connections between political, religious, economic, social and intellectual developments will become clear in the narrative sections of the book. The aims of the next three chapters are to analyse separately some of the major characteristics of the economy, society, Church and government of early Stuart England, and also to address the question of how serious were the strains and stresses that existed in the social, economic, ecclesiastical and constitutional structure of England in the early seventeenth century.

1

The economy of early Stuart England

The population and the economy[1]

For a long time historians have been divided about the state of the early Stuart economy.

> **Historiography**
>
> ### Different views of historians about the performance of the economy of England in the early seventeenth century
>
> There are two different views:
>
> - An optimistic conclusion, based on the assumption that the rising population in England and Wales from the 1520s to the 1650s presented the potential for economic growth. A growing population, it is assumed, could be the source of more and cheaper labour, as well as the basis of an expanding market.
>
> - A pessimistic conclusion, based on the assumption that the sustained rise in population could pose serious problems of economic adjustment, as agriculture struggled to increase its productivity to feed more people and the economy failed to expand sufficiently to employ all of them.

---

[1] With some reluctance I have agreed to make major changes to this chapter as it was in previous editions by cutting out large sections of it. There are two reasons why I have agreed. One is a practical one: to allow more room in later chapters for information about new research that has appeared recently. The other is the sad fact that early modern economic history is currently in the doldrums with few exciting works appearing on it for many years, so that it has lost the interest of teachers and students alike.

One of the keys to resolving these differences – or least to helping you make up your own mind about this issue – is the rapid rise in the population of England and Wales that had been under way since the early sixteenth century and how the economy responded to it. Following the publication in 1981 of the work of the Cambridge Group for the History of Population and Social Structure on parish register statistics, much is now known about short-term and long-term population trends in early modern England and the reasons for these trends.[2] From the early sixteenth century to the mid-seventeenth century, the population of England recovered from the decimating effects of the Black Death of 1348–9 and the long subsequent period of demographic attrition in the later fourteenth and fifteenth centuries.

The Cambridge Group's estimates of the population of England and Wales (millions)

1522–3	2.3
1541	2.774
1601	4.110
1656	5.281

This population growth did not take place at a uniform rate. Spurts of rapid expansion in the early 1550s, 1561–86 and 1601–56 were punctuated by periods of population decline (1556–61) and slower population growth (1586–1601). Indeed in some years (1587, 1591, 1592, 1597, 1623) burial figures in some parishes were as high or higher than baptismal rates. As might be suspected, mortality crises were the principal governing factors behind these short-term population fluctuations, as sharp rises in burial rates were followed by rises in birth rates in subsequent years. This is a process called 'demographic homoeostasis' by historical demographers. The work of the Cambridge Group shows that mortality crises were caused by harvest failure and famine as well as by diseases like bubonic plague. In Cumberland and Westmorland and parts of Durham and Yorkshire, the main cause of mortality crises between 1594 and 1597 was starvation following four successive bad harvests. In Lancashire in 1623, similar evidence of burials peaking during the winter months when the plague virus was inactive suggests that famine temporarily and dramatically reversed population

---

[2] E. A. Wrigley and R. S. Schofield, *The Population History of England 1547–1871* (1981). This is not a readable book, which is a pity because its conclusions are very important. The following are a clearer guide to the work and conclusions of the Cambridge Group: R. M. Smith, 'Population and its geography, 1500–1750' in R. A. Dodgson and R. A. Butlin, eds., *An Historical Geography of England and Wales* (1978); R. A. Houston, *The Population History of Britain and Ireland* (1995). Historical demographers continue to contest and refine Wrigley and Schofield's figures. The population of England and Wales may have been 5.47 million in 1656: J. Oeppen, 'Back projection and inverse projection: members of a wider class of constrained projection models', *Population Studies*, 47 (1993).

expansion in the north-west. Changes in death rates, too, are not surprisingly a major explanation for the long-term population expansion in the century and a half before 1650, when bubonic plague outbreaks were less virulent and largely restricted to towns (unlike plague epidemics of the later Middle Ages).

More surprising, however, is the Cambridge Group's conclusion that changes in fertility levels were more important than mortality factors in explaining the long-term rise in population in the period before 1650. In an age when illegitimacy rates were very low, changing fertility levels were largely controlled by the age at which women married and by the numbers of people who married. The Cambridge Group's estimates show that both figures tended to move together and that both were significantly higher in the period before 1650 than after, indicating that the ensuing rise in the birth rate was a major cause of long-term population growth. This conclusion is supported by the Group's gross reproduction rate figures, which show a fairly rapid rise in the later sixteenth and early seventeenth centuries, coinciding with the dramatic rise in the size of the national population.

How well did the English economy respond to the challenge of this sustained population rise? One of the difficulties in answering that question with any certainty is that a case can be made for both an 'optimistic' and a 'pessimistic' conclusion.

The optimistic case

Those who have put this case have pointed out the differences in the demographic structure of early modern England from modern Third World countries, which suffer from a youthful population, low average expectation of life at birth figures and the predominance of extended families. The Cambridge Group's figures show that the percentage of people in the 0–14 age group was smaller (31.3 per cent) and that the average expectation of life at birth figure was higher (the upper 30s) than was once thought. This means that 'the dependency burden' – the percentage of the population who could not work at full productive capacity – was lighter than in many traditional societies, and did not act as a drag on the productive capacity of the early modern English economy. Nor did it suffer from the presence of large extended family households, in which 'all the family's resources go on supporting an army of relations, many of whom contribute nothing to production'.[3] Instead in early modern England the norm was the nuclear family, consisting only of parents and unmarried children. When a son married he set up his own separate household. Since, as a result, households in this period were small (an average of four or five people), so too was the typical economic unit, the family farm or workshop, the family workforce being supplemented only by a few living-in apprentices, labourers or servants. Though small, the nuclear family is much more likely to produce more than it needs for its own subsistence. This means that many sectors of the economy were organised for production for the market, as they had been since at least the thirteenth century.

---

[3] L. A. Clarkson, *The Pre-industrial Economy in England 1500–1750* (1971), p. 41.

In addition to these arguments, the 'optimists' point to the fact that the early modern English economy was stronger than that of many other contemporary countries, including Scotland, Ireland and France. Contemporary glowing accounts of the English economy were not just written by blinkered, patriotic Englishmen. In England, wrote Paul Hentzner, a visitor from Brandenburg in 1598,

> the soil is fruitful and abounds with cattle, which inclines the inhabitants rather to feeding than ploughing, so that near a third part of the land is left uncultivated for grazing. . . . There are many hills without one tree or any spring, which produce a very short and tender grass, and supply plenty of food to sheep, upon these wander numerous flocks extremely white, and whether from the temperature of the air or goodness of the earth, bearing softer and finer fleeces than any other country.[4]

The 'optimists' also bring forward the ways in which all sectors of the economy responded with some vigour to the challenge of the rise of population and demand for food. Historians have found enterprising farmers like Rober Loder of Harwell in Berkshire and Henry Best of Elmwsell in Yorkshire who had the entrepreneurial skills necessary to bring about changes in farming techniques to increase both food production and their own profits. There is little doubt that under the combined pressure of a rising population, the development of food markets and the example of the Low Countries, English farming made rapid strides forward before 1650 by adopting new crops and techniques, most notably new fodder crops that enabled more animals to be kept alive during the winter and so ensuring a continuing supply of fertilizers, and by extending the area under cultivation, most notably by the reclamation of large expanses of marshland in eastern England using the engineering skills of Dutchmen like Cornelius Vermuyden. The same story has been used regarding England's only commercial manufacture, the woollen cloth industry. English cloth manufacturers were no less sensitive to market forces than English farmers, and in the late sixteenth and early seventeenth centuries there was a remarkable, sustained effort by the English woollen textile industry to respond to changing fashions in European markets, and especially to demands from southern Europe for a new type of cloth. Manufacturers in the West Country, who were the most heavily committed to broadcloth manufacture, found it more difficult to adapt than others, though there were notable successes in this region. In Wiltshire and Somerset a small thriving industry was established, using fine Spanish wool to produce the so-called Spanish medley cloth associated with the enterprise of Benedict Webb, who was not slow to advertise his activities.[5] At the same time, the development of the Somerset serge industry was also a response from within the old broadcloth-producing area to the changes in demand. Manufacturers elsewhere, especially in eastern England, had greater success in producing what contemporaries called 'the new draperies', varieties of lighter, more highly coloured

---

[4] W. B. Rye, ed., *England as seen by Foreigners in the Days of Elizabeth and James I* (1865), pp. 109–10.
[5] Thirsk and Cooper, pp. 206–8; E. A. L. Moir, 'Benedict Webb, clothier', *Econ. H.R.*, 2nd ser., X (1957), pp. 256–64.

and cheaper cloths than the old broadcloths, and produced from longer-staple, coarse wool. Their success must be attributed largely to the influx of Protestant refugees who settled in southern and eastern England after fleeing from the Spanish armies in the Low Countries in the last decades of the sixteenth century.

There seems to be an even stronger case for a more optimistic assessment of the performance of English overseas trade and colonization than of English agriculture and manufacturing by the middle of the seventeenth century. On the face of it, English merchants in the century before 1650 had responded well to the severe trade crisis of 1550–1, which had made apparent the narrow foundation on which English overseas trade was based. By the middle of the sixteenth century, the late-medieval English penetration of the Mediterranean and Baltic trades had ended, and most of English (and indeed European) trade was concentrated on Antwerp, a major entrepôt with sophisticated marketing and credit institutions. Moreover, most English trade went to Antwerp from London, and many English provincial ports (King's Lynn, Boston, Southampton, Bristol) declined. More seriously, this dominating London–Antwerp trade relied almost totally on the export of English cloth, mainly the broadcloths of the West Country and East Anglia, which were exchanged for a variety of goods, including raw materials for the cloth industry (oil, madder, woad, alum), nonwoollen textiles (high-quality silks, velvets, taffetas) and exotic foods and spices brought overland from the East. Much of the trade was regulated by the English Company of Merchant Adventurers, but a large share of English trade was in the hands of alien merchants, especially the Hansards of north Germany, or was carried in foreign-built ships. For much of the early sixteenth century all this had not mattered as English overseas trade boomed. But in 1550–1 cloth sales in Antwerp slumped dramatically, and the effect was to jolt English merchants into an effort to end their dangerous reliance on one trade route, one trade organization and one export commodity.

During the next hundred years it can be argued that English merchants responded energetically to this crisis, and in the process established a new diversified pattern of English overseas trade with new trade routes and new trading companies. English trade to Antwerp never recovered fully after the crisis of the early 1550s, largely because of growing hostility between England and Spain. In 1564 the Merchant Adventurers left Antwerp in the Spanish Netherlands and began to search for new bases in northwest Europe. In the next century Hamburg, Emden and Stade all became, with varying success, alternative outlets for English cloth to the markets of northern Europe. Gradually also English merchants increased their share of the country's trade – in 1597 the Hansards were expelled from London – and the size of England's mercantile marine increased. English merchants, moreover, began to reappear in parts of the world with which they had abandoned direct trade in the fifteenth century. The Baltic countries, which were the major suppliers of corn to Europe as well as sources of naval stores and a potential market for English cloth, drew English merchants through the Sound between Denmark and Sweden. In 1555 the first joint-stock trading company, the Muscovy Company, received its charter, and in 1579 the Eastland Company was formed to trade in the Baltic. English merchants also began to reappear in the Mediterranean, from which they had withdrawn in the fifteenth century. In 1581 the

Levant Company and in 1585 the Barbary Company were established to conduct the carrying trade in fish, grain and cloth to the Mediterranean from northern Europe. English merchants also captured a large share of the intra-Mediterranean trade that had previously gone through the Sicilian entrepôt, which collapsed in the early 1590s.

In the early seventeenth century English merchants penetrated even further afield than the Baltic and Mediterranean. In 1600 exploratory expeditions to the Far East were consolidated by the foundation of the joint-stock English East India Company, which set up trading posts in Indonesia ('the Spice Islands') and in India. Shortly afterwards the search for new trade routes, notably a north-west passage to the East, and colonies across the Atlantic culminated in the establishment of the first English colony at Jamestown in Virginia in 1607. During the next forty years the English Empire in the New World expanded in three areas: Virginia, with the Bermuda islands from 1615 and Maryland from 1633, became the centre of the tobacco colonies of mainland America; Barbados, St Christopher, Nevis and Antigua in the Lesser Antilles in the Caribbean from the late 1620s, after a false start as tobacco islands, developed sugar-based economies; and thirdly, the colonies of New England (Plymouth 1621, Massachusetts 1629, and its offshoots) emerged as farming, fishing and trading communities. It is true that not all these colonies were developed only as a response to England's economic problems. Dislike of the religious trends in Caroline England was a prime motive for the establishment of the New England colonies and of Maryland. But a desire to cure England's overpopulation problem and open up new trades and new markets was a persistent motive behind most of the colonization schemes.

The pessimistic case

This is based on the view that, like some modern underdeveloped economies, the economy of Stuart England was predominantly based on agriculture, chronically unstable and extremely vulnerable to short-term disasters, such as a wet summer and a consequent bad harvest or an outbreak of plague. Professor W. G. Hoskins has demonstrated the large extent to which the stability of the economy of pre-industrial England depended on good harvests. One bad harvest could dislocate the whole economy, especially since even the non-agricultural sectors of it were very dependent on agriculture. As Professor Hoskins has shown, bad harvests were a familiar feature of life in pre-industrial England. He calculated that from 1480 to 1759, 25 per cent of the harvests were deficient and over 16 per cent very bad. The late sixteenth and early seventeenth centuries had an even worse record than that, since in those years bad harvests were bunched together, in the 1590s, the early 1620s, the 1630s and the later 1640s.[6] Not surprisingly, people in the early seventeenth century, even when judged

---

[6] W. G. Hoskins, 'Harvest fluctuations and English economic history, 1480–1619' *Agric. H.R.*, XII (1964), pp. 28–46; and 'Harvest fluctuations and English economic history, 1620–1759', ibid., XVI (1968), pp. 13–31. Hoskins's results are modified slightly in C. J. Harrison, 'Grain price analysis and harvest qualities, 1465–1634', ibid., XIX (1975), pp. 135–55.

by the standards of England's present-day reputation as a weather-conscious nation, were preoccupied with the weather to the point of obsession. The diary of Ralph Josselin, the vicar of Earl's Colne in Essex in the middle of the seventeenth century, bristles with weather notes. 'Among all the several judgements on this nation', he wrote in May 1648, 'God this spring, in the latter end of April, when rye was earing and eared, sent such terrible frosts that the ear was frozen and so died.' A month later he recorded, 'The Lord goeth out against us in the season, which was wonderful wet, floods every week, hay rotted abroad. Much was carried away with the floods, much inned but very dirty and dangerous for cattle. Corn laid, pulled down with weeds. We never had the like in my memory, and that for the greatest part of the summer.'[7] Such comments were ominous for the economy of England and for the standard of living of most of its inhabitants.

Nor do any of the major sectors of the economy show unqualified success. There are reasons to doubt whether, despite the major advances that were made before 1650, English agriculture kept pace with the food requirements of an expanding population. The decisive evidence is the movement of food prices in the century and a half before 1650.

Like demographic history, the history of prices is bedevilled by intractable primary sources and by regional variations. The Phelps Brown price index is the one most commonly used, but it is based on material from southern England and on wholesale prices, and therefore is not an accurate guide to retail price movements in the country as a whole. With all its many defects, however, there is no better alternative as a *rough* guide to price movements. The index indicates a general price inflation of the order of about five times from 1501–10 to 1641–50, but a rise in the price of food in the same period of nearly seven times.

The rise in prices, 1501–1650[8] (food prices with industrial prices in brackets: 1471–1475 = 100)

1501–10	106 (98)	1581–90	389 (230)
1511–20	116 (102)	1591–1600	530 (238)
1521–30	159 (110)	1601–10	527 (256)
1531–40	161 (110)	1611–20	583 (274)
1541–50	217 (127)	1621–30	585 (264)
1551–60	315 (186)	1631–40	687 (281)
1561–70	298 (218)	1641–50	723 (306)
1571–80	341 (223)		

---

[7] Thirsk and Cooper, p. 49. See also *English Historical Documents 1603–60*, document 17.

[8] R. B. Outhwaite, *Inflation in Tudor and Early Stuart England* (Macmillan Studies in Economic History, 2nd edn., 1982), based on E. H. Phelps Brown and Sheila V. Hopkins, 'Wage-rates and prices: evidence for population pressure in the sixteenth century', *Economica*, XXIV (1957), p. 306.

The table indicates that the biggest leap upwards in food prices before 1650 was in the 1590s (coinciding with a series of disastrous harvests), followed by a slower rise in the first thirty years of the seventeenth century. But any attempt to conclude that this reflects the permanent success of English agriculture in meeting demand must explain the further rapid rise in food prices in the next two decades, which brought the long upward movement of prices to an end. The reasons for this 'price revolution' have been the subject of heated controversy.[9] Most historians, however, now generally recognize that, though monetary factors like debasement may have contributed to it, the major force behind inflation was population pressure which outstripped the resources of English agriculture. The best that can be said for English agriculture before 1650 is that it did not fail to increase its output and efficiency. But the price evidence suggests that the demand for food continually outran the supply that English agriculture was able to provide.

The same theme – a spirited response to economic problems that met with overall failure – runs though the history of the woollen cloth industry. In 1550–1 there was the first of a series of major crises which hit the traditional woollen broadcloth industry during the next century. The opening of the Stuart age is deceptive in this respect, because exports of English broadcloths rose for a decade after 1604, largely because the end of the war with Spain in that year, followed by the truce between Spain and her rebellious colony in the Netherlands in 1609, reopened the Spanish and Flemish markets for English cloths. But the recovery was temporary; from 1614 onwards sales of English broadcloths in Europe fell, with especially severe recessions in 1614–17, 1621–4 and 1640–2. It has been estimated that total exports of English broadcloths fell from a value of £1,193,333 early in the seventeenth century to £846,667 in 1640.[10] As is usual in this period, the statistics are probably far from accurate, but they indicate the likely scale of the overall trend. There are various possible reasons for the collapse of the broadcloth industry: the nature of the wool produced in England may have changed, as a result of agrarian improvements, from a short-fibre, fine wool to a long-fibre, coarse wool which was unsuitable for broadcloth manufacture;[11] a Dutch woollen industry developed at Leiden in direct competition to the English industry; and the English industry suffered from unwise state intervention, as the Cockayne Project of 1614–16 illustrates (see below, p. 15). All these factors are important, but often in explaining fluctuations in the fortunes of the textile industry too little emphasis is given to changes in fashion. Quite simply, in the late sixteenth and early seventeenth centuries Europeans seem to have grown tired of heavy broadcloth-type materials and to have demanded instead a lighter, more highly coloured product.

As has been seen, woollen cloth manufactures made a spirited response to this crisis by attempting to supply European markets with the kinds of cloth they demanded.

---

[9] Outhwaite, *Inflation*, is the best summary of this controversy.

[10] J. D. Gould, 'Cloth exports 1600–40', *Econ. H.R.*, 2nd ser., XXIV (1971), p. 251.

[11] This is the suggestion of P. Bowden, 'Wool supply and the woollen industry', *Econ. H.R.*, 2nd ser., IX (1956).

It is likely that the new draperies made rapid progress in the early seventeenth century. Yet the cloth industry as a whole was severely dislocated as it adjusted to changing circumstances. Severe unemployment and distress in the cloth-producing villages of the West Country during the crises of 1614–16, 1621–3 and 1640–2 is sufficient evidence of this. Nor, despite the undoubted proliferation of new consumption industries and the growth of industries like coal and iron smelting, is there much evidence to substantiate a belief that there was a *per capita* increase in industrial production in England before 1650. The best that can be concluded is that industrial developments before 1650 were important for the future. It would be wrong to exaggerate their contemporary significance.

There are also many reasons to doubt that overseas trade and colonization underwent a period of 'expansion'. Despite all the developments mentioned so far, 'the pessimists' argue that English overseas trade by the middle of the seventeenth century was just as insecurely based as it was a hundred years before. It needs to be stressed, though, that, as with many other problems discussed in this book, there is plenty of room for alternative hypotheses. This is generally true of overseas trade in the early seventeenth century because of the lack of customs accounts. From 1604 English customs were collected not by government officials, but by customs farmers, who paid a lump sum to the crown for the privilege of running the customs on a private enterprise basis. It was not until 1696, when an Inspector-General of Imports and Exports was appointed, that a continuous series of customs accounts recommences. It is therefore difficult to assess trends in overseas trade in terms of the value of the goods traded or to quantify changes in the direction of English overseas trade. Yet, taking together the few scattered figures that survive with the qualitative evidence, it seems probable that in the early seventeenth century there was no increase in the total volume of English overseas trade, and that the bulk of trade was still the export of cloth to Europe from London. It is true that now for the first time most of the trade was in the hands of English merchants, and that a growing proportion of the exported cloth was made up of new draperies which were sent to southern Europe, Spain, north Africa and the Mediterranean. Also some provincial ports (notably Exeter and Bristol) slightly increased their share of the trade, especially after the reopening of the Spanish and Mediterranean trades. But the bulk of English overseas trade still went through London, and provincial port resentment at the dominance of London continued unabated. In 1604 this exploded in the misleadingly named 'free trade' debate in parliament; those who represented the views of the outports protested *against* the trade monopoly of London merchants and the Merchant Adventurers, *not* in favour of a free trade ideology.

Moreover, all the 'new' trades were subjected to immense difficulties in the late sixteenth and early seventeenth centuries. Before 1650 in the Baltic, Mediterranean and Far East, English merchants faced and were outbid by Dutch mercantile competition. The one possible exception is the Mediterranean, where the Dutch with their unarmed, large and cumbersome *fluits* were less able than the English to withstand the attacks of pirates based in north African ports. Elsewhere, though, the *fluits* gave the Dutch a tremendous advantage over their competitors in lower freight costs: in the

Baltic they captured the biggest share of the trade in grain and naval stores; in the Far East it was the Dutch who were there first and who inherited most of the trade which the Portuguese were in the process of relinquishing. Although the English East India Company made profits on its early voyages, by the 1620s its fortunes were at a low ebb. The company not only had to overcome the risks of long voyages to the East and Dutch hostility, which in 1623 flared into a skirmish between representatives of the rival companies, the 'massacre of Amboyna', but also opposition at home, directed at the export of silver bullion with which the East India Company paid for its spices and silks. This criticism was misguided in that some of the East India Company's imports were re-exported, making up for the loss of silver. But in the early seventeenth century a contemporary could be forgiven for not seeing the Far Eastern trade as an area of rapid growth. Of course, this pessimistic conclusion was to be disproved later, but at the time the impact of East Indian trade on England's total trade was slight.

The same is true of the trade generated by the American colonies. By the 1620s much of the euphoric expectation raised in the hope of the advantages that colonies would bring had been dissipated. By this time the Virginia Company was split by internal divisions, it had paid no dividends to its investors, and in 1624 it collapsed, forcing the crown to take on temporarily the administration of the Jamestown colony. The colonists were hampered by attacks from hostile Indians – in March 1622 the colony was nearly wiped out by an Indian attack – and by opposition in England to their attempts to establish tobacco as the staple export crop. Respectable opinion in England could not tolerate the foundation of a colony which relied on such a morally dubious crop as tobacco, which in the early seventeenth century had the status and the radical, subversive associations that cannabis has nowadays. Virginia also faced a severe labour shortage, partly because prospective emigrants found Ireland a more attractive destination.[12] These problems were eventually overcome: tobacco was established as a profitable crop, and immigrants were attracted to the colony by the indentured labour system, which gave the new settler the prospect of owning his own land after a period of 'temporary servitude'. Before 1650, however, imports of tobacco from mainland America to England were no more than a trickle. This is true also of sugar, which was to be the key commodity in the later prosperity of the new Caribbean colonies. There the labour shortage problem was not overcome before the mid-seventeenth century, because in the small island colonies there was no reservoir of land to attract indentured servants as in the mainland colonies. Although the trade in African slaves was eventually to provide a solution, there was little hint of this before 1650. Nor were the new colonies either the suppliers of raw materials or the markets for English goods which the enthusiastic propagandists had promised; the total colonial population was only about 48,000 in 1650. Moreover the New England colonies had developed an economic structure which, far from complementing that of the mother country, clearly promised to be its competitor in the colonial trade.

---

[12] See p. 102 and pp. 158–9 in Chapters 4 and 5 for a discussion of early seventeenth-century Ireland.

Recurrent trade crises, especially in 1614–17, 1621–4 and 1640–2, underline the argument that English overseas trade in the early seventeenth century was no more stable than it had been in the mid-sixteenth century. The crisis of 1614–17 was a direct result of the misguided intervention of the crown in the cloth trade.[13] In fairness to James I and his advisers, the scheme put to them in 1614 by Alderman Cockayne and a syndicate of London merchants for a reorganization of the cloth industry and trade was not without some commercial sense. Most of the profit on cloth was from the finishing and dyeing processes. Therefore, since most English cloth was exported unfinished and the Dutch finishing manufacturers took the cream of the profits, Cockayne proposed that the export of unfinished cloth should be banned, that the monopoly of the Merchant Adventurers be rescinded, and that he and his syndicate should establish a new company to take over the profitable dyeing process and control the export of the cloth. The crown, through increased customs duties, would gain from the enhanced value of the trade, and Cockayne also offered James a substantial cash payment. In James's financial predicament it was probably the latter consideration that encouraged him to accept Cockayne's project, rather than its alleged commercial advantages. The latter, in fact, never materialized; the new company lacked the Merchant Adventurers' marketing contacts in Europe and the craftsmen with sufficient skill in the difficult art of dyeing cloth. As with many other manufacturing processes – mining, metal smelting, silk weaving, clock making – the English were technologically backward compared to others on the Continent. Consequently, the Cockayne Project failed badly, and in 1617 the old company was reinstated and the slide in overseas sales of cloth temporarily reversed.

The crisis of 1621–4 was more serious and its causes more deep-rooted. As long as the English cloth trade was directed to and through one market it was vulnerable to changes, beyond the control of English merchants that affected that market. In the early 1620s this northern European market was disrupted not by the Thirty Years War (this may have generated sufficient demand to offset the dislocation it caused), but by a series of currency debasements undertaken by many north German and east European princes, which had the effect of raising the prices of imported goods, including English cloth. The repercussions in the major cloth-producing areas were serious. The threat to order was made clear by a clothiers' petition in May 1622: 'the livelihood of so many thousands being taken from them, we leave it to your honourable discretions to consider how difficult a thing will be like to be to contain them from mutiny and rebellion'.[14] Consequently, as at other times of economic crisis, the government as well as merchants were jolted into an awareness of the unstable nature of English trade. Government commissions were appointed, and a great public debate took place to identify the causes of the crisis. There is no reason to see this debate as part of a

---

[13] For the Cockayne Project and the trade crisis of the early 1620s, see A. Friis, *Alderman Cockayne's Project: the commercial policy of England in its main aspects* (1927) and B. E. Supple, *Commercial Crisis and Change in England 1600–42: a study in the instability of a mercantile economy* (1959).

[14] Thirsk and Cooper, p. 15.

continuous thread of economic policy or economic thought. Once the crisis was over the debate ended. Moreover, it had little impact on the future development of English trade. Contemporary analyses and remedies for the trade depression of 1640–2 are significantly similar to those current in the early 1620s and early 1550s.[15]

The achievements of English merchants in the century before 1650 were not negligible: the capture of English trade from the hands of alien merchants, the export of a greater variety of woollen textiles, the reopening of the south European trade. But it is unlikely that a perceptive observer in 1650 would have been able to forecast the later important shift in the focus of English trade from Europe and the Mediterranean to the Atlantic and the Far East. More obvious to such an observer would have been the recurrent trade crises, and the inferiority complex of early seventeenth-century Englishmen regarding Dutch merchants. Despite the renewed Spanish–Dutch war from 1621 to 1648, Dutch merchants reigned supreme in Europe. Amsterdam not London was the major European commercial entrepôt.

Conclusion

It is difficult to avoid a general pessimistic conclusion about the performance of the English economy before 1650, since most of the economic improvements noted in this chapter were more important for the future than they were for early Stuart England.[16] As has been seen, agricultural productivity barely kept pace with increasing demand for food; English manufacturing was still largely concentrated on the production of woollen cloth, an industry which was in the process of major readjustment and dislocation; and overseas trade was still dangerously reliant on exporting cloth to Europe.

Why did the English economy fail to expand at a greater rate before 1650? Some possible explanations are, at best, only secondary ones. It is doubtful if, as is sometimes suggested, lack of capital held up economic progress. Studies of the landowning classes reveal neither a shortage of surplus capital nor an unwillingness to invest in industry or commerce. What held back investment on a large scale was the obvious unprofitability of mining, manufacturing and colonial ventures. 'Instead of dreining the water', wrote a contemporary about those who invested in mining, 'their pockets are dreined.'[17] In any case, was there a need for large-scale capital investment? When more industrial progress was made in the eighteenth century, manufacturing units were still small, and most of the necessary capital was provided fairly easily from ploughed-back profits and from loans from members of the entrepreneur's family. More serious in holding back economic progress in the early seventeenth century was technological backwardness, which prevented, for example, deep mining. However,

---

[15] Compare the documents in Thirsk and Cooper, pp. 1–15 and pp. 39–46.

[16] For a pessimistic conclusion, see Outhwaite, 'Progress and backwardness', *Econ. H.R.* (1986) and A. L. Beier, 'Poverty and progress in early modern England' in A. L. Beier, ed., *The First Modern Society* (1989).

[17] Quoted in L. Stone, *The Crisis of the Aristocracy 1558–1641* (1965), p. 340.

the importance of this can be exaggerated, as can be seen by the lack of enthusiasm which greeted major technological discoveries, like the atmospheric engine and coke-smelting of iron, in the later seventeenth and early eighteenth centuries. Moreover, although the imperfect state of many roads and rivers hindered economic growth, this was less of a problem in England than elsewhere because of its many navigable rivers and coastal trade. More important probably were the adverse effects of government intervention in economic affairs, which was often motivated by the financial necessity of the crown rather than by consideration of the national interest.

It may be that more crucial than any of these factors in holding back economic growth was the lack of a mass market for anything other than agricultural products. There was as yet no expanding colonial market for English manufactures, the European market was unstable, and the Far Eastern market non-existent: in these conditions the state of the domestic market was crucial. This opens up a large chasm of ignorance in early seventeenth-century economic and social history, but it may be that the majority of most people's incomes was spent on food with little or nothing to spare for other consumer goods. The key to this, and therefore to the failure of the English economy to transform itself by an industrial revolution of the early seventeenth century, is the poor performance of English agriculture. Not until the later seventeenth century, as will be seen in Chapter 14, was there a dramatic increase in agricultural productivity in England. The persistence of small farms in the later sixteenth and early seventeenth centuries contributed to the failure of English agriculture to increase its output greatly.[18] This meant that surplus labour was not released from the land for work in non-agricultural occupations and that insufficient industrial raw materials were produced. It also meant that food prices remained high, inhibiting the development of a mass domestic market for manufactured goods. If this is the case, then England's economic problems before 1650 are closely connected with the condition and standard of living of English people in the early seventeenth century, which is one of the subjects dealt with in the next chapter.

---

[18] Outhwaite, 'Progress and backwardness'.

2

Society in early Stuart England[1]

Historiography

Changing trends in writing on the social history of early modern England

Until the early 1970s, social history held an inferior position amongst English historians. Its reputation was tarnished by the description of it by G. M. Trevelyan, writing in the early twentieth century, as 'history with the politics left out'. This phrase was often used to dismiss social history as unworthy of the interest of professional academic historians. However, from the early 1970s there was a marked improvement in the academic reputation of social history as social historians learned the value of using theoretical concepts and statistical techniques drawn from other disciplines. Historians who approached the history of society in these ways were rightly excited at the prospect of revealing aspects of the lives of people in the past, like their marriage patterns, kinship ties, social and geographical mobility – even their sex lives – that it was once thought would always remain hidden.

---

[1] I was much happier making fundamental changes to this chapter than I was fundamentally revising Chapter 1. Unlike economic history, social history is buzzing. Its fast-moving nature makes it difficult to come to clear conclusions in a book like this, but I have done my best to point out what social historians have achieved in recent years and where they are taking the subject.

Some of the achievements of social historians writing in the 1970s and 1980s are explained in the first part of this chapter.

The year 1990 was another turning point in the study of social history, marked by the publication of Patrick Collinson's *De Republica Anglorum: Or, History with the Politics Put Back*. In it Collinson argued that there are major links between the study of society and the study of politics, and exploring these links has been a major task of historians like Keith Wrightson, Steve Hindle, Mike Braddick and Mark Goldie since the beginning of the 1990s.

This exploration is ongoing, but some of its major achievements so far are outlined in the second part of this chapter.

The achievements of social historians writing in the 1970s and 1980s

Their major achievement was to cause long-held assumptions about the nature of early modern English society to be abandoned. No longer is it possible to hold an idealized, romanticized picture of a society which was markedly different from that in England during and after the Industrial Revolution: a country in which people rarely travelled far afield and married, lived and died in the villages in which they were born; a society in which kinship ties based on large, extended families were much stronger than in nineteenth- and twentieth-century Britain; and a society made up of contented, introverted communities, in which local concerns were more important than what was going on elsewhere in the country.

Migration and mobility

The first and most startling discovery that has destroyed these stereotypes of pre-industrial England is that villages in early modern England were not insular communities from which most people rarely moved. On the contrary, it is now clear that it was more common for men, women and children in the sixteenth and seventeenth centuries to move from their birthplaces than it was to stay at home. That this was so was one of the early discoveries of those working for the Cambridge Group for the History of Population and Social Structure (see pp. 6–7), who, when they began to exploit parish registers as sources for population history, were frequently disconcerted to discover that a series of baptismal, marriage and burial registers for one parish did not produce the expected picture of long-established village family dynasties. Instead, individuals 'disappeared' from the registers; a symptom of large-scale internal migration, conclusive evidence for which has been provided by historians working on many sources. The most useful of these is an unlikely one: the depositions made by witnesses in ecclesiastical courts, who had to make a brief biographical statement before they gave their sworn testimony. These show that most people moved only short distances. Dr Cornwall's study of 206 witnesses before two church courts in Sussex between 1580 and 1640 concludes that over 75 per cent of them no longer lived in their birth-places; most had moved only once and over short distances of up to twenty miles. These witnesses, however, were 'gentry, farmers and respectable tradesmen' from the middling ranks of English society.[2] Long-distance migration was more common among people at the upper and lower ends of the social spectrum. Wealthy landowners, merchants and professional people and their families, as will be seen (pp. 27–8), habit-ually travelled to London to take advantage of the many attractions of the capital; while landless labourers, vagrants and unemployed young people travelled long distances in search of work. Between 1580 and 1640 poor migrants from all parts of Britain poured into three Kentish towns. Some travelled even further afield, emigrating to Ireland or boarding ships at ports like Bristol, taking the hazardous gamble of sailing to the newly established colonies in north America to become indentured servants.[3]

Classifying migrants into two broad categories ('betterment' and 'subsistence' migrants) gives a pattern to what otherwise seems a confusing maelstrom of people continually on the move. 'Subsistence migrants' were those who moved because they were forced to do so as a result of the unstable contemporary agrarian economy, which it has been seen failed to produce adequate employment for people and forced many to tramp the roads looking for work at hiring fairs in arable, 'fielden' areas, or to flock to pastoral, 'forest' regions like the Northamptonshire Forest, the Sussex Weald or the moorland areas of Cumbria. Many subsistence migrants also went to towns, attracted by urban poor relief schemes. 'Betterment' migrants, on the other hand, were those who moved from choice in order to improve their economic and social positions: for example, to serve as apprentices in a neighbouring town or in London, or to get married. As might be expected, subsistence migrants were drawn from the poorer end of society and travelled long distances, while betterment migrants came from more well-to-do backgrounds and travelled short distances.

There was another group of migrants in early modern England that does not fit easily into either of these categories. Ann Kussmaul has estimated that about two-thirds of unmarried adolescents and young adults aged between 15 and 24 worked as domestic or farm servants, commonly on annual contracts, living in the houses of their employers.[4] In this, as in other respects, the family life of Ralph Josselin, the

[2] J. Cornwall, 'Evidence of population mobility in the seventeenth century', *B.I.H.R.*, XL (1967), pp. 143–52.

[3] P. Clark, 'The migrant in Kentish towns, 1580–1640' in P. Clark and P. Slack, eds., *Crisis and Order in English Towns 1500–1700* (1972), pp. 117–63; P. Clark and D. Souden, eds., *Migration and Society in Early Modern England* (1987).

[4] A. Kussmaul, *Servants in Husbandry in Early Modern England* (1981).

mid-seventeenth-century vicar of Earl's Colne in Essex, is typical; all his children left home in their early teens.[5]

The 'European marriage pattern'

That so many young people lived away from their parental homes until they married in their mid or late twenties is consistent with other features of early modern English society which are accepted by most (if not all) social historians: the typicality of the nuclear family, small households and what has become known as the 'European marriage pattern'. The main feature of this 'pattern' is that couples did not marry until they had the resources to establish independent households, causing many people to marry late in life or remain unmarried. Additional features of the 'pattern' are that brides were frequently pregnant when the marriage was entered in the parochial marriage register, and illegitimacy rates were very low.

Not all families in early Stuart England, of course, fit into this 'marriage pattern'. Extended families, large households and arranged child marriages were common among the landed elite. Moreover, as will be seen, illegitimacy rates did occasionally rise to high levels. But these are exceptions to the general rule. There is little reason to doubt the Cambridge Group's estimate that the mean household size in late sixteenth- and early seventeenth-century England was between four and five, that the mean male age at first marriage was between 27.1 and 28.1 years of age, and that the mean female age at first marriage fluctuated between 24.8 and 27 years of age. Not only did most English men and women marry fairly late in life, but a large percentage never married at all. Probably typical is Ealing, where in 1599 one-quarter of the women aged over forty were unmarried.[6] The age at which people married fluctuated in early modern England and, as has been seen, this was the main factor determining rises or falls in national population levels. But people always married much later in this period than they do in modern Britain, which is perhaps a reflection of the fact that in the early seventeenth century population growth outstripped resources and that many people had a pessimistic assessment of their economic future.

One further feature of the 'marriage pattern' is even more difficult to account for. Given the fact that many people married late and spent long periods away from parental supervision, it is slightly surprising that illegitimacy rates only once exceeded 3 per cent in the seventeenth century. This may be a distortedly low figure produced by under-assessment of infanticide and abortion. But a more likely explanation is the power of church courts and communal sanctions. Cohabitation seems to have been common, however, among couples who were already betrothed. Between 1600 and 1649 in twelve widely scattered parishes, 228 per 1,000 babies were born within eight months of marriages being recorded in parish registers. One explanation for this high incidence

---

[5] A. Macfarlane, *The Family Life of Ralph Josselin* (1970).
[6] Smith, 'Population and its geography, 1500–1700' in Dodgson and Butlin, eds., *Historical Geography of England and Wales*.

of bridal pregnancy may be that before the mid-eighteenth century marriage did not begin with a church wedding service; marriage was a process that began from the moment of the betrothal and was concluded by a ceremony in church. As a result, conception often took place before the marriage process ended. This perhaps accounts for the relatively few times when illegitimacy rates rose sharply, as they did in the first years of the Stuart age when circumstances occurred that unexpectedly prevented the marriage process from being completed. It may not be coincidental that the high illegitimacy rates of the late 1590s to early 1600s followed a succession of bad harvests between 1594 and 1597. Of the 82 illegitimate births that are recorded in the Essex village of Terling between 1570 and 1699, for example, 27 took place between 1597 and 1607.[7]

Relationships within families

How were social relationships in early modern England affected by a situation in which most people moved about frequently, married relatively late in their lives and lived in small nuclear families? Given the bewildering diversity of experiences even among a population as small as 4–5 million, answering that question in a general way is extremely difficult. However, two generalizations about relationships in this period have received widespread support in recent years. The first is that relationships within nuclear families, between husbands and wives and parents and children, were no less affectionate or warm than those between members of modern nuclear families. That is not the view expressed in one of the most readable books on the social history of early modern England: Lawrence Stone's *Family, Sex and Marriage in England 1500–1800* (1977). At first sight Stone's thesis is persuasive. Since most people married relatively late in life and the duration of marriages was short and remarriages very common, he argues that marriages were unlikely to have been characterized by deep bonds of love and affection, especially since many were arranged by parents and were made for hard-headed practical reasons rather than for love. Moreover, since infant mortality was high, it follows, he suggests, that parents were inhibited from making an 'emotional involvement' in their children. What is more, some primary source material seems to confirm this picture of cold, unloving relationships between husbands and wives and parents and children: married couples often addressed each other in very formal ways in their correspondence ('dearest madam', 'honoured sir', etc.) and parents often gave the name of a recently deceased infant to a new-born child. Stone's argument is that this situation changed only slowly during the course of the seventeenth century as family life became infused with 'affective individualism', with love and affection, as the English family passed through phases that he calls 'the open lineage family' (1450–1630), 'the restricted patriarchal nuclear family' (1550–1700) and 'the closed domesticated nuclear family' (1640–1800).

---

[7] P. Laslett, et al., eds., *Bastardy and Its Comparative Context* (1980); P. E. H. Hair, 'Bridal pregnancy in rural England in earlier centuries', *Population Studies*, XX (1966); K. Wrightson and D. Levine, *Poverty and Piety in an English Village: Terling 1525–1700* (1979), pp. 127–32.

This is a view, however, which (outside the ranks of the landed elite) has been shown to be at odds with historical reality.[8] This is not to suggest that family tensions and even wife beating, double standards regarding extra-marital sex and child abuse were not as prevalent as they are nowadays. But in the late sixteenth and early seventeenth centuries, young people were normally given much freedom in choosing their marriage partners; a situation which is not surprising given the fact that many young adolescents spent much of their time working away from the close day-to-day supervision of parents. Diary evidence shows many instances of close attachments between husbands and wives and also of close affectionate bonds between parents and children. In August 1659 the death of his eight-year-old son obviously brought deep emotional anguish to the family of Adam Martindale, who recorded in his diary that

> I was gone to Chester when he died, my businesse being urgent, and he in a hopefull way of recovery when I set out, (at least as we thought), and being there I had an irresistible impression upon my spirit that I must needs go home that night, (though I could not ghesse why, for I did not in the least suspect his death) so that I left some considerable businesse undone which I could have brought to an head the next day, and went home that evening, where I found a sad distracted family that needed much consolation and assistance from me; and I do verily believe that strong impression was from some angell that God employed to help me in that worke.[9]

In the present state of knowledge, Stone's hypothesis of a broad change from cold, impersonal relationships within the nuclear family to the later growth of 'affective individualism' seems exciting but without much foundation, while the alternative view of a continuous thread of affectionate relationships within the early modern family is duller, supported by much more evidence, and probably nearer the historical 'truth'.

The importance of neighbourliness

The second generalization about relationships between individuals in early modern England is that bonds with kin outside the nuclear family were not as significant as was once thought. This is, like most historical generalizations, one that needs some qualification. Among propertied groups such as large landowners and merchants, relations within a wide circle of 'cousins' were important when matters like the ownership and descent of property or the pursuit of credit were uppermost. But even among these groups, kinship was not the only – or prime – consideration in their calculations. In constructing their patronage networks, landed gentlemen did not rely solely or mainly on recruiting blood relations; and in getting business or credit, seventeenth-century merchants and manufacturers often tapped a network of co-religionists rather than of kin. Lower down the social scale, relations with kin beyond the nuclear family were of even less significance, as might be expected of a society in which a highly geographically

---

[8] R. Houlbrooke, *The English Family 1450–1700* (1984) and 'Alternatives: the early modern English family', *Early Modern History*, I (1992), pp. 30–1.
[9] Quoted in B. Coward, *Social Change and Continuity in Early Modern England*, 1550–1750 (1988), pp. 109–10.

mobile population was a solvent of close and extensive kinship networks. In times of trouble, the mass of people in Stuart England seem to have looked not to their kin for aid, but to their neighbours and the local community.[10]

Despite the fact that people travelled with some frequency in this period, neighbourhood ties were a strong feature of the popular culture of Stuart England, and were reinforced by many aspects of day-to-day life in English towns and villages. The parish, for example, was the basic unit of local government, which administered both the statutory poor law and private philanthropic schemes. Popular participation in local government through office holding was extensive (see p. 29).

It is now clear that local customs and festivities also had a crucial role in strengthening local ties in early modern England. Sometimes they were used in a menacing manner to help enforce orthodox values, as in the case of 'charivari' or 'rough music'. These were demonstrations of communal disapproval of those thought to be adulterers or cuckolds or other 'deviants', in which the 'culprits' were publicly humiliated and subjected to mocking laughter. More frequently, local festivities were used in less menacing ways to strengthen local social bonds, as in the case of harvest suppers and sheep-shearing feasts or the annual Rogation week perambulations of the parish boundaries.[11]

The strength of these neighbourhood ties, however, should not obscure the fact that for many people in early Stuart England a sense of belonging to one's own local community did not preclude allegiance to other 'communities', whether these were the county or the country or loyalty to one's patron. As will be seen in Chapter 3 (pp. 67–72), allegiance to local communities did not prevent early Stuart men and women participating in a wider national political and religious culture.

Towns and townspeople

Another area of social history in which rapid progress was made in the 1970s and 1980s is the history of towns and those who lived in them. With the exception of the history of London, the subject hardly seems to warrant the attention it has received from urban historians.[12] The growth of towns was not a marked feature of the economy of the Stuart age until the later seventeenth and early eighteenth centuries.

---

[10] K. Wrightson, 'Kinship in an English village' in R. M. Smith, ed., *Land, Kinship and Life Cycle* (1984). For a slightly different emphasis, see D. Cressy, 'Kinship and kin interraction in early modern England', *P. & P.*, CXIII (1986) and M. Chaytor, 'Household and kinship in Ryton', *History Workshop*, no. 11 (1981).

[11] M. Ingram, 'Ridings, rough music and the "reform of popular culture" in early modern England', *P. & P.*, CV (1984); M. Ingram, 'Ridings, rough music and mocking rhymes in early modern England', in B. Reay, ed., *Popular Culture in Seventeenth-Century England* (1985); B. Bushaway, *By Rite: Customs, Ceremony and Community 1700–1880* (1982).

[12] For good recent introductions to urban studies, see Jonathan Barry, 'Introduction' in Barry, ed., *The Tudor and Stuart Town: a reader in English urban history 1530–1688* (1990) and P. Corfield, 'Urban development in England and Wales in the sixteenth and seventeenth centuries' in A. H. John and D. C. Coleman, eds., *Trade, Government and Society* (1976), repr. in Barry, *Tudor and Stuart Town*. See also three Open University books: *Towns and Townspeople 1550–1780*; *The Fabric of the Traditional Community*; and *The Traditional Community under Stress* (1977).

4.   A henpecked husband and his punishment: *Halfe a Dozen Good Wives: All for a Penny* (London, ?1635), in *The Roxburghe Ballads*, ed. W. Chappell and J. W. Ebsworth, 9 vols. (London and Hertford, 1869–99), i, p. 451.

Figure 2.1 A charivari. A husband is being chastised by some women for being a cuckold: that is, for not controlling his wife's extra-marital sexual activities. Often charivari involved more people and threatened more violence. Whatever the scale of the demonstrations, however, all charivari were one of the means by which communities attempted to impose moral codes of conduct.
Source: © GNU Free Documentation License: Wikipedia.

Without any doubt, however, the exception is very important. London grew at an exceptionally rapid rate in the sixteenth and early seventeenth centuries and by 1650 its economic and social importance was greater than before or since. This has become more than ever apparent following the publication of important research on early modern London that plugged a gaping gap in historical scholarship.[13] From 1550 to 1600 the population of the capital rose rapidly from 80,000 to 200,000: that is, at a much faster rate than the national population. In 1650 London's population had reached 400,000, by which time it was about twenty times bigger than the largest English provincial town and was the biggest city in western Europe (Constantinople in

---

[13] A. L. Beier and R. Finlay, eds., *The Making of the Metropolis: London 1500–1700* (1986); J. P. Boulton, *Neighbourhood and Society: a London suburb in the seventeenth century* [Southwark] (1987); S. Rappaport, *Worlds Within Worlds: structures of life in sixteenth-century London* (1989); I. W. Archer, *The Pursuit of Stability: social relations in Elizabethan London* (1991); following the pioneering work of V. Pearl, 'Change and stability in seventeenth-century London', *London Journal*, V (1979) and 'Social policy in early modern London' in H. Lloyd-Jones, V. Pearl and B. Worden, eds., *History and Imagination: essays in honour of H. R. Trevor-Roper* (1981).

Figure 2.2 From 'The Long View of London from Bankside' produced by Wenceslaus Hollar in 1647. Hollar was a Protestant refugee from Bohemia who came to London in the late 1630s in the entourage of the earl of Arundel. In London and later in Antwerp he developed a profitable career selling high-class engravings. This one catered for those both in England and on the Continent who were interested in the emergence of London as the largest city in western Europe.
Source: © Mary Evans Picture Library.

eastern Europe was bigger); it had just overhauled its nearest rival, Paris, and had left other European cities far behind in size: Naples (250,000–300,000), Amsterdam (150,000), Palermo, Venice, Rome, Lisbon (100–125,000).[14]

London had spilled beyond the boundaries of the medieval City so that the familiar pattern was already established of poorer housing to the east and on the south bank of the Thames in Southwark, and superior property development to the west, at first following the river frontage along the Strand towards Westminster, and later expanding northwards to Holborn and westwards to St Martin's Lane. John Evelyn's explanation for this is an attractive one. The better classes built or bought houses to the west of the city 'because the Windes blowing near ³/₄ of the year from the west, the dwellings of the West End are so much free from the fumes, steams & stinks of the whole Easterly Pyle; which when Sea Coal is burnt is a great matter'.[15] But, while this illustrates

[14] I have followed Dr Harding's revisions of some recent estimates of the population of London: V. Harding, 'The population of London 1550–1700: a review of the published evidence', *London Journal*, XV (1990); E. A. Wrigley, 'A simple model of London's importance in changing England's society and economy 1650–1750', *P. & P.*, XXXVII (1967).
[15] Quoted in C. Wilson, *England's Apprenticeship 1603–1763* (1965), p. 47.

London's great dependence on coal from the mines of the north-east, a more accurate – if more prosaic – explanation is probably that the royal court and the law courts attracted the superior houses and shops to the Westminster area. This embryonic West End produced some examples of enlightened urban development, especially the Covent Garden piazza erected on his Long Acre site by the fourth earl of Bedford and the architects Inigo Jones and Isaac de Caux. Most landowners, however, were more interested in the profits of property speculation than the aesthetics of town planning. Most of them gave long 31-year leases of their London estates to builders, allowing them to develop them as they wished.[16] The result was that many tenements were built in the West End that were as squalid as – and in some cases perhaps even more so than – those in the East End.

Why did London grow at such a rapid rate in the century and a half before 1650? London's growth was sustained by continuous, massive immigration from the provinces (and to a much lesser extent from abroad) and not by a superior birth rate; on the contrary, the death rate in London far outstripped the birth rate because of the above-average incidence of plague and other diseases in the insanitary conditions of the capital. Part of the explanation for London's growth therefore lies in the reasons why people came to live there. As at all times, these, of course, varied. Poor 'subsistence migrants' came to the capital because of its superior official system for the relief of poverty, its private poor relief schemes, and the greater opportunities for survival in London by means of part-time employment, begging and crime. The better-off 'betterment migrants' of the Dick Whittington type came to London to serve as apprentices of London merchants and craftsmen, while London's mercantile community expanded because of the capital's role as the centre of England's overseas and internal trade. Aliens sought refuge in London from political and religious persecution in their own countries. Nor was it economic motivation that drew those from higher up the social scale. Typically, the mysogenic James I thought that 'one of the greatest causes of all Gentlemens desire, that have no calling or errand, to dwell in London, is apparently the pride of women: For if they bee wives, then their fathers, must bring them up to London . . .' Landed gentlemen, though, probably did not need nagging into visiting London or into buying a house there. London was the residence of the royal court, where attendance by the politically or socially ambitious was a necessity. The main law courts, to the grievance not only of the radicals of the mid-seventeenth century, were all in London, drawing the members of the litigious propertied classes to them. In the capital, too, there were fine schools: Westminster and St Paul's, and the Inns of Court, the 'third university' of the English landed gentry in this period. In addition, London developed unrivalled social facilities for all tastes, shops, entertainment parks like Paris Gardens in Southwark, and the theatre. Professor F. J. Fisher has argued that to the late sixteenth and early seventeenth centuries can be traced the

---

[16] Stone, *Crisis*; L. Stone, *Family and Fortune: studies in aristocratic fortunes in the sixteenth and seventeenth centuries* (1973), ch. 3.

origins of the London social 'season'.[17] Many people, then, came to London for different reasons, but all (with the possible exception of the numerically insignificant foreign immigrants) have one thing in common: they came to London because it was already a big city with developing facilities of all kinds. In other words, the major reason why London grew bigger at such a rapid rate in the sixteenth and early seventeenth centuries is that it was already big by 1500.

To many contemporaries this was something to condemn. 'It is the fashion of Italy', wrote James I, 'that all the Gentry dwell in the principal towns, and so the whole country is empty. Even so now in England all the country is gotten into London, so as with time England will only be London and the whole country be left waste . . .' Later, in 1641, Sir Thomas Roe wrote dramatically that 'it is no good state of a body to have a fat head, thin guts, and lean members'.[18] It is not easy to judge how justified those fears were. Different conclusions can be drawn from the fact that London's growth was sustained by immigration on a massive scale. Since London was a 'demographic drain', it can be argued that the provinces were thereby stripped of a valuable supply of labour as their able-bodied men and women moved away to London. On the other hand, one could argue that London fulfilled a valuable function in relieving many provincial economies of the excessive pressure put on them by an expanding population. Is it not possible that the growth of London could have had both a beneficial *and* a parasitical effect on the country's economy, depending on different circumstances? Professor Fisher has shown how the market for food and the development of industries in London stimulated agricultural improvements, regional specialization and commercialization, and internal trade in grain, cattle, other agricultural products and coal in many provincial economies. In its role in the organization of English overseas trade and the provision of credit, London became an 'engine of growth'.[19] Significantly, for example, it was a group of London merchants who successfully established a colony in Virginia in 1607, not their West Country-based rivals who did not have the London money market behind them. But in different circumstances London clearly inhibited economic growth. The capital's dominance of English overseas trade was not the sole reason for the decay of provincial ports, like Southampton, but it undoubtedly contributed to it. The London food market, too, was a powerful competitor for sparse food resources in some areas, so depressing the standard of living there. For example, London brewers successfully outbid local rivals for the supply of barley in some Home Counties and diverted precious grain supplies to the capital. Surely London had a multiple impact on the economy of the provinces.

---

[17] F. J. Fisher, 'The development of London as a centre of conspicuous consumption in the sixteenth and seventeenth centuries', *T.R.H.S.*, XXX (1948), pp. 37–50, repr. in E. Carus-Wilson, ed., *Essays in Economic History*, II (1962), pp. 197–207 and in N. Harte and P. Corfield, *London and the English Economy* (1990).

[18] Thirsk and Cooper, p. 45.

[19] F. J. Fisher, 'The development of the London food market', *Econ. H.R.*, 1st ser., V (1935), repr. in Carus-Wilson, ed., *Essays*, I, pp. 135–51 and in Harte and Corfield, eds., *London*; Fisher, 'London as an "engine of economic growth"', in J. S. Bromley and E. H. Kossman, eds., *Britain and the Netherlands*, IV (1971), pp. 3–16.

Work in the 1970s and 1980s also clarified, if it did not solve conclusively, another historical problem about the rapid growth of London, where the growing inequality in the distribution of wealth and social polarization that was taking place in rural areas was proceeding even more rapidly. On the face of it, this situation ought to have been a recipe for the kind of violent social conflict that erupted in some continental cities in early modern Europe: for example, the risings of the *Communeros* and the *Germanias* that caused massive devastation in towns in Castile and Valencia in 1520–1.[20] Yet, although towns in early modern England were no freer from riots than are some nowadays, popular disturbances never escalated into attacks on the existing social and political order. They focused instead on specific targets; usually the scarcity and high price of grain, as in the riots in Maldon, Essex, in 1629.[21] In the same year, 500 rioters attacked and killed Dr John Lambe on the streets of London for his association with the unpopular duke of Buckingham.[22] Urban riots in seventeenth-century England, like popular disturbances elsewhere, were small scale and rioters were motivated by a desire to protect existing rights, not to establish new ones (see p. 37). Recent work on early modern London has, in general, supported Valerie Pearl's optimistic view that, despite the massive influx of poor migrants in the later sixteenth and early seventeenth centuries, life in the capital was remarkably stable. It may be that this view is one seen through the distorting mirror of City of London sources and does not take enough account of what was happening in more volatile, teeming, extra-mural suburbs like Islington, Bermondsey and Lambeth.[23] But, even during the severe economic crisis years of the 1590s and early 1620s, London (both outside and inside the City walls) remained stable.

One explanation for this is that the development of 'residential zoning' (rich and poor living in separate parts of the city) had not proceeded very far or quickly in London by the mid-seventeenth century.[24] Another is that the multiplicity of local government offices made for a high incidence of participation in urban affairs by Londoners, especially men. In the London parish of Cornhill in the 1640s, one in every sixteen inhabitants was an office-holder and elsewhere the ratio was even higher. By this time, too, half the adult males of the London suburb of Southwark were freemen of the City.[25] The result may have been to bridge the gap between the rulers and the ruled of

---

[20] J. H. Elliott, *Imperial Spain 1469–1716* (1963), pp. 141–59.

[21] J. Walter, 'Grain riots and popular attitudes to the law: Maldon and the grain riots of 1629' in J. Brewer and J. Styles, eds., *An Ungovernable People* (1980).

[22] K. Lindley, 'Riot prevention and control in early Stuart London', *T.R.H.S.*, 5th ser., XXXIII (1983), pp. 114–15.

[23] See the works by Pearl, Boulton, Rappaport and Archer cited in note 13 above, and the review article by K. Lindley, 'The maintenance of stability in early modern London', *H.J.*, XXXIV (1991), pp. 985–990.

[24] M. Power, 'East and West in early modern London' in E. W. Ives, et al., eds., *Wealth and Power in Tudor London* (1978).

[25] Boulton, *Neighbourhood and Society* [Southwark], pp. 151–4.

early Stuart London. This tendency was strengthened by the growing sensitivity of the authorities in the capital to the problems of poverty, a phenomenon evidenced by the development of a social policy designed to alleviate them. As will be seen (p. 32), provincial town authorities, too, attacked the poverty problem with some gusto, especially in places like Salisbury (in Wiltshire) and Dorchester (in Dorset) where urban governors' concern for order was reinforced by a godly zeal for reformation.[26] In crisis years of bad harvests, trade depression or plague tensions erupted, as they did in Dorchester in October 1630 when a crowd of women seized a sack of corn in the market and one of them slit it open to prevent the merchant from selling it elsewhere.[27] But generally, urban poor relief schemes in early Stuart England seem to have successfully alleviated the worst effects of poverty and so avoided severe social instability in provincial towns and London alike.

It is easier to make clear generalizations about the history of early modern provincial towns than it is about the history of London. Before 1650 provincial towns were unimportant. Even at the end of the seventeenth century only about 5 per cent of the population lived in towns of over 5,000 inhabitants outside London. Before 1650 there were only a handful of provincial towns in this category, including Norwich and Bristol, which had between 10,000 and 20,000 inhabitants, and Exeter, Plymouth, Worcester, Coventry, Ipswich, Colchester, York and Newcastle upon Tyne with between 5,000 and 10,000. Did the populations and importance of this group of provincial towns with over 5,000 inhabitants increase in the period before 1650? Unfortunately, urban historians have not yet produced a clear-cut answer to that question. Rather they have revealed a vast variety of urban fortunes. Some towns, like Southampton and other provincial ports, were adversely affected as London gobbled up their trade; though clearly not all ports suffered, as those like Bristol and Exeter developed independent trades to southern Europe, and in the case of Newcastle London's demand for coal was the major factor in the rapid rise of that port in the late sixteenth and seventeenth centuries. Some towns, like Coventry, Leicester, Beverley and Lincoln, suffered in the general movement of industry, especially cloth manufacturing, to the countryside; others, however, emerged in the same period as manufacturing and marketing centres of the cloth industry, like Norwich, Exeter and Worcester; and others, like Canterbury and Sandwich, developed crafts brought by foreign immigrants. The economies of some towns, especially those in the hotly contested Severn Valley, like Gloucester and Bristol, were dislocated during the Civil War in the early 1640s;[28] while others, like those in the south-eastern counties which saw less fighting, were able to carry on their trade and industry with less (if not without) disruption. Some expanded as

---

[26] P. Slack, 'Poverty and politics in Salisbury 1597–1666' in Clark and Slack, eds., *Crisis and Order*; D. Underdown, *Fire from Heaven: the life of an English town in the seventeenth century* [Dorchester] (1992), ch. 3.

[27] Underdown, *Fire from Heaven*, p. 87.

[28] Ian Roy, 'England turned Germany? The aftermath of the civil war in its European context', *T.R.H.S.*, XXVIII (1978), pp. 127–44.

administrative centres, like York which was until 1641 the seat of the council of the north, or as the meeting places of quarter sessions and assizes; these 'provincial capitals' with their professional services, social and shopping facilities developed as mini-Londons, expanding, of course, in this respect at the expense of neighbouring towns.

The varying ways in which provincial towns developed before 1650 ought to warn against attempts to maintain generalizations about provincial towns being in a state of 'crisis' in this period, and against seeing the period from 1500 to 1700 compared with the Middle Ages as 'a period of substantial and sustained urbanization'.[29] This should not, though, serve to obscure the facts that, beside the growth of London, the development of provincial towns before 1650 was snail-like, and that, seen in the context of the national economy, their significance was slight. English agriculture had not yet become efficient enough to feed a large urban population. The manufacturing sector of the English economy was not diversified enough to enable many towns to develop as industrial centres. Overseas trade had not yet broken sufficiently away from its London–Europe axis to promote the development of the trade of provincial ports. The English economy needed to expand faster and diversify considerably more before towns other than London could grow. This, as will be seen, like a lot of other economic and social developments, was a phenomenon whose beginnings can be traced more clearly to the later seventeenth century than to the period before 1650.

Social mobility: affluence and poverty

Finally, some historians by the 1980s had reached some widely accepted conclusions about the standards of living of people in this period. Disagreements there were along the way, some of them very major ones,[30] but no one now challenges the view that inflationary and demographic pressures made the period one of great social mobility. Sixteenth- and early seventeenth-century England in no way accorded with the stable, ordered society that many contemporaries would have liked it to be. The prosperous people of the period left monuments to their rising standards of living which still survive: 'prodigy houses', the stately homes of rentier landlords; manor houses built by lesser gentry with profits made from rents and farming; substantial farmhouses of thriving yeomen farmers; funeral monuments and educational endowments of successful merchants and clothiers; and, though less obvious, tucked away as they are in county record offices, probate inventories of well-to-do husbandmen, labourers and craftsmen. William Harrison, writing in the later sixteenth century, noted improved standards in housing and living conditions:

---

[29] P. Clark and P. Slack, *English Towns in Transition 1500–1700* (1976). On this debate see Barry, *Tudor and Stuart Town*, pp. 6–7 and A. Dyer, 'Growth and decay in English towns 1500–1700' in *Urban History Yearbook* (1979).

[30] See for example 'the storm over the gentry' and its aftermath, which is detailed, along with much information about the changing standards of living of social groups in this period, in earlier editions of this book, but which have been deleted from this edition to make way for the new research and new emphases of social historians since the early 1990s.

> There are old men yet dwelling in the village where I remaine, which have noted three things to be marvellouslie altred in England within their said remembrance . . . One is, the multitude of chimnies latelie erected . . . The second is the great (although not generall) amendment of lodging . . . The third they tell of, is the exchange of Vessell, as of treene platters into pewter, and wooden spoones into silver or tin.[31]

Yet Harrison also observed that these improvements were not to be seen 'further off from our southern parts'. The geographical inequality in the distribution of wealth is best illustrated by county subsidy assessments. An analysis of those from 1515 produced the unsurprising conclusion that all but four of the counties with wealth higher than the average lay south of a line drawn from the Severn to the Wash. More startling is the scale of the disparity in the distribution of wealth; in 1515 Lancashire was assessed at £3 8s per 1,000 acres, while Middlesex's assessment was fixed at £238 1s per 1,000 acres.[32] Though the 1515 situation changed during the next century – for example, the West Country and East Anglia declined, reflecting the fortunes of their textile industries – it is likely that the major change was that the rich southern counties pulled even further ahead of the poor north, especially as London grew rapidly. The unequal distribution of wealth among social groups is as striking as the regional differences. Those who became poorer in this period, improvident landlords, small farmers hit by bad harvests or rising rents, unemployed labourers and vagrants, and the urban poor, have left as many enduring (if not as obvious) signs of their presence as their more fortunate contemporaries: almshouses, workhouses, poor law statutes and contemporary comments. Robert Gray in 1609 got right to the heart of the cause of poverty in this period. 'Our multitudes', he wrote, 'like too much blood in the body, do infect our country with plague and poverty. Our land hath brought forth but it hath not milk sufficient in the breast thereof to nourish all those children which it hath brought forth.'[33]

Not the least important indication of the size of the poverty problem in England in the late sixteenth and early seventeenth centuries is the combined effort of officialdom and private individuals to deal with it. Since poverty was more extensive in towns, it was naturally urban authorities which led the way in doing so. During the sixteenth century London and the provincial capitals, which were the main goals of streams of poor migrants, began to make censuses of the poor and build houses of correction in which to provide workhouses and outdoor relief for the young, old and sick. In 1547 London was the first authority to authorize a compulsory poor rate to finance these schemes, and the capital's lead was soon followed by Norwich, Ipswich, Colchester, York and other towns. In most towns expenditure on poor relief rose; the tiny community of Tiverton in Devon more than doubled its financial provision for the poor

---

[31] E. Power and R. H. Tawney, eds., *Tudor Economic Documents* (3 vols., 1924), III, pp. 69–70.

[32] R. S. Schofield, 'The geographical distribution of wealth in England 1334–1649', *Econ. H.R.*, 2nd ser., XVIII, 1965, pp. 505–7.

[33] Thirsk and Cooper, p. 758. See also *English Historical Documents 1603–60*, document no. 17.

between 1612 (£120) and 1656 (£300).[34] At times of severe economic crisis, especially during the early 1620s when trade dislocation combined with plague and bad harvests, the threat of being overwhelmed by hordes of desperate, poor people encouraged some towns to formulate imaginative schemes. The best known is the establishment of a municipally run brewery at Salisbury in the early 1620s, the profits of which were intended to be used to finance poor relief in the town. In addition, no doubt to prevent the poor squandering their dole on municipal ale, the Salisbury authorities issued poor relief tokens which could only be exchanged for goods at a town storehouse.[35]

In all this English towns responded to the poverty problem in ways similar to those of many continental towns. Where England differed is that the State adopted some of the urban poverty relief schemes to establish a national poor relief system. The first major step was an Act of 1572 which established a compulsory poor rate in every parish. The economic crisis of the 1590s prompted parliament in 1598 to produce two statutes which drew on urban experience in coping with the poor, and which were to be the basis of the national poor relief system in England until 1834. The two statutes reflected the way contemporary opinion divided the poor. The first dealt with the able-bodied poor, who were considered to be poor because they were idle and who were therefore undeserving of poor relief; all such 'sturdy beggars' over the age of seven were to be whipped and returned to the parish of their birth if it was known, or, if it was not, to the place where they had last lived for at least a year. A statute of 1610 made further provision for 'sturdy beggars' by ordering each parish to establish a house of correction to employ and punish them. The second Act of 1598 was concerned with the impotent poor, who were poor because of no fault of their own; these old or sick deserving poor were either to be given outdoor relief in the form of pensions, food or clothing, or they were to be put into workhouses. Poor children where possible were to be found apprenticeships. These Acts and a codifying statute of 1601 placed the responsibility for organizing poor relief on the parishes, who were to appoint overseers to administer poor relief and to collect the compulsory poor rate.

Legislation reflects intention not achievement. How successfully did the parish authorities in the early seventeenth century administer the national system of poor relief? Unfortunately the establishment and operation of it was too piecemeal to allow a clear answer. Not all parishes established a compulsory poor rate after the passage of the 1572, 1598 and 1601 legislation, and those that did administered it with varying degrees of efficiency and zeal. Often more energy seems to have been directed by parish authorities into the punishment and resettlement outside their parish of the vagrant poor and into outdoor relief for the deserving poor, rather than into the more compli-cated business of establishing workhouses and employment schemes. Few parishes in the West and North Riding of Yorkshire had stocks of material on which the poor

---

[34] A. L. Beier, *The Problem of the Poor in Tudor and Early Stuart England* (1983); P. Slack, *Poverty in Tudor and Stuart England* (1987); Clark and Slack, eds., *Crisis and Order*, p. 20.

[35] Slack, 'Poverty and politics in Salisbury' in Clark and Slack, eds., *Crisis and Order*, pp. 164–203.

could work until the reign of Charles I.[36] The control of alehouses was also a common concern of both county and parish authorities, partly on moral grounds and because alehouses were seen to be the breeding ground of crime and disorder, but also because alehouses were considered to be a major cause of poverty, as well as providing shelter for wandering beggars. The predominant emphasis of poor law administration in individual parishes was on restricting the numbers of paupers within their jurisdiction and therefore in keeping down the escalating cost of poor relief. Concern at the latter undoubtedly grew; parishioners grumbled at too high assessments, and quarter sessions had to sort out numerous rating disputes. Though there are few instances of blatant inefficiency and corruption in early seventeenth-century poor law administration, this is no doubt a reflection of the available primary sources rather than of reality; overseers' and churchwardens' accounts are hardly likely to record instances of maladministration and corruption. It would be dangerous to argue that none occurred. But perhaps one can be too sceptical. At times of severe distress most poor law authorities acted zealously, although once the immediate crisis was over the authorities probably relaxed their administrative vigilance. This is probably true of the administration of poor relief in the 1630s through the Books of Orders, as will be seen later. With varying results the poor relief system was established in most English parishes in the early seventeenth century, especially from the 1620s onwards. Anthony Fletcher concludes, after a survey of the administration of poor relief in many counties, that 'the serious dearth of 1647 to 1650 was probably the decisive factor in the institutionalization of the poor law where it had not yet occurred'.[37]

It is a mistake to assume from the patchy quality of poor law administration in the early seventeenth century that the major role in the relief of poverty was filled not by the official poor law, but by the philanthropy of individuals. This is Professor W. K. Jordan's contention, which he supports by massive research into all charitable endowments and bequests made between 1480 and 1660.[38] Landed gentlemen considered it their duty to look after the poor by distributing largesse. 'Twice a week', wrote Sir Hugh Cholmondley, a Yorkshire landowner, looking back to the 1630s, 'a certain number of people, widows and indigent persons were served at my gates with bread and good pottage made of beef, which I mention that those which succeed may follow the example.'[39] Even more important was the money poured into poor relief by merchants. Jordan has shown that private charity was important before 1660; he has not, however, proved that it was growing in value or that it was more important than official charity. Indeed, when the fall in the value of money in the sixteenth and early seventeenth centuries is taken into account (which Jordan does not do), the *real* value

---

[36] G. C. F. Forster, 'The English local community and local government 1603–25', in A. G. R. Smith, ed., *The Reign of James VI and I* (1973), p. 203.

[37] A. Fletcher, *Reform in the Provinces: the government of Stuart England* (1986), p. 187.

[38] W. K. Jordan, *Philanthropy in England: a study of the changing pattern of English social aspirations 1480–1660* (1959). See W. G. Bittle and R. Todd Lane, 'Inflation and philanthropy in England: a reassessment of Jordan's data', *Econ. H.R.*, 2nd ser., XXIX (1976) and J. F. Hadwin, 'Deflating philanthropy', ibid., XXX (1979).

[39] J. T. Cliffe, *The Yorkshire Gentry from the Reformation to the Civil War* (1969), p. 114.

of private philanthropy did not grow at all. Moreover, the charities established by individuals were probably no more efficiently administered than those set up by the poor law authorities. Some municipal authorities found irresistible the temptation to dip into charitable funds and use the money for other purposes.

There seems no doubt that the poor law was more important than the erratic contribution of private charity in the relief of poverty in the early seventeenth century. Parochial poor relief was increasingly important, especially for individuals at particularly vulnerable times in their lives: for example, young orphans, widows and the aged. A study of Aldenham in Hertfordshire, where about one-third of the inhabitants during the seventeenth century relied on parochial poor relief at least once in their lives, concludes that 'the cycle of family life had the benefit in times of crisis of a system of support operated over a very wide range of needs by a local authority sensitive to the circumstances of those requiring it'.[40] The undoubted achievements of early Stuart welfare schemes, however, should not be exaggerated. They were at best palliatives, and had no success in significantly reducing the size of the pauper population. As Robert Gray recognized at the time, poverty was deep-rooted in the economic structure of early Stuart England, in which unemployment and underemployment were common. When such an economy was hit by a run of bad harvests, then the condition of life for many people could become very bad indeed. The harvest failures of the 1620s, 1630s and 1640s led Bowden to conclude that these decades 'witnessed extreme hardship in England, and were probably the most terrible years through which the country has ever passed'.[41]

From the 1990s onwards: social history with the politics put back

In what follows the work of social historians since the 1990s to the present day will be praised as path breaking and exciting. But often their attempts to explain what they are doing is so riven by jargon that it might leave readers with a sense of puzzlement. Readers who master the jargon will be well rewarded, however. Another difficulty with their work is that it is so multi-faceted that it is sometimes far from easy to see common threads running through it. However, some do stand out very clearly and are so important that they will appear many times in the narrative sections of this book.

The first is the wide extent of office holding and popular participation in politics in early modern England. In some respects this is not a new insight. Nearly forty years ago Derek Hirst estimated that 27–40 per cent of adult males in England and Wales had the vote: that is, about 300,000 people (or 7–10 per cent of the population) were enfranchised.

---

[40] T. Wales, 'Poverty, poor relief and the life cycle: some evidence from seventeenth-century Norfolk' and W. Newsom-Brown, 'The receipts of poor relief and family situations in Aldenham, Herts., 1630–90' in Smith, ed., *Land, Kinship and Life Cycle.*

[41] P. Bowden, 'Agricultural prices', in J. Thirsk, ed., *The Agrarian History of England and Wales 1500–1640* (1967), p. 621.

For the later period Geoffrey Holmes estimated that by 1715 some 5 per cent of the population of England and Wales (about 20 per cent of adult males) had the vote.[42] The electorate was enlarged as the county franchise, the forty shilling freehold, was greatly increased by inflation and the practice of treating some customary tenants as freeholders; many borough franchises were even wider, bringing a much larger number of the people into the 'political nation' than had once been thought. In 1987 Cynthia Herrup's book highlighted another aspect of the extent of political participation of ordinary people: the ways in which members of local communities took part in the apprehension and prosecution of criminals. Herrup writes that 'the legal system exemplifies the participatory nature of English government in the seventeenth century'.[43] As a result of more recent work by social historians, it is now possible to put all this into a wider context. As Mark Goldie writes, 'an astonishingly high proportion of early modern people held office'. By the end of the seventeenth century there were about 50,000 parish officers in England's and Wales's 9,700 parishes; this means that about one-twentieth of the adult male population were office-holders.[44] What is more, these offices were held by people from all social groups from minor gentry to brickmakers, blacksmiths and tanners, as in Stone in Herefordshire.[45] People sought office as a mark of their social position, but, if necessary, offices were forced on them by local rules that offices should rotate amongst families. Service on local juries was restricted to freeholders, but juries sat frequently at assizes and quarter sessions, hearing local complaints or messages from the crown relayed by the assize judges. Stephen Roberts makes an important point when he writes 'of all the institutions of local representation, the sessions grand jury was the closest thing to a mouthpiece of the yeomanry of the country. It was nearly a parliament of the middling sort'.[46]

One important consequence of all this is that many more people than ever before not only became directly involved in the political process as office-holders, but also were drawn into debates about current political and religious issues by reading and talking about them. This fuelled what has been called the growth of 'the public sphere', dealt with on p. 78 and in many other places in the narrative sections of this book.

A second conclusion, which follows from the first, is that political power was often not wielded by superiors over inferiors without any constraints. Instead its use was negotiated between superiors and inferiors. In other words very often the 'inferior' had the ability to use his or her power

---

[42] These paragraphs rely on the mercifully jargon-free analysis of M. Goldie in 'The unacknowledged republic: officeholding in early modern England' in T. Harris, ed., *The Politics of the Excluded, c. 1500–1850* (2010). D. Hirst, *The Representative of the People? Voters and voting in England under the early Stuarts* (1975). G. Holmes, *The Electorate and the National Will in the First Age of Party* (1976).

[43] C. Herrup, *The Common Peace, Participation and the Criminal Law in Seventeenth-Century England* (1987). Quotation from her 'Law and morality in seventeenth-century England' *P. & P.*, 106, 1985, pp. 102–23.

[44] Goldie, 'Unacknowledged republic' p. 161.

[45] Ibid., p. 163.

[46] S. K. Roberts, 'Juries and the middling sort: recruitment and performance at Devon quarter sessions, 1649–1670', in J. S. Cockburn and T. A. Green, eds., *Twelve Good Men and True: the criminal trial jury in England, 1300–1800* (1988), quoted in Goldie, 'Unacknowledged republic', p. 167.

to put restraints on the apparently all-powerful 'superior'.[47] This can be demonstrated by two examples of the negotiation of power in early modern England: the role of women and the functions of riots.

According to contemporary law and attitudes reflected in conduct books designed to guide people on how to behave, there can have been no more disadvantaged people in early modern England than women. The law gave married women no legal rights; they were seen as the property of their husbands. Conduct books taught that in all respects, intellectually, morally and physically, they were 'the weaker vessels' and that they should serve obediently their male superior whether that should be a father, husband or master. One of the achievements of recent historians is to show how women managed to negotiate a more powerful position for themselves than contemporary official opinion gave them.[48]

They did this by adopting many strategies, like exploiting their position as managers of households (and even of estates in the case of some elite women) or as contributors to the family economy by the by-employments they took on, spinning, weaving and so on, to become partners of their husbands and not their servants, taking a full part in decisions made within families. They also used the female networks (which Capp describes using a contemporary term, 'gossips') they had made outside the home, on the streets and in church, to support them in their complaints against violent men and adulterous husbands, often by shaming their victims publicly and informally, not through the courts. Some women negotiated even more power for themselves, as moneylenders, leaders of riots and disorders, witnesses in court proceedings, and occasionally holders of parish offices.[49]

Largely women negotiated more powerful positions for themselves by informal, non-violent strategies. This clearly cannot be said of those who used riots to put pressure on their governors. Although rebellions against the existing social and political order were largely absent from England before 1640 (unlike contemporary France), riots protesting against the rising price of food, enclosures, fen drainage and forest laws were very common. Using E. P. Thompson's seminal article,[50] which showed the existence of a contemporary view of a 'moral economy' that advocated a 'just' price

---

[47] The best introduction to this aspect is M. J. Braddick and J. Walter, 'Grids of power: order, hierarchy and subordination in early modern society' in their *Negotiating Power in Early Modern Society: order, hierarchy and subordination in Britain and Ireland* (2003).

[48] B. Capp, *When Gossips Meet: women, family, and neighbourhood in early modern England* (2004). There is an excellent summary of some of the themes of this book in his 'Separate domains? Women and authority in early modern England' in P. Griffiths, A. Fox and S. Hindle, eds., *The Experience of Authority in Early Modern England* (1996), on which I have relied a lot when writing this and the following two paragraphs.

[49] See my *Social Change and Continuity: England 1550–1750* (rev. edn., 1997), pp. 25–6; for more examples of women using power against their superiors, see A. Wood, ' "Poore men woll speak one daye": plebeian languages of deference and defiance in England, *c.*1520–1640', in Harris, *Politics of the Excluded*, p. 77.

[50] E. P. Thompson, 'The moral economy of the English crowd in the eighteenth century', *P. & P.*, no. 50 (1971).

for food and the need for customary regulations forbidding merchants from taking grain away from stricken areas in times of bad harvests, more recent social historians have shown how rioters used this concept and the threat of violence to pressurize magistrates to put 'the moral economy' into practice. Riots were often the last resort of those affected by rising food prices. After the failure of petitions to magistrates, the rioters in effect used their positions to negotiate, often successfully, more power for themselves in the local community of the parish.

What is particularly exciting about this work on the negotiation of power is that it encourages us to envisage a new view of the early modern State: to see it not necessarily as an all-powerful centre ordering obedient, subservient local magistrates to perform the tasks given them. Instead, in the work of M. J. Braddick and S. Hindle, it is possible to see the early modern English State as 'to a greater or lesser extent, participatory'.[51] All local officers from magistrates (justices of the peace in counties and mayors and aldermen in towns) to parish officials (churchwardens, overseers of the poor) were in theory 'inferior officers', taking orders from the crown and privy council. But in reality their power, whether to execute those orders or not, was very great. This meant that the crown and privy council, like husbands in areas in which contemporary theory portrayed them as 'superiors', had to restrain their use of power in negotiation with their 'inferiors'. One further consequence of this – the growth of the idea that early modern England was a 'monarchical republic' – will be dealt with later (see pp. 83–4).

Intellectual developments and popular beliefs

There are many aspects of the period before 1650 that seem to be progressive fore-runners of future developments: educational opportunities increased; more people became literate, modern scientific principles were discovered; and Protestantism, a rational and anti-magical religion, was the prevalent ideology. However, it would be misleading to describe these developments in education, science and religion in the early seventeenth century as 'modern' or 'progressive'. Even if more people were becoming literate, it does not necessarily follow that they read or were taught new, 'modern' ideas. Though the scientific discoveries of this period were important for the future development of science, before 1650 few of them were known outside a narrow group of English and European scientists. Furthermore, these men easily combined their work on the new discoveries with equal interest in matters that are nowadays considered to be irrational and superstitious. Nor is it clear that Protestantism, any more than science, was a catalyst of change, a solvent of old attitudes and beliefs. Historians looking back to the period before 1650 are too prone to characterize it as one which makes a clear break with the Middle Ages, in the history of ideas no less than in the history of government. In both cases this approach can produce a distorted

---

[51] M. J. Braddick, *State Formation in Early Modern England, c.1550–1700* (2000); and S. Hindle, *The State and Social Change in Early Modern England, c.1550–1640* (2000). The quotation is from Hindle, p. 23.

picture: what is unusual is highlighted as the norm and the most common ideas and beliefs of the period are obscured.

Education and literacy: an 'educational revolution'?

Educational opportunities for boys were plentiful in England in the late sixteenth and early seventeenth centuries. For the sons of landed gentlemen, education often began at home or in the household of a neighbouring magnate. Some gentlemen employed tutors, though education in large households was not confined to academic subjects. Boys learned how to run households and estates by service as household officials, which was seen as

> a gentlemanly profession. . . . [It] was in no sort servile, nor the paynes belonging it any pennance, but they ioyed as much in their libertie, and flourished as freshe in their profession as any other; their fare was always of the best, their apparell fine, neate, handsome and comely, their credite and esteeme alwayes equall with their birth and calling in good regarde.[52]

For other boys also education often began outside a school. Promising youngsters might be singled out to be taught to read and write by local clergymen or curates. Others who were able attended village 'petty' schools, which attempted to teach basic reading and writing. Naturally, the quality of such schools varied. In the Shropshire village of Myddle there can be little doubt which was the better school: Mr Osmary Hill ran a school at Bilmarsh Farm, which had a good local reputation and 'many gentlemen's sons of good quality were his schollers', while Mr Twyford merely 'taught neighbours' children to read and his wife taught women to sew, and make needle workes'.[53] Only after learning to read was a boy supposed to enter a grammar school to be taught to read and write Latin. Both petty and grammar schools were abundant in the early seventeenth century in all parts of the country that have been studied. Between 1574 and 1628 most Cambridgeshire villages had a schoolmaster; in early seventeenth-century West Sussex there was a petty or grammar school in at least twenty towns and villages; seventy schoolmasters were licensed to teach in Leicestershire between 1600 and 1640; in the same period there were thirty-eight teachers in Canterbury, twelve schools in Faversham and twenty-eight in Maidstone in Kent. It has been estimated that between 1560 and 1640 over £293,000 were given by individuals for the establishment of grammar schools, and that 142 new grammar schools were established between 1603 and 1649. These statistics probably under-estimate the scale of educational provision because many unendowed schools and unlicensed teachers are hidden from the records. There is also some indication that schoolteachers were becoming better qualified; from the 1580s to the 1630s the

---

[52] *A Health to the Gentlemanly Profession of Serving Men by I. M., 1598* (Shakespeare Association Facsimiles no. 3, 1931), sig. C3.

[53] Quoted in D. Hey, *An English Rural Community: Myddle under the Tudors and Stuarts* (1974), p. 189.

percentage of teachers with degrees, licensed to teach in the diocese of London, more than doubled.[54]

Numerous contemporary treatises reflect the high value placed by many on education to produce an educated magistracy and to promote Protestantism by increasing the ability to read and interpret the Bible. Higher education, as well as elementary and secondary education, consequently flourished. New colleges were founded at Oxford and Cambridge: Jesus and Wadham at Oxford in 1571 and 1612, Emmanuel and Sidney Sussex at Cambridge in 1584 and 1596. Even more striking is the apparent increase in the numbers admitted to the universities in the same period, rising from under 800 a year in 1560 to a peak of over 1,200 a year in the 1630s. Professor Stone concludes that this represented a proportion of the seventeen- to eighteen-year-old age group at university that was not exceeded until three centuries later.[55] Many undergraduates did not stay to take a degree. After a year many sons of landed gentlemen went to one of the Inns of Court to gain a smattering of legal knowledge to help them in the administration of their estates. In the early seventeenth century, especially after the establishment of European peace in 1604 and 1609, it was becoming customary for them to complete their education by foreign travel. The Grand Tour was established as a normal part of a gentleman's education, despite great parental concern, due not only to its expense and the opportunities it gave young men to enjoy pleasures forbidden them at home. It was also felt unfortunate that the major European centres of culture were also hotbeds of Catholicism, and in any case early seventeenth-century gentlemen were no less distrustful of foreigners than their descendants in the reigns of William III and Queen Anne. Sir Henry Slingsby of Scriven in Yorkshire told his son in 1610 to 'take heed what companie he keepes in too familiar a fashion for the frenche are of an ill conversacon and full of many loathsome deseases'.[56]

Stone believes that not only were educational opportunities abundant in this period, but there was an increase in the provision and an improvement in the quality of education between 1560 and 1640 that amounted to 'an educational revolution'. This raises two associated questions: how extensive were educational opportunities and how high were educational standards before 1560; and how can one measure changes in educational standards after 1560? Too often the argument that there was a marked improvement in education after 1560 minimizes the later medieval expansion of English education. Between 1350 and 1529 six Oxford colleges and nine Cambridge colleges were founded. Although there are few statistics, many grammar schools were also founded in this period. The historian of education in the later Middle Ages

---

[54] M. Spufford, 'The schooling of the peasantry in Cambridgeshire 1575–1700', in J. Thirsk, ed., *Land, Church and People* (1970), pp. 112–47; A. Fletcher, *A County Community in Peace and War: Sussex 1600–60* (1975), pp. 34–5; B. Simon, ed., *Education in Leicestershire 1540–1940* (1968), p. 41; P. Clark, 'The ownership of books in England 1560–1640: the example of some Kentish townsfolk', in L. Stone, ed., *Schooling and Society: studies in the history of education* (1976), p. 106; Jordan, *Philanthropy*, p. 283; D. Cressy, ed., *Education in Tudor and Stuart England* (1975), p. 10.

[55] L. Stone, 'The educational revolution in England 1560–1640', *P. & P.*, XXVIII (1964), p. 53.

[56] Cliffe, *Yorkshire Gentry*, p. 78.

cannot be more exact because of the scarcity of primary sources. Licensing of schoolteachers and diocesan visitation recording of schools did not begin until the 1550s. Matriculation registers were not regularly kept at Cambridge until 1544 and at Oxford until 1571. The historian of English education from the mid-sixteenth century onwards is consequently faced with an abundance of sources. What he or she must guard against is assuming that this by itself is proof of anything other than an improvement in educational administration and record keeping.[57]

The difficulties of measuring educational changes in the late sixteenth and early seventeenth centuries are illustrated by the research on the extent of literacy in this period. Some of the evidence used for this purpose is of dubious value. Clearly it would be wrong to assume that those convicted criminals who recited 'the neck verse' to prove that they were beneficed clergymen and so exempted from corporal punishment, were actually reading the passage. A more probable indicator of literacy is the ability to write one's name instead of signing documents with a cross mark, especially since it was common in the early seventeenth century to learn to read before learning to write. (One wonders, though, how many people simply learned to write their name and nothing else.) Using a sample of nearly 6,000 signatures to depositions in ecclesiastical courts from 1530 to 1750 as evidence of literacy, David Cressy concludes that there was a marked increase in literacy in the last decades of the sixteenth century until by 1600 one-third of the male population could read and write. But he does concede that over the whole period there was 'no steady cumulative progress', only 'irregular fluctuation'. Moreover, illiteracy persisted among the labouring poor, farmers, skilled craftsmen, and most women. Literacy was confined to the landed elite, wealthy merchants, shopkeepers and professional men.[58] In some Kentish towns more people owned books in 1640 than in 1580, but the ownership of books was restricted to propertied males. When Bartholomew Dann of Faversham found his wife 'reading and leaving her book in some place . . . he would catch the book out of her hands and tear it in pieces or otherwise fling it away'.[59] Significantly, those who had the temerity to suggest that women should be educated had to assure their readers that the male dominance of society would not be thereby disrupted.

> We are not advising that women be educated in such a way that their tendency to curiosity shall be developed, but so that their sincerity and contentedness may be increased, and this chiefly in those things which it becomes a woman to know and to do; that is to say, all that enables her to look after her husband and to promote the welfare of her husband and her family.[60]

---

[57] Elizabeth Russell, 'The influx of commoners into the university of Oxford before 1581: an optical illusion?', *E.H.R.*, XCII (1977), pp. 721–5; N. Orme, *English Schools in the Middle Ages* (1973).

[58] D. Cressy, *Literacy and the Social Order: reading and writing in early modern England* (1980); 'Levels of illiteracy in England 1530–1730', *H.J.*, XX (1977), pp. 1–23 and 'Literacy in seventeenth-century England: more evidence', *Journal of Interdisciplinary History*, VIII (1977), pp. 141–50.

[59] Clark, 'Ownership of books', p. 97.

[60] Cressy, ed., *Education in Tudor and Stuart England*, p. 111.

So in 1657 wrote Jacob Comenius, one of the most liberal men produced by the seventeenth century. The same fears that his words were designed to calm were also felt about the consequences of popular education. Too many schools, felt Sir Francis Bacon in 1611, caused on the one hand a lack

> both of servants for husbandry and apprentices for trade; and on the other side, there being more scholars bred than the state can prefer and employ, and the active part of that life not bearing a proportion to the preparative, it must needs fall out that many persons will be bred unfit for other vocations and unprofitable for that in which they are brought up, which fills the realm full of indigent, idle and wanton people, which are but *materia rerum novarum*.[61]

It is likely that his fears were unfounded. For the mass of English people at that time, the task of gaining enough to eat left no spare time for education. If there was an 'educational revolution' before the middle of the century, it did not extend to women or to the poor.

How 'modern' were the subjects taught in the schools and universities of early seventeenth-century England? This ought to be an easy question, since the curricula they were to adopt were laid down in school regulations and university statutes. However, these were not necessarily adhered to, especially by the universities. One can be more certain about what was taught in grammar schools, in which the curriculum was dominated by religious and classical subjects, especially the teaching of Latin grammar. The same set books recur in early seventeenth-century grammar school syllabuses: the Catechism, Psalter, Book of Common Prayer, Bible, a Latin grammar textbook (usually William Lily's written in the early sixteenth century) and various selected classical authors with 'lewd or superstitious books or ballads' weeded out, and 'all filthy places in the poets' quickly passed over.[62] In vain, some writers urged schools to adopt a more practical and vocation-orientated syllabus. In 1570 Humphrey Gilbert proposed the establishment of a school which would teach mathematics, horse riding, map making, navigation, biology and other subjects.[63] Significantly, reformers in the revolutionary decades of the mid-seventeenth century were still recommending similar things.

What was taught in early seventeenth-century universities is the subject of debate which is difficult to resolve because different types of source material produce conflicting accounts. University statutes and examination requirements indicate that the formal curriculum of universities was dominated by scholasticism, and that new ideas, like those in science, made little headway. It is true that in 1619 Oxford established the Savilian professorship in geometry and astronomy, the Sadlerian chair of natural philosophy and the Tolmins lecture in anatomy. But by and large the formal university

---

[61] Ibid., pp. 24–5.
[62] John Brinsley, in 1612, quoted in ibid., pp. 84, 88.
[63] *The Erection of an Academy in London for Education of Her Majesties Wardes, and Others the Youth of Nobility and Gentlemen*, printed in *Archaeologia*, XXI (1827), pp. 508–20.

institutions ignored the new science. What is less certain is the extent to which individual tutors taught new ideas which were outside the official syllabus. By its very nature such teaching is ill-recorded, but it is known that there were some lecturers who propounded new ideas, such as the mathematicians William Oughtred at King's Hall, Cambridge, and Thomas Allen at Gloucester Hall, Oxford.[64] Many of these had connections with London and with Gresham College. The most famous is Henry Briggs, who in 1620 left Gresham to take the Savilian chair in geometry at Oxford. What one would like to know is how typical such teachers were. The surviving evidence is inconclusive, but if students' notebooks are a guide to what was taught (not always a totally safe assumption!) then the syllabus at Oxford and Cambridge at that time was very conservative and narrow. 'Vera et sana philosophia est vera Aristotelica', jotted down Lawrence Bretton of Queens' College, Cambridge, in his student notebook in the 1630s.[65] Aristotelian philosophy seems to have reigned supreme at the universities before the English Revolution.

The scientific revolution

The concept of 'the scientific revolution' to describe changes in the intellectual climate of the sixteenth and seventeenth centuries is more acceptable than the idea of 'an educational revolution'. It is true that there were medieval scientists, like the thirteenth-century Oxford scholars Robert Grosseteste and Roger Bacon, who emphasized the importance of observation and experimentation. But it was not until three centuries later that more than a handful of scientists began to question long-held conclusions about man and his environment which were based on traditional methodology. Medieval science was rooted in the works of the Greek philosophers Galen and Ptolemy who lived in the second century AD, and Aristotle who lived in the fourth century BC. Medical principles were based on the Galenic concepts of anatomy and physiology: the body was composed of four basic 'humours', phlegm, blood, black bile and yellow bile, and, since both physical and psychological disorders were caused by a superfluity of one of these humours, conventional medical remedies consisted of ways of purging the body of it. Galen had done some dissection, but mainly on apes not humans, and throughout the Middle Ages his conclusions were accepted and not tested by experiments and dissections of the human body. The Ptolemaic view of a finite, earth-centred universe, in which the moon, sun and planets revolved round a stationary earth, was as ancient as Galen's anatomy and as deeply rooted in medieval thought. Both derived heavily from Aristotle's theories about physics and the universe, especially his views that matter consisted of only four elements, fire, earth, water and air, and that bodies moved only in two ways, in straight lines and in circles. The validity of these fundamental principles was tested not by experiment, but by reason, and on

---

[64] M. Feingold, *The Mathematician's Apprenticeship: science, universities and society in England 1560–1640* (1984); C. Webster, *The Great Instauration: science, medicine and reform 1626–60* (1975), p. 126.

[65] H. Kearney, *Scholars and Gentlemen: universities and society in pre-industrial Britain 1500–1700* (1970), p. 84.

the basis of these principles broad theories were built by logical deduction. By the six-teenth century the 'ancients' and their ideas were so revered that the intellectual climate was against discovery; it was believed that there was little left to be discovered about natural phenomena. Any change was likely to be a change for the worse: old ways and old books were the best. This is, of course, the antithesis of the equally unfounded belief in progress and the modern tendency to regard new books as better than old books.

During the sixteenth and seventeenth centuries, scientists began to question the deductive method of Aristotelian philosophy and in so doing they discovered some of the fundamental principles of modern science. The first major developments were in the fields of anatomy and astronomy, which were marked by the publication in 1543 of two treatises, the Italian Vesalius's *De Humanis Corporis Fabrica* and the Pole Copernicus's *De Revolutionibus Orbium Coelestium*. Both were implicit attacks on Greek science. Vesalius's description of human anatomy was based on dissections of the human body, and Copernicus's theory that the sun, not the earth, was the centre of the universe was the result of observation. Copernicus's work was developed by other astronomers, Tycho Brahe, a Dane, Johannes Kepler, a German, and Galileo Galilei, an Italian. It is clear, then, that the emerging scientific movement was a European one, and a notable feature of it is the way scholars of different nationalities freely communicated their research conclusions to each other. The reasons for the timing of these remarkable developments remain controversial, but that they were a European phenomenon suggests that they had more powerful impulses behind them than English Puritanism.

This is not to say that Englishmen did not participate in the European scientific movement. Already by the early seventeenth century much had been achieved in England, notably by mathematicians and astronomers like Robert Recorde, John Dee, Thomas Digges and Thomas Harriot (who carried on his work into the seventeenth century before he died in 1621), and by William Gilbert, whose work on magnetism was published in 1600. One of the most important contributions of Elizabeth's reign to English science in the seventeenth century was the foundation of Gresham College in 1597 under the terms of the will of the financier Sir Thomas Gresham. He stipulated that this London college should have seven professorships, in law, rhetoric, divinity, music, physics, geometry and astronomy, and that lectures should be in both Latin and English. Gresham College was a research and a teaching institution, and many of the notable developments in early seventeenth-century English science were connected with it because of the wide contacts of Henry Briggs, Gresham's professor of anatomy, whom Christopher Hill calls a 'contact and public relations man'.[66] The specific English contributions to European science in the early seventeenth century were in the spheres of mathematics and medicine. A crucial feature of the new science was its reliance on statistics and mathematical logic as the vital proof of truths rather than on deductive logic. Therefore John Napier's invention of logarithms (his *Descriptio* was published in 1614) and its subsequent development and popularization by Henry Briggs were

---

[66] Christopher Hill, *The Intellectual Origins of the English Revolution* (1965), p. 38.

important aids to the new experimental science. Arguably of even greater importance in the history of mathematics is William Oughtred, the clergyman, who invented trigonometry and who had an extensive reputation as a great teacher. William Harvey's discovery of the circulation of the blood (his *De Motu Cordis et Sanguinis* was published in 1628) is the most important English contribution to the new science before the middle of the century. Significantly, it demonstrates the close links of English science with the Continent, since Harvey developed his idea after studying at Padua University where the tradition established by Vesalius was maintained by Hieronymus Fabricius. Unlike all the scientists mentioned so far there is no agreement about the role and significance of Sir Francis Bacon in the scientific movement in the early years of the century. However, one does not have to believe that he was the creator of the new experimental science or that he was very influential before 1640 (the first proposition is certainly wrong and the second very doubtful) to suggest that his views are typical of the new science. He rejected the ideas of 'the ancients' and recommended a search for new scientific explanations by experiment, observation and induction. The results of experiments were to be collected by a 'College of Natural History' with the aim of using scientific knowledge for the progress of mankind. 'The true and lawful goal of the sciences', he wrote, 'is none other than this: that human life be endowed with new discoveries and power.'[67]

The philosophical implications of the new science as illustrated in the writings of Bacon are without doubt one of the greatest developments in modern European thought: the replacement of the passive acceptance of traditional, unchallenged truths, which were revered because they were ancient, by the idea of progress, that man can change his condition and environment for the better. However, important as this is, it would be wrong to exaggerate the modernity of the 'natural philosophers' of the early seventeenth century and the break they represented with the past. Maybe even in this respect, as in some others (as has been seen), 'revolution' is a misleading concept for historians to use. Some historians of science have recently abandoned a 'tunnel vision' approach aimed primarily at discovering the antecedents of modern scientific attitudes and values, and have instead endeavoured to investigate ideas in the historical context in which they were developed.[68] One of the principal discoveries of those taking this approach is that in the late sixteenth and early seventeenth centuries the modern borderline between rational science and irrational, occult and esoteric investigations did not exist. Scientists sought explanations in mystical tradition and experience as much as in the mechanical world. John Dee combined his mathematical work with

---

[67] Quoted in A. R. Hall, *The Scientific Revolution 1500–1800: the formation of modern scientific attitudes* (2nd edn., 1962), p. 165.

[68] The editors' introduction in R. S. Westman and D. C. Lindberg, eds., *Reappraisals of the Scientific Revolution* (1990) is a good guide to recent literature on a subject that is sometimes written about by historians who appear not to attempt to make their subject accessible to those who are unfamiliar with it. The exceptions in this book (in addition to the editors' introduction) are the articles by J. T. Coke, 'The new philosophy of medicine in seventeenth-century England' and M. Hunter, 'Science and heterodoxy: an early modern problem resolved'.

astrology and spiritualism. John Napier used his mathematical talents to unravel prophecies in the Book of Revelation that forecast the struggle against Antichrist and the end of the world, and to calculate the chronology of their fulfilment. William Gilbert, the first person to demonstrate the magneticism of the earth by careful experiments, believed that the earth was alive. 'We consider', he wrote, 'that the whole universe is animated, and that all the globes, all the stars, and also the noble earth, have been governed, since the beginning by their own appointed souls and have motives of self-conservation.'[69] Like many other contemporary European scientists, Gilbert was swept along by a current of belief in magic, the revival of Neoplatonism, 'the last school of ancient pagan philosophy'.[70] Hermes Trismegistus, who was (wrongly) thought to have been a pre-Christian sage, became a cult figure among intellectuals. Hermeticists considered the universe to be animated by spirits, and matter to be possessed of sympathetic and antipathetic influences, and their aim was to discover these by scientific enquiry in order to control natural phenomena. So influential were the magical beliefs of Renaissance Hermeticism that some historians of science have argued that it played the key role in the attack on Greek science.[71] The most notable illustration is the work of the Swiss Paracelsus on chemical remedies for diseases, which owed much to the Hermetic tradition and was a major attack on Galenic medicine. Paracelsian iatro-chemistry was very influential among scientists in the late sixteenth and early seventeenth centuries. Clearly there was a great intellectual gulf between them and the modern professional scientist.

How great was the impact of the new science on early seventeenth-century England? Its significance for the future development of science can tempt one to exaggerate its contemporary importance. After reading Bacon's *Advancement of Learning*, James I is alleged to have remarked that 'it is like the peace of God, that surpasseth all understanding'.[72] There is point to James's witticism. Many of the new ideas were too difficult to follow. It was not until the later years of the century that Harvey's discovery gained wide acceptance, after the Italian Marcello Malpighi, using an improved microscope, confirmed the existence of the capillaries which Harvey had suggested carried blood from the arteries to the veins. Other discoveries, like that of Copernicus, were too revolutionary to gain widespread acceptance. The Ptolemaic view of the universe, in any case, provided satisfactory explanations of visible astronomical features.[73] Even Tycho Brahe did not fully accept the implications of Copernican astronomy. Defenders of the 'moderns' like George Hakewill, whose *An Apologie or Declaration of the Power and Providence of God* was published in 1627, were in a minority, and it is difficult to avoid the conclusion that the 'ancients' had the better of the literary debate.[74]

---

[69]   Quoted in Antonia McLean, *Humanism and the Rise of Science in Tudor England* (1972), p. 158.

[70]   K. Thomas, *Religion and the Decline of Magic* (1971), p. 223.

[71]   See especially the works of Frances Yates.

[72]   Quoted in P. M. Rattansi, 'The social interpretation of science in the seventeenth century', in P. Mathias, ed., *Science and Society 1600–1900* (1972), p. 18.

[73]   McLean, *Humanism and the Rise of Science*, p. 108.

[74]   R. F. Jones, *Ancients and Moderns: a study of the rise of the scientific movement in seventeenth-century England* (2nd edn., 1961), esp. pp. 29–35.

Charles Webster has shown how Gresham College 'was extremely variable in its effectiveness, in both its research and teaching capacities'. Many Gresham professors spent a lot of time on other business. Samuel Hartlib thought that most of them were 'very idle'. John Greaves, the professor of astronomy, went to the Middle East in 1633 and did not return to London until 1640.[75] It is true that some members of the landed elite took a fashionable interest in the new science, and these *virtuosi* began to conduct experiments and collect curiosities. But their activities bore only a superficial resemblance to Bacon's hopes of a massive coordinated research programme. On the contrary, as Professor Stone argues, 'the quest [by the aristocratic *virtuosi*] for rarities, mechanical, natural, or antiquarian, was the very antithesis of the Baconian ideal. . . . So far from conforming to a rational programme of controlled research, it encouraged the mentality of the fair-ground peep-show.'[76] Before 1640 the impact of the new science was slight. Its practical application was confined to improvements in navigation, map making and surveying.

Popular beliefs: magic and witchcraft

The beliefs of ordinary men and women in England in the sixteenth and seventeenth centuries are one of the most fascinating areas of more recent research. There is, though, no point in minimizing the obstacles in the way of such investigation. The major type of evidence available is printed material, which is hardly a perfect source for discovering the beliefs of people, many of whom were illiterate. In any case, at any time common beliefs are not recorded, simply because they are well known. After the work of Keith Thomas and Alan Macfarlane, however, there is little doubt that belief in magic was prevalent in early seventeenth-century society, and that it formed part of a popular subculture, separate and distinct from the Hermeticism and mystical beliefs which it has been seen were current in intellectual circles at this time.[77] In its most striking forms, popular belief in magic in the late sixteenth and early seventeenth centuries manifested itself in two major ways.

The first is evident in the witchcraft accusations brought before the assize courts in this period. In the early seventeenth century the numbers were fewer than in the 1580s and 1590s, which were the peak years in this respect, but there were more cases than in the later seventeenth century. The accusations reveal a belief in witchcraft of a different type than that prevalent in contemporary Scottish and continental witchcraft trials.[78] Very few people in England were alleged to be witches who had made covenants with the Devil or who wore distinctive clothes. Most of those accused of witchcraft in England were women, who were usually older than their accusers and

---

[75] Webster, *Great Instauration*, pp. 51ff.

[76] Stone, *Crisis*, p. 717.

[77] Thomas, *Religion and the Decline of Magic*; A. Macfarlane, *Witchcraft in Tudor and Stuart England* (1970).

[78] For Scotland, see C. Larner, *Enemies of God: the witch-hunt in Scotland* (1983). For continental Europe, see B. Levack, *The Witch-Hunt in Early Modern Europe* (1987) and G. R. Quaife, *Godly Zeal and Furious Rage: the witch in early modern Europe* (1987).

who often lived alone. They were charged with having worked maleficent magic, causing harm to the person of the accuser, or death or illness to the accuser's children, relatives or animals. With the exception of the case of Matthew Hopkins, the professional witchfinder who was active in East Anglia in 1645, the initiative in the prosecution of English witches in this period came from their neighbours, not from the magistrates or the ecclesiastical authorities. The second manifestation of popular belief in magic in this period is the existence of people variously called 'cunning' or 'wise' men and women, 'white witches' and 'wizards', who it was believed had powers to work beneficial magic. Healing, recovering stolen goods and discovering those responsible for thefts recur in the few surviving casebooks of cunning men. Many appear to have operated rather like modern psychiatrists, listening to problems brought to them and sometimes succeeding in providing acceptable solutions simply by confirming what their clients already suspected. Others had some success as faith healers and by prescribing herbal medicines. By such means local men and women gained reputations as wise people who had magical powers. Unlike witches, those believed to possess white magic were largely tolerated and rarely brought before the courts in this period.

There is little doubt that many people in the late sixteenth and early seventeenth centuries believed in magic. However, it is slightly disconcerting that much of the evidence is drawn from a county, Essex, where witchcraft prosecutions were numerous and perhaps exceptionally high. Between 1560 and 1700, 299 people were indicted for witchcraft before the assizes in Essex, but only 91 in Kent, 52 in Hertfordshire, 54 in Surrey and 17 in Sussex appeared before the assizes for the same offence.[79] This discrepancy does raise doubts about the value of witchcraft prosecutions as a gauge by which to measure witchcraft beliefs. At best, they represent only the cases which got to court, and they were dependent on the willingness of the authorities to let them proceed. One cannot, therefore, assume that they are a record of all witchcraft cases, or that when prosecutions became less frequent (from the mid-seventeenth century onwards) popular belief in witchcraft died. Belief in magic was prevalent in the late sixteenth and early seventeenth centuries, but it is not certain that it was more widespread and intense than in earlier or later periods.

Some uncertainty also surrounds attempts to explain the persistent belief in magic. These have been of three major types. First, there are those which attempt to link it to the economic instability of this period. Since population and pressure on resources were increasing in the late sixteenth and early seventeenth centuries, it is argued that people had less and less to give away in the form of charity. Consequently, the medieval tradition of neighbourliness in villages was weakened. Witchcraft cases appear to support this thesis. Many witchcraft accusations arose out of incidents when individuals turned down requests for charity from poor neighbours. As a result, it is argued, the former felt guilty about their callous attitude and, after suffering a misfortune, turned their guilt against those who had been refused charity, by accusing them of witchcraft and of

---

[79] C. L. Ewen, *Witch Hunting and Witch Trials* (1929), p. 99.

being the cause of their misfortune.[80] A major doubt about this line of argument is whether neighbourliness was a reality in medieval villages and whether it was being eroded in villages in this period.

The second type of explanation is more convincing.[81] The starting point is the fact that in the sixteenth and seventeenth centuries tragedies for which there were no rational explanations happened frequently; conventional medicine was unable to diagnose most human and animal diseases, infant mortality was high and bad harvests were frequent. In the absence of mechanical explanations, people felt that the cause lay in the occult. In pre-Reformation England, the Catholic Church – by means of the confessional role of priests, and belief in the healing capacity of saints and the power of holy water and relics – had provided explanations of and remedies for tragedies. But the Reformation 'denied the value of the church's rituals and referred the believer back to the unpredictable mercies of God. If religion continued to be regarded by its adherents as a source of power, then it was a power which was patently much diminished.'[82] With the protective magic of the Catholic Church removed, it is argued that individuals had to attack the agents of maleficent magic, witches, and so began the rash of witchcraft accusations and trials from the mid-sixteenth to the mid-seventeenth centuries. Speculative though this explanation remains, it is an attractive one. Clearly the work of Thomas and Macfarlane has created a new dimension to social history by establishing the central role of magic in people's lives.[83]

The third type of explanation is the more recent emphasis by some historians on the role of the magisterial class in promoting belief in witchcraft. This 'top-down' explanation is based on the argument that the educated elite, drawing on views about witchcraft that were common throughout Europe, had a key role in initiating witchcraft prosecutions and were not simply pressed to do this from below.[84] Their belief in magic and witchcraft, though rooted in different origins, was as strong as that of ordinary men and women in this period.

Religious beliefs

Since most people are themselves genuinely uncertain about their religious faith, it is difficult at any time to discover people's attitudes to religion. In the early seventeenth

---

[80] This is the hypothesis of Macfarlane, *Witchcraft*, pp. 200–6; Keith Thomas presents a slightly modified version of it in *Religion and the Decline of Magic*, pp. 560–9.

[81] Thomas places more emphasis on this second hypothesis in *Religion and the Decline of Magic*. In his 1978 book, *The Origins of English Individualism*, p. 59, Macfarlane concedes that his earlier stress in *Witchcraft* on the transition from neighbourliness to individualism in sixteenth-century communities may have been wrong.

[82] Thomas, *Religion and the Decline of Magic*, p. 77.

[83] A. Gregory, 'Witchcraft, politics and "good neighbourhood" in early seventeenth-century Rye', *P. & P.*, CXXXIII (1991) is a fascinating study of a witchcraft case in 1607 that develops the pioneering ideas of Thomas and Macfarlane. As can be seen from M. Gaskill's article, 'The pursuit of reality: recent research into the history of witchcraft', *H.J.*, vol. 51 (2008), others have tried (and still are trying) to do this. But no clear alternative overall themes have emerged yet to replace Thomas's and MacFarlane's clear conclusions.

[84] J. Sharpe, *Instruments of Darkness: witchcraft in England 1550–1750* (1996).

century this is doubly difficult because religious uniformity was imposed by the State. Given the severe statutory penalties for nonconformity, it is hardly surprising that nonconformists often hid their real faith by occasional attendance at a parish church, or that sympathetic magistrates sometimes did not enforce the penal laws. The recusant Catholic who refused to attend a parish church and was proceeded against by the authorities is relatively easy to identify, but this is not true of those who practised Catholicism in the privacy of their own homes and who also attended a parish church. The problem facing the historian as far as non-Catholics are concerned is one of categorization as well as of identification. Did Protestantism outside the State Church exist, either in its Presbyterian form of a national Church without bishops, or its separatist form of independent congregations following their own forms of worship and liturgy? Among those who were committed to the State Church was there a clear distinction between 'Anglicans' and 'Puritans'? Finally, were there people in the early seventeenth century who were totally indifferent to religion?

Indifference

The last question may seem irrelevant to those accustomed to seeing this as a period in which religion played a central role in everyone's life. Keith Thomas believes that this is a false assumption. 'It can be confidently said that not all Tudor and Stuart Englishmen went to some kind of church, that many of those who did went with considerable reluctance, and that a certain proportion remained throughout their lives utterly ignorant of the elementary tenets of Christian dogma.'[85] There is considerable circumstantial evidence for this view. In many parishes the churches were not large enough to seat all the members of the community. The authorities often tried to impose religious uniformity on 'the better sort', not on the poorer classes. Moreover, it is likely that enforcement of religious legislation was laxer in areas where parishes were large, communities scattered and the power of the Church weak, as in the forest areas of Sussex and Kent and the pastoral regions of the north-west. In 1607 John Norden found that in areas of

> great and spacious wastes, mountains and heaths . . . the people [are] given to little or no kind of labour, living very hardly with oaten bread, sour whey, and goats' milk, dwelling far from any church or chapel, and are as ignorant of God or of any civil course of life as the very savages amongst the infidels.[86]

Of those who attended church, some misbehaved, 'nudged their neighbours, hawked and spat, knitted, made coarse remarks, told jokes, fell asleep, and even let off guns'.[87] 'Some sleep from the beginning to the end [of sermons]', noted John Angier, a

---

[85] Thomas, *Religion and the Decline of Magic*, p. 159. See also Christopher Hill, *Society and Puritanism in Pre-revolutionary England* (Panther edn., 1969), pp. 457–8.

[86] Quoted in Thirsk, *Agrarian History*, p. 411.

[87] Thomas, *Religion and the Decline of Magic*, p. 161.

Lancashire preacher, 'as if they come for no other purpose but to sleep, as if the sabbath were made only to recover the sleep they have lost in the week.'[88]

There is no doubt that religious indifference existed. There is even evidence that some had more serious doubts about Christianity. In 1607 a Wiltshire gentleman, John Derpier of Buttermere, was alleged to have said that 'there was no god and no resurrection and that men died a death like beasts'.[89] But such extreme scepticism was untypical in the early seventeenth century.[90] Moreover, it is possible to exaggerate the extent of popular religious apathy and indifference at this time. Margaret Spufford characterizes the mental world of some Cambridge villagers in the later sixteenth and early seventeenth centuries as 'a society in which even the humblest members, the very poor, and the women, and those living in physical isolation, thought deeply on religious matters and were often profoundly influenced by them'.[91] As will be seen, Protestantism, and to a lesser extent Catholicism, played a great part in the lives of most men and women in early Stuart England.

Catholicism

Among ordinary people in the late sixteenth and early seventeenth centuries, Catholicism was strongest in the areas that contemporaries called 'the dark corners of the land',[92] where there were few Protestant preachers and existing clergymen were poorly paid and educated. In Lancashire there was 'widespread popular Catholicism', and in Wales 'half-understood relics of the missal and breviary survived in the home for generations after they had been banished from the church'.[93] These remnants of unreformed Catholicism in areas where the Reformation had made little impact are often difficult to distinguish from magical beliefs. In 1628 Benjamin Rudyerd talked in the House of Commons about 'the utmost skirts of the North, where the prayers of the common people are more like spells and charms than devotions'.[94] An assault was made on popular Catholicism by a Protestant campaign of evangelization by preachers and lecturers and by endowment of schools in 'the dark corners of the land'. The appointment by some London merchants in the 1620s of trustees, the Feoffees for Impropriations, to buy tithes from landowners to augment church salaries, and the passage of the Act for the Propagation of the Gospel in Wales in 1650 illustrate that the campaign was maintained in the early seventeenth century, and that it was not totally successful. Not all aspects of recent attempts to argue that the process of Protestantization (at the grass-roots, parochial level in post-Reformation England) was

---

[88]   Quoted in C. Haigh, 'Puritan evangelism in the reign of Elizabeth 1', *E.H.R.*, XCII, 1977, pp. 47–8.

[89]   M. Ingram, *Church Courts, Sex and Marriage in England 1570–1640* (1987), p. 95.

[90]   M. Hunter, 'The problem of "atheism" in early modern England', *T.R.H.S.*, 5th ser., XXXV (1985), pp. 135–57.

[91]   M. Spufford, *Contrasting Communities* (1979), p. 350.

[92]   C. Hill, 'Puritans and "the dark corners" of the land', in his *Change and Continuity in Seventeenth-Century England* (1974), pp. 3–47.

[93]   Haigh, 'Puritan evangelism', p. 30; A. H. Dodd, *Studies in Stuart Wales* (1952), p. 53.

[94]   Quoted in M. James, *Family, Lineage and Civil Society* (1974), p. 125.

very slow are convincing. But there is no doubt that England did not become a Protestant country without a long, painful period of adjustment and conversion in the later sixteenth and early seventeenth centuries; nor that Protestant evangelists found it much more difficult to capture popular attention than had Catholic propagandists before the Reformation.[95] Protestants relied largely on words in sermons, lectures, catechisms and Bible readings to get their message across, which did not have the instant appeal of visual aids like paintings, sculptures and woodcut illustrations, as well as pageants, processions and mystery plays which Protestants avoided as 'popish' and 'superstitious'.

Nevertheless, it is likely that the hold of unreformed Catholicism on ordinary people was gradually becoming weaker in the early seventeenth century. This is not true of reformed, Counter-Reformation Catholicism, whose adherents among the landowning classes probably grew in numbers in this period. Clearly the total number of Catholics was tiny: they made up 1.5 per cent of the population of Yorkshire in 1604, and probably amounted to only 35,000 in the whole country. However, by 1640 the total Catholic population had risen to 60,000.[96] Why did reformed Catholicism not only survive, but make 'modest progress' in a country where it was outlawed? The explanation lies mainly in the protection it received from landed gentlemen. Counter-Reformation Catholicism in England was a seigneurial religion, which survived within the shelter of the households of great magnates, some of whom were too powerful to be proceeded against by local magistrates.[97] In some cases the local magistrate was a Catholic: a Sussex Catholic landowner, Sir Henry Compton of Brambletye, was a JP and deputy lieutenant from the 1620s to 1642 in a county where Catholicism had received strong gentry support in the reign of Elizabeth I.[98] In other cases the heads of households conformed while their wives did not, which may account for the comparatively large number of devoted women Catholics in the early seventeenth century. Credit for the survival of Catholicism must also be given to the work of Jesuit, Benedictine and secular priests. In the early seventeenth century the infighting between Jesuits and secular priests, which had absorbed much of their energies in the 1580s and 1590s, was temporarily ended. Moreover, they dropped the role of political activism which some of them had adopted in the reign of Elizabeth I. Professor Bossy calls the Gunpowder

---

[95] The arguments for a 'slow' Reformation are presented in C. Haigh, *The Reformation Revised* (1987) and P. Collinson, *The Birthpangs of Protestant England* (1988), and for a 'quick' Reformation in A. G. Dickens, *The English Reformation* (2nd edn., 1989). A dispassionate assessment can be found in P. Marshall, *Reformation England, 1480–1642* (2003), especially ch. 6; R. O'Day, *The Debate on the English Reformation* (1986); and S. Doran and C. Durston, *Princes, Pastors and People: the Church and religion in England 1529–1689* (1991), ch. 6.

[96] A. G. Dickens, 'The extent and character of recusancy in Yorkshire, 1604', *Yorks. Archaeological Journal*, XXXVII (1948), p. 33; H. Aveling, 'Some aspects of Yorkshire Catholic recusant history 1558–1791', in G. J. Cuming, ed., *Studies in Church History*, IV (1967), p. 110; J. Bossy, *The English Catholic Community 1570–1850* (1975), p. 188.

[97] J. Bossy, 'The character of Elizabethan Catholicism', *P. & P.*, XXI (1962), pp. 39–57; Stone, *Crisis*, pp. 729–33.

[98] Fletcher, *Sussex*, p. 97; R. B. Manning, *Religion and Society in Elizabethan Sussex* (1969).

Plot of 1605 'the last fling of the Elizabethan tradition of a politically engaged Catholicism'.[99] Yet, as Peter Marshall writes in his excellent survey of religion after the Reformation, 'confidence and expansion, rather than ossification or decline from a heroic mid-Elizabethan peak seems to characterize the Catholic experience in the decades before the Civil War. By the 1630s the ratio of priest to people was higher than it was to be for another two centuries.'[100]

Protestantism

The word 'Puritan' causes so much confusion among students of the history of the period from 1558 to 1660 that it is tempting to abandon it. As will be seen, it would be a mistake to do so. Nevertheless, 'Puritanism' is a difficult concept and one which many history students find hard to understand. It was used in the later sixteenth and early seventeenth centuries as a term of abuse: 'that odious and factious name of Puritans', John Pym called it. Consequently, it was not used at the time with any great precision, and some historians, with less excuse, have followed suit in using it to describe individuals and groups with widely varying views. Christopher Hill rightly calls 'Puritanism' 'an admirable refuge from clarity of thought'.[101] Many of the characteristics often described as 'Puritan' were shared by many (perhaps the vast majority) of English Protestants, including the hierarchy of the English State and Church until at least 1625. What were the beliefs which were common to most Protestants in early seventeenth-century England?

Information

Protestants and what they believed

- The majority of Protestant churchmen believed in predestination: that an individual's fate after death was preordained, since the Elect are already chosen. Predestinarianism is based on the doctrine of justification by faith alone. An individual's salvation after death owes nothing to his or her good works on earth but rests entirely on the grace of Jesus Christ.
- Protestants emphasized the centrality of the Bible and its exposition through preaching. They believed that the central point of church services should be the sermon.

---

[99] J. Bossy, 'The English Catholic Community 1603–25', in A. G. R. Smith, ed., *The Reign of James VI and I* (1973), p. 95.
[100] Marshall, *Reformation England*, p. 189. It is not difficult to see why anti-Catholicism was so strong in early Stuart England.
[101] Hill, *Society and Puritanism*, pp. 1–2.

- They believed that everyone should be able to read, and that the clergy should be educated enough to preach eloquent and intelligent sermons.

- Images were viewed with suspicion as violations of the Second Commandment and largely cleared from churches during the reigns of Edward VI and Elizabeth I.

- The most powerful unifying aspect of Protestantism in this period was anti-Catholicism, both apocalyptic and political. The world-view popularized in influential books like John Foxe's *Acts and Monuments* was reinforced from 1618 by the events of the Thirty Years War against the Catholic powers of Europe. European Protestantism seemed threatened by a rising tide of Counter-Reformation Catholicism.

- Most Protestants of the seventeenth century were agreed about the form of church government they wanted: one national Church, a reformed Church but a Church with bishops.

Increasingly during the early seventeenth century, the Church in the form in which it had been established in 1559 gained wide popular acceptance. Martin Ingram's study of church court records in Wiltshire conveys 'the distinct impression that regular attendance at church, and certainly annual participation in the communion, were far more widely accepted by the 1620s and 1630s than they had been in the middle years of Elizabeth I's reign'.[102] The same may have been true of urban attitudes to the Church if the situation in two suburban parishes of London is typical, where between 80 and 98 per cent of all potential communicants received annual communions during the last years of Elizabeth I's reign and the reign of James I.[103] Slow though the process may have been, by the early seventeenth century the Church as it had been established in 1559 (along with its Book of Common Prayer, traditional festivals like Easter, Whitsuntide, Rogationtide and Christmas, as well as its emphasis on a predestinarian theology, sermons, bishops and a potent anti-Catholicism) had sunk deep roots in English popular culture.

Is it then possible, or even useful, to distinguish between Protestant supporters of the established Church and 'Puritans'? Were there real differences between 'Anglicans' and 'Puritans'? As has been emphasized above, a distinction between Anglicans and other Protestants is difficult to draw, and this remained true until at least 1625. But there is a compelling reason to retain the label 'Puritanism': without it, it would be impossible to identify individuals in early seventeenth-century England whose attitudes to life and death were shaped much more strongly than those of other Anglicans by

---

[102] Ingram, *Church Courts*, p. 108.

[103] J. Boulton, 'The limits of formal religion: the administration of Holy Communion in late Elizabethan and early Stuart London', *London Journal*, X (1984).

the Protestant principles outlined above. The differences were 'of degree, of theological temperature, so to speak, rather than of fundamental principle'. What were the characteristics of these Puritans, 'the hotter type of Protestants', or (the word they commonly used to describe themselves) 'the godly'?[104]

Information

Puritans and what they believed

- Godly Puritans had a distinctive lifestyle. Their more intense attitude towards predestinarianism meant that every aspect of their lives was dominated by it.

- They spent their days (and nights) at a high level of spiritual intensity, often undergoing long periods of introspection and self-examination in order to convince themselves that they had been chosen as members of the Elect.

- Prayer and sermons played a major part in the lives of Puritans. Some Puritans travelled outside their own parish to hear a minister whose views they agreed with.

- The godly, too, were much more influenced by anti-Catholicism and millenarianism than most Protestants. This led them to adopt a very militant attitude in seeing the English as the Elect Nation chosen by God to lead the cause of international Calvinism against the forces of Antichrist in the Thirty Years War in the early seventeenth century.

- Puritans believed passionately in the need for a godly reformation. They believed that the Reformation of the mid-sixteenth century was by no means completed and that the Church was, at best, but 'halfly reformed'. 'Popish' relics in church government needed to be abolished, but so also should sin in people's lives. All this was done not out of opposition to enjoyment for its own sake, but in order to secure God's blessing.

In the early seventeenth century Puritans were militant Protestants with distinctive lifestyles, who urged reform of the Church. Some of these characteristics are captured well in the lives of individuals. Katherine Gell regularly consulted the divine, Richard Baxter, as she did in 1655 fearing that God had allowed her 17-week baby boy to die and 'in anger throwne him into hell'. She felt that she 'should shortly follow & soe [she wrote to Baxter] into a sad condition I fell. I saw noe beame of love light of gods

---

[104] P. Collinson, *The Elizabethan Puritan Movement* (1967), pp. 26–7.

countenance nor favour for a long time.'[105] Nehemiah Wallington, a godly wood-turner in early seventeenth-century London, was brought to the brink of suicide by his 'godly doubts'.[106] The godly, too, considered the course of their lives, misfortunes as well as successes, to be dictated by Providence, by the workings of God's will. Robert Loder, a Berkshire farmer, wrote in 1616: 'This year in sowing too early I lost (the Lord being the cause thereof, but that the instrument wherewith it pleased him to work) . . . the sum of £10 at least, so exceeding full was my barley with charlock.'[107] Such anxieties were the product of what has been described as 'experimental' predestinarianism, the belief that every aspect of life was dominated by the predestinarian creed, to be distinguished from the shallow-rooted 'credal' predestinarianism of non-Puritan Protestants.

The sermon-dominated household of the godly and passion for effective preaching can be seen in the lives of other godly people. In 1653 Thomas Taylor instructed all Protestants: 'Let every master of a family see to what he is called, namely to make his house a little church, to instruct every one of his family in the fear of God, to contain every one of them under holy discipline, to pray with them and for them.' Unlike other Protestants, Puritan heads of households carried out this instruction to the letter. In William Gouge's house 'there were prayers twice daily, three times on Sunday: there was Bible-reading, and children and servants were catechized'.[108] Lady Margaret Hoby of Hackness in Yorkshire meditated privately every day, conducted household prayers and attended church several times a week. Her diary for Friday 21 December 1599 reads:

> Afer privat praier I ded a litle, and so went to church: after the sermon I praied, then dined, and, in the after none, was busy tell 5 a clock: then I returned to private praier and examenation: after supped, then hard publick praers and, after that, praied privatly, havinge reed a Chapter of the bible, and so went to bed.[109]

On Sundays, naturally, the routine of prayer, meditation and worship in Puritan households was much more rigorous. It was common to attend three sermons, take notes, and meet afterwards with other godly people to discuss the contents of the sermon. When a local minister's views were not approved of, these private meetings could become especially important and serve as alternative services to those offered in the parish church. Some Puritans might travel outside their own parish – 'gadding' was the buzzword for this among the godly – to hear a minister whose views were more agreeable. In the 1630s, Lawrence Clarkson felt that the minister of his home town, Preston in Lancashire, was 'a pitiful superstitious fellow'. Only occasionally did

---

[105] N. H. Keeble and G. F. Nuttall, eds., *Calendar of the Correspondence of Richard Baxter* (2 vols., 1991), vol. I, p. 191.

[106] P. Seaver, *Wallington's World: a Puritan artisan in seventeenth-century London* (1985), pp. 22–5.

[107] Quoted in Thomas, *Religion and the Decline of Magic*, p. 81.

[108] Hill, *Society and Puritanism*, pp. 440–1.

[109] Quoted in Cliffe, *Yorkshire Gentry*, p. 273.

'true laborious ministers of Christ' visit Preston, 'who when they came, would thunder against Superstition, and sharply reprove Sin, and prophaning the Lords-day; which to hear, tears would run down my cheeks for joy'. So he would often travel to Standish and other places 'where we could hear of a Godly minister, as several times I have gone ten miles, more or less, fasting all the day when my Parents never knew of it, and though I have been weary and hungry, yet I came home rejoycing'.[110]

The life that best captures the passionate zeal for godly reformation is that of Oliver Cromwell. He was not unique, however. He and many other Protestants had a deeply held conviction that without such 'a reformation of manners' to abolish sin in people's lives they and the nation would lose God's support, and that God would (as they graphically put it) 'spit in their face'. Their biblical studies confirmed this view, especially the account they read in the Bible of the eventual success of the Old Testament Israelites in escaping from Egyptian bondage and, after a struggle, inheriting the Promised Land. This triumph was possible only after the Israelites had won God's blessing by expiating their sins. For the godly of late sixteenth and early seventeenth-century England the lesson was clear: like the Israelites, the English would inherit the Promised Land of godly reformation only after they had undergone a spiritual 'reformation of manners'.

This was a mentality that drove some of the godly (including Oliver Cromwell, as will be seen) to become activists. Unlike Catholics, they were not content to practise their religion within their households: Puritans were evangelizers. They wanted to spread their views and to reform the Church and society in accordance with them. Puritans led the demand for an educated clergy: Puritan landlords appointed able preachers to parishes to which they owned the right of presentment; they cooperated with Puritan town corporations in appointing lecturers to preach sermons in addition to those delivered by the appointed minister. Puritans were also zealous reformers; they wanted to rid the Church of what they considered to be popish ceremonies, like bowing at the name of Jesus and the wearing of vestments by clergymen.

However, militant and activist though they were, before 1640 Puritans worked for reform *within* the existing Church. They showed no desire to destroy the framework of the established Church or to get rid of bishops. It was not until the Laudians began to have a real impact on the liturgy and practice of the Church of England in the 1630s that Puritans found themselves in serious conflict with the diocesan authorities.

Were there Protestants in England before 1640 who did not accept the established Church? If there were, they have left few traces. No doubt some of the godly individuals who met together after church services in private religious 'exercises' formed the basis for the independent 'gathered churches' which were established after 1640 (see pp. 271–2). But between the 1590s and 1640 there is little evidence that independent churches existed. The exception is in London, where in 1616 Henry Jacob established an independent church, from which before 1640 developed various offshoots in the

---

[110] Lawrence Clarkson, *The Lost Sheep Found* (1660, published by *The Rota* at the University of Exeter, 1974), p. 4.

City. However, the total membership of those independent churches was never more than 1,000.[111] Perhaps also in the 1630s there began a popular anti-episcopalian movement in response to the policies of the Laudian bishops; in Cheshire there is some evidence of this.[112] But, although these groups are inevitably obscure, there is little doubt that Independency and anti-episcopalianism in terms of numbers and influence were negligible elements in English Protestantism before 1640.

Moreover, even 'the hotter type of Protestants', the Puritans, dissociated themselves from the implication that they intended to change the fundamental structure of the Church or break away from it. It used to be fashionable to stress the revolutionary implications of Puritan ideology, on the grounds that the godly's emphasis on the individual's duty to interpret God's word would create a questioning mentality that, when extended beyond religious topics, would become a radical challenge to the established political and social structure. This is an argument that has now lost a lot of its force, largely because before 1640 the Puritans who can be identified as such were conservative upholders of the status quo. They wanted church reform, but not at the expense of political and social upheavals. When in the early 1640s it appeared that this might be the consequence of reform, many of them drew back even from that. Most Protestants accepted unquestioningly that religious diversity was a sure recipe for anarchy in society. 'If a toleration were granted', wrote Thomas Edwardes in 1646, 'men should never have peace in their families more, or ever after have command of wives, children, servants.'[113] This belief effectively bridled in Puritans any tendency towards radicalism.

Conclusion

Nevertheless, it would be foolish to suggest that the development of many different religious views in post-Reformation England, together with the other major social and intellectual changes that have been discussed in this chapter, did not produce strains and stresses that threatened the stability of early Stuart England. It is important, however, that these destabilizing effects are not exaggerated unduly.

Without any doubt, the religious differences between the godly and non-godly that have been discussed above produced tensions in some English towns and villages in early seventeenth-century England. Many of the reasons for the hostility directed at the godly are reflected in the proceedings of the bishop's court in Wiltshire in 1624. A young Wiltshire woman, Susan Kent, complained against the spiritual intensity of

---

[111] M. Tolmie, *The Triumph of the Saints: the separate churches of London 1616–49* (1977), p. 37. Unlike other London separatists, Jacob maintained contacts with those within the Church. There is evidence of a separatist congregation in Yarmouth and Baptist congregations in London, Lincoln, Coventry, Salisbury and Tiverton from the 1620s onwards: M. R. Watts, *The Dissenters from the Reformation to the French Revolution* (1978), pp. 52–3, 159, 166.

[112] J. S. Morrill, *Cheshire 1603–60: county government during the 'English Revolution'* (1974), p. 20.

[113] Thomas Edwards, *Gangraena*, part 3 (1646), p. 156.

the godly minister in her village, John Lee, rector of Wylye: 'When once he . . . takes his green book in hand', she said, 'we shall have such a deal of bibble babble that I am weary to hear it, and I can then sit down in my seat and take a good nap.' Her reaction to godly preaching is very different from Lawrence Clarkson's ecstatic comment quoted above, and probably more typical of the attitude of a young person in early Stuart England. Susan Kent also reflected the widespread hostility that the godly incurred because of their attacks on popular sports and pastimes on Sundays. 'We had a good parson here before', she is alleged to have said, 'but now we have a puritan . . . A plague or a pox in him that ever he did come hither, and I would have kept our old parson for he never did dislike with [games and dancing]. These proud puritans are up at the top now but I hope they will have a time to come as fast down as ever they come up.'[114] From the other side of the religious fence, in the 1620s the young Richard Baxter felt the force of this kind of anger as he sat in his father's godly household in Eaton Constantine in Shropshire on Sundays, trying to read the Scriptures but being distracted by 'the great disturbance of the tabor and pipe and noise in the street'. Occasionally he was tempted to join the fun outside, but (he later wrote in his autobiography) 'when I heard them call my father Puritan, it did much to cure me and alienate me from them; for I considered that my father's exercise of reading the Scripture was better than theirs, and would surely be better thought on by all men at the last; and I considered what it was for that he and the others were thus derided'.[115] In the early seventeenth-century Dorset market-town of Dorchester, these kinds of tensions were constant undercurrents before 1640. Townspeople resented the restrictions imposed on them by a town government dominated by a godly elite. The tiny Essex village of Terling, too, witnessed such tensions, caused by the attempts of godly local governors to stamp reformation on an apathetic and hostile community.[116]

It is essential for a full understanding of the history of early Stuart England that these kinds of religious friction are added to those causes of disaffection already discussed in this and the previous chapter: that is, those arising from the economic and social changes which took place as a result of dramatic rises in population and prices from the early sixteenth century onwards. The two major social changes that stand out are the growing differentiation in the distribution of wealth as the rich got richer and the poor poorer, and the extraordinary expansion of London. One consequence of these changes, when combined with an agrarian economy that struggled to muster its resources to meet the demands of a rising population, was social problems of poverty and deprivation on a scale unprecedented in England since at least the thirteenth century.

What is less certain is whether the resulting social tensions (seen, for example, in Susan Kemp's frustrated anger at the reforming aspirations of the godly and in the food riots that erupted in this period) were a major threat to the social and political stability of early Stuart England. Attempts that have been made in the past to make

---

[114] Ingram, *Church Courts*, p. 121.
[115] Quoted in K. Wrightson, *English Society 1580–1680* (1982), pp. 183–4.
[116] Underdown, *Fire from Heaven*; Wrightson and Levine, *Terling*.

direct links between some of the major social changes of this period and the extra-ordinary political instability that occurred during the 1640s and 1650s do not find much support among historians nowadays (see pp. 169–70). However, one general interpretation of social trends in the period before 1640, which suggests that a major fracture had opened up in English society by the mid-seventeenth century, has received some acceptance in recent years. It is best illustrated in the words of Keith Wrightson, in one of the best general books on the social history of early modern England written in the 1980s:

> A deep social cleavage of a new kind had opened up in English society. It was not one simply between wealth and poverty, but between respectable and plebeian culture, and it followed the line which divided not the gentry and the common people but 'the better sort' and the mass of the labouring poor. This process of transition was essentially completed by 1660.[117]

The two central propositions on which this hypothesis are based are open to question. Was there 'a deep social cleavage' measured either by wealth or by 'culture' in England by the mid-seventeenth century?

As has been seen, there are many qualifications to be made to an overly pessimistic interpretation of economic and social change in the later sixteenth and early seventeenth centuries. Although the price revolution depressed the standards of living of many (especially small farmers and landless labourers who relied largely on wages for their living), not all small farmers were forced off the land in the period before 1640; nor did all (or indeed most) labourers in this period rely on wages as the sole source of their incomes. Moreover, although the scale of agricultural progress in the century or so before 1640 was not spectacular, it was sufficient to enable England to escape the frequent subsistence crises that hit other parts of Europe in this period. Also, as has been seen, the development of private and public poor relief schemes had some success in cushioning the poor from the worst effects of deprivation. The result was to produce a society in which the divisions between rich and poor were not as polarized or as glaring as those in some parts of contemporary continental Europe, or in Ireland and Scotland.

Similar doubts exist about the reality of a division between an elite and plebeian culture along religious lines. The godly were an embattled minority in early Stuart England, but they were not drawn exclusively from one social group. Puritans can be found in all social groups in this period and not simply among 'the middling sort' or among 'the better sort'. Alongside godly peers can be found godly men and women from humble backgrounds. 'It is premature', writes Patrick Collinson, 'simply to equate the godly elite of early Stuart England with a social elite, or even with the broad band lying across the middle rungs of the social ladder.'[118] This generalization is supported by Martin Ingram's study of two Wiltshire villages, Keevil and Wylye,

---

[117] Wrightson, *English Society*, p. 227.
[118] P. Collinson, *The Religion of Protestants: the Church in English society 1559–1625* (1979), p. 241.

which shows that rector John Lee's godly reform plans (that so offended Susan Kent) 'rapidly ran out of steam'; and that 'the notion that religious commitment was conditioned by social class must be treated with caution'.[119]

In these circumstances it is difficult to make direct or major links of causation between social changes in this period and the political instability that characterized England after 1640. On closer inspection, the threat to the existing political order posed by the economic and social changes surveyed in these first two chapters was, in reality, much less serious than it seemed to some at the time and than it has seemed to others since. This is not to say that the fears and anxieties that gripped some contemporaries in the face of the economic and social changes that were taking place should be ignored. As will be seen in Part 2, they played as important a part in shaping the attitudes of many people to the political events of early Stuart England as did the rumbling fears that (it will be seen in the next chapter) many had about the future of parliaments.

---

[119] Ingram, *Church Courts*, p. 123.

3

The Elizabethan constitution

Summary

The knowledge that the Tudor and early Stuart constitution collapsed in 1640–1 inevitably colours any analysis of early seventeenth-century political, constitutional and religious history. Therefore, historians need to guard against assuming that contemporaries knew of the impending constitutional crisis and that they were preparing for it for many years beforehand. Of course, this is not true. The first part of this chapter points to the most important features of this constitution and emphasizes that it was generally accepted by the political nation and the wider population of the country, a fact often masked by those primarily interested in the early seventeenth century in order to discover the origins of the English Revolution.

But it would be misleading to obscure the stresses and tensions within the constitutional and political structure of England in the early seventeenth century. The second part of this chapter isolates three major features of the early Stuart State that threatened its long-term stability: the problem of ruling multiple kingdoms, which grew more serious with the accession of monarchs who were rulers of Scotland as well as of England, Ireland and Wales; the State's financial weakness; and differing views about the nature of the post-Reformation English Church. These problems did not make inevitable the serious political crisis faced by Charles I in 1640, nor do they 'explain' the outbreak of the Civil War in 1642. However, they did make the task of ruling early seventeenth-century Britain very difficult, since political stability depended more than ever before on monarchs exercising power with great political astuteness.

The framework of government

The king's government

Constitutional history written in terms of institutions rather than of individuals can give the impression that central government in the early seventeenth century was more formalized than it could have been when its focal point was the monarch. This, as has already been seen, is a major point made by social historians of State formation, who have shown that 'institutional histories' of the State can hide its wider participatory nature, which included a large percentage of people who were office-holders (p. 67 below). Such histories too often obscure the personal nature of the government of this period. The personal nature of English government was not new. In fifteenth-century England, for example, one of the main reasons for the contrast between the political troubles of the 1450s that climaxed in the 'Wars of the Roses' and the relative political stability that followed the accession of the Tudors in 1485 was the ineptness of Henry VI and the political acumen of Henry VII. In the seventeenth century the character of government, as well as its efficiency, still depended very much on the personality of the monarch. In this respect James I and Charles I were medieval monarchs: they ruled as well as reigned. Neither claimed absolute power; both normally acted within the common law and respected the inviolability and superiority of parliamentary statute. Yet their powers were theoretically and practically very wide; they appointed their own advisers and officials; they could obstruct parliamentary legislation by veto or by dissolution of parliament; they could dispense individuals from the law; and they took part directly and personally in the initiation of all government decisions. Much has been made by some historians of the ways in which the decisions of James I and Charles I were allegedly influenced by favourites, especially by George Villiers, duke of Buckingham between 1618 and 1628. Yet, it will be seen later that even the power of an important favourite like Buckingham was strictly limited and that both James and Charles made most of the key decisions taken by early Stuart government. 'Government' is an imprecise word at any time. But the monarch was more synonymous with early seventeenth-century English government than is a prime minister or president with governments in modern democratic States, where governmental power is more widely shared.

This is not to deny that James I and Charles I were open to many influences, voiced by different individuals and pressure groups, when they made decisions. The ultimate responsibility for authorizing the Cockayne Project was the king's, but James was persuaded to do so by his advisers, who believed that the project would be very profitable to the crown, and by Cockayne and his fellow merchants, who argued that it would be of commercial benefit to the nation. Early Stuart kings had formal institutions, which had developed in the sixteenth century, to help them make decisions. The first was the office of principal secretary, which had been held by Thomas Cromwell in the reign of Henry VIII and by William Cecil, Lord Burghley in the reign of Elizabeth I. By the early seventeenth century it had become usual for the office to be called secretary of state, and for it to be held by two people, who were theoretically equal in status, though in practice there was a senior and a junior secretary; when in 1600 John Herbert was appointed as 'second secretary' to William Cecil's son, Sir Robert Cecil, he was popularly and scornfully known as 'Mr Secondary Herbert'. Under the Cecils the office of secretary developed a sophisticated bureaucracy and a wide degree of influence; they were the closest advisers of Elizabeth I and James I and the main channels by which the monarchs communicated with their subjects and with foreign powers. Secondly, the early Stuarts inherited the privy council as an advisory, administrative and judicial body, which had developed in the previous century from the royal council of medieval kings.

However, institutional history can hide the realities of where power lay; this is true of the history of the secretaryship of state and of the privy council. The former was important when the Cecils were secretaries because William and Robert were men of outstanding abilities. It became less important from the death of Robert Cecil in 1612 to 1642, when it was held by lesser men than the Cecils. Too much significance can also be attached to the privy council. The fact that it grew in size, from thirteen in 1601 to forty by 1625, increased the likelihood that important decisions would be taken outside meetings of the full council, as was probably also the case in the previous reign. Some matters came to be discussed by small standing committees – on trade, Ireland, the militia and the colonies under Charles I – or by ad hoc committees of privy councillors. One of these meetings of a selected group of councillors met officially to discuss foreign affairs, but in practice it dealt with many other matters. Contemporaries called it 'the cabinet council', though it is doubtful if one could trace (as some historians have hoped to do) a continuous development from it to the later cabinet. As far as early seventeenth-century government is concerned, 'the cabinet council' was only one (and probably not the most important) of many private semi-official meetings between the king and men chosen by him, which are unfortunately not recorded, but which were at the core of decision taking in central government in early Stuart England.

'Policy', like 'government', is also a word that needs to be used with great care in an early seventeenth-century context. It is often assumed that James I and Charles I and their advisers had long-term, coherent plans to initiate changes in contemporary institutions and society. However, it is unlikely that they had such 'policies'. Rather one is inclined to think that early Stuart kings met each situation as it arose and reacted accordingly. Later commentators have sometimes interpreted what were often a series of panic reactions to short-term crises as a long-term strategy. The outstanding example of this is the common belief that sixteenth- and seventeenth-century governments had a 'mercantilist' economic policy. 'Mercantilism', however, was the invention of Adam Smith in the late eighteenth century, who used it to support his belief that State intervention in the economy was harmful. It was later taken up by a protectionist school of historians in Germany and in England in the late nineteenth and early twentieth centuries to support their case in favour of State intervention. 'Mercantilism' is intelligible with reference to the later ideological debate between free trade and protection. It has little to do with the attitudes of early seventeenth-century govern-ments.[1] When James I established committees of merchants and politicians during the severe trade crisis of the early 1620s, he did so in order that they should recommend ways of ending the crisis, not that they should draw up any economic policy document on the future of the English economy.

Information

The royal court

If the king was the focus of early seventeenth-century government, the royal court was the main arena of politics. This has only been fully recognized in recent years. It carried out this function in two principal ways.

- First, by making available royal patronage, both in the concrete shape of grants of offices, money and land, and in the less tangible form of royal support and influence. Successful monarchs were those who used the court as a means of dispensing patronage freely and widely.
- Secondly, by acting as a forum for political debate. Interpretations of early Stuart politics that stress a prevailing consensus are misleading. The court was seldom united, but was the scene of constant competition between factions for the patronage of the king and frequent debates between groups recommending different courses of action to the king. The two often merged.

The bitter quarrel at James's court in the early 1620s between Buckingham and Cranfield, for example, was a personal battle for political survival as well as an argument about the desirability of declaring war against Spain. In these circumstances, bountiful monarchs and divided courts were a normal part of the framework of royal government.[2] As will be seen, abnormal political tensions grew when monarchs were not able to contain political debates within the court, were not bountiful enough, or did not distribute their patronage and favour widely enough.

The formal royal administrative and financial bureaucracy at the disposal of early Stuart kings is an apparent striking contrast with the informal way in which decisions were reached. Professor Aylmer has examined the administrative machinery through

---

[1] D. C. Coleman, ed., *Revisions in Mercantilism* (1969), *passim*.
[2] L. L. Peck, ' "For a king not to be bountiful were a fault": perspectives on court patronage in early Stuart England', *J.B.S.*, XXV (1986); L. L. Peck, *Court Patronage and Corruption in Early Stuart England* (1990).

which early Stuart kings communicated with their subjects and foreign powers – using the sign manual and signet in the secretaries' office, the privy seal held by the lord privy seal, and the great seal held by the lord chancellor – and the formal financial departments: the exchequer, the court of wards, and the duchy of Lancaster.[3] The importance and growth in size of this bureaucracy ought not to be minimized; it formed the basis of a powerful civil service which developed under the last two Stuart kings. But compared with the large numbers of civil servants in the governments of William III and Queen Anne, or even with the sizeable bureaucracy of the French monarchy in the early seventeenth century, there were very few people employed within the early Stuart administrative system.[4] Indeed, it may be misleading to talk in terms of an early Stuart 'administrative system'. Certainly there was no administrative system in the modern sense of a non-political civil service, made up of departments, each with its own separate and jealously guarded areas of jurisdiction. The court was the centre of the king's administration, as well as of politics. There was no division between politicians and administrators in the early seventeenth century. The secretaries of state and privy councillors were the king's political advisers as well as his chief administrators. The concept of government 'departments' is also anachronistic. Administration and financial institutions were called 'courts' or 'councils' and each had overlapping functions and jurisdictions. The exchequer, the major financial 'department', and the chancery, part of the machinery of administration, were both also courts of law. It is true that the machinery for collecting and spending royal revenue was more rigidly organized than the administrative bureaucracy. The exchequer consisted of the upper exchequer responsible for auditing accounts and the lower exchequer for the receipt and expenditure of revenue, and was headed by the lord treasurer and his junior, the chancellor of the exchequer. It dealt with all crown income except royal feudal income, which was administered by the court of wards, and receipts from the duchy of Lancaster. However, the bureaucracy that dealt with the latter ought to be a reminder of the major differences between early seventeenth-century central administration and a modern departmentalized civil service. The duchy of Lancaster was responsible for managing those estates which had come to the crown in 1399, it collected some royal revenues, it was a court of law, and it exercised palatinate jurisdiction in Lancashire by means of a system of courts which duplicated those at Westminster.

Finally, the most striking difference between early seventeenth-century administration and its modern counterpart is that official salaries were very low, ranging from £100 p.a. for secretaries of state to clerks of the signet who received no annual salary.[5] Although official salaries also included pensions, annuities and subsistence allowances, officials were expected to get the bulk of their income from fees and gratuities paid to them by clients. Such payments were an accepted part of the administrative procedure,

---

[3] G. E. Aylmer, *The King's Servants: the civil service of Charles I* (1961).

[4] For the bureaucratic explosion of the 1690s and 1700s, see Chapter 14. In early seventeenth-century France there were 40,000 royal officials, compared with only 1,200 employed in England by Charles I, P. Williams, *The Tudor Regime* (1979), p. 107; Aylmer, *The King's Servants*, p. 440.

[5] Aylmer, *The King's Servants*, pp. 203–4.

but clearly these could (and sometimes did) go over the narrow borderline which separated them from corrupt payments made to bribe officials.

Local government

For most ordinary people in early seventeenth-century England, the king's government was remote. Much more familiar would have been the major officials of local government: lord lieutenants, sheriffs, undersheriffs and justices of the peace in the counties; high constables of the hundreds (or wapentakes or rapes); petty constables (or headboroughs), overseers of the poor, surveyors of highways, and churchwardens in the parishes; officers of town corporations; and officials of the council of the north, the council in the Marches of Wales and the church courts. Indeed, although the major offices were dominated by the landed gentry, men of humbler origins – farmers, tradesmen and craftsmen – were expected to serve in lesser local government posts, especially in parishes and towns. In that sense local government in the early seventeenth century represented a wide segment of the local community. Therefore, tension between the local community and central government was perhaps inevitable in this period, especially when the latter attempted to interfere in local affairs. Not surprisingly, this has been the major theme highlighted by the many local and regional studies on the early seventeenth century which have appeared in the last forty years or so.[6] Inevitably there was a conflict of interests between the government's desire to impose its decision on the country and county communities, which resented interference in their affairs by outsiders.

The extent and seriousness of that conflict, however, can be exaggerated. Indeed, as has been noted already, a predominant feature of English government in the late sixteenth and early seventeenth centuries is the cooperation between the crown and its most powerful subjects among the political nation. Successful kingship in early modern England still depended, as it had in the fifteenth century, on maintaining what K. B. McFarlane, one of the best historians of later medieval England, called 'the community of interests between the crown and baronage'.[7] Nor is this surprising since local government was largely in the hands of locally powerful men. Most lord lieutenants were wealthy noblemen and deputy lieutenants were rich gentlemen with estates within the areas under their jurisdictions. Moreover, although the crown (and later the parliamentary and republican regimes during the 1640s and 1650s) attempted to control justices of the peace by means of assize judges, by the fear of dismissal and by sporadic purges of men considered to be unreliable, county commissions of the peace in the seventeenth century almost invariably reflected the structure of the upper elite of landed society in the English provinces.

By the early seventeenth century, lord lieutenants, deputy lieutenants and justices of the peace were the key officials of English local government. The Tudor origins and development of the office of lord lieutenant are paralleled by the declining power and status of sheriffs.

---

[6] See the Bibliographical note, pp. 517–18.
[7] K. B. McFarlane, 'Service, maintenance and politics', in his *The Nobility of Later Medieval England* (1973).

Information

Sheriffs

Their main duties were:

- to preside over the county court, which had only one important function: to organize the election of knights of the shire (MPs representing the county constituencies). They only wielded significant power at election times, which in the early seventeenth century were infrequent.
- to summon people to attend quarter sessions, to collect fines and to execute writs.

The minor role of sheriffs in county government was in great contrast to the major one they had had in the Middle Ages. By the early seventeenth century not only was the office toothless and tedious but it was also an expensive one to hold. Sheriffs were expected to pay the fees of their under-officers, provide hospitality for visiting assize judges, and to be personally accountable for the money they were charged to collect. During the shrieval year 1637–8 the arrears on the ship money tax in Yorkshire were £1,237, and Sir Thomas Danby, the unfortunate sheriff who was responsible for collecting the tax, was ordered to pay the arrears 'to his great damage'.[8] Not surprisingly, when the time came for the monarch to 'prick' the names of the sheriffs from lists prepared by the privy council, the latter was snowed under with letters from those who were trying desperately to avoid being chosen.

Information

Lord lieutenants

Their main duties were:

- to organize the military defence of groups of counties in times of crisis
- to take on ad hoc duties given them by the crown.

---

[8] Cliffe, *Yorkshire Gentry*, p. 253.

By the late sixteenth and early seventeenth centuries, lord lieutenants had largely taken over the roles and reputations of sheriffs as key local officials. Paradoxically, it was during the reign of the *rex pacificus* (James I) that the lord lieutenant became a permanent part of English local government, wielding real power unlike his modern counterpart. In 1626 there were lieutenants in all counties, although some lieutenants were responsible for more than one county.[9] Naturally, their effectiveness, and that of their deputies, varied. It needs little imagination to realize what must have been the defects of a militia which was starved of money, reliant on people who were mainly farmers to maintain their own arms and to bring them to the musters, and in which most of the training was done by deputy lieutenants who had no professional military experience. This is why during the early seventeenth century there were sporadic efforts to reform the militia and to introduce muster-masters: men who were familiar with the modern techniques in drilling soldiers, new tactics and armaments which were being introduced in continental armies under the inspiration of Gustavus Adolphus. These efforts at reform culminated in Charles I's scheme for an 'exact militia'.

Information

Justices of the peace (JPs)

Important though the lieutenancy was, JPs bore the main burden of local government in the seventeenth century, as in the previous century. JPs were members of commissions of the peace ('the Bench') that were appointed by the crown to serve in all counties throughout England and Wales. The administrative and judicial duties of JPs defy brief description. These duties grew greatly during this period, as did the size of the commissions of the peace. Moreover, in some counties meetings of groups of JPs between quarter sessions, which had often been held informally, received institutional recognition with the development of petty sessions (encouraged by a privy council order of 1605). Given that the duties of JPs were burdensome and that they were carried out without any pay, it is slightly puzzling why a place on the commission of the peace, in great contrast to the office of sheriff, was such a prized one. The answer lies in the fact that gentlemen were taught from birth that it was the duty of a 'perfect gentleman' to serve the community, as well as in the more practical consideration that JPs held high social status and local power.

---

[9] L. Boynton, *The Elizabethan Militia 1558–1638* (1967); J. C. Sainty, *Lieutenants of Counties 1585–1642* (*B.I.H.R.* supplement, 1970), pp. 1–9.

An important function of lord lieutenants, deputy lieutenants and JPs was to act as points of contact between the crown and the localities. They acted as means of channelling to the localities decisions made by the crown and privy council, as well as being essential sources of information for the royal government about opinion in the country.[10] The government also had other means of maintaining contact with the localities and of dispersing and gathering information. The council of the north (based at York and with a jurisdiction covering Yorkshire, Northumberland, Cumberland and Westmorland) and the council in the Marches of Wales (which governed Wales, as well as Shropshire, Glamorgan, Worcestershire and Herefordshire, from its headquarters at Ludlow in Shropshire) were staffed by professional lawyers and local men who were directly responsible to the privy council. The justices of assize, who travelled on their legal circuits hearing cases too serious to be dealt with at quarter sessions, were also used to communicate privy council orders to the localities, to lecture justices of the peace on their duties, and to provide the crown with the names of reliable men to be appointed to local government offices. Lord Keeper Finch told a gathering of justices of assize that they were 'the great surveyors of the kingdom on whom lesser officers should wait as on the king himself'.[11] The Church, too, played an important role in buttressing the authority of the crown, which was very natural at a time when it was believed that religious uniformity was inseparable from political order. Not only could the crown rely on the votes of the twenty-six archbishops and bishops in the House of Lords, but the Church was also the main organ of censorship: all printed books and pamphlets, as well as schoolmasters, had to be approved by it. Not only did the Church control public opinion, it also moulded it. The pulpit was the most important means of disseminating government propaganda and information in the days before the development of other means of mass communication. Bishops, too, were agents of the central government in the localities, another means by which the privy council attempted to get objective assessments of the state of affairs in provincial England.

In these circumstances, when contacts between the crown and the country were so frequent, it would be rash to identify a 'court versus country' divide as a major feature of English government in the early seventeenth century. England's geography and its history militated against the appearance of such a division. In contrast to France, for example, England is a small country, and even northern and western areas of the country that were often referred to as 'isolated' and 'backward' regions (like Lancashire, Northumberland and Cornwall) were only a few days' journey from London by horseback or coach. Moreover, as a group of eminent Anglo-Saxon historians has pointed out, England (in European terms) has a long history as a unified State:

---

[10] K. Sharpe, 'Crown, parliament and locality: government and communication in early Stuart England', *E.H.R*, CI (1986).

[11] Quoted by Ivan Roots, 'The central government and the local community', in E. W. Ives, ed., *The English Revolution 1600–60* (1968), p. 41.

The origins of the security of the English state lie in the length of its history. This is the determinative contrast between England and other great states of Europe. In no other has there been such continuity in the exercise of effective authority over so wide an area for so long. Cnut's writ ran from Yorkshire to Sussex and from Norfolk to Cheshire. So has that of all his successors, brief intervals of civil war apart. Continuity in the exercise of power brought with it, and was sustained by, continuity in the institutions of government.[12]

Ought one, then, to abandon the concept of 'the county community'?[13] It would be unwise to reject the work of many historians who in the 1960s and 1970s stressed the importance of provincial loyalties in explaining the workings of early seventeenth-century politics and government. When people wrote or spoke about their county as their 'country', they were expressing a social and political reality. This is most obviously true of the greater landed gentry in a county like Sussex, for example, where Anthony Fletcher has shown that the gentry were bound together in county-wide relationships of kinship and patronage. In Kent, where 'virtually all the county families could have been incorporated into a single family tree', kinship was a cohesive force behind county unity and insularity.[14] However, common experience of divisions and hatreds within families ought to be a warning that family connections are not necessarily as solid a basis for political and social alliances as bonds based on patronage and clientage.[15] K. B. McFarlane described the relationship between patron and client in the fifteenth century as 'one of mutual convenience and profit'; writing about the sixteenth century, J. E. Neale felt it was 'an association of self-interest, a mutual benefit society. Members expected their patron to sponsor their interests at court and cast his mantle over them whenever the prestige of his name or the cogency of his recommendatory letters might help.'[16] At the time, the phrase most commonly used to describe this relationship was 'good lordship'. In the same way as the crown distributed patronage to its greater subjects, so the latter granted offices, leases of land, protection and help in court cases, and so on, to lesser magnates. McFarlane's colourful description of the system operating in fifteenth-century society applies equally well to the early seventeenth century. 'These busy letter-writers', he wrote of medieval gentlemen, 'cover their crisp sheets of paper, one after another, ladling butter, rolling logs and scratching backs.'[17] Provincial insularity was deep-rooted and persistent in English society.

---

[12] J. Campbell et al., eds., *The Anglo-Saxons* (1982), quoted in P. Corrigan and D. Sayer, eds., *The Great Arch: English state formation as cultural revolution* (1985), p. 15.

[13] C. Holmes, 'The county community in Stuart historiography', *J.B.S.*, XXXVII (1987).

[14] Fletcher, *Sussex*, ch. 2; A. Everitt, 'The county community' in Ives, *English Revolution*, p. 54.

[15] The danger of assuming that family relationships are the basis of political alliances has been well illustrated by work on the politics of the reigns of William III and Queen Anne: see pp. 363–4.

[16] McFarlane, *The Nobility*, p. 113; J. E. Neale, 'The Elizabethan political scene', *Proceedings of the British Academy* (1948), p. 106.

[17] McFarlane, *The Nobility*, p. 114.

Moreover, 'the county community' was a reality for people other than the gentry. Analyses of those who sat on county grand juries, and who participated in the work of county quarter sessions, assizes and county parliamentary elections, suggest that the county was a forum of some importance for the conduct of political affairs in early seventeenth-century England. The 'participants [in county affairs, writes Anthony Fletcher in a perceptive essay on this topic] included numerous yeomen and townsmen, even husbandmen, craftsmen and labourers, as well as the gentry',[18] a point now reinforced by social historians like Braddick and Hindle (see p. 38).

What one should not do, however, is build on the recognition of the reality of 'the county community' the twin assumptions that this was the only (or even the most important) focus of people's loyalties in early seventeenth-century England, or that when people identified with their 'county community' they were uninterested in or hostile to affairs that were taking place in the country at large. When people of all social groups regularly moved about the country (see pp. 19–21) and had a common language and set of political institutions, it is highly unlikely that this would have been the case. Sir Richard Grosvenor, a Cheshire gentleman, was probably not unusual when in the early 1620s he used the word 'country' to mean Cheshire and also 'some concept of the common good that transcended pure localism and instead referred to the national community of which the local formed but a part'.[19] People were influenced at this time (as at other times) by a series of overlapping loyalties: to family, kin, patron, neighbourhood, county and country. They were not insulated from affairs in the country or national political issues. As the political history of the Stuart age that is detailed in the rest of this book demonstrates, awareness of national political issues spread (particularly during the 1620s, 1640s, late 1670s and early 1680s, 1690s and early 1700s) beyond a tiny metropolitan elite deep into the English provinces and among a large section of English society.

In these circumstances it would be wrong to assume that, since local gentlemen were jealous both of their spheres of influence as magistrates and of the independence of their 'countries', they were necessarily 'opponents' of the crown. For much of the early seventeenth century, local magistrates found no difficulty in reconciling their loyalties to the crown and to their 'countries'.

Parliament

Forty years ago it would have been fairly easy to describe the role and the development of parliament in the framework of government in the early seventeenth century. The thesis developed by Professor J. E. Neale in his books on sixteenth-century parliaments, and by Professor Wallace Notestein in his work on parliaments in the early seventeenth

---

[18] A. Fletcher, 'National and local awareness in the county community', in H. Tomlinson, ed., *Before the English Civil War* (1983), p. 152.

[19] R. Cust and P. Lake, 'Sir Richard Grosvenor and the rhetoric of magistracy', *B.I.H.R.*, LIV (1981).

century, was widely recognized as the 'correct' one.[20] The Reformation Parliament of the 1530s, so went the orthodox view, marked a turning point in the history of parliament's place in the constitution. Henry VIII's decision to carry out the Dissolution of the Monasteries and the break with Rome by parliamentary statutes awakened among members of the House of Commons a demand that they should have a more important place in the government of the country. So it was natural that during the reign of Elizabeth I this 'rise of parliament' should continue, and Neale described the way in which it seemed to do so as the House of Commons continually demanded in the late sixteenth century the right to express itself on matters which hitherto had been regarded as the concern solely of the monarch: religion, the queen's marriage and the succession. Moreover, Neale showed how the later parliaments of Elizabeth's reign saw important procedural innovations (the introduction of rules to facilitate orderly debates, voting by formal divisions instead of by acclamation, and the practice of sending bills to committees) and the establishment of special parliamentary privileges (freedom from arrest and freedom of speech for MPs). All this, Neale believed, reflected the attainment by parliament of 'institutional maturity'; by 1597, he wrote, parliament's adolescence was over. Neale's view of Elizabethan parliaments neatly complemented that already current about early seventeenth-century parliaments. In 1924 Notestein had delivered the Raleigh Lecture on *The Winning of the Initiative by the House of Commons*. Although he was careful not to press his argument too far,[21] later writers assumed that he meant that by continuing procedural development, especially the establishment of the Committee of the Whole House, the House of Commons aimed to free itself from royal control and to claim the right to be consulted in the initiation of government policy. This the House of Commons persevered in during the early seventeenth century in the face of determined resistance from James I and Charles I, who would, if they had been given a free hand, have dispensed with parliaments altogether.

As a result of later studies, however, many of the assumptions on which the Neale–Notestein thesis is based are questionable.[22] First, the concept of the 'rise of parliament', of a parliament growing from early sixteenth-century infancy to late sixteenth-century adolescence and early seventeenth-century maturity, is called in question by Professor Roskell's studies of the reigns of Richard II and Henry IV, when parliament played an active political role, claiming to control the crown's finances and ministers.[23] Some historians are too eager to anthropomorphize institutions. Some are also too ready to equate an abundance of records with institutional importance and vice versa. In the

---

[20] J. E. Neale, *Elizabethan House of Commons*; *Elizabeth I and her parliaments* (2 vols., 1953, 1957); W. Notestein, *The Winning of the Initiative by the House of Commons* (1924).

[21] Conrad Russell, 'Perspectives in parliamentary history 1604–29', *History*, LI (1976), pp. 3–4.

[22] Russell, 'Perspectives', pp. 1–27; C. Russell, *Parliaments and English Politics 1621–29* (1979); G. R. Elton, 'Parliament under the Tudors: its functions and fortunes', *H.J.*, XXII, pp. 255–78; M. A. R. Graves, *Elizabethan Parliaments 1559–1601* (1987).

[23] J. S. Roskell, 'Perspectives in English parliamentary history', in E. B. Fryde and Edward Miller, eds., *Historical Studies of the English Parliament* (1971), II, pp. 296–323.

case of parliament and its records this is not necessarily true. Late fourteenth- and early fifteenth-century parliaments left few records, but they were called more frequently and sat for longer periods than two centuries later. Nor are procedural developments or the assertion of privileges indications of enhanced parliamentary power. MPs were not protected by privileges of free speech or freedom from arrest. After many of the parliaments of the reigns of Elizabeth I, James I and Charles I, the crown had no compunction in arresting and imprisoning those MPs with whom it was displeased.

Did MPs in the early seventeenth century want to be consulted in the formulation of government policy, and were they aiming to enhance the constitutional powers of parliament? Since it has already been suggested that the concept of 'government policy' is anachronistic at this time, it is likely that the answer is 'no'. What then, did MPs consider to be the role of parliament in the early seventeenth century? For most MPs, parliament represented the correct, traditional way of securing legislation and the resolution of grievances. They wanted legislation, however, not to bring about fundamental changes in government or society, but to remedy local grievances. Most parliamentary business in the late sixteenth and early seventeenth centuries was concerned with local, private bills. Most MPs also came to parliament to pursue political ambitions at court, to secure office or favours for themselves or for their dependants at home. The demands made on MPs, then, came from a wide section of the local communities. This is why it is often difficult to identify one particular House of Commons' point of view on any issue. On the contrary, the Commons was no more united than was the court, which is one important reason why (as will be seen later) it is too simplistic to interpret early seventeenth-century politics in terms of 'Court *versus* Commons', 'King *versus* Parliament', or 'Government *versus* Opposition' (see below, p. 132).

There are two more assumptions about parliament in the early seventeenth century that are dubious. First of all, it may be that previous historical studies have placed too much emphasis on the House of Commons. The Upper House played a far from subordinate role in the politics of the late sixteenth and early seventeenth centuries. The size of its membership grew from 81 in 1603 to 128 in 1625, reflecting its enhanced importance. It will be seen how often political rivalries at court spilled over into the House of Lords. Certainly contemporaries considered the Upper House to be at least as important as the House of Commons in the early seventeenth century. Finally, it can be too readily assumed that early Stuart kings wanted to get rid of parliaments. There is no evidence for this. For the crown, as for MPs, parliament had important functions. Parliament was necessary to vote taxation, 'extraordinary' supply without which by the early seventeenth century the crown found it very difficult to manage. Above all, however, parliament was, as Professor Elton has called it, 'a point of contact', a place not only where MPs could pursue their political ambitions, but also where the court could gauge opinion in the local communities, and where it could explain the reasons behind its decisions.[24] In 1629, it is true, Charles I decided that the disadvantages of parliamentary

---

[24] G. R. Elton, 'Tudor government: points of contact: Parliament', *T.R.H.S.*, 5th ser., XXIV (1974), pp. 183–200.

government temporarily outweighed its advantages. He did not relish the prospect of meeting parliament again very soon and, not surprisingly after the stormy parliaments of 1626 and 1628–9, he wanted to rule without it for as long as possible. But there is no evidence that Charles I wanted to rule permanently without parliament.

Order and obedience

One beneficial effect of 'revisionism' was to make clear that the large area of common ground between early Stuart kings and their most important subjects is often ignored. The latter were far from being the factious, embryonic rebels they are sometimes portrayed as being. The above description of the framework of early Stuart governments illustrates that the members of the political nation had strong motives of self-interest in the maintenance of the existing system of government. The central government, the court, absorbed their political ambitions and was a lavish source of patronage. The system of local government allowed them to retain power and to benefit from very low taxation. Moreover, existing social and political order was supported by a formidable political ideology, which both early Stuart kings and the majority of their subjects accepted.

As will be seen, there was room for ideological differences about the exact nature of what was generally known as England's 'ancient constitution' and its 'fundamental laws', partly because they had never been defined. When Edmund Waller asked for a definition of 'the fundamental law' in the House of Commons in 1641, he was told that if he did not know the answer, he had no right to sit in parliament.[25] However, the view of the constitution that gained general acceptance was that established by the fifteenth-century lawyer Sir John Fortescue: that 'the ancient constitution' was a balanced one; kings ought to rule not alone (*dominium regale*) but with the consent of the people represented in parliament (*dominium politicum et regale*). Yet everyone accepted the king as 'the head' of the 'body politic' or as 'the key' of 'the arch of government'. Another common metaphor to express the same thing was the Great Chain of Being, which bound everyone in a relationship of inferiority to the person above him in the chain, and of superiority to the person immediately below him. Everyone owed obedience to his superior and protection to his inferior. It was a doctrine well expressed by Sir John Fortescue, who was widely read in the early seventeenth century:

> God created as many different kinds of things as he did creatures, so that there is no creature which does not differ in some respect superior or inferior to all the rest. So that from the highest angel down to the lowest of his kind there is absolutely not found an angel that has not a superior and an inferior; nor from man down to the meanest worm is there any creature which is not in some respect superior to one creature and inferior to another. So that there is nothing which the bond of order does not embrace.[26]

---

[25] J. A. Pocock, *The Fundamental Law and the Ancient Constitution* (1959), p. 48, n. 2.
[26] Quoted in Anthony Fletcher, *Tudor Rebellions* (2nd edn., 1973), p. 5.

There were sound, practical arguments for not breaking the chain; if this happened, the inevitable consequence would be anarchy. Already there was a foretaste of what could happen in the presence in early Stuart England of migrant labourers, masterless men and women, who could not be integrated into the 'great chain' of order and dependence. The need for obedience was reinforced by the teaching of the Church in its role as a mouthpiece of government propaganda. Since 'the powers that be are ordained of God', the Church taught that disobedience to politically constituted authority was not only treason but also sinful. Even rebellion against a tyrant was unjustified. 'Let him [the monarch] rage, kill, massacre, hee is but a storm, sent of God to chastise his children', said William Goodwin in 1614. 'We may not *conspire* against them; our *hands bound* we may not so much as *lift up* our little *finger against them.*'[27] The doctrine of obedience was extended to relations between husbands and wives, parents and children, employers and employees, landlords and tenants. Propertied people, therefore, had strong motives for obeying the old constitution. The inevitable consequences of political change were felt to be escalating disorder.

It is easier to understand why the upper classes accepted the old constitution than it is to explain why the lower orders in early Stuart society did not pose a great threat to it. Despite the enormous inequality in the distribution of wealth, there was no large-scale popular challenge in the early seventeenth century to the established social and political order. It is true that the times were punctuated by riots and popular distur-bances: the Midland rising of 1607 and revolts in Wiltshire in the early 1630s against enclosures; grain riots in many southern counties in 1630–1, popular protests against fen drainage, enclosure and forest laws in the 1630s and early 1640s. But most riots in this period tended to be small scale; in Kent between 1558 and 1640 there was no popular disturbance involving over 100 people.[28] Most also were very limited in aim; it was common, for example, for grain rioters, having prevented grain from leaving their locality, to return it to the authorities. There are as yet only a few tentative answers to explain why there was no great popular rebellion in sixteenth- and early seventeenth-century England against the established political order.[29] It may be that poverty and dearth were such common features of the lives of ordinary men and women in this period that they were accepted stoically. In case they were not, the Church and gov-ernment offered persuasive explanations – bad harvests were punishments for people's sins, while high food prices were caused by the activities of middlemen – which, in explaining the reasons for poverty, perhaps made it easier to bear. Another possibility

---

[27] William Goodwin, *A Sermon . . . 1614*, quoted in M. Judson, *The Crisis of the Constitution* (1949), p. 181.

[28] Peter Clark, 'Popular protest and disturbance in Kent 1558–1640', *Econ. H.R.*, 2nd ser., XXIX (1976), p. 379.

[29] Clark, 'Popular protests'; John Walter and Keith Wrightson, 'Dearth and the social order in early mod-ern England', *P. & P.*, LXXI (1976), pp. 22–42; B. Sharp, *In Contempt of all Authority: rural artisans and riot in the west of England 1586–1660* (1980); J. Walter and J. Morrill, 'Order and disorder in the English Revolution', in A. Fletcher and J. Stevenson, eds., *Order and Disorder in Early Modern England* (1985); J. Walter, 'The social economy of dearth in early modern England', in J. Walter and R. Schofield, eds., *Famine, Disease and the Social Order in Early Modern England* (1989).

is that public and private poor relief, although it did not cure poverty, at least helped to alleviate its worst effects. The authorities did act in times of economic crisis to relieve extreme distress, by controlling grain prices, distributing grain to famine areas and ordering JPs to administer existing poor relief regulations. The Books of Orders in 1630–1 are an example of this (see below, pp. 150–1). The paternal role of early seventeenth-century magistrates may have contributed to the apparent political quiescence of the masses in this period. Yet it is striking that, even when the relief machinery did not work and local people resorted to violence, the main aim of rioters appears to have been to get the authorities to act and to enforce existing regulations. Riots in the early seventeenth century were not directed against the existing social and political order, but on the contrary, were aimed at its maintenance. There is no more striking illustration of the extent to which the doctrine of deference and obedience permeated early Stuart society.

Stresses within the Elizabethan constitution: political and religious divisions and 'the public sphere'

Historical revision which emphasizes the large measure of agreement between the early Stuart monarchy and its subjects is necessary. It can, of course, be carried too far.[30] The Elizabethan constitution did collapse in 1640–1, and the questions of why this occurred and when it became inevitable are among the major ones facing historians of early Stuart England. These are questions that will be fully addressed in Part 2 below. Here the main aim is to pick out three aspects of the framework of government in early Stuart England that threatened to disrupt the harmony between the crown and many of its subjects before 1640: the problems James I and Charles I faced when ruling their multiple kingdoms of England, Ireland and Scotland; the unreformed state of crown finances; and the question of whether further reform of the English Church was necessary. What ensured that all these problems would be difficult to solve without causing political tension is that inherent in the concept of 'the ancient constitution' was the assumption that the existing framework of government was perfect. There was therefore a possibility that anyone who proposed reform was at risk of being smeared as a dangerous 'innovator' who was undermining the framework of 'the ancient constitution' and therefore threatening traditional values. By proposing changes in the methods of government and in the Church in the early seventeenth century, the crown found itself open to these charges. In a reversal of the roles normally ascribed to them by later historians, contemporaries came to see the crown and the court, not the parliamentary classes, as revolutionaries.

What also ensured that the differences rooted in these stresses with the Elizabethan constitution would be deepened was the development of 'the public sphere'.

---

[30] On 'revisionism' and 'counter-revisionism', see the Bibliographical note, pp. 517–18.

Information

'The public sphere'

This is a phrase invented by a German sociologist, Jürgen Habermas, whose work was first published in German in 1965 but was not translated into English until 1989. Habermas used the term to refer to the rise of public opinion in politics, which he dated in England to the early eighteenth century, largely amongst a literate urban bourgeoisie.[31] As many have shown since then, popular political awareness and popular debates about political issues in England long pre-dated the eighteenth century and can be seen from the later sixteenth century onwards. They manifested themselves in the development of the popular press, manuscript newletters, rumour and word-of-mouth gossip, and many other ways (principally by the medium of coffee houses in the seventeenth century).

The problem of multiple kingdoms

The first of the problems facing the early Stuarts was new. It is true that Wales had been effectively integrated into and subordinated to English rule, law and institutions since the early sixteenth century. But, although the Tudors had claimed to be kings of Ireland since 1541, English authority in Ireland during the sixteenth century was continually met by Irish opposition and frequently outright rebellion. Moreover, Scotland before 1603 was an independent country with a long history of hostility to its southern neighbour and with strong connections with England's continental enemies, especially France. In 1603, however, England acquired a monarch who was not only king of England and Wales but also in a position to exercise effective authority over the whole of Ireland, and who was also king of Scotland. The year 1603 therefore marks the advent of a new era, marked by rule of the multiple kingdoms of the British Isles by a single monarch based in London.

The new era brought with it both potential opportunities and problems.[32] One of the most attractive opportunities to the English was that of establishing their authority over Ireland. During the sixteenth century Tudor monarchs had had, at best, patchy success in doing this. The proclamation of Henry VIII as king of Ireland in 1541 was not matched by his success in exercising kingship there, and the subsequent attempts

---

[31] Jürgen Habermas, *The Structural Transformation of the Public Sphere: an enquiry into a category of bourgeois society* (1989).

[32] C. Russell, 'The British problem and the English Civil War', *History*, LXXII (1987).

Figure 3.1 Frontispiece of a pamphlet called *The World is Ruled and Governed by Opinion*, 1641, satirizing the growing importance of public opinion in contemporary affairs. The figure of Opinion sits blindfolded in a tree on whose branches are hung many pamphlets.
Source: © The Trustees of the British Museum. All rights reserved.

of Edward VI and Elizabeth to impose Protestant English rule on Ireland met fierce resistance. Some English 'plantations' (colonial settlements) were established in Ireland in Munster and Connaught, but most were disrupted by Irish rebellions. The most serious rebellions came during England's war with Spain when the Irish rebels received military aid from Spain. During the 1590s, rebellion in Ulster was especially serious, largely due to the charismatic leadership of the rebels by Hugh O'Neill, earl of Tyrone. The earl of Essex's attempt to crush Tyrone's rebellion in 1599 failed miserably. However, Essex's successor as lord deputy of Ireland, Charles Blount, Lord Mountjoy, in the last years of Elizabeth's reign achieved the military success that had eluded Essex and many of his predecessors, and O'Neill surrendered in March 1603. Therefore, in 1603 James I of England and Ireland inherited an Irish kingdom in which outright rebellion had been quashed, although at great cost to the English taxpayer. What James I and his son Charles I made of this situation will be seen in the next two chapters, but the prospects of their success were improved by the fact that they were also kings of Scotland, enabling joint Anglo-Scottish power to be turned against the Irish. The running sore of raids across the English–Scottish border was now healed and James I had access to Scottish troops and (more importantly) Scottish settlers to send to Ireland, giving him the chance to build on the military conquest achieved by Mountjoy and to bring Ireland firmly under British control.

There is no doubt, though, that the problems of ruling these multiple kingdoms far outweighed the opportunities that they offered the early Stuart crown. The European experience of multiple kingdoms was not encouraging. The Spanish monarchy's attempt in this period to subjugate outlying kingdoms and provinces to rule from Madrid led to protests that spilled over into rebellions in the Netherlands, Portugal, Catalonia and Naples. Moreover, it is likely that the British multiple-kingdom problem was more intractable than that facing the Spanish monarchy, which did not have the striking religious diversity in its subject dominions that existed in England, Ireland and Scotland. Both James I and Charles I found serious obstacles in the way of assimilating their kingdoms of Ireland and Scotland with England. Both Anglo-Irish and Anglo-Scottish relations were bedevilled by mutual suspicions and hatreds. Most English thought of the Irish as barbarians and the Irish resented the English as jack-booted conquerors. There were similarly deep-rooted antipathies between the English and the Scots, in this case born out of the Scots' traditional Auld Alliance with France and divergent historical developments which had given England and Scotland completely different legal, political, economic and social structures. The union of the English and Scottish thrones in 1603 failed to overcome these antipathies and indeed may have exacerbated them. No common British machinery of government was erected in 1603 and consequently Scottish (and Irish) suspicions were aroused that, when making decisions, their monarchs were overwhelmingly influenced by English interests at their expense. Interestingly (and paradoxically), another indication of the mutual suspicions that characterized Anglo-Scottish relations is that during James I's reign many of his English subjects felt that their new Scottish king was exploiting English wealth for the benefit of his Scottish subjects.

What, however, made the task of ruling these very different kingdoms more difficult than ever was that each had different religions. Despite conquering and colonizing Ireland, England's success in Protestantizing that country was by 1603 restricted to a small number of so-called 'New English' families, who were an embattled minority that dominated the government of Ireland from Dublin. The vast majority of Irish – whether Gaelic Irish or 'Old English' (see p. 158) – were Catholics. During the later sixteenth and early seventeenth centuries Counter-Reformation Catholicism made great strides in Ireland, further widening the religious gulf between it and England. The recent religious history of Scotland, too, had differed from England's. The Reformation north of the border had proceeded much more quickly than in England, and Presbyterianism had become entrenched in the Lowlands. Only the sparsely populated Highlands remained attached to the old religion.

This mixture of mutual antagonisms, different historical traditions and religious diversity within the multiple kingdoms inherited by the early Stuarts made the task of ruling them very difficult. Were they ungovernable? When 'the British problem' is considered alongside the two other major problems that are discussed below, it is tempting to suggest that they were. This is, however, a conclusion that should not be reached lightly; nor is it one that is supported here. It was not until Charles I attempted to impose religious uniformity on his three kingdoms that he lost control of events in all of them. Before that, the record of James VI and I as ruler of Britain suggests that such an outcome was not inevitable.

The unreformed State

Many of the inadequacies inherent in early Stuart government have already been hinted at. James I and Charles I lacked a professional bureaucracy to execute their decisions. The fact that the king's officials were poorly paid (or unpaid) meant that bribery could become a normal part of the administrative machinery. Local government was in the hands of the rulers of the county communities, who in turn had to take account of the views of borough and parish office-holders, and was therefore not always responsive to the wishes of the monarch. Moreover, both James I and Charles I, like the Tudors, possessed no professional army or police force.

All these inadequacies were the consequences of the poor financial situation which the Stuarts inherited from Elizabeth I. The roots of their financial troubles are not unfamiliar to present-day governments or individuals. The sixteenth and early seventeenth centuries were periods of inflation, and the royal revenue system was incapable of meeting the growing demands on it. The crown had three major sources of ordinary revenue. The first of these – the crown estates – had been greatly enlarged from 1399 to the 1530s, but successive monarchs from Henry VIII onwards, including the early Stuart kings, sold many of them. When the fall in the value of money is taken into account, the decline in income from the crown estates is even more alarming than is apparent from the following figures: the average annual income dropped from £200,000 in the 1530s, to £72,000 in 1619, and to only £10,000 in the 1630s.[33] Even the denuded crown estate did not produce its full potential; many crown tenants held long leases at low rents. The crown similarly found it difficult to increase its income from its two other main sources of revenue, customs and feudal incidents. To collect customs duties efficiently would have necessitated a large bureaucracy, and therefore instead the crown, sporadically in the later sixteenth century and systematically after 1604, farmed customs duties out to private syndicates of merchants, who paid an annual rent to the crown. This meant that it was the customs farmers, not the crown,

---

[33] G. R. Batho, 'Landlords in England: the crown', in Thirsk, *Agrarian History*, pp. 256–76.

who took the cream of the revenue from overseas trade. Finally, as both James I and Charles I found, income from feudal incidents, especially wardships, could only be increased at the expense of raising political opposition. In this situation the early Stuarts, like Elizabeth I, came to rely on parliamentary taxation, which in theory was meant to provide money only for extraordinary needs, as a normal part of their income. However, as has been seen, assessments for parliamentary taxation bore little relation to the true wealth of the country and yields were comparatively small. More and more, James I and Charles I were driven to rely on loans from the City of London for ordinary government expenditure. Leaving aside the question of James I's extravagance, the crown's finances were not geared to meeting the cost of government, even in peacetime, in the early seventeenth century.

It is often assumed that these inadequacies made the collapse of the early Stuart monarchy inevitable. This is not necessarily so. Other contemporary monarchies suffered from similar weaknesses, and, far from collapsing, grew in strength.[34] More-over, as has been seen, the deficiencies of the early Stuart monarchy were a source of political unity between it and its leading subjects, who had a vested interest in maintaining the constitutional status quo. In normal circumstances neither the crown nor its subjects showed any real desire to reform the king's administration; significantly, the major attempts at reform in peacetime in the early seventeenth century, by Sir Robert Cecil and Lionel Cranfield, met with a distinct lack of enthusiasm both at court and in parliament (see pp. 116–21, 125–7).

However, as government costs escalated as a result of inflation and royal extravagance, the pressure for financial and administrative reform in the later sixteenth and early seventeenth centuries became immense; during wartime, and at times when war seemed a distinct possibility, this pressure could not be ignored. Royal income was barely adequate to meet peacetime requirements, hence James I's experimentation with financial expedients like impositions (see pp. 117–18). The problem became particularly acute given the escalating cost of warfare in the later sixteenth and early seventeenth centuries. Therefore the crown in the 1590s and in the 1620s was driven to resort to extraordinary financial measures – forced loans and other forms of extra-parliamentary taxation – and to assert its power more forcibly than in peacetime (see p. 142). As at other times in the seventeenth and early eighteenth centuries, war and the needs produced by war became important catalysts of political change. Like the regimes of the 1640s and 1650s and the governments of William III and Queen Anne in the 1690s and 1700s, the crown in the early seventeenth century discovered that war necessitated the establishment of a strong and efficient central executive.

Inevitably such changes in the royal revenue system in the early seventeenth century were interpreted as threats to the independence of parliament. This interpretation was strengthened by events taking place on the Continent and which heightened contemporary fears for the future of county independence and of parliament. Just as later in the century European events helped to fuel opposition to James II (see

---

[34] H. G. Koenigsberger, 'Revolutionary conclusions', *History*, LVII (1972), pp. 394–8.

p. 349), so in the early seventeenth century the contemporary trend in Europe towards powerful absolutist monarchies and the elimination of representative assemblies had an important impact on English political opinion: fears about the future of the English parliament were apparent in every parliamentary session. Far from wanting to secure more powers for parliament, the limit of the ambitions of most MPs for parliament was to ensure its survival. In these circumstances political opinion represented in parliament became increasingly fearful of the absolutist designs of central government, and such fears, which were especially inflamed during wartime, were a major threat to constitutional harmony.

As will be seen, these fears led to political tension between James I and his parliaments, but their consequences became much more serious after the accession in 1625 of Charles I, who appeared to adopt 'new counsels' aimed at the establishment of royal absolutism. In this situation two distinct, divergent beliefs about the constitution slowly became apparent in the early seventeenth century, representing fundamentally different reactions to the fact that from the 1590s the crown increasingly resorted to raising money without parliamentary consent. One belief emphasized the 'mixed' (*dominium politicum et regale*) nature of the English constitution noted above, and stressed that monarchs should rule with the consent of their subjects, according to the law and through parliament.

Work by Patrick Collinson and Marku Peltonen emphasizing that the view of England's constitution was 'mixed' has been strengthened by two themes that were prominent in late sixteenth- and early seventeenth-century political thought and that have not received sufficient emphasis. The first is the notion that England from the later sixteenth century was 'a monarchical republic', a term coined by Professor Patrick Collinson in 1990 with specific reference to the reign of Elizabeth I. Explaining what he meant by this apparently paradoxical term, he wrote that 'early modern England consisted of a series of overlapping, superimposed communities which were semi-autonomous, self-governing political cultures. They may be called, but always in quotes, 'republics', village republics, in the counties, gentry republics; and at a transcendental level, the commonwealth of England.' This idea fits in what has been seen was the normal pattern of local government in this period, in which monarchs ruled with the active participation and consent of many local office-holders. It can be argued that the idea of England as a 'monarchical republic' persisted in the early seventeenth century.[35]

The second is the extensive familiarity of people in early modern England with the notion of classical humanism and republicanism. This idea has largely emerged from the work of literary scholars and intellectual historians like David Norbrook and Marku Peltonen, who have shown that a knowledge of classical humanism and republicanism encouraged contemporaries to take an active participatory role in civic

---

[35] P. Collinson, 'The monarchical republic of Elizabeth I' and 'De Republica Anglorum: or history with the politics put back' in his *Elizabethan Essays* (1994). The quotation is from p. 16. See also J. F. McDiarmid, ed., *The Monarchical Republic of Early Modern England: essays in response to Patrick Collinson* (2007) for critical analyses of Collinson's idea.

life. This also broke down any inhibitions some may have had about criticizing the court, following precedents in classical history.[36]

It is very doubtful whether such ideas encouraged the development of republican ideas in a modern sense: that is, of a government without a monarchy. But both ideas encouraged an existing trend towards active participation in government and public debates about religion and politics.

Distinct from the 'mixed' view of English monarchy is another belief that emphasized the 'personal' nature of the monarchical constitution, which has also been noted above. Some argued that a monarch's power came from God alone, allowing kings and queens to take emergency measures that might conflict with established parliamentary custom and legal precedent. It would be unwise to inflate these different emphases, reflected in ephemeral parliamentary speeches and clerical sermons, into an assumption that two sharply contrasting political ideologies existed in early Stuart England.[37] They were not expounded in rigorously argued political treatises. It cannot be denied, though, that these ideological differences, though as yet skin deep, were an important consequence of the unreformed structure of the early modern English State. They ensured that the crown's attempts at administrative and financial reform were a potential source of political tension and instability in early seventeenth-century England.

The unreformed Church

The English Church was far from perfect in the early seventeenth century. As has been seen, Puritan demands for reform highlighted its major shortcomings: many clergymen were ill-educated, some held more than one living and did not live in their parishes. Moreover, the ecclesiastical hierarchy was accused of gross worldliness. Cathedrals were considered to be 'dens of loitering lubbers', who were fonder of enjoying the comforts offered by wealthy cathedral foundations than of pastoral work.[38] From the 1570s onwards a principal aim of many Protestants was to bring about 'a godly and learned ministry', and this concern, if anything, intensified in the early seventeenth century.[39] As with the defects of early Stuart government, so the root cause of the Church's problems was financial.[40] The wealth of the Church was very unequally

---

[36] M. Peltonen, *Classical Humanism and Republicanism in English Political Thought 1570–1640* (1995); D. Norbrook, *Writing the English Republic: poetry, rhetoric and politics, 1627–1660* (1999) and D. Norbrook, 'Lucan, Thomas May, and the creation of a republican literary culture' in K. Sharpe and P. Lake, eds., *Culture and Politics in Early Stuart England* (1993).

[37] J. P. Sommerville, *Politics and Ideology in England 1603–40* (1986) and 'Ideology, property and the constitution', in R. Cust and A. Hughes, eds., *Conflict in Early Stuart England* (1989).

[38] C. Cross, 'Dens of loitering lubbers: Protestant protest against cathedral foundations 1540–1640', *Studies in Church History*, IX (1972), pp. 231–7.

[39] Collinson, *Elizabethan Puritan Movement*, pp. 280–2.

[40] C. Hill, *The Economic Problems of the Church* (1959). This and many other aspects of the Church in this period are dealt with in two collections of essays: R. O'Day and F. Heal, eds., *Continuity and Change: personnel and administration of the Church in England 1500–1642* (1976); and F. Heal and R. O'Day, eds., *Church and Society in England: Henry VIII to James I* (1977).

distributed. Most of its estates were held by bishops and by deans and chapters of cathedrals; the only land remaining in the hands of parish churches was glebe land, which rarely extended to a substantial amount. Moreover, a large part of the income which ought to have gone to the parish clergy was received by laymen. The history of tithes lay at the heart of the economic problems of the Church in the early seventeenth century. Tithes, 10 per cent of the income of every parishioner, were originally paid to parish clergy for their maintenance. But even before the Reformation many tithes had been impropriated by laymen, and after the Reformation many more fell into the hands of lay rectors, who, as well as having the right (the advowson) to present nominees to church livings, were obliged to provide for the vicar's support. In practice, many lay rectors took the great tithes of corn and hay for themselves, treating it as an important part of their rental income, leaving only the small tithes of animal produce for the vicar. Small tithes were difficult to assess and collect; moreover, since they had often been commuted to a fixed money payment, their value declined greatly in a period of inflation.

This situation was considered to be scandalous by many sections of opinion in early seventeenth-century England. Puritans were the most vociferous in condemning it, but their concern was shared by many bishops and by both James I and Charles I. One of James I's first decisions on his accession was to promise to restore royal impropriated tithes to their proper use, and he was very sympathetic to many of the aims of Protestant reformers during his reign (see below, pp. 106–10). Under Charles I, too, the crown and bishops were intent on improving the quality of the clergy. Nor were they without some success. By the 1630s most clergymen were graduates;[41] lay patrons, including town corporations, often appointed able preachers to livings and lectureships; and many of the worst manifestations of the plunder of the Church by the crown, which had been common in Elizabeth I's reign, had ended. Yet, as the many complaints about non-preaching clergy in the early months of the Long Parliament illustrate, the achievement fell far short of what the reformers wanted.[42] The reform movement within the Church in the early seventeenth century failed almost as totally as did attempts at administrative and financial reform of the government. The central problem of the early Stuart Church – lay impropriated tithes – remained untouched. Too many people, propertied gentlemen and institutions, had a vested interest in the maintenance of impropriated tithes to allow schemes to restore them for the good of the Church to be successful. The Feoffees for Impropriations in the 1620s and Archbishop Laud's plans in the 1630s to buy back tithes failed as completely as did Cecil's and Cranfield's administrative reforms (see below, p. 154).

The Church, then, remained largely unreformed. This, though, by itself was not dangerous to constitutional harmony in the early seventeenth century. Although many were not willing to give up their property rights which would have ensured its success,

---

[41] R. O'Day, 'The reformation of the ministry 1558–1642', in O'Day and Heal, eds., *Continuity and Change*, pp. 55–75.

[42] Anthony Fletcher, 'Concern for renewal in the Root and Branch debates of 1641', *Studies in Church History*, XIV (1977), pp. 279–86.

the crown, bishops and many laymen were agreed that some reform of the Church was necessary. What made political tension on this issue likely was that by the early seventeenth century two different views about the way the English Church ought to be reformed had emerged. The first, held by 'godly' Protestants, has already been discussed (see pp. 55–8). For them, the lesson of the outbreak of war in Germany in 1618, the invasion and annexation of the Protestant Palatinate by Catholic forces, and the ensuing war between Protestant and Catholic countries in Europe was clear. It was that further reformation of the Church in a Protestant direction was an urgent necessity in order to combat the threat of popery. For them the Thirty Years War was just as powerful in exciting fears about the future of Protestantism as it was in making people fearful about the continuance of parliaments in England.

This Puritan view, however, was not the only vision of how the Church should be reformed that existed in the early seventeenth century. As will be seen, some influential churchmen had begun to formulate ideas about the future development of the Church that were very different from those who advocated an intensification and continuation of the Protestant Reformation. Indeed, some began to question some of the main characteristic elements of the post-Reformation English Church: especially its Calvinist predestinarian theology, preaching and a sermon-orientated church service. Such churchmen are often described as 'Arminians', because their criticisms of Calvinist predestinarianism were similar to those voiced during the reign of James I by Jacobus Arminius, a Dutch theologian at the University of Leiden. However, as will be seen, the views of these English churchmen (like William Laud, Lancelot Andrewes and John Cosin) drew on debates within the English Church that pre-dated those initiated by Arminius, being first apparent in the 1590s. They also extended beyond Arminius's narrow focus on theology to encompass topics like the ceremonial and sacramental role of ministers in church services, the divine origins of episcopacy and the downgrading of sermons and preaching. For these reasons, and because William Laud became the central figure in the promotion of such views in the 1630s, 'Laudianism' rather than 'Arminianism' is the term that is used to describe them in this book.

These Puritan–Laudian disagreements about the future of the Church must be set alongside the developing ideological differences about the constitution that have been noted above as key features of early Stuart England which made the maintenance of constitutional harmony increasingly difficult. It was not inevitable, however, that these disagreements should have provoked serious political tensions. They were capable of being controlled and contained by a politically astute monarch, as the history of the reign of James I largely demonstrates. Their potential for bringing about major political conflicts, however, is illustrated in the reign of Charles I, when the king promoted Laudians and Laudianism in the Church. By doing this, Charles I alienated the crown from the religious mainstream of the country. More seriously for the prospects of continued political harmony, such action ensured that the Laudian threat to the future of Protestantism came to be seen by many as indistinguishable from the threat they imagined to the future of parliament. Part 2 will illustrate how Laudianism played a vital role in bringing about the collapse of the Elizabethan constitution.

PART 2

The reigns of the early Stuarts, 1603–1640

Introduction

The meeting of the Long Parliament in November 1640 marked the collapse of the Elizabethan constitution. At that time Charles I had only a handful of supporters: Laudians, customs farmers, monopolists and a few Catholics.[1] He was alienated from the bulk of the political nation. When and why Charles I found himself in such a weak and vulnerable situation are among the major historical problems of the early seventeenth century. It is tempting to frame one's answer to those problems in metaphorical terms: for example, by arguing that 1640 was the end of 'the high road to civil war' which began in 1529 or 1558 or 1603, and that progress along the road was even and inevitable. This is a temptation to be resisted. It is true (as recent research has demonstrated) that the history of the late sixteenth and early seventeenth centuries is full of political tension, and that James VI and I's success in bringing political stability to his multiple kingdoms was not as great as some revisionist historians have suggested. Yet it is arguable that there was no fundamental break between the English crown and the political nation at least before 1621 and probably much later. During the first thirty years of the seventeenth century, political life in England was not divided into two camps, 'court' and 'country'; on the contrary, there was a great deal of contact between the parliamentary classes and the court, as the careers of most political leaders of the period testify. If this is true, then the oft-repeated belief that James I, by his stupidity, opened up an unbridgeable rift between crown and parliament on constitutional issues must be rejected.

When, then, did the breach which culminated in the constitutional crisis of 1640–1 occur? Much more serious strains were put on the traditional constitutional framework by Charles I after his accession in 1625 than by his father, resulting in the fierce antagonism to royal policies seen in the parliaments of the late 1620s. Was the breach, then, irrevocable by 1629? To such hypothetical questions there can, of course, be no one 'correct' answer. Not everyone became alienated from the Caroline regime at the same time. Nevertheless the physical separation of Charles I from his natural supporters, which was the result of his failure to summon a parliament for eleven years

---

[1] Most Catholics were uncommitted in 1640: K. J. Lindley, 'The lay Catholics of England in the reign of Charles I', *J. Eccl. H.*, XXII (1971), pp. 199–222; idem., 'The part played by Catholics', in B. Manning, ed., *Politics, Religion and the English Civil War* (1973), pp. 126–76.

after 1629, allowed the issues and suspicions dividing them to have full rein. As each of these eleven years went by, the lack of a political forum in which king, royal councillors and parliamentary leaders could meet and discuss current issues increasingly made constitutional deadlock a more distinct possibility than it had been at any time before 1629 and certainly during the reign of James I.

The Stuart Family Tree

4

The survival of the Elizabethan constitution, 1603–1621

Summary

King James VI and I: changing views of historians

King James, who became ruler of England, Wales and Ireland in March 1603 on the death of Queen Elizabeth I, had been King James VI of Scotland ever since the enforced abdication of his mother, Mary Queen of Scots, in 1567. By the time his minority ended in 1584, he had developed a keen interest in scholarship and remarkable political skills that enabled him as an adult king to oversee the development in Scotland of royal, centralized government over Kirk and State. His success in overcoming immense political problems as king of Scotland has generally been recognized by historians. So too has his dynastic success in producing with his wife, Anne of Denmark, whom he married in 1589, two sons (Henry 1594–1612 and Charles 1600–49) and a daughter (Elizabeth 1596–1662). However, in great contrast to his reputation as king of Scotland, James has been one of the most maligned rulers of England. For generations, historians accused him, after the union of the crowns of England, Wales, Ireland and Scotland, of putting the country on to 'a high road to civil war' by the time he died in 1625.

In the following pages it will be seen (following the work of some revisionist historians of the late twentieth century) that in some respects that charge is unfair. However, it will also be seen that, despite his undoubted success as ruler of Britain and Ireland between 1603 and 1625, King James contributed to the continuation (and in some cases the worsening) of political and religious tensions between the crown and its subjects that had existed in the reign of Elizabeth I.

James I and the succession

At the end of the first session of parliament in the summer of 1604, some MPs recounted for the benefit of the new king how they felt on the day he was proclaimed king of England. On 24 March 1603, they wrote, 'a general hope was raised in the minds of all your people that under your Majesty's reign religion, peace, justice, and all virtue should renew again and flourish; that the better sort should be cherished, the bad reformed or repressed, and some moderate ease should be given us of those burdens and sore oppressions under which the whole land did groan'.[1] It was only the passing of time which lent enchantment to the reign of Elizabeth I and allowed the tradition of 'the reign of our late queen of blessed memory' to pass into popular mythology. In 1603 there were few who mourned her passing and fewer who did not welcome the peaceful accession of the new king. J. E. Neale's study of Elizabeth's later parliaments reveals the extent of the disaffection at many aspects of Elizabethan government felt by those represented in parliament, a situation amply confirmed by a recent analysis of an anonymous document, 'the Memorial' of March 1603 addressed to the new king, which catalogued grievances like wardship and purveyance and defects in the Church such as the lack of preaching ministers, pluralism and non-residence, and which amounted (according to Nicholas Tyacke) to 'sweeping plans for change' in both Church and State.[2] Nor had Elizabethan government been a guarantee of political stability, which might have compensated for its defects. Elizabeth's refusal to marry or to name a successor, even on her deathbed, ensured that her reign was dominated by uncertainty, which increased yearly and became the principal domestic issue of her reign. James VI of Scotland was Elizabeth's most obvious successor, but no one in the late sixteenth century could have been certain that his succession would go unchallenged. In 1600 Thomas Wilson tried to console himself with the conviction that James VI would be accepted as king of England, but, looking at the vast range of competing claimants, he wryly commented that 'this Crowne is not like to fall to the ground for want of heads that claime to weare it, but upon whose head it will fall is by many doubted'.[3] James was an alien and a member of a nation hated by the English. Legally his claim was weakened by Henry VIII's will, which debarred from the succession the heirs of Margaret Tudor. A peaceful succession was thus not guaranteed. That the fears of contemporaries did not materialize was due partly to James's diplomatic negotiations with European powers in Elizabeth's last years and, possibly to a greater extent, to the political skill of Robert Cecil in England. Not the least of James's attributes in the eyes of Englishmen was that he already had two sons and that his accession promised an end to the uncertainty over the succession to the English throne which had threatened political stability in England since at least the 1450s.

---

[1] Kenyon, *Stuart Constititution*, p. 30.

[2] Nicholas Tyacke, 'Puritan politicians and King James VI and I, 1587–1604', in T. Cogswell, R. Cust and P. Lake, eds., *Politics, Religion and Popularity in Early Stuart Britain* (2002), p. 42.

[3] F. J. Fisher, ed., *The State of England Anno Dom. 1600 by Thomas Wilson*, Camden Society, 3rd ser., LII (1936), p. 5.

By the middle of the twentieth century, most historians agreed that James's record as ruler of his multiple kingdoms after 1603 was a disaster.[4] Very influential in the formation of the black legend of James I was a book written during James's reign by one of his ex-household officers, Anthony Weldon, called *The Court and Character of James I.* This book contains the infamous 'codpiece' pen-portrait of the king:

> He was naturally of timorous disposition, which was the reason of his quilted doublet; his eyes large, ever rolling after any stranger that came into his presence, insomuch as many for shame have left the room, as being out of countenance. His beard was very thin, his tongue too large for his mouth, which . . . made him drink very uncomely, as if eating his drink, which came out of his cup each side of his mouth. . . . His walk was ever circular, his fingers ever in that walk fiddling with that codpiece; he was very temperate in his exercise and in his diet, and not intemperate in his drinking . . . he would never change his clothes until worn out to very rags.[5]

To that image of a personally repellent, prematurely senile and shabby dirty-old-man, other damaging charges were added and accepted by later generations. It was alleged, for example, that the Scottish king was totally ignorant of conditions in his new southern kingdom and that, as a result, he blundered into making many serious errors after 1603. It was said that he opened up fundamental and permanent fractures in the fabric of the English State because his ruinous extravagance destroyed the already creaking structure of English public finances. He also created, it was alleged, serious divisions along religious lines by his inflexible, uncompromising attitudes to those who demanded further reforms within the Church. This forced godly Puritans to begin to move away from advocating moderate reforms within the Church towards demanding radical measures, like the abolition of bishops. James was also charged with allowing himself to be led by Count Gondomar, the Spanish ambassador in London, into following a pro-Spanish foreign policy that was against England's national interests. As a result, it was argued, in the early seventeenth century the stability of the country was threatened, not only by a constitutionally aggressive parliament and a Puritan ideology that was subversive of the social and political status quo, but also by the accession of an inept and foolish king, 'the wisest fool in Christendom' as Henry IV of France was wrongly thought to have called him.[6] In these circumstances it was accepted by many that England became deeply divided on 'court versus country' lines and that England was firmly set on the celebrated (if mythical) 'high road to civil war'.

Without doubt, most of the charges implicit in the image of James I as 'the wisest fool in Christendom' are unfair, as has been demonstrated by historians since the 1980s.[7] Contemporary accounts of the deterioration in his physical appearance and

---

[4] A view illustrated clearly in D. H. Willson, *James VI and I* (1956, Cape paperback edn., 1963).

[5] Quoted in C. Daniels and J. Morrill, *Charles I* (1988), p. 9.

[6] The phrase was in fact coined by Weldon: Jenny Wormald, 'James VI and I', *Oxford Dictionary of National Biography* (2004–8), p. 59.

[7] Crucial to the process of James's rehabilitation as ruler is the brilliant seminal article by J. Wormald, 'James VI and I: two kings or one?', *History*, LXVIII (1983). See also the books on James by Houston, Lockyer and Durston in the Bibliographical note, p. 521.

habits as an old and sick man in the last five or six years of his life have been used wrongly, out of chronological context. Even his physical decline in his last years can be exaggerated, since right until the end of his life he often got out of bed at dawn to go hunting. James's lively letter in 1624 to an ill duke of Buckingham is hardly one of a man debilitated by senility: 'My only sweet and dear child, Blessing, blessing, blessing on thy heartroots and all thine. This Tuesday morning here is a great store of game, as they say, especially partridges and stone curlews. I know who shall get their part of them.'[8] Above all, Weldon's assessment of James has been taken at its face value, regardless of the fact that Weldon was hardly fitted to be an objective commentator on the king. For one thing, Weldon was violently prejudiced against Scotland and all things Scottish. In his book *A Perfect Description of the People and Country of Scotland*, which Weldon wrote after visiting Scotland as part of James's entourage on a royal tour in 1617, he wrote that Scotland is 'too good for those that possess it, and too bad for others to be at the charge to conquer it. The air might be wholesome but for the stinking people that inhabit it . . . There is a great store of fowl too, as foul houses, foul sheets, foul linen, foul dishes, and pots, foul trenchers and napkins.' In this book, Weldon was careful to distinguish between the mass of Scottish people and the king. 'I do wonder', he wrote, 'that so brave a prince as King James should be born in so stinking a town as Edenburg in lousy Scotland.'[9] Not surprisingly, James was furious and he sacked Weldon from his court office. After that Weldon had no reason not to turn his bitter pen against James as well as the Scots; *The Court and Character of King James* is the result. It is certainly not the piece of objective historical evidence that it is often assumed to have been. An essential starting point for a proper historical assessment of James I is the abandonment of the distorting mirror of English anti-Scottish opinion as seen in Weldon's book or Lady Ann Clifford's diary comment on the Jacobean court: 'We all saw a great change between the fashion of the court as it now is and of that in the Queen's time, for we were all lousy by sitting in the chamber of Sir Thomas Erskine [one of James's Scottish entourage].'[10] Such comments are an interesting reflection of those English views on the Scots that were to block James's plans for a union of his two kingdoms, as will be seen. But they give a very misleading picture of contemporary attitudes to James I. The realization of this has led in recent years to a justified rehabilitation of James's reputation as king of England. James I of England was as successful a monarch as was James VI of Scotland.

As with other aspects of historical 'revisionism', however, it is important that favourable reassessments of James I are not carried too far.[11] As will be seen, some of the origins of the causes of the opposition faced by Charles I before and after 1640 are to be found in the reign of his father; and some of these derived from James's defects as a monarch. Both as a man and as a king he was not without unappealing characteristics, some of which had damaging political consequences. This is not particularly true of James's

---

[8] G. P. V. Akrigg, ed., *Letters of King James VI and I* (1984), pp. 14, 438.

[9] Quoted in Wormald, 'Two kings or one?', pp. 190–1.

[10] Quoted in Willson, *James VI and I*, p. 191.

[11] This is not done by Pauline Croft in her excellent *King James* (2003), or by the contributors to R. Houlbrooke, ed., *James VI and I: Ideas, Authority and Government* (2006); see especially the editor's essay on 'James's reputation, 1625–2005'.

voyeuristic prurience about sexual matters, which led him to visit the bedrooms of newly married courtiers to interrogate them about the intimate details of their first post-wedding nights together, or of the cruel references he made about Robert Cecil's lameness in his 'dear beagle' letters to his chief minister during the first part of his reign. These are more out of tune with modern attitudes than they seem to have been with those of his contemporaries. James's male chauvinism – women, he advised his son, 'are no other thing else but *irritamenta libidinis* [incitements to lust]'[12] – also grates more on twenty-first-century liberal ears than it probably did on those of patriarchally minded early seventeenth-century people. What, however, did contribute to the political tensions (which, it will be seen, are a thread running through the history of Jacobean parliaments) was the fact that James made no attempt to counter the image of his court as decadent and corrupt. His displays of public affection for his male favourites and his occasional bouts of drunkenness were noted disapprovingly in the diaries and letters of his important subjects, along with the sexual and corruption scandals that rocked the Jacobean court in the second decade of his English reign. When his brother-in-law Christian IV of Denmark came to England on a state visit, one report of the masque that was put on for the royal visitor noted that

> the entertainment went forward and most of the presenters went backwards or did fall down. Hope [one of the characters in the masque] did essay [try] to speak but wine rendered her endeavours so feeble that she withdrew . . . Charity . . . returned to Hope and Faith who were both sick and spewing in the lower hall.[13]

Unlike Elizabeth I, who mastered the technique of image projection long before the days of the modern public relations industry, James scorned the task of cultivating his regal popularity. When large crowds came to see him, James is said to have shown his resentment. On one occasion at least, on being told that the people had come to express their love for him, he cried out (fortunately perhaps in an impenetrable Scottish accent), 'God's wounds! I will pull down my breeches and they shall also see my arse.'[14]

James's irritation at popular adulation and his failure (unlike other early modern European monarchs like Louis XIV) to hide the seediness and corruption of the court behind a veneer of glory were matched by his dislike of attending to matters of routine administration. His preference for hunting, while leaving day-to-day government business to others, need not, as has often been assumed, have led to administrative inefficiency. The personal application to routine matters of government practised by Philip II of Spain or Henry VII of England was not necessary as long as monarchs delegated administrative business to capable subordinates; in Robert Cecil, until he died in 1612, and (later) Lionel Cranfield, James had such ministers. Unfortunately, however, James sometimes undermined his ministers' policies (especially their efforts to reform the antiquated royal financial and administrative structure, by his extravagance), so that it

---

[12] Quoted in *Willson, James VI and I*, p. 135.
[13] Quoted in J. Miller, *Bourbons and Stuarts: kings and kingship in France and England in the seventeenth century* (1987), p. 26.
[14] Quoted in Willson, *James VI and I*, p. 165.

will be seen that his ministers' pleas for parliamentary support for administrative reform often got a hostile reception. As will be seen, too, many of James's deeply held beliefs – his willingness to extend a measure of toleration to Catholics and his pacific approach to foreign policy, for example – struck a discordant note in the ears of the political nation. Furthermore, generally successful as were his ecclesiastical policies, sometimes his actions, especially in the last years of his reign, roused rather than calmed anxieties in both England and Scotland, and fuelled a belief in the reality of a 'popish plot' aimed at subverting the Protestant Church in both countries.

Yet recent writing on James I has successfully established two important general points that put James's historical reputation in a much brighter light than the black 'wisest fool in Christendom' legend noted above. The first is that the political tensions of the reign were not caused solely, or indeed mainly, by James I. Elizabeth's legacy to the new king in 1603 was not a good one: a country at war, dissatisfaction in many quarters with the condition of the Church, a royal revenue system in need of radical reform, and grievances over which the late queen had failed to satisfy her last turbulent parliament in 1601. As has been seen at the end of the previous chapter, fears about parliament's future existence in England were already prevalent before Elizabeth died. The queen's attempts to raise extra-parliamentary taxes to finance the expensive wars against Spain and in Ireland, at a time when some continental monarchs were seen to be undermining representative assemblies in their kingdoms, was the main reason for the suspicions many MPs in Jacobean parliaments had of the court's 'absolutist' intentions; and for the expression of coherent constitutional ideologies that asserted parliament's traditional rights and liberties which were felt to be under threat. In these circumstances, the task of governing Britain in 1603 was extremely difficult. The second point in James's favour is that it is now clear that he carried out this daunting task with much more success than he has often been given credit for, using the political skills of flexibility and compromise that he had long deployed in Scotland to defuse some of the fears of his new English subjects. As will be seen, James saw himself as a *rex pacificus* – a peacemaker king – in foreign affairs. He also displayed the same qualities in domestic affairs, in the Church and State. These were seen not on the great public occasions that have often been given prominence in unfavourable accounts of James's reign, when the king could not resist lecturing parliamentary audiences about the divine origins of monarchy. James's qualities of political flexibility and tact are instead to be seen away from the public parliamentary political arena, in a less formal political forum in and around the court.

James's court might have lacked the formal decorum of the courts of Elizabeth I or Charles I, but its informality allowed a wide variety of views to be openly expressed. At his court James was accessible to the representatives of many powerful factions. He was never, even in the most ardent phase of his homosexual relationship with the duke of Buckingham, the prisoner of one faction in the ways that both Elizabeth I in the 1590s and Charles I in the late 1620s were. During James's reign, Buckingham never achieved the dominance of the court that he gained in the late 1620s or that the Cecils had in the 1590s. Significantly, one of James's first actions after his accession in England was to promote the Howards (Henry Howard was created earl of Northampton) to counterbalance the dominant position of the Cecils. James's experience in coping with the factional jungle of Scottish politics made him adept at balancing faction in the English court; and also (as will be seen) at acting as an arbitrator, defusing the factional tensions within the English Church. Moreover, James's 'extravagance', in part, is to be explained by his perceptive recognition that it was essential for successful early modern monarchs to be bountiful.[15] The distribution of royal largesse helped to secure the cooperation between leading magnates and the crown, which it has been seen was vital if the governmental system of late Tudor and early Stuart England was to operate smoothly.

It will be noted in what follows that James's reign did not see the emergence of an unbridgeable gulf between 'court and country'; nor did it see an uninterrupted slide towards the serious political crises of the late 1620s. Yet it will also be seen that James did not make full use of his political skills, or of his insights into the realities of political life in his new kingdom.

Peace with Spain and the settlement in Ireland

Financial considerations alone would have been enough to cause a revaluation of English foreign policy in 1603. With military expenditure escalating, could the country afford to continue the long-drawn-out Spanish war? In James's mind, however, there was more to it than this. In his view of the relationships between nation states, war was to be used only in the very last resort. James's vision of himself as *rex pacificus* and international peacemaker dominated his conduct of English foreign policy. One of his first acts as king of England was to issue a proclamation forbidding the capture of Spanish ships, and in his speech to his first parliament in March 1604 he outlined his pacific philosophy.

> The first . . . of these blessings which God hath, jointly with my person, sent unto you is outward peace . . . which is no small blessing to a Christian Commonwealth, for by peace abroad with their neighbours the towns flourish, the merchants become rich, the trade doth increase, and the people of all sorts of the land enjoy free liberty to exercise themselves in their several vocations without peril or disturbance. Not that I think this outward peace so unseparably tied to my person as I dare assuredly promise to myself and to you the certain continuance thereof; but thus far can I well assure you . . . that I shall never give the first occasion of the breach thereof, neither shall I ever be moved for any particular or private passion of mind to interrupt your public peace except I be forced thereunto, either for reparation of the honour of the kingdom or else by necessity for the weal and preservation of the same; in which case a secure and honourable war must be preferred to an unsecure and dishonourable peace.[16]

James's pacificism, it is often forgotten, had very definite limits.

---

[15] L. L. Peck, '"For a king not to be bountiful were a fault": perspectives in court patronage in early Stuart England', *J.B.S.*, XXV (1986).

[16] Tanner, *Constitutional Documents*, p. 25. See also *English Historical Documents 1603–60*, document no. 51.

Nor should the peace made with Spain in 1604 be seen as a stark reversal of Elizabethan policy. English Protestant hatred of Catholic Spain was still intense, and the generation-long war had developed strong vested interests for its continuance among privateers and merchant-profiteers who supplied the navy. Strategically, too, could the prime purpose of the war, the defence of the Dutch against Spanish invasion, be abandoned? James did not allow his desire for peace to blind him to England's true interests. He eagerly responded to Archduke Albert's peace initiative – with the collapse of Spanish intervention in Ireland in 1601 many on the Spanish side saw little point in continuing the war. But in the peace negotiations James made sure that his commissioners resisted Spanish efforts to prevent continued English unofficial military and commercial help for the Dutch rebels. The Treaty of London in August 1604 extricated England from a costly war without repudiating the interests of her Dutch allies.[17] Even a modern critic of James's conduct of foreign affairs concedes the result as 'a victory for English diplomacy'.[18] While the major reasons for the twelve-year Spanish–Dutch truce of March 1609 lay elsewhere, English mediation played a small part in the conclusion of the Truce of Antwerp, the next step in the establishment of a general European peace.

Immediately it was made, this peace was threatened. Four days before the truce was finally sealed, the death of William, duke of Cleves resulted in a disputed succession to his dukedom which threatened to divide Europe in a line-up that presaged the outbreak of the Thirty Years War nine years later: France against Spain, each supporting respectively the Protestant Evangelical Union and the Catholic Union of German states. James supported Henry IV of France in a frenzy of diplomatic and military preparations designed to prevent Habsburg control of the vital strategic Cleves–Jülich provinces in the Lower Rhine. That the outcome was a peaceful one was largely due to the assassination of Henry IV in May 1610, but in reaching the eventual compromise settlement in 1614 James played the role of international mediator. There is no doubt either that James enjoyed this chosen role or that he ever questioned the feasibility of making permanent peace between France and Spain, Catholic and Protestant Germany, by maintaining his contacts with both power blocs. In this scheme dynastic marriages played a large part. The marriage in February 1613 of his daughter, Elizabeth, to one of the leading members of the Protestant Evangelical Union, Frederick, the elector palatine, was balanced by the soundings made by the English ambassador in Madrid on the possibility of a Spanish bride for the Prince of Wales. James's pacific policy, his efforts to remain uncommitted unreservedly to any European alignment, eventually failed. But its failure was not inevitable and for more than a decade it was carried on very successfully.

---

[17] In this respect Jacobean foreign policy in the first part of the reign had much in common with that followed in the later sixteenth century, a point developed in David Trim, 'Calvinist internationalism and the shaping of Jacobean foreign policy', in T. Wilks ed., *Prince Henry Revived: Image and Exemplarity in Early Modern England* (2007).

[18] Maurice Lee, *James and Henri IV: an essay in English foreign policy 1603–10* (1970), p. 37.

········ Western limit of Cromwellian conquest at end of 1650

The Ulster plantation

Other areas settled or re-settled by English and
Scottish settlers, 1603-40

Map 1 Ireland

James's reputation as a peacemaker was enhanced by his record in Ireland. By surrendering in the last months of Elizabeth's reign, the principal leader of the Irish rebels in Ulster, the earl of Tyrone, had not totally destroyed his power. But in 1607 his dominance was ended when he and the earl of Tyrconnel, demoralized by the lack of Spanish help after the Treaty of London, fled to the Continent. Their flight signalled the end, temporarily at least, of Irish resistance to English rule, and a renewal of the Elizabethan policy in Ireland of consolidating military gains by colonization. As Toby Barnard writes, 'much that happened in seventeenth-century Ireland could be regarded as a simple continuation of Tudor policies'.[19]

James, who showed little interest in the colonizing ventures in the New World, took an active part in the plantation of Ulster, and in the work of the commissioners he appointed in 1608 to supervise the project. The principles for the settlement worked out by the commissioners were almost totally dictated by strategic motives. The native Irish inhabitants were to be forcibly removed from the land and settled separately in the west of Ireland in order to clear the land for English and Scottish settlers. As always in their dealings with the Irish in the seventeenth century, the English considered the Irish to be a barbaric, uncivilized, sub-human species.[20] In order that the settlers would be capable of holding down the country, stringent military conditions were attached to the grants of land. Depending on the amount granted, each proprietor was to build on his estate a military fortification. They were not to alienate their land to Irishmen or even to allow natives to hold land on their estates. In addition a strict plan was laid down for the establishment of twenty-three towns in Ulster (Londonderry, Belfast and Enniskillen were the main ones) and in 1615 a Highways Act provided for the building of roads to facilitate military control. Within this framework the actual process of colonization was left to private enterprise. The most famous is the City of London joint-stock company which acquired the proprietorship of Coleraine and took in hand the settlement of the town and county of Londonderry. But there were other privately organized ventures in Antrim and County Down, the proprietors in turn granting the land to English and Scottish settlers. In one respect the Ulster plantation scheme was not carried out with the severity envisaged by its planners. Lack of enthusiasm for the scheme both by prospective landowners and by settlers forced the crown to amend the regulations in order to allow some grants of land to Irish landowners and of tenancies to Irish farmers. Yet between 1610 and 1640 many English and Scottish Protestant settlers did go to Ireland, thus beginning the Presbyterian domination of that province. The Jacobean Ulster plantation scheme and the injustices it did to the native Irish, of course, contributed directly to the rebellion of 1641. But until then the plantation went on apace peacefully, and was one of the most successful colonization schemes of the reign of James I.

---

[19] T. Barnard, 'The making of Great Britain and Ireland', in B. Coward, ed., *A Companion to Stuart Britain* (2003), p. 26.
[20] Nicholas Canny, *Making Ireland British, 1580–1640* (2001).

Puritans and Catholics

Of all the political problems of his reign, James I undoubtedly dealt most successfully with the dangers of religious nonconformity. One cannot exaggerate just how seriously contemporaries considered the threat which refusal to accept the legally established Church posed to the State. When the head of the State, the monarch, was also head of the Church religious nonconformity was not only heresy, it was treason. 'Although many religious men of moderate spirits must be borne with', wrote Sir Robert Cecil, 'yet such are the turbulant humours of some that dream of nothing but a new hierarchy directly opposite to the state of monarchy, as the dispensation with such men were the highway to break all the bonds of unity, to nourish schism in the Church and Commonwealth.'[21] By 1603, despite the efforts of Archbishop Whitgift since 1583 to enforce religious orthodoxy, there were many of the new king's subjects who were far from happy with the Church to which they were forced to belong.

Most English Catholics since the Reformation had been loyal subjects of the English crown. Especially in the 1570s and 1580s, however, a minority led by the more militant Catholic exiles, Allen and Parsons, had been active in organizing propaganda and, occasionally, armed force against the English crown. But the decade of the 1590s, with its feuding among English Catholics and the death of William Allen, marks the end of 'the heroic age' of English Catholicism. 'What was most obviously new about the English Catholic body after 1603', writes John Bossy, 'was its retreat from the political engagement which had marked the Elizabethan period.'[22] In the first decade of James's reign there were few defenders of the papal deposing power among English Catholics; even Robert Parsons (who died in 1610) no longer urged his co-religionists to support it. In 1603 there were even high hopes among Catholics, fostered by James before his accession, that they would be allowed some relief from the penal laws. Not all were as misguided as one Oxfordshire Catholic lady who rejoiced on Elizabeth's death, 'now we have a Kinge who ys of our religion and will restore us to our rightes'.[23] But James was prepared to make a distinction between Catholics who were 'quiet and well-minded men, peaceable subjects' and those who were 'factious stirrers of sedition and perturbers of the commonwealth'; as to the former, he 'would be sorry to punish their bodies for the error of their minds'.[24] Not all Protestant Englishmen, however, would go this far in extending toleration to Catholics; anti-Catholicism was as deep-rooted and widespread in seventeenth-century England as was anti-Communism in McCarthyite America in the 1950s. As with other issues, the policy dictated by James's personal leanings ran counter to that dictated by political commonsense.

---

[21] Quoted in Gardiner, *History*, I, p. 199.

[22] John Bossy, 'The English Catholic community 1603–25', in A. G. R. Smith, ed., *The Reign of James VI and I*, p. 92.

[23] Quoted in P. McGrath, *Papists and Puritans in the Reign of Elizabeth I* (1967), p. 339.

[24] Tanner, *Constitutional Documents*, p. 29. See also *English Historical Documents 1603–60*, document no. 51.

This is probably why James's public attitude to English Catholics in the first decade of his reign fluctuated from tolerance to severity, which, however, must not obscure his success in allowing a measure of tolerance of Catholics without offending too much the anti-papist prejudices of his subjects. There is ample evidence that James saw the political dangers of a 'soft' policy towards Catholics. One of his earliest proclamations, in May 1603, ordered the collection of recusancy fines. In the 1604 session of parliament he encouraged the progress of legislation against Jesuit priests. Probably to counter suspicions raised by an unofficial embassy to the pope led by Sir James Lindsay, and by Catholic involvement in the Main and Bye Plots, in February 1605 James inaugurated a purge against recusants. Gardiner estimated that 5,560 in all were convicted of recusancy as a result. And in November 1605 came the Gunpowder Plot.

Information

The Gunpowder Plot, 1605

On 5 November, a group of thirteen conspirators, led by Sir Robert Catesby and including Guy Fawkes, attempted to blow up the Houses of Parliament when it was in session. The plot was discovered as Fawkes began to set gunpowder alight in the cellars of the parliament building. Fawkes was cruelly tortured and he revealed the names of his fellow conspirators. Catesby was killed trying to get away from London, but others were also taken into custody and later sentenced to be hung, drawn and quartered. That much is known with certainty about the plot. However, considerable doubt surrounds other aspects of it.

What were the motives of the conspirators? What was the role of Cecil and the government in the conspiracy? The extant historical evidence does not support conclusive answers. The most probable explanation of the conspirators' motives is that they were Catholics, desperate because Spain had recently made peace with England and possibly because of renewed persecution of Catholics. Evidence that Cecil supported the conspiracy in order to implicate prominent Catholics in it, as some Catholic historians have suggested, is slight. Amid the speculation what is certain is that the plot confirmed the suspicions of most Englishmen that all Catholics were potential traitors, a point which both the trials of the conspirators and of Henry Garnet, the Superior of the English Jesuits, and the earl of Northumberland hammered home.[25] Thus, 5 November became an important date in the Protestant calendar (alongside 17 November, Elizabeth I's accession day).

---

[25] M. Nicholls, *Investigating Gunpowder Plot* (1991) and A. J. Loomie, *Guy Fawkes in Spain: 'The Spanish Treason' in Spanish documents* (*B.I.H.R.* supplement 1971) are correctives to the view held mainly by Catholic historians (e.g. Francis Edwards, *Guy Fawkes: the real story of the Gunpowder Plot?* (1969)) that the plot was engineered by Cecil.

Figure 4.1 The Gunpowder Plotters. This woodcut depicting eight of the thirteen plotters is one of the most enduring images of the plot. It was produced first in 1605 and has been reproduced many times since, emphasizing the continuing significance in the British Protestant consciousness of the plot as evidence of Catholic treachery and terrorism. It is even reproduced as a mural at Charing Cross station on the London underground.
Source: © Mary Evans Picture Library.

When parliament reassembled in January 1606, two severe penal laws against Catholics were passed. By the terms of one of them, all recusants were required to take an oath of allegiance that asserted that the papal claim to depose monarchs was 'impious and heretical'.[26] Yet it seems that the anti-Catholic measures were not rigorously enforced. Here James's lack of administrative drive coincided with his own personal inclination and also with the desire not to upset Spain. The result may have been fortuitous, but it took much of the political sting out of the Catholic issue for the time being. While the Catholic minority was allowed to worship in private in peace, and indeed to increase slightly in numbers (see above, pp. 52–3), the anti-Catholic prejudices of Englishmen were appeased, partially at any rate, by the harsh legislation of 1606.

A more potentially explosive issue than Catholicism lay in the existence in early Jacobean England of those who wanted to reform the English Church in a Protestant direction. The problems that arise when using the term 'Puritan' to describe such people have already been discussed. Before 1640 the differences between 'Puritans' and other Protestants were not major ones. Puritans were those whose lifestyles were more influenced than others by Protestant principles and who were more concerned

---

[26] *Statutes of the Realm*, vol. 4, pp. 1071–7.

than others to reform the Church (see above, pp. 55–8). In 1603 it is highly unlikely that there were many Puritans who wanted a disestablished Church, or even a State Church without bishops. Those who had advocated radical measures like these in the later years of Elizabeth's reign had been severely punished. It is not surprising, therefore, that the Puritans who publicized themselves in 1603 held fairly moderate reforming ideas, typified by the so-called Millenary Petition presented to James I on his journey to London from Scotland in 1603. There may, of course, have been Puritans in 1603 who adopted a radical stance, but one has to be satisfied with the conclusion that, if they existed, they were too prudent to show themselves to the authorities – or to the historian. If some of their reforms were open to a radical interpretation, there were few reforms suggested by the petitioners of 1603 or those put forward in the 1604 parliament that posed a fundamental threat to the doctrine or organization of the English Church. There is no reason to challenge the disclaimer of the petitioners that they were 'neither as factious men affecting a popular parity in the Church, nor as schismatics aiming at the dissolution of the state ecclesiastical'.[27] Their requests were moderate: for modifications in the church service (the abolition of the sign of the cross in baptism and the use of the ring in the marriage ceremony, and so on), for the freedom of ministers not to wear church vestments, for an educated, preaching clergy, for the abolition of non-residency, and for the reform of the ecclesiastical courts and church discipline.

It is always difficult to determine the exact nature of anyone's personal faith, even of one's contemporaries, let alone of people long dead. How one envies the certainty of examination candidates who 'know' the religious beliefs of Elizabeth I or James I. Whatever his private beliefs, outwardly at any rate James I appeared to be a Calvinist, a firm believer in predestination, as were most of his subjects. Nor was he unsympathetic to most of the requests of the Puritans at the beginning of his reign. James soon made clear that he wanted to stop one of the great abuses suffered by the Church, the 'plunder' of church property and income by the crown and secular landowners. In July 1603 he announced that all income from impropriated tithes would in future be devoted to paying better salaries to church ministers, and he encouraged the enactment of a statute in 1604 which forbade archbishops and bishops to alienate ecclesiastical property even to the crown.

James was, therefore, fairly well disposed towards the Puritan reformers, and he relished the prospect of presiding over an academic, theological debate when he summoned representatives of the church hierarchy and the reformers to a conference at Hampton Court in 1604 to discuss the Millenary Petition.

---

[27] Kenyon, *Stuart Constitution*, p. 117. See also *English Historical Documents 1603–60*, document no. 152.

Information

The Hampton Court Conference, 1604

What happened at this conference has often been misunderstood by historians, largely because they have relied on an account of it by William Barlow, dean of Chester (later bishop of Rochester and bishop of Lincoln). Barlow represented the conservative wing of the Church establishment and gave the impression that James was hostile to all the Puritan demands for reform and that the conference ended in a series of bitter clashes between the king and the Puritan representatives, notably Dr John Reynolds.

However, other contemporary accounts are not so partisan. They show that the king's notorious allegation that the Puritans' opposition to bishops inclined them to republicanism ('no bishop, no king' is what he is said to have said) was based on a mistaken assumption that Reynolds was advocating the abolition of episcopacy, not a modified form of it. He then allowed himself (as he was prone to do on public occasions) to indulge in discussions about the powers of monarchs. The episode soured relations between the king and the Puritan delegates, but what it did not do was to bring about the end of the conference. This continued with the king agreeing to put into effect some of the Puritans' key demands, including the reform of the court of high commission, the abolition of the powers of chancellors and lay officials to excommunicate, and the introduction of measures to ensure a well-paid, educated ministry, and to promote preaching missions in Ireland, Wales and the northern borders, 'the dark corners of the land'.

It is true that the only permanent achievement of the conference was the beginning of a new English translation of the Bible, the Authorized Version, completed in 1611. James, perhaps because of his administrative laziness, failed to carry out the reforms agreed on at Hampton Court and a major opportunity to reform the Church was lost. But was the failure caused solely by King James?

No is the answer to that question. Behind the clerical Puritan demands in 1603–4 was the support of powerful secular opinion among the landed gentry, and it was they who had it in their power to bring about a Church staffed by well-paid, learned men. Of the 9,244 Church livings in England, 3,849 were impropriated in lay hands, which meant that the majority of the tithes in these cases were paid to the landowners, who also nominated ministers to the church benefices. Too few English landowners were willing to surrender part of their incomes for the good of the Church. In this situation was ecclesiastical reform possible?

For a time after the end of the Hampton Court Conference, James does seem to have lost his enthusiasm for church reform, for which there are at least two possible explanations. The first is that he may have felt that what had been agreed in 1604 was a 'settlement' of religion, following the precedents of religious settlements made by his royal predecessors. What also seems to have turned him temporarily away from reform of the Church was irritation at the continuation of Puritan demands for reform. He considered these unnecessary, given that a reform programme had already been agreed at Hampton Court. When parliament first met in March 1604, Puritan demands were voiced and petitions for reform were circulated, occasioning James's proclamation in July 1604 warning against 'the troublesome spirits of some persons who never receive contentment either in civil or ecclesiastical matters'.[28] In September 1604 James gave his full support to the ecclesiastical canons passed by convocation. To the dismay of godly reformers, these upheld many orthodox doctrines and liturgies of the Church, as well as practices (such as the insistence on clerical dress, the use of the sign of the cross in baptism, and bowing at the name of Jesus) which had been condemned by the godly in the Millenary Petition, at the Hampton Court Conference and in the parliamentary session of 1604. Unfortunately, during a prolonged hunting holiday in the winter of 1604–5 in Cambridgeshire and Northamptonshire, James was pestered with more Puritan petitions demanding church reform. This made him more than ever determined to ensure that what had been agreed at Hampton Court would be the limit of his religious 'settlement'.[29] The appointment of Richard Bancroft as Whitgift's successor at Canterbury – he was consecrated archbishop on 4 December 1604 – was used by James as the occasion to initiate a drive against nonconformity within the Church. Within three weeks of his consecration, acting on James's orders, Bancroft ordered that all beneficed clergy who refused to conform to the canons of 1604 should be expelled from their livings.

Was James, then, guilty of alienating Puritan opinion in England by failure to carry out reforms in the Church and by his support of Bancroft's campaign to enforce uniformity? Certainly the deprivation of ministers by Bancroft caused a great outcry. In the spring of 1605 petitions of complaint flooded in from Northamptonshire, Essex, London, Warwickshire, Leicestershire, Lincolnshire and Lancashire. Sir Francis Hastings, the instigator of the Northamptonshire petition, was placed under house arrest and deprived of the deputy-lieutenancy and his place on the county Bench. Yet Bancroft and James can hardly be said to have created a narrowly based Church by excluding many Puritan ministers and harassing nonconformist opinion. Probably not more than ninety ministers (less than 1 per cent of the total beneficed clergy) were deprived by Bancroft.[30] There was no wholesale purge of Puritan lecturers in London,

[28] J. F. Larkin and P. L. Hughes, eds., *Stuart Royal Proclamations. VII. 1: Royal Proclamations of King James I* (1973), p. 89.

[29] B. W. Quintrell, 'The royal hunt and the puritans, 1604–5', *J. Eccl. H.*, XXXI (1986).

[30] S. B. Babbage, *Puritanism and Bancroft* (1962), pp. 147–219.

and Archbishop Tobie Matthew (appointed in 1606) in the province of York was generally tolerant of nonconformist opinion.[31]

Moreover, what reinforces the view of James's drive for conformity in 1604–5 as a temporary aberration is that, after investigating the demands of the Northamptonshire petitioners, he realized his mistake in labelling them as factious subjects. Showing a political tact and adeptness for which he has not always been given due credit, James publicly acknowledged his error by declaring that the petitioners were 'good and loving subjects, rather blinded . . . with indiscreet zeal than otherwise carried by any disloyal intentions'.[32] What is more, in subsequent years James returned to his earlier commitment to moderate reform of the Church. Unlike Elizabeth I, who had steadfastly refused to budge from the 'settlement' of 1559, James allowed moderate reform beyond the limits of his 'settlement' of 1604. Nothing better underlines this contrast between the two monarchs than Elizabeth's obstinate refusal to allow 'prophesyings' – meetings of clerics and laymen, usually after church services, to discuss sermons – and James's encouragement of 'exercises', by which these means of educating parish clergy and some of their congregations were now known.

The essence of James's ecclesiastical policy for much of his reign, and one explanation for its success, is that he stood above factions within the Church.[33] He did not make the mistake of identifying himself with the new theological reaction against Calvinism among a few Anglican divines like William Barlow, Lancelot Andrewes and Richard Bancroft. James had no sympathy for divines who, like Bancroft, were beginning to believe that the authority of bishops did not depend on the king but existed by divine right. Nor had he any time for the few theologians who questioned the doctrine of predestination and stressed the contrary doctrine of free will. Most of the bishops appointed by James were orthodox Calvinists; in this sense the appointment of Bancroft as archbishop of Canterbury was 'a Jacobean anomaly'.[34] When the novel theological doctrines, which were associated with the views of a Dutch professor, Jacobus Arminius, were discussed at the Synod of Dort in 1619, James enthusiastically joined in the Synod's condemnation of 'Arminianism'. In 1611 James emphasized where he stood by his rejection of Lancelot Andrewes, an Arminian, as Bancroft's successor. Instead he appointed George Abbot, an orthodox Calvinist, as archbishop of Canterbury. Apart from his refusal to countenance parliamentary initiative in ecclesiastical reform, James only occasionally offended Puritan opinion. In this respect James's Declaration of Sports, which he issued in 1618, was an exceptional episode in his reign. The declaration, which condoned selected Sunday amusements, 'such as

---

[31] Paul S. Seaver, *The Puritan Lectureships: the politics of religious dissent 1560–1662* (1970), pp. 201–39; R. A. Marchant, *The Puritans and the Church Courts in the Diocese of York 1560–1642* (1960), p. 29.

[32] Quintrell, 'The royal hunt', p. 54.

[33] K. Fincham and P. Lake, 'The ecclesiastical policy of King James I', *J.B.S.*, XXIV (1985); idem., 'The ecclesiastical policy of James I and Charles I' in K. Fincham, ed., *The Early Stuart Church, 1603–42* (1993).

[34] N. Tyacke, 'Puritanism, Arminianism and counter revolution', in Conrad Russell, ed., *The Origins of the English Civil War* (1973), p. 126.

dancing, either for men or women, archery for men, leaping, vaulting, or any other such harmless recreation',[35] but not bear- and bull-baiting or bowling, alarmed Puritan opinion. But James eventually withdrew his order that it should be read in the churches, and it is significant that, as Gardiner noted, 'during the first ten or twelve years of Abbot's primacy the ecclesiastical history of the country was almost totally barren of events'.[36]

Until at least 1624 James successfully filled the role of arbitrator within the English Church, this remaining a broad one in which diversity of religious views and practices was allowed as long as it did not cause public controversy. As will be seen in the next chapter, James's mediatory stance came under severe strain in the last years of his reign, as Puritan criticism of his foreign policy grew in the early 1620s. But even then, religion never became the major divisive issue between crown and parliaments that it was to be during the reign of Charles I.

James's first parliament, 1604–1610

The case of the Buckinghamshire election, 1604

However, given the existence of the kind of grievances detailed in 'the Memorial' of March 1603 (see p. 94), political friction between James I and his subjects was rarely absent, especially since many English MPs were determined that the English parliament should not suffer the fate of other European representative institutions whose powers were being taken away by absolute monarchs (see above, p. 83). In at least one county, Norfolk, Elizabeth's attempts to bypass the usual channels of local government by imposing 'prerogative' government had raised a political storm in her last parliament.[37] Fears about the continuing existence of parliament go a long way to explain why the mood of the House of Commons which assembled on 19 March 1604 resembled that of its immediate predecessor in the last parliament of Elizabeth's reign in 1601: resentment at outstanding grievances, like wardship, purveyance and monopolies, combined with an ultra-sensitivity about its institutional status and privileges. However, James's handling of the House of Commons, which differed markedly from that of Elizabeth I, contributed to the discord of the session. In part this was due to James's failure to take full advantage of the political experience of the man who was his principal adviser at the start of the reign, Robert Cecil.[38]

---

[35] Tanner, *Constitutional Documents*, p. 56. See also *English Historical Documents 1603–60*, document no. 167.

[36] Gardiner, *History*, III, p. 252.

[37] A. Hassell Smith, *County and Court: government and politics in Norfolk 1558–1603* (1974), *passim*.

[38] P. Croft, 'The reputation of Robert Cecil: libels, political opinion and popular awareness in the early seventeenth century', *T.R.H.S.*, 6th ser., 1 (1991), and 'Robert Cecil', *Oxford Dictionary of National Biography*, (2004–8).

Biography

Robert Cecil (1563–1612)

Cecil's physical defects, his splayed legs and humped back, did not prevent him from becoming one of the most powerful men in late Elizabethan–early Jacobean England before he died in 1612. The only son of Elizabeth's long-serving minister, William Cecil, Lord Burghley, he became secretary of state to Queen Elizabeth in 1596, prompting the jibe that England had become 'regnum Cecilianum'. After his father's death in 1598 and the execution of his rival, the earl of Essex, in 1601 Cecil enjoyed unrivalled influence during Elizabeth's last years and he played a major role in facilitating James's accession as monarch of Britain and Ireland in 1603. For this he was showered with rewards, becoming James's principal secretary and ennobled as Lord Cecil of Essendon, 13 May 1603, Viscount Cranborne, 20 August 1604, and earl of Salisbury, 4 May 1605. On the death of the earl of Dorset in 1608 he became James's lord treasurer, a position he held until he died in 1612.

Cecil sat in the Lords, which, as yet, was in need of little management. The failure to ensure that experienced privy councillors sat in the Commons meant that there was no one there to take the initiative in raising non-controversial topics or to lead debates away from politically sensitive areas such as the extent and scope of the royal prerogative. An even more important reason why James contributed to political tensions in the English parliament was that he took some time to get used to the differences between the largely quiescent behaviour of MPs in Scottish parliaments and the vociferous, outspoken words, albeit clothed in a rhetoric of subservience, voiced by some MPs in English parliaments, which (like his son after him) James interpreted as signs of disloyalty or even sedition.

Typically, too, James, when given a public platform in parliaments (just as he had at the Hampton Court conference) could not resist allowing debates on specific topics to broaden out into discussions on fundamental constitutional principles. Indeed, he seemed to revel in the ensuing theoretical discussion. In so doing James gave an opportunity for the submerged fears about the future of parliament to surface. This is why the disputed Buckinghamshire election became the major political topic of the first session of James I's first parliament.[39] On the first day of parliamentary business

---

[39] On the attitude of the Commons to their privileges in this and other cases in the early seventeenth century, see Derek Hirst, 'Elections and the privileges of the House of Commons in the early seventeenth century: confrontation or compromise?', *H.J.*, XVIII (1974), pp. 851–62.

the Commons learned that the election of Francis Goodwin as one of the MPs for Buckinghamshire had been annulled by the court of chancery on the grounds that Goodwin was an outlaw; and that at a second election Sir John Fortescue, a privy councillor, had been returned in Goodwin's place. With European and recent Elizabethan precedents in mind, many English MPs needed little persuading that this was a clear case of undue royal interference with parliamentary business. After hearing Goodwin at the bar of the House, the Commons voted to reinstate him as an MP, and refused to discuss the matter any further with the Lords. Yet given careful handling perhaps Goodwin's case could have been settled without controversy. James's tactics made the incident into a much more serious one than it need have been.

James's first move was irreproachable. Because he felt that the Commons had acted illegally in allowing an outlaw to sit as an MP, he asked them to confer with the Lords and to get legal advice. But instead of restricting the debate within narrow legal limits, he chose to raise wider constitutional issues when he told the Commons that 'they derived all matters of privilege from him and by his grant'[40] and that all disputed elections ought to be decided by the court of chancery not the Commons. 'Now the case of Sir John Fortescue and Sir Francis Goodwin has become the case of the whole kingdom', said one MP in the excitement of the ensuing debate. Not quite. James's *public* intervention had raised a political storm, but his handling of it *in private* revealed his ability to defuse political controversies by hammering out behind-the-scenes compromises. On 11 April the king did 'meet us half way', by suggesting that both Goodwin and Fortescue should be unseated and a writ issued for a new election. In return for the Commons' acceptance of this suggestion, James acknowledged their claim to be a court of record and the judge of election returns; a right the House proceeded to exercise in two outstanding disputed election cases.[41]

Historical hindsight gives greater significance to the Goodwin case than it perhaps deserves. While it illustrates the Commons' sensitivity about status and privileges and the fears that lay behind that sensitivity, which were exacerbated by heavy-handed dealings with the Commons,[42] it does not mean that from the outset of the reign parliamentary government was impossible. Yet recent research on this period rightly warns against underestimating the extent and seriousness of the opposition to the crown at the start of James's reign as king of Britain and Ireland. The king's refusal to allow the Commons to introduce ecclesiastical reforms irritated some MPs, as has already been seen, although James was merely continuing the Elizabethan precedent of maintaining the royal prerogative right to decide religious questions. There were also rumblings of discontent on wardship and purveyance, and deep suspicions were voiced when the question of union between England and Scotland was suggested; all

---

[40] Tanner, *Constitutional Documents*, p. 204. See also *English Historical Documents 1603–60*, document no, 53.

[41] L. L. Peck, 'Goodwin v. Fortescue: the local context of parliamentary controversy', *Parliamentary History*, III (1984).

[42] For a different view of James's handling of the case, see R. C. Munden, 'The defeat of Sir John Fortescue: Court *vs* Country at the hustings?', *E.H.R.*, XCIII (1978), pp. 811–16.

became major constitutional issues in later sessions, as will be seen. *The Form of Apology and Satisfaction*, which was drafted by a group of MPs at the end of the 1604 parliamentary session, is one of the best illustrations of the threats to parliamentary liberties that some felt existed at this early stage of the reign. 'The prerogatives of princes may easily and do daily grow', wrote the drafters of *The Form of Apology*; 'the privileges of the subject are for the most part at an everlasting stand . . . they may be by good providence and care preserved, but being once lost are not recovered but with much disquiet.'[43] It is true that near the end of the parliamentary session most MPs voted against presenting *The Form of Apology and Satisfaction* to the king. Nor should it be assumed that the document represented the opinion of all MPs.[44] But the significance of the fear that parliamentary liberties were threatened by the crown should not be underestimated. Moreover, unfortunately for James in later sessions of the first parliament it became clear that there were two royal proposals which, if they were debated long enough, would produce something like a united opposition to them: the proposal for a union of England and Scotland, and that for a reform of the king's finances.

Union of England and Scotland

In the early sessions of James's first parliament the Commons clearly took the procedural initiative. It did not win (nor probably were many members seeking) initiative in the making of policy.[45] Yet opinion in the parliament was very influential in shaping and, sometimes, in negating royal policy, as is illustrated by the fate of James's hope that he might make England and Scotland one country. This plan was part of his grand design for his new kingdom: internal peace, as well as peace abroad, an end to civil war and an end to Anglo-Scottish wars. And were there not strong strategic arguments for a union of England and Scotland: 'if 20,000 men be a strong army, is not the double thereof, 40,000, a double the stronger army?'[46] Unfortunately, most Englishmen did not see a union with Scotland in the terms outlined by James's statistics, a union of equals. 'This Kingdom the more glorious the more honourable',[47] jotted down the clerk of the Commons in the *Commons Journal* in an attempt to summarize the reaction

---

[43] Tanner, *Constitutional Documents*, pp. 222–3. See also *English Historical Documents 1603–60*, document no. 61.

[44] G.R. Elton, 'A high road to civil war?' in C. H. Carter, eds., *Essays in Honour of Garrett Mattingley* (1966).

[45] Conrad Russell, 'Parliamentary history in perspective 1604–29', *History*, XLI (1976), pp. 1–27. See pp. 72–5 above.

[46] Tanner, *Constitutional Documents*, p. 26. See also *English Historical Documents 1603–60*, document no. 51.

[47] Quoted in S. T. Bindoff, 'The Stuarts and their style', *E.H.R.*, IX (1945), p. 194. For the proposed union see B. Galloway, *The Union of England and Scotland 1603–08* (1986); B. P. Levack, 'Towards a more perfect union: England, Scotland and the union' in B. Malament, ed., *After the Reformation* (1980); B. P. Levack, 'English law, Scots law and the Union' in A. Harding, ed., *Law Making and Law Makers in British History* (1980); B. P. Levack, *The Formation of the British State: England, Scotland and the Union 1603–1707* (1987); N. Cuddy, 'Anglo-Scottish union and the court of James 1603–25', *T.R.H.S.*, 5th ser., XXXIX (1989), pp. 107–24.

of MPs in April 1604 to James's proposal to unite the two kingdoms under one name, Great Britain. It did not augur well for James's hopes that merely the suggested name of the new united kingdom encountered intense opposition, especially when in April 1604 the judges gave their support to a widespread fear that a union of the two countries would destroy the laws of England. 'The first hour wherein the Parliament gives the name Great Britany', they ruled, 'there followeth necessarily . . . an utter extinction of all the laws now in force.'[48] By May 1604, according to a Commons' committee, the name 'Great Britain' became 'a thing left, and no more to be spoken of'. But at least parliament agreed in June 1604 to an Act appointing commissioners, including Francis Bacon, who were to discuss with Scottish delegates the means to 'perform and accomplish that real and effectual Union already inherent in his Majesty's Royal Blood and Person'. After the prorogation James took every step he could to further the union. By a proclamation of 20 October 1604 he declared himself 'King of Great Britain, France, and Ireland, Defender of the Faith, etc.' On 16 November he announced the issue of a union currency, beginning with a 20 shilling gold piece to be called, prophetically he hoped, a 'unite'. On 12 April 1606 all British ships were ordered to carry a new union flag devised by the College of Arms.

The union commissioners had their report ready for the third session of parliament in November 1606. The debates on the union dominated the whole session, during which it became crystal clear that few English MPs were enthusiastic about uniting with a long-established enemy and one that many Englishmen considered to be a nation of barbarians. 'They have not suffered above two Kings to die in their Beds, these two hundred Years. Our King hath hardly escaped them', sneered Christopher Piggot, MP for Buckinghamshire.[49] As in other cases of racial hostility, irrational intolerance had some economic logic, which in this case was expressed in Nicholas Fuller's parable in the full-scale Commons debate of February 1607:

> one Man is owner of two Pastures, with one Hedge to divide them; the one Pasture bare, the other fertile and good: A wise Owner will not pull down the Hedge quite, but make Gates, and let them in and out etc. If he do, the Cattle will rush in Multitudes, and much against their Will return.[50]

In this mood the Commons would only confirm a minor proposal of the union commissioners: the repeal of mutually hostile legislation. There was bitter opposition to the commissioners' plan for a commercial union and for the naturalization of Scotsmen in England and vice versa. The Commons heeded Sir Edwin Sandys's advice to 'proceed with a leaden foot'. It was Sandys who was instrumental in bringing about the collapse of the proposals when he introduced a scheme for a 'perfect union' which was idealistic and impractical. When Sir William Maurice tried to revive the union proposals at the beginning of the fourth parliamentary session in February 1610, he was greeted with

---

[48] Quoted in R. Lockyer, *The Early Stuarts: a political history of England 1603–42* (1989), p. 162.

[49] *The Parliamentary or Constitutional History of England*, V (1763), p. 178.

[50] *Commons Journals*, I, p. 334. See also *English Historical Documents 1603–60*, document no. 65.

whistles of derision.[51] All that was salvaged from James's dream was the repeal of some mutually hostile laws in 1607, an extradition agreement binding the English authorities to hand over to Scotland criminals who sought refuge in the English border counties, and, finally, a union flag which was flown by English ships until 1634.

Financial reform and the Great Contract

James regretfully had to withdraw his proposals for union. Much more serious for him was the cool parliamentary reception for his requests for help with his financial difficulties. The failure to reach a parliamentary solution to them was the prime reason for the temporary breakdown of parliamentary government in 1610.

The seriousness of the financial situation and its implications for continued political and constitutional stability have already been emphasized (pp. 81–4). Elizabeth I had only kept the royal debt down to manageable proportions at great political cost: her extreme parsimony strained the patience and loyalties of some of her courtiers and officials, and forced them to resort to extortion and corruption to supplement their meagre salaries; her extra-parliamentary taxation caused political uproar in her last parliaments; and her massive land sales eroded the crown's capital assets. In 1603, although £300,000 of the subsidy granted in 1601 had still to be collected, the crown debt was £400,000. The fundamental reasons for the insufficiencies of English public finance in the early seventeenth century have already been considered: a royal revenue system badly in need of reform, and escalating government costs to which James added by his financial extravagance. However, some of the blame that has been heaped on James for this is unfair. As a married man he had additional financial burdens; Lord Treasurer Dorset estimated that because James had a wife and family his ordinary expenses were £80,000 p.a. greater than Elizabeth's.[52] As has been seen, too, there were political reasons why James should bring an end to Elizabeth's parsimony. Even Robert Cecil, who tried to curb James's expenditure, recognized that 'for a king not to be bountiful were a fault'. Bounty and patronage were crucial elements in the contemporary political system and, when he became king of England, James had to distribute money, land and offices in order to secure the loyalties of his English subjects.

All this, though, is not an adequate defence of James's extravagance in the face of the crown's financial problems. Only a mere eighteen months after James's accession the aged Matthew Hutton, archbishop of York, was writing reproachfully to the king about popular fears 'that his excellent and heroical nature is too much inclined to giving, which in short time will exhaust the treasure of this kingdom and bring many inconveniences'.[53] In the first five years of his reign James's wardrobe expenditure increased fourfold compared with the previous four years. The treasurer of the chamber

---

[51] W. Notestein, ed., *The House of Commons 1604–10* (1971), p. 256.

[52] J. P. Cooper, 'The fall of the Stuart monarchy', in Cooper, ed., *The New Cambridge Modern History, IV: 1609–1648/59* (1970), p. 544.

[53] *H. M. C. Salisbury*, XVI, pp. 220–1.

spent 40 per cent more in the same period. Some increase in royal largesse to ministers and courtiers was perhaps inevitable, but the scale of gifts (£68,153) and pensions (nearly £30,000 p.a.) in the first four years of his reign was excessive.[54] Moreover, James compounded a financial fault by the political folly of making many gifts to Scottish favourites, notably to successive masters of the wardrobe, George Home, earl of Dunbar, and James Hay (later viscount Doncaster and earl of Carlisle). But, although parliamentary critics singled these out, James was lavish in his gifts to English courtiers as well, especially the Howards (the earls of Northampton, Suffolk and Nottingham). James was quite right when he told Cecil in 1610 that 'the English have tasted as much, and more, of my liberality than the Scots have done'.[55] Office-holders were expected to exploit their privileged position for their own private pockets, but James put no limit on this practice. Sarcastic commentators nicknamed Thomas Sackville, earl of Dorset, the lord treasurer, 'Lord Fill-Sack'. The great Jacobean palaces built by courtiers, Hatfield, Knole, Audley End, Northumberland House, are monuments to private greed and to James's failure to curb public expenditure.

On the death of Dorset in 1608, Cecil was appointed lord treasurer, combining the office with his duties as principal secretary. Cecil's administrative ability has never been in doubt. What is less clear is whether a man with Cecil's vested interests in the existing royal revenue system, especially in the customs farms, could possibly succeed in reforming it. Nevertheless, his tenure of the treasurership saw the first systematic attempt to curb expenditure and increase royal income for over half a century. By 1608 the crown debt had risen to £597,337, and after much private pleading, as his private correspondence reveals,[56] in November Cecil succeeded in extracting a public declaration from the king that he would curtail his gifts of land. Six months later James made a more sweeping promise not to alienate any crown land without the consent of the principal privy councillors, or to grant any sources of revenue as gifts or pensions. Promises, promises. James realized what the remedies were, but he failed to carry them out. This was hardly Cecil's fault; nor was the fact that his attempt to raise an economic rent from the crown estates met with only limited success. In 1608 he ordered a survey to be made of all crown lands, with the ultimate aim of revising the crown's leasing policy. This was clearly a task beyond the capability of the bureaucratic machinery of the early Stuart State. The survey was not completed; those surveys which were produced were inaccurate. Cecil had to resort instead to short-term expedients of raising money, continuing the Elizabethan sales of crown estates and the established practice of deficit borrowing: a system of financial juggling, by which old debts were

---

[54] M. Prestwich, *Cranfield: politics and profit under the early Stuarts* (1966), pp. 12–14. Mrs Prestwich amends the figures of James's expenditure in F. C. Dietz, *English Public Finance 1558–1642* (1932). See also the figures of household expenditure in P. R. Seddon, 'Household reform in the reign of James I', *B.I.H.R.*, LIII (1980).

[55] Akrigg, *Letters of King James*, p. 317.

[56] P. Croft, ed., 'A collection of several speeches of the late Lord Treasurer Cecil . . . given to King James concerning his estate and revenue in the years 1608, 1609 and 1610', Camden Miscellany, vol. XXIX (1987).

repaid by taking on new ones.[57] In the early part of the reign, until the City fathers discovered the worthlessness of royal credit, the biggest source of crown loans was the City of London; in 1608 a loan made by the City in 1604 was repaid largely because a new loan of £69,000 was being negotiated from the same source.

In this situation the prospect of a new source of income for the crown was very welcome, and this seemed to be at hand as a result of a decision in the court of exchequer in 1606 in the case of John Bate.

Information

The case of John Bate, 1606

This originated in the refusal of John Bate, apparently with the support of his fellow merchants trading to the east Mediterranean, to pay the import duty – the 'imposition' – of 5s 6d on each hundredweight of currants he imported from the Levant. Since this was in direct contravention of the crown's long-established right to levy impositions, the decision of the judges against Bate was not surprising, and raised little contemporary controversy outside that portion of the mercantile community whose pockets were hit. But what made Bate's case of political importance and caused it to be widely discussed in political circles was that one of the judges in the case, Chief Baron Fleming, as well as affirming the crown's right to levy impositions went on to make a crucial distinction between two branches of the royal prerogative. Not only did the monarch have an 'ordinary' prerogative, defined and limited by common law and parliamentary statute, but, he asserted, the crown also had an 'absolute' prerogative, which was not guided by rules 'which direct only at the common law'.[58] The impact of this judgment on a political nation that was already hypersensitive about threats to parliamentary liberties cannot be underestimated, especially when Cecil advised James that the judges' decision gave the crown the right to levy impositions both as a source of revenue and as a means of regulating trade.

In July 1608, in the first major revision of English customs duties since the marquis of Winchester's reforms in the 1550s, Cecil issued a new Book of Rates which levied impositions on 1,400 items, with a projected income for the exchequer of between £60,000 and £70,000. Something which in 1606 affected a few merchants' profits, in

---

[57] R. Ashton, 'Deficit finance in the reign of James I', *Econ. H.R.*, 2nd ser., X (1957), pp. 15–29.
[58] J. P. Kenyon, *The Stuart Constitution* (1st edn., 1966), p. 55.

1608 became a constitutional issue affecting the liberties of parliament. It is true that the Commons' petition in 1610 against impositions emphasized the commercial damage that they caused: 'the overthrow of merchants and shipping, the causing of a general dearth and decay of wealth among your people'.[59] Yet many saw impositions as a major threat to the existing constitution. Impositions contravened the 'old fundamental right' of parliament that 'no such charges should ever be laid upon the people without their common consent'.[60] 'If this power of imposing were quietly settled in our Kings,' commented James Whitelocke in parliament in 1610, 'considering what the greatest use they make of assembling Parliaments, which is the supply of money, I do not see any likelihood to hope for often meetings in that kind because they would provide themselves by that other means.'[61] No doubt it was as a result of this kind of reasoning that some began to think of ways of ensuring parliament's permanence. Significantly, between 1614 and 1621 a tract called *Motives to Induce an Annual Parliament* was being circulated among the parliamentary classes.[62] The furore stirred up by the Bate case and the Book of Rates illustrates a central theme of importance in James's reign: that finance, unlike religion, was a major political issue. A permanent solution to the crown's financial problems had to be one approved of by parliament. This Cecil realized and it accounts for his efforts to find such a solution in the fifth parliamentary session of James's reign in 1610.

At the beginning of the 1610 session, Cecil spelled out to a conference of both Houses the seriousness of the king's financial position. Despite massive land sales since 1609, the crown debt was £280,000, with current annual expenditure running at £511,000. If Cecil hoped to shock the Commons into agreeing to his request for a subsidy of £600,000, he was disappointed. Instead the House proceeded to debate possible sources of revenue other than a subsidy. One suggestion, that of collecting more fines from Catholic recusants, satisfied anti-Catholic prejudices as well as fears of higher taxation. Another, that of curbing royal expenditure, had already been tried by Cecil. He realized, just as much as radical parliamentary critics like Mr Thomas Wentworth, that by itself increased revenue was not enough,

> except it would please the King to resume his pencions granted to cortiers out of the exchecquer, and to diminish his charges and expences. For (sayes he) to what purpose it is for as to drawe a silver streame out of the country into the royall cisterne, if it shall dayly runne out thence by private cocks.[63]

The proposal which found most favour in the Commons became known as the Great Contract.

---

[59] Ibid., p. 73

[60] Ibid., p. 72.

[61] Tanner, *Constitutional Documents*, p. 262.

[62] P. Croft, 'Annual parliaments and the Long Parliament', *B.I.H.R.*, LIX (1986).

[63] S. R. Gardiner, ed., *Parliamentary Debates in 1610* (Camden Soc., 1st ser., LXXXI 1862), p. 11.

Information

The Great Contract, 1610

Its central feature was that, in return for the king's agreement to abolish wardships (the monarch's feudal right to become guardian, arrange the marriages, and administer the estates of tenants-in-chief who inherited their estates as minors), and purveyance (the right of the crown to buy goods and transport at below-market prices), parliament would grant an annual sum of money to him. James had forbidden discussions of the topic in the parliamentary sessions of 1604 and 1606 on the grounds that his feudal revenue was a prerogative matter and no concern of MPs. But on 12 March 1610 he gave way and after months of intense haggling £200,000 was being considered as a possible annual payment. The contract had a lot to recommend it both to the king and to MPs:

- From the point of view of the king, although under Cecil's mastership the revenue from the court of wards increased substantially, the actual profit for the crown was small. Revenue leaked into the pockets of officials rather than the royal exchequer, while wardships themselves brought much political opposition.

- From the point of view of landowning MPs, the abolition of wardships was considered (in the words of Sir Edwin Sandys in the parliament of 1604) 'but a restitution unto the original right of all men, by the Law of God and Nature, which is that children should be brought up by their parents and next of kin and by them be directed in their marriages'.

Negotiations for the Great Contract seemed to be going quite smoothly. James's concession on the discussion of wardships pleased the Commons. The king, with considerable political adroitness, also dealt with some other grievances. He agreed to suppress Dr Cowell's book, *The Interpreter*, a law dictionary which had caused some offence by, for example, defining 'King' as someone who 'is above the law by his absolute power'. More significantly, he listened favourably to many of the Commons' long-standing demands for ecclesiastical reform: better execution of the recusancy laws, the reinstatement of deprived ministers, the end of pluralities, non-residency, excommunication for trivial offences and prohibitions. However, the real obstacle to the successful conclusion of the contract was the opposition to impositions levied by Cecil's Book of Rates. When the Commons' committee of grievances considered the matter, James, on 11 May, announced that all discussion of the matter was to end, and ten days later he addressed the Commons personally, defending his right to levy impositions. Not surprisingly, given the precedents of Elizabeth's later parliaments, the Commons considered this an attack on the 'ancient, generall, and undoubted right of parliament to debate freely all things properly concerning the subjects, and theyre rights and interests'. The negotiations over the contract were thus jeopardized. But James smoothed the path by removing his ban on discussion of impositions and by making it clear that any MP was welcome to approach him privately 'without using ceremonies and compliments', to thrash out any grievances. Moreover, in late June and early July he promised to agree to an Act which would prevent him from levying impositions in future without parliamentary consent. Since this left untouched those impositions already in existence, James's concessions could hardly have satisfied the Commons completely. But perhaps they had done enough to divide the House and gain some support for the contract. By the time parliament was prorogued on 23 July, the prospects for a successful conclusion of the contract seemed good. A subsidy was agreed, a bill prohibiting impositions passed the Commons, and agreement was reached on £200,000 as an acceptable compensation for the abolition of feudal tenures and wardships.

Why, then, did the Great Contract fail? When parliament reassembled in October most MPs were quite clearly dragging their feet. A week after the appointed starting date of the session, only one hundred MPs were present and penalties were proposed for non-attendance. One explanation for the change of mood is that it was a reflection of opinion in the constituencies. Could James be trusted to redress the Commons' grievances as he had promised he would do in July? 'If we should now return into our country', said one MP, 'with nothing for the good of the commonwealth, they would say we have been all the while like children in ketching butterflies.'[64] In any case how would the £200,000 p.a. be raised? By a permanent land tax? 'It is impossible to rayse 200,000 *li* out of the land onely', said another MP, 'the rest out of merchandise and a running subsidy from the monied men.' 'If we go forward,' said Sir Thomas Beaumont, 'wee are undone, charging the land so deeply as is desyred.'[65] More seriously, would not a permanent addition to the royal revenue make the king independent of parliament at a time when other representative assemblies in Europe were losing any power they had to absolutist monarchs?

But it was not only MPs who had had second thoughts during the recess. Sir Julius Caesar, the chancellor of the exchequer, questioned whether the financial gains to the king from the abolition of feudal tenures would be very great. Since the king would lose an estimated £115,000 p.a. which he got from his feudal rights, the actual increase in revenue would only be £85,000 p.a., which was hardly sufficient to meet a total debt of £600,000 and high current expenditure. An equally serious defect of the Great Contract from the crown's point of view was that the agreed compensation of £200,000 payable to the crown for the abolition of feudal tenures was a fixed one, its

---

[64] Quoted in Prestwich, *Cranfield*, p. 29.
[65] Gardiner, ed., *Parliamentary Debates in 1610*, p. 129. See also *English Historical Documents 1603–60*, document no. 222.

value gradually being eroded in an inflationary age. The crown, too, would lose a valuable source of patronage. The Great Contract, concluded Caesar, 'wilbee the most unprofitable bargaine that ever King made, to part with most of the greatest pre-rogatives of gaine and honor which he hathe, and not to relieve that want which was the onelie motive of that resoluccion'.[66] There were others on the king's side who had more selfish motives than Caesar to poison the king's mind against the contract; many had much to lose if the sale of wardships was abandoned. Robert Carr, James's Scottish favourite, who was the butt of much of the anti-Scottish feeling in the Commons, aligned himself against the contract and the continuation of parliament. Not for the last time, division among James's courtiers was reflected in events in parliament. In addition, by the autumn James, with a newly negotiated City loan of £100,000 in his pocket, felt more financially secure. As a result when the negotiations on the contract were resumed in November, both sides raised their terms and the contract quickly collapsed. Parliament was prorogued until February 1611, but before that James dissolved his first parliament.

How serious was this failure of parliamentary government? How deep and wide was the gulf between James and the parliamentary classes in 1610? Events since 1603 showed that there were large areas of agreement between him and his leading subjects: the king's foreign policy had been successful; on religious questions the king generally took an uncontroversial stance; and he had shown that even on the issues of impositions and parliamentary freedom of speech he was willing to listen to reason. The attachment of the political nation to the monarchy and the old constitution was still strong in 1610. Yet James had failed either to satisfy many grievances or to calm the widespread fears about the future of parliament in the constitution. The events of the next eleven years were to inject more tension into the political life of Jacobean England.

Rule without parliament, 1610–1621

The Howards and the ruin of the royal finances, 1610–1618

Despite the City loan of 1610, the failure of the Great Contract left James desperately short of money. More than ever in the following years he was ready to listen to anyone who had a scheme to raise extra-parliamentary revenue. The result was a succession of financial expedients which did not raise enough money either to meet the king's escalating costs or to compensate for the injury they did to the crown's reputation. Some of the money-raising ventures were well-used ones, such as continuing the sale of crown estates and monopolies, increasing the price of wardships and levying a forced loan (in 1611), but the fact that they were not new (indeed, all of them had been used by Elizabeth I) did not make them any more popular.

---

[66] Ibid., p. 176. See also *English Historical Documents 1603–60*, document no. 222.

Perhaps the most damaging to the crown was a scheme certainly not resorted to by the late queen, the sale of honours. Elizabeth I exercised just as much tight-fisted control on the creation of new titles of honour as she did on royal expenditure. In his wholesale creation of knights on his accession, James I was therefore simply giving way to the pent-up demands of many gentry for outstanding recognition of their social status. James, however, went too far. By permitting courtiers to sell knighthoods he allowed the rank to fall into popular disrepute. 'Two walking espyed one a far off', began a popular joke; 'the one demanded what he should be, the other answered he seemed to be a gentleman; no, I warrant you, says the other, I think he is but a knight.' The devaluation of the knightage provided the opportunity for James to take up one of the many ideas being mooted for the creation of a new hereditary dignity. In 1611 the order of baronets was established, to consist of 200 members, and, although James promised that only those from worthy, ancient families would be chosen, little care was taken in this regard. Baronetcies were sold to anyone who could afford the £1,095 purchase price, bringing in a revenue to the crown by March 1614 of £90,885.[67] Thereafter the income to the crown from the sale of baronetcies fell rapidly, as James allowed courtiers and others to sell them for services rendered. The baronetcy, like the knightage before it, became devalued, which struck at the roots of a society which valued the stability brought by respect for order, 'degree' and precedence. Nor were these financial expedients sufficiently successful in their primary aim. In August 1612 James established a special commission, headed by Sir Thomas Roe, whose terms of reference were to devise yet more money-making projects.

In the years after 1610 the Howards slowly increased their influence at the Jacobean court. Cecil's failure to secure the Great Contract marked the end of his special relationship with the king. Before and after his death in May 1612, his enemies at court lost no opportunity to attack him and his reputation. Yet with all his faults and limitations Cecil's death in 1612 was a great loss to the crown. There was no one of equal administrative ability to replace him, which perhaps James, to his credit, recognized. He put the treasury into commission and made no appointment to Cecil's other office of secretary, which must have been a great blow to the Howards, who hoped to benefit from Cecil's death. Their setback was short-lived, however. In 1613 the divorce of Lady Frances Howard, the earl of Suffolk's daughter, and the earl of Essex enabled Lady Frances to marry the king's youthful favourite, Robert Carr, now earl of Somerset. James intervened personally to secure the divorce against the opinion of Archbishop Abbot. The marriage signalled the triumph of the Howards' political ambitions.

Although it is now clear that the Howards, and especially Henry Howard, earl of Northampton, do not deserve the bad reputation they have had as the source of corruption and decay at the Jacobean court in the second decade of the Stuart age,[68] the period when their influence was strongest was marked by the temporary collapse

---

[67] L. Stone, *The Crisis of the Aristocracy 1558–1641* (1965), p. 85.
[68] L. L. Peck, 'Problems of Jacobean administration: was Henry Howard, earl of Northampton, a reformer?', *H.J.*, XIX (1976); L. L. Peck, *Northampton: patronage and policy at the court of James I* (1982).

of effective reform measures. Northampton in 1608 and 1613 headed commissions to investigate abuses in the navy, which was administered by his cousin Charles Howard, earl of Nottingham. His reports revealed examples of gross corruption and fraud, but nothing was done to put a stop to them. Northampton, like Cecil before him, found that James failed to give his full support to his reforming ambitions. Without this support, the plans for financial reforms produced by a treasury commission in 1613 inevitably remained paper schemes. James was reduced to the plight of borrowing from courtiers (in 1613 he borrowed £25,000 from Somerset) and selling more crown lands. So, despite Howard opposition, the pressure for calling another parliament became intense, and James gave way in February 1614. But the Howards were more successful in blocking concessions on grievances, such as impositions and monopolies, urged on the king by Sir Henry Neville and Francis Bacon. Nor, as ten years earlier, were provisions made to provide official leadership in the Commons. James appointed Ralph Winwood as secretary only seven days before parliament met in April 1614. While it is not surprising that in these circumstances the Commons proved intractable, it is ironic that the fiercest opposition developed because of suspicions that there had been too much royal influence before parliament met. Hard on the heels of the grievances about the activities of royal 'undertakers' (seen in the Commons' attacks on Parry and Bacon) came the more predictable stormy outcry against impositions, which (as in 1610) developed into a debate on MPs' freedom of speech, issues which (unlike 1610) now received significant support in the Lords as well as in the Commons as members of both Houses were outraged by Bishop Neile's 'noli tangere' ['do not touch'] speech, in which he claimed that impositions were an untouchable part of the royal prerogative. The 1614 parliament well deserves its nickname 'the Addled Parliament'.[69] It was dissolved on 7 June, having passed no legislation and, more seriously for James, no subsidy. Why did it fail? Was it due entirely to lack of royal management and the failure to remove outstanding grievances before parliament met? It may be that some royal advisers did not want the parliament to succeed and worked hard behind the scenes for its failure, perhaps by encouraging rumours of the activities of royal 'undertakers'. The Piedmontese ambassador thought that 'the dissolution of Parliament is not displeasing to many of the more important councillors, since it appears that there was to be an investigation of some of them, which would have caused them much trouble and embarrassment'.[70]

James's celebrated outburst to Gondomar, venting his frustration at parliament in 1614, is often used as evidence of James's ultimate ambition never to call parliament again. There is little corroboratory support for this. In the following years serious consideration was frequently given to summoning parliament, as the search for ways to pay the mounting royal debts became more desperate. Because royal credit was so bad the City dried up (temporarily) as a source of loans; in June 1614 it made James

---

[69] T. Moir, *The Addled Parliament of 1614* (1958), C. Russell, *The Addled Parliament of 1614: the limits of revisionism* (1992).

[70] Quoted in Clayton Roberts, *The Growth of Representative Government in Stuart England* (1976), p. 22.

a free gift of £10,000 rather than lend him £100,000. The king, however, had not lost everyone's goodwill. When he appealed for a voluntary loan or 'benevolence' there was some resistance, but it was far from universal. Thomas Wentworth in Yorkshire, for example, spoke in its favour and there is evidence that some MPs towards the end of the Addled Parliament had been willing to vote a subsidy to prevent the dissolution.[71]

But other financial expedients after 1614 did have more serious consequences. The Cockayne Project for the reorganization of the cloth trade, which has already been mentioned, is not the only example of this (see pp. 15–16). The real aim of the commission set up in May 1615, despite its overt town-planning motives and James's protestations, was not to prevent further building in London but to raise money by collecting fines for evading the ban on building. The irritation felt at this, though, was a pinprick compared with the sale of peerages which began in 1615. The gains were lucrative (earldoms went for £10,000 each) but a lot of the profit was syphoned off by intermediaries, and the sales were naturally resented by the established aristocracy. Nor was the increase in crown revenue sufficient to meet the crown's expenditure. By 1617 the royal debt was £726,000 and James had great difficulty in paying for his visit to Scotland in that year. One man had even been willing to bet that it (and Raleigh's trip to Guiana, and the Spanish marriage) would never take place.[72] So suspicious was the City of the soundness of royal credit that it would lend James £100,000 for one year only; it surrounded the loan with unprecedented guarantees and still the City authorities had great difficulties in forcing merchants to contribute to it.

Not only the royal credit (in the financial sense) was brought low during the supremacy of the Howards; so too was its general 'credit', its reputation. The revelations and allegations in 1615 of the earl and countess of Somerset's role in the murder in 1613 of Sir Thomas Overbury, who had opposed Lady Frances's divorce, and the subsequent investigation and trial formed one of the seamier scandals of Jacobean England.[73] The Howards were also the centre for another *cause célèbre* in 1618 when the earl of Suffolk (lord treasurer since 1614) and his wife were tried for financial corruption, and their fall brought the disgrace of many important Howard clients, including William, Lord Knollys and Sir Thomas Lake. By this time the Howards could be forgiven for feeling they were the subject of a witch-hunt, because in a sense they were. The attack on them was pressed home by an anti-Howard faction at court (including Archbishop Abbot, Lord Ellesmere who died in 1617, Sir Edward Coke, and the earls of Southampton and Pembroke). It was they who promoted George Villiers in his attempt to replace Somerset in the king's affections. Their (and his) success is charted in the rapidly rising fortunes of George Villiers.

---

[71] J. P. Cooper, ed., *The Wentworth Papers 1597–1628*. Camden Society, 4th ser., XII (1973), pp. 79–80 and 80 n. 1.

[72] Gardiner, *History*, III, p. 82.

[73] A. Bellamy, *The Politics of Court Scandal in Early Modern England: news culture and the Overbury affair, 1603–1660* (2002).

Biography

George Villiers, duke of Buckingham (1592–1628)

Villiers's career demonstrates that it was possible to rise to political power in early Stuart England from fairly lowly social origins. He was the second son of a minor Leicester gentleman but yet had a meteoric rise to power from royal cupbearer in 1614 to duke of Buckingham in 1623. This is to be explained by the fact that James liked him (his relationship with the king was probably a homosexual one) and because he secured the backing of the anti-Howard faction at the Jacobean court.

Villiers also became a favourite of Prince Charles, whom he accompanied on his visit to Madrid in 1623. When Charles became king, Villiers wielded even more influence than he had done before 1625. As lord of the admiralty he had a major role in the war against Spain and France and monopolized royal patronage for his own advantage. This and the failure of the war effort made him the focus of massive parliamentary opposition in Charles's first parliaments. Charles saved him from parliamentary impeachment, but he could not shield him from the anger of John Felton, a disgruntled army officer, who assassinated him at Portsmouth on 23 August 1628.

Buckingham, Cranfield and reform, 1618–1621

Able men round James, like Sir Francis Bacon who became lord chancellor in January 1618, saw that reform was necessary in order to restore royal credit, financially and otherwise, from the low point to which it had been reduced in recent years. Buckingham rose to a powerful position as a protégé of this reforming, anti-Howard faction, and soon he was secure in James's favour. 'Christ had his John', James is alleged to have said, 'and I have my George.' Buckingham, however, had little reason to desert those who were working for financial reform, especially since reform was a useful stick with which to beat the Howards. As a reformer, Buckingham found an ally not only in the lord chancellor but also in Lionel Cranfield.

Despite snobbish jibes at his mercantile 'apprentice-boy' background, Cranfield had carved out a useful career for himself at court: in 1615 he became surveyor-general of the customs and in 1616 master of the court of requests. An astute, careful business-man in the running of his own personal and business affairs, he was ideally suited to cutting out wasteful and needless public expenditure. This was the aim of what turned out to be a series of investigatory commissions into the running of royal departments of state. The first, concerned with the royal household, was intended to be 'the beginning for the Reformation of all the heads of his Majesty's expense'. Cranfield and

Sir Richard Weston, together with officials from the exchequer, painstakingly examined the household consumption of food, drink, fuel and clothes. No detail was beneath them; Cranfield even investigated the waste of unburnt candle ends. At the end of their investigation the commissioners issued a new Book of Orders for the running of the household which effected an estimated saving of £10,000 p.a. In June 1618 another commission with Cranfield prominent in its membership began to investigate the administration of the navy, revealing similar waste and corruption to that in the household. Buckingham also took a first-hand interest in the work of this subcommission, and with his support (in January 1619 he replaced Nottingham as lord admiral) the programme of retrenchment met with a great deal of success. In the treasury the blatant peculation, which resulted in the disgrace of the Suffolks and their colleagues, was uncovered by yet another team of investigators led by Cranfield. The reform of two other departments was Cranfield's own personal triumph. As master of the wardrobe from September 1618, he halved royal expenditure; and he increased the revenue of the court of wards by one-quarter after he became master of the court in January 1619.

Impressive as was Cranfield's work in its thoroughness in rationalizing the existing administrative system, it was not a permanent solution to James's shortage of money. Why could even an administrator of the proven ability of Cranfield (and Cecil before him) not achieve the reform that James needed? The Stuarts' lack of a large and experienced bureaucracy is only part of the answer. Even if there had been the necessary administrative machinery, was fundamental reform of the crown's finance and administration possible? It is significant that there was a great deal of powerful opinion against reform; too many people had a vested interest in the existing system. Buckingham's very presence at court meant that royal largesse, in the form of grants of offices, pensions and monopolies, went on unabated. Despite his adopted role, Buckingham's powerful position (and that of his mother and brothers) depended far too much on the court system for the duke to be a serious reformer. It is difficult to escape the conclusion that for Buckingham reform was valued as a political weapon against the Howards rather than a desirable end in itself.[74] The influence of Buckingham's mother, Lady Compton, was all-pervasive, building up a Villiers connection so impressive that Gondomar, the Spanish ambassador, wrote home ironically to his masters in Madrid that he had more hope than ever of the conversion of England, since he found that there were more prayers and oblations offered to the mother than to the son.[75] The Villiers were a serious obstacle to reform. So too was Cranfield himself. How serious depends on whether or not one considers the private fortune he made as a royal servant justified as a reward for his administrative ability and technical expertise in dealing with customs farmers and other financiers. One is left with the impression that both inside and outside the court circle there was a general unwillingness to countenance radical and administrative reform. It is easy to understand why courtiers resented the imposition of irksome

---

[74] G. Aylmer, 'Buckingham as an administrative reformer?', *E.H.R.*, CV (1990).

[75] Gardiner, *History*, III, pp. 207–8.

economy measures and the pruning of valuable sinecures and pensions by a man they considered to be a social upstart. Yet the same is true of the man making his career at court and the man living on his country estates in the early seventeenth century: both saw the court as the fount of honour and advancement. Courtier and parliamentarian, royal administrator and country gentleman must have had an ambivalent attitude to reform. Was it only James's extravagance, aided and abetted by the Howards, Villiers and others at court, that frustrated the reforming efforts of the two men with most administrative ability in James's reign, Cecil and Cranfield? Or is it justifiable to place part of the blame, at least, at the door of the whole political nation? It is possible that some of those who demanded reform, administrative as well as ecclesiastical, in the early seventeenth century had in their own hands the means to carry it out.

It was inevitable, therefore, that at some stage James would have to recall parliament. What finally ensured that it was called were international developments which threatened the European peace established in 1604 and 1609. As has been seen, James believed that he could play a vital role in maintaining this peace by not aligning himself solely either with France or with Spain, either with the Protestant or with the Catholic sides in Germany. He hoped that his daughter's marriage to the Protestant Elector Palatine would be balanced by a Spanish Catholic marriage for his son. This is why James's negotiations with Spain became the keystone of his foreign policy in his later years. As he saw it, Spain must not be allowed to feel isolated in Europe; by keeping diplomatic channels open, James could use his influence to defuse international crises. His attachment to this policy, contrary to the traditional view, owed little to the influence of the Spanish ambassador, Gondomar – James's foreign policy was his own – and even less to the Spanish pensions paid to Somerset, the Howards, Buckingham and others. James was not alone in his financial difficulties; quite often the Spanish pensions were never paid. And as Professor C. H. Carter notes, 'Spain, far from being in control of its hirelings, was rather in the position of a hapless diner who must "bribe" a surly waiter with tips to avoid soup getting spilled on him.'[76]

Even after his son-in-law's rebellion – in September 1619 Elector Palatine Frederick accepted the rebels' offer of the Bohemian crown – James tried to maintain an uncommitted position. Despite the pressure of some of his advisers, led by Archbishop Abbot, for stronger action, James continued to rely on a diplomatic solution. The marriage negotiations in Madrid continued, and in Brussels Sir Richard Weston and Sir Edward Conway were sent to argue against the invasion of the Palatinate. Even after this happened at the end of August 1620, and even after Imperial troops won a crushing victory outside Prague at the Battle of White Mountain on 29 October 1620, forcing Elector Palatine Frederick and his queen, James's daughter, to vacate their recently occupied throne in Bohemia and flee into exile, James did not abandon his diplomatic contacts with Spain. But the invasion of the Palatinate did

---

[76] C. H. Carter, *The Secret Diplomacy of the Hapsburgs 1598–1625* (1964), pp. 126–7; C. H. Carter, 'Gondomar: ambassador to James I', *H.J.*, VII (1964).

force him to consider the possibility, at least, that he might have to go to war against Spain; as he had made clear in 1604, James's pacific philosophy did not rule out the use of war as the last resort when diplomacy failed. War preparations meant the need for parliamentary finance, and writs for parliamentary elections inevitably followed Spinola's invasion of the Lower Palatinate. The always close connection between foreign policy and domestic history is nowhere better illustrated. It is no coincidence that England's temporary involvement in the Thirty Years War in the 1620s was a crucial period in England's domestic political history.

5

The breakdown of the Elizabethan constitution, 1621–1640

Historiography

Changing explanations for the unpopularity of Charles I by 1640

For many years the unpopularity of Charles I and the crown by 1640 were seen as the result of long-term developments. However, during the last quarter of the twentieth century many of these were shown by 'revisionist' historians to be flawed. The major long-term explanations were:

- 'The rise of Parliament' argument (see Chapter 3). This collapsed when it became clear that most MPs in later Tudor and early Stuart parliaments were merely determined to safeguard existing parliamentary liberties, not to win new ones.

- 'The rise of Puritanism' argument (see Chapter 2). Doubt was cast on this by the realization that most Puritans in late sixteenth- and early seventeenth-century England merely wanted reform within the national Church and were staunch upholders of the existing social and political order.

- 'The rise of the gentry' argument. There is little evidence that the gentry were driven to oppose the crown in order to gain new political powers for themselves to match their improved economic and social status.

> 'Revisionist' explanations for the growth of opposition to Charles I therefore emphasized short-term, contingent, factors, principally the fact that Charles I had few of the attributes that had enabled his father to be a successful ruler. Despite some recent attempts to rehabilitate Charles's reputation (see the works by Sharpe and Kishlansky in the Bibliographical note, p. 521), it seems likely that the new king contributed personally to the predicament he found himself in by 1640.

Students need to consider whether Charles's weakness as a king is the sole (or main) cause of the crisis faced by Charles I and the crown by 1640. As has been seen in previous chapters, there were long-term factors rooted in the existing political, constitutional and religious situation that constantly threatened the stability of later sixteenth- and early seventeenth-century England. Moreover, although during the first eighteen years of his reign James I was much more successful than he has often been represented in preventing these tensions from erupting into major crises (most notably in his handling of ecclesiastical affairs), political conflict was always just below the surface calm of life in Jacobean England. Even though there is no evidence that James I intended either to rule without, or to erode the power of, parliaments, fear and mistrust of the 'absolutist' intentions of the monarchy remained very much alive throughout his reign.

This can be seen after the outbreak of the Thirty Years War in 1618 and the eruption of a severe economic crisis in 1621–3, which intensified the tensions that had long threatened to destabilize the early Stuart State. As in an earlier period of war and economic crisis in the 1590s, England in the 1620s underwent a period of intense political instability. The conflicting conspiracy theories – of a 'Popish Plot' and a 'Puritan Plot' – that were to be so divisive in the early 1640s can already be seen. During the last few years of his reign, James I found it more difficult than ever to maintain harmony between the crown and the parliamentary classes.

Yet, in this task he had more success than his son, Charles I, who succeeded his father as king in 1625. There are three principal reasons for this. The first is that Charles I had little of his father's political ability and proved to be inflexible and uncompromising to the point of ineptness, whereas James's innate political shrewdness and flexibility enabled him to ride out political storms in a way that was later characteristic of Charles II. Secondly, whereas James I tried (not always with total success, as will be seen) to act as an impartial arbitrator between different factions within the English Church, his son abandoned any such attempt with the result that religion became a serious divisive issue for the first time in early Stuart England. Thirdly, unlike his father, Charles I failed as ruler of his multiple kingdoms. The contrast between father and son as kings of Britain is clearest in the case of Scotland. Charles's blundering policies north of the border had the catastrophic consequence of uniting against him not only most of his English subjects but also many of his Scottish ones.

1621–1624: the emergence of conflicting conspiracy theories[1]

In 1621 there were many things which the leaders of English landed society found distasteful in the events since the dissolution of the Addled Parliament in 1614. The image that recurs in Jacobean literature of a corrupt and decadent court had gained some substance through the financial and sexual scandals that had brought many prominent courtiers to the Tower by 1621. No doubt William Davenport in Cheshire was not the only country gentleman to note disapprovingly in his commonplace book such court scandals as the Essex divorce and the Overbury murder.[2] The 'inflation of honours', too, was felt to be undermining the prestige of the landed elite and this may have contributed to the new, more critical, role of the House of Lords in the constitutional conflicts of the 1620s. The increasing use of patents and monopolies, as well as the collection of impositions, also kept alive the image of a court that was a threat to parliamentary liberties.

In the early 1620s another, even more potentially damaging, source of dissatisfaction with the court became prominent: James's persistent diplomatic negotiations for a marriage between Prince Charles and the Spanish Infanta at a time when many of his subjects, and especially the godly, were urging him to aid his Protestant son-in-law against the rampant Catholic Habsburg forces in the Palatinate. The effect was to cause mutual mistrust to grow between James and some of his vocal subjects both inside and outside the court. In 1620, Thomas Scott in a controversial pamphlet, *Vox Populi*, denounced the king's pro-Spanish policies, using the full range of Protestant anti-papal polemic, and adding yet more fuel to a growing debate in 'the public sphere'.[3] Scott was forced to flee to the Low Countries to escape James's wrath, but his fears that James might not be the 'godly prince' he had appeared to be for most of his reign hitherto were shared by prominent courtiers like Archbishop Abbot and the earl of Pembroke. Moreover, what fuelled such fears were alarming indications not only that James was doggedly pursuing the reviled Spanish match negotiations but also that he seemed to be moving towards the 'Laudian' group within the Church.[4] As in 1604–5

---

[1] For the enormous influence of conspiracy theories in early modern England and continental Europe, see the essays in B. Coward and J. Swann, eds., *Conspiracies and Conspiracy Theory in Early Modern Europe; from the Waldensians to the French Revolution* (2004). For the importance of conspiracy theories in early Stuart England, see R. Cust ' "Patriots" and "popular spirits": narratives of conflict in early Stuart England', in N. Tyacke, ed., *The English Revolution c.1590–1720* (2008).

[2] J. S. Morrill, *Cheshire 1603–60: county government during the 'English Revolution'* (1974), pp. 21–2; Bellamy, *Politics of Court Scandal in Early Modern England*.

[3] P. Lake, 'Constitutional consensus and puritan opposition in the 1620s: Thomas Scott and the Spanish match', *H.J.* (1982); T. Cogswell, 'England and the Spanish Match' in R. Cust and A. Hughes, eds., *Conflict in Early Stuart England: studies in religion and politics 1603–42* (1989).

[4] See p. 86 and pp. 152–3 for the reasons why 'Laudian' rather than 'Arminian' or 'anti-Calvinist' has been chosen to describe members of this group and their beliefs.

James found exceedingly irritating the persistent demands of Puritans – this time that he should align himself militarily with the godly cause in Europe – and he correspondingly found attractive the views of those Laudian divines who supported his diplomatic negotiations with Spain. Until now, James's ecclesiastical policies had been characterized (as has been seen) by a desire to help Protestants who disagreed with each other to 'meet in the middest which is the centre and perfection of all things'.[5] In allowing divines like William Laud, bishop of St David's, greater prominence in theological debates at court, and in 1624 not censoring Richard Montague's publication of a Laudian tract, *A New Gag for an Old Goose,* James seemed to be wobbling from his position as arbitrator within the English Church. The parallel with 1604–5 can also be seen in the way in which in 1622 James banned sermons on controversial matters. As at the start of his reign, he again considered Puritan demands irresponsible and dangerous disturbances of the political order, while James's restrictions on sermons reinforced Puritan suspicions that he was straying from the godly path. This was the view that spread amongst godly Protestants in Scotland as well as in England when in 1618 James exerted great pressure on a general assembly of the Scottish Kirk to accept five ceremonial and liturgical changes (the Five Articles of Perth), including kneeling at communion, which were seen by some as a dangerous move towards Catholicism.[6] The result was to inject into the political climate of the last years of James's reign a new ideologically divisive issue.

It would, though, be wrong to characterize these divisions simply as those between 'court and country', 'king and parliament' or 'crown and opposition'. Such analyses are too simple and cut-and-dried to take account of the numerous political alliances of courtiers, privy councillors and parliamentary leaders that were made in the early 1620s. MPs could ill afford lightly to cut themselves off from the prospects of court office or court patronage, without which their local prestige would suffer. When and why most of them did break with the court are, of course, crucial questions in explaining the collapse of the old constitution and the crisis of 1640–1. It does not seem, though, that many were forced into taking this drastic course in the last years of James's reign. The reasons behind the political battles in his last parliaments of 1621 and 1624 are to be found in differences between royal councillors as well as in 'country' mistrust of 'court' policies.[7]

The parliament of 1621 began fairly well for the crown. In February, in only the third week of the opening session, James was offered a grant of two subsidies (about £140,000), which, though not enough to pay for an army, did not preclude the possibility of a further

---

[5] Quoted in T. H. Wadkins, 'The Percy–"Fisher" controversies and the ecclesiastical politics of Jacobean anti-Catholicism 1622–25', *Church History*, LVII (1988), p. 153. See also Fincham and Lake, 'Ecclesiastical policy of King James'.

[6] A. R. Macdonald, *The Jacobean Kirk, 1576–1625: sovereignty, polity and liturgy* (1998) and his article, 'James VI and I: the Church of Scotland and British ecclesiastical convergence', *H.J.*, vol. 48, (2005); Laura Stewart, '"Brothers in treuth": propaganda, public opinion and the Perth Articles debate in Scotland' in Houlbrooke, ed., *James VI and I*; and her *Urban Politics and the British Civil Wars: Edinburgh 1617–53* (2006).

[7] D. Hirst, 'Court, country and politics before 1629', in K. Sharpe, ed., *Faction and Parliament: essays in early Stuart history* (1985).

grant. Unfortunately, though, the privy council, although much better represented in the Commons than in any previous Jacobean parliament, was deeply divided. The crown's leading advisers, Bacon, Coke and Cranfield, treated each other with mutual wariness. Already the royal preparations for the parliamentary session (which were much more thorough than in 1614) had been hindered by opposition in the privy council, led by the Villiers connection and by Coke, to Bacon's proposal to withdraw some patents of monopoly before parliament met and so remove this source of grievance. Sir Edward Coke's antipathy to Bacon was due to a mixture of long-standing professional rivalry, personal incompatibility and differing views on the independence of the judiciary, for his defence of which Coke had been dismissed in 1616 as chief justice of the King's Bench. In 1617 he was restored to the privy council and was hopeful of preferment as lord treasurer. In these circumstances the appointment in December 1620 to the treasurership of Sir Henry Montague, who had replaced Coke as chief justice in 1616, was, to say the least, ill-timed, and partly accounts for Coke's criticism of royal policies later. If Coke hated Bacon, Cranfield's mercantile origins and his continuing reform programme left him isolated at court. It is a tragedy that he was unable to find any common personal ground with Bacon, who also had plans for reform.

Members of parliament were treated to the unusual[8] sight of privy councillors, Coke and Cranfield, encouraging them from the start of the parliamentary session to enquire into royal grants of patents of monopoly. They found willing support among MPs in making this the dominant issue of the session (30 January to 4 June 1621) for two main reasons. First, parliament met at a time of grave economic crisis and MPs did not need convincing that monopolies had been injurious to trade. The patent of the monopoly of gold and silver thread, for example, it was said in the Commons on 26 February, 'did waste 200,000*l* of our coin, and stayed the importation of 20,000*l* more in bullion brought in from Venice in that commodity', thus contributing to the 'want of money' which contemporaries believed to be at the root of the crisis.[9] Moreover, many monopolies seemed to have been granted to courtiers who could pay for a patent, regardless of good commercial sense. The Cockayne Project was still fresh in people's memories. Secondly, not all patents were grants of a commercial monopoly; James I, like Elizabeth before him, entrusted specific administrative functions of government to patentees, a system which bypassed the normal local government process and which was open to the charge of being 'government by patentees'. Two such grants, giving the right to commissioners to license inns and alehouses respectively, had caused special annoyance to local magistrates and the Commons began proceedings against Giles Mompesson and Sir Francis Michell, the chief patentees. Mompesson was especially singled out for attack, because he was both a multiple monopolist (as well as the patent for inns, he was involved in the patent for the manufacture of gold and silver thread and for the concealment of crown lands) and an MP and therefore vulnerable to the process of

---

[8] Elizabethan privy councillors had sometimes encouraged parliamentary opposition to royal policies but never as blatantly as in 1621.

[9] Thirsk and Cooper, p. 3. See above, p. 15.

existing parliamentary judicature. Ominously for the crown, a subcommittee of the Commons began systematically investigating any royal patent or monopoly which was referred to it, questioning the patentee and deciding on its validity.

Not only were these novel incursions into judicial spheres by the Commons directly encouraged by privy councillors, but Coke and Cranfield were also involved in promoting an attack on their rival, Bacon, which was of even greater constitutional significance. The lord chancellor had been one of the referees who had sanctioned the grants of patents, and, with vocal support from Coke and Cranfield, the demand grew for punishment of the referees as well as the patentees, so that 'the Saddle [may be] set on the right Horse'.[10] The willingness of the House of Lords to cooperate with the Lower House in the proceedings against Bacon was crucial. Hitherto in previous Jacobean parliaments, opposition in the Lords had been fairly unimportant, but in 1621 the leadership of the earls of Southampton and Oxford, who were in close contact with the Commons' campaign against Bacon, swayed the Lords, many of whom were dismayed by Buckingham's domination of the king. Nor did James do anything to protect his lord chancellor. In addition to making it known, as he did on 10 March, that he would listen favourably to a bill against monopolies, he also allowed Bacon to be sacrificed. Lacking the king's support, Bacon submitted to the Lords on a charge of having accepted bribes in his position as a judge, and he was fined, imprisoned and excluded from office.

These events clearly threatened Buckingham and his brothers, who were involved in many patents. Therefore, soon after the parliamentary recess Sir Edwin Sandys and the earls of Southampton and Oxford were arrested in an attempt to frighten the parliamentary leaders. There was also a concerted attempt to conciliate them. On 10 July a royal proclamation cancelled eighteen monopolies and promised to review seventeen others; a privy council standing committee began an investigation into the causes of the economic crisis; and the outports were allowed to trade in the new draperies, despite the monopoly of the Company of Merchant Adventurers.

Unfortunately, although the arrested MPs and other political prisoners (including the ninth earl of Northumberland, who had been in prison since 1605) were released in a general amnesty suggested by the new lord keeper John Williams, the damage to parliamentary liberties had been done. What is more, James again seemed to threaten these liberties in the second session of parliament, when he refused (as had Elizabeth I) to allow the Commons to discuss foreign policy. It is probable that this by itself would have raised the Commons to a strong protest. James made this inevitable by foolishly accompanying his ban on discussion with a theoretical statement claiming that parliament's privileges originated in a royal grant and that they had not held them for ever. Historically he was right; politically he was foolish, especially since he made clear that he 'never meant to deny them (the Commons) any lawful privileges that ever that House enjoyed in our predecessors' times'.[11] This gloss failed to allay MPs' fears. On 18 December they passed a Protestation that their privileges were 'the ancient and

---

[10] Quoted in C. Tite, *Impeachment and Parliamentary Judicature in Early Stuart England* (1974), p. 89.

[11] Tanner, *Constitutional Documents*, p. 287.

undoubted birthright and inheritance of the subjects of England'.[12] The adjournment followed on the next day and the dissolution soon after. Coke was quickly arrested and imprisoned; Sir Robert Phelips and William Mallory followed him; John Pym was placed under house arrest. Other 'ill-tempered spirits' from the Commons arguably fared even worse; they were sent as royal commissioners to Ireland.

For James's finances, dissolution without further supply was a blow. Cranfield's campaign of economy measures was continuing (in 1621 he became lord treasurer and earl of Middlesex) but by now was suffering from the law of diminishing returns. Some minor increases in impositions were made and a benevolence levied after the dissolution brought in only the equivalent of one subsidy. Parliamentary finance was needed, but what determined the calling of parliament at the end of 1623 was Buckingham's and Charles's changed view of the Spanish marriage, which came about as a direct result of their visit to Madrid in the spring and summer of 1623.[13]

Information

The visit of Prince Charles and Buckingham to Madrid, 1623

The Madrid visit is one of those 'truth-is-stranger-than fiction' episodes that seem to have been rooted in a novelist's imagination rather than in reality. Early in 1623 Charles and Buckingham became convinced that the only way to conclude the Spanish match quickly was for them to go to Madrid and for Charles to woo the Spanish Infanta in person. Spurning the advice of both career diplomats in Spain (like Cottington and Digby) and the king, the two young men rode on horseback to Madrid, part of the way disguised with false beards and calling themselves Thomas and John Smith, taking a mere sixteen days to cover the journey of nearly 1,000 miles. In Madrid, Charles's youthful expectations received a rude jolt. His attempt to see the Spanish Infanta in private by climbing a wall into a secluded garden horrified her and offended the protocol of the Spanish court. Charles and Buckingham spent a long, hot summer kicking their heels in Madrid, during which their romantic dreams collapsed in frustration. Inevitably they found themselves at a disadvantage in dealing with the Spaniards, who humiliated Buckingham and foisted a disadvantageous marriage treaty on Charles. Their return to England in the autumn met with popular rejoicing: 'When Israel came out of Egypt and the house of Jacob from among the barbarous people', sang the choir in St Paul's in celebration.

---

[12] Ibid., p. 289. See also *English Historical Documents 1603–60*, document no. 97.
[13] G. Redworth, *The Prince and the Infanta: the cultural politics of the Spanish match* (2003); A. Samson, ed., *The Spanish Match: Prince Charles's journey to Madrid, 1623* (2006).

The principal consequence of the visit was to convert prince and duke to a war policy against Spain. They overcame the objections of James and those in the privy council like Cranfield, who pointed out the financially ruinous consequences of a war, and at the end of the year writs went out for a new parliament.

It soon became clear that James's hopes of the new parliament were very different from those of Charles and Buckingham, who were keen to get England involved in a war against Spain, following Elizabethan precedents, at sea. The king, however, although he talked of war, meant a land war in the Palatinate and intended to use the expected parliamentary demands for war to increase the diplomatic pressure he was exerting on Spain to complete the Spanish marriage alliance.[14] This is why, at the opening of the 1624 parliament on 19 February, he asked for parliament's 'good and sound advice'[15] on foreign policy. Meanwhile Buckingham and Charles had been formulating a parliamentary alliance with Sandys, Digges, Phelips and Eliot in the Commons and with the earl of Pembroke in the Lords, coordinating tactics for the new session. As proof of their good faith, Buckingham and Charles brought to prominence at court (like producing a trump card from their sleeve) the Puritan divine, John Preston, who had been Charles's chaplain since 1621 and Buckingham's client since October 1622. It was a parliamentary alliance based on a common hatred of Spain and of popery. In the 1621 parliament the Lords had set aside a Commons' sentence of a £1,000 fine and the pillory on a Roman Catholic barrister who had made offensive references to the elector palatine and his wife and replaced it with one of branding and whipping, a fine of £5,000 and life imprisonment. In 1624 the Commons was alive with rumours of a second gunpowder plot, and elated with the long-awaited opportunity to join the Protestant campaign in defence of the usurped elector palatine. In the foreign policy debate in March in the Commons, Buckingham's and Charles's parliamentary allies called for an end to the Spanish negotiations and for a declaration of war against Spain. Ominously though for the alliance, the Commons only granted £300,000. When John Glanville, the lawyer, suggested a higher grant he was sharply reminded by Thomas Belasyse, the landowner, that 'subsidies come not in so easily as fees'.[16] Others, like Eliot, believed that a naval war against Spain would bring its own profits. And for the moment Charles and Buckingham put their full support behind this naval war strategy, with dire consequences for the future, as will be seen. A more immediate consequence was the impeachment of Cranfield. Once again courtiers and parliamentarians cooperated in legal proceedings against a king's minister; and Cranfield, who was not only opposed by Charles and Buckingham for following an anti-war line, but was also hated by Sir Edward Coke (who felt that Cranfield's successful career at court had blighted his own), stood no chance of beating off the impeachment against him.

---

[14] T. Cogswell, *The Blessed Revolution: English politics and the coming of war, 1621–24* (1989); and see his 'A low road to extinction? Supply and redress of grievances in the parliaments of the 1620s', *H.J.*, XXXIII (1990).

[15] Kenyon, *Stuart Constitution*, p. 44. See also *English Historical Documents 1603–60*, document no. 99.

[16] Quoted in R. E. Ruigh, *The Parliament of 1624: politics and foreign policy* (1971), p. 222.

The 1624 parliament illustrates the extent and limitations of James's political success by the end of his reign. Some of his actions had reinforced a conspiracy theory that was emerging amongst some outside the court that there was 'a Popish Plot' afoot to subvert the English Church and parliament. An equally powerful solvent of political stability was James's encouragement at court of a different conspiracy theory: that at the root of contemporary political tensions was 'a Puritan Plot', organised by a small group of militant Puritans, 'ill-tempered spirits [that] had sowed too many tares among the corn' (as he called them in his proclamation explaining why he had dissolved the parliament of 1621). These contrasting and competing conspiracy theories were to be a major cause of the huge rifts that had appeared in English politics by 1640, but their origins lay in the political debates of James's reign.

But in 1624 their disruptive impact on political instability was not yet as great as it was to be in a few years' time. At the end of James's reign there is no evidence of a crown versus parliament split. The importance of the device of appropriating the subsidy to treasurers appointed by parliament and for specific uses laid down by parliament can be exaggerated, since it was suggested by James and Buckingham and not by a constitutionally aggressive parliament, as was once thought. James had kept the control of foreign affairs securely in his grasp. While he lived, diplomatic relations with Spain were never cut, nor was war with Spain officially declared. Moreover, by making judicious compromises on this and other issues James defused the political tension. Under pressure from Charles and Buckingham he conceded a Monopoly Act, which forbade royal grants of monopolies to individuals but left the crown free to make grants to corporations. Also the Commons' committee on trade and the privy council's commission on trade worked together to combat the economic crisis, and the crown made some concessions to the outports' demands for free trade in non-white clothes. James's last parliament provided promising signs of continued cooperation with the crown. Fortunately, it is not the job of the historian to indulge in problematic speculative 'what-might-have been' questions, such as what might have happened if James I had lived longer. The possibilities are infinite. Yet it is hardly likely that, if James had not died in 1625, the country would have been plunged so quickly into deep political turmoil as it was within weeks of the accession of Charles I.

The prerogative 'extended . . . beyond its just symmetry', 1625–1629

The accession of Charles I marks a definite turning point in the history of the 1620s. After 1625, although many people in parliament retained contacts with the court, ever hopeful of court office and patronage, it is clear that the parliamentary leaders were finding it harder than ever both to cooperate with royal ministers and to keep their local prestige. Why were the prospects of parliamentary cooperation with the crown bleaker after 1625 than before? The most obvious reason, though not the most important, was the personality of the new king. A great contrast to his father, Charles was a shy man of few words, possibly as a result of a speech defect. 'I mean to show what I should speak in actions', he told his second parliament. Consequently, his contemporaries (like historians) found that he was unapproachable and, what was worst, uncommunicative, especially in parliament, where his intentions and his actions often went unexplained, leaving others free to interpret them to his disadvantage. Charles also showed that he possessed none of his father's political shrewdness or flexibility. He did not appear to know the meaning of the word 'compromise' and often adopted extreme positions. He seemed unable to understand viewpoints that differed from his own, he interpreted the slightest hint of criticism of him as tantamount to sedition, and in dealing with opponents he was not above using very dishonest (and in some cases, as will be seen, illegal) tactics. It is difficult not to sympathize with the judgement that Charles I was the most inept monarch to have occupied the English throne since Henry VI in the fifteenth century.[17]

Not only did father and son differ greatly in personality and political ability, so too did the courts over which they presided. Whereas James's court was, if fairly disorderly, open and accessible to all kinds of factional and ideological views, Charles's court increasingly came to represent a narrowing range of interests. This was as a result partly of Charles's introverted character and partly of his love for order and decorum. Just how suddenly things changed at court was commented on by contemporaries. The London gossip John Chamberlain wrote to a correspondent only two weeks after Charles's accession that 'the King shows himself very graceful and affable, but the court is kept more straight and private than in former times'. The Venetian ambassador also noted the new privacy of the court. Writing in the first weeks of the new reign, he noted that 'the King observes a rule of great decorum. The nobles do not enter his apartments in confusion as heretofore, but each rank has its appointed place. . . . The King has also drawn up rules for himself, dividing the day from his very early rising . . . it is said that he will set apart a day for public audience, and he does not wish anyone to be introduced to him unless sent for.'[18] The result was (as even hostile observers like the godly Lucy Hutchinson conceded) to change dramatically the moral tone of the court, which soon shed its Jacobean air of seediness and corruption. But the change also had damaging political consequences in that the court no longer filled as fully as it should have done the vital role of communication between court and country, so further increasing the possibilities of misapprehension and misunderstanding of the king's actions and intentions.

Both Charles's political ineptitude and the damaging consequences of an increasingly closed court are well illustrated in the ways in which in the later 1620s Charles foolishly

---

[17] I have not been persuaded to change this view by K. Sharpe, 'Private conscience and public duty in the writings of Charles I', *H.J.*, 40 (1997) and Mark Kishlansky, 'A case of mistaken identity', *P. & P.*, 189 (2005). My view has been confirmed by reading recent biographies of Charles by Durston, Young and Cust (see Bibliographical note, p. 521) and C. Holmes's critique of Kishlansky, 'Debate: A case of mistaken identity', *P. & P.*, no. 205 (2005).

[18] Quoted in J. Richards, ' "His nowe Majesties" and the English monarchy: the kingship of Charles I before 1640', *P. & P.*, CXIII (1986), p. 78.

allowed Buckingham a predominant role in the management of royal patronage, although not the control of royal decision-making as some have thought. Charles was responsible for the course of royal policies from the very beginning of his reign. He never allowed Buckingham in the 1620s, or Laud and Wentworth in the 1630s, to take from him the key role of making all major executive decisions. What Charles did do, however, was to allow Buckingham to control the distribution of royal bounty. This had the disastrous consequence of ensuring that it was channelled to only a few, to the benefit of Buckingham's family and the Villiers family clientage. As has been seen, it was essential for successful kingship in early modern England that monarchs should distribute their patronage freely and widely. Buckingham's monopoly of royal patronage in the later 1620s forced natural allies of the court, like Thomas Wentworth (the future earl of Strafford), to look not to the court but to parliament as a forum in which to pursue their own and their localities' interests. It also accelerated the tendency for disputes between courtiers to be carried on in parliament. Not surprisingly in these circumstances, one of the key charges against Buckingham when impeachment proceedings were brought against him in the late 1620s was that he had not left the king 'to be the master of his own liberality'.

One final major difference between James I and Charles I that boded ill for political harmony in England might be noted: Charles's abandonment of his father's conciliatory role in international affairs and in the Church. Charles's accession signalled the involvement of England in war, first against Spain and later against Spain and France. Financial and military necessities caused the crown to wield its emergency 'prerogative' powers on a scale and with an intensity unparalleled since the last years of the Elizabethan war against Spain. As a result, the already hypersensitive fears of many of Charles's subjects about creeping royal 'absolutism' were even further inflamed. Finally, although the full force of its impact was delayed, Charles's accession also signalled an important religious change. As has been seen, although James had wobbled a little from his arbitrating role between different strands of opinion within the English Church and had shown some favour to 'Arminian' divines in his last years, he never completely abandoned his ecumenical attempt to preside over a broad Church. Charles, on the other hand, placed his full support behind a group within the English Church whose views were generally felt to be at odds with the most deeply held beliefs of practically the whole of the political nation.

Even before the death of the old king in March 1625, the parliamentary alliance of 1624 was breaking up. In November 1624 a French alliance, providing for the marriage of Prince Charles and Henrietta Maria, was concluded at a high price: the suspension of the recusancy laws in England and English help for the French against the Protestant Huguenot rebels at La Rochelle. Moreover, the money granted in 1624 appeared to have been wasted. A force of pressed Englishmen under the German mercenary Mansfeld, which set off for the Palatinate in January 1625, was reduced by poor supplies, bad weather and French lack of cooperation from 12,000 to 3,000 men only a few days after crossing the Channel. By May 1625 Charles was committed to spending £20,000 a month supporting Danish involvement in the war, as well as a similar sum pledged to Mansfeld. The war promised in 1624 had not yet been declared; instead a costly fleet and army of 10,000 men was being assembled at Plymouth. More seriously for the prospects of political harmony when parliament should next meet, the war that was in prospect was not the war that many MPs, Charles and Buckingham had planned in 1624. As a result of the French alliance, despite the repeated promises that they had given in the 1624 parliament that the war they would wage would be a cheap naval one, Charles and Buckingham only a year later found that they had no alternative but to embark on an expensive land campaign in Europe.

With a planned expenditure of £1 million, Charles needed cooperation from his first parliament which met on 18 June 1625. Given the waste of money on a continental war strategy, the broken promises and the pro-Catholic nature of the French alliance, he was not likely to get it, especially when he refused to explain his position to parliament or even to ask for a specific subsidy. A measure of the Commons' distrust was the grant of a paltry two subsidies (about £140,000) and tonnage and poundage for one year only instead of for the king's life. As far as the Commons were concerned, Charles's foreign policy was misdirected and mishandled.

In addition, the serious implications of Charles's conversion to theological beliefs which most of the political nation found abhorrent became apparent in the case of Richard Montague. Montague was a divine who in 1624 published a tract, *A New Gag for an Old Goose*, which rejected the predestinarian Calvinism which had been accepted by the English Church since the Elizabethan Settlement. Charles signalled his support for Montague's radical beliefs by making Montague his chaplain in 1625, when the Commons began proceedings against him. This, together with the appearance at court of William Laud, foreshadowed the Laudian supremacy in the Church which became a reality in the 1630s. When in August the parliament of 1625 met in Oxford after an adjournment, there may have been an attempt at conciliation with Buckingham by the duke's ex-parliamentary allies, led by Sir Nathaniel Rich and the earl of Warwick in the Lords.[19] But Charles would make no concessions, and personal criticism of Buckingham in the Commons by more extreme MPs like Seymour and Phelips made the dissolution inevitable.

Unfortunately for the court, the events of the autumn and winter of 1625 illustrated Buckingham's incompetence. After the fleet finally sailed in September it failed even to take the poorly manned town of Cadiz, let alone capture the Spanish treasure fleet. More English troops were lost from lack of food and too much local wine than from enemy gunfire. To this disaster Buckingham seemed to be adding the prospect of a French war as well, as he tried to please his parliamentary critics by ordering punishment of recusants and threatening to return the English ships being used against La Rochelle. Even with the prominent parliamentary critics of 1625 removed by the ingenious device of picking as sheriff men like Seymour, Phelips, Coke and Wentworth, the parliament planned for February 1626 would be stormy. Yet all hope of cooperation was

---

[19] Christopher Thompson, 'The origins of the politics of the parliamentary middle group 1625–29', *T.R.H.S.*, 5th ser., XXII (1972), p. 76.

not gone on the parliamentary side. At the request of the earl of Warwick, Buckingham chaired a theological debate at York House on 11 and 17 February 1626 on the writings of Richard Montague, hoping to wean Charles away from Laudianism. The task was hopeless; in order to retain the king's favour, John Preston was discarded and William Laud adopted. Buckingham rarely allowed attachment to principle to get in the way of his political ambitions. He now had few supporters in the Commons; his former parliamentary clients and allies, Eliot, Digges, Sandys and Phelips, encouraged by Buckingham's enemies in the Lords, began impeachment proceedings against him. In vain, Charles tried to stop the impeachment by a thinly veiled threat in which he described the fate of European countries where kings ruled without parliaments, whose subjects are 'like so many ghosts, and not men, being nothing but skin and bones, with some thin cover to their nakedness, and wearing only wooden shoes on their feet, so that they cannot eat meat or wear good clothes, but they must pay and be taxed unto the King for it'.[20] The only way he could protect his favourite was by dissolving parliament.

The political consequences, though, were very damaging to Charles's reputation and could perhaps have been avoided by someone who did not respond to criticism in the inflammatory way that Charles had done. It is hard to avoid the conclusion that James I's political shrewdness would have dictated a more judicious reaction. Given that MPs were already fearful that Charles was considering ruling without parliaments, it was the height of political folly to allow his secretary of state, Dudley Carleton, to threaten them by reminding them of the fate of representative assemblies that had once existed in some countries until their rulers, 'seeing the turbulent spirits of their parliaments . . . began to stand upon their prerogatives, and at last overthrew the parliaments throughout Christendom, except here only with us'. It is not surprising that suspicions grew that Charles was thinking of turning to 'new counsels', following the suit of his fellow monarchs on the Continent.[21] What gave weight to these suspicions was that, with the country at war and in severe financial difficulties, Charles began to exercise the crown's emergency powers. To many they were seen as dangerous innovations, threatening the traditional government process and the right of the propertied classes. It is arguable that between the dissolution of the 1626 parliament and the end of 1627, opposition to the Caroline court reached a peak it was not to reach again until the late 1630s. The refusal of the city to lend more than £20,000 and the 'colossal failure'[22] of a free gift immediately after the dissolution prompted the crown to order a forced loan.[23]

---

[20] Kenyon, *Stuart Constitution*, p. 45.

[21] Ibid., p. 45. See R. Cust, 'Charles I, the privy council and the forced loan', *J.B.S.*, XXIV (1985) for perceptive comments on Charles's mood in 1626 that led him to consider 'new counsels' advocating rule without parliaments.

[22] T. G. Barnes, *Somerset 1625–40: a county's government during the 'Personal Rule'* (1961), p. 163.

[23] For the striking success in collecting the forced loan and for a full analysis of the opposition to it, see R. Cust, *The Forced Loan and English Politics 1626–28* (1987). For the Yorkshire refusal to collect the loan, see J. T. Cliffe, *The Yorkshire Gentry from the Reformation to the Civil War* (1967), p. 292; and for the quotation from the manuscript pamphlet probably written by the earl of Lincoln, see Cust, *Forced Loan*, pp. 173–4.

Information

The forced loan, 1626

The forced loan ordered by Charles I in September 1626 was different from forced loans collected by earlier monarchs who had demanded loans only from a few wealthy subjects. The forced loan of 1626–7 was to be paid by all people who normally paid parliamentary taxes. It was the equivalent of five parliamentary subsidies. Although within ten months £240,000 had been collected, the forced loan caused massive opposition:

- Five prominent men who refused to loan money were imprisoned and at their trial – the Five Knights' case – the judges of the King's Bench in November 1627 upheld the king's prerogative right to imprison them without trial.
- Chief Justice Carew refused to endorse the loan's legality and was dismissed.
- Archbishop Abbot was suspended for refusing to license Robert Sibthorpe's sermon defending the loan.
- Yorkshire deputy lieutenants and JPs refused to collect the loan because 'haveing noe legall power to Levie the same upon the subject wee dare not presume to doe itt'.[24]
- An anonymous manuscript pamphlet (probably written by Theophilus Clinton, earl of Lincoln) trumpeted that 'if this cause be not withstood, but take effect, we shalbe ourselves the instruments of our own slavery and of the loss of the priviledge which we have hitherto enjoyed, that our goods cannot be taken from us without consent of parliament'.[25]

What confirmed the view of many, especially in maritime counties in south and south-western England, that Charles's government was undertaking a concerted attack on people's liberties is that, in addition to mustering troops for the war against France, deputy lieutenants began to billet forcibly in private houses soldiers of the army that had failed to take the island of Rhé off La Rochelle in October. To the burden of increased militia payment was added the imposition of martial law and the enforced billeting of troops. 'Every man knowes there is no law for this', complained the recorder of Taunton. 'We know our houses are our castles.'[26]

---

[24] Cliffe, *Yorkshire Gentry*, p. 292.

[25] Quoted in Cust, *Forced Loan*, pp. 173–4.

[26] Barnes, *Somerset*, p. 218.

For all the financial – if not political – success of the forced loan, Charles eventually had to fall back on parliamentary taxation. Sources of extra-parliamentary revenue were drying up. A new City loan of £120,000, being negotiated at the end of 1627, was only secured in return for the transfer of extensive crown estates to the City. Soon after parliament met in March 1628, a grant of five subsidies was resolved on but was not even recorded until the king should satisfy their grievances. The extension of prerogative government 'beyond its just symmetry' since the last parliament moved the emphasis in the Commons away from attacks on Buckingham to a united demand that the king recognize the illegality of extra-parliamentary taxation, billeting, martial law and imprisonment without trial.

What made the Commons' opposition to Charles particularly bitter and decided many MPs to support drastic measures against him was the revelation of the illegal action Charles had taken in the wake of the decision in the Five Knights' case. Controversy at the time and since has surrounded this decision.

Information

Differing views about the judicial decision in the Five Knights' case, 1627

Charles claimed that the judges had declared that he had a general right to imprison people without giving any other cause than 'reasons of state'.

Many of Charles's subjects, however, believed the judges had decreed not that the king had a *general* right to imprison without showing good cause; they had simply declared that the king had the right to imprison in this *particular* case of the five loan refusers. They also believed that after the judgment had been made Charles had allowed Sir Robert Heath, the attorney-general, to falsify the legal records in which the judgment was enrolled; in effect changing the ruling into one that upheld the king's *general* right to imprison without trial.[27]

Mark Kishlansky, as part of his attempts to rehabilitate Charles's reputation, denies that Charles falsified the official legal record in the case but most historians have accepted the view taken by many of Charles's subjects.[28]

It is not surprising that, soon after parliament met in March 1628, many MPs were united in demanding action be taken to prevent such activities on the part of Charles I in the future. However, there were differences among the parliamentary leaders about

---

[27] J. Guy, 'The origins of the Petition of Right reconsidered', *H.J.*, XXV (1982).

[28] M. Kishlansky, 'Tyranny denied: Charles I, Attorney General Heath and the Five Knights' case', *H.J.*, 42 (1999).

how this should be done. The course proposed by more extreme MPs like Selden, Coke and Eliot, a statutory Bill of Rights, would have led to a head-on clash with the king and would probably have been rejected by the Lords. The device of proceeding by petition, supported by Rich and Digges, though not welcomed by Charles, was more traditional and conciliatory, and Lord Saye and Sele was able to persuade the Lords that the petition was not a revolutionary limitation on the royal prerogative. Under the threat of further proceedings against Buckingham on 7 June 1628, Charles gave his formal assent to the Petition of Right, and the Commons passed the subsidy bill.

Information

The Petition of Right, 1628

The Petition of Right made three demands:

- The king should never again levy taxes without parliament's approval.
- No one should be imprisoned without either cause being given or being brought to trial.
- Soldiers and sailors should not be billeted in private houses by martial law.

Notwithstanding its long-term significance as one of the great landmarks in England's constitutional development, the Petition of Right had less immediate significance. Despite the king's acknowledgement of the illegality of his recent activities and the removal of Buckingham by the assassin Felton in August, when parliament reassembled for a second session in January 1629 the political crisis continued, characterized by a high degree of popular political debate, especially in London.[29] Why did the Petition of Right fail? It left unresolved two fundamental points of disagreement between Charles and the parliamentary leaders. First, since the petition did not explicitly mention impositions or tonnage and poundage, Charles was able to claim that he had not surrendered his rights to levy these customs duties without parliamentary consent. During the recess in the summer and autumn of 1628, merchants who refused to pay the duties were imprisoned. Secondly, the petition made no attempt to express the Commons' distaste at the growing influence of the Laudians in the Church and at court, especially those divines like Roger Mainwaring, who was impeached by parliament in June 1628 for supporting the forced loan. In these circumstances Charles's favour to Laudians in the summer of 1628 was inflammatory. Noted Laudians were

---

[29] A. Bellamy, ' "The brightnes of the noble lieutenants action": an intellectual ponders Buckingham's assassination', *E.H.R.*, 118 (2003); and 'The murder of John Lambe: crowd violence, court scandal and popular politics in early seventeenth-century England', *P. & P.*, 200 (2008).

appointed to bishoprics, including Laud as bishop of London and Montague as bishop of Chichester. Mainwaring (like Montague condemned by parliament) was pardoned and given a lucrative benefice in Essex.

Even so, the disquiet aroused by Laudianism *at this stage* can be exaggerated. It is noteworthy that those moderate parliamentary leaders, led by Rich in the Commons and by Saye and Sele and Warwick in the Lords, who had worked for conciliation with the court in recent previous parliaments, were still anxious not to force a breach with the king. They failed because of the intransigence, on the one hand, of MPs like Eliot and Selden who persisted in pressing opposition to extra-parliamentary tonnage and poundage as well as to Laudianism, and, on the other, of the king. On 25 February parliament was adjourned for a week, during which the king in private negotiations with the parliamentary leaders refused to make any concessions on his interpretation of the Petition of Right. He thereby played into the hands of Eliot and his allies who organized the famous demonstration in the chamber of the House of Commons on 2 March. Speaker Finch was forcibly prevented by Denzil Holles and Benjamin Valentine from reading the royal order to adjourn until the Commons had passed three resolutions, expressing opposition to extra-parliamentary tonnage and poundage and to innovations in religion. The dissolution followed two days later.

One of the great mistakes in analysing any historical development is to assume that events proceed evenly along an unbroken line. That there is abundant evidence of widespread popular opposition to the crown in the late 1620s does not necessarily mean that the strength of the opposition was maintained in the years immediately following. There is some evidence of a royalist 'backlash' in reaction to the attacks on the crown by Eliot and his allies in 1628 and 1629. Even in the debate on 2 March, some MPs expressed doubts about the wisdom of Eliot's criticism of the new lord treasurer, Sir Richard Weston. Sir Simonds D'Ewes felt that 'the cause of the breach and dissolution was immaterial and frivolous, in the carriage whereof divers fiery spirits in the House of Commons were very faulty and cannot be excused'.[30] After 1629 many critics of the crown in the parliaments of the 1620s were willing to work in central and local government. Wentworth was already reconciled to the court after the Petition of Right had been accepted; in December 1628 he became lord president of the council of the north. Others followed him later. William Noy became attorney-general in 1631. Phelips found that in the early 1630s there was not the same conflict between cooperating with royal government and retaining his local prestige in Somerset which had driven him into opposition in the parliaments of the late 1620s. This is true also of future anti-royalists of the 1640s like William Brereton of Handforth, who worked loyally in Cheshire local government in the 1630s. The allegations by the prosecution at the trial of Eliot, Holles and Valentine in 1630 that 'there was a conspiracy between the defendants . . . to raise sedition and discord between the King, his peers and people'[31] was exaggerated, but many contemporaries undoubtedly felt that it contained a germ of truth.

---

[30] J. O. Halliwell, ed., *The Autobiography and Correspondence of Sir Simonds D'Ewes* (2 vols., 1845), I, p. 402.

[31] Kenyon, *Stuart Constitution*, p. 46.

In the period immediately after the dissolution of parliament in 1629 it was not yet clear that Charles's unapproachability, his financial policies and especially his religious beliefs would eventually make it impossible for people to be loyal both to the court and their 'countries'. The date when this sank in differed, of course, from individual to individual. However, it may be that for the majority of the political nation this did not happen until the late 1630s. Some MPs who went to Westminster in April and in November 1640 probably assumed that they would still be able to preserve their double loyalty to court and 'country'. Some did not face up to the choice between the two until 1641 and 1642, and a few, even then, sought to postpone the decision.

The Personal Rule, 1629–1640

Historiography

Differing historical interpretations of the Personal Rule

There have been two main interpretations:

- as an 'Eleven Years' Tyranny' in a country seething with rising opposition to rule without a parliament and the imposition of extra-parliamentary taxation and excessive use of the royal prerogative;
- as a benevolent paternal government, ruling effectively, initiating reforms and looking after the poor by Books of Orders.

Neither of these interpretations ought to be treated as the 'correct' one. The 'Eleven Years' Tyranny' view of the 1630s relies excessively on hindsight, on a biased identification with the 'winners' in history (i.e. the opponents of the king). It blinds historians to the positive aims of Charles's government and pre-dates the development of serious opposition to the crown. The view of royal government in the 1630s as benevolent and paternal, while recognizing that there was a genuine attempt by the crown to produce some effective reformative measures, fails to emphasize that the achievements fell far short of the aims. More seriously, because Charles and his court became increasingly isolated from the mainstream of contemporary religious, intellectual and cultural life, the policies pursued by Charles and his ministers went unexplained and were consequently often misunderstood. As often in history, what people believed to be true was more important than the truth itself in influencing the course of events.

Financial expedients, 1629–1637

The immediate effect of the failure to secure parliamentary subsidies in 1628 and 1629 was to bring home to the king and his advisers, Lord Treasurer Weston and Chancellor of the Exchequer Cottington, the serious financial situation. Historical judgements of the financial administration of Weston and Cottington have too often been coloured by the disparaging way in which Laud and Wentworth referred to them in their correspondence as 'Lady Mora and her waiting-maid'. In fact, before Weston's death in March 1635, the pair fared no better and no worse than Cecil or Cranfield before them in meeting the perennial problems faced by all early Stuart administrators: the need to cut expenditure and increase revenue. When Laud initiated an enquiry into Weston's treasurership in 1635, he may have been disappointed to find little evidence of financial mismanagement. The crown's debt was still large, but the current annual deficit had been reduced to only £18,000. How was this achieved? Even with parliamentary subsidies in the 1620s, England could not afford an active foreign policy; without parliamentary supply, withdrawal from the Thirty Years War was inevitable, and peace treaties were made with France (1629) and Spain (1630). In an attempt to reduce expenditure even further, Weston inaugurated the first concerted attempt since Cranfield's fall to reform the royal spending departments. From 1629 to 1632 the navy, ordnance and royal household departments were investigated, revealing that much of the earlier economies had been undone. Short-term savings were therefore possible in the household, which soaked up over 40 per cent of the royal revenues. Expenditure on food and drink and expensive entertainment fell significantly in 1629–30, but in the following year had doubled.[32] Once again administrative reformers in the early seventeenth century came up against a fundamental obstacle: that inevitably a permanent reduction in the size of the household, in pensions or in offices, curtailed the extent of crown patronage and therefore hit the vested interests of both patron and clients. This attempt at administrative reform failed; but Weston and Cottington were more successful in increasing royal revenue and it can be argued that they did so without causing too much resentment. Resistance to tonnage and poundage collapsed in 1629 and customs duties became an important part of the royal revenue in the 1630s. The increase in income from recusancy fines from an average of £5,300 p.a. in the late 1620s to £26,866 in 1634 could hardly offend violent anti-Catholic contemporary opinion.[33] Even the levying of ship money by the sheriffs in maritime counties in October 1634 was successful and almost the full amount was collected.[34] In Yorkshire, for example, Sir John Hotham, who had been imprisoned in 1627 for his opposition to the forced loan, cooperated as sheriff in the collection of the tax. Elsewhere also there seemed no reason to oppose a tax which was based on precedent, and was apparently an expedient to deal with the menace of pirates off the south and west coasts of England.

---

[32] G. E. Aylmer, 'Attempts at administrative reform 1625–40', *E.H.R.*, LXXI (1957), p. 252.

[33] M. J. Havran, *Caroline Courtier: the life of Lord Cottington* (1973), p. 121.

[34] £79,000 out of £80,609. M. D. Gordon, 'The collection of ship money in the reign of Charles I', *T.R.H.S.*, 3rd ser., IV (1910), p. 143.

More resentment was caused in the early 1630s by the activities of commissioners appointed in 1630, who were to fine anyone holding land worth £40 p.a. or more who had not received a knighthood. In August 1630 the exchequer barons confirmed that the crown was legally entitled to do this, although the precedents for it were hardly recent and dated back to the mid-sixteenth century. The tax was a heavy one; most fines were of £10, but they could be as high as £70. It also involved the local commissioners in a lot of hard and distasteful work; though often they were probably able to shift the tax on to minor gentry, sometimes they had to squeeze it from their fellow JPs, and the privy council, supported by the court of exchequer, inflicted heavy fines on dilatory commissioners. That the exchequer court had to proceed against such offenders is evidence of some resentment at distraint of knighthood, but not of serious opposition. Sir David Foulis's attempt to rally gentry opinion in Yorkshire against the tax fell flat. Foulis, an expatriate Scot, scolded his Yorkshire neighbours for no longer being 'stout-spirited men' who 'stood for their rights and liberties . . . but now in these days Yorkshiremen were becoming degenerate, more dastardly and more cowardly than the men of other countries'. Elsewhere too – across the Pennines in Cheshire, for example – those liable for the tax grumbled but paid up.[35] Weston also offended sections of mercantile opinion, especially by reviving grants of industrial and commercial monopolies to corporations, exploiting a loophole in the Monopoly Act which had only forbidden grants to individuals. That the only consistent element behind such grants was to gather revenue was revealed by the restoration in 1634 of the Merchant Adventurers' monopoly, partially lost in 1624, and the incursion into the East India Company monopoly by a grant of 1635 to the courtier, Endymion Porter, and the merchant, Sir William Courteen, to trade in the Indian Ocean. Not only did the grants seem arbitrary to those merchants involved, but one, the grant in 1632 of a monopoly in soap manufacture to a syndicate with strong Roman Catholic affiliations, roused popular opposition, at least in London, as well as the opposition of those soap manufacturers who had been left out of the monopoly. Even an officially sponsored demonstration in December 1633 by two washerwomen (using an advertising technique beloved by the modern detergent industry) failed to convince anyone that clothes washed in 'Papist soap' 'were as white and sweeter than' those washed by the washerwoman using an unnamed brand.[36]

More annoyance was given to landowners and merchants by revenue-raising schemes after Weston's death than in the early 1630s. The crown's claim that in all of them it was acting within the letter of the law was no doubt true, but this was scant compensation to those who were told that they had transgressed not only against long-forgotten obligations to be knights, but also against enclosure laws; that their estates were within the royal forest; that wardship fines were to be drastically increased; and on top of all this, that ship money was to become a permanent land tax. From 1635 the long-dormant forest courts were revived patently for fiscal purposes. Landowners,

---

[35] Cliffe, *Yorkshire Gentry*, p. 300; Morrill, *Cheshire*, p. 27.
[36] Gardiner, *History*, VIII, p. 73.

great and small alike, who had estates within their jurisdiction were deemed to have encroached illegally on the royal forest and were subsequently fined. Nor was there any pretence that the commission on depopulation set up in the same year was anything other than a device to sell licences confirming enclosures. What is more, the government proved efficient in collecting revenue; fines were exacted, enclosures were sought out and Cottington as master of the court of wards raised the revenue from wardships to £61,900 by 1637, nearly treble the level in 1613.[37]

It is not surprising that the decision to extend the demand for ship money to inland counties from June 1635 met with more disapproval than meets most new tax demands. It now appeared to be a permanent land tax; in December 1635 the judges declared that the king was acting legally, and successive new ship money writs were issued in each year from 1636 to 1639. Moreover opposition to ship money may have extended below the substantial freeholder classes. Although there was some confusion about the basis on which the sheriffs were to make the assessment for the tax, most sheriffs seem to have taken personal, as well as real, property into account (in Cheshire the sheriff turned to the mise roll used for levying the local poor rate[38]); the result was that the new tax directly affected more people than a parliamentary subsidy. To the taxpayers also the new tax seemed difficult to justify on the grounds of dire necessity; there seemed to be no immediate threat of invasion in the mid-1630s. This was perhaps the strongest argument used by Oliver St John in 1637 at the trial of John Hampden for refusing to pay ship money, and five out of the twelve judges gave their verdict against the crown, which stiffened the resolve of many to oppose the tax.

What is difficult to determine is the extent and seriousness of the opposition to ship money before 1638. Opposition on constitutional grounds was not very apparent before that date, and between 1634 and the end of 1638, 90 per cent of the tax was paid; a remarkably high collection rate when set against (for example) modern attempts to collect unpopular taxes like the British poll tax in the late 1980s. Perhaps, though, the lack of both vocal, principled opposition to and non-payment of ship money should not be equated with its general acceptance. In the absence of sessions of parliament, there was no forum for anyone to express constitutional disquiet without exposing themselves to royal wrath. Even so, there are indications in Cheshire and Kent that ship money was discussed as an attack on parliamentary liberties.[39] Nor is this surprising. What would have been surprising and unlikely is that the awareness of political issues, which had grown in the hothouse atmosphere of the late 1620s when news of the controversies surrounding the forced loan and the Petition of Right was widely disseminated by newsletters, should have been forgotten and left attitudes in

---

[37] Havran, *Cottington*, p. 138.

[38] Morrill, *Cheshire*, p. 28.

[39] P. Lake, 'The collection of ship money in Cheshire during the 1630s: a case study of relations between central and local government', *Northern History*, XVII (1981); K. Fincham, 'The judges' decision on ship money in February 1637: the reaction of Kent', *B.I.H.R.*, LVII (1984).

the 1630s unaffected.[40] Nevertheless, opposition to ship money did not become overt on a large scale until Charles's and Laud's religious policies brought England and Scotland to the verge of war in 1638.

The Books of Orders and the 'exact militia'

It is tempting to treat the administrative activities of the king's government during the Personal Rule as a coherent policy of 'thorough'. It may be that Laud and Wentworth would have liked to achieve effective paternalistic government, not by any radical departure from, but by a stricter enforcement of existing legislation and methods. However, there is little evidence that they were able to put such policies into effect in the 1630s. Rarely does it seem that Caroline government succeeded in breaking free from the normal pattern of ad hoc decision-making. Most of the efforts of Charles I's government to increase administrative efficiency in local government were made in response to immediate crises, and, once these were over, the privy council relaxed its pressure on the localities and programmes of reform were not sustained.

The decision to issue Books of Orders in 1630 and 1631 is a good illustration of these generalizations. Successive harvest failures in 1629 and 1630 prompted the privy council to undertake what Professor Barnes considers to be 'the most concerted effort, almost until our own times, to make the statute book an effective reality'.[41] Soaring corn prices and unemployment in the cloth manufacturing areas, exacerbated by the politically motivated refusal of merchants to export cloth in 1629 and by outbreaks of plague, threatened law and order. There were food riots in the worst affected areas in the West Country. As a direct result, on 5 January 1631 most of the members of the privy council were appointed commissioners to see that the laws concerning poor relief were put into force and that 'other public services for God, the King and the Commonwealth, are put into practice and executed'.[42] On 31 January steps were taken to give teeth to the conciliar commission: 314 printed Books of Orders were sent to the sheriffs for distribution to JPs and municipal authorities, setting out the scope of the authority and duties of local officials in executing legislation on all subjects, not just on poor relief. Similar books had been issued in the 1570s and 1580s, but what was novel about the books of 1631 was the procedural machinery laid down in them: JPs were to meet monthly in each hundred to supervise the work of the hundred and petty constables, churchwardens and overseers of the poor; the JPs were to send reports to the sheriffs, who in turn reported to the assize judges on circuit, who were the direct agents of the conciliar commission. It is often difficult to unravel the process by which Stuart governments made decisions, but in this case it seems fairly certain

---

[40] Cust, *The Forced Loan*, pp. 334–5; R. Cust, 'News and politics in early seventeenth-century England', *P. & P.*, CCII (1986), pp. 60–90.

[41] Barnes, *Somerset*, p. 178.

[42] Kenyon, *Stuart Constitution*, p. 452.

that the earl of Manchester was an influential voice in the privy council in favour of the Books of Orders. He was closely in touch with his brother, Lord Montague, a Northamptonshire JP, and they discussed the practicability of the scheme.[43] The Books of Orders, then, originated in a time of economic crisis, and they were the blueprint for a permanent reform of local government, reinvigorated by centralized conciliar direction.

How successful were the Books of Orders in practice? A simple answer cannot be given. Historians are divided. Professor Barnes feels that 'throughout the 1630s the contents of the books was effectively translated into reality': while Professor Jordan reaches the opposite conclusion.[44] Firm generalizations about the success of the books are difficult to make because few private papers of the JPs active in the 1630s survive, and therefore detailed knowledge of the working of the Books of Orders is often lacking. Undoubtedly the books made a significant impact in alleviating the worst effects of the 1629–30 economic crisis in those places which have been studied. They also helped to regularize meetings of petty sessions, and procedures for licensing alehouses and apprenticing poor children.[45] However, once the worst of the crisis was over, it is hard to imagine, even given the maintenance of its supervisory powers, that the privy council could have kept JPs up to the mark.

A similar gulf between reforming aspirations and achievements is evident in the efforts made by the Caroline government to reform the militia.[46] The defects of the militia were patent, and during the last fifteen years of James I's reign the privy council had initiated sporadic attempts to remedy the militia's lack of professional training and its chronic shortage of money. From 1624 to 1627 these efforts were stepped up as the country became involved in wars against France and Spain. Charles and his advisers began to talk about producing an 'exact militia', and like the Books of Orders, this scheme had a lot to recommend it. Why, then, did it meet with a hostile reception in many counties? In 1604 the parliamentary statutes passed in the reign of Mary Tudor regulating the militia were repealed. Consequently, from now on lord lieutenants and their deputies derived their authority directly from the crown, and this enabled people to question the legality of their activities. As early as 1620 John Bishe of Brighton refused to attend the militia musters on the grounds that 'there was no law to enforce him'.[47] During the war years of the late 1620s, such opposition became more pronounced. When the officers of the lieutenancy began administering unpopular policies like forcible billeting, gentlemen curried popular favour, as did Sir Robert

---

[43] P. Slack, 'Books of Orders; the making of English social policy 1577–1631', *T.R.H.S.*, 5th ser., XXX (1980); B. W. Quintrell, 'The making of Charles I's Book of Orders', *E.H.R.*, XCV (1980); R. B. Outhwaite, 'Dearth and government intervention in English grain markets 1590–1700', *Econ. H.R.*, XXXIV (1981).

[44] Barnes, *Somerset*, p. 196; W. K. Jordan, *Philanthropy in England: a study of the changing patterns of English social aspirations 1480–1660* (1959), pp. 133–6.

[45] See especially Anthony Fletcher, *A County Community at Peace and War: Sussex 1600–1660* (1975), p. 224.

[46] L. Boynton, *The Elizabethan Militia 1558–1638* (1967), pp. 244–97, for the 'exact militia'.

[47] Fletcher, *Sussex*, p. 187.

Phelips, by denouncing 'the oppression of the deputy lieutenants'.[48] Opposition to the exact militia was focused especially on muster-masters, professional soldiers appointed to train the local militia.[49] Not only were these men appointed by the lieutenants, but (unlike during the reign of Elizabeth) they were paid out of rates levied locally on no authority other than that of the royal prerogative. Opposition to muster-masters (as to many other things in the early seventeenth century) was fed by depleted purses, as well as by injured principles and local independence. How effective such opposition was in preventing the foundation of an exact militia is not clear. In Cheshire and Sussex more reforms were achieved than in Somerset.[50] Yet, as in the case of the Books of Orders, the vigilance of the privy council was short-lived. Its energy aimed at producing an exact militia was at its height in the late 1620s; after 1630 when peace was concluded its pressure was relaxed. It is true that Charles's exact militia was never given a test like a patriotic war against a universally hated enemy; by the late 1630s the Scots were far from being that. However, there is little doubt that by that time many county militias fell far short of their exact ideal.[51]

Laudianism and isolation

There were, of course, many reasons for the growing dissatisfaction with Charles's personal government, but it is likely that the king's attachment to Laudianism made the greatest contribution to it. It has been usual for historians to label Charles's religious preferences as 'Arminianism'. As has been noted before (see p. 86), there are many problems associated with using this term. It implies that Charles's religious views were identical to those of Jacobus Arminius, a Leyden divine, and that, like him, Charles's religious views were characterized principally by a theological alternative to Calvinist predestinarianism. In fact, Charles's religious views were based on ideas that had been debated in England within the Church since at least the 1590s, well before Arminius published his doctrines. Nor were Charles's religious views concerned solely with theology. He aligned himself with views that were associated increasingly by the late 1620s and 1630s with an ambitious divine, William Laud. Laud's views, like those of others before him, including Richard Neile, Lancelot Andrewes and John Buckeridge, were characterized not only by theological concerns but also by 'the propagation of a vision of a visible Church and the Christian community radically different from that implied

---

[48] Barnes, *Somerset*, p. 257. Phelips's stance loses its force as an alleged illustration of a 'court versus country' episode by the fact that a few months later he accepted the post of deputy lieutenant: ibid., p. 266.

[49] Opposition to muster-masters was not new. See the controversy in Wiltshire in 1603–6: W. P. D. Murphy, ed., *The Earl of Hertford's Lieutenancy Papers 1603–12* (Wiltshire Record Society, XXIII, 1969), pp. 11–13. For the opposition to muster-masters faced in the 1630s by the lord lieutenant of Leicestershire and Rutland, see T. Cogswell, *Home Divisions: aristocracy, the state and provincial conflict* (1998), pp. 165–200.

[50] Morrill, *Cheshire*, p. 26; Fletcher, *Sussex*, p. 184; Barnes, *Somerset*, pp. 258–71.

[51] For a different view, see H. Langeluddecke, ' "The chief strength and glory of this kingdom": arming and training the "perfect militia" in the 1630s', *E.H.R.*, 118 (2003).

by Calvinist orthodoxy'.[52] Hence, there is a case for preferring 'Laudian' and 'Laudianism' over 'Arminian' and 'Arminianism' to describe the religious views that Charles adopted and the churchmen he patronized during the first fifteen years of his reign.

However, adopting Laudianism as the label for Charles's religious views does not obviate the problem of defining what these were. What was Laudianism? When he was asked what Laudians held, a contemporary tried to get round this question by saying that they held all the best bishoprics and deaneries in England. One difficulty in going further than that is that Laudianism in the sense of a group of people all holding exactly the same set of beliefs did not exist. Moreover, the gulf between Laudians and other Protestants on some issues can be exaggerated. It is not hard to find 'puritanical' traits in the life of William Laud. When William Cavendish (later earl of Newcastle) broke his horse's neck in a fall on Good Friday, Laud noted in his diary, 'should not this day have other employment?'[53] Moreover, was not Laud's concern to reform the Church by recovering ecclesiastical endowments from lay hands in order to finance an educated clergy similar to that of many 'Puritan' reformers since the reign of Elizabeth I?

Information

Why were Laudians hated by most Protestants?

- Laudians believed in the doctrine of free will, that God's grace was open to all and that an individual could attain salvation by good works. In the early seventeenth century this theology found favour with a minority of Jacobean bishops (including Neile, Andrewes and Buckeridge) and a younger generation of clerics, principally William Laud. This was seen as an attack on the doctrine of predestination held by most English Protestants.

- In church services, Laudians highlighted the sacramental and ceremonial aspects and the vicar's role in them. This posed a challenge to the emphasis placed by most clerics and laymen in the late sixteenth and early seventeenth centuries on the scriptures and on their dissemination in church services.

- Some – though not all – Laudians even went so far as to claim that the existence of bishops depended not on the king's grant but on divine right.

---

[52] P. Lake, 'The impact of early modern Protestantism', *J.B.S.*, XXVIII (1989), p. 302. See the Bibliographical note (pp. 518–19) for widely differing interpretations of Laudianism amongst historians.

[53] Quoted in H. R. Trevor-Roper, *Archbishop Laud* (2nd edn., 1962), p. 159. See also C. Carlton, 'The dream life of Archbishop Laud', *History Today*, XXXVI (1986) and his *Archbishop William Laud* (1987). W. Lamont, *Godly Rule: politics and religion 1603–60* (1969), p. 69, calls Laud's diary 'an authentic puritan document'.

What convinced most people that Laud was a dangerous innovator[54] was that after he became archbishop of Canterbury in 1633 he and Charles carried into practice this theoretical assault on predestination and preaching, as well as attacking vested property interests. What caused most controversy was the Laudian attempt to move the communion table from its accustomed position in the nave of most parish churches to the east end of the church, where (as in most cathedral churches) it was to be surrounded by rails. Why did this, apparently slight, internal reorganization of churches cause great contemporary furore? For one thing the change, by emphasizing the sacrament of the altar, was a sign of the Laudian attack on the doctrine of predestination that everyone could recognize. By reviving the annual archiepiscopal metropolitan visitations, Laud attempted to enforce uniformity in this respect. Moreover, no one seeing the change needed an understanding of doctrinal niceties to see it as an innovation. Indeed, to most people the railing off of the communion table must have seemed, as it did to the Root and Branch petitioners of 1640, 'a plain device to usher in the Mass'.[55] What is more, the removal of family pews, which was sometimes necessary to accommodate the communion table in its new 'altar-wise' position and to enable the congregation to see the communion being celebrated, was a clear instance of how Laudian innovations could upset the social status quo. Nor was any effort made to convert people to the wisdom of the changes. On the contrary, the published reason for the change appeared to be to bring about uniformity for its own sake. The canons of 1640 reiterated Laud's opinion that the repositioned communion table 'doth not imply that it is or ought to be esteemed a true and proper altar whereon Christ is again really sacrificed'. A high price was paid in renewed opposition and distrust for something which was 'in its own nature indifferent'.[56]

Also controversial was the fact that Laud's accession as archbishop coincided with the republication of James I's Declaration of Sports, permitting secular activities on the sabbath, and with an intensification of the campaign against unlicensed preaching which had begun in December 1629. Significantly, the fact was forgotten that bishops were also told to live in their dioceses and not alienate their episcopal estates. Instead the measures that caused offence were those which attempted to deter the appointment of nonconformist lecturers, by ordering that only those who read the prayer book in a surplice and hood could deliver the sermon. In 1633 Laud succeeded in abolishing (via star chamber) the Feoffees for Impropriations, a group of Puritan London merchants and landowners founded in 1625, which was beginning to buy livings and appoint Puritan preachers to them. The episode reveals the Laudian dilemma: Laud abolished a reforming organization, whose aim, the recovery from lay ownership for the Church of tithes and livings, was identical to his own.

---

[54] Much the best and most influential works that explain this point are by Nicholas Tyacke: see especially 'Puritanism, Arminianism and counter-revolution', *passim*; and *Anti-Calvinists: the rise of English Arminianism c.1590–1640* (1987).

[55] Kenyon, *Stuart Constitution*, p. 156. See also *English Historical Documents 1603–60*, document no. 464.

[56] Kenyon, *Stuart Constitution*, p. 153.

One did not need to be a sophisticated theologian or ardent Puritan to recognize Laud as a threat. Landowners could see their possession of tithes and control over advowsons in danger. Nor did the court of high commission, its powers strengthened, make any social distinctions when prosecuting defendants under Laud's guidance. Great and small, men and women alike, were hauled before the ecclesiastical courts, which in the early seventeenth century had a wide jurisdictional sphere. The ownership of tithes, probate of wills, the payment of alimony, 'adultery, whoredom, incest, drunkenness, swearing, ribaldry and usury', activities not confined to any particular social group, were all matters for the ecclesiastical courts. The growing interference of clerics in secular affairs was resented, whether it was Laud's influence on financial expedients like the commission for depopulation, Bishop Juxon's appointment in 1636 as the first ecclesiastical lord treasurer since the fifteenth century, or clerical nominations to county benches.

A significant result was to weaken the attachment of contemporaries to episcopacy, which had never been seriously questioned since the 1580s. It may be that the anti-episcopal movement found most support among the ranks below that of gentleman (given the lack of sources on these groups before the 1640s it is impossible to be certain).[57] Certainly the revival of radical sects in the late 1630s suggests this was the case. Propertied men, after all, had a vested interest in the maintenance of episcopacy – 'no bishop, no magistrate'. But the activities of Laud and those Laudian bishops in key positions (Neile at York, Wren at Ely, Pierce at Bath and Wells, for example) undermined that attachment. The savage star chamber punishment in 1637 of three authors of anti-episcopal pamphlets, Prynne, Burton and Bastwick, aroused fairly universal horror (in contrast to Prynne's earlier ear cropping in 1632). It mattered little that some felt horror at the physical punishment of gentlemen by branding and ear cropping, rather than sympathy for their anti-episcopal views. Prynne especially won popular acclaim for himself and hatred for Laud: his brandmark S. L., he wrote, stood not for 'seditious libeller' but for '*stigmata Laudis*'. By the late 1630s Calvinist episcopalianism no longer had the almost universal support it had had even a decade earlier.[58]

So the contemporary caricature of Laudianism was formed. Although Laud himself might claim otherwise, his attempts to reform the Church came to be seen as signs

---

[57] Popular discussion and debates about religion were rife in early seventeenth-century London, as was popular criticism of bishops: D. R. Como, 'Predestination and political conflict in Laudian London', *H.J.*, 46 (2003); D. R. Como, *Blown by the Spirit: Puritanism and the emergence of an antinomian underground in pre-Civil War London* (2004); P. Lake and M. Questier, *The Antichrist's Lewd Hat: Protestants, Papists and plays in post-Reformation England* (2002); *The Boxmaker's Revenge: 'orthodoxy' and 'heterodoxy' and the politics of the parish in early Stuart London* (2001). See 'the public sphere' (above, p. 78).

[58] The extent of anti-episcopal sentiment before 1640 can be exaggerated, see pp. 57–8. Sir Robert Phelips in 1637 wrote to Laud congratulating him for dealing with those 'lunatics', Burton, Bastwick and Prynne. I am grateful to Conrad Russell for this information. The important work of K. Fincham and N. Tyacke in *Altars Restored: the changing face of religious worship, 1547–c.1700* (2007) shows that the unpopularity of the Laudian emphasis on imagery and ritualism can be exaggerated. See A. Cambers, 'Pastoral Laudianism: religion, and politics in the 1630s: a Leicestershire rector's annotations', *Midland History*, 27 (2002) for one man's positive reaction to Laudianism.

of encroaching Catholicism. Even in the eyes of a future Cheshire royalist, Laudianism was 'a plotting, undermining and dangerous sect'.[59] In the eyes of its critics it was, paradoxically, at the same time a means by which an independent Church would dominate the secular State and lay magistracy, and a source of theoretical support for the claims of royal absolutism. Might it have been otherwise? If the contacts between the court and the parliamentary classes which had been maintained in the 1620s had not been cut in the 1630s, might one side have appreciated the common ground it had with the other? Fortunately, might-have-beens are not the primary concern of the historian. Anyway the fact is that the Caroline court, instead of being a forum in which royal policies could be explained and the views of the political nation listened to, became increasingly alien. Some even became more convinced than ever that there was a Popish Plot at court, now with Charles's wife, Henrietta Maria, at its centre. She gained a reputation as an evil papist and foreigner, a Lady Macbeth-type figure seducing her husband away from Protestantism and towards Rome.

It is important that the black image that the Caroline court came to have in the minds of many English people by the later 1630s should not be equated with historical reality. The court of Charles I was not the monolithic, Catholic-dominated court that its critics from outside thought it. It was one in which, like other early modern European courts, factional competition was rife and in which the queen was only one of many players in the factional game. Indeed, during the 1630s, rather than being the pro-Spanish queen of legend, at the centre of a clique of crypto-Catholics, Henrietta Maria was part of an anti-Spanish court faction in which Protestant courtiers, such as the future parliamentarian earls of Northumberland and Holland, played a key role. She worked closely with those who were anxious to secure French support for the Protestant cause of Charles's sister Elizabeth in the Palatinate, as well as with those godly Protestants connected with the Providence Island Company who were anxious to gain French support for a war in the Caribbean against Spain.[60] Nor does the image of a cultural split between court and country seem to have had as much substance in reality as was once thought. Future parliamentarians like the earl of Warwick as well as court acolytes had their portraits painted by the Catholic Anthony Van Dyck. The architectural styles used by Inigo Jones in designing the Banqueting House in Whitehall and the Queen's House at Greenwich do not seem to have caused the hostility it was once assumed they did. A travelling provincial gentleman described a new house he visited in 1634 as 'not much unlike in that goodly and magnificent Building the Banqueting House in Whitehall'; while Sir Simonds D'Ewes, a godly critic of the court in the early 1640s, had to ask in the first session of the Long Parliament who Inigo Jones was.[61] Moreover, Martin Butler's work on the theatre in the 1630s has

---

[59] Morrill, *Cheshire*, p. 28.

[60] R. M. Smuts, 'The puritan followers of Henrietta Maria in the 1630s', *E.H.R.*, XCIII (1978), pp. 26–45.

[61] J. C. Robertson, 'Caroline culture: bridging court and country?', *History*, LXXV (1990), p. 408. See also R. M. Smuts, *Court Culture and the Origins of a Royalist Tradition in Stuart England* (1987) and K. M. Sharpe, *Criticism and Compliment: the politics of literature in the England of Charles I* (1987).

revealed a more complex picture than that of a gaping gulf between courtly masques and popular London drama.[62]

Nevertheless, increasingly from the 1630s a more simplistic, Popish Plot image of the court became popular in the country, in which Henrietta Maria's role was seen to be especially pernicious.[63] What gave support to this was that in 1628 relations between Charles and his wife had changed dramatically. For the first four years of their marriage Charles and his teenage bride had found each other's company at best irksome. Stories of public quarrels between them were commonplace in the later 1620s. After one quarrel in 1626, Henrietta Maria smashed the window of a room with her bare fist and threatened to go home to France.[64] In 1628, however, coinciding with the assassination of Buckingham, dramatically husband and wife fell suddenly, deeply in love. For a time they seem to have found it difficult to be apart. When Charles visited Scotland without her in 1633, Henrietta Maria was said to have been 'in extremity'. The 1630s were punctuated by a series of royal pregnancies, resulting in a miscarriage in May 1629, and the births of Charles (the future Charles II) in May 1630, Mary in 1631, James (the future James II) in 1633, Elizabeth in 1635, Ann in 1637, a stillborn girl in 1638 and Henry in 1640.[65] The queen later wrote in an autobiographical fragment that during the 1630s 'I was the happiest and most fortunate of queens, for not only had I every pleasure the heart could desire I had a husband who adored me.' However, the public perception of the marriage was far different from this story of private bliss. Henrietta Maria's close relationship with her husband was seen in the context of her Catholic associations: the Catholic clauses of the 1624 marriage treaty; her establishment of Catholic chapels at St James's and elsewhere; and her patronage of twelve Capuchin monks at Somerset House after 1629. By this time, a London preacher railed against a queen who 'has wounded [Jesus Christ] with her infidelity, Superstition and Idolatory'.[66] Later these Popish Plot suspicions were strengthened as Henrietta Maria in 1637 broke with her old court allies and associated more closely with those bent on undermining plans for a pro-French coalition: first Gregorio Panzani, papal agent at court since 1634; and then from 1636 his successor, a canny Catholic Scot, George Con, who worked with court Catholics like Francis Windebank. Against the background of what looked like Laudian attempts to reverse the Reformation in the Church, the evidence of creeping Catholicism at court to many seemed believable and increased the distrust they felt for royal policies that seemed both 'popish' and 'absolutist'. Given the lack of parliamentary sessions, there are few sources that reveal the growing mistrust of the court in provincial England. This has enabled some historians to argue that none existed, but it may be that the evidence in the diaries of Thomas Dugard, a Warwick schoolmaster and preacher, and Robert Woodford, the

---

[62] M. Butler, *Theatre and Crisis 1632–42* (1984).
[63] C. Hibbard, *Charles I and the Popish Plot* (1983).
[64] C. Carlton, *Charles I: The Personal Monarch* (1983), pp. 58–9.
[65] Their last child, Henrietta, was born in 1644.
[66] Carlton, *Charles I*, p. 142.

steward of Northampton, were not untypical. Dugard was part of a circle of godly men and women, including Lord Brooke, who met frequently and who were antagonistic to the ideals of Charles I and Laud; and Woodford's diary 'demonstrates that the theory of a popish plot to subvert England's religious laws had by 1637 percolated down to the provinces'.[67]

The 'British' context to the Personal Rule

Despite the growing opposition in England to Charles's financial and religious policies, in 1637 the king had no reason to contemplate the end of his personal rule without parliament. It was Charles's policies in Ireland and Scotland that precipitated the collapse of the Personal Rule in the late 1630s.

Wentworth, as lord-deputy of Ireland from 1633, was more consistently successful in imposing administrative efficiency in Ireland than was the privy council in England in the 1630s.[68]

Information

Factions in early seventeenth-century Ireland

Complicating the task of those who attempted to govern early modern Ireland was the tripartite divison of Irish society:

- The 'mere Irish': those whose ancestry pre-dated the English colonization of Ireland.
- 'The Old English': the Catholic descendants of those who had settled in Ireland before the Reformation.
- 'The New English': the Protestant landlord-undertaker class who had spearheaded late sixteenth- and early seventeenth-century colonization of Ulster and Munster.

Wentworth's first task was to impose his own authority on the Dublin council. Whereas previous lord-deputies had been parties to faction rivalries in Ireland,

---

[67] A. Hughes, *Politics, Society and Civil War in Warwickshire 1620–60* (1987), pp. 71–80 and her 'Thomas Dugard and his circle in the 1630s: a parliamentary–puritan connection?', *H.J.*, XXIX (1986); J. Fielding, 'Opposition to the Personal Rule of Charles I: the diary of Robert Woodford 1637–41', *H.J.*, XXXI (1988). See P. Lake, 'Puritanism, Arminianism and a Shropshire axe-murder', *Midland History*, XV (1990) for a dramatic illustration of the tensions caused in England by the promotion of Laudian policies.

[68] H. F. Kearney, *Strafford in Ireland 1633–41: a study in absolutism* (1959): T. W. Moody, F. X. Martin and F. J. Byrne, eds., *A New History of Ireland, III: Early Modern Ireland 1534–1691* (1976), pp. 243–69.

Wentworth stood outside them. When the Irish parliament met in 1634, therefore, Wentworth was able to play the time-honoured political game of divide and rule. Having granted three subsidies in the first session they learned that Wentworth refused to remedy their grievances. The 'graces' which had been promised were not conceded. Having secured control and money, Wentworth proceeded to press ahead successfully with the colonization of Ireland at the expense not only of the native 'mere' Irish, whose interests had never been considered, but also of the Catholic 'Old English'. Wentworth's plantation of Connacht involved the confiscation of the estates of the most eminent 'Old English' aristocrat, the earl of Clanricarde.

The 'New English' also stood in the way of Wentworth's plans. This group had become very rich, as well as very powerful in the Dublin administration. In trying to reform both the financial administration and the Church in Ireland, Wentworth could not fail to attack this class who had benefited at the expense of both. The crown's income was augmented considerably by a revivified court of wards and liveries; the Statute of Uses which Wentworth guided through the Irish Parliament in 1634 prevented Irish landlords from evading their feudal obligations, something which Henry VIII had failed fully to do in England by a similar statute a century earlier. What really offended the 'New English', though, were Wentworth's ecclesiastical reforms. Even the powerful Richard Boyle, earl of Cork was forced to disgorge his ex-ecclesiastical property to its former owner. Moreover, the high commission in Ireland began to impose on the Protestant landlord class, as well as on Presbyterian settlers, a Laudian uniformity, which seemed to them indistinguishable from Catholicism. By the late 1630s Wentworth had doubled the revenues of the Irish administration and rid the Irish Church of many abuses, but only at the expense of uniting in an unnatural alliance 'Old' and 'New' English, Catholics and Protestants.

In many respects, Charles's handling of Scottish affairs mirrors the mistakes he made in England. Just as he attempted to impose order and uniformity on his court and on the English Church (indeed, the emphasis of Laudianism on order may have been its greatest attraction to the king), so Charles foolishly attempted to impose religious uniformity on Scotland and England, countries with very different religious situations.[69] Moreover, just as he cut himself off from powerful English opinion, so Charles remained ignorant of Scottish opinion. His advisers were anglicized Scots and his policies were consequently misdirected and misunderstood. This is illustrated by his precipitate announcement, without explanation, in November 1625 that he intended to revoke all crown gifts of royal and Kirk property made since 1540. In fact his intentions were not so radical as this announcement implied. Although landowners were to lose their tithes (which were to be commuted) and the feudal dues attached to the land, Charles intended to confirm the grants in return for compensation to the crown.

As in England, though, Charles's greatest blunder was in promoting Laudianism in Scotland, thereby upsetting the ecclesiastical *modus vivendi* developed by his father.

---

[69] C. Russell, 'The British problem and the English Civil War', *History*, LXXII (1987).

Despite Jacobean policies in Scotland like the promotion of the Five Articles of Perth[70] that fuelled opposition to the court in Scotland, James had made significant progress in making episcopacy acceptable to the majority of Scots people, by erecting a system of Church government which combined elements of episcopacy and Presbyterianism. By identifying Scottish bishops with Laudian policies, Charles succeeded, as in England, in forcing into more radical opposition those who previously had been willing to accept episcopacy. By increasing the secular power of bishops in government, Charles and Laud strengthened the anti-episcopal movement in Scotland as well as in England.

Laud urged Charles to introduce the English prayer book into Scotland as early as 1629, but it was not until after the king's visit to Scotland in 1633 that the fatal decision seems to have been taken. All protests from Scotland against introducing the prayer book were ignored or suppressed; Lord Balmerino was sentenced to death in 1634 for possessing a copy of a petition concerning the religious grievances. No attempt was made to consult Scottish opinion, apart from the bishops, thus infusing a strong nationalist anti-English element into the opposition. Charles did not deviate from his plan. In 1635 he issued a new book of canons, based on the English canons of 1604, and the Scottish privy council were ordered to command the use of the new prayer book when it was ready early in 1637. In the face of the king's uncompromising attitude, Scottish moderates were forced into allying with radical elements like Archibald Johnston, Laird of Wariston, heirs of a long apocalyptic tradition in Scotland which professed 'a verie near paralel betwixt Izrael and this Churche (of Scotland), the only two suorne nationes of the Lord'.[71] This powerful nationalist and radical religious opposition stirred up by Charles culminated in prearranged demonstrations against the prayer book when it was first used in July 1637. The furious violent scene in St Giles Church in Edinburgh on 23 July was characterized by the leadership of formidable Edinburgh 'matrons'. As in some riots in early seventeenth-century England, women played a prominent part in these Scottish demonstrations. Robert Baillie, fortunately for him, turned down the bishop of Glasgow's request that he conduct a service in the city using the new prayer book. He later reported that 'at the outgoing of the church about 30 or 40 of our honestest women, in one voice, before the Bishop and Magistrates, did fall in railing, cursing, scolding with clamours on Mr. William Annan [his replacement]' and that night 'some hundreds of enraged women, of all qualities, are about him, with fists, and staves, and peats [but] no stones: they beat him sore'.[72]

Defiance always made Charles more uncompromising and he made clear his decision to continue with a policy which was clearly impractical. The reaction from Scotland was an organized petitioning movement and in November the petitioners elected a permanent representative body, which in February 1638 drew up the National Covenant. Even now there were still supporters of limited episcopacy in Scotland; the

---

[70] See p. 132 in this chapter.

[71] Quoted in S. A. Burrell, 'The apocalyptic vision of the early covenanters', *Scottish H.R.*, XLIII (1964), p. 17.

[72] Quoted in J. McCoy, *Robert Baillie and the Second Scots Reformation* (1974), pp. 29–30.

Covenant, though denouncing the canons and the prayer book, did not mention bishops. Charles's stubbornness and insincerity in the next ten months cut the ground from beneath the feet of the moderates. When the Glasgow assembly met in November 1638 episcopacy was abolished. In effect the king's power had been directly challenged and undermined. The 'Scottish revolution' had begun. Both sides began to prepare for war.

The end of the Personal Rule

The lack of enthusiasm in England for war against the Scots is a measure of the opposition Charles faced at home. Laud had achieved the impossible: to make himself more hated in English eyes than the Scots. Hatred of Charles's policies even drove some English peers, including William Fiennes, Viscount Saye and Sele, to begin secret communication with Scottish Covenanters, who shared their godly commitment.[73] Charles's command to call out the trained bands released a flood of complaints about the cost and legality of the militia. Although the king's mobilisation of a large army of 15,000 men in 1639 was a notable achievement,[74] he found that his financial position, though improved by increased rents from the customs farmers after the renegotiation of the great and petty farm of the customs in the winter of 1637–8, was not adequate for wartime needs. Appeals to the City, its Irish estates confiscated by the crown, brought no offers of a loan. By now too the yield of ship money fell dramatically; only 20 per cent of the expected receipts from the 1639 writ was actually paid to Sir William Russell, the treasurer of the navy.[75] The incidence of violent assaults on the tax collectors increased; George Vernon of Whatcroft in Cheshire 'drew out his knife and threatened the constable to whett it in its gutts'.[76] Charles had little choice but to negotiate with the Scots army and conclude a truce at Berwick on 18 June 1639, agreeing to a meeting of the Scottish assembly and parliament and the disbandment of both armies.

But the truce settled nothing. The covenanters did not disband their army and the Edinburgh assembly and parliament which met in the autumn completed the ecclesiastical and constitutional revolution and repudiation of royal control. When Wentworth returned from Ireland in September realizing that the projected cost of the war of £300,000 could not be met by loans from privy councillors and customs farmers alone, he advised the king to call an English parliament, which eventually met

---

[73] P. H. Donald, 'New light on the Anglo-Scottish contacts of 1640', *Historical Research*, LXII (1989) and his *An Uncounselled King: Charles I and the Scottish Troubles 1637–41* (1990). Jason Peacey in 'The outbreak of the Civil Wars', in Coward, ed., *Companion to Stuart Britain*, p. 297 argues cogently that these contacts were not new but built on 'profound and long-standing cross-border Puritan connections, and of an Anglo-Scottish Protestant culture based upon both print and personal contacts'. These contacts and the role in maintaining them of Sir John Clotworthy, the brother-in-law of John Pym, are discussed in John Adamson, *The Noble Revolt: the overthrow of Charles I* (2007), pp. 36–9.

[74] M. C. Fissel, *The Bishops' Wars: Charles I's campaigns against Scotland, 1638–40* (1994).

[75] Gordon, 'The collection of ship money', pp. 143–4.

[76] Morrill, *Cheshire*, p. 29.

on 13 April. Was the failure of this Short Parliament inevitable? Undoubtedly, as Derek Hirst and others have shown,[77] some candidates in 1640 were elected on a popular anti-court platform, which presupposes widespread opposition to Caroline government among the electorate. The flood of local petitions to parliament, cataloguing the grievances of the 1630s, indicates some degree of organization behind the opposition. Yet the picture of a united opposition developing in the 1630s, using colonizing and trading organizations, such as the Providence Island Company, as a front for its political activities, is too simplistic. Not all elections in 1640, by any means, were dominated by national issues; nor were MPs united on the tactics needed to secure a redress of grievances; nor was Charles entirely devoid of support. On the contrary, in the Short Parliament the king could count on a majority in the Lords in favour of voting him subsidies. And his announcement of the illegality of ship money must have won him support in the Commons, despite John Pym's long tirade against the record of Caroline government since the 1620s.[78] The issue which in the end seems to have turned the Commons against granting the king subsidies was that of military charges for the Scottish war. These were to continue and were much heavier than ship money. The Yorkshire MP, John Hotham, pointed out that, whereas Yorkshire's ship money assessment was £12,000, coat and conduct money levied on the county was £40,000.[79]

By 1640 the old constitution was still intact. However, after the dissolution of the Short Parliament in May 1640 it is difficult to see any possibility of Charles securing enough support to avoid a serious constitutional crisis. What little chance of cooperation remained he threw away by arresting Warwick, Brooke, and Saye and Sele, and the leading parliamentary spokesmen in the Commons, and, despite Laud's conciliatory advice, ordering the continuation of Convocation, which proceeded to adopt new canons, embodying the Laudian innovations of the 1630s. A vain attempt was made by Cottington to salvage Charles's financial position by an ingenious commercial deal involving the purchase and resale of over 600,000 pounds of pepper, which raised over £50,000. But the City again refused to lend the crown any money until a parliament was called. The militia in many counties was undisciplined and more inclined to pull down communion table rails and enclosure fences than march against the Scots.[80] In Yorkshire the gentry petitioned the king against the expense of billeting the troops there. The Scots, therefore, met little resistance when they crossed the Tweed on 20 August 1640, and within ten days, after a minor skirmish at Newburn, they occupied

---

[77] Derek Hirst, *The Representative of the People? Voters and voting in England under the early Stuarts* (1975), *passim*.

[78] M. Kishlansky in 'A lesson in loyalty: Charles I and the Short Parliament', in J. McElligott and D. L. Smith, eds., *Royalists and Royalism during the English Civil Wars* (2007) takes this point further than I am willing to go, arguing that Charles I in his dealings with this parliament was much more politically astute and less duplicitous than he is often said to have been, and that the main reason for the parliament's failure was the intransigence of leading MPs.

[79] Cliffe, *Yorkshire Gentry*, p. 518.

[80] J. Walter, 'The politics of popular iconoclasm in England, 1640–42', *P. & P.*, 183 (2004); and 'Popular iconoclasm and the politics of the parish in eastern England, 1640–42', *H.J.*, 47 (2004).

Newcastle. If Charles's military standing was weak, his diplomatic and political position was worse. The Council of Peers which met at York on 24 September refused to cooperate until Charles called a new parliament. So did the authorities and the moneylenders of London. Charles had little choice but to issue writs for a new parliament and to accept humiliating conditions as the basis for a truce with the Scots. His commissioners agreed at Ripon on 21 October 1640 to pay the Scots army £850 a day while they occupied English soil. This alone ensured that the second parliament of 1640 would not be got rid of as easily as the first.

PART 3

The English Revolution, 1640–1660

Introduction

Was there an 'English Revolution' in the middle of the seventeenth century? It is an open question whether the exciting events that happened after 1640 merit being given the label 'Revolution' or even 'English'. As will be seen, events during the 1640s and 1650s were shaped by conservatism – sometimes militant conservatism. For this and other reasons, earlier historians preferred to call the period 'the Great Rebellion' rather than 'the English Revolution'. More recently, historians, especially the proponents of 'the new British history', have been very keen to see what happened after 1640 in a wider context than merely an English one, accounting for the appearance of labels like 'the War of the Three Kingdoms' (of Scotland and Ireland as well as England and Wales), and even 'the British Revolution'. As has already been seen, events in Scotland and Ireland, as well as in England, influenced greatly the timing and the nature of the political crisis of 1640–1, as they did too the way that crisis developed in succeeding years. The importance of both conservatism in the events of the 1640s and 1650s and of the 'British context' in understanding those events will not be ignored in what follows.

Yet I will also be careful, in doing this, not to downgrade too much the radical nature and the English origins of what happened in the middle of the seventeenth century. The dramatic and unique nature of those events is incontrovertible. Within less than a decade the power of the monarchy was first drastically reduced, and then extinguished, the king executed and monarchy abolished, along with the other pillars of traditional society, bishops and the House of Lords. The downfall of the crown and the established Church meant the collapse of effective censorship of the press, and the emergence of radical ideas about religious toleration, political democracy, economic reform, fundamental restructuring of education and the law, and the imposition of new social values. What is more, these ideas were often voiced by men and women of low social status, whose views were only rarely heard in England before 1640 and after 1660. Moreover, many of these ideas were rooted in England well before 1640, as were the causes of what happened in England after 1640. The impact on each other of events in England, Ireland and Scotland is important, but this is by no means the only or primary explanation of those events. In these circumstances, 'the English Revolution' does not seem to be an unreasonable term to use. This assertion bears directly on the hotly disputed question, what were the causes of this English Revolution?

6

The making of the English Revolution, 1640–1649

Historiography

The causes of the English Revolution

The following three causes of the English Revolution are now rejected by most historians:

- *Whig explanations* are based on the assumption that the parliamentary leaders in the 1640s were consciously aiming at something like the nineteenth-century British constitution.
- *Marxist explanations* are based on the belief that the events of the 1640s were the direct result of social and economic changes in the preceding century.
- *Geographical and 'ecological' explanations.* The old assumption that royalism was more common in the north and west of England and parliamentarianism in the south and east has disintegrated as historians have found many exceptions to that generalization. The more recent equation by historians (see the Bibliographical note, section 3) between royalism and arable areas, and between parliamentarianism and pastoral areas, has been less decisively rejected, but it too tends to fall down in the light of detailed local studies of both kinds of 'ecological' community.

Having cast serious doubts on these once popular long-term causes of the English Revolution, some so-called 'revisionist' historians in the last decades of the twentieth century tended to explain what happened in the 1640s in terms of *short-term and 'functional' explanations*, notably Charles's ineptness and events in Scotland and Ireland.

Were there, then, any long-term causes that help to explain why people took different courses of action in the 1640s? In this chapter it will be suggested that there were. The dramatic course of events after 1640 was greatly influenced by different constitutional and religious attitudes and aspirations (reflected in different conspiracy theories) that had emerged in the early seventeenth century.

The constitutional crisis, November 1640–September 1641

Unity

As has been seen in the previous two chapters, two different views had emerged about political and constitutional developments during the early seventeenth century: 'constitutional parliamentarianism' and 'constitutional royalism'.

Constitutional parliamentarianism and belief in a Popish Plot

The determination of some MPs and their constituents to safeguard parliamentary liberties and Protestantism (a determination which, it has been seen, existed in parliaments from at least the 1590s and had intensified during the late 1620s) was still prevalent in the 1640s. People who held these views were not united on everything. As in the late 1620s, some people were willing to pursue those aspirations more zealously than others and were less willing to trust the king than others. Moreover, for some religious reformation was not central to their political aims; there were ungodly parliamentarians. Henry Marten, the womanizing Berkshire lawyer, is an example (if an extreme one) of those MPs whose memories were indelibly marked by recollections of Charles's contempt for the law in the aftermath of the Five Knights' case in the 1620s and his resurrection of antiquated feudal rights in the 1630s. But more typical of those who remained committed against the king for much of the 1640s were people for whom the godly and the parliamentary causes were inextricably intertwined. One of the lessons learned by zealous Puritan gentry like Robert Harley, Sir Thomas Pelham, Lord Brooke and Sir Nathaniel Barnardiston in the late 1620s was that the fortunes of parliaments and Protestantism were linked; both would sink or swim together. The strongest ideological drive behind the opposition to the king in the 1640s was religious zeal. This helps to explain the otherwise surprising commitment to parliament in the Civil War of a conservative, antiquarian lawyer like Sir Simonds D'Ewes, who was hardly the stuff of which revolutionaries are made. At crisis points in 1641 and 1642 he showed himself to be a very timid man, leaving the chamber of the Commons complaining of a cold during the Grand Remonstrance debates in November 1641 when tempers flared dangerously, and going home to make his will after the king's attempted arrest of the Five Members in January 1642 threatened to plunge the country into premature civil war. Yet when the Civil War did begin, D'Ewes supported parliament, stiffened in his resistance to the king by a godly zeal to rescue him from a Popish Plot and to complete the uncompleted Reformation. What put the fire of resistance into the bellies of many of the people who opposed Charles in the 1640s was the chance they saw to bring about, through parliament, the godly reformation that they and their predecessors had been campaigning for since at least the 1580s. 'Constitutional parliamentarianism' – the desire to safeguard parliament's place in the constitution from the creeping threat of royal 'absolutism' that had seemed to be prevalent since at least 1626 – often went hand in hand with a craving for godly reformation which also had its roots in the decades before 1640.

Constitutional royalism and belief in a Puritan Plot

As the parliamentary leaders soon found in the early months of the Long Parliament, not all those who were united with them in 1640 shared these attitudes and aspirations. MPs like Sir Edward Hyde who wanted to undo Caroline and Laudian 'innovations' soon began to fear that some of their colleagues wanted to go further; that parliamentary, rather than royal, 'absolutism' was the greater threat to the ancient constitution. They also began to believe that the consequences of further reformation of the Church would be religious diversity and the collapse of the traditional ecclesiastical order. Consequently, they began to express an alternative ideology to that of godly constitutionalism: 'constitutional royalism'. This comprised a desire to safeguard the balanced ancient constitution from the creeping threat of parliamentary and 'popular-puritan' incursions into the royal prerogative, combined with an attachment to a Church with bishops, with a Book of Common Prayer and with a liturgy centred on traditional festivals like Easter and Christmas. For royalists, unlike parliamentarians, the pre-Laudian Church as it had developed by 1625 was truly reformed and, for some, was worth fighting for. Once Charles I abandoned Laud in 1640 and in 1641 began to claim that he was the only true defender of the Elizabethan Church and the ancient constitution, both of which were threatened by parliamentary innovations, he began to gain support for ideological as well as functional reasons.

When the Long Parliament first met on 3 November 1640 these differences in attitudes and aspirations were not yet clearly apparent. Inevitably, given an electorate that (as Derek Hirst has shown) had grown rapidly in numbers and independence during the early seventeenth century (see pp. 35–6), there were people in the constituencies, as well as in parliament, who had vastly differing aims and expectations of the new parliament. But these were not visible; in November 1640 the political nation appeared united. Both inside and outside parliament there was a dominant, unifying optimism that the new parliamentary session would have a cathartic effect. Wildly optimistic, millenarian aspirations were voiced in some quarters in 1640. Anna

Temple, a Warwickshire lady, wrote excitedly to her daughter, 'Wee shall see idolatory and superstition rooted out and God's ordinances set up in the puritie and power of them.' Thomas Knyvett made the same point more prosaically: 'Now reformation goes on again as hot as toast.'[1] England became a magnet for European radicals, reformers and idealists who hoped that they would now have an opportunity to try out their ideas in practice. That both parliamentary leaders and some rank-and-file MPs were affected by this exciting atmosphere is not in doubt. Reformers like Samuel Hartlib, John Comenius and John Dury were patronized by important political leaders like the earl of Bedford in 1640; a 'godly reformation' was prayed for by preachers of some of the fast sermons to parliament which were given the seal of official approval and were ordered to be printed.[2] However, the immediate aims of the majority of MPs as they rode to Westminster for the new session seem to have been to get rid of the men and the measures that had caused such offence in the 1630s. Their principal targets were Laud, Strafford and the judges who had declared for the king in the ship money case in 1637 and the religious and fiscal innovations they had counselled the king to introduce. Future royalists in the Civil War were as vocal in condemning them as future parliamentarians. Sir Henry Slingsby, a Yorkshire MP, noted in his diary:

> Great expectance there is of a happy Parliament where ye subject may have a
> total redress of all grievances: and here they apply them to question all delinquents,
> all Projectors and Monopollizers, such as levi'd ship money, and such Judges as gave
> it law.[3]

With their grievances resolved, most MPs expected, with John Culpepper, that

> then by the Blessing of God we shall return with an Olive branch in our Mouths, and a
> full Confirmation of the Privileges which were received from our Ancestors, and owe to
> our Posterity, and which every Free-born Englishman hath received with the Air he
> breatheth in.[4]

All factions and shades of opinion were united on an immediate programme of dismantling the worst features of Caroline government. It was not until the question arose of what to put in their place that serious divisions emerged.

---

[1] Quoted in A. Fletcher, *A County Community at Peace and War: Sussex 1600–60* (1975), p. 25; and A. Fletcher, *The Outbreak of the English Civil War* (1981), p. 2.

[2] H. R. Trevor-Roper, 'Three foreigners: the philosophers of the Puritan Revolution', in his *Religion, the Reformation and Social Change* (1967), pp. 237–93 and 'The fast sermons of the Long Parliament', in his *Essays in British History* (1964), pp. 85–138; P. Christianson, 'From expectation to militance: reformers and Babylon in the first two years of the Long Parliament', *J. Eccl. H.*, XXIV (1973), pp. 225–44; J. F. Wilson, *Pulpit in Parliament* (1969); E. W. Kirby, 'Sermons before the Commons', *American H.R.*, XLIV (1938–9), pp. 528–48. From its first meeting the Long Parliament ordered that occasional days should be set aside as fast days. Beginning on 23 February 1642 regular fasts were held on the last Wednesday of every month, when two preachers invited by the Commons delivered sermons, one in the morning and one in the afternoon.

[3] Quoted in R. Ollard, *This War Without an Enemy* (1976), p. 42.

[4] John Rushworth, *Historical Collections* (1659–1701), IV, p. 34.

It is, however, possible to underestimate the radical nature of the programme of the king's parliamentary opponents in the first months of the Long Parliament. Prominent amongst these opponents were rich and powerful aristocrats, notably the earls of Bedford, Warwick and Essex, and lords Saye and Sele, Mandeville and Brooke, who worked with John Pym, Oliver St John, John Hampden, Denzil Holles, Nathaniel Fiennes and William Strode in the Commons.

Biography

John Pym (1584–1643)

Pym's rise to political prominence was based on his position as receiver of the king's estates in Hampshire, Wiltshire and Gloucestershire and the patronage he secured from the earls of Bedford and Warwick. In the parliaments of the 1620s he gained a reputation as a fierce opponent of Laudians in the Church and State. He also played a leading role in the impeachment of the duke of Buckingham. During the 1630s life was difficult for him as a known opponent of Laudians and he sought the protection of Sir Richard Knightley of Fawsley in Northamptonshire. He was also treasurer of the Providence Island Company, a colonizing venture aimed at the establishment of commercially viable colonies in the Caribbean and godly commonwealths in New England. This was the time that he forged very close links with all the men who were to be parliamentary leaders in 1640, all of whom were members of the company.

When parliament met again in 1640, Pym took a key role in voicing grievances that many had against the crown, and in the early 1640s before he died in 1643 of bowel cancer he had an equally key role in constructing an effective parliamentary war effort with new financial expedients, more efficient administration by the use of county committees and an alliance with the Scots (made in 1643 by the Solemn League and Covenant).

A key question about Pym is: how important was his role in the parliamentary politics of the early 1640s? Was he 'King Pym' or was his role overshadowed by that of others like Warwick?

What is certain is that he shared the driving revolutionary religious zeal of many others on the parliamentary side.

Most of the parliamentary leaders were men driven to take radical actions by the ideology of constitutional parliamentarianism defined above: an amalgam of a desire to safeguard parliamentary liberties and a burning zeal for godly reformation. What gave their radical campaign an added impetus is the fact that it was not just a 'noble revolt', but one that reflected and was sustained by extensive popular support.[5]

Undeniably, though, the king's opponents were also pushed to pursue radical courses by the need to meet pressing practical problems. Amongst these was the need to raise money to carry on government and pay the Scots, which was partly and temporarily met by the negotiation of a City loan in November and a parliamentary grant of two subsidies in December. Undoubtedly, however, a more pressing and more serious problem was their own security, which is why in the first week of the Long Parliament Strafford was arrested and the drafting of charges against him became the main business of parliament during the whole of November 1640.

Biography

Thomas Wentworth, earl of Strafford (1583–1641)

He was the eldest surviving son of a wealthy Yorkshire landowner near Sheffield. In the parliaments of the 1620s he opposed crown policies (including the forced loan), and the duke of Buckingham for his excessive use of the royal prerogative in the 1620s.

The assassination of Buckingham in 1628 marked a major turning point in Wentworth's career as he believed that it removed the source of the policies he had opposed. In 1628 he was made Viscount Wentworth and appointed lord president of the council of the north. In the north Wentworth proved to be a firm supporter of the crown, using his position to promote royal policies in an authoritarian way.

These qualities were evident in and after 1632 when Wentworth was appointed lord-deputy of Ireland. In Ireland he took on leading New English magnates like Richard Boyle, earl of Cork, promoting assiduously royal Laudian policies and the confiscation of the estates of New and Old English landowners.

When the crisis exploded against the crown in 1639, Charles turned to Wentworth as his chief adviser, making him earl of Strafford in 1640. Given the threat he posed to the parliamentary leaders by his control of royal armies in England and Scotland, it is not surprising that proceedings were begun against him when the Long Parliament met in 1640. After a long legal struggle, he was brought to trial. This failed to find convincing evidence to prove a charge of treason against him, and the parliamentarians resorted to a bill of attainder that simply asserted – but did not prove – Strafford's guilt. Charles reluctantly gave his assent to that bill and Strafford was executed on 12 May 1641.

---

[5] John Adamson, *The Noble Revolt: the overthrow of Charles I* (2007) is good on the radical nature of the aims of the parliamentary leadership to curb the powers of the monarch but pays insufficient attention to the religious zeal and popular support that lay behind those aims.

A. Doctor Vsher, Lord Prima:
te of Ireland,
B the Sherifes of London,
C the Earle of Strafford,
D. his kindred and friends.

Figure 6.1 'The true manner of the execution of Thomas, earl of Strafford . . . 12 May 1641'
by Wenceslaus Hollar perhaps exaggerates the ordered nature of the crowd but not its size.
Both that and Hollar's annotations in German illustrate that this event was seen to be of major
importance in England and also throughout Europe.
Source: © Mary Evans Picture Library.

It is true that other leading ministers in Charles's government were proceeded
against; the ship money judges impeached, and Laud imprisoned and his impeachment voted. But the haste behind Strafford's prosecution is unique and testifies to the
separate category of fear and hatred in which he was held.

By the time of Strafford's execution on 12 May 1641, most of the alleged perpetra-
tors of the 'abuses' of the 1630s were dead, in prison or in exile; the next step was to
get rid of the abuses themselves. Judging by the volume of petitions to parliament and
parliamentary speeches, support for this course was unanimous. Gardiner called the
great debate on grievances at the beginning of the parliament on 7 November 'one
long outburst of suppressed complaint'.[6] The comprehensiveness of the legislation of
the first session of the Long Parliament and the speed with which it was enacted (the
last major measures were passed in August 1641) testify to the strength and unity of
agreement among MPs in favour of abolishing the royal financial expedients of the
1630s (tonnage and poundage without parliamentary consent, ship money, forest fines,
distraint of knighthood, monopolies) and the prerogative courts (star chamber, council
of the north, the ecclesiastical court of high commission). They also amount to a
sustained attack on the royal prerogative, suggesting that the leaders of the king's
opponents were driven by an ideology of 'constitutional parliamentarianism' as well as

---

[6] Gardiner, *History*, IX, p. 224.

by functional pressures. The validity of this suggestion is strengthened by the passage of two Acts that made fundamental incursions into the crown's hitherto undisputed right to call and dismiss parliaments. The Triennial Act (15 February) set a maximum gap of three years between parliaments. More drastically, a brief Act on 10 May declared that the present parliament should only be dissolved when it, and not the king, saw fit.[7]

The legislation of 1641, however, left unsolved a central problem of the 1640s: how could the parliamentary leaders ensure that the redress of the grievances and constitutional concessions they had obtained in 1641 would be permanent? Until November 1641 the parliamentary leaders were not prepared to commit themselves to a radical and effective solution to that problem. In the meantime they appear to have believed that the guarantee of 'good government' in the future was for Charles to give them and their allies important state offices, enabling them to wield influence in the privy council and with the king. This is certainly in line with the activities of some members of Bedford's circle in the parliaments of the 1620s (see above, pp. 136, 145). There is little reason to doubt the accuracy of Clarendon's account of Bedford's suggestion in April 1641 that in return for his support in parliament for merely removing Strafford from office the earl should be made lord treasurer, Saye and Sele master of the court of wards, Pym chancellor of the exchequer, and Denzil Holles secretary of state.[8] Charles appears to have seriously considered this proposition to end the crisis (as he saw it) by buying off the opposition; already he had offered St John the solicitorship, and later Saye and Sele became master of the court of wards. The Bedford group had a detailed programme of financial reforms worked out to give the crown an adequate extra-parliamentary revenue. With this, and with themselves in power, they hoped to ensure that royal government would once again work as they wanted it to do.[9] The practicality of the scheme is open to question; neither Laud in the 1630s nor Digby in the 1640s was able to use their positions in office to control Charles's activities. Some parliamentarians, too, found it difficult to accept a scheme that allowed a dangerous man like Strafford to live. 'Stone dead hath no fellow', said the earl of Essex when Hyde told him what was being proposed, and no doubt others agreed with this sentiment that the only good Strafford was a dead Strafford. In any case, with the revelations of an army plot on 3 May, the death of Bedford on 9 May, and the continuation of Charles's hopes that he could defeat the opposition by other means, the scheme was doomed, paving the way for the more radical solutions to control the king adopted in November 1641.

---

[7] Only two major grievances were not dealt with in the first session of the Long Parliament. Purveyance was declared illegal in December 1642, and the court of wards and liveries and all feudal tenures were formally abolished in February 1646.

[8] Clarendon, *History*, I, pp. 280–2. See Clayton Roberts, 'The earl of Bedford and the coming of the English Revolution', *J.M.H.*, XLIX (1977) pp. 59–76.

[9] Conrad Russell, 'Parliament and the king's finances', in Conrad Russell, ed., *The Origins of the English Civil War* (1973), pp. 111–13; Conrad Russell, *The Fall of the British Monarchies, 1637–42* (Oxford, 1991), chapter 6.

As yet all groups within parliament were united. Future royalists, like Sir Edward Hyde (later earl of Clarendon) and Viscount Falkland, supported the legislative programme of 1641, and in some cases took a leading part in it, as did Hyde in securing the abolition of the council of the north. The unity was in part a function of the universal agreement on what was wrong with royal government as it had developed in the 1630s; it was also partly a result of the skilful political tactics of the Bedford group and especially of Pym in the Commons. By careful planning and coordination of tactics, by securing the control of key Commons' committees, Pym and his lieutenants were able to give the Commons something like 'front-bench' leadership to steer the business of the House as they wished and certainly to avoid potentially divisive issues whenever possible.[10] Nor did the parliamentary leaders shrink from encouraging popular participation in politics. Petitioners and mass demonstrations in favour of parliament were actively solicited. On key occasions, for example when in May 1641 the Commons' approval was being sought for the Protestation and the bill for the attainder of Strafford, Pym used his contacts with radical groups in the City to organize marches of apprentices and others to Westminster.[11] The best example of Pym's skill in maintaining parliamentary unity in the early months of the Long Parliament is his expert use of the revelations of an army plot in May 1641.[12] Details of the plot to bring the English army southwards and take control of the Tower and release Strafford were not hard to come by; both Charles and Henrietta Maria made little attempt to keep them secret. Pym's skill was not in uncovering the conspirators' plans but in the use he made of what he knew to convince sceptics that there was a Popish Plot. For Pym the revelation about the army plotters' activities was confirmation of his conviction that the king was the victim of a Popish Plot and was being manipulated by papist 'evil councillors' to use Catholic troops from the Scottish Highlands and Ireland to impose Catholicism on both England and Scotland.[13] In the middle of the Commons' debate on the army plot, Pym's allies dramatically proposed an oath of association to be taken by all MPs, swearing their allegiance to 'the true reformed religion . . . against all Popery and Popish innovations'. All the key elements of the alleged Popish Plot were skilfully interwoven in the preamble to this Protestation Oath:

---

[10] See J. H. Hexter's brilliant exposition of the work of Pym in his *The Reign of King Pym* (1941). On the dangers of exaggerating Pym's influence, see John Morrill, 'The unweariableness of Mr Pym: influence and eloquence in the Long Parliament' in S. D. Amussen and M. A. Kishlansky, eds., *Political Culture and Cultural Politics in Early Modern England: essays presented to David Underdown* (1995); and Austin Woolrych, *Britain in Revolution, 1625–60* (2002), pp. 165–6.

[11] Naturally the evidence for this is not very clear: if the demonstrations were organized, those responsible were hardly likely to do so openly. Therefore, it is possible to argue that the marches of apprentices and others at this time were spontaneous.

[12] C. Russell, 'The first army plot', *T.R.H.S.*, 5th ser., XXXIX (1988).

[13] Pym also believed that there was a second possible explanation for Charles's activities: that the king was mentally deranged: J. Adamson: 'Pym as a draftsman: an unpublished declaration of March 6 1643', *Parliamentary History*, VI (1987).

The designs of the priests and Jesuits, and other adherents of the see of Rome, have of late been more boldly and frequently put in practice than formerly, to the undermining and danger of the ruin of the true Reformed Religion . . . There hath been, and . . . still are . . . endeavours to subvert the fundamental laws of England and Ireland, and to introduce the exercise of an arbitrary and tyrannical government by most pernicious and wicked counsels, practices, plots and conspiracies; and that the long intermission and unhappier breach of parliaments hath occasioned many illegal taxations . . . and that divers innovations and superstitions hath been brought into the Church, multitudes driven out of his Majesty's dominions, jealousies raised and fomented between the King and people, a popish army levied in Ireland, and two armies brought into the bowels of this kingdom, to the hazard of his Majesty's royal person . . . and . . . endeavours have been, and are used, to bring the English army into misunderstanding of this Parliament, thereby to incline the army by force to bring to pass those wicked counsels.[14]

By these means, for a time the flagging belief of some MPs in a Popish Plot was re-invigorated. In this the parliamentary leaders were undoubtedly helped by the activities of Charles and his wife. Henrietta Maria's contacts with Catholic foreign powers and elements in the army were fruitless and did little but enable the details to be fed into the parliamentary propaganda machine to help persuade moderate opinion to swallow the incursions that had been made so far into the royal prerogative, and to maintain parliamentary unity.

Too much, however, should not be made of the ways that the king's opponents in parliament manipulated opinion to their advantage. It is probably more accurate to see them reacting to and interacting with the pressure of popular opinion outside parliament. What is striking from the work of David Cressy is how wide was the public arena in which the revolutionary changes took place as ideas and events were discussed and reported in pamphlets, newspapers and satirical libels that poured from an unfettered press.[15] Even more riveting is John Walter's evidence of the ways in which in Essex an energetic local campaign in 1641–2, often organised by politicized clergymen, to get all adult males to subscribe to the Protestation, interacted with and strengthened what he calls 'a pro-Parliamentarian popular political culture' that in August 1642 was to flare into an extraordinary outbreak of popular violence in the Stour Valley in Essex.[16]

Disagreements

Even in the first session of the Long Parliament, however, it became clear that unity amongst the king's opponents in 1640–1 was only skin deep. The first signs of a breach in parliamentary unity came paradoxically in the discussions on the method to be used to get rid of Strafford. Soon after Strafford's trial began on 22 March 1641 it became

---

[14] Kenyon, *Stuart Constitution*, p. 200; See also *English Historical Documents 1603–60*, document no. 419.

[15] David Cressy, *England on Edge: crisis and revolution 1640–42* (2006); 'The Protestation protested, 1641 and 1642', *H.J.*, 45 (2002).

[16] John Walter, 'Confessional politics in pre-Civil War Essex: prayer books, profanations and petitions', *H.J.*, 44 (2001).

obvious that it would not be a straightforward affair. For one thing, it was clearly difficult to make stick a charge of treason against a man who still had the king's confidence. 'Almost every article set forth a new treason that I never heard of before', mocked Strafford at his trial.[17] And, on the principal count against him, his alleged intention to bring over an Irish army to 'reduce' England, the evidence of the only witness, Sir Henry Vane senior, was ambiguous. As a result the Commons voted, against Pym's advice, to proceed against Strafford by a parliamentary bill of attainder. Many wanted to get rid of Strafford without delay. The earl of Essex rejected Bedford's proposal that Strafford should be removed by imprisonment rather than by execution, with a cryptic 'Stone dead hath no fellow.' 'We give law to hares and deer, because they be beasts of chase,' St John is reported to have said when he defended the legality of the bill of attainder, 'it was never accounted either cruelty or foul play to knock foxes and wolves on the head as they can be found, because they be beasts of prey.' A significant minority had qualms, not surprisingly given arguments like St John's, that the execution of Strafford had been justified as an act of necessity rather than an act of law. Perhaps the division, noticed by contemporaries, between a large body of 'anti-Straffordians' and a few 'Straffordians' was not serious, but it was the first real breach in parliamentary unity and provided the king with his first significant convert from the opposition, Lord George Digby.

It was the issue of church reform, however, that revealed much more serious disagreements within the parliamentary ranks. After Laud and Laudianism were officially swept away there was little agreement on what to put in their place. Some radical groups hoped that there could now be a 'godly reformation' and an end to all bishops. Popular anti-episcopalianism has been noted in Cheshire, Kent, London and elsewhere in 1640–1; but Laudian bishops had done little to endear themselves to gentlemen either. Certainly in the elections of 1640 some MPs had given radical religious views their tacit blessing either to gain electoral support or because the radical social implications of 'root and branch' abolition had not yet sunk in. The former rather than the latter (despite his later pleas) seems to have been the explanation for Sir Edward Dering's otherwise surprising support for the London Root and Branch petition (11 December 1640) which catalogued the alleged evils of bishops and demanded that 'the said government [of bishops] with all its dependencies, root and branches, may be abolished'. In January 1641 Dering also presented a Kent petition against bishops, and in May 1641 actually moved a Root and Branch bill in parliament. Later, in 1642, he claimed that the radical intentions of the Root and Branchers had not been clear in 1640 and 1641, and that he did not realize that their aim was not a modified form of episcopacy, but a wholesale reconstruction of the Church, involving popular participation by congregations in church affairs, especially in the nomination of their ministers.[18]

---

[17] Quoted in Fletcher, *The Outbreak*, p. 12.

[18] Derek Hirst, 'The defection of Sir Edward Dering 1640–41', *H.J.*, XV (1972), pp. 193–208; W. Lamont, *Godly Rule: politics and religion 1603–60* (1969), pp. 83–93.

That there was strong opposition to the abolition of bishops among MPs became clear in the Commons' debates in early February 1641 on the London Root and Branch petition, despite strong pleas on its behalf by religious radicals like Nathaniel Fiennes, younger son of Lord Saye and Sele. In parliamentary debates and printed pamphlets a multitude of different plans for church reform were canvassed, but few envisaged the abolition of bishops.[19] During 1641 pro-bishops petitions flooded into parliament to stiffen the resistance of MPs to root and branch reform, reinforcing the suggestion 'that an alternative view of the Church from the Puritan one was very firmly held by substantial numbers of people in the country'.[20] Why was there such strong support for bishops, despite their close association with the hated church policies of the 1630s? In the early 1640s it was feared by many that James I's maxim of 'no bishop, no king' would be extended quite validly to 'no bishops, no king, no magistrate'. The political and social implications of the de facto collapse of ecclesiastical hierarchical discipline and relaxation of censorship laws could already be seen. Reports of altar rails and 'images' being ripped down and of interruptions to services using the Book of Common Prayer were common. The violent actions and language of religious radicals (a Cheshire Puritan minister was reported to have said that the Book of Common Prayer 'doth stink in the nostrils of God and hath been the means of sending many souls into hell'[21]) produced an inevitable reaction in favour of bishops. In Cheshire this was led by Sir Thomas Aston, whose *Remonstrance against Presbytery*, the printed version of his petition presented to parliament on 27 February 1641, expressed the social and political fears of conservatives. 'Freedom of their consciences and persons is not enough, but they must have their purses and estates free too . . . Nay they go higher, even to the denial of the right to proprietie in our estates.' The aim of the reformers, the *Remonstrance* alleged, was to 'pull down 26 bishops and set up 9324 potential Popes' (one in each parish).[22]

The equation that religious freedom equalled social disorder also received confirmation (quite wrongly) from the rash of outbreaks of riots which were not directly concerned with religious matters. Reports of popular disturbances against enclosures, the drainage of sluices by fen-dwellers in Lincolnshire and disorder among the inhabitants of Windsor Forest were grossly exaggerated by paranoid gentlemen whose fears of 'the many headed monster' were already heightened by the growth of poverty after a century of inflation.[23] Moreover, the riots that did take place had more to do with a recurrence of economic crisis as bad as that in the early 1620s than with the collapse

---

[19] J. P. Cooper, 'The fall of the Stuart monarchy', in Cooper, ed., *The New Cambridge Modern History, IV: 1609–48/59* (1970), pp. 571–2; S. R. Gardiner, *Constitutional Documents of the Puritan Revolution 1625–60* (3rd edn., 1906), p. 167; A. Fletcher, 'Concern for renewal in the Root and Branch debates of 1641', in D. Baker, ed., *Studies in Church History*, XIV (1977), pp. 279–86.

[20] Fletcher, *The Outbreak*, p. 288.

[21] Quoted in J. S. Morrill, *Cheshire 1603–60: county government during the 'English Revolution'* (1974), p. 35.

[22] See J. Maltby, *Prayer Book and People in Elizabethan and Early Stuart England* (1998), and Fletcher, *The Outbreak*, for analyses of conservative religious opinion. Quotation from Morrill, *Cheshire*, p. 50.

[23] J. Morrill and J. Walter, 'Order and disorder in the English Revolution', in A. Fletcher and J. Stevenson, eds., *Order and Disorder in the English Revolution* (1985); K. Lindley, *Fenland Riots and the England Revolution* (1982).

of ecclesiastical discipline. But this was not a distinction made by those who, like Dering, were dissuaded from supporting anti-bishop factions at Westminster and in the constituencies in the summer and autumn of 1641. As a result the debates on church reform in 1641 were barren. All that the Commons could agree was that the secular powers of bishops should be curtailed and an Exclusion Bill to this effect was sent up to the Lords in March 1641. But the Lords would not even go this far; they objected especially to the bill's proposal to exclude bishops from the Lords and rejected it on 8 June 1641. The religious issue was shunted off the parliamentary stage by the decision to set up an assembly of divines to discuss it. This was announced in the Grand Remonstrance in November 1641, but the Westminster Assembly of Divines did not begin work until July 1643. In this way the clash was postponed, not resolved.

By the summer of 1641 Charles must have seen these disagreements among his opponents as promising signs that the end of the crisis was in sight. Where he had had few supporters a year ago, moderate opinion was now moving in his favour. With the major grievances legislated away, attendance in the Commons became thin; the euphoria of the previous winter was evaporating. An accommodation between king and parliament, though, was not a practical possibility. Charles's announcement in June that he intended to go to Scotland to ratify the treaty between the two countries made clear that the gulf of distrust between king and parliament was still much wider than that opening up between factions among the king's opponents. In Scotland, Charles hoped to appeal to a body of potential royalists who objected to the course the Scottish revolution had taken since 1637. So great was the distrust of Charles in England that he might attempt to mobilize an army in Scotland, that when the king left for Scotland in August a parliamentary committee of defence was appointed and commissioners were selected to accompany the king to keep a watch on his activities. Yet much more than the fears generated by the Scottish visit prevented an end to the crisis, as can be seen by the Ten Propositions sent to the king in June 1641 as the basis for a negotiated settlement.

Information

The Ten Propositions, 24 June 1641

Its main proposals were that:

- Charles's visit to Scotland should be postponed until his armies were disbanded.
- Charles's 'evil councillors' should be removed and replaced with officers of state 'as his people and Parliament may have just cause to confide in'.
- Military officers should be 'faithful and trusty' to parliament.
- Catholics should be excluded and Protestants appointed as advisers of the queen and those responsible for the education and upbringing of the royal children.

Charles would not have found it easy to control his wife and her Catholic connections. But he would have found it even harder to accept the proposed limitations on the king's hitherto unrestrained choice of advisers and control of the army, even though they were not spelled out as starkly as they were to be in future negotiating proposals. These incursions into the royal prerogative would have been an obnoxious dose for any seventeenth-century monarch to accept, let alone anyone as unwilling to compromise as Charles I.

The crisis becomes a civil war, September 1641–July 1642

The extent to which opinion in England polarized for and against the king and parliament after the autumn of 1641 is uncertain. As will be seen, there was some confusion about allegiances, and a determination to attempt not to get involved in the Civil War when it began was common. Yet it may be that some historians have exaggerated the numbers of those who remained (or attempted to remain) aloof from the growing conflict.[24] During the early months of the second session of the Long Parliament, opinion amongst MPs at Westminster polarized for and against king and parliament more clearly than ever before. What is more, some recent local studies have demonstrated that, as before in the early seventeenth century, people outside Westminster were not insulated from events taking place elsewhere in the country, as well as in Ireland and Scotland, and that they were as engaged with and as divided by current controversial issues as seriously as MPs at Westminster. Two major questions present themselves about the period immediately before the outbreak of the Civil War. First, why were the supporters of parliament, who in 1640 and early 1641 had wanted only moderate constitutional and ecclesiastical reforms, now pushed into accepting more radical measures and finally into the drastic step of taking up arms against the king? Secondly, why did the king get a party, when by the summer of 1641 there had only been a few signs that opinion had begun to swing in his favour? Clues to the answers to both these questions lie in events in Scotland and Ireland at the end of 1641. As in 1639 and 1640, events in those two countries, while not causing the crisis to erupt in England, ensured that it became more serious than ever.

The impact of events in Scotland and Ireland

In 1641 conditions in Scotland were ripe for a counter-revolution. The unity of the Scots covenanters, like that of the English parliamentarians, was fragile. For many Scotsmen, radical lay covenanters, like Johnston of Wariston, had gone too far too quickly in abolishing episcopacy and in proceeding unconstitutionally in defiance of royal authority. Although the covenanters acquired a moderate leader in the earl of

---

[24] See, for example, John Morrill, *The Revolt of the Provinces: the people of England and the tragedies of war, 1630–48* (2nd edn., 1999), pp. 52–9.

Argyll, opposition to them began to crystallize when in August 1640 the earl of Montrose and seventeen other Scottish nobles signed the Cumbernauld Bond, protesting at the 'particular and indirect practising of a few'.[25] The allegation was not quite true: the covenanters had fairly widespread support, but it was not total. The opposition, however, was hindered by Charles's failure to give it support at the right time. 'It was ever his [Charles's] constant unhappiness to give nothing in time', said Robert Baillie.[26] This was borne out when Charles arrived in Scotland in August 1641. His concessions were granted too late and with such apparent reluctance that his sincerity was doubted. On 16 September, Charles agreed in principle that his nominations of officers of state in Scotland should be confirmed by the Scottish parliament; he then indicated that he had no intention of keeping to the spirit of this declaration by appointing the royalist earl of Morton as his chancellor. What, however, really destroyed Charles's chances of gaining much support in Scotland was the revelation of a plot, the 'Incident', by some of the more extreme Scottish royalists led by the earl of Crawford, to seize the covenanter leaders, Argyll and Lanark, as well as the king's one-time agent in Scotland, the duke of Hamilton. The extent of Charles's complicity is not known; what is, is that most people believed he was deeply implicated, a feeling which he hardly dispelled by attending parliament in Edinburgh on 12 October to proclaim his innocence, accompanied by a force of armed royalists. The 'Incident' destroyed any hopes Charles might have had of gaining support in Scotland; before he returned south on 17 November 1641, he had to appoint all the leading covenanters to key offices in Scotland. In England the 'Incident' intensified the mistrust of the king in the eyes of many parliamentarians: might not Charles attempt a similar coup in England? When the English parliament reassembled after the recess on 21 October, one of its first acts was to appoint a hundred men to stand guard in the Palace Yard at Westminster.

The repercussions of events taking place in Ireland at the same time were even more disastrous than those in Scotland for the hopes of a settlement between king and parliament. The fall of Strafford had resulted in the collapse of the unnatural coalition between the Catholic 'Old English' and the Protestant 'New English' which had developed in Ireland by 1640. Hatred of Strafford was the only thing that had kept the alliance together, and the grievances of the 'Old English' were intensified by the negotiations of the 'New English' lords justices in Ireland, Sir William Parsons and Sir John Borlase, with the English parliamentary leaders for measures to be taken against Irish Catholicism. Irish Catholics were also encouraged to rebel by Charles's negotiations with the 'Old English' leaders, the earls of Ormonde and Antrim, in order to recruit a royalist army in Ireland. The negotiations were not pursued, but when the Irish Rebellion began in October 1641, many who joined it felt they did so in the name and in the defence of King Charles.[27]

---

[25] Quoted in G. Donaldson, *Scotland: James V to James VII* (1965), p. 328.

[26] R. Baillie, *The Letters and Journal of Robert Baillie* (3 vols., 1841), II, p. 373.

[27] A. Clarke, 'The genesis of the Ulster Rising of 1641', in P. Roebuck, ed., *Plantation to Partition* (1981); D. Stevenson, *Scottish Covenanters and Irish Confederates* (1981).

Information

The Irish Rebellion

It is very difficult indeed to discover what happened in Ireland in the winter of 1641. What is known is that:

- The rebellion began as conspiracies by Ulster Catholic landowners, especially Sir Phelim O'Neill, to put pressure on the English and Dublin authorities to meet their grievances, especially over their confiscated estates, by capturing Dublin and key towns in Ulster.
- The plot to capture Dublin was discovered and was a flop.
- O'Neill succeeded in capturing key Ulster towns, including Charlemont on 23 October. A week or so later he produced a document purporting to be a commission to him from the king.
- The rising then spiralled out of O'Neill's control as many Irish Catholics spontaneously attacked and killed English and Scottish Protestant settlers in Ulster. Soon this popular rising spread to most parts of Ireland.
- These risings prompted violent retaliatory attacks on Irish Catholics.

Very soon, however, what happened in Ireland in 1641 became distorted by English propaganda, in two key respects:

- The king's pleas that the commission produced by O'Neill was a forgery (a claim now known to be true) was ignored.
- The numbers of Protestant settlers who were massacred were grossly exaggerated. Modern estimates vary between 4,000 and 7,000; contemporary English commentators put the numbers very much higher. Sir John Temple in his *Irish Rebellion* (1646) claimed that 300,000 Protestants were massacred between October 1641 and September 1643.

In England, though, appearances were of more importance than reality. Fear of popery was diffused throughout seventeenth-century English society. 'Talk of "popery",' writes John Morrill, 'is not a form of "white noise", a constant fuzzy background in the rhetoric and argument of the time . . . This falsifies the passionate belief . . . that is the ground of action, that England was in the process of being subjected to the force of Antichrist, that the prospects were of anarchy, chaos, the dissolution of government and liberties.' Robin Clifton describes fear of popery as 'a latent force; buried beneath

Figure 6.2 A Protestant propaganda image of the Irish Rebellion, 1641. One of many allegations of atrocities committed by Catholics on Protestants in Ireland in 1641.
Source: © Topfoto/Fotomas.

the day-to-day business of living until a crisis burst upon the country'. In England at the end of 1641 there were panic-laden rumours of imminent invasion by the Irish rebels; recusants were arrested and night-watches organized. At Pudsey (Yorkshire) the church service was interrupted by someone who 'came and stood up in the chapel door and cried out with a lamentable voice. "Friends," said he, "we are all as good as dead men, for the Irish rebels are coming; they are come as far as Rochdale . . . and will be at Halifax and Bradford shortly".' Joseph Lister, a Bradford clothier who was in the church, was naturally alarmed, 'for we must needs go to Bradford, and knew not but Incarnate Devils and Death would be there before us'.[28] The 'Irish rebels' in this

---

[28] J. Morrill, 'The religious context of the English Civil War', *T.R.H.S.*, 5th ser., XXXIV (1980), p. 173; R. Clifton, 'The fear of popery' in Russell, ed., *Origins of the English Civil War*, pp. 165–6; J. T. Cliffe, *The Yorkshire Gentry from the Reformation to the Civil War* (1969), p. 329.

case were probably Protestant refugees from Ireland, but it needed little to trigger off anti-Catholic scares whether in Pudsey or in Westminster.

In this rumour-laden atmosphere, for many Charles's credibility was now destroyed, and it is not surprising that, when he proposed to raise an army against the Irish, many feared he would use it instead against parliament. Just as fear forced the attainder of Strafford through parliament, so the pressure of events forced the parliamentary leadership to take radical steps they would not have even considered twelve months before. However, what gave a new and much sharper sense of urgency, bordering on panic, to their actions was a heightened fear of popery in the wake of events in Ireland. The main impact of the Irish Rebellion on England was to emphasize, although not to create,[29] the ideological as well as the functional nature of the crisis of 1641.[30] On 8 November, after a fierce political struggle against moderate opinion led by Hyde and supported by Sir Simonds D'Ewes, Pym secured majority support (151/110 votes) for an 'additional instruction' to be sent to the parliamentary commissioners in Scotland. As a condition of helping Charles raise an army against the Irish, the king must employ 'only such councillors as should be approved of by Parliament'; otherwise parliament 'should take such a course for the securing of Ireland as might likewise secure our selves'. This looked forward to a second radical step: parliamentary control of the army. At the same time as the 'additional instruction' was being discussed, parliament appointed the earl of Essex to the command of the trained bands south of the Trent, and an Impressment Bill was introduced which proposed to take away the king's power to order men to serve outside their own counties. More radically, on 7 December, Sir Arthur Hazelrige introduced a bill which would take the command of the trained bands out of the king's hands altogether: army commanders were to be appointed by parliament.[31]

Polarization in England and slide towards civil war

This was a move which was temporarily resisted by the Lords. But it was not only the members of the Upper House who were worried by the tactics of the king's opponents. The polarization of opinion that was taking place in the Commons can be seen in the debates late in November on the Grand Remonstrance, a statement of the grievances of parliament. Though they disliked its violent language, it was not just the contents of the Remonstrance that the moderates objected to. What was also alarming to them about it was its intention to be a direct appeal to the people. The chaotic scenes in the Commons on the night of 22 November took place *after* the Grand Remonstrance had been approved by the narrow margin of 159/148, on the question of whether or not

---

[29] E. Shagan, 'Constructing discord: ideology, propaganda, and English responses to the Irish Rebellion of 1641', *J.B.S.*, 36 (1997).
[30] C. Russell. 'The British background to the Irish Rebellion of 1641', *HR*, LXI (1988). Russell, *Fall*, pp. 414–21.
[31] W. H. Coates, ed., *The Journal of Sir Simonds D'Ewes* (1942), pp. 104, 244–5.

the Remonstrance should be printed. 'When I first heard of a Remonstrance,' said Dering, 'I presently imagined that like faithful councillors we should hold up a glass to His Majesty . . . I did not dream that we should remonstrate downwards and tell stories to the people.'[32] No matter that Dering and others had been 'remonstrating downwards' since the 1640 elections. By now he and others backed away from the constitutional and religious radicalism that the popular participation in politics encouraged by the parliamentary leadership seemed to entail.

Consequently, when Charles returned to London from Scotland at the end of November 1641, he found he had more supporters in England than when he had left. On 25 November the City aldermen gave him a lavish welcome, to which Charles responded by promising to return the City's Londonderry estates which he had confiscated in the 1630s. In his public pronouncements in December, Charles was able to pose convincingly as the defender of the 'fundamental law' against the parliamentary revolutionaries. He it was, he said, who stood between the Church and 'the irreverence of those many schismatics and separatists, wherewith of late this kingdom and this city [London] abounds, to the great dishonour and hazard both of Church and State, for the suppression of whom we require your timely aid and active assistance'.[33] This was a tempting appeal to which 'constitutional royalists' like Hyde, Falkland and Culpepper responded, especially when their fears seemed to become reality. On 21 December 1641 the ruling oligarchic clique in the City of London was defeated in City elections by a faction which had close ties with the parliamentary leadership, and which had not scrupled to organize mass demonstrations in support of its policies.[34]

The growing support for him at Westminster and the county petitions in favour of episcopacy perhaps persuaded Charles that the time was ripe for a coup against the parliamentary leaders.[35] Obviously the timing was crucial; and in late December 1641 there were signs that the royalist 'backlash' was on the wane. Certainly, Charles's misguided choice as lieutenant of the Tower on 23 December, Sir Thomas Lunsford, a man outlawed by respectable gentry society in his native Sussex,[36] rebounded against the king. Most seriously of all, dramatically, the breach between the Lords and Commons on the Impressment and Militia Bills was temporarily healed. After a popular demonstration had prevented the bishops from attending the House of Lords, they returned on 29 December and moved that all the Lords' proceedings during their absence should be declared null and void. The majority in the Lords interpreted this as a breach of their privileges and accepted from the Commons a vote of impeachment against the bishops. Before events moved further out of control, Charles decided to

---

[32] John Rushworth, *Historical Collections* (1659–1701), IV, p. 425.

[33] The king's answer to the petition accompanying the Grand Remonstrance, 23 December 1641, in Gardiner, *Constitutional Documents*, p. 235.

[34] V. Pearl, *London and the Outbreak of the Puritan Revolution: city government and national politics 1625–43* (1961), especially, pp. 132–45.

[35] C. Russell, 'Charles I's financial estimates for 1642', *B.I.H.R.*, LVII (1985) suggests that Charles may also have been pushed into action by news of his grim financial situation.

[36] Fletcher, *Sussex*, pp. 54–5.

act. On 3 January he announced the impeachment of Pym, John Hampden, William Strode, Hazelrige, Denzil Holles and Lord Kimbolton, and on the following day, his attempt to arrest them in the chamber of the Commons failed disastrously. A Commons' committee sitting in the Guildhall declared these events a violation of parliamentary privileges, and Philip Skippon was appointed sergeant major-general of the City trained bands as a defensive measure. On 10 January Charles, possibly physically frightened by the popular outburst against him and alarmed for his own and his wife's safety, retreated to Hampton Court; and on the following day the five MPs returned in triumph to Westminster. For many MPs the incident was the final confirmation of the king's untrustworthiness, and it hastened the slide to civil war. It is difficult to see that, even if the coup had succeeded, there could have been any other result. If Pym had been removed, would the parliamentary cause have collapsed?

The immediate aftermath of the attempted coup was to strengthen the parliamentary leadership in its determination to carry out the radical programme which had emerged during the last few months: press for the removal of 'evil councillors' round the king, secure parliamentary approval of the commanders of the militia, forts and the Tower, and force an Exclusion Bill preventing bishops from sitting in the House of Lords through the Upper House. Popular support for this programme was actively encouraged. In January and February 1642 there is every sign of an organized petitioning movement in the counties in support of the programme of the parliamentary leadership, again reinforcing the point that there was no artificial divide between Westminster and public opinion in the wider 'public sphere' of the country in the 1640s. Often the presentation of these petitions was made the occasion for mass demonstrations. When, on 11 January 1642, one of the first county petitions was presented, 4,000–5,000 supporters are said to have accompanied it from Buckinghamshire to Westminster. Coinciding with Lord Brooke's nomination as lord lieutenant of Warwickshire early in February 1642, his followers brought a petition to London with 'many hundreds of the gentry and freeholders of the best rank . . . riding orderly, all well mounted, two in a rank, through the city to the old Exchange'.[37] Other county petitions followed, blaming every evil from the violation of parliamentary privileges to the 'decay of trade' on evil councillors, bishops and popish lords. What added to the effectiveness of the petitioning campaign was that behind the ritualized ceremonial lay the menace of violence. At one huge demonstration on 31 January in Moor Fields, London, these petitioners threatened that unless bishops were removed 'your petitioners shall not rest in quietness'.[38]

Under this kind of pressure the opposition in the Lords collapsed: on 5 February they accepted the Exclusion Bill and on 15 February approved the Commons' Militia Ordinance. The actual ordinance was not finally issued until 5 March, significantly without the king's approval. As common lawyers like John Selden pointed out, there

---

[37] A. Hughes, *Politics, Society and Civil War: Warwickshire 1620–60* (1987), p. 135.

[38] Quoted in B. Manning, 'The outbreak of the English Civil War' in R. H. Parry, ed., *The English Civil War and After 1642–58* (1970), p. 11. See also Fletcher, *The Outbreak*, ch. 6.

was a legal case for the Militia Ordinance; the repeal of the Marian legislation governing the militia in 1604 had meant that the powers of lieutenants and their deputies had rested on a very obscure base, and it was claimed that the new ordinance provided the necessary legal backing.[39] But such claims did little to counter the horror that many constitutionally minded gentlemen felt at these novel measures. Not only had parliament made a significant attack on the power of bishops but it was now claiming the power to legislate without the king, as well as the right to usurp the crown's control of the militia. The situation also demanded novel financial measures to supplement City loans and parliamentary subsidies. A poll tax levied in the summer of 1641 had produced only £169,000 because potential taxpayers desperately, and successfully, tried to pay less than the amounts demanded. As a result in March 1642 parliament approved a proposal to raise £400,000, ironically on the ship money principle of fixed assessments from each county. Also like the majority of ship money assessments, the so-called Act of £400,000 was very effective: Sussex, Anthony Fletcher calculates, contributed over half as much as a result of that Act in 1642 as it had done to all kinds of taxation in the war years of the 1620s.[40]

Information

The Nineteen Propositions, June 1642

These were another set of proposals sent to the king in the 1640s as the basis for a negotiated settlement. Their severity, however, indicated that parliament had no intention of concluding such a settlement. The terms were harsh ones:

- Charles I was to approve the appointment of all privy councillors and all the major officers of the State and Church. Moreover, their offices were to be held *'quam diu bene se gesserint'*: that is, as long as they performed their duties satisfactorily, they could not be removed by the king.
- The children of the king and all Catholics were to be brought up as Protestants.
- The king was to accept the Triennial Act and the Militia Ordinance.
- He was also to accept any reform of the Church dictated by parliament.
- He was also required to ally with European Protestant powers, especially the United Provinces.

---

[39] R. Tuck, '"The ancient law of freedom": John Selden and the Civil War' in J. Morrill, ed., *Reactions to the English Civil War* (1982).

[40] Fletcher, *Sussex*, p. 210.

Given the almost total unanimity of opposition to the king in 1640 and the cumulating evidence since then of Charles's intention not to accept the constitutional legislation of 1641, it is easier to understand the reasons for the adoption of radical measures by parliament than why the king gained supporters from parliament in 1641 and 1642. Yet for the growing numbers of 'constitutional royalists' like Hyde, attacks on bishops and novel parliamentary claims to choose the king's advisers, control the army and enact legislation without the king were unacceptable constitutional innovations and their consequences more to be feared than the events of 4 January 1642. Others had more than constitutional qualms about the direction of events. Not only did the parliamentary financial measures seem indistinguishable from the centralized government of the 1620s and 1630s, but the political crisis was associated more and more with the breakdown of order, with huge political demonstrations, enclosure riots and disturbances in churches. These fears were skilfully exploited by the king's reply (drafted by Culpepper and Falkland) to the parliamentary Nineteen Propositions in June 1642. Not only would the parliamentary proposals be 'a total subversion of the fundamental laws', but eventually they would encourage the common people

> to set up for themselves, call parity and independence liberty, devour that estate which had devoured the rest, destroy all rights and properties, all distinctions of families and merit, and by this means this splendid and excellently distinguished form of government end in a dark, equal chaos of confusion, and the long line of our many noble ancestors in a Jack Cade or Wat Tyler.[41]

Gardiner believed that, after parliament rejected a petition from Kent in favour of bishops and against the Militia Ordinance at the end of March 1642, civil war was inevitable. Within a few weeks, well before the official declarations of war in August, it had in fact begun. Mostly it was a war of words as royal declarations were met with parliamentary replies in an unprecedented public political debate. The central issue was the legality of the Militia Ordinance, and this was a question which could not be confined to the realms of debate. Local gentlemen had to choose whether or not to obey the orders sent to them to secure the local militia for parliament. Their dilemma became much harder from June, when the king began to send out commissions of array to local gentlemen, empowering them to control the local militia. For those who received orders from both king and parliament, the choice was well nigh impossible to make, as the tortured comment of Thomas Knyvett to his wife demonstrates: 'Oh sweete hart, I am nowe in a great strayght what to doe.'[42] Nor is this surprising. Not only were there doubts about the legality of the Militia Ordinance, which had not received the royal assent, but commissions of array were also legally dubious. No commissions had been issued since the early sixteenth century and so Charles's commissions in 1642 were widely seen as a departure from the traditional militia

---

[41] Kenyon, *Stuart Constitution*, p. 20.

[42] J. Morrill, *The Revolt of the Provinces: conservatives and radicals in the English Civil War 1630–50* (1980), p. 136.

organization by lieutenants. To many they were seen as showing the same disregard for the law as had Charles's measures of fiscal feudalism in the 1630s. Not surprisingly, armed conflict resulted as both sides tried to get control of local stores of ammunition. Inevitably the attention of historians has focused on the king's attempt in April to seize control of the garrison at Hull (so important as a store of ammunition for the Scottish war and as a strategic post for supplying armies in the north) and the successful defence of the town by Sir John Hotham. But this was only one of many similar skirmishes in the spring and summer of 1642: the most serious were the marquis of Hertford's confrontation with Alexander Popham in Somerset, and Lord Strange's failure to secure the Manchester magazine, a skirmish in July 1642 which parliamentary propagandists claimed was 'the start of the civil war'. As will be seen, enthusiasm for the war was rare. The language of politics for so long had been couched in terms of king *and* parliament that it took an enormous mental adjustment to come to grips with the concept of a parliament in arms against a king. But Charles's declaration of war by raising his standard at Nottingham on 22 August 1642 only made official the slide into civil war which had been apparent for months.

The first civil war, 1642–1646

Commitment and neutralism, 1642–1643

It is easier to be certain about what the roots of royalist and parliamentary commitment at the outbreak of the Civil War *were not* than what they *were*. Explanations based on alleged social, economic and geographical divisions have proved to be very unsound. Those who have made detailed studies of the members of the Long Parliament have found no evidence that the way MPs divided in 1642 depended in any respect on social status or wealth.[43] Similarly, the once-popular analytical model of a royalist north and west of England versus a parliamentary south and east has collapsed under the weight of local studies that show that both royalist and parliamentary commitment existed in all parts of the country in 1642. The reasons why people chose sides at the outbreak of the Civil War are too varied and complex to fit into universal 'models' like these. Yet, as has been suggested at the beginning of this chapter, there may have been two broad, separate categories of motives for making a commitment to king or parliament in 1642. The first consists of 'functional' or negative reasons. Royalists were driven to support the king partly by the fear of parliamentary absolutism, religious radicalism and popular rebellion; while parliamentarians remained committed against the king through fear of royal absolutism, fuelled by mistrust of Charles I and the belief that the king was either the victim of a Popish Plot or mentally deranged.

The second category of motives consisted of ideological or positive reasons for commitment. Royalists were driven by an ideology of constitutional royalism, a desire

---

[43] E.g. D. Brunton and D. H. Pennington, *Members of the Long Parliament* (1954).

to protect a balanced constitution of king, Lords and Commons that seemed to them to be threatened by a rising tide of parliamentary radicalism between 1640 and 1642. They were also concerned to protect the Church that had been established in 1559, a Church which retained bishops, clerical vestments, the Book of Common Prayer and traditional Christian festivals. The ideology that drove others towards the parliamentary cause, on the other hand, was one which derived from a belief that both the constitution and the Church were not safe in the hands of the king and his evil councillors. Parliamentarians took to the battlefield to safeguard parliamentary liberties and to continue the godly Reformation.

Information

Popular parliamentarianism in action in Essex

Given the evidence seen in previous pages that the religious and political issues that were causing divisions in the early 1640s were discussed by a much wider number of people than was once thought, it is not surprising that historians are discovering examples of the consequences of what popular political awareness could lead to at the start of the war. The most thorough study is of events in Essex and Suffolk in August 1642. On 22 August a 5,000-strong crowd attacked the house of Sir John Lucas near Colchester as he set off to join the king. Lucas had long been the focus of popular local hostility as a zealous ship money sheriff and a patron of Laudian divines. Having seized Lucas, the crowds then plundered his house and property. This was the first of a series of attacks by crowds during the next few weeks on the houses of prominent supporters of Charles I and Catholics in Essex and Suffolk. These have often been seen as attacks on the rich by mobs motivated by class hatred. But John Walter in his study *Understanding Popular Violence in the English Revolution: the Colchester plunderers* (1999) persuasively shows that, although the effect of the economic distress suffered by local people because of the depression in the cloth industry cannot be discounted, the dominant motive behind these outbreaks of popular violence was anti-popery: the same combination of loathing of popery and zeal to protect parliament and Protestantism that can be seen in the pronouncements of the parliamentary leaders at Westminster, and which were reflected in the Protestation Oath of May 1642.

Commitment to the king and to parliament, however, was not the only reaction to the coming of civil war in most areas of the country. Undoubtedly, some resisted committing themselves to any side. Neutralism just before and in the early stages of the war took many forms. In some places, individuals grouped together and made neutrality pacts, agreeing not to support either side. Cheshire is the best-studied example of this type of organized neutralism, which culminated in an agreement on 23 December 1642 at Bunbury (Cheshire) between royalist and parliamentarian gentry who agreed to disarm and disband their troops. Similarly, at the Staffordshire quarter sessions on 15 November 1642 a group of gentry committed themselves to the demilitarization of the county. Probably, however, a more common neutralist response to the coming of the war was passive neutralism. Significantly, in some counties neither the Militia Ordinance nor the commission of array was put into operation until the local gentry were forced to do so. Often the choice of sides was determined, not on grounds of principle, but by whether the region was controlled by royal or parliamentary troops. In some cases, individuals made clear their non-commitment by supporting with men and money both sides at the same time. In part, the lack of enthusiasm for the war can be explained by the fact that literate Englishmen had at hand in the well-reported war in northern Europe evidence as to what disruptive effects war could have. 'Oh lett the miserable spectacle of a German devestation', said a Norfolk petition of January 1643, 'persuade you to decline those perilous casualties which may result from a civil war.'[44]

The current economic crisis was linked in many people's minds with the breakdown of political order. Petitioners agreed that the restoration of political and economic order would go hand in hand. Similarly, many believed that the breakdown of political order was responsible for social and religious radicalism. Sir John Hotham, for example, argued that, if an agreement with the king was not reached, then 'the necessitous people of the whole kingdom will presently rise in mighty numbers and whatsoever they pretend for at first, within a while they will set up for themselves to the utter ruin of all the nobility and gentry of the kingdom'.[45] 'They would take advantage of these times', some anti-enclosure demonstrators were alleged to have said, 'lest they have not the like again.'[46] Very often the anti-war sentiments of 1642–3 sound like crypto-royalism, echoing the sentiments already quoted in the king's answer to the Nineteen Propositions, and it is likely that some episodes of 'neutralism' were in fact examples of covert royalism, reinforcing the suspicion that some historians have exaggerated the extent of non-commitment at this time. But undeniably the peace petitions of the summer and autumn of 1642 and the winter of 1642–3 reflected a desire of many people up and down the country to maintain what some called 'the peace of my country'.

Given that there was no real divide between politics at Westminster and in the English localities, it is not surprising that in the second half of 1642 the desire for peace was as strong at Westminster as in the country at large. Denzil Holles later explained that he became the leading spokesman in parliament in favour of a speedy settlement with the king, because he was afraid that in the train of political instability would come

---

[44] Quoted in C. Holmes, *The Eastern Association in the English Civil War* (1975), p. 44. For the impact that reports of the Thirty Years War had on English opinion, see B. Donagan, *War in England, 1640–49* (2008), ch. 2, esp. pp. 278–92.

[45] Quoted in Cliffe, *Yorkshire Gentry*, p. 341.

[46] Quoted in Holmes, *Eastern Association*, p. 44.

a social revolution, when 'Servants should ride on Horses' and 'the meanest of men, the basest and vilest of the nation, the lowest of the people, have got the power into their hands; trampled upon the Crown; baffled and misused the Parliament; violated the Laws; destroyed, or suppressed the Nobility and Gentry of the kingdom'.[47] Holles, however, wrote that comment when in exile in 1646–7, when he had more reason than in 1642 to connect war with the appearance of popular radicalism. In 1642 shocked reaction at the horror of war probably played a greater part in the desire of Holles (and others) for peace. Holles was present at the siege of Sherborne castle in September 1642, when, as soon as the royalist cannons were fired, the frightened untrained parliamentary soldiers ran, or so said the earl of Bedford, 'as if the devil had been in them'.[48]

Not surprisingly, in these circumstances the early military engagements of the war (like the battle of Edgehill, 23 October 1642) were indecisive. The failure of either side to win a decisive battle gave force to the growing peace movement, especially in the House of Lords among people like the earls of Pembroke, Holland and Northumberland. On 29 October 1642 the Lords proposed that negotiations be opened with the king, and, under pressure from opinion in the City and country, on 2 November the Commons agreed. Even Charles's continued march along the Thames Valley towards London, despite his agreement to open peace negotiations, did not stop the pressure for peace on the parliamentary side. After the king's march had been halted by the London trained bands at Turnham Green (13 November 1642) peace petitions were received sympathetically at Westminster. In December parliament agreed on peace proposals, and negotiations on them between commissioners from both sides began at Oxford on 1 February 1643 and lasted until 14 April. With hindsight one can see that the Oxford 'treaty' negotiations, the peace petitions and neutrality pacts of 1642 and early 1643 were the culmination of a great effort to end the war. Their collapse marks the definite end of the first phase in the war.

The collapse of neutrality pacts and of the Oxford 'treaty', 1643

Neutralism was never totally extinguished during the civil war. In 1643, though, it temporarily lost its political force and it became increasingly difficult to be neutral or to be in favour of peace negotiations without appearing to be a royalist 'delinquent'. Charles as usual did not help his own cause; he did little to dispel either the suspicions raised by his attempted coup in January 1642 or the impression that Henrietta Maria's Catholic circle had more influence with the king than Hyde. The king's march on Brentford and Turnham Green in November 1642 was used to great propaganda effect against him, as evidence that he was not serious in wanting peace. This was supported by the prevarication of the royal commissioners at Oxford, and confirmed later in the year when it became known that Charles was negotiating with the Irish

---

[47] Denzil Holles, *Memoirs*, in F. Maseres, ed., *Select Tracts Relating to the Civil Wars in England* (1815), p. 191.

[48] Quoted in D. Underdown, *Somerset during the Civil War and Interregnum* (1973), p. 41.

rebels, negotiations which culminated in the Cessation Treaty between the king and the Irish in September 1643.

What really destroyed the peace hopes of the early part of the war, however, was not Charles's duplicity, which, after all, was not revealed for the first time in 1643. The changed political climate was primarily caused by a new military situation: in the spring and summer, the royalist armies threatened both to carry all before them and to enable the king to set aside the reforms of the Long Parliament. It is not often before 1645 that one can talk in terms of either side as having and carrying out a nationwide war strategy. But in 1643 Charles *seemed* to have achieved just that. His three armies appeared to be acting in accordance with a preconceived strategic scheme: the northern army under the earl of Newcastle would occupy Yorkshire and march south through East Anglia to Essex; Sir Ralph Hopton and the king's western army would march through the south-western counties towards London, both armies acting out a kind of pincer movement on the capital, while the king's forces kept the main parliamentary army under the earl of Essex occupied in the Thames Valley. In fact, as will be seen, both sides were so reliant on local commanders that overall strategies never got beyond the discussion stage. However, in the spring and summer of 1643 it must have seemed to many (albeit wrongly) as if the king did have a three-pronged strategy that was succeeding beyond all expectations. In February 1643 Henrietta Maria landed at Bridlington with arms and money which she had collected during her year's absence on the Continent. She joined Newcastle's army at York and the royalist army proceeded to conquer the whole of Yorkshire apart from Hull, where the Fairfaxes held out. By the end of July, Newcastle had taken Gainsborough (Lincolnshire) and was threatening to push southwards into East Anglia. Meanwhile Hopton, having already captured Cornwall, overran Devon (except Exeter and Plymouth) and in Somerset he joined forces with the marquis of Hertford and Prince Maurice. This combined force decisively defeated the parliamentary commander in the west, Sir William Waller, at Roundway Down near Devizes (Wiltshire) on 13 July 1643, a battle which delivered nearly all of south-west England into royalist hands and made Prince Rupert's siege of Bristol an easier task than it might otherwise have been. The parliamentarians were understandably shattered by the surrender of Bristol on 26 July 1643, and subsequently court-martialled the governor of Bristol, Nathaniel Fiennes. Fiennes, however, had had little support. Waller by this time had abandoned Bath and was retreating eastwards slowly towards London. Nor did the earl of Essex help Fiennes or parliamentary morale. His only success was the capture of Reading in April 1643 (resulting in the royalists' court-martialling of the governor, Colonel Fielding), but Essex made little further progress. Tied down in the Thames Valley, he was so disillusioned that by July 1643 he suggested reopening peace talks with the king.

Such a course, however, was not now practical. The possibility now arose of an unconditional royalist military victory, the consequent return of the king to the power and position he had in 1639, and the loss of the constitutional gains of 1640–1. Significantly, to support the polarization which was taking place, political ideologies began to be formulated on both sides.[49] The ablest exponents of the royalist brand of political theory were Henry Ferne and Dudley Digges, who erected a theory of constitutional royalism which had first been outlined in Falkland's and Culpepper's Answer to the Nineteen Propositions: that the king rules not by arbitrary power but under the law and limited by parliament, but still retains necessary prerogative powers over foreign affairs, sole control of the militia, and the right to appoint his own advisers and officers, and to call and dismiss parliament. The theory allowed that the crown was but one of three estates, but it was the supreme one, and in challenging it, parliament was guilty of treason and rebellion. Parliamentary political theorists had therefore to formulate a justification for taking up arms against the king. This, as elaborated by Henry Parker and others, came to be that government rests on popular consent and that, since Charles had betrayed the trust given him by his people, rebellion was justified. The obvious charge against this theory of parliamentary sovereignty (and the royalists were not slow to make it) was that parliamentary rule would be as arbitrary and unchecked as that of an individual tyrant. Parker in perhaps his most important work, *Observations*, argued that the safeguard against arbitrary rule by parliament was its representative nature. Parliament, wrote Parker, is 'so equally and geometrically proportionable' that it took 'away all jealousies'.[50] Other pamphleteers at this time took these ideas much further; the anonymous author of *Plaine English* published in January 1642 (perhaps written by Edward Bowles, the chaplain of the earl of Manchester) even argued that the people had the right to act against the three estates of king, Lords and Commons if necessary.[51] As the political crisis escalated, there was no shortage of justifications for rebellion, an ideology to stiffen the resistance of those who baulked at the necessary step of fighting the king if all that had been gained was not now to be lost.

Parliamentary factions and the management of the war, 1643–1644

Faced with the possibility of a long-drawn-out civil war, from 1643 onwards opinion on the parliamentary side on how the war should be conducted was divided. The divergences of opinion among parliamentarians have been matched by the division of opinion among historians in describing them. Parliamentarians were not agreed on short-term objectives (should peace negotiations be carried on during the war or should a total military victory be secured first?), let alone on what should be their long-term objectives regarding a political and religious settlement. The problem for the historian is to put these divergences of opinion into an analytical framework. The belief that the parliamentarians during the war divided into two groups along religious

---

[49] M. Judson, *The Crisis of the Constitution* (1949), chs. 9 and 10; A. Sharp, *Political Ideas of the English Civil Wars* (1983).

[50] Quoted in Judson, *Crisis*, p. 431.

[51] David Wootton, 'From rebellion to revolution: the crisis of the winter of 1642–3 and the origins of Civil War radicalism', in R. Cust and A Hughes, eds., *The English Civil War* (1993).

lines (religious presbyterians who were moderate in politics and 'doves', and religious independents who were political radicals and 'hawks') was first brilliantly and persuasively exploded by Professor J. H. Hexter in an article in 1938–9. Although it has proved more difficult to get agreement on what new analysis to put in its place, the dust has now settled on the 'Presbyterian–Independent' controversy.[52]

Information

Parliamentary factions in 1642–1643

With few exceptions most historians now agree that political groupings in the early 1640s were ephemeral. However, at least three political groups can be identified in the war years:

- *'The peace group'* led by Denzil Holles and Philip Stapleton. They advocated a settlement with the king at any price, except perhaps that of agreeing to a return to Laudianism in the Church. Their fear of the social and religious radicalism brought by the war made them willing to trust Charles to maintain the legislation of 1641 without any safeguards. Until such a settlement was negotiated, they advocated a purely defensive war policy, as was being followed by Essex in the Thames Valley.

- *'The war group'*, amongst which were prominent MPs such as Sir Henry Vane jnr, Henry Marten and Arthur Hazelrige. Their enemy, Clarendon, alleged that they aimed to 'change the whole frame of the government in State as well as Church'.[53] 'The war group' advocated an offensive strategy, aimed at a total military victory and carried out, if necessary, by new generals. Until this was achieved there should be no negotiations with the king at all.

- *'The middle group'*, whose principal members were John Pym (until his death in December 1643), Oliver St John, Viscount Saye and Sele and Lord Wharton.

---

[52] See the Bibliographical note, p. 526, for the major contributions to this debate. The only significant dissenters from the interpretation of parliamentary factions in the early 1640s given here are L. Mulligan (née Glow) and J. R. MacCormack. I have not been convinced by the doubts also cast on it recently by David Scott, *Politics and War in the Three Stuart Kingdoms, 1637–49* (2004), pp. 40–3, following John Adamson, 'Parliamentary management, men-of-business and the House of Lords, 1640–49' in C. Jones, ed., *A Pillar of the Constitution: the House of Lords in British Politics, 1640–1784* (1989).

[53] Clarendon, *History*, III, p. 492.

> Unlike 'the peace group', they wanted an unconditional military defeat of the king. Consequently, they allied with 'the war group' in securing parliamentary approval for measures for an effective prosecution of the war. Yet, unlike 'the war group', 'the middle group' wanted an eventual constitutional settlement that incorporated the novel features introduced in 1641 but that was not as radical as that apparently envisaged by 'the war group'.

Right from the beginning of the war, some MPs had battled against the desire for a settlement with the king. But they had few successes: new fiscal measures were bogged down in Commons' committees and the only progress towards a Scottish alliance was parliament's approval of a letter to be sent to the Scots agreeing to the abolition of episcopacy, as a bait for a military alliance. It was not until February 1643 that the political climate at Westminster and in the country changed and that 'the middle group' was able to push through reforms and overcome what Professor Hexter called the '"heartburnings" and the symptoms of a slightly dyspeptic conservatism' of most MPs. The 'heartburnings' are not surprising. It is one of the great paradoxes of the 1640s that the parliamentary leadership adopted a programme of centralized government and high taxation, in many respects identical to that which in 1640 they had been determined to abolish.

The first priority for an effective war strategy was money. Already parliament had departed from traditional channels of public finance in the so-called Act of £400,000 of March 1642. But more radical measures were needed and resulted in a remarkable series of financial Ordinances in 1643 instituting weekly assessments (February), sequestrations (March), compulsory loans (May), and the excise (July). The weekly assessments (later monthly assessments) became the backbone of parliamentary finances both during and after the Civil War. The irony was probably not lost on some that the new tax continued the ship money principle of fixed county assessment: a connection that was very clear when (as in Cheshire) ship money assessments were used as the basis for collecting 'the weekly pay'. The advantage to the government was that the new tax, again like ship money, hit a much wider section of society than did parliamentary subsidies. It was more geared to tapping the true wealth of the country: the more prosperous south and east counties were more heavily assessed than poorer ones. Despite some complex technical provisions in the Ordinance which hindered its administration, the weekly assessment was a major improvement in public finance and the contrast in receipts from it and from parliamentary subsidies was staggering. The second plank of the new parliamentary financial system was the sequestration of the property of the king's supporters. The Ordinance was enacted on 27 March 1643 at a time when it was clear that the Oxford 'treaty' was on the brink of collapse. Only then would a majority in parliament accept a measure which could force a deep rift in county society. These 'delinquents', whose estates were to be taken over by local commissioners and the profit forwarded to a central committee in Guildhall, would in all probability be the friends, relatives or dependants of those who had voted for, or who would have to administer, the sequestrations. Compulsory loans introduced by Ordinance in May 1643 were equally distasteful, reminiscent as they were of the earlier hated forced loans. All those worth £10 p.a. in land or £100 p.a. in goods were to lend a maximum of one-fifth of the annual revenue of their estates or half the value of their goods, repayable 'upon the public faith'. Already the worthlessness of that promise had become apparent through the workings of an Ordinance of November 1642, which allowed commissioners for provisions to requisition food, fuel and horses for parliamentary garrisons in return for chits promising repayment. Easily the most hated of the new financial expedients was the excise tax, a purchase tax on a very wide range of consumption goods and therefore one which affected everyone. To collect the new taxes (apart from the excise) local committees were appointed, often staffed (at least at first) by the old local government officials, deputy lieutenants, sheriffs and justices of the peace. The extent of the powers of the parliamentary county committees varied, but generally their administrative and judicial functions were wide and efforts were made to see that they were made up of 'well-affected' men. As will be seen, the financial and administrative reconstruction in 1643 did not fulfil all the hopes of its creators, but undeniably that it was created at all was a major achievement.

If the war was to be won, there had also to be some military reorganization. The defects of the militia were plain. Organized on a county basis, it suffered from entrenched localism, and prevented the execution of a national war strategy. Looking at the military history of Staffordshire, Pennington and Roots could see no strategic pattern: 'its military history is largely one of sporadic and gentlemanly conflicts between garrisons and leaguers, and between the small companies that often seem to be moving about the county with as little coordinated purpose as ducks on a pond.'[54] The same was true of the country as a whole: Hopton, for example, found that his Cornish levies fought keenly in Cornwall, but were very reluctant to cross the Tamar into Devon. Both sides attempted to overcome this obstacle by organizing counties into regional groups. But even those considered local defence rather than cooperation on a national strategic plan to be their main function. The parliamentary Eastern Association of Norfolk, Suffolk, Essex, Cambridgeshire and Hertfordshire established on 20 December 1642 under Lord Grey of Warke refused to support the earl of Essex in the Thames Valley, and Oliver Cromwell's regiment in the association was depleted because of the 'eronious opinion . . . of our unexperienced country soldiers that they ought not to be drawn or ledd . . . beyond the bounds of the five counties'.[55] Faced with these frustrations, some on the parliamentary side (though not Pym) began to campaign for the replacement of Essex by Waller as the chief parliamentary general, in the belief that Essex was only concerned to reach a negotiated peace with the king.

---

[54] D. H. Pennington and I. Roots, eds., *The Committee at Stafford 1643–5* (1957), p. lxi.

[55] Quoted in Holmes, *Eastern Association*, p. 85.

Pym instead, in an effort to develop an army responsive to central commands, supported two important ordinances which were passed on 10 August 1643: an impressment ordinance ending the reliance of the parliamentary armies on volunteers; and an ordinance reorganizing the Eastern Association under the earl of Manchester, who was empowered to impress 20,000 men.

Desperate measures were needed to deal with the dire plight of the parliamentary armies in eastern England in 1643. Given his military inexperience, the parliamentary cavalry commander in East Anglia, Oliver Cromwell, had done well in slowing down the southward advance of the royalist army led by the earl of Newcastle. But by July 1643 Newcastle's army threatened to invade the heartland of the Eastern Association. The reorganization of the army of the Eastern Association grew out of this desperate military situation. Even the August 1643 ordinance did not lead to significant improvements. Cromwell's letters to middle group politicians in the autumn of 1643 ring with panic. Manchester's 'force will fall if some help not', he wrote to St John on 11 September 1643. 'Weak counsels and weak actings undo all. Send at once or come or all will be lost, if God help not.'[56] So bad was the situation by the end of the year that Manchester and Cromwell temporarily left the battlefield for London to press for a political solution to their problems. There they allied with middle group politicians St John, Saye and Sele, and Wharton, and in January 1644 pushed through parliament a financial ordinance increasing by 50 per cent monthly assessments levied on the individual counties of the Eastern Association and putting the money in the hands of a committee at Cambridge under Manchester's control. Not only did his army now have an effective financial system for the first time, but Manchester also began to choose his officers more for their previous military experience than for their local affiliations and social origins. Significantly, though, he was not interested in mercenaries: immoral, though efficient, officers were expelled; 'godly' soldiers were promoted. All were welcomed, said Manchester, who 'love Christ in sincerity', though 'differing in judgement to what I profess'. With its new leader, a reorganized financial and administrative structure, and a high ratio of committed and professional officers, the army of the Eastern Association was the most effective army to take the field so far in the Civil War.

From an English Civil War to a War of Three Kingdoms

Pym's last contribution to the parliamentary cause was to secure a military alliance with the Scots. The difficulty was not in getting Scottish agreement: the Scots covenanters knew that the permanence of the 'Scottish Revolution' depended on the victory of the English parliament over the king. Within ten days of their arrival in Scotland on 7 August 1643, the English commissioners had reached agreement with the Scots and signed the Solemn League and Covenant.

---

[56] W. C. Abbott, ed., *The Writings and Speeches of Oliver Cromwell* (4 vols., 1937–47), I, p. 259.

Information

The Solemn League and Covenant, 1643

Its main features were:

- An oath to be sworn by all subjects in England, Scotland and Ireland to ensure 'the preservation of the reformed religion in the Church of Scotland, in doctrine, worship, discipline and government, against our common enemies; the reformation of religion in the kingdoms of England and Ireland, in doctrine, worship, discipline and government, according to the Word of God and the example of the best reformed Churches'.
- A commitment 'to bring the Churches of God in the three kingdoms to the nearest conjunction and uniformity in religion': that is, to bring religious uniformity in Britain and Ireland on the Scottish model. This was the major price those English parliamentarians who did not favour such a model had to pay for acquiring Scottish military support.
- A commitment to 'endeavour the extirpation of Popery [and] prelacy'.
- A commitment to preserve the rights and privileges of parliaments in both England and Scotland.

When the Covenant was brought before the English parliament for ratification, however, it met intense hostility, and not only from 'peace group' MPs. English contempt for Scots and all things Scottish was not new; it was now reinforced by detestation of Scottish Presbyterianism which the Scots, with missionary zeal, hoped to bring to England. The ecclesiastical supremacy of the Kirk in secular affairs was too reminiscent of Laudianism for most Englishmen of whatever religious persuasion. Significantly, before the alliance was ratified on 7 September, the English parliament deleted the description of the Scottish Church as being established 'according to the Word of God'. Robert Baillie, one of the Scottish commissioners who came to England as a result of the alliance, was quite right: 'The English were for a civill League, we for a religious Covenant.' The differences were ominous, but temporarily were consigned to the Westminster Assembly. The parliamentary committee of safety was transformed into the committee of both kingdoms. This was finally approved by the Lords on 16 February 1644, cementing the Anglo-Scottish alliance.

More importantly, the differences between English parliamentarians and Scottish covenanters were overshadowed by confirmation of the king's negotiations with the Catholic Confederation of Kilkenny in Ireland. These had been going on since April

1643 by virtue of the king's commission that he had sent to his principal agent in Ireland, the earl of Ormonde. In the following months Henrietta Maria encouraged the earl of Antrim to cooperate with Scottish royalists and pursue negotiations with the Confederation of Kilkenny. Antrim's plans came to nothing but Ormonde's resulted in the signing of a truce with the Kilkenny Confederation on 15 September 1643, aimed at releasing Irish troops to help the royalist cause in England. When these troops arrived they were too few to be of significant military help. More seriously for the royalist cause, Antrim's negotiations and the Cessation Treaty soon became public knowledge, enabling the parliamentarians to stiffen the determination of their supporters to oppose the king by yet more evidence of Charles's negotiations with Catholics.

Although, as will be seen, the parliamentarians' alliance with the Scots also had serious political consequences for their war effort, it did bring immediate and dramatic, if only short-lived, advantages. Together with the fiscal, administrative and military innovations of 1643, the Scottish alliance brought about the crushing victory at Marston Moor on 2 July 1644 when the combined armies of the Scots, the Yorkshire troops of Sir Thomas Fairfax and the army of the Eastern Association under Manchester and Cromwell decisively defeated the forces of Prince Rupert and the earl of Newcastle. The royalist threat from the north-east, which had been there since the beginning of 1643, was ended; Newcastle went into exile.

But the battle was far from being the turning point in the war that it is often said to have been. The royalists were still strong in the south-west where Prince Maurice and Hopton were assembling armies. The king was having no difficulty in holding out in Oxford against Essex. And the parliamentary euphoria after Marston Moor was soon dissipated by subsequent military failures, as well as crippling internal divisions exacerbated by the alliance with the Scots.

Military deadlock, 1644

Why had a state of military deadlock been reached by the end of 1644 despite the parliamentary victory at Marston Moor? Part of the answer lies in the fact that neither side was able to maintain adequate communications with its army commanders in the field. Beset by conflicting advice, the king gave his generals no clear directives. The committee of both kingdoms also proved ineffective in organizing coordinated military action. The members of the committee were split on the conduct of the war, and the command chain from the committee to the armies was too long; local army commanders were often left following a course dictated by local and personal considerations rather than the orders of the Westminster strategists. Even the militant Warwickshire county committee under Lord Brooke (until he died in March 1643) and William Purefoy was not anxious to allow its local forces to join parliamentary armies outside the county.[57]

---

[57] Hughes, *Warwickshire*, pp. 212–13.

Part of the answer is also to be found in the fact that parliament's superiority in the early stages of the war was illusory. Before 1645 the royalist war effort was much stronger and the parliamentary war effort less efficient than some accounts have suggested. Ronald Hutton's analysis shows that the royalist war machine was underpinned by measures that were remarkably similar to those devised by Pym and the parliamentarians: county committees, weekly contributions, forced loans, sequestrations and the excise. These were introduced later and less systematically by the royalists than were the parliamentary measures, but they were by no means totally ineffectual in squeezing money out of the inhabitants of the areas under royalist control. Moreover, in at least one respect the royalist war effort was improved ahead of its parliamentary counterpart. As will be seen, the parliamentarians did not introduce measures to professionalize their armies until 1645. The royalists did this in 1643 and 1644 by replacing militarily inexperienced territorial magnates like the earl of Derby in north-western England with professional soldiers like the king's nephew, Prince Rupert. By 1644 the latter controlled a vast military empire in Wales and western England, and in turn appointed experienced soldiers who were not hindered by local interests.[58]

The parliamentary war effort, on the other hand, was not immediately transformed by the programme of reorganization worked out in 1643. Though not totally effective (this varied naturally from area to area depending on the efficiency and incorruptibility of local officials), the yield from the new taxes compared favourably with that from traditional methods of taxation. What must have been a disappointment to the parliamentary leaders, however, was that the bulk of the receipts from taxation (apart from excise) never reached London, but was used locally. Sometimes the taxation revenue was not even seen by the local county treasurers, but was requisitioned by garrisons and troop commanders in the areas where it was collected. John Morrill calculates that only 2 per cent of the money raised before March 1645 in Cheshire left the county.[59] As a result, money was not always channelled where it was needed most. Army pay in some regiments got into arrears and in 1644 and 1645 there were outbreaks of mutinies and disorders in the parliamentary armies, as well as cases of plundering and desertion, the first signs of army discontent that increased in scale and in political importance at the end of the Civil War.

Nor did the military measures adopted in 1643 fully live up to the expectations their backers had of them. The programme of 1643 – impressment, the Scots alliance, reliance on the armies of Essex and the Eastern Association – proved to have serious drawbacks. Impressment was not designed to produce willing or manageable soldiers, a situation which was not improved by the poor rates of pay in the parliamentary armies. Foot soldiers were still only paid at the Elizabethan rates of 8d a day (against 1s 6d a day for dragoons and 2s a day for cavalry troopers). Desertion was therefore probably highest in the infantry regiments, and sometimes took place on a large scale. The earl of Bedford calculated that over half of his force deserted during the

---

[58] R. Hutton, *The Royalist War Effort 1642–46* (1982), parts 2 and 3.
[59] Morrill, *Cheshire*, p. 100.

Sherborne campaign of September 1643.[60] One-tenth of five infantry regiments in the army of the Eastern Association ran away between 7 June and 1 October 1644.[61] Disease, especially typhus and other infectious diseases, probably accounted for even more losses than desertion, a generalization supported by evidence from European armies in the Thirty Years War.[62]

Cromwell's claims that his regiments, not the Scottish army, won the battle of Marston Moor are naturally biased. However, there is some evidence to suggest that the Scottish army may have been a paper tiger in 1644. It was badly supplied; so much so that in January 1644 its general, Alexander Leslie, earl of Leven, ordered it to march south into England to prevent it disintegrating in the Border counties. Nor did the army have a united nation behind it. Royalist support in Scotland, centred on the marquis of Montrose, was fostered (belatedly, as usual) by Charles, who in February 1644 appointed Montrose lieutenant-general of the king's forces in Scotland. In April Montrose's invasion failed, but Leven could never commit himself totally to an English campaign without looking back over his shoulder towards Scotland. In the autumn of 1644 his fears were realized when Montrose returned, joined a Scottish force which had returned from Ireland led by the earl of Antrim, and won a battle at Tippermuir on 1 September 1644. From now on the Scottish covenanters were fighting the war on two fronts: in the Highlands as well as in England. Equally seriously, the Anglo-Scottish alliance was shot through with distrust because of the religious differences between the two countries. The Scots made no secret of their disgust at the slowness of the Westminster Assembly in recommending the introduction in England of 'rigid' Scottish Presbyterianism. Meanwhile the English parliamentarians began to suspect that the Scots' military backwardness grew out of a desire to negotiate a peace with Charles in return for his acceptance of Scottish Presbyterianism. The alliance was soured, and the committee of both kingdoms rendered ineffective.

The events of the summer of 1644 also gave good reason for St John and his allies to doubt the wisdom of continuing Pym's policy of shielding Essex from the efforts of the 'war group' to get rid of him. Essex's remarkable decision, taken against the advice of the committee of both kingdoms and without the support of any other parliamentary force, to march westwards against Prince Maurice and Hopton, was fatal. As he marched further and further into enemy territory, with his supply lines stretched behind him, he found himself isolated in Cornwall. At Lostwithiel at the end of August his army was decimated and Essex forced to escape ignominiously in a fishing boat, his military reputation in shreds. Equally ominously for the parliamentary cause, the autumn of 1644 proved that the military effectiveness of the army of the Eastern Association was being undermined by politico-religious rifts within its ranks. Cromwell's first-hand experience on the Marston Moor campaign of the determination of the Scots to export their brand of Presbyterianism to England seems to have been

---

[60] Underdown, *Somerset*, pp. 41–2.
[61] Holmes, *Eastern Association*, p. 168.
[62] C. Carlton, *Going to the Wars: the experience of the British Civil Wars 1638–51* (1992).

at the root of his public quarrel with the Scottish major-general in the Eastern Association army, Lawrence Crawford, who accused Cromwell of purging his regiments of Presbyterians and packing them with 'such as were of the Independent judgement'. Cromwell's conversion to more militant religious radicalism undoubtedly frightened the earl of Manchester, which probably accounts for the earl's transformation by the autumn of 1644 from the dynamic, win-the-war general of the summer into the indecisive leader at the second battle of Newbury (27 October 1644). It would be wrong to swallow whole the charges of Manchester's ineptitude in failing to cash in on the parliamentary army's superiority in numbers at the battle. His enemies from the right (Essex) and left (Cromwell) wanted a scapegoat. Lack of finance, poor morale among the troops, a high level of desertion and a divided strategy contributed to the military failure. But Manchester did not hide his conversion to a defensive military strategy and peace negotiations. 'If we beate the King 99 times', he said at the post mortem on the Newbury campaign, 'he would be King still, and his posterity, and we subjects still; but if he beate us but once we should be hang'd, and our posterity be undonne.'[63] By the end of 1644 the policies pursued by Pym and his political heirs lay in ruins. All semblance of unity among parliamentary supporters was gone: the quarrel between Cromwell and Manchester was bitterly fought out at Westminster. The victory hoped for by the 'middle' and 'war' groups seemed further away than ever.

The impact of the war

It is fairly commonly believed that, as long as they had the good fortune not to be recruited into one of the numerous armies, the Civil War passed most people in England by. This is a view that historical research is bringing increasingly into doubt.[64] Of course, the extent to which individuals were affected by the war varied, depending for one thing on the proximity of their home to the fighting. Those, for example, who lived in East Sussex, out of the war zone, suffered much less than those in West Sussex where the bulk of the fighting was concentrated.[65] Yet as the war dragged on it became increasingly difficult for anyone, even those not directly affected by the fighting, to insulate their lives from the effects of the war.

---

[63] J. Bruce, ed., *The Quarrel between the Earl of Manchester and Oliver Cromwell*, Camden Society, new series, XII (1875), p. 93.

[64] A. M. Everitt, *The Local Community and the Great Rebellion* (1969), pp. 24–6 reflects the older view which has been overtaken by research reflected in the following: Carlton, *Going to the Wars* and Donagan, *War in England*. The following two articles were path breaking in opening up news ways of looking at the impact of the Civil War: I. Roy, 'The English Civil War and English society', in B. Bond and I. Roy, eds., *War and Society: a yearbook of military history* (1975), pp. 24–43; I. Roy, 'England turned Germany? The aftermath of the Civil War in its European context', *T.R.H.S.*, 5th ser., XXVIII (1978), pp. 127–44. See also C. Carlton, 'The impact of the fighting', in J. Morrill, ed., *The Impact of the English Civil War* (1991); and D. Pennington, 'The war and the people' in Morrill, ed., *Reactions*.

[65] Fletcher, *Sussex*, p. 270.

Vastly increased taxation demands were one obvious offshoot of the war which hit everyone. As has been seen, parliamentary war taxation represented a far heavier financial burden for all classes than any other previous taxation. Royalist administration was perhaps not quite so effective, but 'step by step the King kept pace with Parliament, introducing the same measures, overriding property rights without Parliamentary assent'.[66] The 'contribution' agreements (the royalist equivalent of weekly assessments) made with royalist-controlled areas represented a massive increase on earlier taxation levels. The £61,000 annual 'contribution' levied on royalist Oxfordshire was ten times bigger than the county's assessment for the parliamentary subsidy of 1641.

Great as was the impact of direct taxation, it is highly likely that it was surpassed (as in those areas of northern Europe ravaged by the Thirty Years War) by the cost of providing armies with free quarter and supplies, and by making good the damage to property done by ill-disciplined, ill-paid, plundering soldiers. Both sides freely billeted soldiers on civilians and requisitioned food, fuel and horses in areas under their control. Constables of each village were supposed to record the cost of providing lodgings and meals to soldiers according to scales of compensation. From these records it is clear that the sums involved were very large and that, except in cases where they had caused severe hardship, they were seldom repaid. In Cheshire, John Morrill estimates that the cost to the county of providing free quarter may have been £120,000 as against a total of £100,000 raised in direct taxation during the war.[67] The cost of plunder by the armies of both sides is impossible to quantify. Both military and civilian authorities vainly tried to maintain discipline in their armies. Largely because the soldiers of both sides were ill-paid, petty thefts by passing bands of soldiers were common. More serious, if not as widespread, are the recorded instances of large-scale pillaging, carried out by troops usually after they had won a victory, when the generals proved unable to prevent their junior officers and rank and file taking their share of the spoils. Essex's army after the siege of Reading in April 1643, and Rupert's army after the siege of Bristol three months later, went on the rampage for days before normal military discipline was reimposed. Even this was overshadowed by the plunder and indiscipline of the royalist troops of Lord Goring – 'Goring's Crew' – in the south-western counties. Without any doubt the most dramatic illustration of the devastating impact of the war is Charles Carlton's estimate of the numbers killed in battles and from diseases created by the war. Although it must be treated as a very rough estimate, given the uncertain nature of the evidence, his guess is that the total war mortality in England amounted to 3.7 per cent of the population, a proportion of the total population of England greater than the 2.6 per cent killed in the First World War.[68]

Apart from the effects on village economies of the loss of small husbandmen, craftsmen and labourers killed in the war or taken away by impressment, other economic

---

[66] Ian Roy, 'The English Civil War and English society', p. 29.

[67] Morrill, *Cheshire*, p. 108.

[68] Carlton, *Going to the Wars*, p. 214. He also estimates that the percentages of people killed were even higher in Scotland (6 per cent) and Ireland (41 per cent).

effects of the war are less identifiable. To what extent can the war be blamed for the 'decay of trade' complained of in the 1640s? Certainly the fact that roads from London to Bristol and the west, and from London to the north-east, were controlled in places by royalist garrisons must have hit metropolitan trade,[69] as well as disrupting more localized markets and trade. The economies of towns and villages in the war zones must have been hit, especially when a town was besieged and the suburbs demolished as the garrison retreated into a more defensible position inside the town.

It is not surprising that quite soon popular enthusiasm for the war, even where it existed, was converted to at best sullen apathy, or at worst open opposition to the manifestations of the war. The passive neutralism of 1642 (noted above) persisted: people 'swimming with the tide', obeying the power that happened to be stronger and then, apparently, 'changing sides' when the control of the locality changed from one side to the other. More interesting are the more militant expressions of anti-war opinions in the early 1640s. It is only recently that the significance of these before 1645 has been recognized. But civilian protests at the war were a major factor that both armies had to contend with even before the better-known manifestation of anti-war opinion in 1645, the Clubmen movement. Dr Ian Roy, for example, has documented the remarkable way in which armed groups of dairy farmers in Gloucestershire protected themselves against Prince Rupert's ill-disciplined troops after the fall of Bristol in the autumn of 1643. In September they even ambushed an eighty-strong royalist troop of 'crack cavalry', killing six of them.[70] Also in 1643 moderate gentry in Kent led a rebellion against the imposition of the Presbyterian covenant and high war taxation. There is no evidence that either the Gloucestershire farmers or the Kent gentry rebelled respectively for parliament or for the king. Their activities were essentially negative, neutralist, anti-war in character.

The impression that incidents like these were not uncommon even in the early part of the war must await confirmation. It is not until 1645 that there is strong evidence of widespread concerted civilian resistance to the armies of both sides by the Clubmen of central-southern and south-western counties of England and in South Wales, significantly areas with long histories of riots and disorder. Despite recent work on the Clubmen movement, there are a lot of questions still to be answered about it.[71] To what extent was it 'a movement' in terms of contacts between different groups? Were the Clubmen used and infiltrated by the politically committed for their own ends?

---

[69] B. Coward, 'London and the English Civil War', *The Historian*, vol. 99 (2008); B. Coates, *The Impact of the Civil War on the Economy of London, 1642–50* (2004); S. Porter, 'The economic and social impact of the Civil War upon London', in S. Porter, ed., *London and the English Civil War* (1996).

[70] Ian Roy, 'The English Civil War and English society', pp. 35–42.

[71] There is no lengthy study of the Clubmen. Good starting points are M. Braddick, *God's Fury, England's Fire: a new history of the English Civil Wars* (2008), ch. 15; Morrill, *Revolt in the Provinces*, pp. 132–51 (the first edition of this book, *Revolt of the Provinces*, pp. 196–200, is still useful since it prints the text of Clubmen manifestos that are omitted from the 2nd edition); and D. Underdown, 'The chalk and the cheese: contrasts among the English Clubmen', *P. & P.*, LXXXV (1979). Significantly Braddick remarks that 'comparatively little is known about the Clubmen' (p. 414), leaving much room for different interpretations.

Fairly certainly most Clubmen groups grew out of incidents of spontaneous civilian resistance to pillaging or outrages committed by soldiers of both sides. Thereafter the leadership passed often to men of gentry origins, who organized their followers, called mass meetings and drew up resolutions to protect themselves from 'plunder and all other unlawful violence'. Both parliamentary and royalist armies were attacked by Clubmen in an effort to protect 'the peace of my country'. Unlike the Clubmen of Dorset and Wiltshire, the Clubmen of Somerset, however, allied with Fairfax and the New Model Army. In making these decisions, as their manifestos make clear, they were not unaware of issues of national importance. They were not simply a 'localist', introverted movement. Yet, the Clubmen movement makes more sense, not as a crypto-parliament or crypto-royalist movement, but as a cry of resentment against the disruptive effects of war.

The end of the war, 1645–1646

Why did the royalists lose the Civil War?[72] Given the deadlocked military situation and parliamentary disunity at the end of 1644, the parliamentary victory in the Civil War came remarkably quickly. In the summer of 1645 the New Model Army won what proved to be decisive battles at Naseby and Langport, and in the following spring Charles gave up the military struggle. The reorganization of the parliamentary armies in 1645 and the creation of the New Model Army undoubtedly helped to bring about this transformation. Although it is not the sole – or even perhaps the major – cause of the royalist defeat in the Civil War, it is the best place to begin the explanation of how this came about.

The New Model Army emerged out of a crucial change in parliamentary politics at Westminster. Until the end of 1644, St John, Lords Saye and Sele, and Wharton and the 'middle group' had held out against drastic reorganization of the parliamentary armies. But in November, when it became known that the Scots were offering to make peace with Charles on the basis of Scottish Presbyterianism, their growing disillusionment with the Scots alliance was complete. In December, too, there were indications that Essex and some of the leading 'peace group' MPs were willing to sink their religious differences with the Scots and accept the prospect of the unconditional return of the king in order to halt the religious radicalism of the sects, and especially the influence of 'that darling of the sectaries', Cromwell. Once again, as so often in the recent past, the Scottish factor proved to be a major divisive one in English politics. From now on St John and his aristocratic allies had little alternative but to combine much more closely than hitherto with the 'war group' to advocate new measures to win the war: the removal of the discredited military leaders and the reorganization of the army. For a time it is difficult to identify specific 'middle group' policies, and the political activists of Westminster do seem (temporarily at least) to polarize into two groups: Political Presbyterians and Political Independents.

---

[72] See C. Holmes's essay 'Why did Parliament win the Civil War?' in his *Why was Charles executed?* (2006).

Information

Political Presbyterians and Political Independents

The main Political Presbyterians were the earls of Essex and Manchester, Denzil Holles and Philip Stapleton, who had been prominent members of the old 'peace group'. They were agreed on:

- support for Manchester in his savage attack on Cromwell in the Lords at the end of 1644

- a willingness to ally with the Scots, with whom they worked closely from the end of 1644

- support of an intolerant Presbyterian church settlement, in order to prevent any moves towards liberty for tender consciences, which they believed would lead to the collapse of the social order

- a desire for a defensive war strategy, combined with the rapid conclusion of a negotiated peace settlement with the king.

The major Political Independents were Viscount Saye and Sele, Oliver St John, Arthur Haselrige and Oliver Cromwell, who had been members of the old 'war and middle groups'. They were distinguished from the Political Presbyterians by:

- support in the Commons at the end of 1644 for Cromwell's scathing indictment of Manchester's 'averseness to action' on the battlefield

- mistrust of Scottish intentions to impose Scottish Presbyterianism on England by their negotiations with the king

- a desire to establish a more tolerant independent national Church than either English or Scottish Presbyterians and to allow some diversity of Protestant religious opinions

- a common aim to prosecute the war vigorously by the introduction of measures aimed at the reorganization of the parliamentary armies.

The completion of the military reorganization, however, did not take place until after the failure of another attempt to reach a settlement with the king. Many parliamentarians were no doubt sincere in their desire for peace, but it is difficult to see how the Uxbridge 'treaty' negotiations, which began at the end of January 1645, could have succeeded. The programme for a settlement offered by the parliamentary commissioners was an uncompromising one, and Charles was never the person to make compromises at the right time. The failure of the Uxbridge 'treaty' weakened the Lords' opposition and paved the way for the acceptance of the New Model Army Ordinance on 17 February and the Self-Denying Ordinance on 3 April. Both of these important measures originated directly in the highly charged political atmosphere at Westminster during the winter of 1644–5. The idea of a Self-Denying Ordinance, which would make it illegal for any member of the Commons or Lords to hold an army command, was first floated by Cromwell (acting in alliance with his Political Independent friends) in a speech in the Commons on 9 December 1644, partly to deflect the campaign of the Political Presbyterians against them. It was calculated to gain wide support because it appealed to the Puritan belief that drastic measures of self-denial were necessary in order to win back God's blessing, the loss of which, it was believed, was the cause of the political and military crisis in which they now found themselves. It was also designed to get the backing of MPs of all political inclinations, who would support it as a means of ensuring the expulsion of their opponents from the army. Yet the principal motive behind its introduction was the Political Independents' aim to expel Essex and Manchester from the army, even at the cost of losing Cromwell's military command as well. The fact that Cromwell survived was purely fortuitous and could not have been foreseen by him or his allies when the Self-Denying proposal was first made in December 1644. His eventual promotion in June 1645 to the rank of lieutenant general in the remodelled parliamentary army was due to the military needs of the moment and not to his Machiavellian guile. The consequence of the passage of the Self-Denying Ordinance was the reorganization of the army. The New Model Army Ordinance merged the armies of Manchester, Essex and Waller into an army of ten cavalry regiments (later another was added) of 600 men each, twelve foot regiments of 1,200 men, and one regiment of 1,000 dragoons. Fairfax was appointed its commander-in-chief and Philip Skippon its major-general.

Information

Why was the New Model Army so successful?

- The New Model Army contained a larger number of ideologically committed soldiers and officers of proven military ability than any other army that had taken the field so far in the Civil War. This has been contested by Mark Kishlansky in his *The Rise of the New Model Army* (1979). He argues that the New Model Army was made of parts of existing armies and therefore contained many conscripts who were not motivated to fight for a cause and who owed their positions to social standing not military ability. This has been effectively countered by Ian Gentles in his *The New Model Army* (1991) and others. They have shown that

> many New Model Army officers were Political Independents, well motivated to fight. Moreover, the New Model Army included soldiers from cavalry regiments from the army of the Eastern Association, who had volunteered to fight for the cause of godly reformation.

- It was also better paid (and therefore better disciplined) than some other contemporary armies. This was largely because, from March 1645, royalist composition fines were paid direct to Goldsmiths' Hall and not, as in the case of royalist sequestrations, swallowed up locally. Payments did get into arrears (with tremendous political results, as will be seen), but the New Model Army was more regularly paid than other armies.

- Its commanders were careful never to enter a major engagement with the enemy unless their own forces were much greater in numbers. When the New Model Army won its famous victory at Naseby (near Leicester) on 14 June 1645, its forces were nearly double (14,000 against 7,500) those of the royalist army.

There is no denying the importance of the New Model Army or of the parliamentary navy,[73] in securing victory for the parliamentarians in the Civil War. Too often, though, this has led some to play down – or even neglect – other significant reasons for the war's eventual outcome. Amongst these is the fact that the parliamentarians had access to superior resources, men and money, to fight the war.[74] As has been seen, the financial and administrative reconstruction of the parliamentarians' war effort begun in 1643 did not bring immediate benefits (see above, p. 203); but eventually they proved to be decisive. Although the royalists introduced similar measures, these were not as effective as the parliamentarians', which were more organized, systematic, and perhaps more ruthlessly administered,[75] than the comparatively uncoordinated measures of the royalists. What gave the parliamentarians an even more crucial advantage in terms of resources is that throughout the whole of the war they had access to the only major source of men and money that existed in mid seventeenth-century England, which was London. This had three major consequences. First, it gave the parliamentarians the support of the London militia, its trained bands, which enabled it, for example, by sending these trained bands to join the earl of Essex's army in the West Country in 1643, to prevent the royalists from taking Gloucester, and then probably taking over the whole of south-west England for the king. Secondly, London,

---

[73] B. Capp, 'Naval operations', in J. Kenyon and J. Ohlmeyer, eds., *The Civil War: a military history of England, Scotland and Ireland 1638–60* (1998). M. Wanklyn and F. Jones in *A Military History of the English Civil War 1642–46: strategy and tactics* (2005) play down the importance of parliamentary control of the navy.

[74] Here I am resisting M. Wanklyn's argument in his *The Warrior Generals: winning the British Civil Wars* (2010), pp. ix–x and *passim* that individual events and decisions made on battlefields were more important than anything else in determining the outcome of the war. In my view, 'off the battlefield' factors like those dealt with in this and succeeding paragraphs are the most important contributors to the war's outcome.

[75] A. Hughes, 'The king, the parliament and the localities during the English Civil War', *J.B.S.*, 24 (1985).

given its great size and mercantile wealth, was a major source of tax revenue. It is probable that Londoners paid as much as one-quarter to one-third of all the money received by the parliamentarians from its new taxation system.[76] Thirdly, and of most importance, London was a major source of loans. The great corporate and livery companies of London were the only sources of large-scale credit in seventeenth-century England, enabling parliamentary treasurers to tap into these sources to bridge the gap between expenditure and irregular flows of income. The king, in contrast, had to rely on loans from individuals, who simply did not have the resources of the scale provided by the City.

Not only did the parliamentarians command more financial and human sinews of war, they made better use of their resources than did the royalists. In this respect the king ought to have been in a better position than his opponents, who (as has been seen) were bitterly divided amongst themselves. Charles ought to have capitalized on the fact that he was in sole command of the royalist war effort. Unfortunately, he failed to prevent the royalist council of war from being rent apart by major divisions amongst his councillors, a situation that led to serious strategic errors.[77] One of the most disastrous was the indecision before the battle of Naseby when the king failed to choose between competing strategies that were floated in his war council. The upshot was the fatal decision to order Prince Rupert to engage the New Model Army in battle at Naseby on 5 June 1645, although the royalist forces were half those of the parliamentarians. Ronald Hutton's claim that 'the royal army command committed suicide at Naseby' may be too harsh a verdict,[78] but it can hardly be said that the king made effective use of the resources at his command at Naseby.

Finally, more needs to be made than has been done in the past of the impact of the king's 'British' policies in weakening his cause in England by giving the parliamentarians a massive propaganda advantage. It is true that the parliamentarians' British policies (in this case their alliance with the Scots) did not bring unqualified benefits to their war effort, as the Solemn League and Covenant not only brought military support but also opened up damaging internal divisions (see pp. 200–1). It is also true that the royalists did not lose the war of propaganda entirely. Indeed in the early stages of the war, the royalists had a superb propaganda expert in John Berkenhead. The royalist newspaper he edited weekly from Oxford from January 1643 to September 1645, *Mercurius Aulicus*, was the envy of its parliamentary rivals. One of these, *Mercurius Britannicus*, in 1643 claimed that *Aulicus* 'had as exact intelligence from some of the close committee and both Houses as can be wished', and the Commons initiated an enquiry into how *Aulicus* knew 'some Things privately passed in the House?'[79] But this early advantage

---

[76] S. Porter, 'Introduction', in Porter, ed., *London and the English Civil War*, p. 10. See also B. Coward, 'London and the English Civil War', *The Historian*, vol. 99 (2008).

[77] I. Roy. 'The royalist council of war, 1642–46', *B.I.H.R.*, 35 (1962).

[78] Woolrych, *Britain in Revolution*, p. 316 thinks that Hutton's verdict in his *Royalist War Effort*, p. 178 is too harsh.

[79] P. W. Thomas, *Sir John Berkenhead 1617–79: a royalist career in politics and polemics* (1969), pp. 41–4. K. Sharpe believes that royalist propaganda became increasingly effective as the war progressed; see his *Image Wars: promoting king and Commonwealth in England 1603–60* (2010).

was lost by the damage done to the royalist cause by the king's Irish policies. Already the king had begun to pay a high political price for the Cessation Treaty he had made in 1643 with the Catholic Confederation of Kilkenny and for his association with plans in 1644 to send Catholic troops from Ireland led by Alasdair MacColla, largely men drawn from the Irish MacDonnell clan, to join Montrose in the western Highlands of Scotland. They were to aid their Gaelic kinsmen, the McDonalds, in their fight against their clan enemies, the Campbells, who were led by the earl of Argyll, a leading Scottish covenanter. To many in England these events provided confirmation of their belief that Charles I was at the heart of a Catholic plot to use his British kingdoms to destroy parliament and Protestantism in England. Further evidence of this appeared in 1645 when Charles sent the earl of Glamorgan, the Catholic son of the earl of Worcester, to Ireland to negotiate again with the Confederation of Kilkenny. The outcome was a treaty by which the Confederation promised to provide 10,000 soldiers for the king's use but at the very high cost of Charles's promise to grant toleration for Catholics in Ireland. Charles tried to distance himself from the treaty (in fact he briefly imprisoned Glamorgan), but the damage had been done, especially when after the battle of Naseby Charles's private papers were captured, amongst which were incriminating letters revealing the king's part in these negotiations (as well as with other foreign Catholic powers). When these were published by the parliamentarians, they further blackened Charles's claim to be a Protestant monarch.

Consequently, in the post-Naseby campaign the royalist army was at a grave disadvantage, short of money and supplies, beset by conflicting advice, and the cause for which it fought damaged by the revelations in the captured royal documents. In order to try to stem the tide of defeat, royalist commanders in the west were forced to impose heavier and heavier burdens on the localities in which their armies were garrisoned. One result was that in some areas, like Glamorganshire, the gentry raised irregular armies, forcing the king to remove his regular troops and thus accelerating the spiral of royalist defeats.[80] The defeat of Goring at the battle of Langport (10 July) opened up the south-west to the New Model Army, which was able to consolidate the victory in a way that had not been possible after Marston Moor. After the surrender of Bridgwater (23 July) and Bristol (11 September), Charles ordered the Prince of Wales, who was in nominal command in the south-west, to leave for France. Hopton still held out, but in March 1646 surrendered. In the north, the crucial battle was at Rowton Heath (near Chester) on 24 September 1645; it prevented Charles from linking up with the Scots. In any case, Montrose's defeat at Philiphaugh (13 September) had already weakened the chances of Scottish royalist support, and Charles fell back on Oxford, which finally fell to parliamentary forces on 24 June 1646. Before that Charles had recognized the inevitability of defeat: on 27 April he left Oxford in disguise. But the fact that he chose to surrender to the Scottish army in Nottinghamshire rather than to the parliamentary army indicated that, for Charles, the struggle with parliament was far from over.

---

[80] Hutton, *Royalist War Effort*, p. 184.

Map 2 The English Civil War, 1642–1646: principal battles and garrison towns

The search for a settlement: king, parliament, the army and the Scots, 1645–1649

This period after the end of the Civil War has a claim to be one of the most exciting in the history of seventeenth-century Britain, beginning as it did with the New Model Army becoming a major political force and ending with Charles I's execution at Whitehall on 30 January 1649. Intriguing historical questions are raised: when and why did the New Model Army become politicized? Why did the search for a settlement with the king fail? Why was the king executed? These are questions to which there are no generally accepted answers. One of the reasons why they are so difficult to answer is that events immediately after the end of the war seemed to be moving inexorably in the king's favour. Ironically, Charles I was more popular immediately before, at and after his execution than at any other time in his life. So why did events turn out as they did?

In explaining the failure of the search for such a settlement, historians have rightly emphasized the important roles of Charles's continual refusal to negotiate seriously and the deep divisions among his opponents. The political ineptness of Charles I in failing to capitalize on a situation that was running strongly in his favour is very evident in post-Civil War England. The violence and radicalism produced by the war, and the fear of further violence that might happen, combined to accelerate the conservative reaction in his favour that had been evident since 1641. Moreover, the divisions among his opponents that had appeared during the war also became more serious. Lord Astley was not the only royalist to predict, rightly, that it would not be long before the military victors fell out amongst themselves. They were not only divided on simple parliament versus army versus Scots lines, but there was little measure of agreement among parliamentarians, among soldiers or among Scotsmen on the means of transforming the military victory into a political one. The nature of these disagreements can be seen by looking at the four chronological phases of post-war English politics: the parliamentary constitutional and religious discussions from 1645 to early 1647; the first political intervention of the army from the spring of 1647; the Scots' decision at the end of 1647 to ally with the king, which precipitated the so-called 'second civil war' (March to October 1648); and the last attempt at a settlement with the king, which was forestalled by the second major political intervention of the army at the end of 1648.

Presbyterians, Independents and counter-revolution, 1645–1647

At the end of the Civil War (as before and later) there were no clear-cut party divisions. The vast majority of MPs remained uncommitted and therefore uncataloguable. Yet the polarization of political opinion which had occurred in late 1644 to early 1645 still held good after the war. At one end of the political spectrum was a minority of hardliners, who wanted cast-iron limitations on Charles's power before disbanding the army; at the other extreme were those who were willing to accept the king's return with minimal conditions. In this sense the terms 'Political Independents' and 'Political Presbyterians' represent the extreme poles of political opinion among parliamentarians in the late 1640s. The use of the adjective 'Political' in both cases is advisable when using these labels, because the prime differences between the two groups were political not religious. Political Presbyterians, of whom the earl of Essex in the Lords and Denzil Holles in the Commons were the most influential, were willing to accept the return of the king to power on minimal terms; while Political Independents, a coalition of former middle group and war group men (of whom St John in the Commons and Viscount Saye and Sele and Lord Wharton in the Lords were the leading lights) demanded that Charles agree to firm limitations on his power before the army should be disbanded and a settlement made with the king. Religious divisions did not correspond exactly with these major political divisions. Not all Political Presbyterians were religious Presbyterians and not all Political Independents were religious Independents. Yet, as earlier in the 1640s, one of the prime causes of political action was religious zeal. As time went on, more and more Political Presbyterians, though not doctrinaire religious Presbyterians, supported a Presbyterian Church settlement in order to cultivate the support of both the Scots (who were eager to export Presbyterianism to England) and powerful interests in London (who were becoming converted to the idea of a national Presbyterian Church by the arguments of Scots like Robert Baillie and by the belief that the erection of a Presbyterian ecclesiastical discipline would be a bulwark against a slide into religious diversity and anarchy).[81] On the other hand, although not all Political Independents were committed to full-blown religious Independency (i.e. the right of each congregation to decide its own form of worship), many were in favour of some measure of religious freedom within the confines of a loosely organized national Church.

There are many indications that opinion in the country was likely to favour the soft political line adopted by the Political Presbyterians for an expeditious 'safe and well-grounded settlement'. The reasons for the disillusionment with the parliamentary management of the war and the forms it took varied from area to area, but everywhere there was a strong conservative reaction to the violence, high taxation and disruption caused by the war, which had already provoked the Clubmen movement, as has already been seen. The serious harvest failures and consequent high prices after the wet summers of 1646 and 1647 also resurrected fears of food and enclosure riots, and an eagerness among the propertied classes for the restoration of political order. The assorted strands of anti-war sentiment came to be focused on the parliamentary county committees and the army. The county committees were the agents of the 'arbitrary'

---

[81] See A. Hughes, *Gangraena: the struggle for the English Revolution* (2004) and E. Vernon, 'The ministry of the gospel: the Presbyterians during the English Revolution' in C. Durston and J. Maltby, eds., *Religion in Revolutionary England* (2006) for the view that the Presbyterians were primarily motivated by a vision of radical change not conservative fears.

policies of parliament (the intrusion of central government into local affairs, high taxation and imprisonment without trial) which to many seemed identical with those adopted by Charles in the 1620s and 1630s. In addition, the county committees came to be infiltrated by men from outside the traditional ruling borough and county elites. The Isle of Wight county committee, sneered the snobbish royalist Sir John Oglander, was dominated by 'Ringwood of Newport, the pedlar; Maynard, the apothecary; Matthews, the baker, Wavell and Legge, farmers, and poor Baxter of Hurst Castle'.[82] Too much, however, can be made of the low social origins and radicalism of the 'new men' (John Pyne in Somerset, Sir John Gell in Derbyshire, Anthony Weldon in Kent, Herbert Morley in Sussex, Sir William Brereton in Cheshire and Staffordshire, for example). They were not often members of the major magnate families, but nevertheless they were prosperous propertied gentry. And often their radicalism consisted only of sub-ordinating local interests in favour of a more effective prosecution of the war. Sometimes, though, they were set apart from most of the traditional rulers of the country by their radical religious beliefs, their commitment to a 'godly reformation'. They and the county committees came to be an embattled minority in the face of (sometimes organized) county opinion for a return to the running of society as it had been in pre-war days. The army was an equally obvious target of the peace movement of 1645–7, especially when unrest in the army grew in scale towards and immediately after the end of the war. Dr Morrill found that by late summer 1646 twenty-two counties had reported cases of army mutinies, in addition to organized plundering by unpaid regiments who were now unemployed but still not disbanded.[83] By the end of the war, the best-paid parliamentary army, the New Model, was owed £601,000 in arrears of pay. A conservative estimate of the total arrears due to all the parliamentary forces from 1642 to 1647 is around £2.8 million.[84] Not surprisingly, indiscipline in the army was rife. In July 1646 the Nantwich garrison threw members of the local sequestration committee into gaol until the county committee promised to do something about the garrison's arrears of pay. Incidents like this were frightening to the gentry, especially when the mutinies appeared to be led and organized from within the ranks and in defiance of the officers.

Two factors, however, frustrated the overwhelming desire for a return to the traditional political order. First, the split in the parliamentary ranks deepened as from 1645 onwards, for the first time since 1640–1, the religious issue moved to the centre of the political stage at Westminster. Ever since 1640 any religious agreement among parliamentarians had been on the negative grounds of what to abolish, rather than on any constructive proposals. On the whole the divisions had been relegated to the

---

[82] F. Bamford, ed., *A Royalist's Notebook* (1936), pp. 110–11.

[83] J. S. Morrill, 'Mutiny and discontent in English provincial armies 1645–7', *P. & P.*, LVI (1972), p. 53.

[84] I. Gentles, 'The arrears of pay of the parliamentary army at the end of the 1st Civil War', *B.I.H.R.*, XLVIII (1975), p. 55. Professor Gentles calculates that half these arrears were owed to the non-New Model Army parliamentary soldiers, and that of those arrears owed to the New Model Army three-fifths originated from the period before it was founded: *The New Model Army* (1991), pp. 49–52.

Westminster Assembly of Divines, where a vocal minority, the Dissenting Brethren, had upheld the cause of religious toleration and Independency against majority support for Presbyterian uniformity. In January 1645 parliamentary approval was given for the abolition of the Book of Common Prayer and its substitution by the Presbyterian Directory of Worship. With the encouragement of the Scottish representatives, however, the Westminster divines also came out in favour of the Scottish system of appointing elders and ministers by the church authorities not the State. This was obviously anathema to most English MPs, who considered that its logical outcome was that 'the whole nobility, gentry, and Commons must be brought under the power of the clergy'.[85] As a result the ordinance establishing Presbyterianism in England (finally approved by the Lords in March 1646) gave parliament the supreme voice in church affairs. 'A lame Erastian Presbytery' the Scot, Robert Baillie called it. But the unity of most English MPs extended only as far as a hatred of Scottish Presbyterianism and support for a parliament-controlled state Church. The key controversial issue was how extensive should be the interference of state control in the doctrinal and liturgical practices of individual congregations. Support for some measure of toleration was not confined to the Dissenting Brethren and those sects who were already establishing their independent gathered churches. Fast-day sermons to parliament proposing limited toleration in 1646 and 1647 were received sympathetically.[86] Former 'middle group' men like St John were in contact with Cromwell, who made no secret of his pro-toleration views. 'He that ventures his life for the liberty of his country, I wish he trust God for the liberty of his conscience, and you for the liberty he fights for', he wrote to the Speaker of the Commons after Naseby.[87] St John's commonplace book shows that he was in favour of some form of toleration[88] and, although the Political Presbyterian majority at Westminster deleted Cromwell's appeal for 'liberty for conscience' from the officially printed version of his Naseby letter, his political allies printed the offending section privately, and Viscount Saye and Sele published a defence of Cromwell against the charges being made by Political Presbyterian MPs that religious liberty would open the floodgates to social and political radicalism. Parliament's failure to present a united front on its proposals for a religious settlement seriously hindered the prospects of agreement with the king.

More seriously, so too did the mistrust of Charles's sincerity which was confirmed by the publication of the Naseby and Digby 'cabinets', the captured correspondence of the king and Digby, which revealed the king's treacherous negotiations with the Irish and other foreign powers during the Oxford and Uxbridge 'treaties'. All this

---

[85] Quoted in V. Pearl, 'The "Royal Independents" in the English Civil War', *T.R.H.S.*, 5th ser., XVIII (1968), p. 92.

[86] W. Haller, *Liberty and Reformation in the Puritan Revolution* (1955), pp. 247–9.

[87] Abbott, *Writings and Speeches*, I, p. 360.

[88] V. Pearl, 'Oliver St John and the "middle-group" in the Long Parliament', *E.H.R.*, LXXXI (1966), pp. 500–1.

helped to strengthen the position of the Political Independents in the Derby House Committee[89] and to ensure that the Propositions of Newcastle, which were sent to the king in July 1646, represented no 'sell-out', and that they would be unacceptable to Charles.

Information

The Propositions of Newcastle, July 1646

These proposals for a settlement (which were very similar to those offered to the king in the Uxbridge 'treaty' negotiations) were by far the most harsh, punitive and humiliating that the king was offered in the 1640s.

- Parliament was to nominate all the major officers of state in perpetuity.
- Parliament was to control the militia for twenty years.
- The king was to accept the Solemn League and Covenant, i.e. accept the abolition of episcopacy and religious uniformity in Britain and Ireland on the Scottish Presbyterian model.
- 58 royalists were exempted from pardon and a long list of others were declared dismissed from office for life.

The growing chorus of demands in 1646 from all parts of the country for the reduction of high taxation, the demobilization of much of the army, and the abolition of the county committees, however, ensured that the political initiative was held by the Political Presbyterians. This was symbolized by the elaborate funeral of the most eminent Presbyterian, the earl of Essex, in September 1646 and the Presbyterian victory in the London common council elections in December 1646. During the winter of 1646–7, Political Presbyterians began, under the guidance of Holles and Stapleton, to advocate a consistent programme: demobilize the army, keeping only a smaller force for service in Ireland; create an alternative 'safe' army, based on the London trained bands purged of Independents; and reach a settlement with the king on the basis of a revised version of the Newcastle Propositions. It was this attempted 'counter-revolution' that provoked the political intervention of the army.

---

[89] I. Gentles, 'The politics of Fairfax's army, 1645–9', in J. Adamson, ed., *The English Civil War* (2009), p. 184.

The army and the Levellers, 1647

On the face of it, the political intervention of the New Model Army ought to have accelerated the process that ended with the failure of plans to reach a settlement with the king and his execution. That is not what happened in 1647. As has been seen, the parliamentary armies had a lot to complain about at the end of the Civil War. Their wage arrears amounted to nearly £3 million; it was likely that most regiments would be disbanded before these arrears were settled; and for some officers there was the prospect of being found guilty of treasonable acts committed during the war. These material grievances were the dominant motive behind the army mutinies of 1646 and 1647. But at some stage in 1647 radical ideological religious and political demands became inextricably bound up with the army's professional grievances. Both the timing and significance of this process are unclear.[90] A key question for historians is: how important was the influence of London radical opinion (principally that of the Levellers) in this process? In the past many historians believed that these metropolitan radicals were the prime source of the army's emergence as a political force.

The capital was a hothouse for the growth of radical ideas in the 1640s. Hierarchical social discipline was much laxer than in many rural areas (especially arable); and the economic dislocation caused by the war was felt very severely in London. During the war years the radical movement was probably not as well organized as it was later, but it had thrown up a trio of influential pamphleteers, John Lilburne, Richard Overton and William Walwyn, who, despite differences in temperament and religious beliefs, had in common a disillusionment with the failure of the Long Parliament and the Westminster Assembly to bring about 'a godly reformation'. The titles of some of their pamphlets alone express this: Lilburne's *London's Liberty in Chains* (November 1646), Overton's *An Arrow against all Tyrants* (October 1646) and Walwyn's *England's Lamentable Slaverie* (October 1645). Inevitably their demands for greater political and religious liberty were not popular with the parliamentary and City authorities, but repressions and imprisonments only stimulated them to organize themselves and to demand economic, legal, educational, as well as political and religious reforms. 'Wee still find the Nation oppressed with grievances of the same destructive nature as formerly though under other notions', said the Leveller Large Petition (March 1647). Arbitrary judicial power was exercised not by star chamber, but by parliament; religious nonconformists were oppressed not by bishops, but by Presbyterian clergy. The law and penal system were unreformed; tithes and monopolies still in existence; and 'thousands of men and women are permitted to live in beggery and wickednesse all their life long'. Not surprisingly, the Commons ordered the petition to be burned.

Undoubtedly, some London radicals attempted to make links with discontented elements in the army. A pamphlet of 26 March 1647, *An Apollogie of the Soldiers*, protested at the imprisonment of 'those honest people [Lilburne and Overton] who have shown

---

[90] The best modern account is Gentles, *The New Model Army*, ch. 6.

themselves with us'.[91] But there are many reasons to doubt whether these attempts were very successful throughout the spring and summer of 1647. Writings on the Levellers in the past have exaggerated the support the Levellers had – they were, after all, confined to London and only found support there amongst small tradesmen and craftsmen, not the bulk of London's population; nor was the label 'Levellers' attached to them until November 1647. Considerations like these have caused many historians to look for the main impetus behind the dramatic politicization and radicalization of the New Model Army early in 1647; to attribute it not to infiltration and indoctrination of its ranks from *outside*, but to reactions *within* the army to the harshness and unfairness with which they were treated by parliament.

As soon as the Civil War ended, the Political Presbyterians began a political campaign against the New Model Army, which they disliked as a major obstacle to a settlement with the king and as the seedbed of religious extremism. In December 1646 a City of London petition demanded that parliament disband the New Model Army because it was the refuge of heretics. Once the Scots left England in February 1647, Denzil Holles and his Political Presbyterian allies appear to have committed themselves to a single-minded campaign against the New Model Army, and, as they gained control of the capital's pulpits, press and militia, as well as the key parliamentary Derby House Committee, they pushed through parliament in February and March 1647 measures to reduce the New Model Army in size without satisfying its demands for payment of wage arrears or for indemnity against prosecution for actions committed during the war. On 18 February the Commons decided to reduce the army to only 5,400 horse and 1,000 dragoons, and on 8 March voted that only Presbyterians and non-MPs should be officers in the new army. Despite negotiations between parliamentary commissioners and army officers at Saffron Walden in March and April, an army petition of 21 March, which drew on the demands of many manifestos that had come from the junior officers and rank and file of many regiments, was condemned as treasonable in what became known as 'the declaration of dislike'. Unpopular Presbyterian generals (Skippon and Massey, not Cromwell and Fairfax) were appointed to lead the army to Ireland, and the City authorities were allowed to purge the London trained bands of Independents. In the face of this provocation, eight militant cavalry regiments at the end of April elected 'agitators' to represent their views. The final breach between the mutinous army and parliament came in May. On 18 May the Commons accepted the king's third reply to the Propositions of Newcastle, in which Charles conceded Presbyterianism for three years and parliamentary control of the militia for ten years, as the basis for reopening negotiations. With the prospect of a settlement before them, the Presbyterian leaders decided to break with the army. On 25 May the Commons voted to disband the New Model infantry regiments with only eight weeks' arrears of wages paid. Four days later Fairfax, who probably took a more prominent

---

[91] G. E. Aylmer, ed., *The Levellers and the English Revolution* (1975), pp. 75–81 (the Large Petition), pp. 22–3. This is the best introduction to the Levellers.

role in events at this time than he indicated in his later memoirs,[92] ordered a general rendezvous of the army at Newmarket, and on 2 June Cornet Joyce seized the king from his parliamentary guards at Holmby House (Northamptonshire) and took him to Newmarket.

The army had now committed itself to political action, and all the indications are that it was done on rank-and-file initiative and that the officers had to choose between following or resigning their posts. Joyce's capture of the king is a case in point. As Christopher Hill points out, Cromwell, who had now thrown in his lot with the army again, knew and approved of Joyce's plans to replace the king's parliamentary guards with New Model Army men, but there is no evidence that he initiated them.[93] Nor was Cromwell the main author of the army's subsequent manifestos, which were largely drafted by his son-in-law Henry Ireton. The army's *Humble Remonstrance* (4 June) agreed that the army should not disband until its grievances were met. In the meantime an army council was to sit, consisting of two commissioned officers and two 'agitator' privates from each regiment. Slowly the army began to march towards London, rejecting parliament's minor concessions. In a development unique among sixteenth- and seventeenth-century European armies, the New Model Army now became politicized. Although in continental armies mutinies about wage arrears and poor conditions were common, none developed into a political movement. On 5 June the New Model Army announced in *A Solemn Engagement* that it refused to disband until its grievances were met. Nine days later in *A Representation of the Army*, drafted by Ireton, Cromwell and Lambert at St Albans, the army announced that it was 'not a mere mercenary Army', but a political force with a political programme: a purge of the present parliament; future parliaments of fixed duration; guaranteed right of the people to petition parliament; liberty of tender consciences. They were an army dedicated to 'the defence of our own and the people's just rights and liberties'.[94] It would be easy to see these documents as milestones on the army's road to regicide and republic. This is wrong. As will be seen, the army was still intent on securing a monarchical post-war settlement.

During the next few weeks, the army's political aims became even clearer because during July they were incorporated in *The Heads of the Proposals*, which were intended to be presented to the king as the army's terms for a settlement. Instead of marching directly on London, the army fell back on Reading, where in July *The Heads* were debated in the army council, now consisting of agitators as well as officers.

---

[92] A. Hopper, *'Black Tom': Sir Thomas Fairfax and the English Revolution* (2007), chapter 4.

[93] C. Hill, *God's Englishman: Oliver Cromwell and the English Revolution* (1970), pp. 88–9. This is a view supported by Gentles, *New Model Army*, p. 169 and Woolrych, *Britain in Revolution*, p. 363.

[94] A. S. P. Woodhouse, ed., *Puritanism and Liberty, Being the Army Debates, 1647–9* (2nd edn, 1974), pp. 401–3 (A Solemn Engagement), pp. 403–9 (A Representation of the Army).

Information

The Heads of the Proposals, 1647

These were published on 2 August, and were largely the work of Henry Ireton, reflecting not only his views and those of his father-in-law Oliver Cromwell but also those of their Political Independent civilian allies, with whom they remained in close touch during this period. Both Wharton and Saye and Sele were at Reading early in July and their collaboration with Cromwell and Ireton continued throughout the summer.

The Heads of the Proposals is an explicit statement of 'the cause' which the army and its Political Independent allies were working to achieve:

- a constitutional settlement with the king that provided for regular biennial parliaments
- rational reform of parliamentary representation which was linked accurately to regional variations in population and wealth
- parliamentary control of the army and navy, and parliamentary appointment of the great officers of state for ten years
- a religious settlement that maintained a national Church with bishops, but the bishops were to be stripped of their coercive powers, and all laws enforcing attendance at parish churches were to be abolished, leaving all Protestants free to worship in their own ways
- as a bait to the king to accept it, an Act of Oblivion that exempted only a few noted royalists.

It was the most generous settlement the king had yet been offered, much more so than the Propositions of Newcastle of July 1646.

What raised the hopes of both military and civilian Political Independent leaders that Charles would accept the document was the fact that for much of the summer the army seemed united behind this programme. The agitators showed little unease at Cromwell's negotiations with the king at Caversham (near Reading) and as the army slowly marched towards London in July. The only chink in army unity at this stage was caused by the speed of the march towards London. Cromwell advised against a speedy occupation of the capital, which might seem as if the army was dictating a settlement. 'Whatsoever you get by a treaty, whatsoever comes to be settled upon us in that way, it will be firm and durable, it will be conveyed over to posterity . . . that which you have by force, I look upon it as nothing.'[95] But the agitators wanted an immediate march on London to take vengeance on the Eleven Members (including Holles) whom the army had singled out for impeachment because they were believed to be behind the anti-army measures passed earlier in the year.

Events in London soon forced the army leaders to agree. The conservative reaction which swept the country after the Civil War also made a deep impression on many in London who were as anxious as anyone for a return to political normality. Many believed that this was the major remedy for 'the decay of trade'. Conservative popular sentiment, as well as fear of army retaliation, encouraged Holles and his colleagues to step up their plans for a Presbyterian counter-revolution. At the end of July their plans culminated in a series of organized popular demonstrations in favour of peace and settlement, and against a Militia Bill designed to restore Independents to the London militia. On 26 July, apparently with the connivance of Holles, Waller and Sir John Clotworthy,[96] a mob invaded the chamber of the Commons and forced the House to pass a resolution inviting the king to come to London. Eight days later the army assembled on Hounslow Heath. Significantly, the Political Independent MPs joined it, rather than support a Presbyterian sell-out to the king. On 6 August the army, without any resistance, occupied Westminster, and on 8 August the City.

The occupation of London, however, did not cause the army to deviate from its efforts, in cooperation with the Political Independents, to secure the king's agreement to *The Heads of the Proposals*. Negotiations with Charles continued and in parliament most of the major provisions of *The Heads* were discussed in the form of parliamentary bills. The memoirs of John Berkeley, one of the intermediaries between the king and the army, make it clear that Charles (as always) never intended to reach a settlement, but that was not known at the time. The main obvious obstacle to a settlement on *The Heads* was the opposition of John Lilburne and the Levellers, who feared that the 'grandees' (the name they disparagingly gave to the senior army officers) intended to allow the king back unconditionally. The army's occupation of London allowed the Levellers for the first time to influence sections of opinion within the army on a significant scale. In October, agitators who had close links with the Levellers appeared in five cavalry regiments.[97] Together with John Wildman, the new agitators drafted *The Case of the Armie Truly Stated*, a long indictment of the 'grandees' for backsliding. It urged the army to adopt the radical religious and constitutional programme of the Levellers. This was presented to Fairfax on 18 October and a week later was followed by a detailed plan for a constitutional and religious settlement, *The Agreement of the People*,

[95] Abbott, *Writings and Speeches*, I, pp. 481–3.

[96] V. Pearl, 'London's counter-revolution', in G. E. Aylmer, ed., *The Interregnum: the quest for settlement 1646–60* (1973), p. 52.

[97] A. Woolrych, *Soldiers and Statesmen: The General Council of the Army and its Debates 1647–8* (1987), pp. 203–6. This and Gentles, *The New Model Army*, chs. 6 and 7, are the best detailed accounts of these crowded months. More succinct but equally useful is I. Gentles's article in Adamson, ed., *The English Civil War*.

which differed significantly from *The Heads* and threatened to disrupt the army unity on *The Heads* programme which had been maintained throughout the summer.[98]

The disruptive effects became apparent when Fairfax referred *The Case of the Armie Truly Stated* to the general council of the army at its meetings at the army headquarters in Putney at the end of October.

Information

The Agreement of the People, October 1647

Unlike *The Heads*, this proposed a completely new constitution to be approved by the people.

- The current parliament was to be dissolved 'to prevent the many inconveniencies apparently arising from the long continuance of the same persons in authority'.
- Future parliaments should be elected once every two years.
- Parliamentary constituencies should be reorganized 'according to the number of inhabitants', although nothing was said about who should have the vote.
- The powers of the single-chamber parliament thus elected were deemed to be 'inferior only to theirs who choose them', and included the making of laws, appointing officers of state and making peace and war.
- Parliaments, however, should have no power to interfere with 'our native rights', which included people's freedom of religion, immunity from conscription and equality before the law.

The Agreement thus represented a direct attack on the New Model Army's political programme.

So began the famous Putney Debates in the general council of the army, which took place largely in Putney church between 28 October and 8 November, and which are well known because of the discovery in the late nineteenth century in Worcester

---

[98] The authorship and the significance of *The Case* and *The Agreement* have been hotly debated in recent years. Some historians, notably John Morrill and Phil Baker, argue that these documents did not come from Leveller sources but from within the army: Morrill and Baker, 'The Case of the Armie truly restated' in M. Mendle, ed., *The Putney Debates of 1647: the army, the Levellers and the English State* (2001), and E. Vernon and P. Baker, 'What was the first Agreement of the people? *HJ*, 53 (2010). I have not been persuaded by their arguments.

College Oxford of the shorthand notes of the debates made by William Clarke, secretary to the general council.[99] In one sense Clarke's account of the debate on 28 October masks the fundamental disagreement between the Leveller representatives (John Wildman and Maximilian Petty and the agitators who had emerged a few weeks earlier) and the leaders of the New Model Army. This is so because the debates focused largely on the question of the 'engagements' entered into by the army in May and June: grandees and agitators taking different views about whether the engagements were binding. But the root of these differences became clearer in subsequent debates as army leaders like Cromwell and Ireton indicated their lack of interest in the kind of wide-ranging constitutional changes some Levellers hoped for. The most dramatic example of these differences is the debate that took place on 29 October (interestingly, probably not in Putney church but in the nearby quartermaster-general's lodgings)[100] on the question of who should have the vote. In what proved to be a tactical error, Cromwell and Ireton allowed a debate on the franchise, and the exchange between the army Leveller, Colonel Thomas Rainsborough, and Ireton has lost none of its significance in illustrating the gulf that had opened up within army ranks as a direct result of Leveller influence:

> *Rainsborough*: For really I think that the poorest he that is in England hath a life to live as the greatest he; and therefore truly, sir, I think it's clear, that every man that is to live under a government ought first by his own consent to put himself under that government; and I do think that the poorest man in England is not at all bound in a strict sense to that government that he hath not had a voice to put himself under . . .
> *Ireton*: . . . I think that no person hath a right to an interest or share in the disposing of the affairs of the kingdom, and in determining or choosing those that shall determine what laws we shall be ruled by here – no person hath a right to this, that hath not a permanent fixed interest in this kingdom.[101]

In the debates in the first week of November, more serious divisions opened up between grandees and agitators on the question of continuing negotiations with the king. In Cromwell's absence, on 5 November Rainsborough secured a vote in favour of sending a letter to the Speaker of the Commons giving the impression that the army was no longer in favour of negotiating a monarchical settlement. This vote was subsequently overturned, but by 8 November Cromwell and Fairfax had decided that the debates must end and army unity be reimposed. Accordingly, agitators were no longer admitted to debates of the army council and the army was ordered to disperse and meet at three separate rendezvous.

Whether or not Cromwell engineered the escape of Charles I from Hampton Court on 11 November is uncertain. He may have done so, since it certainly helped

---

[99] A. S. P. Woodhouse, ed., *Puritanism and Liberty, being the Army Debates 1647–9* (3rd edn. 1985, reissued with new preface 1992); L. Le Claire, 'The survival of the manuscript' in Mendle, ed., *Putney Debates*.
[100] A. Woolrych, *Soldiers and Statesmen*, pp. 230–1.
[101] Woodhouse, ed., *Puritanism and Liberty*, pp. 55–6.

the grandees to reimpose military discipline and close the rifts in the army's ranks. However, what makes it unlikely that Cromwell was behind Charles's escape is that it ended the hopes of reaching a settlement on *The Heads of the Proposals* which Cromwell and his allies had been working to achieve for months. In the face of the renewed threat posed by the king, the army closed ranks. Leveller dissatisfaction at the failure to get the support of the 'grandees' for *The Agreement of the People* at Putney produced only a ripple of opposition in the army. At Corkbush Field near Ware (Hertfordshire) on 15 November, a Leveller-inspired mutiny in two regiments was crushed efficiently and brutally, but also easily.[102] Discussions of religious and constitutional issues were temporarily abandoned. The army was again united behind the grandees, but now with the aim not of reaching a settlement based on *The Heads of the Proposals*, but of defeating another wave of counter-revolution.

Charles, the Scots and the second civil war

Before he escaped from Hampton Court, parliament sent Charles another set of proposals for a settlement with him, the Four Bills.

Information

The Four Bills, December 1647

The first four proposals were to be converted into bills to receive Charles's assent – 'the Four Bills':

- Parliament was to control the militia and navy for twenty years, and thereafter the king's decisions were to be ratified by parliament.
- All declarations made against parliament and its supporters were to be annulled.
- All peerages granted since May 1642 were to be cancelled.
- The present parliament was allowed to meet anywhere in England it chose.

Annexed to these proposals were others that included the king's approval for the abolition of bishops and the Book of Common Prayer, and the exclusion from pardon of as many royalists as had been excluded in the Propositions of Newcastle.

---

[102] M. Kishlansky, 'What happened at Ware?', *H.J.*, XXV (1982) denies that Cromwell was there. But for a convincing argument to the contrary, see Woolrych, *Soldiers and Statesmen*, pp. 281–4.

Charles, however, gave them no more serious consideration than he had previous proposals. Instead after he escaped he rejected the Four Bills and concluded an 'Engagement' with the Scots, promising to establish Scottish Presbyterianism in England for three years. The Engagement represented a victory for a conservative faction in Scotland led by the marquis of Hamilton, who from the beginning had questioned the wisdom of allying with the English parliament. Now these doubts were confirmed by the victory of the anti-Presbyterian army in England, and radical covenanters, like Argyll and Johnston of Wariston, who had supported the alliance, consequently lost a great deal of influence in Scotland. At this time, too, the threat of a military offensive against the English parliamentarians was intensified by royalist hopes of bringing the Irish Confederates into a pan-British alliance against their English opponents. This failed largely because of the military weakness of the Confederates at this time. But that was not yet clear and English opinion united in a backlash of anger at Charles's attempts to use two of his 'British' kingdoms against them. This is the context for the passage in the English parliament early in January 1648 of a vote that 'the Lords and Commons do declare that they will make no further addresses or applications to the King', the so-called Vote of No Addresses, seemingly another 'signpost' or 'milestone' in these crowded post-war months on the road to regicide and republican rule.

This one, however, proved to be as misleading as previous ones in this regard. The finality of the Vote of No Addresses was blunted by the continuing evidence that the prevailing sentiment of the majority in England was in favour of a settlement, a return to pre-war order in society and government. The reasons had been apparent since 1645, as has been seen, and were reinforced by the events of 1647. Dislike of high taxation, centralization, arbitrary rule by low-born county committeemen and disorders provoked by the army, recurred in the local protests (the first and most dramatic being the Christmas Day riots at Canterbury in 1647), and county petitions received by parliament in December 1647 and the first part of 1648. In south Wales and in the heavily taxed south-eastern counties of Essex and Kent, this desire for a return to traditional forms of government exploded in April, May and June into a series of rebellions against parliament and its county committees. Off the Kentish coast the parliamentary navy revolted against its Leveller admiral, Rainsborough, and reinstated its old Presbyterian commanders. In the north the major garrisons were taken over by pro-royalist forces. Generally, though, there is little evidence of ardent royalist fervour among the rebels of 1648.[103] Like the Clubmen of 1645 they were more concerned to demonstrate their dislike of the political programme, and especially the religious aims, of the New Model Army. This series of uncoordinated risings hardly deserves being called a war. The superior coordinated forces of the New Model Army (Hardress Waller in Cornwall, Cromwell in south Wales and John Lambert in the north) soon

---

[103] Morrill, *Revolt*; D. Underdown, *Pride's Purge: politics during the Puritan Revolution* (1971), ch. 4. For a different view of the second civil war, which emphasizes the royalism of the army's opponents, see B. Lyndon, 'The second civil war', *History* (1986) and 'Essex and the king's cause in 1648', *H.J.* (1986).

restored army control. The Scottish invasion, too, when it came early in July proved a minor threat. The weakness of the Scottish army reflected the internal divisions in Scotland; it was badly led by Hamilton and ill-supplied. Cromwell's victory at a series of battles round Preston (Lancashire) from 17 to 19 August paved the way for Hamilton's surrender on 25 August, and Cromwell's expedition to Scotland, where he allied with the enemies of the 'Engagers', Argyll and Johnston of Wariston. Pontefract in Yorkshire held out until March 1649, but by October 1648 the 'war' was over.

The risings of 1648 and the Scottish invasion reunited the army, but widened the gap between it and most parliamentarians. The longing of most people outside the army for a treaty with the king had increased. Even the Political Independent MPs who had supported the army in 1647 (Valerie Pearl calls them 'royal Independents')[104] now broke with the army and supported the movement in parliament for a reconciliation with the king in the summer and autumn of 1648: the revocation of the Vote of No Addresses, the readmittance of the Eleven Members, and the preparations of proposals to be put to the king at Newport on the Isle of Wight in September.

Given all this, what determined a small minority (largely, though not exclusively, in the New Model Army) to maintain their opposition to the king to the point of revolution? Why was Charles I executed less than six months later?

One possibility is that the 'revolutionaries' of 1648–9 were driven by a republican ideology. However, there is no evidence that any of them (with the exception of Henry Marten and Edmund Ludlow) held republican ideas that envisaged a State without a monarchy. But before this idea is discounted totally, it is worth considering the extent to which there was a 'republican' tradition in English political thought in this period, not an anti-monarchical republican tradition, but one that has led some historians to call England 'a monarchical republic' (see above, pp. 83–4). There is no evidence that republican ideas of any kind played a *direct* part in bringing about the king's execution,[105] but it may be that the power of the monarchical republican idea (noted by Patrick Collinson) and the wide interest in classical humanism and republicanism (noted by Marku Peltonen) may have at least eased the way towards an acceptance of what happened on 30 January 1649. One historian who has developed this idea is Ann Hughes in an excellent article on the execution of Charles I on the BBC history website. In it she writes that 'my argument is that regicide was not simply a result of the impasse of 1648 but a solution made thinkable by longer-term aspects of English political culture and history'.[106]

Another idea that has some force is the possibility that Charles himself contributed to his own fate. It may be that his failure to negotiate seriously with his opponents in the 1640s was rooted not only in his expectations that one day his enemies would fall

---

[104] Pearl, 'The "Royal Independents"', pp. 69–96.

[105] See D. Norbrook, *Writing the English Republic: Poetry, Rhetoric and Politics, 1627–60* (1999) for a different view.

[106] Ann Hughes, 'The execution of Charles I', **www.bbc.co.uk/history/british/civil_war_revolution/ charlesi_execution_01.shtml**.

out, allowing him to be restored unconditionally to power, but in his plan to fashion himself as a royal martyr on whose image the monarchy would be rebuilt more strongly than ever – as indeed did happen. In the last months of his life, Charles seems to have made little effort to hide his attempts to escape (his coded ciphers on this topic sent by his confidante Jane Whorwood were easily broken, unlike the more carefully constructed ones he used to write to Jane on their personal relationship).[107] There is much evidence to support the view that Charles hoped to become a royal martyr, thereby contributing to his own downfall.[108]

A much more powerful reason for Charles's fate in my view is the religious ideology of the men who brought him to the scaffold. They had supported a settlement with the king at the Putney Debates only just over a year before, but were now driven to take revolutionary action. For those who executed the king, the events after his escape from Hampton Court, and especially his use of a pan-Britannic alliance against England, were indisputable proof that a settlement with Charles I would never be made because he had no intention of ever making one. But what made their opposition to Charles even more deadly was that to these realpolitik considerations were added 'ideological' arguments of 'providence'. At an army council prayer meeting at Windsor on 29 April 1648, Cromwell urged his fellow officers

> to a thorough consideration of our actions as an army, as well as ways particularly as private Christians, to see if any iniquity could be found in them, and what it was, that if possible we might find it out and so remove the cause of such sad rebukes which were upon us by reason of our iniquities.[109]

During the second civil war, some soldiers became convinced that the cause of their 'sad rebukes' was the leniency shown to the 'contrivers' of the renewed war. As Cromwell said, 'their fault who have appeared in this summer's business, is certainly double to theirs who were in the first, because it is the repetition of the same offence against all the witnesses that God has borne'.[110] This feeling explains why the army's treatment of the defeated rebels in 1648 was much harsher than that meted out to those who had opposed it during the first civil war. After the defeat of the Essex and Kent rebels at the siege of Colchester in August 1648, Fairfax had two of the rebellion's leaders shot after a summary court martial. Gradually during the summer the anger of the army leaders came to be directed at the king as 'the man of blood', 'the capital and grand author of all our troubles'.[111] What precipitated the 'revolutionaries' to violent action was the conviction that Charles I not only would never make any agreement with them, but also was a sinful man whose death was required to remove the cause of

---

[107] S. Poynting, 'Deciphering the king: Charles I's letters to Jane Whorwood', *The Seventeenth Century*, 21 (2006).

[108] See Sharpe, *Image Wars*, p. 289, for his recent support for this long-established idea.

[109] Abbott, *Writings and Speeches*, I, pp. 598–99.

[110] Ibid., I, p. 691.

[111] Kenyon, *Stuart Constitution*, p. 288.

their 'sad rebukes' and thus regain God's blessing. On 27 December 1648, Thomas Brook delivered a sermon in the House of Commons on the Old Testament Book of Numbers text, chapter 35 verse 33:

> Ye shall not pollute the Land wherein ye are; for blood it defileth the Land, and the Land cannot be cleansed of the blood that is shed therein, but by the blood of him that shed it.[112]

That was a sentiment shared by those who signed the king's death warrant a few days later. Religious zeal was as prominent at the climax of the English Revolution in 1649 as it was at its start in 1640.

1648–1649: the English Revolution

The English Revolution – the purge of parliament in December 1648 and the trial and execution of the king in January 1649 – was carried out by a tiny clique against the wishes of the vast majority in the country. By October 1648 this clique included Ireton among the 'grandees' (though not yet Cromwell, who was in the north), rank-and-file supporters of the agitators in the army, civilian republicans, like Henry Marten and Edmund Ludlow, in parliament, and their militant supporters in the counties, like John Pyne, the 'boss' of the Somerset county committee. On 18 November, with the evidence sent to him in regimental petitions that opinion in the army was running strongly against the king, Ireton persuaded the army council (now shorn of the agitators) to accept his *Remonstrance of the Army*, calling for a purge of parliament and the king's trial,[113] under the threat that the Newport negotiations were going to succeed: indeed, on 15 November the Commons had voted to accept Charles's request to come to London. Also early in November Ireton began negotiations with the civilian Leveller leaders, which culminated in the so-called Whitehall Debates early in December and two revised versions of *The Agreement of the People*. The debates revealed grave differences between Levellers and 'grandees' on the extent of religious toleration desirable, as well as on constitutional issues as seen at Putney earlier. But they did ensure, temporarily, Leveller support for the army's slow march on London. Ironically, the Newport proposals were finally rejected by Charles at the same time as the army entered Whitehall for the second time on 2 December.

Obstinately, the Commons continued to discuss the Newport treaty, and on 5 December actually voted, by 129 to 83 votes, to continue the negotiations with the king. Army retaliation was inevitable; the only hesitation appears to have been on the question of a purge or a dissolution of parliament. Wisely, Ludlow advised Ireton against a dissolution and new elections, which would only have ensured the return of

---

[112] R. M. Jeffs, ed., *The English Revolution: fast sermons to parliament* (35 vols., 1971), XXXII, p. 81.

[113] It is difficult to accept the suggestion that the *Remonstrance*'s call for capital punishment upon 'the principal authors' does not refer to the king. For another view see Braddick, *God's Fury, England's Fire*, p. 556.

another set of MPs hostile to the army. In the purge, which began on the morning of 6 December when Colonel Pride and Lord Grey of Groby stood at the door of the Commons, about 110 MPs were forcibly excluded and about 260 other MPs voluntarily withdrew (of the latter, about a hundred returned after February 1649).

Many, of course, though supporting the purge, refused to accept that the next step would be the trial and execution of the king. After Cromwell returned to London on 6 December, he was at the centre of yet more negotiations with the king.[114] Exactly when he decided that these were fruitless is uncertain, but by the end of December he seems to have been converted to the view that such negotiations could not succeed, and that the king should be removed from the political scene by deposition or by execution (I think the latter). The military threat of Ormonde in Ireland may have been a contributory (but surely not the main) factor in this conversion.[115] Others took a less decisive line, leading Sean Kelsey to the plausible (but I think unconvincing) view that, even after the trial began, the king's execution was not inevitable, but the trial was meant to press Charles to reach a settlement that would have allowed him to live.[116] That, of course, did not happen, and Charles was executed outside the Banqueting Hall on 30 January 1649.

The fact that the events of December 1648 to January 1649 were carried out by a minority drawn largely from outside the traditional ruling elite in England and against the wishes of that elite goes a long way towards explaining the eventual failure of the new English republic. Yet, paradoxically, the history of the republic confirms that only a limited political revolution had taken place in 1648–9, and one that was reversed in 1660. The basic structure of society remained unaffected. But it is surely semantic quibbling to deny the unique revolutionary nature of the abolition of episcopacy, monarchy and the House of Lords, the involvement in politics of masses of people from outside the normal political sphere, and the ventilation of radical ideas of universal importance in the late 1640s. What was done was not as wide-ranging as the Russian Revolution or as permanent as the French Revolution, but if there ever has been an English Revolution, it surely took place from December 1648 to January 1649.

---

[114] See Braddick, *God's Fury, England's Fire*, p. 564 for the details of these negotiations.

[115] J. Adamson, '"The frighted junto": perceptions of Ireland and the last attempts at settlement with Charles I', in J. Peacey, ed., *The Regicides and the Execution of Charles I* (2001).

[116] S. Kelsey, 'The death of Charles I', *H.J.*, 45 (2002); S. Kelsey, 'The trial of Charles I'. *E.H.R.*, 118 (2003). Kelsey's argument receives the support of Braddick, *God's Fury, England's Fire*, ch. 20.

7

The search for a new settlement, 1649–1660

Summary

Conservatism and radicalism in the English Revolution

The 1650s saw a constant tension between those who wanted a return to political and social normality and those who wanted to follow up the political revolution of 1648–9 with sweeping legal, social and religious changes. By the late twentieth century most historians agreed that conservatism not radicalism was the dominant characteristic of the 1650s. This view is reflected in the two titles that I gave this chapter 7 in previous editions of this book: 'Retreat from revolution' (1980) and 'The failure of revolution' (1994 and 2003). This is a view that will be questioned in this chapter.

But its main aim is to examine the attempts of the republican regimes of the 1650s to find policies that would satisfy both the demands for a return to stability and the desire of radicals for further reform.

From 1649 to 1660 major efforts were made to find such policies by:

- the Commonwealth government of the Rump Parliament between 1649 and 1653
- the Barebones Parliament from July to December 1653
- the Cromwellian Protectorate from December 1653 to May 1659

- the many short-lived regimes that were established between May 1659 and the restoration of the monarchy in May 1660.

As will be seen, this search failed. Yet the regimes of the 1650s ruled more successfully, pursued a more radical agenda, and came nearer to achieving a permanent political-constitutional framework which would comprehend revolutionary radicalism and conservative traditionalism than is generally recognized. It is important to understand the reasons for the eventual failure of the republican regimes of the 1650s, but it is equally important that their achievements should not be overlooked.

The search for a 'godly reformation'

The Civil War and its aftermath released radical demands that were far removed from the moderate, constitutional aims of many parliamentarians of 1640–2. In the beginning, conservatives and 'middle-group' politicians had been willing to use popular radicalism for their own immediate political purposes. But soon most of the parliamentary leaders of Westminster, and the gentry rulers in the localities, shied away in horror from the extreme ideas which had been allowed to flourish by their initial tolerance and by the collapse of the old political order. From 1640 until the early 1650s, parliamentary ordinances attempting to suppress pamphlets and books were largely ineffective; the State as well as the Church was in no position to clamp down on the free expression of opinion as it had done before 1640 and as Cromwell was to do after 1655. The collection of pamphlets made in the 1640s and 1650s by a London bookseller, George Thomason, is a good indicator of the quantity of material printed in those two decades. Although he did not get his hands on everything published, Thomason, a fanatically keen bibliophile, collected over 18,000 items between 1640 and 1655, after which the flow diminished; between 1655 and 1660 he collected over 3,000 printed works.[1] The Thomason Collection, which is still intact in the British Library, is a monument to the intellectual activity released by the English Revolution, from the lively, scurrilous and libellous, to the serious, high-minded and academic. It also gives a unique insight into the normally unrecorded beliefs and aspirations of ordinary men and women.

The reforming and radical ideas which flourished in the ideal climate of the 1640s and early 1650s do not fall easily into separate neatly labelled categories, 'economic', 'social', 'religious', 'political'. Individual thinkers and writers moved easily from one topic to another. Samuel Hartlib, for example, appears in the catalogue of the Thomason Collection as the author of tracts on many subjects including Church reform, agriculture, medicine and the creation of a Utopia called Macaria. Even the Levellers, who in the

---

[1] G. Fortescue, *Catalogue of the Pamphlets, Books, etc., Collected by George Thomason 1640–61* (2 vols., 1906), I, p. xxi; II, p. 590.

winter of 1647–8 developed an unusually elaborate internal organization, included people with different views on a wide range of topics. Individual Levellers differed not only on the exact nature of the franchise, but also on religious doctrine: Lilburne for most of his life was an orthodox Calvinist predestinarian; Walwyn propounded the doctrine, often known as antinomianism, that God's grace and salvation were potentially available to all believers. Nor did Leveller pamphlets concentrate solely on demands for political and religious liberty for the individual, but covered a wide range of topics from proposals for prison reform to the evils of monopolists and patentees.

Despite the disparate nature of radical individuals and groups in the 1640s and 1650s, the frequent recurrence of ideas common to them all is as striking as the differences among them. What undoubtedly bound them all together was the popular mid-seventeenth-century belief that the establishment of the perfect society was imminent. Defined in this broad, general sense, there is now little doubt that millenarianism, far from being the creed of a few cranks, was part of the mainstream of English intellectual life in the first half of the seventeenth century, and was widely diffused throughout society at all levels.[2] The belief in the Second Coming, the reign of King Jesus, was widespread among the people at large, as well as among those intellectuals who read the works of influential millenarian writers like Thomas Brightman. Because historians in the past have failed to appreciate this, groups like the Fifth Monarchists have commonly been dismissed as fanatical eccentrics.[3]

Information

The Fifth Monarchy Men

The Fifth Monarchists flourished in the early 1650s and especially among the clothworkers of London. Central to their philosophy were the biblical prophecies in the Books of Revelation and Daniel, which had been the subject of ingenious speculation for centuries. The Fifth Monarchists interpreted the prophecy in Daniel chapter 7, that after the rise and fall of four great empires a kingdom would be established that would last for ever, to mean that Christ's kingdom – the Fifth Monarchy – would follow the collapse of the four great empires of Babylon, Persia, Greece and Rome. Using this and other imaginative interpretations of key Old Testament prophecies (King Charles was the 'little horn' of Revelation, and so on), John Rogers and his followers proclaimed that the execution of Charles was the sign for the establishment of the reign of King Jesus.

---

[2] Lamont, *Godly Rule*, *passim.*; C. Hill, *Antichrist in Seventeenth-Century England* (1971).
[3] For a fundamental revision of this sect, see B. S. Capp, *The Fifth Monarchy Men: a study in seventeenth-century millenarianism* (1972).

Eccentric as these ideas now seem, they were well in line with those held by many people in the mid-seventeenth century. The uniqueness of the Fifth Monarchists lies only in the detailed way they elaborated the structure of the new kingdom of Christ. They had detailed plans:

- for an interim government controlled by a minority, based on the Jewish Sanhedrin, until King Jesus should return to rule in person
- to abolish the legal profession and establish the Mosaic Law, and
- to bring about the millennium by force and to establish the reign of King Jesus over all the world.

Other individuals and groups were less precise than the Fifth Moanarchists about the shape that the millennium should take and the way in which it should be brought about, but were no less sincere that a new age was at hand.

The millenarian ideal of a 'godly reformation' was most commonly expressed in religious terms. The astounding proliferation of religious sects in the 1640s and 1650s can be confusing to the student who is confronted with an array of apparently exotic sects – Particular Baptists and General Baptists, Grindletonians and Muggletonians, Quakers and Ranters – with widely differing theological standpoints – adult or infant baptism, predestinarianism or free will.

Information

The Baptists

These were undoubtedly the most successful of the new religious sects, whose only rivals in terms of popularity were the Quakers. By the late 1640s there were 35–40,000 Baptists, scattered throughout England and Wales, less numerous than the Quakers in the latter's heartland of northern England, but very strong in London, southern England and Wales, with especially strong support in the parliamentary armies.

There were two types of Baptist, each with their own organizations: the General Baptists who believed that God's grace was open to all, and Particular Baptists who held predestinarian beliefs that only a minority were chosen for salvation.

All Baptists, however, shared the belief that baptism should take place not immediately after birth but only when the person to be baptised was fully aware of and had agreed to the decision that he or she had made to enter the Church.

The differences between the new religious sects are important, but all were united in developing and extending two beliefs that it has been seen were characteristic of Puritanism from the late sixteenth century onwards. The first was the belief that God worked through the individual. The Protestant Reformation had challenged the notion that the interpretation of the word of God in the Bible was the preserve of the priesthood. The radical sects of the mid-seventeenth century took this a step further and claimed that 'a poor plain countryman by the spirit which he hath received, is better able to judge of truth and error touching the things of God than the greatest philosopher, scholar or doctor in the world that is destitute of it'.[4] Since this conviction was common to most religious sects of the period, each developed a very similar programme of religious reforms. The belief in the primacy of the inner spirit of every individual precluded any concept of a national, uniform Church imposed on the individual by the State, and also meant a drastic reduction in the power of the clergy over the individual. It was also compatible with a wide extension of religious toleration, at least for all Protestants, although most sects qualified this by maintaining that individuals in each congregation must abide by the interpretations decided on by that congregation. Since there was to be no state Church and individual congregations were to be autonomous, ministers were to be elected by congregations and (to emphasize their rejection of a clerical elite) were to be one *of* the congregation. As if all this (the abolition of the state Church, religious toleration, congregationalism) were not radical enough, most radical sects also demanded the abolition of tithes (so attacking the property rights of landowners who received the most valuable tithes in the form of rent) and advocated the rights of women to take part in church government and sometimes to preach (so striking at the roots of the traditional, hierarchical and patriarchal society).[5] Closely related to these ideas was a second belief that united many religious reformers in the 1650s: that there was an urgent need for 'further reformation' and especially for 'a reformation of manners' to eliminate sin from people's lives (see pp. 262–3). In the 1640s this had led parliament to undertake not only a godly programme of reform of church government and liturgy (including the abolition of bishops, the Book of Common Prayer and traditional festivals like Christmas, Easter, Whitsuntide and Rogationtide, and the destruction of 'popish' statues and other images in churches), but also measures to encourage the abolition of immorality, which was considered vital (as the 1642 ordinance abolishing stage-plays said) 'to appease and avert the Wrath of God'.[6]

Increasingly, measures that in the 1640s had helped to unite godly MPs lost their unifying force among propertied, conservative MPs because of their association with the radical demands of the religious sects that have just been discussed. However,

---

[4] C. Hill, *The World Turned Upside Down: radical ideas during the English Revolution* (1972), p. 80, quoting William Dell.

[5] For the role of women and contemporary attitudes to them, see E. M. Williams, 'Women preachers in the civil war', *J.M.H.*, I (1929), pp. 561–9; K. Thomas, 'Women and the civil war sects', *P. & P.*, XIII (1958), pp. 42–62; Patricia Higgins, 'The reactions of women, with special reference to women petitioners', in B. Manning, ed., *Politics, Religion and the English Civil War* (1973), pp. 179–222.

[6] C. H. Firth and R. S. Rait, eds., *Acts and Ordinances of the Interregnum* (2 vols., 1911), I, p. 26.

it is arguable that the subversive implications of this programme would not have become apparent or abhorrent to conservative opinion but for the activities of those associated with the Quakers, who developed that programme in a very extreme way indeed.

Information

The Quakers

George Fox and the early Quakers of the 1650s were very different from their respectable, pacific successors. They were also very successful. By 1660 there were an estimated 400,000–600,000 Quakers.[7]

The Quakers of the 1650s carried the Puritan emphasis on the primacy of individual conscience ('the inner light') much further than any other organized religious sect in this decade, arguing that what their consciences told them were 'right' thoughts and actions were lawful regardless of what church ministers or anyone else decreed. This radical doctrine, voiced as it was by the middling and lower sorts of English society, frightened the wealthy and propertied. The dangerous implications for social and political order of their stress on the primacy of 'the inner light' was confirmed by their campaign for the abolition of tithes, their refusal to take off their hats in the presence of social superiors and (as will be seen) their close involvement with political radicalism. Given all this, the savage treatment meted out by the first Protectorate Parliament in 1656 to one of the principal Quaker leaders, James Nayler (see below, p. 278), is hardly surprising. Nor is the horrified reaction of respectable opinion to the militant and violent activities of some Quakers in 1659. This undoubtedly contributed to the support for the restoration of Charles II in the following year (see below, p. 283).

A few people in the early 1650s may have taken the emphasis on the primacy of 'the inner light' even further than did the Quakers. In 1650, hostile contemporaries began to publish lurid pamphlets with eye-catching titles like *The Ranters Religion, Or a Faithfull and Infallible Narrative of Their Diabolicall Opinions*, complete with woodcut drawings of naked men and women.

---

[7] Barry Reay, *The Quakers and the English Revolution* (1985).

Information

Who were the Ranters?

Ranters were said to hold two distinctive beliefs:

- antinomianism (the belief that God's salvation is open to all believers)
- pantheism (the belief that God is not only the creator of all things but in all things; and therefore that sin, which is the negation of God, cannot exist).

To demonstrate these beliefs, it was said, Ranters indulged freely in sexual promiscuity, swearing, drunkenness and all activities that others considered to be sinful.

Since most sources for studying the Ranters are hostile ones, it is not known how extensively such views were held or even whether the Ranters existed at all. There is no Ranter writing that puts forward a full-blown philosophy combining all the elements of antinomianism and pantheism, as well as advocating the practical expression of that philosophy, in ways that hostile pamphleteers and journalists alleged. Enterprising journalists undoubtedly used their imaginations to write newspaper articles and pamphlets that would increase their circulation figures, and orthodox churchmen were not unwilling to use stories of Ranter excesses to frighten back to the fold anyone tempted to stray from orthodox Protestantism. This has led at least one historian, J. C. Davis, in *Fear, Myth and History: the Ranters and historians* (1986) to suggest that the Ranters did not exist. Yet, although it is fairly certain that there was no organized Ranter sect with a coherent ideology and the mass support enjoyed by Quakers, it is highly likely that a few enthusiastic radicals (like Abiezer Coppe, the author of *A Fiery Flying Roll*) voiced antinomian and pantheistic views in the 1650s.

Often interwoven with, and gaining its force from, the same millenarian aspirations as religious radicalism in the 1640s and 1650s was a strand of secular radicalism, which was also as bewilderingly diverse in the range of ideas it dealt with and the number of thinkers it threw up. It is hardly an exaggeration to say that every institution and aspect of life was subjected to minute and often drastic criticism. Apart from the political reforms proposed by the Levellers, however, two major spheres absorbed a large part of the energies of the radicals: reform of the law and of education. Many of the radicals' complaints about the law – its slowness, expense and unintelligibility – might well have been written in the early nineteenth century. Throughout their writings

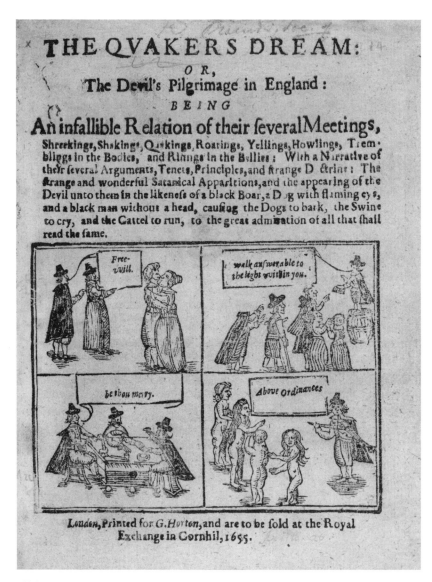

Figure 7.1 Frontispiece of *The Quakers Dream*, 1655.
Source: © British Library Board/Thomason Collection: E.833.14.

two principal proposals for reform recur: first, decentralization of the law courts and abolition of unwieldy and inefficient central courts like chancery, to make justice available locally and cheaply; and secondly, codification of the law in English, so that it might be freely and intelligibly available to all. Professional groups, like lawyers and clerics, were prime targets for the radicals; so too were university teachers 'which occasions all the trouble in the world'. There exists a vast corpus of writings pillorying universities and university teachers (like lawyers) for hindering rather than serving the cause for which they were established. 'The secrets of the creation', wrote Gerrard

Figure 7.2 Frontispiece of *The Ranters Religion*, 1650. Both Figures 7.1 and 7.2 show how printers and publishers cashed in on contemporary fears of radical groups like the Quakers and Ranters, no doubt exaggerating their views and lifestyles in order to boost sales of their pamphlets.
Source: © British Library Board/Thomason Collection: E.619.8.

Winstanley, 'have been locked up under the traditional, parrot-like speaking from the universities and colleges for scholars.'[8] Universities were to be reformed as part of a fundamental restructuring of education, establishing universal education for both sexes to the age of eighteen years, and university training for those suitable. But in this educational utopia the university curriculum was to be stripped of its emphasis on the classics and divinity, and was to concentrate on vocational and scientific subjects.

Often, of course, reform of the law and education was only part of much wider schemes for reforming society as a whole. Many moderate social reformers were simply concerned to attack the symptoms of the acute economic crisis of 1649 by providing

---

[8] Quoted in J. C. Davis, *Fear, Myth and History: the Ranters and historians* (1986), pp. 242, 244.

labour exchanges, which was one of the functions of Hartlib's proposed 'Office for Addresses'.[9] Other radicals, however, were not content with reform within the existing structure of society. Gerrard Winstanley is important as a political theorist of the stature of contemporaries like James Harrington and Thomas Hobbes, and his writings illustrate the way in which 'secular'-looking ideas were inextricably rooted in religious thought.[10] But what makes Winstanley particularly interesting is that not only was he a religious visionary who advocated the restructuring of many major aspects of society, government, law and education, but also he tried to put that formula to the practical test. Developing the 'Norman Yoke' idea common to other contemporary radical thinkers – the idea that before the Norman Conquest there existed a golden age, when men lived freely and equally under the law and the earth was 'a common treasury of all mankind' – Winstanley argued that the conquest established the existing social and political structure which he wanted to overthrow and, in its place, establish a state of pure communism, in which the land would be owned communally, in which there would be no need for law or the State, and in which there would be universal education. Later he compromised by envisaging a transitional stage in which magistrates would temporarily be necessary,[11] but he went further than any other thinker towards a total reappraisal and subversion of the traditional society. For a year from April 1649, Winstanley and his followers (their enemies called them the Diggers, they called themselves 'True Levellers') attempted to set up a commune on the commonland of St George's Hill at Walton, and later at Cobham Heath, Surrey.[12] Their efforts were tragic and pathetic and stood no chance of success in the face of violent opposition from local landowners and tenant farmers. It remains to be seen to what extent and why not only the True Levellers, but the hopes of many radicals for the creation of a new society, a 'godly reformation', were disappointed following the execution of the king.

The Rump Parliament, 1649–1653

Conservatism and the Rump

In the weeks following the execution of the king, the government of the country passed into the hands of the Rump Parliament, those members of parliament who had survived

---

[9] C. Wilson, 'The other face of mercantilism', *T.R.H.S.*, 5th ser., IX (1959), pp. 81–101, repr. in D. C. Coleman, ed., *Revisions in Mercantilism* (1969), pp. 118–39.

[10] The best introductions to Winstanley are C. Hill, ed., *Winstanley: The Law of Freedom and other writings* (1973) and J. Gurney, *Brave Community: the Digger Movement in the English Revolution* (2007).

[11] J. C. Davis, 'Gerrard Winstanley and the Restoration of the True Magistracy', *P. & P.*, LXX (1976), pp. 76–93. Davis qualifies Hill's analysis of Winstanley's writings, as do Lotte Mulligan, John K. Graham and Judith Richards, 'Winstanley: a case for the man as he said he was', *J. Eccl. H.*, XXVIII (1977), pp. 57–75.

[12] Hill, *World Turned Upside Down*, pp. 86–103. Although the evidence is thin, Dr Hill thinks that other Digger colonies were established in Northamptonshire, Kent, Buckinghamshire, Hertfordshire, Middlesex, Bedfordshire, Leicestershire Gloucestershire and Nottinghamshire.

Pride's Purge in December 1648. They were to hold supreme legislative and executive power until they were expelled by the army in April 1653. The Rump faced opposition from conservative opinion in the country. Pro-royalist sentiment in the country was revived by the publication of *Eikon Basilike*, purportedly the work of Charles I, which portrayed the king in the image of 'the royal martyr' he had fashioned for himself in the last part of his life. In the months following the execution of the king, royalist sentiment reached unparalleled heights.[13] But the Rump's most vociferous critics came from the radicals.

In their first few months of power, radical expectations were at fever pitch. 'Me thinks I see the kingdom of Jesus Christ begin to flourish, while the wicked . . . do now perish and fade like a blowne-off-blossom', wrote William Rowse to Speaker Lenthall. When the rule of the saints had been established in England, believed John Owen, God would 'sooner or later shake all the Monarchies of the Earth'. 'Beware of Nol Crumwel's Army', John Spittlehouse warned Rome, 'lest Hugh Peter come to preach in Peter's Chaire.'[14] Disillusionment came less rapidly for some than others. In 1650 Winstanley the Digger still advocated supporting the Rump as a lesser evil than the restoration of the monarchy,[15] as did many other radicals. It was the Levellers who led the way in denouncing the new regime, undoubtedly because the Rump's extremely narrow representative nature offended their democratic aspirations. John Lilburne's two-part pamphlet, *Englands New Chains Discovered* (February and March 1649), sneered at 'this new kind of liberty' offered by the Rump, which was no liberty at all:

> A Councel of State is hastily erected for Guardians thereof, who to that end are possessed with power to order and dispose all the forces appertaining to England by Sea or Land, to dispose of the publicke Treasure, to command any person whatsoever before them, to give oath for the discovering of Truth, to imprison any that shall dis-obey their commands, and such as they shall judge contumatious. What now is become of that liberty that no mans person shall be attached or imprisoned, or otherwise dis-eased of his Free-hold, or free Customs but by lawful judgement of his equals?[16]

By 1653 radical disillusionment was complete. It is a measure of Cromwell's ability to straddle conservative and radical opinion that in 1649 he was denounced by the Levellers, and in 1653 was a mouthpiece of the radicals' disappointment at the Rump. According to Whitelocke's account of the dissolution of the Rump on 20 April 1653, Cromwell 'told the House, that they had sat long enough . . . that some of them were whoremasters . . . that others of them were drunkards, and some corrupt and unjust

---

[13] Sharpe; *Image Wars*, ch. 12; B. Worden, 'The royalism of Andrew Marvell,' in J. McElligott and D. L. Smith, eds., *Royalists and Royalism during the English Civil Wars* (2007).

[14] Quoted in Capp, *Fifth Monarchy Men*, pp. 55, 53.

[15] G. E. Aylmer, ed., 'England's spirit unfoulded', *P. & P.*, XL (1968), pp. 3–15.

[16] Aylmer, ed., *Levellers*, pp. 143–4.

Figure 7.3 Frontispiece to *Eikon Basilike*, 1649. Often reproduced, singly as well as in *Eikon Basilike*, this image of Charles I as a royal martyr resonated loudly in succeeding decades, promoting royalist support. Charles is shown leaving the adversities of the world (on the left), putting aside his earthly crown (at his feet) and about to wear, Christ-like, a crown of thorns (in his hand) and an eternal divine crown (above his head).
Source: © The Trustees of the British Museum. All rights reserved.

men and scandalous to the profession of the gospel, and it was not fit that they should sit as a parliament any longer'.[17]

This kind of exaggerated language is explained by the Rump's failure to bring about the 'godly reformation' hoped for by the Levellers, religious sects and many in the army. It is true that the political changes introduced by the Rump were dramatic enough. Immediately after the execution of the king, the Rump ordered the seclusion of any MP

---

[17] Quoted in B. Worden, *The Rump Parliament* (1974), p. 1.

who had voted on 5 December for continuing negotiations with the king. On 4 January 1649 the Rump passed some startling resolutions 'for settling the kingdom' as follows:

> Resolved that the Commons of England, in parliament assembled, do declare that the people are, under God, the original of all just power.
>
> And do also declare, that the Commons of England, in parliament assembled, being chosen by and representing the people, have the supreme power in this nation.
>
> And do also declare, that whatsoever is enacted and declared for law, by the Commons in parliament assembled, hath the force of law, and all the people of this nation are concluded thereby, although the consent and concurrence of king or House of Peers be not had thereunto.[18]

On successive days (6 and 7 February) the Rump went even further, abolishing the House of Lords and the monarchy, and with them disappeared the apparatus of monarchical government: the privy council and the prerogative courts. The administrative departments (the exchequer, the admiralty) were replaced by a council of state and a whole host of subcommittees with wide executive powers. But dramatic and radical as these changes were, some historians have considered that they were effected with a great show of reluctance. The legislation enacting the abolition of the monarchy and the House of Lords did not appear until over a month after the votes of early February. The Act declaring England to be a Commonwealth was not passed until the middle of May. Even the Engagement (2 January 1650) which the Rump ordered to be taken by all males over eighteen years of age, promising obedience to 'the Commonwealth, as it is now established, without a King or House of Lords', owed little to ideological enthusiasm. Indeed, Blair Worden considers that 'the engagement was imposed on the nation chiefly out of panic'.[19]

The council of state and the Rump soon signalled their conservative disposition by their repression of Levellerism. The alliance between the Leveller leaders and senior army officers in late 1648 had collapsed before the execution of the king. The Whitehall Debates produced no consensus version of *The Agreement of the People*: the Levellers' second *Agreement* (15 December) and the officers' *Agreement* (20 January) differed fundamentally, especially on the extent of religious freedom to be allowed. By February and March 1649 the breach was public; and on 28 March Lilburne, Walwyn, Overton and the Levellers' treasurer, Thomas Prince, were arrested. This did not prevent the spread of Leveller pamphleteering (especially a marvellous piece of political polemic, *The Hunting of the Foxes*, and the third *Agreement*, smuggled out of the Tower), and Leveller-inspired mutinies in the army. As in 1646–7 these were triggered off by a threat to send the army to Ireland. But there were major differences between the army disorders of 1646–7 and 1649. The 1649 mutinies were smaller (in Whalley's regiment in London led by Robert Lockyer, and in two regiments in Salisbury and north

---

[18] *Commons Journal*, vol 6, p. 133; *English Historical Documents 1603–60*, document no. 380.

[19] Ibid., p. 227.

Oxfordshire led by Robert Thompson); they were not connived at or encouraged by senior army officers; and they were efficiently suppressed. Lockyer was executed at the end of April; Cromwell and Fairfax pursued the Salisbury mutineers to Burford (Oxfordshire) and shot the ringleaders on 14 May; and Thompson was killed later in Northamptonshire. The vital difference was that the Rump, unlike the parliamentary leaders of 1646–7, was willing and able to satisfy the wage grievances of the army rank and file. In 1649 the soldiers were paid in debentures, entitling them to ex-crown land, which they sold (often regiments acting collectively) and the cash was distributed.[20] The coincidence of the demise of Levellerism and the payment of army wage arrears reinforces the view that political and religious radicalism, as well as having only limited support in London, had very shallow roots in the army. Lilburne gloriously survived his trial in September and was acquitted; but by then Levellerism in the army was dead. 'Posterity', said Lilburne, 'shall reap the benefit of our endeavours what ever shall become of us.'[21] That is as good an epitaph for the Levellers as any.

If confirmation were needed of the Levellers' views of the new regime, it was received in the autumn. After the last Leveller outbreak in the army (at Oxford in early September) had been crushed, the Rump passed an Act on 20 September severely restricting the liberty of the press. A formidable pair, Thomas Scott and Elizabeth Atkin, 'Parliament Joan', searched out and suppressed all unauthorized printing presses. From December 1649 until January 1653 when his blindness forced him to resign, John Milton inspected all printed matter and acted as 'a kind of propaganda minister and censorship minister combined'. A few pamphlets got through the net; it was not until 1655 that Cromwell made government censorship completely efficient. But there was now no rival to the government newspaper, *Mercurius Politicus*, launched in June 1650 and edited by Marchamont Needham, who only a year before had been arrested for editing a royalist newspaper, *Mercurius Pragmaticus*. Needham's journalistic talents transformed what could have been a dull official newspaper into a brilliant exercise in successful propaganda and a landmark in English literature.[22]

For many radicals, though, especially anti-democratic religious groups, like the Fifth Monarchists, the suppression of the Levellers and the reimposition of censorship would have been unimportant if the Rump had made any serious steps towards the 'godly reformation' they hoped for. Unfortunately, reform came no easier to the immediate heir of the revolution than it did to early seventeenth-century pre-revolutionary governments. The Rump's major reform achievements were carried out under strong army pressure after the army's victory at Dunbar (3 September 1650) and were pitifully few in number. On 27 September 1650 the Rump repealed all statutes compelling people

---

[20] H. J. Habakkuk, 'The parliamentary army and the crown lands', *Welsh H.R.*, III (1966–7), pp. 403–26; I. Gentles, 'The management of crown lands 1649–60', *Agric. H.R.*, XIX (1971), pp. 25–41.

[21] Aylmer, ed., *Levellers*, p. 146.

[22] P. W. Thomas, ed., *The English Revolution, iii: Newsbooks, 5, I, Mercurius Politicus* (1971), pp. 1–8; J. Raymond, ed., *Making the News: an anthology of newsbooks of revolutionary England, 1641–60* (1993); J. Raymond, *The Invention of the newspaper: English newsbooks, 1641–9* (1996).

to attend the national Church. Later in 1650 the Rump, by converting all proceedings in law courts into English from Latin and into ordinary handwriting from court hand, went some way towards making the law more intelligible to laymen and breaking through the mumbo-jumbo thrown around the law by lawyers. Yet, despite a lot of discussion, little further religious or ecclesiastical reform was achieved. The Presbyterian system set up from 1646 to 1648 remained unrepealed, and moves to abolish tithes received little support. Although there was general concern that the clergy should be well paid and educated, the Acts for the Propagation of the Gospel passed by the Rump to effect this applied only to Wales, Ireland and selected parts of England. There was no national Act and even the Act for Wales was not renewed when it expired in 1652. To add to the radicals' fury, the Rump passed severe measures in the summer of 1650 against religious nonconformity, and revealed its obsessive fear and hatred of the excesses of the Ranters by enforcing observance of the sabbath, suppressing 'the detestable sin of prophane swearing and cursing', and prescribing the death penalty for those guilty of adultery, fornication and incest. Sweeping reforms of the law progressed no further than the discussion stage. Significantly, the Hale commission on law reform, which from January to July 1652 produced a string of radical law reform proposals, was only appointed by the Rump after Colonel Pride 'attended at the door while this was in debate';[23] equally significantly, not one of Hale's recommendations was put into effect.

It was the Rump's dilatory record on constitutional reform that led directly to its dissolution. As with other matters, the Rump talked a lot but did little. It considered a multitude of schemes for redistribution of parliamentary seats and decided in principle to alter the qualification for the franchise in county elections from possession of a forty shilling freehold to £200 in real or personal property. But little was done to put any proposal into effect. Like other measures considered by the Rump, what was known as 'a Bill for a new representative' was committed and recommitted, amended and revised, but in this case the Rump appears to have been on the brink of passing a bill which provided for its immediate adjournment until elections were held in November, when the Rump would reassemble, vet the new MPs and then hand over power to the new assembly. This was the bill killed by Cromwell's dissolution of the Rump on 20 April. After four and a half years the hoped-for millennium seemed further away than ever. Monopolies were unchecked; the grievances of the depressed rural classes not even considered. Again, as in 1647 and 1648, the army was provoked by civilian conservatism into entering the centre of the political arena.

Reasons for the Rump's conservatism

Before the autumn of 1651, the Rump had sound reasons to explain its failure to act quickly and effectively to remedy the grievances of the soldiers and saints. The new regime was launched during what was arguably the worst economic crisis of the

---

[23] Quoted in Worden, *Rump*, p. 271.

seventeenth century. Nor was the security situation conducive to a period of social experimentation. The most immediate danger came from Ireland, which had been in revolt since 1641 and was a potential launching-pad for an invasion of England. Hyde, at the exiled court of Charles Stuart, believed that Ireland rather than Presbyterian Scotland was the more favourable starting point for a Stuart restoration. In January 1649 Ormonde, the king's lieutenant in Ireland, concluded an agreement with the Confederate Catholics of Ulster, who were to provide the men for an expeditionary force to England under naval cover provided by Prince Rupert. Not only was this a serious military threat to the new regime; it also added to the Rump's already large financial problems. Despite an assessment of £90,000 per month from March 1649, the continuation of the excise, and the sale of crown and dean and chapter lands from April 1649, the Rump was never free of crushing financial demands.

Throughout the rebellion the Irish cause was held back by divisions among the confederate rebels: the pro-royalist Old English had only their Catholicism in common with the Ulster Catholics led by Owen O'Neill. The leadership of the Protestant Ormonde was not likely to smooth over these divisions. It was ominous for Charles that in May 1649 George Monck, at the head of the parliamentary army in Ireland, induced O'Neill to sign a secret armistice, which, although later denounced by the Rump, gave Cromwell in England a much-needed breathing-space to organize his army for Ireland. The fate of earlier English armies in the bogs of Ireland meant that Cromwell's success was not assured. His victories in Ireland were not simply due to the disunity of his opponents; Cromwell was careful to make painstaking preparations before he left. By appointing Lord Broghill, the son of Richard Boyle, earl of Cork, to a command in his army he won over some English Protestant settlers in Ireland to his cause. He also ensured that before he left for Ireland the wage arrears of his army were paid, and that he was guaranteed sufficient financial provision by the Rump. Cromwell and his well-paid and disciplined army were also encouraged by a racial contempt and hatred for the Irish. 'I had rather be overrun with a Cavalierish interest, than a Scotch interest; I had rather be overrun with a Scotch interest, than an Irish interest; and I think of all this is the most dangerous . . . all the world knows their barbarism', said Cromwell, who had swallowed whole the horror stories of Irish atrocities against English settlers in 1641.[24] Only this can explain Cromwell's justly infamous behaviour in Ireland, especially when he condoned the massacre of the civilian populations of Drogheda (September 1649) and Wexford (October 1649). Otherwise his intolerance and bigotry on his Irish campaign stands out starkly from his record of tolerance of the opinions of others in England and in Scotland.

Hardly had the Irish expedition been organized and financed than the infant English republic was faced with another major crisis, in Scotland. There Charles Stuart, the dead king's eldest son, who had been on the Continent since 1646, was preparing to regain his throne. Cromwell's victories in Ireland in the autumn of 1649 forced Charles into a very irksome course of action: negotiations with the dominant

---

[24] Abbott, *Writings and Speeches*, II, pp. 38–9.

Presbyterian party in Scotland, who were in the process of defeating the Scottish royalists and hanging his chief supporters, Hamilton, Montrose and Huntly. Even early in his career Charles never let principle stand in his way. In June 1650 he arrived in Scotland, swore an oath of loyalty to the Covenant and denounced his parents. So only a month after returning from Ireland in May 1650, Cromwell (Fairfax having turned down the command) headed north with Fleetwood, Lambert and an expeditionary force against the Scots. As in Ireland, success was due to Cromwell's political and organizational, as well as military, talents. He followed up his victory at Dunbar (3 September 1650) against heavy numerical odds (11,000 English against some 22,000 Scots) by skilfully widening the political and religious divisions among the Scots. Cromwell, said Whitelocke, 'sought to win them by fair means rather than to punish them'. In contrast to his intolerance of Catholics in Ireland, he won over moderate Scots opinion by his willingness to listen to the Presbyterian case. It was a divided enemy that Cromwell fought after Dunbar and decisively defeated at Worcester, exactly a year after Dunbar.

Before Worcester the Rump was faced by the prospect of invasion and with almost universal international hostility provoked by the execution of Charles I. The pursuit of international respectability and adequate defence were consequently given a higher priority than the creation of a utopia. But it is fairly certain that this alone does not adequately explain the Rump's reactionary record. By 1650 the immediate economic crisis was over, and after Worcester there was no longer the excuse of imminent royalist or foreign invasion. Recent studies of the Rump have emphasized the unrevolutionary nature of its members.[25] Older views of the Rump made two false assumptions: that Pride at the end of 1648 purged all religious Presbyterians from parliament, and that all religious Independents were political radicals. On the contrary, there were few MPs in the Rump, whether religious Independents or religious Presbyterians, who held revolutionary opinions. Twenty-two of the forty-one members of the council of state, among which may be expected to be found the most committed republicans, refused to swear an oath approving of the execution of the king and the abolition of the House of Lords and the monarchy. Pragmatic, rather than ideological, considerations induced most people to support (or at least not to oppose) the Rump. Whitelocke's reasoning was typical: although 'a strict formal pursuance of the ordinary rules of the law . . . hath hardly to be discerned in the late proceedings on either side . . . unavoidable necessity hath put us upon these courses, which otherwise perhaps we should not have taken'.[26]

For Whitelocke, who became a commissioner of the great seal, and for many others the Rump was highly preferable to rule by the army. The antipathy between the Rump and the army was possibly the major factor in the Commonwealth's dismal failure to produce far-reaching reform. As a result, religious Independents, as well as Presbyterians, opposed any extension of toleration. The activities of the Quakers and Ranters made many fearful that moderate reform would be the thin end of the wedge:

---

[25] Worden, *Rump*; D. Underdown, *Pride's Purge*, especially pp. 208–96.
[26] Bulstrode Whitelocke, *Memorials of the English Affairs* (4 vols., 1853), II, p. 523.

'If a toleration were granted', believed Thomas Edwardes, 'they shall never have peace in their families, or ever after have command of wives, children, servants.'[27] Similarly, not only lawyers resisted changes in the law. So too did many Rumpers who had no vested interest in the legal status quo, but for whom moderate legal reform came to be associated with army rule and extremism. Would not moderate legal reform be the first step towards the eventual overthrow of the common law, when views like those of the Fifth Monarchist, John Rogers, were ventilated? 'It is not easy to change some of these Lawes, and so to reform them', wrote Rogers. 'O no: that will be to poor purpose, and it is not your worke now, which is . . . bringing in the Lawes of God given by Moses for Re-publique Lawes.'[28]

What was the role of Cromwell in the Rump's failure to introduce reforms? As usual, it is not easy to slot Cromwell into any one category. He frequently called on the Rump to adopt radical measures; he was also a notable force behind the moderation of the Rump. In the crucial early weeks of the Republic he worked behind the scenes for the return of the secluded MPs, building political bridges between Presbyterians and Political Independents. Cromwell's religious confidant, John Owen, on the day after the king's execution, urged the Commons in a fast sermon to 'labour to recover others, even all that were ever distinguished and called by the name of the Lord, for their late fearful and sinful returning to sinful compliance with the enemies of God and the nation'. So anxious was Cromwell for a rapprochement with the moderates that in April 1649 he even urged that 'the presbyterian [church] government might be settled, promising his endeavours thereto'. Such political tactics might be justified by the dangers of 1649–51. What then, of Cromwell's continued contacts with conservative MPs after the battle of Worcester? Cromwell appears to have been a fairly close political ally of Oliver St John after Worcester, and apparently approved of St John's reforming, but limited, programme. At one meeting after Worcester, St John came out clearly in favour of the superiority of monarchical over republican government. Cromwell agreed, against the republican views of Desborough and other army officers: 'I think', he said, 'if it may be done with safety, and preservation of our Rights, both as Englishmen and Christians, that a Settlement with somewhat of Monarchical power in it would be very effectual.'[29] It is highly likely that, despite Cromwell's denunciations of the Rump's conservatism, he was partly responsible for its failure to bring about a 'godly reformation'.

The Rump's achievements

In the eyes of radicals like the Levellers, and those in the religious sects and the army, the Rump did not seem to be a revolutionary regime. To them, too, it seemed to be a corrupt regime, full of men who subordinated public concerns to their own private

---

[27] Quoted in Worden, *Rump*, pp. 13–14.
[28] Quoted in Capp, *Fifth Monarchy Men*, pp. 74–5.
[29] Quoted in Worden, *Rump*, p. 276; Abbott, *Writings and Speeches*, II, p. 507.

interests. These criticisms are reflected in Cromwell's scathing words denouncing the Rumpers on 20 April 1653 quoted above (pp. 243–4), and are echoed in the words of Clement Walker, an MP excluded by Pride in 1648: 'the Rump is a parliament with corrupt maggots in it'. But was the Rump as corrupt and as slow to bring about change as these criticisms of it implied?

There are many reasons to think that descriptions by the Rump's enemies, like Cromwell and Walker, are in need of modification. In terms of corruption, 'by the standards of the time the Rumpers as a body do not come out badly', writes Austin Woolrych. Like all office-holders in the seventeenth century they made sure they profited personally from their official positions, but fewer did so as excessively as many MPs in earlier and later parliaments in this period.[30] Nor were the Rumpers inactive in governing the country. Led by a group of committed republicans round Henry Marten and Thomas Chaloner, the Rump set about putting into effect very successful foreign and commercial policies. It is likely that the foreign and commercial policies pursued by the Marten–Chaloner group received *general* support in the Rump, because they gained enormous international prestige for the new regime.

It was a well-known seventeenth-century maxim that 'power and profit are jointly to be considered'; national greatness and commercial property go hand in hand. This was the reason for the establishment of the council of trade appointed in August 1650 by the Rump to find remedies for the trade depression. The most notable product of the council, before its demise in December 1651, was the Navigation Act (9 October 1651), by which all imports to England had to be in English ships or in ships of the country where the imported goods originated. Both the authors and the purpose of the Act have been the subject of historical debate,[31] but there seems little doubt that its major aim was to attack the Dutch hegemony of the carrying trade. It was not the sole reason for war with the Dutch which began in 1652. An attempt by the Rump to effect a full union – 'a confederacy perpetual' – with their fellow Protestants in 1650–1 met with an angry response from the Dutch. But commercial hostility between the two nations was uppermost. There was a long history of commercial rivalry in the East and West Indies, in North America and in West Africa between the Dutch and English, but the Act hardly helped Anglo-Dutch relations. The war was received enthusiastically in England for a variety of motives: the Fifth Monarchists hated the Dutch for their Presbyterianism, as well as for their dominance of the cloth markets (many Fifth Monarchists were clothmakers and clothworkers); civilian Rumpers saw the war as a test of national republican prestige. Even conservative Presbyterians, who were uneasy about a war against co-religionists, saw the war as an assertion of national power and a means of diverting attention away from domestic reform.

---

[30] Woolych, *Britain in Revolution*, pp. 555–6; Worden, *Rump*, pp. 93–102; and G. E. Aylmer, *The State's Servants: the civil service of the English Republic 1649–60* (1973), pp. 139–55, 341–3.

[31] See J. P. Cooper, 'Social and economic policies under the Commonwealth', in Aylmer, ed., *Interregnum*, pp. 134–5; S. Pincus, *Puritans and Patriotism: ideology and the making of foreign policy, 1650–68* (1996). See B. Coward, *The Cromwellian Protectorate* (2002), pp. 125–7 for a summary of the historical debate.

War at sea, of course, required a strong navy, and in this respect too the Rump had some success in reorganizing the naval command and vastly increasing the size of the navy, laying the foundation for the naval successes of what (slightly misleadingly) has been called 'Cromwell's navy'.[32] Much the same can be said of the Rump's legacy to the Protectorate in Ireland and Scotland. By 1653, for the first time ever, the whole of the British Isles had been brought under one unified rule. By the time of its dissolution the Rump had laid the foundation for the union of England and Scotland that was completed by the Protectorate; and in August 1652 it passed an Act of Settlement in Ireland, which, though very punitive in its treatment of most Catholics in the country, was accompanied by a reorganization of the government of Ireland, ensuring that, like Scotland, Ireland was put firmly under English control.

Perhaps the most notable achievement of the Rump was not its foreign, 'British' and commercial policies, but that, despite high odds against it, it made republican government tolerable to many. There was much that the traditional rulers of England found hateful in the Rump; it was a regicide regime, which continued to exact high taxation and to interfere in local affairs. In some counties, prominent opponents were removed from the commission of the peace in the purges of 1650 and 1651, and the powers of a minority of radical activists strengthened. The council of state appointed the commissioners of the new county militias, created in July 1650. Yet significantly the Rump met no serious opposition. Partly this was due to its moderation: the purges of JPs were only partial, and only the most prominent royalists were executed (the earls of Holland and Derby). Partly also, the Rump produced a persuasive theoretical justification for accepting a de facto regime in the works of Francis Rous, Marchamont Needham and John Dury. Mainly, however, most people came to see the Rump as the only practicable government. There was little enthusiasm for the return of the monarchy, and the only alternative to the Rump was the army. The prevalence of 'loyalism' was based on the belief that the Rump was the upholder of law and order and the bulwark against radicalism; it had ridden out a severe economic crisis; and it had enhanced England's international prestige in an immensely successful war.

There is one other question that needs to be considered when reassessing the Rump's reputation: were the Rumpers 'reluctant revolutionaries'? Certainly, as has been seen, they seemed to be so in the view of many radicals in and outside the army. But, judging by what they did and said, many in the Rump did have a vision of a permanent British republic, based in part on its resolutions passed on 4 January 1649 (quoted above, p. 245), as well as on its abolition of the monarchy and the House of Lords. This vision can be seen also in the ceremonials put on by the Rump, like that to celebrate Cromwell's return to London after his great victory at Worcester in September 1651. In a procession through the capital's streets, Cromwell paraded 4,000 Scottish prisoners of war in a display that a government newspaper trumpeted as showing 'the cavaliers a true copy of the king's countenance in his gallant design to over-run the Nation at once with barbarism and tyranny'. This does not sound like the

---

[32] B. Capp, *Cromwell's Navy: the Fleet and the English Revolution, 1649–60* (1989).

GREAT SEAL OF THE COMMONWEALTH.

Figure 7.4 The Great Seal of the Commonwealth, 1651, can be seen as a triumphant declaration of the republicanism of the regime established after the abolition of the monarchy in 1649. On one side the emphasis is on the regime's basis in parliamentary sovereignty and individual freedom (see the motto 'In the Third Year of Freedom by God's Blessing Restored'); on the other side, the implicit message is the regime's determination to promote the naval defence of England and Ireland (note that Scotland is deliberately excluded from the map on this side of the seal). *Source*: © Mary Evans Picture Library.

voice of a regime ashamed of its republicanism. On the contrary, these public spectacles and the iconography of the Rump trumpeted its republicanism. The official great seal of the Rump showed the House of Commons in session surrounded by the motto 'In the First Year of Freedom by God's Blessing Restored', hinting at a kind of calendar used by the revolutionaries in late eighteenth-century France. Up and down the country also the Rump ensured that images of monarchy were destroyed, as, for example new town and city maces were made bearing the insignia of the republic not the crown.[33]

The dissolution of the Rump

For many in the army, what was uppermost in their minds were not these achievements, but the Rump's failure to carry out the army's hoped-for godly reformation. In late 1652 both Cromwell and the army made clear how deep was the rift between them and the Rump. A few month later, on 20 April 1653, Cromwell took a file of musketeers into the chamber of the Commons and forcibly brought its proceedings to an end. Why he did that has been the subject of much debate, in part because it is now

---

[33] S. Kelsey, *Inventing a Republic: the political culture of the English Commonwealth, 1649–53* (1997). The quotation is on p. 73.

clear that two commonly accepted reasons for his decision do not hold water.[34] Cromwell did not dissolve the Rump in order to seize power for himself, since there is in no evidence that he had made any plans to bring this about after the dissolution. Nor did he dissolve the Rump because he believed that the constitutional bill being considered by the Rump in the spring of 1653 provided merely for by-elections to fill vacant seats in parliament: a bill, in other words, that was intended to perpetuate the Rump's power. What has destroyed that hypothesis is Blair Worden's convincing argument that the constitutional bill being considered by parliament did provide for new elections.[35] Why, then did Cromwell dissolve the Rump when it was apparently bowing to the wishes of the army? There are various possibilities. One (Worden's suggestion) is that in 1653 Cromwell was gripped by a bout of millenarian enthusiasm. Another is that Cromwell was not aware of the provisions of the constitutional bill until he read them after he had dissolved parliament. Another is that perhaps the new elections provided for in the constitutional bill were to be supervised by members of the Rump, which would ensure that only those hostile to the army's reform programme would be elected. Finally, it is likely that by the spring of 1653 Cromwell realised that he was no longer able to keep the loyalty of the army *and* maintain his contacts with the parliamentarians of the Rump. The rift between the Rump and the army was now so wide that Cromwell had to take an unequivocal stand on the side of the army and reform. It remains to be seen how permanent this would be.

Barebones Parliament, July–December 1653

Cromwell's public statements after the dissolution of the Rump give the impression that he had thrown all political caution to the winds and surrendered himself to millenarian enthusiasm. 'Truly you are called by God to rule with Him, and for Him', he told Barebones Parliament when it assembled on 4 July 1653.

> I confess I never looked to see such a day as this . . . when Jesus Christ should be so owned as He is, at this day . . . this may be the door to usher in the things that God has promised; which have been prophesied of . . . we have some of us thought, That it is our duty to endeavour this way; not vainly to look at that prophecy in Daniel.[36]

These were 'Overturning, Overturning, Overturning dayes', some London Fifth Monarchists told the members of Barebones Parliament, urging them to 'indeavour the erecting of the Kingdom of Jesus Christ to the uttermost parts of the earth'.[37] With

---

[34] Woolrych, *Britain in Revolution*, for the latest and best discussion of this debate.

[35] See Worden, *Rump*, especially pp. 345–8, and A. Woolrych, *Commonwealth to Protectorate* (1982), ch. 3, for a radical revision of the older view. See also S. Barber, 'Irish undercurrents to the politics of April 1653', *Historical Research*, LXV (1992).

[36] Abbott, *Writings and Speeches*, III, pp. 61, 63–4.

[37] Quoted in Capp, *Fifth Monarchy Men*, p. 67.

some justification the hopes of the Fifth Monarchists were high. Cromwell had turned down John Lambert's proposal that a council of twelve should rule temporarily in the political hiatus created by the dissolution of the Rump, and listened favourably to the Fifth Monarchist Thomas Harrison's idea that a larger assembly of godly men should meet, based on the Jewish Sanhedrin. Not surprisingly, the decision to summon an assembly of men 'of approved fidelity and honesty', to whom were to be transferred supreme authority to make a new constitution, was interpreted by Lambert as a victory for Harrison and extreme radicalism.

Information

Barebones Parliament

This was the nickname given (after one of its members, a London leather-seller, Praise-God Barebone), to the nominated assembly of 138 men, 121 from England, 5 from Scotland, 6 from Ireland and 6 from Wales. Many commonly accepted assumptions once made about the assembly have now persuasively been called into question.

- First, that Barebones Parliament was a crucial stage in putting Fifth Monarchy plans into action. In fact, Cromwell ensured that the assembly was not simply a gathering of 'saints' – radical idealists inexperienced in government.

- Secondly, that most members of Barebones Parliament were unfitted to rule because, in Clarendon's words, 'much the major part of them consisted of inferior persons, of no quality or name, artificers of the meanest trades, known only by their gifts in praying and preaching'. London Baptists were represented; so too were the Fifth Monarchists, but the majority of members were the usual type of seventeenth-century MPs: university and Inns-of-Court educated, drawing their wealth mainly from the land, and serving on the commission of the peace in their home counties.

- Thirdly, that Barebones Parliament was only a forum for the discussion of impractical and idealistic schemes. In fact, much time was spent in Barebones Parliament in the discussion of sensible measures of reform.

Barebones Parliament spent a lot of its brief life discussing reforms that were uncontroversial and designed to remedy widely recognized imperfections in the machinery of government, the Church and the law. The abolition of the church courts had left a huge vacuum to fill, and Barebones Parliament established machinery for the probate of wills and for registering births, marriages and deaths. Civil marriages, solemnized by JPs, were legalized. Measures were proposed to rationalize the revenue system, including the abolition of the hated excise. Many of the law reforms proposed by Barebones Parliament were uncontroversial. It was hardly shocking to suggest that the debtor's law should discriminate between genuine and fraudulent bankrupts, that punishments should match crimes, or that the law should be made intelligible to litigants as well as to lawyers. Enlightened Acts were passed for the relief of creditors and poor prisoners, and to regulate conditions under which idiots and lunatics were kept. Even the discussions on finding a more reasonable method than tithes for paying church ministers were not at first unwelcome. After all, this was a problem that had concerned people since the Reformation, because poor salaries ensured an ill-educated, inadequate clergy. Better salaries, whether guaranteed by the State or by individual congregations, were seen as a possible remedy for many of the ills of the Church. Barebones Parliament, too, was just as concerned as the Rump had been with national prestige. Despite Cromwell's peace moves, it continued the popular Dutch war and went ahead with proposals for the union of England and Scotland, taking care that Scottish interests would be subordinated to those of England.

Why, then, did Barebones Parliament fail to persuade the political nation to forget the traumatic events of 1649? Its task was greater than that of the Rump. The dissolution of 20 April 1653 isolated the republican regime even further than before from the mainstream of political opinion. Rumpers could not forgive what they saw as a violation of parliamentary privileges by the army in 1653. From July to October 1653, many JPs who had supported the Rump were ejected from commissions of the peace, leaving fewer greater gentry on them than ever before. Nothing was more symbolic of the alienation of moderate opinion from the republic in 1653. What frightened moderates most of all were the activities in Barebones Parliament of the Fifth Monarchists and members of other radical sects, who, although only few in number, were very well organized. They planned their political tactics in Arthur Squibb's house in London, and at times were able to push through the parliament very controversial measures: a vote to abolish the court of chancery (5 August), a vote to allow the introduction of a bill to abolish lay patronage of church livings (17 November), and on 10 December the rejection (by 56 votes to 52) of a committee's report to retain tithes. These were brief, temporary and narrow victories for the radicals, but they were enough to frighten moderate opinion that property and society as they knew it were in danger. This was no way to heal the wounds of 1649, and Cromwell's conservative instincts for the preservation of the regime were alarmed. He later said that, if Barebones Parliament had continued, the result would have been 'the subversion of the laws and of all the liberties of this nation, the destruction of the Ministry, of this nation, in a word the confusion of all things'.[38] Cromwell may not have initiated the device on 12 December, by which the moderates in Barebones Parliament met very early one morning and outvoted the radicals to hand power back to him; but he certainly needed little persuasion to accept it. The civilian radicals by now had little time

---

[38] Abbott, *Writings and Speeches*, IV, p. 489.

for Cromwell and the army. Christopher Feake, a Fifth Monarchist, called Cromwell 'the man of sin, the old dragon'; and some suggested that the expenditure on the army be drastically cut and that senior army officers receive no pay for a year. One can imagine the relish with which the radical minority were dispersed by the soldiers from Westminster on 12 December 1653. For Cromwell and the army, though, the end of Barebones Parliament solved nothing. The dilemma of the revolution remained, and was neatly encapsulated in two questions asked by a contemporary pamphlet: 'whether the old Parliament [the Rump] was not turned out for leaving undone what they ought to have done,' and 'whether the little Parliament [Barebones] was not turned out for doing what the others left undone'.[39]

Oliver Cromwell

Biography

Oliver Cromwell (1599–1658)

Oliver Cromwell was born on 25 April 1599 in Huntingdon, the second son of Robert Cromwell and his wife Elizabeth Steward. For the first forty years of his life he was a political nonentity. For a time he was a farmer in East Anglia. Although he was elected MP for Huntingdon in 1628 and for Cambridge in 1640, his rise to political prominence was brought about solely by his success as a soldier in the English Civil War. He had no previous military experience but he became parliament's premier cavalry commander in the army of the Eastern Association and New Model Army. After the end of the Civil War he played second fiddle to his son-in-law Henry Ireton in the politicization of the New Model Army in 1647 and (arguably) in the events that led to the trial of Charles I.

After the establishment of the republic in 1649 there is no doubt, though, that further military victories in Ireland, Scotland and England made him the most prominent politician in the country. His reputation among the Irish never recovered from his brutal treatment of his enemies at Drogheda and Wexford in 1649, but his political reputation in England soared to new heights.

During the rest of his life he was the dominant political figure in Britain: dissolving the Rump Parliament by force on 20 April 1653, establishing the government of Barebones Parliament (July to December 1653) and on 16 December 1653 becoming Lord Protector of Britain and Ireland under a new constitution, the Instrument of Government, a position he held until his death on 3 September 1658, when he was succeeded as Protector by his eldest son, Richard Cromwell.

---

[39] Quoted in G. D. Heath, 'Making the Instrument of Government', *J.B.S.*, VI (1967), p. 17, n. 10.

Figure 7.5(a) 'Oliver Cromwell Between Two Pillars', 1658.
Source: © Imagestate/The Print Collector/Heritage Images.

'Without doubt', wrote Clarendon of Oliver Cromwell,

> no man with more wickedness ever attempted any thing, or brought to pass what he
> desired more wickedly, more in the face and contempt of religion, and moral honesty;
> yet wickedness as great as his could never have accomplished those trophies, without
> the assistance of a great spirit, an admirable circumspection and sagacity, and a most
> magnanimous resolution . . . he will be looked upon by posterity as a brave bad man.[40]

Cromwell is one of the great personalities of the past about whom it is more than
usually difficult to be objective or to get a clear idea of his character and his aims.

---

[40] Clarendon, *History*, VI, pp. 91, 97.

Figure 7.5(b) 'The Royal Oake of Brittayne', 1649. These illustrations show that opinion about Oliver Cromwell was as divided while he lived as it has been ever since. 7.5(a) is full of images portraying Cromwell's rule as one of peace and prosperity. 7.5(b), created by Clement Walker, is full of images of destruction as Cromwell oversees the end of the 'Royal Oake' and texts like Magna Carta, statutes and *Eikon Basilike*.
Source: © British Library Board: E.1052.2.

During his lifetime he aroused intense emotions, leaving for historians biased political memoirs, whether from Clarendon on the royalist side or from the civilian republican Edmund Ludlow, and propaganda-laden newspapers and pamphlets. What is even more frustrating for historians is that Cromwell himself rarely made his own motives clear. Unlike his son-in-law Henry Ireton, Cromwell was not an ideologue who delighted in disentangling and analysing his ideas. Consequently, though masses of his letters and speeches survive, his references in them to his aims are often couched in very general terms. He often talked only vaguely of his desire to secure 'the good things' or 'to reap the fruit of all the blood and treasure that had been spent in this cause'. Moreover, at key points in the 1640s and 1650s Cromwell often remained enigmatically silent or away from the centre of events, leaving a host of questions unanswered. Did he encourage the development of the agitating movement in the army in the spring of 1647 or was he swept along by it? Did he engineer Cornet Joyce's seizure of the king from the parliamentarians in June 1647 and Charles's escape from Hampton Court in November 1647? What was his attitude in the last months of 1648 to the army's demands for a dissolution or purge of parliament and the trial of the king? How deeply committed was he to the radicalism of the junior army officers in the early 1650s? Was he the instigator of the coup in December 1653 which led to the collapse of Barebones Parliament? Did he encourage the second Protectorate Parliament to offer him the throne? Why did he reject the chance to become King Oliver?

So ambiguous is the evidence about Cromwell's character and activities that it is possible to portray two very different historical images of the man. One is a dynamic and impetuous character, who in the late 1630s made some very rash and risky decisions. In 1631 he took the extraordinary decision to sell his properties in Huntingdon and move to nearby St Ives where he became a working farmer. Between 1636 and 1638 his economic fortunes were salvaged by his inheritance of leases in Ely from his maternal uncle, but only, according to Simon Healy's research, after a bitter dispute in which Cromwell attempted to get his uncle declared a lunatic, an event which may have been the occasion of Cromwell's letter to Mrs St John in 1638 in which he declared that he had been 'a thief, the chief of sinners' but was now casting that life aside as one of the Elect chosen for eternal salvation. Moreover, in 1640 he sold the inheritance he had received from his wife's uncle in order to concentrate on political activities.[41]

In the 1640s he was totally committed against Charles I both on the battlefield ('it's no longer disputing, but out instantly all you can. Raise all your hands . . . get up what volunteers you can; haste your horses . . . Lord Newcastle will advance into your bowels', he wrote excitedly in 1643 to less keen parliamentarians) and off it ('We will cut off his head with the crown on it', the impetuous Cromwell is said to have cried when doubts were expressed about the legality of what was being done on 30 January 1649).[42] This image of a man full of zeal and fire persists on many occasions in the 1650s; on 4 July 1653 when he addressed Barebones Parliament with millenarian enthusiasm, tears rolling down his cheeks; he angrily dismissed three parliaments in 1653, 1655 and 1658; in 1656 he brushed aside considerations of legality, saying 'if nothing should be done but what is according to law, the throat of a nation may be cut, till we send for some to make a law'.[43] Alongside that exciting, man-of-action impression can be set another, duller image: a man who spent long periods carefully building political alliances based on compromises and conciliation, as he did in 1647 and for much of 1649; a man who was sometimes, as in early 1653 and during the kingship crisis in 1657, as tortured by indecision as ever Elizabeth I was.

How can one harmonize these contrasting images? Two popular explanations for the ambiguities of Cromwell's character need to be treated with great caution. The first is the allegation made by the Leveller Richard Overton that

---

[41] S. Healy, '1636: the unmaking of Oliver Cromwell?' in P. Little, ed., *Oliver Cromwell: new perspectives* (2009).

[42] Abbott, *Writings and Speeches*, I, pp. 251, 736.

[43] Ibid., IV, p. 275.

you shall scarce speak to Crumwell about anything, but he will lay his hand on his breast, elevate his eyes and call God to record, he will weep, howl and repent, even while he doth smite you under the first rib.[44]

This charge that Cromwell clothed selfish ambition in the guise of pious principles has received much support during the centuries since it was first made in 1649, largely because so often events went his way: miraculously, it seemed, he overcame body blows like the Self-Denying Ordinance in 1645 and the rifts in the army ranks at Putney in 1647. It is easy to see why he had such a strong belief in Providence and why both royalists and republican observers condemned him as a hypocritical politician who only used radical sentiments for his own ends (the royalist view) or to prevent a wide-ranging revolution (the republican view). In arguing against this view, it is important not to fall into the trap of portraying Cromwell as what Patrick Little has called 'a somewhat other-worldly figure',[45] a man concerned with ideals and not at all with the political graft needed to put these ideals into practice. By the 1650s he was a master of political guile, willing to use propaganda ('spin') against his political enemies and to promote his idealistic vision. Cromwell wanted power and was willing to use low political means to get and retain it. But he wanted power not for its own sake but to do something positive with it.

Another explanation of Cromwell's apparently ambivalent attitude to radicalism has been that at some stage he underwent a transformation from youthful idealism to middle-aged pragmaticism; that, like a lot of radicals, he spurned his one-time radical allies and beliefs, when he came face to face with the day-to-day problems of government. This explanation has the merit of reconciling Cromwell, the man who in the early 1640s proclaimed that his goal was to attain 'godly rule', with Cromwell, the man who in the late 1640s negotiated with Charles I until weeks before his execution; who ruthlessly suppressed the Levellers, his former allies; and who in the 1650s nearly accepted the title of king. On this view the only matter of dispute is when the change took place: was it at Putney in 1647 when he realized that some of his fellow saints were intent not only on establishing 'godly rule', but also on attacking property as well? But Cromwell's career does not fall into the neat progression from radicalism to pragmaticism that this view presupposes. At times in the 1650s he appeared more radical than he had been a decade earlier.

A more promising approach to the problem of explaining Cromwell's career is to see him not as a self-seeking hypocrite or disillusioned idealist, but as someone who was driven by two very different aims reflecting the contrasting aspirations which had surfaced since 1640: a yearning for the return of social stability, political normality and constitutional respectability, and a passionate zeal for godly reformation. This duality of aim is neatly described by Blair Worden as 'ideological schizophrenia'.[46]

---

[44] D. M. Wolfe, ed., *Leveller Manifestoes of the Puritan Revolution* (1967), p. 370.

[45] P. Little, Introduction, to the edited collection of essays, *Cromwell: new perspectives*, p. 1. This is a trap that Little neatly avoids falling into.

[46] Worden, *Rump*, p. 69.

The first of these is more straightforward and easier to understand than the second. Cromwell himself often called it his desire for 'settlement' or 'healing and settling', by which he meant his wish to reconcile horrified conservative opinion to the traumatic events through which the country had gone since 1642 by restoring something like political and social normality. This is well in line with Cromwell's pragmatic behaviour both in the post-Civil War years (when he tried desperately, with his Political Independent allies, to conclude a settlement with Charles I) and immediately after the execution of the king in January 1649 when he worked equally assiduously to restore those MPs excluded from the Rump Parliament by the army. As will be seen, as Lord Protector from 1653 to 1658 Cromwell continued to woo the traditional parliamentary classes. Despite his dramatic break with his civilian Political Independent allies in 1648, Cromwell as Protector was still influenced by the aspirations that were reflected in *The Heads of the Proposals* of 1647. The four fundamental principles he laid down in 1654 are very like those which underlay *The Heads of the Proposals*: first, government by a single person and parliaments; secondly, parliaments of limited duration; thirdly, liberty of conscience; and fourthly, the militia to be jointly controlled by parliament and the head of State. As will be seen, the Instrument of Government (the written constitution of the new Protectorate), though drafted by a soldier, John Lambert, had many characteristics that were not new. Its provision for the rule of a single person whose powers were limited by the council of state and who was forced to rule through regular parliaments reflected principles to which Cromwell had demonstrated his commitment throughout the 1640s and which were designed to contribute to the success of his 'healing and settling' ambitions.

Alongside Cromwell's yearning for 'settlement' was a thrusting, intense zeal for 'reformation' which had two broad aspects. The first derived from the fact that Cromwell was a militant Protestant who shared many of the aspirations and attitudes of Puritans described in Chapter 2 (pp. 55–8), especially the craving for 'further reformation' by converting the Reformation begun in the sixteenth century into a true reformation of the hearts, minds and lives of every individual, an idea first apparent in his letter to Mrs St John in October 1638.[47] During his speech at the opening of the first Protectorate Parliament he set out his ambition to bring about 'a reformation of manners', his hope

> that Jesus Christ will have a time to set up his reign in our hearts, by subduing those corruptions and lusts and evils that are there, which reign now more in the world than (I hope) in due time they shall do.[48]

The way Cromwell tried to achieve this, as will be seen, was by an alliance of godly magistrates and a reformed educated ministry, and with a loosely organized national Church within which individuals would have the freedom to find God for themselves.

---

[47] See the box on Cromwell, p. 257.
[48] Abbott, *Writings and Speeches*, III, p. 437.

This Cromwellian commitment to liberty of conscience, though, was not identical to that understood by a modern definition of religious toleration. Cromwell excluded not only Catholics and Anglicans from his 'toleration', but also extreme Protestant groups like the Unitarians and Quakers. The Instrument of Government expressly said that toleration should not be extended to 'popery and prelacy [nor] to such as under the profession of Christ hold forth and practise licentiousness' or to those 'that abuse the liberty to the civil injury of others and to the actual disturbance of the public peace'. Moreover, Cromwell's godly reformation was not intended to promote the religious diversity allowed by modern regimes that practise religious toleration. Cromwell's ideal was the maintenance of Protestant unity within a national Church. One of the ironies of his life is that Cromwell, who was smeared by his enemies as 'the darling of the sectaries' (see p. 208), abhorred sectarianism. He wanted to prevent what was happening: the splintering of Protestant unity and the growth of separate religious denominations. However, the united Church he created had broad, if finite, limits. In the clearest definition of his religious goal in a speech of September 1656, he said

> Undoubtedly this is the peculiar interest all this while contended for. [That] men that believe in Jesus Christ . . . men that believe the remission of sins through the blood of Christ and free justification by the blood of Christ, and live upon the grace of God, that these men are certain they are so, are members of Jesus Christ and are to him the apple of his eye.

He also made clear that his central concern was the reformation of inner beliefs, not the imposition of types of church government. His toleration included 'whoever hath this faith, let his form be what it will if he be walking peaceably without the prejudicing of others under another form'.[49]

The second aspect of Cromwell's vision of a reformed England also drew on aspirations that were not new in the 1650s. Rather, they were rooted in ideas developed by the 'Commonwealth' writers of the sixteenth century, who accepted that it was right that wealth and power in the Commonwealth (the State) should be distributed unequally, but maintained that everyone – including the rich and privileged – had duties and responsibilities to the Commonwealth as a whole. The keynote of this ideal is what is nowadays called 'social justice': the idea that private greed should not be allowed to become public injustice, corruption and unalleviated poverty. Cromwell shared this ideal, which led him during the Protectorate to attempt to make the legal system of the country fairer, central and local government less corrupt and education more accessible. It was an aim Cromwell expressed most clearly in a letter he wrote in September 1650 after his miraculous victory over the Scots at the battle of Dunbar. He urged MPs to

---

[49] Ibid., III, pp. 271–2.

own His people more, for they are the chariots and horsemen of Israel. Disown ourselves, but own your authority and improve it to curb the proud and the insolent, such as would disturb the tranquillity of England, though under what specious pretences soever; relieve the oppressed, hear the groans of poor prisoners in England; be pleased to reform the abuses of all professions; and if there be anyone that makes many poor to make a few rich, that suits not a Commonwealth.[50]

Cromwell was not alone in sharing these dual hopes for 'settlement' and 'reformation'. However, during the 1640s and 1650s many Puritan gentlemen who had once shared his hopes that there would be created a godly Commonwealth within the traditional political and social structures abandoned them as they became associated with army revolts, regicide, religious radicalism and threats to turn the world upside down. What makes Cromwell unusual and helps to explain the great political difficulties he faced as Protector is that he did not abandon reformation; indeed, his commitment to it seems to have become greater as he got older. Why did he take this difficult and increasingly lonely road of reformation?

A popular explanation for this is fear of what the army might have done if he had abandoned the Good Old Cause. Would army retaliation not have been swift and deadly? The problem with this explanation is that Cromwell often showed that he was not afraid of the army: for example, at Ware in 1647 and at Burford in 1649, when he suppressed army mutinies, and in February 1657 when he outfaced a hostile crowd of army officers who were angry at the consideration Cromwell was giving to abandoning the Instrument of Government. This is not to suggest that Cromwell's military experiences are not part of the explanation for his undimmed, burning desire for reformation. He never forgot the camaraderie of the army camp, which reinforced his desire to create a post-Civil War land fit for heroes to live in. And, if he seemed to stray from that aim, his one-time army comrades were not slow to bring him back to it. Early in 1657, during the kingship crisis, William Bradford wrote to him as someone who, he said, had gone along with Cromwell 'from Edgehill to Dunbar', and he made a powerful conscience-stabbing point:

the experiences that you have had of the power of God at these two places and betwixt them, methinks, should often make you shrink, and be at a stand in, this thwarting, threatened change.[51]

This, however, was only part of the reason why Cromwell's commitment to reformation remained firm. It was not fear of the army's wrath that explains this, but fear of the wrath of a being much more powerful and awesome: God. Drawing on a biblical parallel commonly used by the godly, Cromwell considered that England in the 1650s faced a situation comparable to that faced by the Israelites in Old Testament days; when they only succeeded in leaving the wilderness, finally and permanently escaping

---

[50] Ibid., II, p. 325.
[51] Ibid., IV, p. 448.

from Egyptian bondage and inheriting the Promised Land, after they had won God's blessing by expiating their sins. Cromwell was convinced that for the English the path of moral purity was the only one that would lead to a permanent escape from the bondage of Archbishop Laud and Charles I which had been temporarily achieved during the Civil War. To inherit the Promised Land of godly reformation, the English had now to undergo a process of spiritual cleansing. What we do not want, he told the second Protectorate parliament in September 1656, is

> a captain to lead us back into Egypt, if there be such a place – I mean metaphorically and allegorically so – that is to say, returning to all those things that we have been fighting against . . . I am confident [he went on], that the liberty and prosperity of this nation depends upon reformation . . . Make it a shame to see men to be bold in sin and profaneness, and God will bless you . . . Truly these things do respect the souls of men, and the spirits, which are the men. The mind is the man. If that be kept pure, a man signifies somewhat.[52]

Godly reformation was at the centre of Cromwell's vision for England. He wanted to reconcile 'settlement' and 'reformation'. 'He sings sweetly', he said, 'that sings a song of reconciliation betwixt these two interests'. But when the two conflicted, he did not jettison reformation, which is surely the strongest argument against those who accuse Cromwell of self-aggrandisement. Instead, he often put the godly cause above that of a parliamentary settlement. 'Civil liberty . . . ought to be subordinate to a more peculiar interest of God', he declared on 3 April 1657.[53] It was a brave judgement but one that was to bring him untold political troubles.

Cromwellian government, 1653–1658

Opinions about the Protectorate differ almost as greatly as do those about the Protector himself. At one extreme the period is seen as one approaching anarchy in which central government all but collapsed; at the other it is considered to have been a repressive, military dictatorship. Both views agree that the 1650s were an irrelevant, unnecessary interruption in the long-term development of the English constitution. That this was so, the argument goes, was recognized by the logic of events in the 1650s: an inevitable reactionary progression from experiments with new forms of government to the adoption by Cromwell in his later years of monarchical government in all but name. This view of the Protectorate is based on two questionable assumptions: that the republic was bound to fail because it lacked enough political support in England, since most people were yearning for a return to monarchical rule; and that the Protectorate was a conservative regime that had abandoned aspirations for reform,

---

[52] Ibid., IV, pp. 263, 273–4.
[53] Ibid., IV, p. 445.

a view of the 1650s that is characterized by William Lamont as 'years of retreat, the successive stages in the process as sell-out, by which the monarchy is restored in all but name well before 1660'.[54] What casts doubt on the first assumption is that Charles Stuart received little support in England in 1651, the royalist risings of the mid-1650s were damp squibs, and Sir George Booth's royalist rebellion in August 1659 was a complete failure. The explanation for these royalist debacles lies only in part in differences among royalists, in the incompetence of their leaders, and in the military strength of the Cromwellian regime. It is also explained by the fact that before the middle of 1659 there is very little evidence of widespread enthusiasm for the return of the Stuarts. It is difficult to know what the masses felt about the Protectorate; though one can speculate with a fair degree of certainty, for example, on what the popular reaction was to the closure of many alehouses in the 1650s. The key problem is to analyse the reactions of the traditional rulers of the counties and boroughs to Cromwellian government. The weakness of the Stuart cause in the 1650s suggests that there were aspects of Cromwellian government that they found attractive. The first of the next two sections isolates some of those aspects. Government during the 1650s did not break down. In some respects it was very efficient and went some way towards satisfying the craving of the political nation for a return to stable, ordered government.

Yet the Protectorate was also a regime that did not lose touch with the revolutionary ideals of the Good Old Cause and 'godly reformation'. Unlike many others in England, Cromwell's zeal for reformation was never extinguished. As a result, the Protector often found himself out of sympathy with mainstream political opinion in the 1650s. The second section shows how Cromwell's pursuit of reformation caused major political conflicts between Protector and Protectorate parliaments, and why despite its achievements Cromwellian government secured the enthusiastic loyalty of only a minority; so that Oliver Cromwell's legacy to his son Richard, if not hopeless, was very insecure.

The achievements of Cromwellian government[55]

Immediately after Cromwell was installed as Lord Protector of the British republic on 16 December 1653, he devoted a large part of his political energies to wooing the political nation by securing peace and stability and returning to at least a semblance of constitutional normality. Even the choice of 'Lord Protector' as Cromwell's title and 'Commonwealth' for the official designation of the republic may have been made in an attempt to obscure the revolutionary constitutional changes that had taken place. The Instrument of Government, the constitution of the new Protectorate, was a victory for the conservative wing of the army. John Lambert, now back in London, had a decisive role in drafting the Instrument. True to his Political Independent past, Cromwell

---

[54] W. Lamont, 'The Left and its past: revisiting the 1650s', *History Workshop*, XXIII (1987), p. 142.

[55] For a different, more critical assessment of these achievements, see B. Worden, 'Oliver Cromwell and the Protectorate', *T.R.H.S.*, 6th ser., 20 (2010).

welcomed some of its major constitutional provisions, especially its insistence on the important role of parliaments.

Information

Instrument of Government, December 1653

The main provisions were as follows:

- Single-chamber parliaments representing England, Ireland and Scotland were to be elected every three years; parliaments were to sit for a minimum of five months; and machinery was established for local officials to send out writs to summon a new parliament if the central government failed to do so.

- All Christian religions were to be tolerated except those which practised Catholicism, had episcopal church governments and threatened to disturb the peace.

- Executive power was held by a Lord Protector and council, both elected by parliament. Protector and council could issue ordinances when parliament was not in session.

- The Protector had to rule with the council of state, especially in key matters like finance, the appointments of senior officers of state and control of the armed forces.

Cromwell later complained that these limitations made him like 'a child in its swaddling clothes. . . . By the [Instrument of] Government, I can do nothing but in ordination with the Council.'[56] This is a case of Cromwellian exaggeration, but it contains a core of truth: councils of state during the Protectorate had a much more prominent constitutional role than did royal privy councils before and after this period.[57] Yet it is now clear from the work of Blair Worden that this is a case that can be taken too far. On many occasions it was Cromwell and not the council that made major decisions of government. 'The destiny of Cromwellian England', writes Worden, 'lay not at the council table but in the decisions of the generals and of the captains and soldiers behind them . . . The council, however valuable to Cromwell as a source of assistance, mattered as a locus of power because the generals sat on it.'[58] The Cromwellian

---

[56] Abbott, *Writings and Speeches*, III, p. 488.

[57] P. Gaunt, '"The single person's confidants and dependants": Oliver Cromwell and the protectorate councillors', *H.J.*, XXXVI (1989).

[58] B. Worden, 'Oliver Cromwell and the council', in P. Little, ed., *The Cromwellian Protectorate* (2007), p. 104.

Protectorate is well named; Cromwell had *the* predominant role in decision-making during the Cromwellian Protectorate.

In choosing members of the new council, a major aim was to reassure conservative opinion about the intentions of the new regime. Eight of the fifteen members of the first council were civilians and only three (John Desborough, Charles Fleetwood and John Lambert) can be categorized definitely as 'soldiers'; later nominations to the council increased its civilian flavour. One of the earliest acts of the new Protector and council was to abolish the oath of Engagement which forced men to recognize the abolition of the monarchy and House of Lords. The 'loyalism' which had induced moderates to support the Rump was transferred to Cromwell, who sought to acquire its mantle as the bulwark against radical change. One of Cromwell's themes in his speeches to the first Protectorate parliament when it met in September 1654 was the need for 'healing and settling'. 'Remembering transactions too particularly (at least in the hearts of many of you)', he said, 'may set the wound fresh a-bleeding.' As part of the healing process, sequestrations (which had opened up deep wounds in county society) were reduced, and Cromwell frequently interfered personally to protect individual ex-royalists from the vengeance of sequestration commissioners. In the early phase of the Protectorate, too, Cromwell used to good effect a political ploy he had employed in 1649, depicting his regime as the saviour of the country from dangerous threats like Levellerism. Was not the country before the Protectorate was established, he asked MPs in the first Protectorate parliament, 'almost trampled under foot, under desire and contempt by men of Levelling principles . . . for the orders of men and ranks of men, did not that Levelling principles tend to the reducing all to an equality?' He followed that with a declaration of his support for the established hierarchical social order: 'a nobleman, a gentleman, and a yeoman. (That is a good interest of the nation and a great one.)'[59]

These were soothing noises to gentlemen whose fears of the imminence of social disorder and perhaps full-scale popular rebellion were now at fever pitch. Not only had recent events from the execution of the king in 1649 to the radical proposals discussed in Barebones Parliament been deeply disturbing for them, but also the aftermath of one of the worst economic crises of the sixteenth and seventeenth centuries had brought major social problems that threatened to spill over into attacks on property. Between 1646 and 1650 the harvest failed in successive years, bringing high food prices, escalating poverty, food riots and the prospect of popular rebellion. Moreover, as has been seen, the paranoia of the gentry was further heightened by exaggerated stories of Ranters and religious radicalism that were disseminated in the early 1650s. In these circumstances, the signals that came from London at the beginning of the Protectorate were designed to calm gentry fears. So too was the fact that the new regime did not continue the drastic purges of JPs undertaken during Barebones Parliament. Commissions of the peace still consisted far more than before the Civil War of men from outside the old county elites, but established gentry began to drift back to act as JPs and assessment

---

[59] Abbott, *Writings and Speeches*, III, pp. 435, 438.

commissioners. As will be seen, the major-generals' interlude in 1655–6 slowed down the process, but only temporarily. The Protectorate, writes Professor Underdown, 'was moving in the right direction, towards a reunion of the nation and of the local communities of which it was made'.[60]

Not only did the new regime interfere as little as possible with the personnel of local government, it also (with the outstanding exception of the rule of the major-generals) allowed local officials a large amount of freedom to get on with administering the areas under their control. Nor was this a recipe for the breakdown of local government, which it is often assumed took place in the 1650s. On the contrary, the normal administrative and judicial processes of local government in those counties which have been studied continued with remarkably little interruption. Indeed, the administration of the poor law, which was the biggest task of seventeenth-century local authorities, appears to have been carried out in the 1650s more efficiently than ever before. Far from being abandoned, as older historians like E. M. Leonard believed, the poor laws were enforced in the 1650s, outdoor relief granted, pauper children apprenticed and educated, and provisions made in workhouses, hospitals and almshouses for the aged and infirm. In other spheres, too – road maintenance, criminal jurisdiction, the control of wages and of the prices of consumption goods – the record of local government in the 1650s seems to have been no worse, and in some cases much better, than at other times in the seventeenth century.[61]

It was not the desire for the return of efficient local government that contributed to the downfall of the Protectorate. Nor was it the lack of firm central government. The Cromwellian government satisfied the requirements expected of seventeenth-century governments, whether monarchical or republican: the regulation of the domestic economy and overseas trade, and the maintenance of internal law and order, England's defence against invasion and the country's international prestige. In many respects, government in the 1650s did this in just as muddled and inconsistent a way as before. This is true of the regulation of the economy, for example; this was no embryonic age of economic *laissez-faire*. The Cromwellian government's interference in the economy was as misdirected and unsuccessful as had been that of earlier governments.[62] In two respects, however, the record of the Cromwellian government seems to have been superior to that of the Stuarts. It was less corrupt and the most obvious administrative wrangles were stamped out.[63] Secondly, its handling of foreign affairs was admired even by its enemies. The hoary examination question often asked about

[60] D. Underdown, 'Settlement in the counties 1653–8', in Aylmer, *Interregnum*, p. 177.

[61] The view of E. M. Leonard, *The Early History of English Poor Relief* (1900) is not upheld by A. L. Beier, 'Poor law in Warwickshire 1630–60', *P. & P.*, XXXV (1966), pp. 77–100; Aylmer, *State's Servants*, pp. 308–11; Morrill, *Cheshire*, ch. 6; G. C. F. Forster, 'County government in Yorkshire during the Interregnum', *Northern History*, XII (1976), pp. 84–104 and Hughes, *Warwickshire*, pp. 277–82.

[62] G. D. Ramsay, 'Industrial *Laissez Faire* and the policy of Cromwell', *Econ. H.R.*, 1st ser., XVI (1946), pp. 93–110.

[63] Aylmer, *State's Servants*, especially pp. 139–67, 328.

Cromwell's foreign policy, whether it was dominated by commercial or religious motives, is really irrelevant. Not only are the two motives not always incompatible, but the question presupposes that foreign policy is made in a vacuum. In reality, foreign policy is made up of a succession of day-to-day decisions, one decision forcing another. In making peace with the Dutch in April 1654, Cromwell had little option but to choose a French alliance not a Spanish alliance, because of the current Franco–Dutch friendship. Motives are often superimposed on foreign policy by historians. What is remarkable about Cromwell's foreign policy is that it was as successful as it was. There were few among Cromwell's entourage who had much expertise in international affairs. In these circumstances, failures could be expected. The Western Design, an attempt to break into the Spanish Caribbean Empire, was a fiasco. The combined land and sea expeditionary force lacked Cromwell's usually meticulous attention to detail; it was badly supplied, and led by two men, one from the army and one from the navy, who differed about both the aims and methods of the Design. Its one success, the capture of Jamaica, so highly prized in the eighteenth century, was seen in the 1650s as scant reward for the expenditure on it of men and money. Yet elsewhere much seemed to have been achieved. English rule was firmly established in Ireland and Scotland. The Dutch peace was very advantageous to England and rid Charles Stuart of a Dutch base and support. The Protector signed a series of commercial treaties with European powers, which were as important as indicators of England's standing as for their content. England's reorganized navy under Admiral Robert Blake was busy sweeping nests of pirates and royalists off the seas, and the Spanish war, though expensive, was popular as a patriotic war against England's national and religious enemy. In the second half of the seventeenth century, the 1650s were looked back to as a time when England's diplomatic standing in the world was very high.

The Protectorate's success in appealing to moderate opinion inevitably meant that its achievements as a reforming regime were limited. Its record in this respect, though, is not totally barren. Certainly it fell far short of the reforming ideals Cromwell had seemed to champion earlier. The reforming ordinances issued by the Protector and council of state before the first parliament met in September 1654 were pale shadows of the sweeping reforms many in the army had wanted. The difficulties, of course, were immense, as the history of the Rump and of Barebones Parliament had demonstrated. Even Cromwell's ordinance to make the access of litigants to chancery easier and cheaper – a 'milk-and-water ordinance' compared with the radicals' dream of abolishing chancery – met with fierce opposition from lawyers in the first Protectorate parliament.[64] There was also the problem of priorities. Given the vast financial and constitutional problems of the regime, educational schemes, like the proposed new university of Durham, inevitably suffered. It is a tribute to Cromwell's sincere desire for reform that projects like this were considered, and, as in the case of the Durham college, sometimes completed.

---

[64] I. Roots, *The Great Rebellion* (1966), p. 175. See also I. Roots, 'Cromwell's ordinances: the early legislation of the Protectorate', in Aylmer, ed., *Interregnum*, pp. 143–64.

Cromwell's most appealing and successful achievement was in the organization of religious life in England.[65] During the Protectorate only a minimum of state control over religion was exercised. In keeping with Cromwell's strategy of appealing to the pre-Civil War rulers of the counties, most of the State's control was exercised by local commissions of 'ejectors', set up by an ordinance of August 1654, who had the power to expel ministers they felt unfit to hold office. An earlier ordinance of March 1654 set up a general commission of 'triers' in London who were to approve the appointment of all ministers. No doubt to the relief of many landowners, the 'triers' made no attempts to question their right to present nominees to livings in their possession. The only other intervention made by the State was by trustees, set up by an ordinance of September 1654, who were to supplement the income of poorly endowed clergy from the income of ex-ecclesiastical estates. As has been emphasized above, Cromwell and the council did not aim to establish the kind of religious toleration that developed in nineteenth- and twentieth-century Britain. Nevertheless, within this loose framework of state control a vast diversity of religious practices was tolerated. For the first time in England the initiative which determined the form of worship in each parish came from below, from the individual ministers and congregations, and not from above, from the established Church and State. In the majority of parish churches this probably meant that there was no great change: congregations continued to worship with ministers ordained before 1640 as they had in the days before Laud's innovations. The biggest difference was the substitution of the Presbyterian *Directory of Worship* for the Book of Common Prayer, but, as Dr Cross explains, the *Directory*

> offered a guide to the form of service to be performed by the incumbent but did not prescribe set forms of prayer. Few Calvinists could have disagreed with its theology and probably the majority of English parish ministers who remained in their livings still were under the influence of Calvin and his popularisers.[66]

In some parishes, congregations went further towards the establishment of a Presbyterian system with lay elders, and even the development of interparochial classical organizations in some parts of the country. The Cromwellian Church also included more radical Protestants than Presbyterians. At the Restoration well over a hundred Independent ministers were ejected from the parochial livings into which they had been accepted by the Cromwellian general commission of 'triers' in London. Other religious groups, at both ends of the doctrinal spectrum, though not given the official seal of approval by the 'triers', were allowed to worship without any harassment from the government. At the radical end, separatist Protestant churches of every conceivable variety flourished during the Protectorate: gathered churches in which the form of worship and often the ministers were chosen by the individual congregations, and which only sixty years before had been ruthlessly suppressed by Elizabeth I. In these circumstances of diverse

---

[65] J. R. Collins, 'The Church settlement of Oliver Cromwell', *History*, 87 (2002).

[66] C. Cross, 'The Church in England 1646–60', in Aylmer, ed., *Interregnum*, p. 107.

doctrines and personalities, it was not easy to organize associations of similar churches, but some gathered churches did so, the most outstanding examples being the General Baptists and the Particular Baptists who developed regional organizations in the 1650s.[67] Some even began to work for cooperation among ministers and congregations of different types in a genuine ecumenical spirit. The most famous example, Richard Baxter's Worcestershire Association, included Independents, episcopalians and 'men of no faction nor siding with any party, but owning that which was good in all as far as they could discuss it'. Baxter later felt that England was on the road 'to have become a land of saints and a pattern of holiness to all the world, and the unmatchable paradise of the earth'.[68]

Even the minority of High Church episcopalians and Catholics in England were given remarkable freedom from persecution by Cromwell's government, as long as they did not threaten public order. For this reason sects, such as the Quakers, Socinians and Ranters, whose activities were often violent and antisocial, were persecuted more than those Catholic priests and Laudian clerics whose activities were confined to the houses of their landed patrons. It is the tolerance of Cromwell and his regime that stands out: in Oliver's conversations with the Quaker leader George Fox, his friendship with the Catholic Sir Kenelm Digby, the readmission of the Jews, and so on. What substance is there in the popular legend of the intolerant, 'kill-joy' aspects of the Protectorate? This seems to be rooted in the hopes of achieving a moral reformation, common to all the regimes of the 1650s, and which resulted in the campaigns to suppress alehouses and Sunday sports, for example. Such aspirations were widely shared, certainly by many gentry, for security as well as moral considerations. Too often, they have been used to erect Cromwell into a caricature of an intolerant philistine 'Puritan', against music, dancing, painting and the arts. Enough is now known of Cromwell's weakness for his long weekends at Hampton Court, his patronage of secular music and dancing, artists and writers, to explode that myth for ever.[69] Indeed, one of the great achievements of recent Cromwellian studies has been to underline that point. Paul Hunneyball has shown that the Protectorate spent more than the government of Charles I in the 1630s on the refurbishment of ex-royal palaces like Whitehall and Hampton Court, as well as on tapestries, statues and paintings. Particularly interesting are the purchases on Cromwell's direct orders for his own apartment at Hampton Court of Gentileshi's painting of *Basheba Washing Herself* and Schiavona's *Madonna and Child*. Patrick Little has also written persuasively about Cromwell's love of music, horses and hunting, putting Cromwell firmly in the context of the gentry culture of seventeenth-century England.[70]

---

[67] B. R. White, 'The organization of the Particular Baptists 1644–60', *J. Eccl. H.*, XVII (1966), pp. 209–25.

[68] Richard Baxter, *Autobiography* (N. H. Keeble, ed., 1974), p. 84.

[69] Hill, *God's Englishman*, pp. 197–9.

[70] P. Hunneyball, 'Cromwellian style: the architectural trappings of the Protectorate regime', in Little, *Cromwellian Protectorate*; P. Little, 'Music at the court of King Oliver', *The Court Historian*, 12 (2007); P. Little, 'Cromwell and falconry', *Cromwelliana*, ser. II, no. 5 (2008); P. Little, 'The culture of the Cromwellian court', *Cromwelliana*, ser. II, no. 6 (2009).

As will be seen, Cromwell's excessive tolerance went too far for many contemporaries. But he was always careful not to offend respectable contemporary opinion. His church settlement respected local interests and property rights. As it evolved in the 1650s it had many elements desired by many moderate parliamentarians of the 1640s: a loose form of state control, retention of lay patronage and tithes, and toleration of those Protestant sects which did not disrupt public order.

> Had Cromwell lived for a further decade [in the opinion of Dr Cross] perhaps many of the Independent churches and some of the Baptist churches on the periphery of the national church might have been more fully comprehended within it. With the deaths of the remaining Laudian bishops perhaps some modified form of episcopacy, as envisaged by Ussher and Baxter, might possibly have been voluntarily adopted as a means of unity by the national church.[71]

The failures of Cromwellian government

Whatever case can be made out for the Cromwellian government (and it is likely that future research may have yet more to say in its favour), Cromwell, like every regime since 1640, failed to find an acceptable constitution to replace the one overthrown in 1640. Consequently, the achievements outlined in the previous section were short-lived. Professor Trevor-Roper suggested that Cromwell, like James I and unlike Elizabeth I, 'failed through lack of . . . parliamentary management by the executive'.[72] As he must have known, there was more to it than that. Cromwell failed because, despite his genuine desire for 'healing and settling', he often gave priority to his aim of achieving a godly reformation and to succeed in that aim he needed the support of the army. Unfortunately for the prospect of political harmony, by 1653 the traditional rulers of England were at one in seeing the army as the prime danger to everything they held dear: rule through parliament, their own supremacy in their localities, low taxation, and their control of the Church, their wives, children, servants and tenants. In spite of Cromwell's efforts to woo the parliamentary classes, his only slim chance of getting a cooperative parliament elected on a propertied franchise (as Cromwell made clear at Putney and later he was not willing to consider any other kind of franchise) was to cut his links with the army, risking an army revolt, the reversal of much that had been achieved so far and (above all) the end of his hopes for further reformation. In 1657 the offer of the crown to Cromwell as part of a new constitutional package, the Humble Petition and Advice, presented him with a chance of taking the road towards 'settlement'. But by rejecting the crown Cromwell signalled his unwillingness to take that road if it meant endangering the prospects of 'reformation'. In so doing, however, he increased the magnitude of the political task facing him, which points towards the

---

[71] Cross, 'The Church', in Aylmer, ed., *Interregnum*, pp. 119–20.

[72] H. R. Trevor-Roper, 'Cromwell and his parliaments', in his *Religion, the Reformation and Social Change*, p. 388.

fundamental reason for his failure to establish a lasting constitutional settlement. His task was almost impossible: to rule as an army leader and secure the confidence of a political nation which would not tolerate the intervention of the army in politics.

Despite Cromwell's conciliatory speech to parliament when it met in September 1654, in which he emphasized his desire for a settlement, his conservative social prejudices and his achievements in the last ten months, his position as Protector came under strong attack in the first week of the session. This was not simply a result of his failure to manage the House, although the redistribution of seats and new franchise under the Instrument of Government made its management a great deal harder than previously: compared with the Long Parliament there was a massive increase in the numbers of country MPs at the expense of borough MPs. Nor was the opposition to Cromwell simply from hardened civilian republicans like Hazelrige, Thomas Scot and John Bradshaw, who could never forgive and forget the dissolution of the Rump; many of these withdrew after Cromwell's dramatic intervention in parliament on 12 September, when he forced MPs to sign a 'Recognition', promising not to alter the government 'as it is settled [by the Instrument of Government] in a single person and a Parliament'. Nevertheless parliamentary opposition continued. Not all features of the Instrument of Government were objectionable to MPs: the executive authority of a single person with constitutional checks, and the guarantees of regular parliaments were welcomed. What few MPs could accept were the powers given by the Instrument to Cromwell and the army, especially the Protector's authority to enact ordinances when parliament was not in session. In the few short weeks of its life, parliament voted against these and other rights which the Protector had been granted by the Instrument. Even the Protector's control of the army was questioned; it was proposed that after Cromwell's death the army should be controlled by parliament alone, and in the meantime there should be an immediate reduction in the army establishment. In the first Protectorate parliament, the root of the difference between Cromwell and the parliamentary classes was laid bare. The Instrument of Government perpetuated the power of the army and there would be no parliamentary cooperation until the Instrument in that respect was amended.

Moreover, another source of major disagreement between Protector and MPs surfaced during the first Protectorate parliament. It soon became apparent that Cromwell differed greatly from most MPs on the extent of religious liberty that could be allowed without endangering political stability. As has been seen, Cromwell's commitment to religious liberty was far from total and it is possible to exaggerate his distaste for the orchestrated campaign of religious intolerance that had been under way since 1650, in which the Ranters had been used as bogeymen to frighten people back into the ranks of Protestant orthodoxy. He had little sympathy for the view of the Socinian divine, John Biddle, whom parliament imprisoned and whose books, which argued against the divinity of Christ, were ordered to be burned by the common hangman. Nevertheless, the Biddle case (and the more famous one of James Nayler in the second Protectorate parliament) highlighted the danger that parliamentary religious intolerance might be extended to religious groups with which Cromwell did sympathize.

A parliamentary committee appointed in December 1654 with the daunting task of enumerating all 'damnable heresies' showed disconcerting signs that it might include Independent and Baptist views in its list. Cromwell's commitment to religious liberty was far greater than that of the majority in parliament. 'Where shall we have men of a Universal Spirit? Everyone desires to have liberty but none will give it', he is reported as saying in December 1654. On 22 January 1655, Cromwell impatiently dissolved parliament, interpreting the minimum parliamentary session decreed by the Instrument of Government as five lunar not calendar months. In his dissolution speech he unleashed the full force of his anger at MPs because they had not 'given a full liberty to Godly men of differing judgements'. 'Nothing will satisfy them, unless they can put their fingers upon their brethren's consciences, to pinch them there', he berated them. 'What greater hypocrisy than for those who were oppressed by the Bishops to become the greatest oppressors themselves, as soon as their yoke was removed.'[73]

In March 1655 a royalist rising in Wiltshire led by Penruddock was easily suppressed by Desborough, who was appointed 'Major-General of the West' for the purpose. This, and the discovery of paper plots by the royalists in other parts of the country, was made the occasion for the appointment later in 1655 of eleven major-generals, and England and Wales were divided amongst them.[74] By October they had received their instructions and were on their way to their 'cantons'. Like a lot of other things about the major-generals experiment, though, the reasons for it are not clear. Perhaps hindsight puts the royalist threat in 1655 into a perspective not possible at the time; but John Thurloe and his government spies were always one step ahead of the plotters, and Cromwell knew how divided amongst themselves they were. It may be that, as well as royalist insurrections, the major-generals were designed to solve the Protectorate's growing financial problems. To get the support of the landed classes Cromwell had to reduce taxation, which meant reducing expenditure on the army. This may have been the intention behind the local volunteer militias, to be organized by the major-generals and financed by a 'decimation' tax of one-tenth of the estates of known royalists worth over £100 p.a. in lands and £1,500 p.a. in goods. Not only would the new militia be cheaper than the professional army, but it was to be locally run by commissioners appointed to assist the major-generals. Security would be tightened up, and the standing army replaced by a cheaper, locally run militia.

Much more than this, however, lay behind the decision to appoint the major-generals. It was also made because during the course of 1655 Cromwell's desire to secure a godly reformation reached new heights. To achieve this, he was more willing than ever to use autocratic methods if necessary. Even before the establishment of the major-generals, in the aftermath of the disillusionment that followed the failure of the first Protectorate parliament, Cromwell indulged in iron-fisted tactics against those

---

[73] C. H. Firth, ed., *The Clarke Papers* (4 vols., 1891–1901), II, pp. xxxiv–xxxvii; Abbott, *Writings and Speeches*, III, p. 586.

[74] The best starting point for the major-generals is C. Durston, *Cromwell's Major-Generals: godly government during the English Revolution* (2001). See also I. Roots, 'Swordsmen and decimators – Cromwell's major-generals', in Parry, ed., *English Civil War*, pp. 78–92.

who questioned the legality of his rule. The outstanding example is the case of George Cony, a merchant who had been imprisoned in November 1654 for refusing to pay customs duties on imported silk, for forcibly preventing customs officers from seizing his property, and for refusing to pay the fine imposed on him. The argument used by Cony's lawyers on their client's behalf was that the customs dues were illegal because they had been levied by order of the Protector and council but not endorsed by parliament. When the case came before the court of upper bench in May 1655, the Protector and council ordered that Cony's lawyers were to be imprisoned for having the effrontery to challenge the protectoral prerogative. Moreover, in a manner not unlike Charles's disregard for the law in the Five Knights' case in 1627 (see p. 143), Lord Chief Justice Rolle was hauled before the council for allowing Cony's case to proceed and, under this pressure, he resigned.

A few weeks later Cromwell received news of a disaster that seems to have convinced him still further that extraordinary measures needed to be taken. On 24 July 1653, news of the defeat three months earlier of the Western Design expeditionary force at San Domingo in the Caribbean reached London. The effect on Cromwell was catastrophic; it raised the dreadful possibility that God's blessing, which he believed he had hitherto enjoyed, was now lost. His letters during the next few weeks reiterate his providential interpretation of what had happened in the Caribbean. The message was a harsh one. 'We have cause to be humbled for the reproof God gave us at San Domingo, upon the account of our sins, as well as others', he wrote on one occasion. Another letter was even more bitter: 'We have provoked the Lord and it is good for us to know so, and to be abased for the same . . . we should . . . lay our mouths . . . in the dust.' Yet, as so often in moods of depression, Cromwell saw grounds for hope. 'Though God has torn us yet He will heal us; though He hath smitten us, yet He will bind us up; after two days He will revive us, in the third day He will ease us up, and we shall live in His sight.' But for this to happen it was essential first that 'all manner of vice may be thoroughly discountenanced and severely punished; and that such a form of government may be exercised that virtue and godliness may receive due encouragement'.[75]

The principal effect on Cromwell of the failure of the Western Design was thus to reinforce his view that 'the liberty and prosperity of the nation depends upon [moral] reformation', which accounts for his determination to use the major-generals as agents for promoting it. Even the first draft of the instructions to the major-generals on 22 August 1655 reflected the need 'to encourage and promote godliness and virtue and discourage all profaneness and ungodliness'. During the next few weeks, coinciding with Cromwell's crisis of conscience triggered by the news from the Caribbean, the council reinforced the major-generals 'moral order' functions. Their final instructions, issued in October 1655, included orders to put into effect 'the Laws against Drunkenness, Blasphemy, and taking of the name of God in vain, by swearing and cursing, Plays

---

[75] Abbott, *Writings and Speeches*, III, pp. 857–8, 859, 756, 860, 585.

and interludes, and prophaning of the Lord's day, and such like wickedness and abominations'. They were also instructed to control the number of alehouses and suppress gaming houses and London brothels. 'The sole end' of the major-generals experiment, Cromwell said later, 'was the security of the nation and the suppression of vice and encouragement of virtue, the very end of magistracy'.[76]

The experiment was not a total failure. Part of the odious reputation of the rule of the major-generals owes more to the jibes of their enemies than to historical accuracy. Their social backgrounds were different from those of the gentry with whom they came into conflict in the localities, but they were not all low-born nonentities, the 'silly mean fellows' of Mrs Hutchinson's sneer. Although their enemies labelled them as dictatorial 'satraps' and 'bashaws', most acted in strict accordance with the law and their instructions.

The striking fact that emerges about the major-generals, when some of the myths about them have been stripped away, is the differences among them. This is certainly true about their effectiveness. All faced enormous difficulties: non-cooperation of local people, too-large areas under their control and, often, a central government insensitive to their needs. How they coped with these difficulties depended on their strength of character. William Goffe, the major-general of Sussex, Hampshire and Berkshire, was 'temperamentally unsuited to the administrative task set him'.[77] Consequently, his constructive impact on local administration was slight. Major-General Worsley, on the other hand, had none of Goffe's timidity and lack of self-confidence. He is said to have closed 200 alehouses in Blackburn Hundred (Lancashire) alone. His dynamic administration in Lancashire, Cheshire and Staffordshire was sometimes embarrassing even for the government, which intervened to moderate his enthusiasm.[78] Their differences apart, however, what united the major-generals was the hatred they roused in the localities. They represented an experiment in direct rule from Westminster. Outsiders were imposed on the localities and provincial resentment, so strong in the sixteenth and seventeenth centuries, was roused. Not only this, but the major-generals began to reopen the wounds in county society, inflicted in the 1640s. Operating the decimation tax meant unearthing royalist pasts which many were trying to forget. The local communities closed their ranks, and in the elections to parliament in August 1656 demonstrated their total opposition to the centralization, high taxation and army rule represented by the major-generals, who failed dismally to persuade the electors to send pro-Cromwellian MPs to the new parliament. Provincial England never forgot the major-generals, and the political nation became even more determined to oppose the political role of the army.

The prospects of cooperation were, therefore, not bright when the second Protectorate parliament met in September 1656, even though Cromwell and the council excluded over a hundred MPs thought likely to be critics of the regime.

---

[76] Ibid., IV, pp. 377–8.
[77] Fletcher, *Sussex*, p. 307.
[78] Aylmer, *State's Servants*, p. 313; Morrill, *Cheshire*, pp. 276–87.

Surprisingly, however, this does not appear to have caused much initial opposition in parliament. The Protector's tirade against 'Papists and Cavaliers' as 'un-Christian' and 'un-English like' seems to have been received enthusiastically, and he gained support for the war against Spain. Progress, too, was made with legislation to regulate alehouses, set the poor to work, abolish 'undecent fashions' among women and other matters dear to the hearts of the godly. MPs even made progress on legal reforms, taking up Lambert's proposals for a court of law and equity at York, and discussing plans to establish regional registry offices for proving wills and for country land registries.

What put an end to the brief period of harmony was the case of James Nayler, which became a *cause célèbre* in the winter of 1656–7, and which revealed again the serious differences between Protector and most MPs on the extent of religious liberty that could safely be allowed without upsetting the existing social and political order.

Information

The case of James Nayler, 1656

James Nayler was an ex-soldier from Lambert's northern army who in the 1650s became a leading Quaker evangelist. The 'crime' for which Nayler was savagely punished was that, as part of a revivalist evangelical tour of the West Country, he rode into Bristol on an ass, re-enacting Christ's entry into Jerusalem. For this he was brought to London, found guilty by parliament of 'horrid blasphemy' on 8 December 1656 without a division, and sentenced to be branded, bored through the tongue, flogged twice and then imprisoned for life.

Behind this violent intolerance lay the fact that, as has been seen, the Quakers had become a prime focus of conservative fears that religious diversity would lead to social subversion and political radicalism. Their refusal to pay tithes or take off their hats before magistrates, and their habit of violently disrupting church services, lent weight to such fears. Cromwell does not appear to have had much sympathy for Nayler's views. He distanced himself publicly from Nayler; writing to the speaker of parliament on Christmas Day 1656, he commented that 'if this [Nayler's activities] be liberty, God deliver me from such liberty'. Cromwell's definition of religious liberty did not extend to groups like the Quakers who disturbed the public peace. But that was the limit of Cromwell's agreement with MPs on the Nayler case. What worried him was that MPs, as they had shown in the earlier case of John Biddle, made no distinction between Socinians like Biddle or Quakers like Nayler and more moderate religious groups like Baptists and Independents. This was a point he put to a meeting of army officers on 27 February 1657: might not 'the case of James Nayler . . . happen to be your own Case?'

Nayler's case had another consequence apart from disrupting cooperation between Protector and MPs. It was probably the reason why Cromwell decided to abandon the Instrument of Government, which had failed to give him the means to check parliamentary religious intolerance. The existing single-chamber parliament, Cromwell told the army officers on 27 February, 'stood in need of a check or balancing power (meaning the House of Lords or a House so constituted)'.[79] This is why Cromwell cooperated with moves early in 1657 to end the major-generals experiment and introduce a new constitution, the Humble Petition and Advice.

Information

The Humble Petition and Advice, 1657

The main provisions of the Humble Petition and Advice were:

- Cromwell was to be king not Lord Protector.

- He was to be advised by a privy council not a council of state.

- Parliaments were to meet regularly as under the Instrument of Government but were now to consist of two Houses, including an upper chamber known as 'the other House', consisting of 40–70 men appointed by Cromwell and approved by the Commons.

- The religious provisions were similar to those of the Instrument of Government apart from the inclusion of additional penalties for blasphemy.

There is little doubt that Cromwell connived at the defeat of Desborough's bill to continue the decimation tax in January 1657; his son-in-law, John Claypole, led the successful attack on it in parliament. Nor was he unaware of discussions for a new constitution. During recent months he had been forging closer links with civilian interests among his advisers. More and more, Lambert, Fleetwood and Desborough found that they had to compete for the Protector's ear with civilians like Lord Broghill, Sir Charles Wolseley and Viscount Fauconberg.[80] Ominously for the 'grandees', the

---

[79] Abbott, *Writings and Speeches*, IV, p. 417.

[80] Austin Woolrych, 'Last quests for a settlement 1657–60', in Aylmer, ed., *Interregnum*, pp. 183–204.

assessment to support the army was drastically cut in 1657 to £35,000 a month from its level of £60,000 a month from 1654 to 1657 and £120,000 a month during 1653 and early 1654.[81] The Humble Petition and Advice was the culmination of these 'civilianizing' tendencies. Most of the constitutional and religious clauses of the new constitution were not unwelcome to Cromwell. Its provisions for parliamentary limitations on the executive (parliament had to approve the great officers of state, for example) echoed *The Heads of the Proposals* of 1647. Moreover, the second chamber, 'the other House', whose members were to be nominated by Protector and council, promised to be, in the words of Cromwell's principal secretary John Thurloe, 'a great security and bulwark to the honest interest' against religious intolerance.[82] Nor were the limitations put on religious freedom by the new constitution out of line with Cromwell's definition of religious toleration. All of these aspects of the Humble Petition and Advice Cromwell could accept. What he could not stomach was the associated offer to him of the crown.

Information

Why did Cromwell reject the offer to become King Oliver I?

This is a much-disputed question to which historians have produced two main answers:

- Fear of the army's reaction was a prime consideration.
- Fear of what God would think weighed much more heavily with Cromwell.

As with most historical questions, the answer to this one probably contains elements of both explanations. But the view argued here is that Cromwell feared God much more than he did the army.

It is difficult to believe that, given his bravado performance in outfacing hostile army officers on 27 February 1657 and at other times in his career, fear of the army was a prime consideration. Cromwell's fear that he was someone whom 'God has no pleasure in' had been heightened by the failure of the Western Design. Would his fears not become realized if he restored the monarchy that had been abolished with

---

[81] M. Ashley, *Financial and Commercial Policy under the Cromwellian Protectorate* (1934), p. 77.
[82] T. Birch, ed., *A Collection of State Papers of John Thurloe* (7 vols., 1742), IV, p. 93.

> God's blessing in 1649? This is the providential reason for his rejection of the crown, which he explained on 13 April to a delegation of MPs:
>
> Truly the providence of God has laid this title aside providentially . . . God has seemed providentially not only to strike at the family [i.e. the Stuarts] but at the name [i.e. monarchy itself]. God . . . hath not only dealt so with the persons and the family, but he hath blasted the title . . . I would not seek to set up that that providence hath destroyed and laid in the dust, and I would not build Jericho again.

In June 1657 Cromwell was installed again as Lord Protector under the amended Humble Petition and Advice. His rejection of the crown, however, showed that he was still committed to reformation and that he would not be shackled by constitutional chains.

One of the greatest unanswerable puzzles about Oliver Cromwell is whether, given more time, he would have been able to pursue reformation with the support of the army and at the same time have won more enthusiastic civilian support. The evidence is inconclusive; Cromwell died on 3 September 1658, having failed. But the last part of Cromwell's life does not prove that, given more time, he would not have succeeded. It was the republican MPs excluded in 1656 who returned to parliament in the second session in 1658 and dynamited the new constitution, and forced Cromwell to dissolve his last parliament in February. Despite Lambert's resignation Cromwell still retained the loyalty of the army, as well as of the civilian Cromwellians. Yet there is precious little evidence, either, that Cromwell would have succeeded. By the end of his life the extent of committed civilian support at his court and in the country was small. The most that one can say is that Cromwell was the only man who could possibly have retained the support of the army, while broadening the base of his political party in the country. What happened to a Protector who took an alternative course and cut his links with the army is seen in the brief reign of Oliver's son, Richard.

The end of the Good Old Cause, 1658–1660

The question usually asked about the closing stages of the Interregnum – why was the monarchy restored in 1660? – ignores the equally important question: why was the monarchy *not* restored until nearly two years after Oliver Cromwell's death? Amid the confusion and complexities of post-Cromwellian politics one fact shines out: the lack of widespread enthusiasm for the Stuarts. Most Englishmen continued to hope that an alternative constitutional settlement to Stuart monarchy could be found. As in 1651 and 1655, the planned nationwide royalist rising in the summer of 1659 was a total failure. All this makes explaining why the Stuart monarchy was restored (and restored unconditionally, as will be seen) in 1660 more difficult than it might seem.

This difficulty is compounded by the fact that one explanation often given for the collapse of the republic – the inadequacy as a ruler of Oliver's successor, Richard Cromwell – has been persuasively questioned in recent years. The image of Richard Cromwell as 'Tumbledown Dick' who lacked the training and aptitude for government will no longer hold water.[83] Contemporaries, like Bulstrode Whitelocke, commented favourably on the new Protector, who 'did carry himself better than was expected.[84] During the first six months of the new Protectorate between September 1658 and March 1659 he displayed political skills designed to contain the army and the Commonwealthsmen who were a potential threat to the Protectorate. His handling of the third Protectorate parliament, which met at the end of January 1659, was efficient, and at least some of the blame for its eventual failure must lie at the door of the senior army officers, 'the Wallingford House grandees' (named after Fleetwood's London residence).

It is true that the grandees had grounds for fearing that they were losing influence. Although Richard made a serious effort to gain army support, he also relied for advice on civilian Cromwellians. These fears were confirmed when Richard allowed the civilian Cromwellians in parliament to lead the conservative majority there in support of measures to restrict both the extent of religious toleration and the army's freedom to indulge in political activity. The army responded to parliament's votes of 18–20 April, which would have stripped the army of all political power, by forcing Richard to dissolve parliament on 21 April.

It is not certain that the grandees would have taken such immediate and drastic action if left to themselves. The senior officers, however, were faced with a situation very like that in 1647. Early in 1659 there was a resurgence of radicalism within the junior ranks of the army, calling for many of the reforms demanded in 1647, and fuelled by the same sort of material grievances. As in 1647 the grandees were faced by pressure from below to take more radical action than they really wanted. The most bizarre element in this reincarnation of 1647 was the alliance between the army radicals and the republicans. The hatred between the army and Rump Commonwealth was forgotten, and ironically the army, which had dissolved the Rump in April 1653, now recalled it on 7 May 1659. It is a measure of the diminishing political options left open to the army that the Rump, which had disappointed radical expectations in 1649, was recalled on a wave of renewed radicalism ten years later. What would have happened if the grandees had resisted the pressure from within the army, as Oliver Cromwell had done in 1657, is not known. But what seems likely is that their failure to do so weakened the republic. So too did the failure of succeeding republican regimes to come up with a workable constitutional settlement.

---

[83] Coward, *Cromwellian Protectorate*, pp. 94–5, 101–12 and especially J. Peacey, 'The Protector humbled: Richard Cromwell and the constitution' in Little, *Cromwellian Protectorate* and 'The upbringing of Richard Cromwell', *Cromwelliana*, ser. II, no. 7 (2010), works that hopefully will be followed by a major reassessment of Richard Cromwell. See also the essays by P. Gaunt, D. L. Smith and M. Malins on Richard Cromwell in *Cromwelliana*, ser. II, no. 7 (2010).

[84] Coward, *Cromwellian Protectorate*, p. 104.

Information

The post-Protectorate republican regimes, 1659

The republican regimes of 1659 consisted of the following:

- Rule by the Rump Parliament again between May and October 1659, as Richard Cromwell began a long period of retirement from public life (he died in 1712). It spent the summer in long sterile constitutional debates and in demonstrating the antipathy felt by civilian republicans for the army.

- Rule by the army between October and December 1659 through a committee of safety ruling as an interim government. The committee proved to be as barren of successful constitutional ideas as its civilian predecessors. It also failed to maintain even the loyalty of the armies in Scotland, Yorkshire and Ireland, and the navy in the Downs. The coincidence of a government which lacked effective support combined with renewed acute trade depression undoubtedly convinced many that the republic could no longer guarantee law and order. Faced with the growing demands for a 'free' parliament or the return of the secluded members of 1648, and with organized threats to withhold taxes, Fleetwood panicked and on 24 December resigned and handed over his powers to the Rump.

- Rule by the Rump again between December 1659 and March 1660.

Beset by major rifts between republican groups and the lack of a political leader with the qualities of Oliver Cromwell to keep them in check, none of these regimes provided the guarantee of political stability that many wanted, and so some began to consider the return of the Stuarts as a possible guarantee of political and social order.

But was this fear of impending political and social chaos justified? Only very briefly in the two weeks after the army's committee of safety abdicated power in December 1659 were there significant signs of a breakdown of order, and these were short-lived and temporary. Why, then, were some people gripped by a mood of panic in the winter of 1659? The first reason is that these months saw another bout of economic depression that periodically affected the seventeenth-century English economy (as has been seen). As a result, the ever-present fear of the propertied at the prospect of riots by the 'many-headed monster of the poor' became greater. There were in fact hardly any riots, but (as usual) what people feared was the case was more important than what actually was the case. What heightend this fear was an outbreak of anti-Quaker hysteria, fuelled by the popular press, which portrayed Quakers as 'the enemy within', subverting respectable society. Barry Reay puts the point neatly: 'in 1659, as part of a more general fear of sectaries, hostility towards Quakers persuaded many to look to the monarchy as the only salvation from social and religious anarchy'.[85]

Fleetwood's resignation paved the way for General Monck, who, as the Rump reassembled, began his march south into England. Viewed with the benefit of hindsight, Monck appears wiser and surer of his goal than he probably was. Yet he was enough of a political realist, after being in London for three weeks, to grasp that the Rump was too unpopular, and the army too divided, to rule; that there was no other alternative but the restoration of the Stuarts. On 21 February, under Monck's protection, the return of the secluded MPs of 1648 to parliament made that inevitable, especially given the conciliatory noises that came from the Stuart court in exile early in 1660 (as will be seen in the next chapter). The republicans of the Rump were now easily outvoted, and on 16 March the Long Parliament, which had first met nearly twenty years before, declared itself dissolved and ordered the meeting of a Convention Parliament to deal with a future constitutional and religious settlement. In April 1660 the republic collapsed because it no longer, unlike the regimes of the Rump and of Oliver, *seemed* to provide stability and security.

---

[85] Barry Reay, *Quakers and the English Revolution*, p. 81. See also B. Coward and C. Durston, eds., *The English Revolution* (1997), pp. 208–13.

PART 4

The reigns of Charles II and James II, 1660–1688

Introduction

There is hardly any more agreement among present-day historians about the consequences of the English Revolution than there is about its causes. The main difference amongst historians has been whether the English Revolution was a major turning point in the history of Britain.

'The turning-point view' was particularly popular in the 1960s and 1970s, when its major proponent was Christopher Hill. He and others argued that not only was the English Revolution brought about by powerful and deep-rooted historical processes but its effects on the country's constitution and Church were correspondingly clear-cut, decisive and permanent. The events of the 1640s and 1650s, it was believed, so weakened the powers of the restored monarchy that England's constitutional development after 1660 diverged permanently from the general European trend towards absolutism, so that the country was irrevocably set on the road which eventually led to constitutional monarchy. 'The sixteen-forties and fifties', according to Christopher Hill, 'marked the end of medieval and Tudor England.'[1] Such historians also believed that 1660 marked an equally decisive turning point in the role of religion in the political and social life of England. They argued that from now on religious indifference grew, and religion was no longer either the great motive force or divisive issue in politics and society that it had been for a long period before 1660. It was therefore held that the early years of the Restoration witnessed the beginning of the slow but inevitable rise of religious toleration, shaped by growing religious indifference, in England.

In the last decades of the twentieth century this turning-point view was challenged by revisionist historians. They argued that, although some of the legislation of 1641 remained in force in 1660, the royal financial expedients of the 1630s remained illegal and the royal prerogative courts remained abolished, and the memory of what had happened to Charles I on the scaffold on 30 January 1649 probably served as a salutary lesson to later Stuart monarchs that there were limits to what they could do. Yet in many other respects the English Revolution may have strengthened the monarchy by bringing about a conservative backlash in its favour. As will be seen, the Convention and Cavalier Parliaments of the 1660s and 1670s left most of the crown's powers

---

[1] C. Hill, *Reformation to Industrial Revolution: a social and economic history of Britain 1530–1780* (1967), p. 106.

intact. Revisionist historians also showed that after the Restoration religion, far from losing its importance, remained a powerful political and social force.

Currently, this continuity view still has much support amongst historians, who recognise that the monarchy, though strengthened by a conservative backlash in its favour in the early 1660s, faced the same problems it had faced before 1660: the triple problems of finance, ruling multiple kingdoms and religious divisions. They also rightly emphasize that religion was a (perhaps the) primary force in the politics of Restoration England.

Yet it is now becoming clear that continuity can be carried too far. Some historians have redefined 'politics' so that it does not focus solely on institutions like parliament. According to John Miller, politics should be seen 'in a wider sense than [that used by] most political historians, a sense closer to that employed by social historians interested in power relationships and dispute resolution, often within small communities'.[2] Historians like Miller have shown that popular participation in and awareness of political issues increased greatly after 1660. This development of 'the public sphere' was not, of course, new. As has been seen, it was significant in the politics of late Elizabethan and early Stuart England. Yet the popular participation in politics and the ideological divisions (principally over religion) that had characterized the 1640s and 1650s intensified after 1660 and were carried over to shape the partisan politics of Restoration England. This was arguably one of the major consequences of the English Revolution.

Before beginning a narrative analysis of Restoration politics, it is worth saying a little more about the current views briefly described above. First, it is important to stress *the continuing strengths and weaknesses of the monarchy*. Britain in the late seventeenth century was still a personal monarchy. Like their Tudor and early Stuart predecessors, later Stuart monarchs ruled as well as reigned. Like its predecessor too, the later Stuart monarchy had a central role in the politics of the country (arguably this is true until well into the ninteenth century). Although some of its powers were stripped away from it by the parliamentary legislation of 1641, the monarchy was restored unconditionally in 1660. Attempts to impose on Charles II limitations like those set out in the Treaty of Newport of 1648 and in earlier parliamentarian proposals for a settlement with the king – principally, parliamentary control of the militia and appointment of state officials – came to nothing. Furthermore, their fear and hatred of regicide and republicanism drove many MPs in the Cavalier Parliament to approve legislation outlawing numerous claims made by parliaments during the revolution, including the right to legislate without the king and to call parliaments without the king's consent. It will be seen that the Cavalier Parliament gave Charles II massive powers of censorship, left untouched many of the king's prerogative powers, and even allowed him to keep a standing army. Above all, within just over a decade of the Restoration, the royal government's financial problems were considerably eased.

---

[2] J. Miller, *After the Civil Wars* (2000), p. 3.

Many of the weaknesses of the Stuart monarchy, however, also remained after 1660. Chief among these was the persistent fear that the crown was intent on promoting 'absolutism'. As in the early seventeenth century, it is questionable whether in fact English monarchs had a coherent 'policy' aimed at strengthening the power of the crown at the expense of parliament. The lack of an efficient central bureaucracy and the dependence of the government on the personality and ability of the monarch for the time being meant that only rarely did later Stuart governments have coherent 'policies' about domestic or foreign affairs.[3] But after 1660, as in the early part of the Stuart age, what people perceived to be the case was at least as important (and often more so) than historical reality. One of the principal reasons why many people believed that the monarchy was intent on absolutism after 1660 grew out of the crown's financial weakness, which (at least before the 1680s) was as severe as it had been in the early seventeenth century. Consequently, like his predecessors, Charles II was sometimes forced to try to secure revenue outside parliament by trying to control town governments or commissions of the peace, or inside parliament by manipulating opinion amongst MPs. Not surprisingly, these measures were interpreted as part of a concerted 'absolutist' campaign to erode parliament's place in the constitution. This belief was strengthened by a second factor which continued to destabilize politics in England after, as before, 1660: the impact of events in Scotland and Ireland. What Charles II and James II as kings of England did as rulers of their other British kingdoms had as great an impact in fuelling mistrust of them among their English subjects as had Charles I's unfortunate intrusion into Scottish affairs in the late 1630s and his negotiations with Irish Catholics in the 1640s.

Secondly, *religion continued to play an important role in politics and society*. The history of Restoration England makes it clear that religion, far from losing its importance, remained a powerful political and social force. In a great wave of militant Anglicanism, some local gentlemen suppressed conventicles and ejected church ministers even before the Cavalier Parliament met in 1661, and when it did meet it put a savage, repressive code (the Clarendon Code) on the statute book, directed at all those who refused to conform to the established Church. But as in the constitutional sphere, the effects of the English Revolution were diverse. The history of the patchy way in which the Clarendon Code was put into practice makes clear that not everyone was sympathetic to the intolerant aspirations of militant Anglicans and that some were more sympathetic to the long post-Reformation tradition of a comprehensive Church, broken by Charles I and Laud in the 1630s and revived by Cromwell in the 1650s, than they were to the narrow Church erected in the early 1660s.

In contrast a third issue is *the transformation of politics*. Here the impact of what happened in the 1640s and 1650s is very marked. In a wide-ranging study of the political history of towns from 1650 to 1720, P. D. Halliday notes the creation from the mid-seventeenth century of a 'world that played a different kind of politics, one

---

[3] J. Miller, 'The crown and the borough charters in the reign of Charles II', *E.H.R.*, C (1985), *passim*.

that permitted, or even encouraged, the exclusion from government of some with the proper credentials because their political loyalties or religious sympathies made them suspect'.[4] He depicts a political culture that was becoming more deeply riven than ever before by ideologically based controversy. What is more, he and others have noted how this development was complemented by an increase in the numbers of people involved in government and in debates about political issues. Building on what had happened before the mid-seventeenth century, it seems as if political debates were now never restricted to a narrow wealthy, educated social elite. Two pieces of research illustrate the increase in popular participation in government and in political debate in the mid-seventeenth century. 'It seems likely', according to John Morrill, 'that [in the 1650s] the bureaucracy of local government – the hordes of assessors, collectors, commissioners, over and above the traditional officers of the civil parish (the constables, overseers and churchwardens) – spread responsibility more widely than ever before, especially among those groups on the margin of literacy.'[5] Ann Hughes strengthens the point by suggesting that, in considering complex legal matters like indemnity cases during the Protectorate, more people than ever came to discuss 'questions of legality and necessity, justice and tyranny'.[6] In addition, coffee houses, which were the centre of religious and political debate, flourished in London and other provincial 'capitals' from the 1650s onwards. This new political world is one that was to characterize Restoration politics, a world that both the crown and its opponents entered, using the written word, sermons, ceremonials and so on to denigrate their opponents and promote their own causes. It is also the world which is the context for explaining why the later Stuarts failed to capitalize on the strong position they had inherited in 1660. Why that was thrown away, resulting in the massive opposition that Charles II faced and culminating in the Exclusion Crisis of 1679–81 and the expulsion from the throne of his brother James II in 1688–9, is one of the questions that helps to bind together the often complex politics of the period between the Restoration and the Glorious Revolution.

---

[4] P. D. Halliday, *Dismembering the Body Politic: Partisan Politics in England's Towns 1650–1720* (1998), p. 64.

[5] John Morrill, 'The impact of society', in John Morrill, ed., *Revolution and Restoration: England in the 1650s* (1992), p. 110.

[6] A. Hughes, *Politics, Society and Civil War: Warwickshire 1620–60* (1987), pp. 302–4.

8

The failure of 'the Restoration Settlement', 1660–1667

The Convention Parliament, 1660: old wounds reopened and old problems unsolved

Summary

This chapter is concerned with two main questions:

- Why is 'the Restoration Settlement' a misnomer? The series of ad hoc decisions made in the early 1660s by the Convention and Cavalier Parliaments, which are traditionally called 'the Restoration Settlement', settled very little.
- To what extent did this contribute to the escalating political instability and growing conflict not only between Charles II and parliament but also between the crown and wide sections of the nation between 1660 and 1667? In 1667 the king only averted a serious constitutional crisis by deserting his principal minister, Clarendon.

The main task facing the Convention Parliament,[1] which met on 25 April 1660, was that which had faced every regime since the 1640s: to continue the search for 'settlement'.

---

[1] In June the Convention passed an Act legitimizing itself as a parliament.

Unfortunately, the MPs of 1660 were no more united on what form a settlement should take than the victorious parliamentarians of 1646. Not only was the Convention split on religious lines – Anglicans, Presbyterians and Independents – but political divisions were sharpened by the bitterness of civil war and regicide. There was a wide gulf between those who had remained committed royalists throughout the revolution and those who had collaborated with the republican regimes of the 1650s and who had only supported the Restoration as a means of ending the political anarchy of the months following Oliver's death. Charles II was only recognizing political realities when he included representatives of both groups in his new privy council: consistent royalists like Hyde (the new lord chancellor, created earl of Clarendon in 1661), Sir Edward Nicholas, and the duke of Ormonde, alongside men who had only recently served the Cromwellian government, notably Monck (now duke of Albemarle), Edward Montague (now earl of Sandwich), and Anthony Ashley Cooper (later earl of Shaftesbury). Seen in this context it is perhaps not surprising that the Convention failed to solve problems which had defeated earlier regimes.

Information

The Declaration of Breda, April 1660

The Declaration of Breda was a skilfully assembled package with three major promises which contained something for every political faction in England.

* By leaving the problem of confiscated estates to parliament, the declaration raised the hopes of royalists that their lost lands would be restored.
* By promising 'liberty to tender consciences', the declaration held out the prospect to Independents, especially the sectaries in the army, of the continuation of the religious toleration of the 1650s.
* The fears of those who had collaborated with the regicide regimes of a reign of terror were calmed by the declaration's promise of a free and general pardon for all except those to be named by parliament.

In these ways, the Declaration of Breda eased the transition to the new regime.

Within a week of its first meeting the Convention resolved that government ought to be in the hands of king, Lords and Commons, and agreed that a fleet (with the politically agile Ashley Cooper on board) be sent to bring Charles Stuart back to England. Why was Charles II allowed to return unconditionally, with the Nineteen Propositions, the Propositions of Newcastle and the 'treaties' of Oxford, Uxbridge and

Newport apparently forgotten and certainly not mentioned publicly?[2] Partly it was a recognition that there was no alternative to the monarchy as a basis for political stability. Partly also it was a result of Charles's declaration issued from Breda, which was read to the Convention when it first met.

What the Declaration of Breda did not do was provide a blueprint for a constitutional and religious settlement. Nor did the Convention. The divisions within it and the weight of more immediate problems facing it ensured that fundamental questions concerning the respective powers of crown and parliament were not resolved, and that Charles II was restored in 1660 free of limitations such as parliamentary control of the army and of his ministers, without which many MPs in the Long Parliament would have thought the restoration of the monarchy inconceivable.

Since money had been a major source of political friction in the early seventeenth century, it was essential for constitutional harmony that crown and parliament agree on a workable financial settlement in 1660. Why did this not happen? Uppermost in the minds of some MPs was the fear that generous financial provision for the crown would make it independent of parliament. But of greater importance was the fact that the intricacies of public finance were unintelligible to most MPs in 1660 and in the following years. (With the notable exception of Professor Chandaman, this stricture applies to many historians as well.[3]) As a result, even the parliamentary grant for paying the arrears of the navy and army, which most MPs of course wanted to disband quickly, was £375,000 short of what was needed. In addition, Charles never received another £550,000 which he had spent in payment of his own and his father's debts. Nor did the Convention provide a settled income of £1,200,000 p.a., which was calculated as the sum necessary for ordinary royal expenditure and which curiously remained as an unquestioned figure in the subsequent negotiations. In September the Convention's financial committee estimated that, if the crown were compensated by a grant of £100,000 p.a. for the loss of its feudal revenue from wardships which were not renewed in 1660, the crown's annual revenue would fall short by £425,000 p.a. of the agreed £1,200,000 p.a. Two months later, when the matter was discussed again, the Convention decided to grant the Commonwealth liquor excise to Charles for life, assuming that this was adequate compensation for both the abolition of wardships and the deficiency of £425,000 p.a. Clearly, as Professor Chandaman has shown, this was a false assumption, of which both Clarendon and the new lord treasurer, the earl of Southampton, were aware, but which they failed to explain to parliament.

All the parties to the financial negotiations in 1660 can be excused in some measure for their failure to produce a reasonable financial provision for the crown. MPs, apart from lacking the necessary knowledge of public finance, could not have foreseen that

---

[2] The council of state, which ruled the country between the dissolution of the Long Parliament and the meeting of the Convention (17 March to 25 April 1660), believed that Charles would have to accept conditions; it spent a week examining the 'treaties' of the 1640s: D. Ogg, *England in the Reign of Charles II* (2 vols., 1955), I, p. 27.

[3] The figures in the rest of this paragraph are from C. D. Chandaman, *The English Public Revenue 1660–88* (1975), pp. 196–202.

an army would be retained and Tangier garrisoned at a minimum cost of £140,000 p.a.[4] Charles's ministers, on the other hand, had good reasons for refraining from asking the Convention for more money. The period before 1660 had been one of unprecedented high taxation. It must have seemed easier to borrow than to risk discontent by imposing further financial burdens. However, in doing this the court allowed MPs to disband in 1660 thinking that the revenue problem had been solved. It had not: by the end of 1660 the crown was saddled with debts of £925,000 and an ordinary revenue that was at least £300,000 short of the magic figure of £1,200,000 p.a.

Of equal significance for later English history was the Convention's failure to provide a religious framework which most English Protestants would accept. On the face of it this did not seem a likely outcome. There was a section of opinion in England in 1660 in favour of erecting a wide comprehensive Church. Some churchmen and moderate Presbyterians resurrected Archbishop Ussher's scheme of the early 1640s for modified episcopacy. Charles appeared to support this move to reconcile opposing Protestant factions and in this he was assisted by Clarendon. Prominent non-Anglicans (Richard Baxter, Edmund Calamy, Simeon Ashe and Thomas Reynolds) were appointed royal chaplains. Moreover, during the parliamentary recess in September 1660, Charles and Clarendon made a determined effort to get some kind of agreement between Anglicans and Presbyterians. This culminated on 25 October in a meeting between Charles and some Presbyterian leaders at Clarendon's lodgings, Worcester House, after which the king issued a declaration proposing a Church settlement in which the powers of bishops were to be limited by councils of presbyters and in which contentious matters of liturgy and ceremony were to be referred to a committee of divines 'of both persuasions' and a national synod. At the same time, bishoprics were offered to leading Presbyterians. Whether or not Charles or Clarendon were sincere in wanting a comprehensive Church is not known. The evidence is inconclusive and has led to divergent interpretations. There is less doubt about Charles's sincerity than Clarendon's.[5] As will be seen, the king for much of the first half of his reign inclined to a policy of reconciliation with dissenters. It will be argued later that he did so largely to erect an alternative political alliance to that of the crown and Church (see below, p. 303). Clarendon, too, may have been sincere in 1660 in wanting comprehension. With the army not yet demobilized, the government had good reason to want to avoid antagonizing non-Anglican opinion. Why, then, did schemes for a comprehensive Church come to nothing in 1660, leaving the way clear for the restoration of an intolerant Church? Perhaps the division of religious opinion represented in the Convention is enough to explain why, despite meeting once

---

[4] John Childs, *The Army of Charles II* (1976), p. 47. I am grateful to Professor K. H. D. Haley for bringing this reference to my attention.

[5] R. S. Bosher, *The Making of the Restoration Settlement: the influence of the Laudians 1649–62* (1951) argues that Clarendon was a consistently intolerant Anglican. G. R. Abernathy, *English Presbyterians and the Stuart Restoration*, Trans. American Philosophical Society, LV, part 2 (Philadelphia 1965), attacks this view of Clarendon. See also Anne Whiteman, 'The re-establishment of the Church of England, 1660–63', *T.R.H.S.*, 5th ser., V (1955); Idem., 'The restoration of the Church of England, in G. F. Nuttall and O. Chadwick, eds., *From Uniformity to Unity* (1962); and Ian Green, *The Re-establishment of the Church of England 1660–63* (1978).

a week from 6 July until the adjournment of 13 September 1660 as a Grand Committee to discuss religion, nothing was decided. But probably of more importance in explaining the failure of comprehension in 1660 is the influence of the government, which, like the political leaders of the early 1640s, wanted to postpone decisions on this explosive, divisive issue until the new regime was more firmly established. Charles also probably wanted to keep the settlement in his own hands. As will be seen, in this aim he was totally unsuccessful. It very soon became clear that so strong was intolerant Anglican opinion in the country that comprehension of non-Anglicans in the state Church was not a practicable possibility.

It has long been recognized that the Convention was more successful in dealing with immediate problems than with fundamental constitutional, financial and ecclesiastical issues. Many of its day-to-day decisions were moderate and sensible compromises. It resisted the extreme demands of Cavaliers and passed Acts confirming judicial decisions made during the Interregnum and continuing those already in progress; it approved an Act of Indemnity which pardoned all but a few who had been closely connected with the execution of Charles I; and it worked out a settlement of confiscated estates and forced sales of land that attempted to alienate as few interests as possible. But it has perhaps not been emphasized enough that all this did not mean that the bitterness that had its roots in the 1640s and 1650s had been forgotten. On the contrary, the debates on the Indemnity Bill revealed the depths of hatred felt by many (including William Prynne[6]) for those who had been associated with the regicide regimes, hatred which was not appeased by the Act's moderation and which found expression in the grisly exhumation of the bones of Cromwell, Pym, Blake and others, even those of Cromwell's mother. In many counties, royalist vindictiveness was directed against prominent parliamentarians and Cromwellian collaborators under the guise of proceedings against suspected conspirators. As Professor Roots says, 'there was only a smear of blood at the Restoration, but a whole streak of meanness'.[7] The land settlement was a valiant attempt to appease different interests.[8] The confiscated estates of crown and Church were restored (by clauses in the Act of Indemnity and the Act for the Confirmation of Judicial Proceedings), as were those of some royalists (by private Acts of parliament and by separate orders of the House of Lords to sheriffs). But nothing was done to help those royalists who had sold estates to enable them to pay composition fines, even though as one prominent royalist, the eighth earl of Derby, caustically said, such sales were no more voluntary 'than when a man beset with robbers delivered them 9 parts of his goods to save the 10th and perhaps his life'.[9] Consequently, the land settlement was a compromise that failed: it inflamed rather than soothed old wounds. It was, wrote Thomas, earl of Ailesbury later,

---

[6] W. Lamont, *Marginal Prynne 1600–69* (1963), pp. 206–7.

[7] I. Roots, *The Great Rebellion 1640–60* (1966), p. 261.

[8] Joan Thirsk, 'The restoration land settlement', *J.M.H.*, XXVI (1954); H. J. Habakkuk, 'The land settlement at the Restoration of Charles II', *T.R.H.S.*, 5th ser., XXVIII (1978), pp. 201–21.

[9] Lancashire Record Office DDK 1602/9.

the source of what was termed in years following 'Whiggism', and it really sprang by degrees from the discontent of noble families and of many good families of the first gentry in the Counties whose ancestors were sequestered, decimated and what not on account of their steadfast loyalties, and so many losing their lives also.

Royalist hopes of receiving reward from a grateful king were not fulfilled. Instead Charles II cynically rewarded 'his enemies to sweeten them, for that his friends were so by a settled principle, and that their loyalty could not be shaken'.[10] The Convention was dissolved on 29 December 1660. Its successor, the Cavalier Parliament, which met first on 8 May 1661, was to show that Anglicans and royalists were determined to get their revenge for the humiliation they felt they had suffered.

The Cavalier Parliament and the restored monarchy, 1661–1664

The elections which followed the dissolution of the Convention reflected the tide of pro-royalist feeling in the country. Gentry memories of the way parliamentary county committees and major-generals had undermined their power combined with continued fears of political instability, which appeared to be the only alternative to monarchical rule. Venner's Rising (see below, p. 300) was contemporary with the elections, and the government had little difficulty in maintaining an atmosphere of panic as it made public its spies' reports of meetings of conventicles and allegedly seditious meetings. It is possible, though, to exaggerate the militant royalism of the Cavalier Parliament even in 1661. One hundred of the new MPs had sat in the Long Parliament, and this legacy of a fund of parliamentary experience alone ensured that the Cavalier Parliament would not be willing to fill the role of rubber stamp for royal authority. Nor, even in the atmosphere of royalist euphoria of 1660–1, were MPs prepared to abandon all the constitutional gains of the early 1640s. Charles I's financial expedients of the 1630s remained illegal, and star chamber, the court of high commission, the council of the north, court of wards and feudal tenures remained abolished. It is often, correctly, said that the monarchy that was restored in 1660 was that of 1641 not 1640.

Yet the powers of the monarchy that the Cavalier Parliament did restore are as significant as those that it did not. The attempt which had been initiated in the winter of 1641–2 to impose two principal limitations on the power of the monarchy was abandoned in the 1660s. The Cavalier Parliament made no attempt to challenge the king's right to appoint privy councillors and state officials or fill Church and local government posts. And in the Militia Acts of 1661 and 1662 the Cavalier Parliament in effect conceded that the crown (not parliament as claimed by the Militia Ordinance of March 1642) should have sole control of the militia. As further evidence of reaction against the pretensions made by parliament during the revolution, an Act of 1661 laid

---

[10] W. E. Buckley, ed., *Memoirs of Thomas Earl of Ailesbury, Written by Himself* (2 vols., Roxburgh Club, 1890), I, pp. 6–7.

down the penalty of praemunire[11] for anyone who claimed that parliament had legislative powers without the king. In addition the Triennial Act of 1664 repealed its 1641 predecessor and replaced it with an emasculated version, which simply declared that the maximum period between parliaments ought to be three years: it did not maintain the 1641 machinery for enforcing this if the king ignored it, as in fact Charles II did at the end of his reign, as will be seen. Further Acts against 'tumultuous petitioning' (1661) and in favour of censorship of the press (1662) emphasized the reaction in the crown's favour at this time. The powers of the restored monarchy were still enormous: the power of vetoing legislation, of dispensing individuals from parliamentary statutes or suspending statutes completely, of dissolving and calling parliaments, of making foreign policy. The royalist reaction produced by the recent memories of sequestrations and decimation taxes helped Charles II to inherit a position *potentially* as powerful as that of Louis XIV in France.

In the early 1660s, however, two things prevented Charles II from developing his power as Louis XIV was doing in France: Charles had neither the ability nor the financial resources of his brother monarch across the channel.[12] The views of historians about Charles II differ greatly.[13] He has had his ardent admirers as well as stern critics. Although it is difficult to take seriously the case for Charles as a great king, his detractors have sometimes criticized him for the wrong reasons, judging him on high-minded moral grounds rather than in the light of whether or not he was an able and effective ruler. His extra-marital adventures are fascinating for the scope and catholicity of the king's sexual appetite and taste which they reveal: in Professor Kenyon's words, in these matters Charles 'was not a gourmet so much as a gourmand'.[14] Although Charles's mistresses were of some political importance, as will be seen, it is possible to place too much emphasis on them in accounts of the political history of this period. Mistresses and effective monarchical rule, as Louis XIV's activities illustrate, were not incompatible in the seventeenth century. None of Charles's mistresses had much political influence on the king.[15] Nor did they cause his public attachment to his wife and family to waver, even when a divorce might have been the way out of the serious succession crises of his reign. Even his habit of seeing ministers in his mistresses' apartments is not *necessarily* evidence that Charles ignored affairs of State, merely that he preferred to conduct government business informally. The tittle-tattle related by that arch-gossipmonger Pepys is too often used to argue that Charles's pursuit of women was the root cause of his neglect of state affairs. Pepys's amusing story about Charles trying to catch a moth in Lady Castlemaine's room while the Dutch fleet sailed up the Medway is guaranteed

---

[11] Forfeiture of lands and goods, life imprisonment and inability to sue for one's rights at law.

[12] A third, equally important reason – Charles's religious polices – will be dealt with on pp. 302–3.

[13] See the biographies by A. Fraser, J. R. Jones, R. Hutton, J. Miller and A. Keay listed in the Bibliographical note, p. 530, and K. H. D. Haley, *Charles II* (Historical Association pamphlet, general series no. 63, 1966).

[14] J. P. Kenyon, *The Stuarts* (Fontana edn., 1970), p. 105.

[15] This was not the view of the earl of Rochester, a contemporary of Charles II, who wrote that Charles's 'scepter and his prick are of a length/But she who plays with one may sway the other': T. Harris, *Restoration: Charles II and his kingdoms* (2006), p. 72.

to appear in a large percentage of examination answers on Charles II, but the story is unsupported and probably apocryphal. Moreover, criticisms of Charles's undoubted cynicism and unprincipled behaviour are often also moral rather than political judgements. His cynical treatment of his friends and enemies alike, his double-dealing and resort to short-term political expediency were just the amoral qualities required by Machiavelli in a successful ruler. As will be seen, Charles's political sense in knowing when a position could no longer be held, regardless of the principle involved, was his greatest strength.

Yet it cannot be denied that many of Charles's activities and his lifestyle were detrimental to the efficient running of the king's government and to good political relations with the parliamentary classes. He did prefer the racecourse and associated pleasures of Newmarket and the brothels of Covent Garden to the day-to-day tedium of government. Royal government suffered in consequence because there was no one at Westminster to supervise administrative details for him. Not even Clarendon in the early 1660s had enough of the king's confidence to take his place. Similarly, the one man who might have been able to do this after Clarendon's downfall, Danby, was rarely taken into the king's secret counsels. Indeed, Charles and Danby often followed contradictory policies, with each detesting that of the other. Perhaps Charles's greatest defect as a ruler was his financial extravagance. To that extent his profligate lifestyle was politically important: his mistresses and his bastards (of whom fourteen were acknowledged) had to be paid for. His Catholic mistresses, especially Barbara Villiers, countess of Castlemaine, Frances Stewart and Louise de Keroualle, duchess of Portsmouth, were also used by those who claimed that Charles's lifestyle was degrading the monarchy. Moreover, his extravagance and dissolute living made it increasingly hard for ministers to persuade MPs to grant the king more money. Above all, Charles's extravagance was not confined to what Professor Chandaman calls his 'harem finance'.[16] Like James I, there was an unbridgeable gulf between Charles's attitude to money and the retrenchment schemes that were dreamed up in the lord treasurer's department. Given the financial resources of the Stuart monarchy this was disastrous, and never more so than in the 1660s.

Even without the king's extravagance the royal financial position would have been poor. Although the Cavalier Parliament recognized soon after it met that the Convention had not provided the king with enough permanent ordinary revenue, it never made good the deficit.[17] The Cavalier Parliament's own addition to the crown's permanent revenue, the hearth tax, in May 1662, was an ingenious device, but raised insufficient for the purpose. Even on the best parliamentary estimate, the crown's ordinary revenue barely reached £1 million. It is true that in the short term the crown's total revenue was boosted by grants of massive parliamentary subsidies and did reach an average of £1,200,000 p.a. from 1660 to 1664. But there was no doubt that parliament would not be willing to maintain such levels of taxation, especially after the high tax years of the 1650s, and especially when the bulk of revenue seemed to be spent on Charles's

---

[16] Chandaman, *English Public Revenue*, p. 271.

[17] Ibid., 203–9.

extravagant lifestyle. More seriously, the feeling grew among MPs that (despite the evidence of financial experts, including their own) the crown now had a sufficient permanent revenue. By 1664, however, Charles's debts had risen to £1.25 million and the likelihood was that the position would get worse. The causes were diverse: from the inadequacies of Lord Treasurer Southampton to Charles's extravagance. But it is difficult to escape the conclusion that at this stage the major reason was an inadequate parliamentary grant of permanent revenue to the crown, which grew out of the ignorance of most MPs of public finance. This by itself was enough to ensure deteriorating relations between king and parliament. The shape of the restored Church proved to be an even greater divisive issue.

The Cavalier Parliament and the restored Church, 1661–1664

No greater contrast could have been devised than that between the broad, tolerant Cromwellian Church and the narrow, bigoted Anglican Church that was restored in the early 1660s. The hopes of some non-Anglicans that they might be included in the new state Church were kept alive by the Savoy Conference, which took place at the bishop of Lincoln's lodgings in the Strand from 5 April to 23 July 1661, between Anglican and Presbyterian representatives. However, by this stage comprehension was clearly a lost cause. As in 1660 both Charles II and Clarendon wanted to include Presbyterians in the Church of England, but the religious situation was now beyond their control. Already, regardless of official pronouncements the Anglican Church was being restored willy-nilly. During the winter of 1660–1 Anglican ministers who had been ejected in the 1640s returned to their livings under the patronage of Anglican gentry patrons. Anti-Puritanism was not confined to the gentry, but was reflected in harsh, popular satirical plays and broadsheets directed against Presbyterians, Baptists and Quakers, with titles like *The Lecherous Anabaptist or The Dipper Dipped*. Ben Jonson's *Bartholomew Fair* was revived in 1661 for the first time since the 1620s and Samuel Butler produced his popular anti-Puritan diatribe, *Hudribras*, between 1662 and 1678. Nor was violence against Quakers, Baptists and other nonconformist sects uncommon in the early 1660s. It is arguable that fear of the more extreme sects, like the Quakers, was the strongest bond uniting people of many different kinds in favour of the restoration of the monarchy in 1659–60.[18] In the months immediately before and after the Restoration there were sporadic popular attacks on Baptists and Quakers in London. On the first two days of May 1660, in a foretaste of more extensive anti-dissenter riots in London in 1710 (see pp. 447–8), Baptist meeting houses in the capital were attacked by a 'rude multitude', who not only took away 'all the doors, seats and windows, Gallerys and floors etc. to the value of above £200',

---

[18] B. Reay, 'The Quakers, 1659, and the restoration of the monarchy', *History*, LXIII (1978).

but also threatened to treat other meeting houses in London in a similar fashion.[19] Dissent and republicanism were seen as interchangeable. According to a popular broadsheet ballad:

> A Presbyter is such a monstrous thing
> That loves democracy and hates a King
> For royal issue never making prayers,
> Since kingdoms (as he thinks) should have no heirs,
> But stand elective: that the holy crew
> May, when their Zeal transports them, choose a new.[20]

If religious nonconformity and political sedition were not already identified closely enough in the popular mind, then this was the lesson for many of Venner's Rising in January 1661. Thomas Venner was closely associated with the Fifth Monarchy men, some of whom were undoubtedly planning to resist the new regime. But in fact Venner posed no real threat. His active followers were perhaps as few as fifty and certainly no more than three hundred, and he was ignored by the army, which anyway was demobilized completely (apart from one regiment of foot and one troop of horse) by February. However, as so often in politics, the cliché – in this case dissent equals sedition – was more important to contemporaries than hard facts.

When the Cavalier Parliament met on 8 May 1661, therefore, despite the presence in the House of Commons of some MPs sympathetic to protestant dissenters,[21] a majority were determined to crush religious and political nonconformity at the same time. Within ten days of its first meeting, bishops had been restored to the House of Lords, and the House of Commons voted by 228 to 103 votes that the Solemn League and Covenant should be burned by the public hangman, and that all MPs were to take the sacraments according to the Church of England. Exactly what form this should take still had to be decided. But it was Convocation not the Savoy Conference that completed the revision of the prayer book by December 1661, and predictably the revised prayer book, which was accepted by parliament in April 1662, was as obnoxious to many dissenters as the Elizabethan Prayer Book. The Cavalier Parliament then proceeded to enact a series of statutes – the so-called Clarendon Code – designed to impose severe penalties on those who refused to conform to the new state Church. Doubts about the chancellor's position there may be (as has been seen) but clearly Clarendon was not the initiator of the Clarendon Code. On the contrary until the end of 1663, most notably in his unsuccessful attempts in the House of Lords in 1661 and 1662 to make the Act of Uniformity less severe on dissenters, Clarendon tried to stem the tide of Anglican reaction. This he failed to do.

---

[19] T. Harris, *London Crowds in the Reign of Charles II: propaganda and politics after the Restoration until the Exclusion Crisis* (1987), p. 52.

[20] C. E. Whiting, *Studies in English Parliament from the Restoration to the Revolution 1660–88* (1931), pp. 111, 425–8.

[21] D. R. Lacey, *Dissent and Parliamentary Politics in England, 1661–89* (1969), p. 30 and appendix 2.

Information

The Clarendon Code

This is the name commonly given to five acts of parliament passed between 1661 and 1665:

- *The Corporation Act (1661)* set up commissions empowered to evict all municipal officials who did not swear oaths of allegiance and non-resistance, declare the Solemn League and Covenant invalid, and take the Anglican sacraments.

- *The Act of Uniformity (1662)* forced all church ministers to swear an oath giving their consent to a new prayer book which contained many features unacceptable to most dissenters. Bartholomew's Day (24 August) 1662 was chosen as the final date by which oaths should be sworn, rather than Michaelmas Day as in the original draft of the bill, because MPs wanted to prevent nonconforming clergy from receiving their Michaelmas tithes before they were ejected. The exact number of English clergy who left their livings by St Bartholomew's Day 1662 is not known, but was probably 1,909. These included 149 ejected from universities and schools.[22]

- *The Quaker Act of 1662* forbade Quakers from not taking necessary oaths and from attending a meeting of five or more Quakers. Penalties for those who transgressed the Act included large fines and even transportation.

- *The Conventicle Act (1664)* prohibited all assemblies not held in accordance with the Book of Common Prayer and attended by five or more adults who were not members of the household in which the service was conducted.

- *The Five Mile Act (1665)* forbade all preachers and teachers who did not take the necessary oaths and declarations from coming within five miles of any town or city, and all ejected clergy from travelling within five miles of the parish where they had been incumbents.

After his failure to amend the Uniformity Bill, Clarendon must have realized the political wisdom of becoming a 'Clarendonian'. Government support for the Clarendon Code was part of the bargain which produced the grants of parliamentary supplies in the early 1660s (which have already been noted). Probably also Clarendon realized just how valuable a supporter of the restored monarchy the restored Church could be.

---

[22] A. G. Matthews, *Calamy Revised, Being a Revision of Edmund Calamy's account of the Ministers and others ejected and silenced, 1660–62* (1934), pp. xiii–xiv.

So enthusiastically royalist was the Restoration Church that it carried the theories of the divine hereditary right of kings and the sinfulness of rebellion to established order to the ultimate absurdity of erecting the executed Charles I into a Holy Martyr. 'The Church of England', sermonized Dr Robert South in November 1661, 'glories in nothing more than she is the truest friend of kings and kingly government, of any other church in the world; that they were the same hands that took the crown from the king's head and the mitre from the bishops.'[23] The restored Church and the restored monarchy must stand together. Sheldon and Sancroft, archbishops of Canterbury from the Restoration to 1691, as well as Clarendon, recognized the force of this. One of the major puzzles of the Restoration period is why Charles II, until the last years of his reign, did not. Why did he persist in pursuing a policy that effectively undermined the alliance of Church and monarchy?

As will be seen, Charles never stood firm on the principle of toleration, but the first twelve years of his reign are peppered with efforts to bring about a general toleration for Protestants and Catholics (1660, 1662, 1663, 1668, 1672). On 26 December 1662, despite the clear evidence of the Cavalier Parliament's fervent Anglicanism which had produced the Corporation and Uniformity Acts, Charles issued a declaration announcing that he intended to honour his Breda promise of 'liberty to tender consciences' by asking parliament to allow him to dispense individuals from the penal laws. It is true that Charles was under some pressure to curb the vindictive nature of the Act of Uniformity. Clarendon continued to advise him that, if the Act was put into effect, it might cause moderate dissenters to consider rebellion. Henrietta Maria, the earl of Bristol and Sir Henry Bennet urged toleration in favour of Catholics, while the king also received petitions against the Act of Uniformity from Presbyterians and Independents. However, the parliamentary storm which followed Charles's declaration could surely easily have been foreseen. Already, before the new parliamentary session began in February 1663, the bishops began to coordinate opposition to Charles's plans. Although a bill embodying his December proposals received some support in the more tolerant Lords, the Commons refused to discuss it, and at the beginning of April Charles was forced to withdraw it, issue a new proclamation against priests and Jesuits, and condone the passage in the Commons of bills against both Protestant and Catholic dissenters. Why did Charles pursue such an obviously unpopular policy instead of taking the easier course of swimming with the Anglican tide? There is no easy answer to this question. It certainly does not seem to be rooted in any strong religious views held by the king. Although he probably did declare himself a Catholic on his death-bed, this was probably, as Professor Charles Firth said, 'fire insurance'. Charles seems to have preferred Catholicism as a religion which supported absolute monarchies, but it is difficult to find evidence that he felt strongly enough about Catholicism to cause him to take extremely unpopular measures to promote it. His religious apathy is well captured

---

[23] Quoted in G. V. Bennett, *The Tory Crisis in Church and State 1688–1730: the career of Francis Atterbury Bishop of Rochester* (1975), p. 5, and see pp. 475–80 below.

in a story about Dr Robert South who, when he was preaching to Charles II and his court, noticed that most of his congregation had gone to sleep.

> Stopping and changing the tone of his voice, he called thrice to Lord Lauderdale, who, awakened, stood up: 'My Lord', says South very composedly, 'I am sorry to interrupt your repose, but I must beg that you will not snore quite so loud, lest you should awaken his majesty,' and then as calmly continued his discourse.[24]

A more likely explanation is that Charles had no wish to become dependent on over-bearing Anglican clergymen and that (like James II in 1686–7) he toyed with the alternative policy of allying with dissenters and Catholics. Certainly this is well in line with Charles's dislike of being dominated by others in his policy-making, whether it be by Clarendon or Danby. Whatever the explanation, it was a policy that only succeeded in souring his relations with parliament and the Church, as will be seen.

Despite Charles, the Anglican Church which had been reduced to ruins in the early 1640s emerged triumphant in the early 1660s. The Church's lands and revenues were restored, and the church courts were once again active. It is worth emphasizing also that many of the defects of the old Church were also restored, especially the system of lay impropriation of tithes and benefices, and the inequality in the distribution of wealth within the Church, resulting in a badly paid clergy who too often had been appointed with no reference to their qualifications for their positions. The Church that was restored in the 1660s did not, however, have exactly the same position as in 1639. In great contrast to the days before 1640, the Clarendon Code, scant comfort though it was to those it persecuted, did give legal recognition to Protestant dissent. The persecution of Protestant dissenters, especially of the Quakers and Baptists, after 1660 is well recorded.[25] What is less often emphasized is that Protestant nonconformity, which had flourished and spread in the 1640s and 1650s, survived after 1660 despite the efforts to eradicate it. The way in which it survived has many parallels with the continued existence of Catholicism in very similar circumstances in late sixteenth-century England, when Catholicism, like Protestant dissent later, was very closely associated in the minds of the authorities with political subversion. Restoration Protestant dissent could not have survived without the patronage and support of powerful landowners and merchants. The political and social pressures on the gentry to conform were great and most undoubtedly succumbed. Not all landowners in Restoration England, however, fall into the 'church and king' stereotype. One example of a man who does not is Lord Wharton, whose house at Woburn near High Wycombe (Buckinghamshire) became a haven for nonconformist divines after 1660. There were other Puritan gentry who in

---

[24] Quoted in *The Times Literary Supplement*, 28 January 1977, review of Irene Simon, ed., *Three Restoration Divines: Barrow, South, Tillotson, selected sermons*, 2 vols. (1977). R. Hutton, *Charles II: King of England, Scotland and Ireland* (1991), p. 456, thinks that Charles's attitude to religion 'centered upon his own interests'.

[25] See e.g. Whiting, *Studies*, especially pp. 54ff, 98ff; M. R. Watts, *The Dissenters from the Reformation to the French Revolution* (1978), pp. 221–62.

1660 became dissenters and who also helped keep the Puritan tradition alive.[26] The Conventicle Act (1670) implicitly admitted that the Clarendon Code had not always been enforced: penalties were enacted against officials who turned a blind eye to the activities of dissenters. JPs and parish and town officials alike often found it difficult to see their inoffensive nonconformist friends and neighbours as the evil, seditious plotters official propaganda portrayed them to be. Even bishops sometimes tried to moderate the persecution of the Clarendon Code.[27] The exact extent of Protestant dissent in Restoration England is impossible to estimate. The religious census ordered by Danby and Sheldon in 1676 calculated that of the adult population over the age of sixteen, 2,477,254 were conformists, 108,676 were nonconformists and 13,656 were papists, and that nonconformists were much stronger in the south and eastern parts of England than in the north and west.[28] Since Danby's purpose was to minimize the number of dissenters in order to convince Charles of the futility of relying on their support, it is not unduly critical to question the accuracy of the census. Clearly it underestimated the strength of nonconformity, especially since a lot of nonconformists probably conformed simply for the sake of the census. Occasional conformity was not new even in the 1670s. Whether openly or not, what is certain is that the Puritan spirit which had played a major role in late sixteenth- and early seventeenth-century society survived the difficult years immediately after the Restoration in the guise of Protestant dissent.

This had many important consequences for the later development of English social and political as well as religious life (see pp. 480–2). One effect needs to be mentioned here because it is crucial to understanding the growth of political divisions during the reign of Charles II. Studies of provincial and urban England show that after the Restoration the most important divisive issue was the attitude to dissent. In Restoration Herefordshire, for example, there was simmering tension as former Presbyterian gentry like Sir Edward Harley and Colonel Birch tried to restrain the vigorous persecution of dissenters by other local gentry.[29] In Glamorgan in the 1660s, too, a similar fault-line appeared in local society as the views of one group of gentry who had political links with Archbishop Sheldon were contested by others whose connections at Westminster were with Lord Wharton and who feared that a policy of intolerance towards dissenters would play into the hands of local Catholics and crypto-Catholics.[30] Nor was this division confined to the elite of landed society. Similar differences of attitude to the

---

[26] R. A. Beddard, 'Vincent Alsop and the emancipation of Restoration Dissent', *J. Eccl. H.*, XXIV (1973), p. 169; G. F. Trevallyn Jones, *Saw Pit Wharton: the political career from 1640 to 1691 of Philip, fourth Lord Wharton* (1967); Whiting, *Studies*, pp. 415ff and 432ff; Anthony Fletcher, *A County Community in Peace and War: Sussex 1600–60* (1975), pp. 123–4.

[27] Whiting, *Studies*, pp. 18–19.

[28] A. Whiteman, ed., *The Compton Census of 1676* (British Academy Records of Social and Economic History, new ser., X, 1986).

[29] N. E. Key, 'Comprehension and the breakdown of consensus in Restoration Herefordshire', in T. Harris, M. Goldie and P. Seaward, eds., *The Politics of Religion in Restoration England* (1990).

[30] P. Jenkins, *The Making of a Ruling Class: the Glamorgan gentry 1640–1790* (1983), pp. 121–4.

persecution of dissenters have been found in Restoration London and Bristol, embracing wide sections of urban society.[31] Though not yet serious, these differences reflected religious tensions that were to become an important reason for the later development of political divisions along Whig and Tory lines.

The second Dutch war and the downfall of Clarendon, 1664–1667

'In 1661 the House of Commons was a house of courtiers; by 1667 it was becoming a house of critics', wrote David Ogg in one of those neat sentences which make his *England in the Reign of Charles II* a pleasure to read.[32] As has been seen, the major reasons for the Cavalier Parliament's increasing opposition to the court were the king's apparent preference for a policy of toleration and his continual demands for money. What made matters worse was that Charles's extravagance gave point to the recurrent complaint of backbench MPs in the seventeenth century of administrative waste and corruption. Moreover, the early years of the Restoration were for most landowners a time of economic difficulties. Not only had some royalist landowners got heavily into debt during the revolution, but there was now an almost universal belief that rents were falling after a long period of rising rent-roll incomes before 1640 (see below, pp. 501–2). There was a great fear that the subsequent fall in land values would strike at the roots of landed society, which explains why the Cavalier Parliament was obsessed with what seem unimportant campaigns, such as that aimed at banning the import of Irish cattle into England. It is not surprising that in these circumstances many MPs were loath to vote taxes to be squandered on a dissolute court. The importance of the second Dutch war (1665–7) in the politics of the reign of Charles II is the role it had in intensifying the sense of puzzlement and distrust of the court that was developing among many MPs in the 1660s. However, it would be wrong to equate this with the emergence of a 'country opposition' to the crown. Despite their growing uneasiness at court policies, most MPs were nevertheless wholly behind the king.

As far as one can judge, the second Anglo-Dutch war, which effectively began in the summer of 1664, but which was not officially declared until 22 February 1665, was not unpopular in England. It represented no radical change of direction in English foreign policy and it appealed to the same mercantile interests in England as did the first war begun by the Rump in 1652. Such was the wealth of commercial grievances between the two countries that, despite an Anglo-Dutch treaty of September 1662, a recurrence of war seemed inevitable. Not only did the expansion of extra-European trade in the second half of the seventeenth century (see pp. 494–8) automatically

---

[31] Harris, *London Crowds, passim.*; J. Barry, 'The politics of religion in Restoration Bristol' in Harris et al., eds., *Politics of Religion.*

[32] Ogg, *Reign of Charles II*, p. 321.

intensify competition for the carrying trade to and from West Africa, the West Indies, North America and the East Indies, but also the Convention Parliament in 1660 produced a Navigation Act that was much more effectively directed against the Dutch than its 1651 predecessor. By enforcing the registration of all foreign-built ships owned by English merchants, the new Act made it much more difficult for foreign-owned ships to escape its provisions. It was also more specific in that it named the goods that had to be imported from the Continent in English ships or in ships of the country from which the goods originated. Similarly, certain other 'enumerated' goods could only be carried to England from the colonies in English or colonial ships. In 1663 the Staple Act went further in attempting to drive the Dutch out of the colonial trade, by forcing English colonists to import European goods only from England and only in English ships. Of the pressure groups clamouring for war with the Dutch, the most vociferous was the East India Company, which had a history of conflict with its Dutch counterpart going back to the beginning of the century, and incidents like the 'massacre' at Amboyna in the East Indies in 1623 acquired increasing importance in the escalating English propaganda against the Dutch. In March and April 1664 a committee of the House of Commons came out in favour of the war, and its report was endorsed by the whole House. Also in March 1664 Charles added to the likelihood of war by granting New Amsterdam at the mouth of the Hudson river (the site of the present New York) to his brother, James, duke of York. As usual, Charles's advisers were not united and their enthusiasm for the war varied. Clarendon, and perhaps Sir William Coventry,[33] realizing the financial implications of war, argued against it, but were overruled by Henry Bennet, Thomas Clifford, the duke of York, and eventually also by Charles himself. In the summer of 1664 the king borrowed £200,000 from the City of London for war preparations, and he endorsed the piratical expedition of Captain Robert Holmes against the trading stations of the Dutch West India Company in West Africa. Possibly the deciding factor for the king was the prospect of huge profits from the capture of Dutch merchant ships, which in the war of 1652–4 had possibly doubled the tonnage of the English merchant fleet.[34]

Although Clarendon was now clearly finding it difficult to maintain his primacy at court, his advice was taken on the tactics to be adopted in the new parliamentary session which began in November 1664. Sir Robert Paston, a Norfolk MP who had not hitherto been associated with the court, agreed to propose a large parliamentary war grant of £2,500,000. It could hardly be expected that agreement on such an unprecedented sum would be easy. Many backbench MPs in Charles II's reign seemed unaware of the high cost of war. One MP, Edward Vaughan, suggested that £500,000 would be sufficient to finance the war, which eventually cost over ten times that amount. That parliamentary sanction for the grant of £2,500,000, which was to be

---

[33] D. T. Witcombe, *Charles II and the Cavalier House of Commons 1663–74* (1976), pp. 26–7, note 6. This book and P. Seaward, *The Cavalier Parliament and the Reconstruction of the Old Regime 1661–67* (1989) are the best guides to the politics of this period.

[34] Chandaman, *English Public Revenue*, p. 223 note.

spent over three years, was delayed, however, was due mainly to the abhorrence MPs had of adopting the method of collecting the sum by means of county assessments, which had proved to be so effective in the 1640s. It was undoubtedly this aspect of it (its effectiveness) as well as its associations with the revolution that MPs in the 1660s found distasteful. But eventually the superiority of monthly assessments in certainty and predictability of yield over the older parliamentary subsidies determined its acceptance, albeit reluctantly, in February 1665. Parliament met again next in the autumn, in Oxford to escape the plague in London. Within days of the opening of parliament, the Commons agreed on a further grant of £1,250,000, again to be raised by monthly assessments. The subsequent adoption of Sir George Downing's proposal that the grant should be appropriated as the Commons directed is often, wrongly, interpreted as an indication of parliamentary distrust of the crown. It is more signifi-cant both in the history of public finance and as another illustration of Clarendon's growing isolation at court than of parliamentary assertiveness. Downing introduced it with the full backing of Charles, Bennet (now earl of Arlington) and Sir William Coventry, but without consulting Clarendon or Lord Treasurer Southampton. Its aim was to appropriate the new parliamentary grant, which would take two years to collect, in order to repay the crown's debtors in strict rotation. Downing hoped that this would encourage smaller investors to have more confidence in lending money to the crown.[35] In the parliamentary sessions of 1664–5 the relative absence of parliamentary criticism of government policy is striking. A Commons' bill (October 1665) against the embezzle-ment of prize goods, aimed at the earl of Sandwich, was one of the rare sour notes in these sessions. With the later grant in the parliamentary session of September 1666 to February 1667 of £1,800,000 and other minor extraordinary sources of income, Professor Chandaman calculates that parliament provided £5,367,000 for the war, which cost the English government £5,250,000.[36] The bargain was not all one-sided – the Five Mile Act was passed in October 1665 – but the court had succeeded in extracting from parliament adequate provision for the war.

How, then, can one account for the great contrast between the 1664–5 parliamentary sessions and the stormy ones of 1666–7? The answer seems to be that, instead of the victory that many MPs expected their unprecedented grants would bring when they dispersed at the end of October 1665, the next twelve months brought naval disasters, diplomatic isolation and near financial collapse for the government. At first the war had seemed to go well. Of the first great naval battle, off Lowestoft on 3 June 1665, Pepys said 'a greater victory [was] never known in the world',[37] and perhaps his ex-aggeration is understandable. But soon doubts began to rise, especially when what had seemed a victory was not followed up, and in August 1665 reports came in of a bungled, treacherous attack in the neutral port of Bergen by English ships on a Dutch fleet returning from the East Indies. Early in 1666 France and Denmark joined the war

---

[35] Seaward, *Cavalier Parliament*, pp. 126–7.
[36] Chandaman, *English Public Revenue*, p. 211
[37] Quoted in Ogg, *Reign of Charles II*, p. 288.

against England and in April England's one ally, the bishop of Münster, defected. The French in fact gave little help to their allies, but it was fear that they might do so that decided Prince Rupert and the duke of Albemarle, the commanders of the English navy, to divide their fleet in anticipation of a French attack and so weaken it considerably in the Four Days' Battle with the Dutch in the Channel (1–4 June 1666). Despite heavy Dutch losses, even English propaganda could not portray the deaths of two admirals, the loss of 8,000 men and the destruction of twenty ships as a 'victory', although at a later engagement at the mouth of the Thames on 25 July 1666 (the St James's Day Battle) Rupert and Albemarle do seem to have had a more unqualified success.

The government's prospects for renewed supply were, therefore, not good when parliament met again in September 1666, and it is not surprising that the war failures and financial losses were blamed on maladministration in the navy and corruption in the government. It is perhaps a commentary on the divisions at court that little effort seems to have been made to put forward an alternative, more respectable, explanation for the need for more money: that the crown's ordinary revenue, especially its income from customs, had been drastically reduced not only by the dislocation of trade by war but by the Great Plague of 1665 and the Great Fire of 1666. The effects of the Great Plague, which was at its height in the summer and early autumn of 1665, can perhaps be exaggerated. The extent of mortality was, of course, high (there were perhaps 70,000 deaths in 1665, although the primary source material, especially the London Bills of Mortality, on which this estimate is based, are notoriously limited). But plague, especially in the towns, was a fairly common phenomenon before 1665 and, though familiarity did not lessen its virulence, it is likely that it had its greatest impact on the poor rather than on the trading and governing classes. Without doubt the economic and social effects of the Great Fire were much more serious. The capital still controlled a disproportionate, if decreasing, amount of the nation's trade and disruption of trade in London therefore had wide economic repercussions. Though most of the newly developed areas nearer to Westminster in Holborn and Covent Garden escaped, contemporaries estimated that the five-day fire (2–6 September 1666) gutted most of the City, and destroyed 13,200 houses, 89 churches and goods valued at £3.5 million.[38] The fire's long-term importance in allowing the rebuilding of London on radical lines is well known: not only wider streets and buildings made of stone and brick resulted, but also the acceleration of the development of the West End of London.[39] Its immediate impact on the crown's ordinary revenue was equally, if not as excitingly, dramatic. For the three financial years from Michaelmas 1662 to Michaelmas 1665 the crown's permanent ordinary revenue averaged over £824,000 p.a.; during the next two years the average fell to nearly £647,000 p.a.[40] In the absence of this explanation from the court for the king's financial difficulties, MPs at the end of 1666 began to look for scapegoats. On 26 September the Commons ordered the officers of the navy, ordnance

---

[38] Ibid., p. 305.
[39] T. F. Reddaway, *The Rebuilding of London after the Great Fire* (1940).
[40] Chandaman, *English Public Revenue*, p. 332.

and stores to bring in their accounts for inspection, and MPs attacked the maladministration of officials, especially Sir George Carteret, the treasurer to the navy board. As has been seen, the Commons agreed on a grant of £1,800,000, but this time, against the wishes of the court, it was proposed to tack on to the grant a clause setting up a commission to examine the public accounts. Charles's anger appears, though, to have been caused by the attempt to *force* him to appoint a commission. When the Lords on 19 December 1666 petitioned him to do this, he gave his assent.[41] But the Supply Bill did not finally pass until January 1667 and not before Charles had addressed the Commons personally and agreed to the passage of a bill prohibiting the import of Irish cattle.

Charles began to negotiate a peace in January 1667; and in March the Dutch agreed to begin peace discussions at Breda. In anticipation of an early peace, the latest parliamentary grant was diverted from war expenditure to paying off the earlier war deficit. So sure were ministers of an early peace that some ships and crew were paid off and economies were made in repairing ships and shore defences. As a result, de Ruyter's daring raid up the Medway in June 1667 and his attack on the naval base at Chatham were devastatingly successful. Despite Clarendon's objections, parliament was recalled in July, earlier than had been intended, in order to pay for an army hastily mobilized after the Medway disaster. The chancellor's attitude is understandable. All that the five-day parliamentary session achieved was to add one more grievance, a standing army, to the parliamentary catalogue against him. The session also gave the chancellor's enemies at court, Arlington, Sir William Coventry and Buckingham, more ammunition to use against him. Unlike 1663, when the earl of Bristol attempted to impeach him, Clarendon was now isolated both at court and in parliament: his only hope was for a successful conclusion to the war. However, when peace with the Dutch was eventually concluded by the Treaty of Breda, the gains to England were seen to be minimal: in contemporary terms, the acquisition of New York and New Jersey was insignificant.

Charles II was never known for his gratitude to those who had given him good service. Moreover, Clarendon had failed to stem the Cavalier Parliament's intolerant Anglicanism, and Charles's dislike of the chancellor's criticism of his personal behaviour was well known. Yet perhaps it was for political, rather than private, reasons that Charles gave way to the pressure to dismiss Clarendon and asked for his resignation on 30 August 1667: might not Clarendon's dismissal end the political crisis? In any case it is difficult to see how Clarendon could have survived politically after the Medway debacle. When parliament assembled again in October 1667, articles of impeachment were brought against him. Yet what was not inevitable was that he should end his life in exile as he did, dying in Rouen in 1674. The House of Lords refused to commit Clarendon to custody as the Commons wished, and it is difficult to see how the charge of treason could have been upheld in any court of law. Why then did Clarendon flee

---

[41] Extracts from the Act establishing the commission are printed in Kenyon, *Stuart Constitution*, pp. 366–70.

to France? His own explanation was the public-spirited one that by going abroad good relations between Lords and Commons could be restored. However, with the king supporting his enemies, it would have taken a lot of courage for Clarendon to stay. He probably had a clear recollection of the fate of Strafford in 1641. Undoubtedly he was right in that his departure did help to reduce the political temperature. Relations between crown and parliament in the parliamentary sessions of 1670–1 were perhaps the most harmonious of the whole reign. What destroyed the chances of parliamentary cooperation permanently were the activities of Charles and his brother immediately after the fall of Clarendon. The effect of these, when they became widely known, was to revive anti-Catholicism as the dominant issue in politics for the next fifteen years.

9

'Catholic' or 'Cavalier' policies, 1668–1674

With hindsight one can see at various times in the past certain alternative courses of action which, if followed, might have changed the course of events dramatically and thereby obviated the consequences of decisions that were in fact taken. The six years after 1667 fall into this category. After the downfall of Clarendon two distinct courses of action were open to Charles II, which can be labelled 'Cavalier' and 'Catholic'.

Summary

What were 'Cavalier' and 'Catholic' policies?

- Cavalier polices entailed unqualified support for the restored Anglican Church, the suppression of all nonconformity as seditious by the enforcement of the Clarendon Code, and (though less important at the beginning) a Protestant foreign policy.
- 'Catholic' policies, on the other hand, combined toleration for Protestant and Catholic nonconformists at home with alliance with France abroad.

It would be simplifying things too much to suggest that the choice between 'Cavalier' and 'Catholic' policies was clear-cut. Charles and his ministers sometimes followed both policies simultaneously. Yet, as will be seen, by making the treaties with France in 1670, and by issuing the Declaration of Indulgence and declaring war on the Dutch in 1672, Charles committed himself to 'Catholic' policies at a time when it was suspected (and in 1673 confirmed) that the heir to the throne, James, duke of York, was a Catholic. Charles thus aligned the English monarchy in the eyes of many Englishmen with popery and absolutism, and so ensured that it would be much harder to gain parliamentary cooperation in the 1670s than in the 1660s.

It therefore becomes of prime importance to try to understand why Charles chose a set of policies that could be smeared as papist and absolutist, and rejected policies that might have produced a cooperative parliament.

It is important to stress that Charles himself was responsible for policy-making. After the fall of Clarendon there was no 'cabal' of ministers – an embryonic prime-ministerial cabinet – advising Charles, as was often thought in the past. Even the use of 'cabal' as a mnemonic (the initial letters of five of Charles's ministers after 1667, Clifford, Arlington, Buckingham, Ashley Cooper and Lauderdale, spell 'cabal') can be misleading, since it omits other influential men who were also around the king at this time, including Sir William Coventry until 1669, Sir George Downing and Heneage Finch. It also wrongly suggests that the five men were of equal political importance and were agreed on public policy. Nothing could be further from the truth. The two principal characters at court from 1667 to 1673, Arlington and Buckingham, hated each other, and politics at court and in parliament were often expressed in terms of this rivalry, which was sharpened by striking personal differences between the two men. Arlington's correct behaviour reflected his diplomatic and administrative background; he was the type of royal servant who is often willing to subordinate his own ideas in order to carry out his master's policy. On the other hand, Buckingham, the son of Charles I's favourite, was an independent man who associated with unorthodox freethinkers. Both men differed above all in their religious views. Arlington was a crypto-Catholic, whose deathbed conversion to Catholicism was probably entered into with more sincerity than was Charles II's; while Buckingham's aim seems to have been to bring about a toleration within or outside the established Church of as wide a cross-section of Protestant views as had Oliver Cromwell in the 1650s.[1] Arlington, with Clifford, was taken into the king's confidence in the making of the secret Treaty of Dover; the king's other ministers, like everyone else, knew nothing of it. If anyone was in control of policy in England after 1667, it was the king himself.

Immediately after the departure of Clarendon there was as yet no overt sign of Charles's preference for pro-French policies. On the contrary, in January 1668 England

---

[1] Harris, *London Crowds*, p. 86.

joined the United Provinces and Sweden in a formal anti-French treaty. The Triple Alliance had its origins in the situation on the Continent and especially in the Dutch republic, which, under the leadership of Johan de Witt as Grand Pensionary, was still very powerful, especially at sea. The English had failed in the second Dutch war to make any impression on Dutch commercial supremacy. But Dutch naval and mercantile strength contrasted with the country's military weakness. Earlier this had not mattered because of the Franco-Dutch alliance of 1662, but just when the war with England was being concluded, this situation changed. Louis XIV began to claim the neighbouring Spanish Netherlands by the so-called right of 'devolution' which, it was claimed, was vested in his wife, daughter of Philip IV of Spain. In May 1667 the French general, Turenne, invaded and soon overran the Spanish Netherlands. It was this threat to the United Provinces posed by French expansion which forced de Witt to abandon the French alliance and look to England. Arlington seems to have welcomed the prospect of the Dutch alliance, which was concluded by Sir William Temple. Charles's motives and attitude are, as usual, less obvious. Did he agree to the Triple Alliance as a step on the road to a French alliance, as a means of forcing on Louis XIV the need to detach England from the United Provinces? Certainly the Triple Alliance seems to have had this effect, since in August 1668 Louis sent Charles Albert de Croissy (the brother of his famous minister, Colbert) as ambassador to London with instructions to propose an alliance with England.

If Charles was not yet definitely committed to alliance, he was ready to press for a measure of religious toleration. The events of the next two parliamentary sessions again drove home to the king the unacceptability of this to the parliamentary classes. When parliament met in February 1668, Charles (as in 1660 and 1662) spoke in favour of toleration. The House of Commons responded by refusing to make the customary vote of thanks for the king's speech at the opening of the session, and by pointedly beginning work on another bill against conventicles to replace the 1664 Act, which had lapsed. This, together with accusations of maladministration of the Dutch war, was revived in the next parliamentary session of October–December 1669. The two sessions produced supply totalling only £300,000 at a time when the crown's financial situation was extremely serious. Despite the work of the treasury commission, which had taken over after the death of Southampton in May 1667, in instituting a new credit order system and a retrenchment scheme, Charles's extravagance prevented an overall improvement.[2] Consequently, in the parliamentary recess (December 1669 to February 1670) the decision was taken to revert to the Cavalier policies which had been so successful in gaining supply from 1661 to 1665. The details are necessarily difficult to discover (behind-the-scenes political compacts are never very well documented), but in discussions with some parliamentary leaders Charles appears to have agreed to a new Conventicle Bill in return for supply.[3] In addition, contemporaries believed that during the next session Arlington, with Clifford as 'bribe master general', anticipated the

---

[2] Chandaman, *English Public Revenue*, pp. 212–19.
[3] Witcombe, *Cavalier House of Commons*, p. 98.

methods later used by Danby to manage the House of Commons.[4] As a result the two parliamentary sessions of February to April 1670 and February to April 1671 produced 'the most generous additional supplies of the reign', a massive increase in indirect taxation with new duties on wines, legal proceedings and an additional excise.[5] However, despite this clear evidence of the gains that came with Cavalier policies, Charles had already begun to commit himself to alternative 'Catholic' policies.

Ever since de Croissy's arrival in England in August 1668, negotiations had been proceeding in secret for an alliance with France. Charles had also been promoting a French alliance by means of his correspondence with his sister, Henrietta, the wife of the duke of Orleans, Louis XIV's brother. By October 1669 the main lines of an agreement had been worked out, and at Dover on 22 May 1670, under the cover of Charles's meeting with his sister, Arlington, Clifford and de Croissy signed the secret Treaty of Dover.

Information

The secret Treaty of Dover, 1670

The treaty contained the following provisions:

- Both kings agreed 'their joint resolution to humble the pride of the States General, and to destroy the power of a people which has . . . shown ingratitude to those who have helped it to create its republic'.

- Louis was to pay Charles £225,000 p.a. during the ensuing war against the Dutch.

- More surprisingly, the treaty declared that Charles, 'being convinced of the truth of the Roman Catholic religion is resolved to declare it, and to reconcile himself with the Church of Rome as soon as his country's affairs permit'.

- In order to meet the opposition which, not surprisingly, such a declaration was expected to raise, Louis agreed to pay Charles £150,000 and to provide and pay 6,000 troops 'for the execution of this design'. 'The time for the declaration of Catholicism', asserted the treaty, 'is left entirely to the discretion of the King of England.'[6]

---

[4] A. Browning, *Thomas Osborne Earl of Danby and Duke of Leeds 1632–1712* (3 vols., 1944–51), I, p. 83, n. 4.

[5] Chandaman, *English Public Revenue*, p. 221.

[6] A. Browning, ed., *English Historical Documents, VIII: 1660–1714* (1953), pp. 863–7.

Given the secrecy of these negotiations and their controversial nature, Charles and his closest advisers naturally did not make clear their thoughts and motives in 1670. Consequently, it is impossible to know certainly what his intentions were, and historians have put forward various alternative hypotheses. One is forced to suggest motives for the making of the Dover policy on the basis of very little direct evidence.

The easiest part of this difficult task is to try to explain *Charles's motives in allying with France*. Even Charles was probably not so foolish as to think that the promised French subsidy offered a way out of his financial predicament, as some historians have argued in the past. Professor Kenyon's comment on the later subsidies Charles received from Louis applies equally to this first one: 'It is only a strange persistence in thinking of *livres tournois* as directly equivalent to pounds sterling that has led so many historians to brand Charles II as a remittance man of France.'[7] Charles may have had a financial motive in making the French alliance: he got total subsidies of £375,000 and there was the prospect of profits from prizes on the same scale as those taken in the previous two Dutch wars. Probably far more important, however, in Charles's mind were two other factors. First was the prospect of allying with a country that Charles had always admired and whose king seemed to have found a way of getting rid of a representative assembly, whose English counterpart had become extremely troublesome to a man who liked a quiet life. Secondly, Charles responded to that part of public opinion in England that wanted revenge for the Medway disgrace. Moreover, the war of 1665–7 had done nothing to resolve the commercial rivalry between the two countries. With hindsight, especially with the knowledge that France was to be a major threat to English security and the English Empire, the wisdom of Charles's French alliance can be called into question.[8] As early as 1670 some perceptive observers did see the dangers to England of French conquests in the Low Countries and of French commercial expansion. But in fairness to Charles, few people saw this and it is highly likely that, if it had not become bound up with Protestant fears, the third Dutch war and the French alliance would not have been unpopular.

The real problems surrounding the Dover policy are to explain why Charles insisted on associating with it the Catholic clause in the secret treaty, and why he later (in March 1672) published the Declaration of Indulgence two days before declaring war on the Dutch. It was these, and especially the latter (since the secret clauses of 1670 were never officially made public) that helped to make the new trend in policy so unpopular. There is no really satisfactory explanation why Charles insisted, despite Louis's reservations, on including the Catholic clause in the secret treaty. It is fairly certain that the answer is not that he was a sincere convert; nor, as has been suggested, need he have included the clause to get Arlington's support for the French alliance; Charles was not the man to let a minister stand in his way. A subsidiary motive may have been that Charles saw the Catholic clause as a means of forcing Louis to raise the French subsidy by £150,000, as did in fact happen. However, this was not his main

---

[7] Kenyon, *The Stuarts*, p. 135.

[8] See Haley, *Charles II*, pp. 18–19, for a forthright condemnation of the French alliance.

motive. It is more likely that he considered the major purpose of the Catholic clause as providing a personal link between the two kings – a kind of 'special relationship'.[9]

Even this, though, seems insufficient reason for taking such a grave political risk. Yet the Catholic clause in the Dover treaty is, if anything, easier to explain than Charles's Declaration of Indulgence of March 1672, which suspended all the penal laws, allowed Roman Catholics to worship in their own homes, and offered licences to Protestant dissenters to hold public worship. Given the more tolerant attitude to Protestant dissenters in the last parliamentary session, by itself the latter part of the declaration might have been acceptable. But it is difficult to imagine how Charles could have expected that parliament would swallow any measure of toleration for Catholics. Charles's motives (as usual) are clouded in doubt. One possibility is that the declaration was intended to persuade Louis XIV to push ahead more quickly with preparations for war against the Dutch; the French king was using Charles's failure to declare himself a Catholic as an excuse for delaying a war declaration.[10] Another is that a reluctant Charles was persuaded to issue the declaration by Ashley and Buckingham, who wanted to help Protestant dissenters, and by James, Clifford and Arlington, who wanted to help Catholics.[11] Probably the most telling consideration from the king's point of view, as far as domestic policies is concerned, is that Charles was again gambling on an alliance of Catholics and dissenters against Anglican opinion. Arlington thought that the aim of the declaration was to conciliate dissenters 'that we might keep all quiet at home whilst we are busy abroad'. Even without the benefit of hindsight that must have been a very vain hope. As will be seen, the Declaration of Indulgence united most of the political nation, not against the Dutch, but against Charles and his ministers.

It is easier to defend Charles's Dover policy against the charge that he ought instead to have persevered with Cavalier policies because the financial prospects for the crown were now much better than in the 1660s. It is certainly true that the trend of the crown's permanent ordinary revenue from 1668 onwards was upwards, and with the addition of parliamentary supplies the situation was, of course, even healthier (see below, pp. 326–7). In the 1670s, even without parliamentary supplies, financial solvency for the crown became a possibility. Yet it is perhaps not surprising that Charles was not attracted by this improving financial situation. Even if he understood it, which is doubtful (the permanence of the increase in revenue was not, after all, immediately obvious in 1670), he would still have had to curtail his expenditure severely. 'A long-term programme of recovery involving undeviating effort and frugality'[12] was hardly one to attract someone of Charles II's temperament. Moreover, in the early 1670s the *immediate* financial

---

[9] This is the view of Haley, *Charles II*, p. 17, which seems to me very plausible. See Hutton, 'The making of the secret treaty of Dover', *H.J.*, XXIX (1986) for a survey of different views, including Professor Hutton's own, on this question.

[10] John Miller, *Popery and Politics in England 1660–88* (1973), p. 115.

[11] Hutton, *Charles II*, p. 285.

[12] This is Professor Chandaman's assessment of what Charles needed to do to attain financial solvency for the crown: *English Public Revenue*, p. 274.

situation was very serious indeed. The total royal debt, which had been rising since the Restoration because of Charles's prodigality, now escalated because of the expense of war preparations. In addition, the credit order system begun in 1667 put too great a burden on the exchequer. So serious was the short-term position that on 7 January 1672 Charles and his advisers were forced to suspend for a year most repayments of the capital of loans to government creditors. After this 'Stop of the Exchequer', the way was cleared for the full implementation of the Dover policy, the Declaration of Indulgence (15 March 1672) and the formal declaration of war on the Dutch (17 March 1672).

Charles's gamble that the combination of the Stop, toleration and war against the Dutch would be a way out of his difficulties was doomed to disappointment. For one thing, the third Dutch war, like the second, went badly for England. The English navy's attack on the returning Dutch Smyrna fleet in March 1672 was bungled, and the naval battle off Southwold Bay on 28 May 1672 was indecisive. Although English propaganda could persuasively argue that the English and French navies had 'won' the battle of Southwold Bay, it could not hide the fact that the victors of the war appeared to be, not the English, but their allies the French. In the early part of June 1672, Turenne and Condé crossed the Rhine and occupied Utrecht. The effect in the United Provinces was to precipitate the bloody downfall of Johan de Witt and his brother, and the appointment of William of Orange as Stadhouder. In England the effect of the French victories was to turn public opinion for the first time against the French alliance. The potential threat to English national security from French expansion in the Low Countries, which only a few had seen in 1670–1, now became apparent to all. But, as yet, the greatest criticism in England was reserved for the Declaration of Indulgence. It is striking that, when parliament met in February 1673 for the first time since April 1671, even with the evidence of French expansion in the Low Countries nine months old, Charles's foreign policy was not yet directly challenged. On the contrary, within two weeks of its first meeting the Commons voted in principle to grant a supply of £1,126,000 by means of eighteen monthly assessments. The main parliamentary attack was directed against the Declaration of Indulgence, which most speakers in the Commons saw as being designed to encourage the growth of popery, and as a major threat to parliament because of Charles's intention arbitrarily to suspend parliamentary legislation. On 14 February the Commons voted *nem. con.* that 'penal statutes in matters ecclesiastical cannot be suspended but by an Act of parliament'.[13] In the counties, too, anti-Catholicism again reared its head and resulted in the most determined effort to enforce the recusancy laws since the Restoration. In some counties the numbers of convicted recusants increased dramatically: in Wiltshire more papists were convicted in 1673 than in the previous twelve years since the Restoration.[14]

The hysterical anti-Catholicism seen in the parliamentary debates of February and March 1673 is not surprising. What perhaps is, is the first signs that the divisions within the Protestant ranks were beginning to close in face of the alleged Catholic menace.

---

[13] Quoted in Witcombe, *Cavalier House of Commons*, p. 133.
[14] Miller, *Popery and Politics*, p. 132.

Even some Protestant dissenting MPs spoke against the Declaration of Indulgence, and on 14 February a bill for the relief of Protestant dissenters, which was on roughly the same lines as the Toleration Bill enacted in 1689, was introduced into the House of Commons. Arguments for the toleration of Protestant dissenters were voiced in parliament that would have been unthinkable in the 1660s.[15] Ominously for Charles and for James, the spring parliamentary session of 1673 showed that in the face of the common fear of Catholicism and absolutism, Anglicans and Protestant dissenters could sink their differences. This was to be the lesson of 1688, as will be seen. Unlike his brother later, however, Charles recognized the strength of this alliance, and on 8 March 1673, despite contrary pressure in the privy council from James, Clifford and Shaftesbury, Charles announced the cancellation of the Declaration of Indulgence, and a few days later he gave his assent to a Test Act, which excluded all non-Anglicans from holding public offices.

Charles tried to gain every political advantage he could from his apparent reversion to 'Cavalier' policies in England. His attempt to dissociate the French alliance from its damaging Catholic and absolutist associations was, however, foiled by two factors in the summer of 1673: the spread of effective Dutch propaganda and the public admission of James's conversion to Catholicism. William of Orange's rise to power in the United Provinces in the revolution of 1672 not only strengthened Dutch resistance in the war, but also resulted in the emergence of what Professor Haley calls 'political warfare',[16] directed by William, with the aim of undermining English support for the French alliance. Soon after his appointment, William and Gaspar Fagel, the new Grand Pensionary of Holland, recognizing the importance of public opinion in the politics of the period, began to encourage the dissemination of Dutch propaganda in England, alleging that the principal aim of the Anglo-French alliance was to spread Catholicism in England. This was the theme of the most effective pamphlet published in 1673, *England's Appeal from the Private Cabal at Whitehall to the Great Council of the Nation*, probably written by Peter du Moulin, a close associate of William of Orange. *England's Appeal* was published in England in late February 1673, too late to have much impact on the spring parliamentary session. But it was widely circulated and read in the late spring and summer of 1673. Its effect was to make 'France, popery and absolutism' as inseparable and as powerful a political cliché in the 1670s as 'dissent and sedition' had been in the 1660s. If the Dutch propagandists had known of the secret Catholic clause in the Treaty of Dover, their allegations would have been even more telling. As it was, soon after the appearance of du Moulin's pamphlet, they received what was arguably as big a boost as the revelations of the Dover Catholic cause would have been. In June 1673 the suspicions raised by Dutch propagandists were amply confirmed when, under the terms of the Test Act, Clifford and James resigned their respective offices of lord high treasurer and lord high admiral. James had been a secret Catholic since at least

---

[15] Witcombe, *Cavalier House of Commons*, p. 134.

[16] K. H. D. Haley, *William of Orange and the English Opposition 1672–4* (1953), p. 10.

the beginning of 1669, but the first public affirmation of his conversion was his failure to take the Anglican sacraments at Easter 1673. After James's resignation in June, his Catholicism was not in doubt, especially when in September 1673 he married a Catholic princess, Mary of Modena. (His first wife, Anne Hyde, had died in 1671.) The Catholicism of the heir to the throne was to be the prime political issue of the next fifteen years.

The immediate effect of Dutch propaganda and James's conversion was to make the parliamentary sessions of October–November 1673 and January–February 1674 the stormiest of Charles's reign to date. Whereas in the spring session of 1673 opposition had been confined in the main to the Declaration of Indulgence, it now widened to encompass a vast range of issues, many of which had not been raised before: the French alliance was now directly criticized; so was James's marriage (in October 1673, the Commons voted belatedly against the marriage taking place); a new Test Act was proposed, designed to prevent Catholics from sitting in both Houses of parliament; in January and February 1674 a long list of bills was drafted to limit the power of future Catholic monarchs, including provision for the Protestant education of the king's children; and, finally, the king's principal ministers were attacked as popish and dangerous. It was resolved that Lauderdale and Buckingham be removed from the king's council, and articles of impeachment were brought in against Arlington. Ashley Cooper (since 1672 earl of Shaftesbury and lord chancellor) no longer supported government policy. Although in February 1673 in his famous *Delendo est Carthago* speech he had defended the government's record, the events of the following summer convinced him that Charles did intend to promote Catholicism and of the need to guard against a Catholic successor. Shaftesbury's first reaction was to press Charles to divorce Catherine of Braganza and remarry with the hope of producing a Protestant heir, a project which seems to have first been discussed at court in 1669 when Catherine had a miscarriage.[17] Then and later Charles would have nothing to do with the divorce plan; on this, unlike many other issues, he refused to make any concessions. Instead on 9 November 1673 he dismissed Shaftesbury from his office of lord chancellor, and in the following May he expelled him from the privy council and the lord-lieutenancy of Dorset. From this date Shaftesbury's efforts to secure the dissolution of the Cavalier Parliament and the exclusion of James from the throne began.

In this, though, Shaftesbury was out on a limb; until the Popish Plot 'revelations', few MPs supported his extreme tactics. Not exclusion but the securing of limitations on a Catholic monarch, on the lines laid down in the parliamentary session of January–February 1674, was the programme of most MPs from 1673–4 to 1678. This was enough of a coherent programme to make historians suspect a more than usual degree of coordination behind parliamentary tactics in the sessions of late 1673 and early 1674. Although one needs to beware of describing this development as though it were the beginning of the organized political parties we have today, political friendships had

---

[17] K. H. D. Haley, *The First Earl of Shaftesbury* (1968), pp. 276–80.

inevitably been forged in the frequent parliamentary sessions since 1660, which had also given many MPs a greater wealth of parliamentary experience even than MPs in the 1620s and 1640s. Although the evidence is slight, there are brief glimpses of MPs in the early 1670s meeting to coordinate tactics before and during parliamentary sessions. Inevitably, those who did this were usually those who were critical of the court, echoing the crown's critics before 1640, accusing it of corruption and extravagance at the expense of impoverished gentry, and of harbouring conspiracies to introduce absolutism. Sir Thomas Meres's fears of what might be the consequences of raising an army to fight the Dutch, which he expressed in the Commons in 1673, illustrate that anxieties which had emerged in early Stuart England were still very much alive. 'It brings in the billeting of soldiers, against the Petition of Right', he alleged. 'You are told also of martial law, made for the governing these men, against the laws of England. Martial law has arbitrary principles and arbitrary power.'[18] By 1674 there was a hard core of such 'opposition' MPs, including Sir William Coventry, Lord Cavendish, William Russell, Sir Thomas Meres and William Sacheverell; in addition, from the summer of 1673 there was a strong political issue – James's Catholicism – round which opposition groups could coalesce. To that extent by 1673–4 a 'country party' had emerged.[19]

In February 1674, in the face of this hardening opposition, Charles, as in the previous year, withdrew by making peace with the Dutch by the Treaty of Westminster (9 February 1674) which made no major changes in the pre-war situation. The 'country party' had thus won two major victories: Charles had torn up the Declaration of Indulgence and abandoned the Dutch war. But the events after the prorogation of parliament on 24 February 1674 showed just how insubstantial as yet was the 'country party'.

> This sudden prorogation [reported a correspondent of du Moulin] caused many of the guilty Commons (Lord St John, Sir Thomas Lee, Sir Robert Thomas, Sir N. Carew, Sir Elias Harvey, Sacheverell, and many others) who had bespoken a large dinner for that day at the Swan Tavern in King Street, to leave . . . and to haste away (some by coach, some by water) into the city, suspecting themselves . . . unsecure in the suburbs.[20]

As after the dissolutions of the parliaments of 1621 and 1624, the king still held the whip-hand. And at this stage Charles acquired a minister, Sir Thomas Osborne (later earl of Danby), who had the necessary qualities to enable the crown to recover the political initiative. It remains to be seen whether Charles's choice of 'Catholic' policies in the crucial preceding six years had made Danby's eventual failure inevitable.

---

[18] Quoted in P. Seaward, *The Restoration 1660–88* (1991), pp. 32–3.
[19] See Haley, *Shaftesbury*, pp. 351–2; Witcombe, *Cavalier House of Commons*, pp. 58–60 and Seaward, *Cavalier Parliament*, pp. 94–9, 279–301 for discussions of 'the country party'.
[20] Quoted in Haley, *William of Orange*, p. 191.

10

Anti-Catholicism and exclusion, 1674–1681

Summary

The decision of Charles II to pursue 'Catholic' policies in the 1670s and the revelation of the conversion to Catholicism of his brother and heir to the throne, James, duke of York, ensured that anti-Catholicism became once again a powerful force in English politics.

In this chapter it will be argued that anti-Catholicism ensured that the attempts of Charles's chief minister in the early 1670s, Danby, to gain support for the crown failed and (more dramatically) it brought about the biggest threat to the monarchy since the mid-century: the Popish Plot and the Exclusion Crisis.

Anti-Catholicism

One of the most striking features of seventeenth-century England is the strength and persistence at all levels and among all classes of society of anti-Catholicism, which from the early 1670s came to play an increasingly important part in politics. Robin Clifton has shown that in the early seventeenth century there were frequent local outbreaks of panic that Catholics were about to murder and pillage the community, notably in 1605 and 1641–2.[1] Despite the growing strength of the intellectual case for toleration, there is very little sign that popular hatred of popery diminished in the second half of the century. William Prynne believed that the New Model Army in 1647–8 had been infiltrated by Catholics and that Pride's Purge and the execution of Charles I were 'nothing else but the designs and projects of Jesuits, Popish priests and recusants'.[2] If Prynne and sober respectable people like Richard Baxter could believe nonsense like this, then the common, uncritical assumption that Catholics were behind the Great Fire of 1666 and the widespread belief in Titus Oates's 'revelation' in 1678 of a Catholic conspiracy to kill the king are more easily understandable. Henry Care's lurid description of an imaginary Catholic England reflects many of the elements in the seventeenth-century anti-Catholic tradition: the men

> forced to fly destitute of bread and harbour, your wives prostituted to the lust of every savage bog-trotter, your daughters ravished by goatish monks, your smaller children tossed upon pikes, or torn limb from limb, whilst you have your own bowels ripped up . . . or else murdered with some other exquisite tortures and holy candles made of your grease (which was done within our memory in Ireland), your dearest friends flaming in Smithfield, foreigners rendering your poor babes that can escape everlasting slaves, never more to see a Bible, nor hear again the joyful sounds of Liberty and Property. This gentlemen is Popery.[3]

The paradox of English anti-Catholicism is that it grew at a time when there were very few Catholics in England. Given the outlawed position of Catholics, it is not surprising that estimates of the size of the Catholic community in late seventeenth-century England vary wildly. John Miller's estimate of 66,000 (just over 1 per cent of the total population), based on the Danby ecclesiastical census of 1676, is probably nearest the truth. Even if this is an underestimate, Catholics almost certainly made up no more than 5 per cent of the population. Not only was the size of the Catholic lay community small, but its political activism was a myth (as it had been in the early part of the century). Nor was there much substance behind the often-hysterical fears of the subversive activities of the Catholic clergy. One can be no more certain about their numbers than one can about the Catholic population as a whole; the most widely accepted estimate, that of Claudius Agrette, a papal agent, in 1669, of 230 secular clergy and about 255 regular clergy (mainly Jesuits, Benedictines and Carmelites) hardly substantiates contemporary allegations of thousands of Catholic priests in the English mission.[4] Nor were those Catholic priests who were at work very well organized. They were split by a long-standing antagonism between seculars and regulars, and lacked

---

[1] Robin Clifton, 'The fear of Catholicism during the English Civil War', *P. & P.*, LII (1971); idem., 'Fear of popery', in Conrad Russell, ed., *The Origins of the English Civil War* (1973).
[2] Quoted in Miller, *Popery and Politics*, p. 85. See Lamont, *Prynne*, for Prynne's obsession with Jesuit plots.
[3] Quoted in Miller, *Popery and Politics*, p. 75.
[4] Ibid., pp. 9–10, 40.

any clear leadership from the papacy. So distrustful was the papal curia of the efforts of some Catholic secular clergy (especially the so-called Blackloites) to secure a rapprochement with Cromwell and, later, Charles II, that it failed to appoint a bishop in England after 1655. The political indecisiveness of the Jesuits and the papal curia in the late seventeenth century, which amounted at times to ineptitude, contrasts sharply with the Protestant caricature of Jesuit and papal guile and political sophistication. For example, at a time when most Englishmen saw James, duke of York's marriage to Mary of Modena as part of a cunning papal-inspired design to convert England to Catholicism, the papal curia could not make up its mind about the marriage, and its bureaucratic incompetence nearly prevented the marriage from taking place. What makes English anti-Catholicism even more inexplicable is that, for the most part, there was little tension between Protestants and Catholics in the local community. This is most easily demonstrated among the landowning classes. Catholic and Protestant gentry shared the same life-styles and met each other socially, and sometimes their families intermarried. Catholic neighbours were not considered to be dangerous papal agents and this (as much as administrative inertia) accounts for the lax enforcement of penal legislation against Catholics in the late sixteenth and seventeenth centuries. Seventeenth-century Englishmen had a schizophrenic attitude to Catholics. While the earl of Anglesey was preparing a book against the Jesuits in the 1670s, he spent his spare time dining with and calling on his Catholic neighbours. How can one, then, account for the hatred and fear of Catholics in seventeenth-century England?

By 1660 Englishmen had been subjected to over a century of Protestant propaganda that the Catholic religion was abhorrent and more evil than the worst type of heresy. 'In pamphlet and sermon, popery was presented as essentially the *debasement* of Christ's teaching, a total and blasphemous perversion of Apostolic practice.'[5] Easily the most important literary contribution to this view and one of the most popular books of the late sixteenth and seventeenth centuries was John Foxe's *Acts and Monuments*, first published in 1563. Foxe not only recounted the martyrdom of about 300 people during the reign of Mary Tudor, he also portrayed the burnings at Smithfield as one episode in a developing struggle between true Christianity and the forces of evil represented by Rome. Later writers interested in eschatology followed Foxe and used the prophecies in the Book of Revelations to identify Rome as the Antichrist and England as the 'Elect Nation' chosen by God to fight and defeat the 'Whore of Babylon'. As with all general theories of historical development, it was then possible to find events that 'supported' this interpretation. Were the St Bartholomew's Day Massacre of French Huguenots in 1572, the Gunpowder Plot in 1605, the Irish Rebellion in the 1640s and the Great Fire in 1666 not simply further episodes in the struggle between Christ and Antichrist?

Protestant propagandists also had answers to Catholic apologists who rightly argued that English Catholics had always been demonstrably loyal during times of national crisis, from the Armada onwards, and that Catholics during the seventeenth century

---

[5]   Clifton, 'Fear of popery', pp. 146–7.

had withdrawn from the political arena. William Blundell, a Lancashire Catholic, argued that 'all Catholic subjects of a lawful Protestant king (such as king Charles the 2nd) are obliged faithfully to adhere to that king in all invasions, whatsoever, though made by Catholic princes or even by the pope himself'.[6] Many Protestants, however, found more convincing the standard anti-Catholic jibe that Catholicism 'draweth with it an unavoidable dependency upon foreign princes'.[7] After all, were there not Catholic conspiracies against the state, from the Ridolfi Plot to the Great Fire, to support this? Especially serious was the refusal of many Catholics to take the Oath of Allegiance of 1606. Their refusal to swear that their faith was 'impious', 'heretical' and a 'damnable doctrine' is understandable, but those who did so laid all English Catholics wide open to the charge of sedition. Nor did English Protestants have much time for those who argued that Catholics could not be a threat because there were not many of them. On the contrary, their enemies countered, were Catholics, though numerically insignificant, not very well represented among powerful groups like the aristocracy and gentry? The most damning charge of all (one which James II believed just as much as the Protestant polemicists) was that thousands of Catholics conformed to the Church of England and were only waiting for the right moment to declare their true allegiance. By its very nature this was a charge that was difficult to refute, and was not shown to be groundless until James II's reign when the hoped-for rally of Catholics to the 'true faith' failed to materialize.

Catholicism, maintained a Commons' petition of December 1621, 'hath a restless spirit, and will strive by these gradations: if it once get but a connivancy, it will press for a toleration: if that should be obtained, they must have an equality: from thence they will aspire to superiority, and will never rest till they get a subversion of the true religion'.[8] This point was often made in the later seventeenth century, as it had been in the 1630s and early 1640s, and it seemed to be confirmed by what was happening at the English court, in Ireland and in Europe. Henrietta Maria provided a personal link between fears of Popish plots at the courts of Charles I in the 1630s (see pp. 156–8) and of Charles II in the 1660s. It was well known that she pressed her son, as she had her husband, to give favour to Catholics and that she was supported in this by Catholic and crypto-Catholic courtiers like the earl of Bristol, Lord Arundell of Wardour, Clifford and Arlington. These Catholic trends at court were, of course, amply confirmed by the duke of York's conversion. As in England before the Civil War, too, events in Ireland supplemented the image of the galloping Catholicization of Britain. Looked at from the Irish point of view, the policies of the restored monarchy must have seemed very hostile as Cromwellian conquest was followed by a systematic (if not total) expulsion of Irish Catholic landowners. But, as in the early 1640s, events in Ireland during the early 1670s were looked at very differently through the eyes of the English since, after the removal

---

[6]   Quoted in Miller, *Popery and Politics*, p. 32.
[7]   Tanner, *Constitutional Documents*, p. 277.
[8]   Ibid., p. 277.

of the duke of Ormonde as lord lieutenant of Ireland in 1669, restrictions on the Catholic Church in Ireland were relaxed and Irish Catholics were admitted to office.[9]

But, as in the reign of Charles I, the main cause of fear of popery in England was what was happening in Europe, and especially in France. The effect on European Protestant opinion of Louis XIV's often savage persecution of his Protestant Huguenot subjects cannot be exaggerated. The Revocation of the Edict of Nantes in October 1685, which took away the limited toleration enjoyed by French Huguenots, reinforced anti-Catholic propaganda. Without the revocation, it will be argued later, the successful intervention of William of Orange in England in 1688 (and therefore the 'Glorious Revolution') would have been impossible. As Huguenot refugees came to England, first in a trickle and then, after 1685, in a flood, they brought concrete proof, in Louis XIV's *dragonnades*, of the truth of Protestant allegations of the cruelty and intolerance of rampant Catholicism. It was this powerful hatred of popery that Charles II's decision to ally with France and the announcement of James's conversion to Catholicism brought to the centre of the English political stage for much of the 1670s and 1680s, and with which Charles II and Danby, and later James II, would have to contend.

Danby, 1674–1678

The immediate aftermath of the dramatic revelation of James's Catholicism was a political vacuum at court. Shaftesbury and Buckingham joined the ranks of the government's critics, Lauderdale spent most of his time in Scotland, Arlington lost most of his political influence, and Clifford resigned and died (probably by committing suicide). Clifford was replaced as lord treasurer by a Yorkshireman, Sir Thomas Osborne (created earl of Danby in June 1674, marquis of Carmarthen in 1689, and duke of Leeds in 1694). Although Danby (like everyone else) could never be certain of Charles's continued support, for at least three years from the end of 1674 his power as leading minister of the crown was fairly secure. During that time he followed distinct policies aimed at restoring the crown's financial position after the debacle of the Stop of the Exchequer, and at establishing permanently good relations between crown and parliament by returning to 'Cavalier' policies: unqualified support for the Church of England, persecution of Protestant and Catholic dissenters, and hostility to France. As will be seen, he was not wholly unsuccessful in these aims. During his tenure of the treasurership, the total revenue of the crown increased dramatically. Moreover, the crown's critics in the four parliamentary sessions held in 1675, 1677 and 1678 did not have any impact on government policy to match their success in forcing Charles to cancel the Declaration of Indulgence in 1673 and to end the Dutch war in 1674.

---

[9]   J. G. Simms, 'The Restoration 1660–85', in T. W. Moody, F. X. Martin, F. J. Byrne, eds., *A New History of Ireland, III: Early Modern Ireland 1534–1691* (1976).

Yet Danby did not improve the overall financial position of the crown; nor did he reduce parliamentary distrust of the crown and its policies. Could he have succeeded more completely than he did? Like so many historical questions, this one is capable of different answers. Yet an analysis of the reasons for Danby's failure suggests that his task was hopeless from the start. After 1670–3 the political situation changed dramatically and permanently. Danby had to accept the consequences of the fact that the heir to the throne was now a Catholic. Nor could he detach the king from his preference for an alliance with France. Indeed, given Louis XIV's ability to reveal the Catholic clause in the secret Treaty of Dover, it is difficult to see how Charles, even if he had wanted to, could have permanently abandoned the French alliance. It is ironic that Charles's choice of policies that were (in part at least) aimed at strengthening the monarchy arguably delayed the creation of a strong monarchy for at least a decade. A Catholic heir and a pro-French foreign policy raised a barrier of mistrust between crown and parliament that even Danby's 'Cavalier' policies could not breach.

Danby and the royal finances

When he became lord treasurer in 1673, Danby inherited what appears to have been a hopeless financial situation. The suspension of the repayment of the capital on loans decided on by the Stop of the Exchequer, which had been intended as a temporary measure, was extended. In addition, parliamentary supplies (£1,800,000) for the Dutch war fell short by £443,000 of total war expenditure.[10] Yet Danby's chances of improving the crown's finances were considerably greater than the possibility of his securing a cooperative parliament. The late 1660s and early 1670s were a turning point in the development of public finance as well as in political history. Danby was fortunate in that his period at the treasury coincided with an improvement in the collection of three major branches of the revenue: the hearth tax, the excise and the customs. Undoubtedly the most important of these, from the long-term point of view, was the last. From the late 1660s England entered a period of commercial prosperity, which continued (though with periodic interruptions) for most of the century. Customs revenue increased in proportion, and, moreover, the benefit to the crown was greater than it might have been, because in September 1671 the crown had taken over the direct administration of the customs as in the sixteenth century, so that the full benefit of the trade boom accrued not to customs farmers, but to the exchequer. Nor did the third Dutch war dislocate trade to the same extent as the second Dutch war. Danby's contribution to the improvement in the revenue was to bring his considerable financial experience to the treasury. As a protégé of Buckingham he first came to the forefront in politics as joint treasurer of the navy in 1668, and in 1671 he was promoted sole treasurer. The effect of the fortuitous combination of Danby's financial expertise and the rise in customs revenue can be seen in the following table.

---

[10] Chandaman, *English Public Revenue*, p. 229.

Net government income, 1668–1679[11]

Financial year	Permanent ordinary revenue (£)	Total revenue with parliamentary and non-parliamentary additions (£)
1663–9	873,174	883,605
1669–70	953,813	990,323
1670–1	840,170	1,165,554
1671–2	1,000,432	1,902,180
1672–3	1,006,860	1,363,395
1673–4	1,027,653	1,342,417
1674–5	1,138,010	1,430,183
1675–6	1,027,427	1,420,963
1676–7	1,042,815	1,409,508
1677–8	1,026,020	1,360,060
1678–9	1,063,723	1,325,894

Unfortunately for the crown and for Danby, as revenue increased so did royal expenditure, and at an even greater rate. When Danby left the treasury in March 1679 he bequeathed a floating debt of about £750,000 greater than he had faced in 1674, with the result that the overall financial position of the crown in the 1670s was, if anything, slightly worse than in the 1660s. Yet the similarity ends there. Whereas the crown's financial difficulties in the 1660s were largely due to the failure of the Convention and Cavalier Parliaments to provide the monarchy with an adequate permanent ordinary revenue, in the 1670s the major cause was Charles's extravagance: 'the simple Caroline law that the extravagance of the king tended to increase in proportion to his resources'.[12] In 1675 and 1677 Danby initiated drastic retrenchment schemes with the privy council's and Charles's approval. But Charles, like his grandfather in similar circumstances, ignored his promises. It seems hard to blame Danby for his failure to cut his master's spending. He depended totally on Charles for his political position, and, like Cecil and Cranfield in the reign of James I, was in no position to enforce rigid economy on the king. His failure, however, was a major factor in retarding the growth of strong monarchy in England in the late seventeenth century. It made the crown more than ever financially dependent on parliament, and increased the importance of Danby's task of securing a cooperative parliament.

---

[11] Ibid., p. 332.
[12] Ibid., p. 235.

Danby and parliament

To overcome parliamentary distrust of royal intentions, caused by the French alliance and a Catholic heir, Danby had two major parliamentary strategies: first to develop the art of parliamentary management, and second, to persuade Charles to adopt Cavalier policies which would appeal to the intolerant prejudices of Anglican MPs. Although the importance of Danby's 'party organization' has been exaggerated in the past, it is important for the insight it gives into the working of politics in the reign of Charles II.[13] Both Clarendon and Clifford had previously made rudimentary and haphazard efforts to coordinate support for government policies in parliament. Danby was much more systematic. His first attempt to influence MPs in favour of his policies grew out of his success in improving the collection of the excise. A by-product of this was that he, and not the excise farmers, secured control of the payment of pensions drawn on the excise revenue, and he began to distribute these pensions to MPs in the hope of consolidating support for the crown in parliament. By the autumn of 1675 pensions on the excise totalling £10,000 p.a. were being paid to between twenty-three and thirty-four MPs. Other MPs were appointed customs commissioners or officials of the Irish revenue. Danby also placed a lot of emphasis on approaching MPs directly to ask for their support. He extended the system of sending letters to potential supporters just before a session, reminding them of the necessity of attending. His agent, Sir Richard Wiseman, tirelessly canvassed opinion, drew up endless lists of MPs who might be persuaded to support the government if approached personally, and organized dinners to woo supporters. The extent of Danby's activities in organizing parliamentary support for the court is reflected in his surviving letters and papers.[14] But did he succeed in organizing a 'court party'? There are many reasons for doubting that he did. Payment of 'bribes' in the seventeenth century, whether paid by Gondomar, the Spanish ambassador in the reign of James I, Danby, or Barrillon, the French ambassador in the 1670s and 1680s, rarely seem to have persuaded anyone to change their opinions or influenced anyone's activities. Moreover, what could be achieved by the distribution of offices was limited, because Danby had nothing like the government resources of patronage, not to mention electoral connections, that were at the disposal of Walpole or Newcastle in the eighteenth century. Most important of all, the effectiveness of Danby's 'party organization' was limited because it tended to be resented. For example, his attempt to suppress coffee houses, which were places where government critics met and read anti-government pamphlets, and which were (as has been seen) a major component of the widening popular participation in politics in this period, roused great opposition. His intervention was resented and in the end he was forced to withdraw the ban. Danby's organization never produced a solid block of supporters in either House on whom he could rely, and his activities tended to help his

---

[13] A. Browning, 'Parties and party organisation in the reign of Charles II', *T.R.H.S.*, 4th ser., XXX (1948); Browning, *Danby*, I, pp. 167–72, 191–3, 201–7.
[14] Many of these are printed in Browning, *Danby*, III, pp. 33–151.

opponents, who portrayed them, as did Shaftesbury, as a 'conspiracy' to raise the power of the monarchy and Church, and abolish Magna Carta and 'the rights and liberties of the people'.[15]

Danby's greatest political quality was that he was thoroughly acquainted with the mood of the mass of country MPs, and he sympathized with their desire for a return to the policies of the Clarendon Code and for the court to cut its ties with Louis XIV. The clearest exposition of his Cavalier philosophy is in a memorandum he drafted for Charles II at the end of 1674 or the beginning of 1675. He proposed that the crown ought to align itself firmly alongside the Church of England in penalizing dissent by enforcing the Corporation and Five Mile Acts. The king should also reward Anglican Cavaliers by promoting them to the commission of the peace and lieutenancy, so that 'preference in all counties may be given to those . . . who have actually been in armes or sufferers for your majestic or royall father, and to the sons of such'. He even proposed that recusancy fines should be used to pay salaries to sheriffs, JPs and 'officers of the militia'.[16]

In the autumn of 1674 Danby began a series of conferences with bishops, which resulted in the following February in a privy council order that all the measures designed to preserve the monopoly of the Anglican Church should be rigorously enforced. To publicize this policy he released plans for the rebuilding of St Paul's, for the erection of a brass statue of Charles I at Charing Cross, and for a ceremony to re-inter the 'Martyr King'. At the opening of the parliamentary session in April 1675, Charles's speech pushed home the point further: 'I', said Charles, who never minded lying for the sake of political expediency, 'will leave nothing undone that may show any zeal to the Protestant religion, as it is established in the Church of England, from which I will never depart.'[17] Two days later Danby introduced into the Lords a Test Bill, which proposed that all MPs and office-holders make a declaration of non-resistance and swear never to try to alter the established government in Church and State.

Yet the two parliamentary sessions of 1675 were not a success. In the first session (April–June) the Commons attempted to remove Lauderdale and articles of impeachment were brought against Danby. Although both were unsuccessful, they were hardly the responses Danby had hoped for. Even after the vigorous effort to mobilize support in the summer, the second session (October–November) produced only a grudging supply of £300,000 for the navy, far short of what the court wanted to pay off all anticipations on the revenue. A motion that all the money should be paid into and administered by the Chamber of the City of London, and not the exchequer, was only defeated by a narrow majority of eleven. When a clause was tacked on to the Supply Bill appropriating all the customs revenue to the navy, parliament was prorogued for fifteen months. Partly the explanation for the failure of Danby's parliamentary policies in 1675 lies in the fact that the extreme Anglican measures proposed roused

---

[15] Quoted in Haley, *Shaftesbury*, p. 390.
[16] Browning, *Danby*, III, pp. 65–6.
[17] Quoted in Haley, *Shaftesbury*, p. 374.

the resistance of MPs who were beginning to find the persecution of dissent distasteful. According to Burnet, the Test Bill was vigorously opposed from 15 April to 2 June by Shaftesbury, Buckingham and Halifax, and produced the greatest and longest debate in the House of Lords 'that he could remember'.[18] It was even rumoured that Danby's Anglicanism forced Shaftesbury and the duke of York to consider a political alliance to defend the dissenters and Catholics. Partly also many MPs opposed Danby because they considered his efforts to build up a court party to be a threat to parliamentary independence. At the end of April 1675 there was an unsuccessful move in the Commons to prevent placemen sitting in parliament or at least to force them to seek re-election. Danby's failure, however, is largely to be accounted for by the fact that he had failed to overcome the suspicions of most MPs of Charles's pro-French and Catholic leanings. In January 1675, Charles told parliament that 'I know you have heard much of my alliance with France, and I believe it hath been very strongly misrepresented to you, as if there were certain articles of dangerous consequence, but . . . I assure you there is no other treaty with France . . . not already printed, which shall not be made known to a committee of this house.'[19] But this blatant lie failed to dampen the growing suspicions of many MPs at the direction of royal policies. In the 1675 parliamentary sessions this can be seen especially in the great opposition to Charles's apparent reluctance to recall English soldiers still serving in the French army. In fact, parliament's suspicions of Charles were well grounded. Charles's negotiations with Louis XIV culminated in two secret agreements in August 1675 and February 1676, by which Louis agreed to pay Charles a subsidy of £112,000. Danby disapproved of the continuation of the French alliance, but his failure to persuade Charles to abandon Louis and make an alliance with the Dutch undermined all the good done by his pursuit of Cavalier policies at home.

Despite Danby's failure in 1675, it is difficult to accept the views of older historians that by this date parliamentary politics had already polarized 'into two fairly well-defined parties with a voting strength of rather more than 150 each'.[20] It has already been suggested that Danby's attempts to produce a 'court party' were largely unsuccessful; there is very little sign yet of a 'country party' either. Certainly there was no generally recognized opposition leader. Shaftesbury, who was to fill this role during the Exclusion Crisis, was as yet too extreme for most MPs. His attempt in 1675 to force Charles to dissolve parliament by exploiting the inter-House dispute, *Shirley* v. *Fagg*, received little support in the Commons. Few MPs were anxious to face the electorate and perhaps lose their seats. 'I am afraid of a dissolution, because God is my witness, I am afraid the next will be worse.' Sir John Berkenhead's comment in parliament was laughed at, but it expressed what a lot of MPs feared. Indeed, when parliament reassembled after fifteen months' prorogation (November 1675 to

---

[18] Quoted in ibid., p. 381.
[19] Quoted in J. Scott, 'England's troubles: exhuming the Popish Plot', in Harris et al., eds., *Politics of Religion*, pp. 117–18.
[20] Browning, *Danby*, I, p. 173. For a similar view, see Ogg, *Reign of Charles II*, p. 535.

February 1677) and Shaftesbury, Buckingham, Salisbury and Lord Wharton claimed that parliament was dissolved on the grounds that a statute of Edward III declared a prorogation of more than twelve months illegal, they were sent to the Tower by the Lords, and received little sympathetic support in the Commons. Danby was able to seize the initiative and secure promises of large parliamentary supplies: a seventeen months' assessment calculated to yield £585,000, renewal of the expiring additional excise, and approval of the government's plan to borrow £200,000 on the security of the excise. Moreover, an attempt to attach an appropriation clause to the Supply Bill was heavily defeated. In return Danby gave government support for a programme of limitations on a Catholic successor, which government critics had been proposing since 1673. Danby and the Cavalier majority in the Commons were closer than at any other time since his rise to power.

Yet the extent of the mistrust of Charles and the court felt by many at this stage should not be underestimated. Danby's militant pro-Anglican policies not only offended those who hoped to extend toleration to moderate Protestant dissenters, or even to bring them within the Church; but they seemed to substantiate allegations made by Shaftesbury in 1675, in *A Letter from a Person of Quality to his Friends in the Country*, that there was an episcopal plot to introduce arbitrary government. Events in Scotland appeared as further confirmation: news of the earl of Lauderdale's ruthless campaign against nonconformists north of the border in the 1670s neatly supplemented Shaftesbury's coherent conspiracy theory. What, however, caused most distrust of the crown at this stage was Charles's continued attachment to the French alliance. Danby's failure to alter this proved to be as decisive as his inability to curb the king's extravagance in determining the shape of England's future political development. The ignorance of many MPs about foreign affairs in the reign of Charles II matched their misunderstanding of public finance. On hearing of the fall of Ghent to French troops in February 1678, Colonel Birch said in the Commons, 'I know not this Ghent, but 'tis said to be a great place.'[21] Yet, even if some MPs were hazy about the details, they were clear by 1677 both that they wanted a Dutch alliance and that they feared and detested the spread of French power. These fears increased in the spring of 1677 as the French army swept into Flanders. The Commons, consequently, with Danby's support, demanded that Charles take action to defend the Spanish Netherlands against France. Charles responded by adjourning parliament on 28 May and it did not meet again until January 1678.

Yet, as Danby knew, the adjournment did not change anything. 'Till hee [the king] can fall into the humour of the people hee can never bee great nor rich', noted Danby in a memorandum just after the adjournment.[22] Danby now also had personal reasons which made it more urgent than ever to persuade Charles to abandon France and secure a cooperative parliament. In the summer of 1677 the treasurer's position at court, which had been supreme since early 1675, was being slowly undermined as a result of a reconciliation between Charles and Buckingham, who was now released

---

[21] Quoted in Browning, *Danby*, I, p. 262 note.
[22] Ibid., II, pp. 69–71.

from the Tower. It was this which forced Danby's conversion to the project of a marriage between William of Orange and James's elder daughter, Mary; this would, Danby hoped, be a preliminary to a military alliance with the Dutch; it would also have the advantage of proclaiming to suspicious MPs the court's commitment to Protestantism abroad as well as at home. Mary was in no position to refuse to agree, although so distressed was she at the prospect of marrying the tiny, hunchbacked William that she is said to have wept for one and a half days. What is not clear is why Charles agreed to the betrothal in October 1677. There are various explanations. He undoubtedly saw the political advantages of the marriage at home; the announcement of the marriage was greeted with public rejoicing and bonfires. David Ogg thought that Charles also agreed to spite his brother, whom he disliked, by imposing 'a brusque and ambitious son-in-law on him'.[23] Yet, although military preparations were made in the winter of 1677–8 for war against France, and Laurence Hyde was sent to the United Provinces to negotiate a Dutch alliance, it is difficult to believe that Charles ever seriously considered the marriage as the first step to such an alliance. It is doubtful, in any case, given the 1670 Catholic clause, whether Charles *could* have abandoned Louis; in the spring of 1678 he was negotiating another secret agreement with the French king.

The most likely explanation is that Charles intended to use the marriage as a means of persuading Louis to make peace, in the hope that this would defuse parliamentary opposition to the government's foreign policy.[24] If this was Charles's scheme, it failed totally: Louis refused to make peace, and when parliament reassembled in January 1678 it became clear that Charles's apparent change of foreign policy had done nothing to remove parliamentary suspicions.

The parliamentary session of January to July 1678 was marked by intensified distrust of the court. The Commons voted (by a poll tax of March 1678) inadequate war supplies that would produce nowhere near the £1 million promised by an earlier vote on 18 February. Not surprisingly, many MPs were sceptical of the sincerity of Charles's about-turn in foreign affairs, a view they would certainly have held even without the campaign of propaganda and bribery conducted by the French ambassador, Barrillon, aimed at undermining Danby's position. There was widespread fear that the army being raised supposedly to fight the French would be used instead against parliament. All these doubts and fears were crystallized in Andrew Marvell's *An Account of the Growth of Popery and Arbitrary Government* which was written late in 1677 and was now published. Its opening sentence put into words what many felt: 'There has now for divers years a design been carried on to change the lawful government of England into an absolute tyranny, and to convert the established Protestant religion into downright Popery.' Consequently, after news of an armistice between the French and Dutch reached London, the Commons early in June voted £200,000 for the disbandment of the army. Yet the army was not disbanded because, according to the official explanation, European peace was not formally concluded (this was not done until the Treaty of Nijmegen, 31 July 1678). Many MPs, however, feared that the real

---

[23] Ogg, *Reign of Charles II*, p. 547.
[24] K. H. D. Haley, 'The Anglo-Dutch rapprochement of 1676'. *E.H.R.*, LXXIII (1958), pp. 614–48.

reason was that the court was planning a military *coup d'état*. When parliament was prorogued on 15 July 1678, therefore, many feared the imminent establishment of popery and absolutism backed by an army of around 30,000 men. There is no better demonstration of the failure of Danby's parliamentary policies; but it is arguable that, until Charles dissolved parliament at the end of the year, the opposition to the court was as powerless as in February 1674. How important was the 'Popish Plot' in transforming the fortunes of the 'country party'?

The Popish Plot

Information

The Popish Plot

There was no Popish Plot. Most of the details of a conspiracy masterminded by the Jesuits to assassinate the king had their origins in the twisted minds of Titus Oates and Israel Tonge.

Their allegations were first made known to the king on 13 August 1678 and were passed to Danby for further investigation. In the following weeks Oates and Tonge added more details of the 'plot' in a deposition before a justice of the peace, Sir Edmund Berry Godfrey. Partly at the instigation of James, duke of York, the matter was then brought before the privy council, when Oates and Tonge produced a new version of their allegations.

The 'plot', they said, had been finalized at a Jesuit 'consult' at the White Horse Tavern on 24 April 1678, when plans had been made to shoot the king, and, if that failed, for the queen's physician, Sir George Wakeman, to poison him. Though the details were vague, the sequel to Charles's death was intended to be a Catholic uprising in Ireland and in England, and possibly an invasion from France.

After the privy council's investigations, Charles and the Tory propagandist Roger L'Estrange made fun of the internal inconsistencies and absurdities of the 'revelations'. Yet within ten days of its reassembling on 21 October 1678 the Cavalier Parliament recorded its unanimous conviction 'that there hath been and still is a damnable and hellish plot contrived and carried on by the popish recusants for the assassinating and murdering the King, and for subverting the government, and rooting out and destroying the Protestant religion',[25] and anyone who dared to cast doubts on the plot's authenticity was in danger of his life.

---

[25] Quoted in J. P. Kenyon, *The Popish Plot* (1972), p. 96.

The first important question about the Popish Plot is: why were allegations that were patently false so universally believed?

The most important explanation lies in the anti-Catholic tradition which it has been seen was so strong in seventeenth-century England. Many people found the Popish Plot story convincing because it was unoriginal and incorporated much English anti-Catholic mythology. To Oates's and Tonge's audience the present 'plot' was an obvious sequel to the Catholic conspiracies in the early seventeenth century, including the Gunpowder Plot, the outbreak of the Civil War, the 'murder' of Charles I and the Great Fire. In the summer of 1678, political events had intensified people's fears of Catholicism; Oates and Tonge could not have produced their story confirming those fears at a more propitious moment. In the early stages also Titus Oates convinced many sceptics by his confident performance before the privy council and at the bar of the House of Commons. (This was less true later on, when at some of the trials of alleged conspirators he seemed to lose his nerve.) It was difficult to disbelieve someone who 'remembered' dates and places of conspiratorial meetings in such an authoritative way. This helps to explain why the privy council was so impressed when Oates at the council meeting on 28 September identified the Jesuit authors of five incriminating letters received by Thomas Bedingfield, James's confessor, even though he was only shown a line or two of each letter. The obvious explanation – that Oates or Tonge had forged the letters – was ignored. The privy council was 'amazed' and from then on 'this very thing took like fire, so that what he said afterwards had credit'.[26] Oates was also fortunate that among those he implicated in the 'plot' was an ex-secretary to James and his wife, Edward Coleman, who for many years since 1673 had corresponded with Jesuits and French agents discussing wild schemes to help the Catholic cause in England. When Coleman was arrested and his correspondence seized, the fact that Oates failed to recognize Coleman when they first met was forgotten. The Coleman papers appeared to substantiate the Popish Plot story. What finally dispelled all doubts was the news of the disappearance on 12 October of Sir Edmund Berry Godfrey, the JP who had taken Oates's original depositions, and the discovery five days later of his body, which had been strangled and stabbed with his own sword. Later investigators have spent a lot of time speculating about the unknown cause of Godfrey's death; was it suicide, or murder by strangulation or by a sword, or a suicide made to look like murder?[27] What is more important than discovering how Godfrey died is that at the time most people believed he had been killed by Catholics to silence a man who might make more damaging revelations against them.

For a few months at the end of 1678 and the beginning of 1679 there is a lot of evidence that the country was gripped by a wave of anti-Catholic hysteria and panic like that of 1640–2. Letters of the time are full of rumours that the French and Spanish had landed, that 'night riders' had been seen, that Catholics were arming themselves

---

[26] Quoted in ibid., p. 80.

[27] See ibid., pp. 302–9, appendix A, 'The murder of Sir Edmund Berry Godfrey', for an historiographical survey.

secretly, that bombs had been placed under churches. Poor communications and the lack of official pronouncements (the details of the 'plot' were not released until April 1679) allowed the spread of wild rumours that had not even occurred to Oates's fertile imagination. Panic was greatest and lasted longest in London, where fear of another fire was endemic. Everywhere the authorities searched the houses of known Catholics for arms, and called the militia out. In London chains were put across the major streets and the trained bands kept on the alert day and night. The panic was reflected in parliament, where various committees heard more witnesses and added more allegations and names to the already long list of Catholic 'crimes' and 'conspirators'. In November and December 1678, Coleman and three others were tried and executed for their alleged part in the 'plot' and articles of impeachment were brought against five Catholic peers named by Oates as deeply implicated in the 'conspiracy'. From the end of 1678 until the beginning of 1681 about thirty-five people were tried and executed for their alleged part in it.[28]

Yet it is clear that the effects of the 'Popish Plot' can be exaggerated. The wave of anti-Catholic hysteria it produced was short-lived; even in London it is difficult to find evidence of it after the spring of 1679, especially as the cumulative effects of one unfounded rumour after another became apparent. Also during the winter of 1678–9 the appearance of new informers with further allegations produced a diminishing impact. Indeed, the attempt of William Bedloe (closely followed by Oates, who did not relish being upstaged) to implicate the queen in the planning of Godfrey's murder produced a 'backlash' in favour of the court and did much to weaken both Oates's credibility and people's belief in the imminence of a Catholic uprising. Too much can perhaps be made also of the political effects of the 'Popish Plot'. Although Danby at first encouraged the investigation into Oates's allegations in the hope that they might unite Protestants and monarchy against the Popish menace, the 'plot' undoubtedly harmed the court. Oates had at first been careful not to attack James directly, but Coleman's letters did implicate his ex-master in his plans and emphasized the Catholic danger at court. But even without the 'Popish Plot', Danby and the court would have met a storm of opposition in parliament, since the army was still in being, despite the grant of parliamentary supplies for its demobilization in June. Nor were the demands for limitations on a Catholic successor or for anti-Catholic legislation new or unexpected. Moreover, despite the 'plot', Charles had a great deal of success in taking the sting out of the parliamentary opposition by a policy of limited concessions.

> I am come to assure you [he told parliament on 9 November], that whatsoever reasonable bills you shall present to be passed into laws, to make you safe in the reign of my successor, so as they tend not to impeach the right of succession, nor the descent of the crown in the true line, and so as they restrain not my power, nor the just rights of any Protestant successor, shall find from me a ready concurrence.[29]

---

[28] G. N. Clark, *The Later Stuarts* (1955), pp. 94–5.
[29] Quoted in Kenyon, *Popish Plot*, p. 103.

To prove his point Charles reissued anti-Catholic proclamations, encouraged local officials to carry them out (convictions of recusants in some counties rose sharply),[30] and gave his assent to a Test Act excluding Catholics from parliament. His strategy worked and gained him enough support to get a narrow majority (158 to 156) in favour of a proviso excluding James from the Test Act. The opposition in parliament had so far been contained. The prime targets were still Danby and the standing army, and the extremists, Shaftesbury in the Lords and Russell in the Commons, had not succeeded in weaning the majority away from pressing for limitations on a Catholic successor to the more explosive issue of exclusion.

The revelations of Ralph Montagu changed the political scene much more fundamentally than did those of Titus Oates. They led directly to the dissolution of the Cavalier Parliament. Montagu had little reason to like Danby, who early in 1678 had vetoed his appointment as one of the secretaries of state and who had been instrumental in ending his appointment as the English ambassador at Paris in June. With the encouragement of Barrillon and Shaftesbury, Montagu returned to England determined to secure Danby's downfall by revealing letters written by Danby in January and March 1678 and containing details of the secret subsidy negotiations with Louis XIV. Before he could be stopped, Montagu produced the letters in the House of Commons on 19 December 1678. The effect was dramatic. Two days later the House agreed to draw up articles of impeachment against Danby and all other parliamentary business came to a standstill. On 30 December, Charles prorogued the session, and on 24 January 1679, to prevent further damaging revelations of his French treaties, he declared the Cavalier Parliament dissolved. Montagu had brought about what the extreme opposition had been trying to do since 1673.

It is tempting to emphasize the contrast between the new parliament – the First Exclusion Parliament which met from 6 March to 27 May 1679 – and the last sessions of the Cavalier Parliament. Shaftesbury estimated that there were about 302 'worthy' and 'honest' MPs as against only 158 courtiers in the new parliament, a much higher anti-court majority than in the old parliament.[31] The new House of Commons voted for two readings of a bill to exclude a Catholic from the English throne, something which had never even been discussed in the Cavalier Parliament. Yet for the first two months of its session the new parliament followed very closely the pattern of the old, concentrating on getting rid of the army, securing the impeachment of Danby and imposing limitations on a Catholic monarch. And like its predecessor it had only limited success in all three aims: the army was not disbanded until the summer; Danby, unlike Clarendon, stayed to face the proceedings against him and both articles of impeachment and a bill of attainder directed at him failed (though he spent the next five years in the Tower); and the opposition's only success in protecting personal liberties against arbitrary government was the Habeas Corpus Amendment Act. Although

---

[30] Miller, *Popery and Politics*, pp. 164–5.
[31] J. R. Jones, 'Shaftesbury's "worthy men": a Whig view of the parliament of 1679', *B.I.H.R.*, XXX (1957), pp. 232–41.

in retrospect this Act, requiring judges to bring a prisoner to trial within a specific period, was a great step forward in the progress of human rights, at the time it was of negligible significance in the opposition's aim of tying the hands of a Catholic monarch. The slow progress made in this direction may have contributed to the growing support among MPs for exclusion at the end of April 1679. Many also may have been at last convinced by the arguments of the extremists that, if they were put in the statute book, limitations would be ignored by a Catholic king. They would be, as one MP had said in 1677, 'like empty casks for whales to play with, and rattles for children to keep them quiet'.[32] The immediate reason, though, for the conversion of many hitherto moderate MPs to exclusion was the public disclosure in April 1679 of part of Coleman's correspondence which seemed to implicate James in negotiations with Rome, and therefore, most people assumed, in the 'Popish Plot' as well. On 11 May, Thomas Pilkington moved that James be impeached of high treason, and on 15 May the first Exclusion Bill was read, providing that on Charles's death the crown should not pass to James, but to the next in succession. On its second reading the bill passed by a majority of 207 to 128. Two weeks later Charles prorogued (and later dissolved) the parliament.

The Exclusion Crisis, May 1679–March 1681

A few years ago it would have been possible to begin this section on the Exclusion Crisis with a simple sentence like: 'for two years from the spring of 1679 the political nation was seriously split on the question of exclusion'. Now, however, that is not possible, since some historians have rejected the label 'Exclusion Crisis' on the grounds that the politics of the period were not dominated by the issue of exclusion and that 'crisis' exaggerates the seriousness of the situation facing the crown. They argue that the opponents of the crown were concerned with the threat from popery and absolutism *in the present* and not with what might happen if a Catholic were to succeed to the throne *in the future*.[33] This is surely carrying revisionism too far. Those who opposed the crown, who came to be called Whigs, were intensely fearful of *current* trends – of a perceived Catholic conspiracy by bishops who it was thought were intent on undermining the English Church, of the Catholic threat from a resurgent French monarchy under Louis XIV, of the toleration of Catholics in Ireland after the removal of Ormonde as lord lieutenant in 1669, and of the attempted absolutist policies being pursued in Scotland by Lauderdale. There is no doubt that the Whigs were fearful of current trends in favour of popery and absolutism. Nor are there any doubts that supporters of the monarchy, who were labelled Tories, were driven in part by current preoccupations, in their case a desire to protect the Church against dissenters, who they thought

---

[32] Quoted in Haley, *Shaftesbury*, p. 423.

[33] J. Scott, *Algernon Sydney and the Restoration Crisis, 1677–83* (1991); M. Knights, *Politics and Opinion in Crisis (1678–81)* (1994).

were a threat to parliamentary government. But for both Whigs and Tories the loom-ing probability *in the future* of a Catholic successor in the shape of James, duke of York was never far from the front of their minds between 1679 and 1681. For them, exclu-sion was a major issue.

Yet does the period deserve to be called a 'crisis'? To compare 1679–81 with 1641–2 is to exaggerate the seriousness of the crisis.[34] As will be seen, the English monarchy was in a much stronger position in 1679 than in 1641 and the opposition to it was much weaker. Charles's eventual victory was not a foregone conclusion, but it was easier to achieve than is often recognized. It is important, however, not to min-imize the seriousness of the crisis too much, and the ways in which public opinion had become involved in it.

Information

The extent of popular participation in the Exclusion Crisis

The extensive popular participation in the Exclusion Crisis is the best example during the reign of Charles II of the way that public opinion was now a major feature of politics. The Whigs were well organized and used political clubs, often held in London coffee houses, as a means of coordinating tactics and of drawing a wider public into current political debates. The most famous is the Green Ribbon Club in Chancery Lane, but there were many others in London and in provincial towns like Bristol, Norwich and York. The press too was used to alert readers to the dangers of popery and absolutism. Whig periodicals and newspapers grew in number, unrestricted now by the Licensing Act that had lapsed in 1679. So too did the publication of political ballads and satirical prints, making it difficult for anyone to be unaware of the political crisis and giving them the opportunity to participate in subsequent debates.

From 1679 to 1681 the opposition to the crown appeared to be very strong, and in the parliaments of October 1680 to January 1681 and March 1681 the Whigs secured majorities in the House of Commons for bills excluding James from the throne. Some of the credit for this is due to the earl of Shaftesbury, who for the first time since he had left the court in 1673 emerged at the forefront of the opposition. Dryden's descrip-tion of Shaftesbury in his *Absalom and Achitophel* as an unprincipled, power-grasping man is, as one might expect from such a piece of propaganda, a caricature. As has been seen, many of his class had, like Shaftesbury, changed sides since the 1640s,

---

[34] For a different view, see Harris, *Restoration*, pp. 190–201.

supporting parliamentary, royalist and Cromwellian regimes alike and welcoming the Restoration. Throughout his career he remained true to certain principles: toleration for Protestant dissenters, but not for Catholics; and government by king in parliament, but not by the masses. Neither Shaftesbury nor the Whigs were the forerunners of the nineteenth- and twentieth-century concept of liberal democracy. 'There is no prince', wrote Shaftesbury, 'that ever governed without nobility or an army; if you will not have one, you must have the other, or the monarchy cannot long support, or keep itself from tumbling into a democratical republic.'[35] Shaftesbury considered that James's accession would end all hopes of toleration and herald the imposition of arbitrary rule. To prevent this he was willing to use unscrupulous methods. It is fairly clear that Shaftesbury did not instigate Oates's and Tonge's (and later Bedloes's) allegations, but he did patronize these and other inventors of plot stories, and encouraged people to believe them.

Not all the Whigs' tactics, though, were crude. In the two general elections of August–September 1679 and the early months of 1681, Shaftesbury and his supporters developed a political organization that became increasingly sophisticated and effective.[36] Significantly, in both elections local interests and family connections played a lesser part than ever before. Charles's serious illness at the end of August 1679 helped the Whigs to focus the attention of the electorate on exclusion, and the Whigs' use of the press, coffee houses and political clubs to disseminate pamphlet literature emphasizing the dangers of a Catholic monarch has already been seen. Just how substantial Whig organization was in many constituencies can be seen in the election of 1681, when many MPs were presented apparently spontaneously with instructions purporting to be from their constituents and insisting that they grant no parliamentary supply unless the king conceded exclusion and a guarantee of frequent parliaments. So similar were the demands in these instructions that it is likely that they were copies of a model drafted by the Whig leadership in London.

Equally impressive were the Whig efforts to maintain the political tempo supporting exclusion during the long prorogation of parliament from May 1679 to October 1680, at a time when anti-Catholic hysteria associated with the 'Popish Plot' had dwindled. Using very similar tactics to those of the parliamentary leadership of the early 1640s, the Whigs initiated a sustained campaign of bombarding the king with petitions for the early recall of parliament. Printed petition forms were distributed in London and the counties, where Whig supporters collected signatures. In January 1680, Charles was presented with two petitions from London and Wiltshire signed by a total of about 90,000 people. Less important were the mass pope-burning demonstrations organized on 5 and 17 November 1679 and 1680. Like other crowds in the seventeenth century, the demonstrators of 1679–80 were not the violent rabble that Tory propagandists at the time made them out to be. They showed a great respect for property, and at the

---

[35] Quoted in ibid., p. 395.
[36] The best study of this is by J. R. Jones, *The First Whigs* (1971).

end of the day they dispersed peacefully. But the demonstrators of 1679–80 illustrate the capacity of the Whigs to mobilize support outside as well as among the parliamentary classes.

The position of the Whigs, however, seemed stronger than it actually was. Their most serious weakness was the lack of an obvious candidate for the succession if James were to be excluded. The result was to open up divisions among the Whigs about who should succeed Charles II. The two most obvious candidates had alarming drawbacks. James Scott, duke of Monmouth, might have been Charles II's son, but he was illegitimate. James's elder daughter, Mary, appeared to be a more suitable successor, but she was married to William of Orange, who it was feared (wrongly) was too dependent on his Stuart uncles, and (rightly) was likely to drag England into an expensive, continental war against France. It is not clear whether even Shaftesbury at the Oxford Parliament in 1681 ever publicly committed himself to Monmouth as Charles's successor. Consequently, the Tories were able to exploit this basic weakness in the Whig position. The absence of an acceptable alternative successor to James partly explains why a substantial majority of the parliamentary classes still supported a policy of limitations, despite its obvious drawbacks. Many, however, were simply repelled by the revolutionary implications of exclusion. If the right of legitimate succession to the throne was overturned, might this not be but a preliminary to challenging the right of legitimate succession to property? If James was excluded, would the country not be torn again by civil war between the supporters of James and those of other claimants? 'Acts of Parliament', said Henry Coventry in 1680, 'have not kept the succession out of the right line but brought in blood and sword . . . show me one man excluded . . . that had right of descent but has come in again.'[37] Roger L'Estrange and other Tory propagandists were able to make great play with the fact that the Whigs' appeal to the people, like that of Pym in 1641–2, would end in the destruction of the Church and the monarchy.

The position of the crown and the Tories was much stronger than that of the Whigs. Although their electoral and parliamentary support was never so well organized as the Whigs', the Tories did have a rudimentary political organization. In 1679–80 there was a rash of Tory petitions 'abhorring' those of their rivals, and in 1680–1 pamphlets and sermons joined in a vociferous anti-exclusion chorus. Charles II too, unlike his father, responded cleverly to this conservative reaction. He remained firm in his insistence on his brother's right to succeed, but made many strategically timed concessions. In April 1679 he greatly enlarged his privy council to include many of his brother's opponents including the earl of Shaftesbury. Since Charles was not willing to concede the principle of exclusion, the new privy council was an empty gesture. But for a time it disconcerted the opposition and it produced one notable permanent convert from the Whigs, the marquis of Halifax. The king's most notable political victory was the defeat of the second Exclusion Bill in the House of Lords in November 1680, which may have been

---

[37] Quoted in J. R. Western, *Monarchy and Revolution: the English State in the 1680s* (1972), p. 40.

The following labels appear within the woodcut:

The Common wealth ruleing with a standing Army

The Fruits of a Common wealth.

Laws Customs

Statutes

Episcopy

Monarchey

Magna Charta prerogative privileges Libertiis

Church Lands & tythis

Nobility & House of peers

gaine

Food for a Com=men wealth.

Figure 10.1 'The Commonwealth Ruling with a Standing Army', 1683. Negative images of the Commonwealth and Protectorate regimes of the 1650s were still alive in Restoration England and used (as in this woodcut) by the Tories to imply that support for the Whigs would mean a return to military rule. What this meant – the end of monarchy, episcopacy, law and custom, and Magna Carta, and the imposition of heavy taxation and arbitrary rule – is illustrated in this powerful cartoon. *Source*: © The Trustees of the British Museum. All rights reserved.

achieved as much by Charles's presence in the House during the debate as by Halifax's speeches in favour of limitations.

Undoubtedly though, Charles would not have defeated exclusion if the political tide had not been running in his favour. The monarchy was much stronger than in 1641–2. Scotland and Ireland were subservient. The revolt of the Scottish Covenanters in June 1679 was easily suppressed by Monmouth at Bothwell Bridge, and James quickly reasserted royal control in Scotland. Although Shaftesbury had strong support in the City of London, he never controlled the City as Pym had done, nor was there in 1679–81 a radical revolution in the City; Charles II retained control of the London trained bands.[38] Indicative of his hold on the country is the ease with which from 1680 to 1682 he purged leading Whigs, like the earls of Suffolk, Manchester and Essex, from the lieutenancy and the commission of the peace, though not yet from the boroughs. The judiciary, too, was staunchly behind the king. Since 1660 Charles had filled the Bench with lawyers of authoritarian leanings, men like Lord Chief Justice Kelyng who in 1667 called Magna Carta 'magna farta'.[39] In great contrast to his father's position

---

[38] David Allen, 'The role of the London trained bands in the Exclusion Crisis, 1678–81', *E.H.R.*, LXXXVII (1972), pp. 287–303.

[39] Quoted in Western, *Monarchy and Revolution*, p. 56.

forty years earlier, Charles's greatest asset was his financial strength, which allowed him in 1681 to dispense with parliament. The contribution of French subsidies to the crown's new financial independence was slight; it was brought about much more by the work of the new treasury commissioners (especially Laurence Hyde, earl of Rochester) who took over after the fall of Danby in March 1679. It was they who at last persuaded Charles to curb his expenditure and allow the monarchy to benefit from the full effect of the improvement in crown revenue which had been under way for nearly a decade. The response of the Whigs to the king's dissolution of parliament in March 1681 typifies their inherent weakness. They dispersed to prepare for new elections which Charles never intended to authorize. The armed men they had brought with them to Oxford were not used. The Whigs were no more willing than the Tory magnates to plunge the country into another rebellion and civil war.

11

The trend towards absolutism, 1681–1688

Summary

After the dissolution of the Oxford Parliament in March 1681 the English monarchy was in a strong position, and during the early 1680s it grew even stronger. England seemed set to follow the trend of other European states, in Germany, France, Sweden and Denmark, towards strong, centralized authoritarian government.[1] Even the accession of a Catholic king in 1685 was accepted by a fiercely anti-Catholic country. The first part of this chapter examines how this strong position was achieved.

---

[1] Although I have used 'absolutism' in the title of this chapter, I have preferred this more cumbersome phrase here because 'absolutism' is a misleading term. During recent years, when some historians have argued that the later Stuart monarchy became more 'absolutist' on the French model, historians of early modern France have been cautious about describing Louis XIV as an 'absolutist' king since, like English monarchs, he needed to secure the cooperation of his most powerful subjects. Nevertheless, in many European states, including England, the 1680s saw a strengthening of royal government at the expense of representative assemblies, J. Miller, 'The potential for "absolutism" in later Stuart England', *History*, LXIX (1984); J. Miller, ed., *Absolutism in Seventeenth-Century Europe* (1990); J. Miller, *Bourbons and Stuarts: kings and kingship in France and England in the seventeenth century* (1987). See N. Henshall, *The Myth of Absolutism* (1992) for an extreme revisionist view of 'absolutism'. I am grateful to Dr Julian Swann for drawing this book to my attention.

> But the next three years were to show not only that there were limits to what James II could do, but also how the king managed to throw away the strong position he had inherited in 1685. The second part of the chapter examines the major reasons why that came about and why he lost his throne in 1688.
>
> In particular, a major question will be raised. Which reason is more important: the loss of support from many of James's subjects, not only amongst the political elite but also amongst ordinary men and women, opposition which plunged James's regime into a major crisis by 1688; or the role played by William of Orange?

The strengthening of royal authority, 1681–1685

Charles II, in the declaration he ordered to be read from the pulpits of all churches after the dissolution of the Oxford Parliament, recalled the horrors of the Civil War when 'religion, liberty and property were all lost and gone, when the monarchy was shaken off, and could never be revived till that was restored'. So Charles and the Tories successfully smeared the Whigs with the taint of republicanism; moreover, the Whigs themselves by their extremist tactics lost the support of many of the propertied classes. In any case, with parliament dissolved the Whigs were stripped of their one chance of reviving support, by using their electoral organization, which had worked so efficiently in the elections of 1679 and 1681. All this partly accounts for the ease with which Charles crushed the Whigs after 1681. He was also helped by the criminal law, which in the seventeenth century was weighted against defendants, especially those charged with treason and felony, who were allowed neither legal advice nor prior view of the charges and the list of witnesses against them. For opponents of the crown, the situation was made even more threatening by the dismissal of judges who resisted royal wishes. The trials and executions in 1681 of Edward Fitzharris, an informer used and then abandoned by the court, and of Stephen College, a Whig supporter, illustrate the usefulness to the crown, as well as the intrinsic unfairness, of the late seventeenth-century legal process. The earl of Shaftesbury, who was imprisoned in the Tower early in July 1681 on a charge of treason, only escaped execution because the grand jury that considered the charges against him at the end of November 1681 was nominated by two Whig sheriffs.

It is a measure of Shaftesbury's desperation that he now seemed to pin his hopes totally on Monmouth, who in the autumn of 1682 toured Cheshire canvassing support among Whig magnates in a way that looked suspiciously like preparations for rebellion. Shaftesbury's flight to Holland in November 1682 was a recognition by him of the hopelessness of opposition to the regime in the face of the loyalist reaction. He died in exile two months later. In the next few months the government used its control of the judiciary to get rid of the remaining major Whig leaders, William, Lord Russell and Algernon Sidney, who were executed in 1683 for their alleged part in the so-called Rye House Plot to assassinate the king on his way to the races at Newmarket. A third Whig, the earl of Essex, committed suicide in the Tower before his trial. As in the case of the Popish Plot, it did not matter that the evidence for a conspiracy was so circumstantial, vague and contradictory that one wonders whether there was a Rye House Plot at all.

In the early 1680s the crown not only harassed the Whigs but intensified and extended its campaign to prevent the Whigs from ever again controlling parliamentary elections as they had done during the Exclusion Crisis. As has been seen, the crown had begun to purge county government in 1679. Like the Elizabethan efforts to purge the commission of the peace, the later effort to curb county independence was probably not completely effective. To claim as much would be to underestimate both local resistance to central government in the seventeenth century and the extent to which the Whigs and Whig organization survived. Yet by 1682–3 county government was as tractable as it had ever been. The early 1680s were punctuated by organized loyal addresses to the king containing thousands of signatures, on the dissolution of parliament in 1681, after the disclosure of the Rye House Plot in 1683, and on the accession of James II in 1685. Significantly, there were no Whig counter-addresses. The government had even more success in purging its opponents from municipal government. There was a long previous history of intervention by the central government in municipal affairs, in Elizabeth I's reign, the 1620s, the 1640s and immediately after the Corporation Act of 1661. Yet arguably the *quo warranto* campaign against municipal independence in the 1680s was more extensive than any of these.[2] *Quo warranto* writs compelled boroughs to substantiate the legality of their charters; since lawyers could easily find technical flaws in them, proceedings invariably resulted in the law courts declaring that borough charters were forfeit. This was the lesson other boroughs drew from London's unsuccessful defence of its charter. Although the crown's victory was hard-won – the *quo warranto* action against London was begun in December 1681 and not completed until June 1683 – the final judgment was for the crown. From now on the king's approval was required for the appointment of the lord mayor, sheriffs and all London's other major office-holders. Many other boroughs took the hint from London's defeat and voluntarily surrendered their charters to the crown. Others fought the writs in the courts and lost. All were given new charters which enabled the crown's Tory supporters to entrench themselves in power. From 1681 until Charles's death, fifty-one new charters were issued, fourteen before and thirty-seven after 1683. From James II's accession in February 1685 until parliament met in May 1685, another forty-seven new charters were granted.[3] Not only the law helped the crown to undermine municipal independence in this way: county landowning gentry, who since at least the sixteenth century had considered the towns to be within their legitimate spheres of

---

[2] Miller, 'The crown and the borough charters, pp. 53–84; J. H. Sacret, 'The Restoration government and municipal corporations', *E.H.R.*, XLV (1930), pp. 232–59.

[3] J. R. Jones, *The Revolution of 1688 in England* (1972), p. 46.

influence and who often were the agents and beneficiaries of royal policy against the towns, gave the crown their enthusiastic support.

The financial 'sinews of monarchy' were also considerably strengthened in the 1680s. A combination of Charles's conversion to relatively restrained expenditure in his old age, increased revenue from the customs during a decade of commercial prosperity, and increased yields from both the hearth tax and the excise from 1683–4, when the crown began to collect these taxes directly and efficiently, enabled the crown's permanent ordinary revenue to soar beyond the £1,200,000 agreed in 1660–1. By 1684–5 it had risen to £1,370,750, and was still increasing.[4] The improving financial position of the crown was symptomatic of the development of administrative efficiency within central government that was to become a marked feature of England after 1689, as will be seen. But even before then the increase in size and efficiency of executive departments, especially the treasury under a succession of able heads, notably Danby and Rochester, was a significant addition to the power of the crown in the 1680s (see above, pp. 326–7).

Frequently during the course of his reign, Charles II had abandoned the Church of England in his pursuit of religious toleration. But in the last years of his reign he at last harnessed the power of the crown with that of the Church of England. Albeit belatedly, Charles took the advice of Clarendon and Danby. From 1681 to 1685, especially after the Rye House Plot, Tory magistrates persecuted Catholic and Protestant dissenters, spurred on by the privy council.[5] This was often done with some brutality as dissenters were fined and imprisoned for attending conventicles instead of the parish church. This has led one historian to conclude that this was 'the most sustained and most intense period of religious persecution in English history'.[6] As Dr Robert South had pointed out in 1661, the alliance of monarchy and Church of England was potentially very powerful. With the addition of vastly improved royal financial resources it was a recipe for the establishment of authoritarian government in England in the 1680s. By exploiting the divisions among his Protestant subjects, Charles bequeathed his brother an apparently strong political position. In 1684 there was no outcry when, despite the Triennial Act, Charles did not call parliament, James was restored to the privy council, and Danby was released from the Tower. Loyal addresses greeted James's accession in February 1685. It remains to be seen how James II transformed this situation. Within three and a half years he had forced Anglicans and Protestant dissenters to forget their differences temporarily, and to unite against him.

---

[4] Chandaman, *English Public Revenue*, pp. 254–5.
[5] Miller, *Popery and Politics*, pp. 191, 193–4.
[6] Harris, *Restoration*, p. 300.

James II and Protestant unity, February 1685–June 1688

Historiography

James II: changing views of historians

Until the 1970s the most common view of James II was that of a wicked king, anxious to establish a Catholic despotism in England. This was a view propounded by Whig, Protestant historians like T. B. Macauley and G. M. Trevelyan.

In the 1970s, however, historians began to rehabilitate James's reputation. They portrayed a king whose aim was not to establish Catholicism as the sole religion of the country, or to rule without parliament. He resisted many of the extremist plans projected by his Catholic advisers to impose Catholicism with French help. James continually attempted to assert his independence of France. In reality, James's aims were much more moderate and limited than many contemporaries and later historians have thought. He simply wanted to establish the rights of English Catholics to worship without persecution and to take full part in the political life of the country. This could be done by repealing the penal laws, the Corporation Act of 1661 and the Test Acts of 1673 and 1678. Once this was done, he believed, Catholicism would triumph without any compulsion by the State.

More recently, some historians have begun to question this view of James as a monarch who only used legal and constitutional methods to achieve his aims. As will be seen, there were times when James was willing to bend the law to do this. But this is a view that (as yet) only qualifies – and does not demolish – the image of James II as a constitutional monarch.

Historians may have rescued James II from the charge of extremism. What they have not done is to show that his aims were anything other than impracticable, foolish and misguided. James was often unable to understand the views of those with whom he disagreed. He completely misunderstood the strength of the attachment of most of his contemporaries to anti-Catholicism, which made the defeat of his plans inevitable. As during previous popish plot crises in the late 1630s and early 1640s, and between 1678 and 1681, fear of Catholicism was indistinguishable in most people's minds from hatred of absolutism. James II might not have been aiming to become an absolutist monarch, but that is what many people thought he was doing. For this reason he demonstrably failed to persuade the majority of Anglicans in the first phase of his reign (1685–6) and Protestant dissenters in the second (1687–8) to accept even limited toleration for Catholics.

The strength of the Anglican–Tory reaction following the Exclusion Crisis is reflected in the composition of the parliament which met in May 1685. Secretary of State Sunderland was very active during the elections, and of the 195 MPs returned by boroughs with remodelled charters, only nine have been identified as Whigs.[7] 'Such a landed Parliament was never seen', wrote the earl of Ailesbury. It would be a mistake, though, to assume that this parliament, even in its first session (19 May to 2 July 1685), was totally submissive to the new king. Like the Cavalier Parliament elected in 1661, it was Anglican as well as royalist. Early in the session it passed resolutions in defence of the Church of England and in favour of executing the penal laws. Nor were all MPs happy about granting the crown its hereditary revenues for life; some were in favour of a temporary grant 'to be renewed from time to time that parliament might be consulted the oftener'.[8] However, these doubts were not reflected in the financial settlement of 1685. This 'landed parliament' was less anxious about granting taxes on trade than on land. As well as a life grant of the crown's hereditary revenues, James was amply supplied by additional revenues from customs duties. Any doubts MPs might have had about the wisdom of generosity were overcome by their recognition of the crown's need for money to suppress the rebellions of Argyll and Monmouth in the summer of 1685. Monmouth drew most of his support from social groups outside the political nation. Contemporaries reported thousands of farmers and clothworkers joining Monmouth as he marched through Dorset and Somerset in June to his final defeat at the battle of Sedgemoor on 5 July. Although there were more craftsmen and townsmen than farmers in the rank and file of Monmouth's army, Dr Peter Earle's systematic study of Monmouth's supporters largely bears out this conclusion about the types of people attracted by the duke. It may be that the area from which the rebels came – Somerset, west Dorset and east Devon, where Protestant dissent flourished in cloth-working villages – was a natural recruiting ground for those in the middle ranks of society who feared the imposition of Catholicism and absolutism.[9] What is certain is that Monmouth, unlike William of Orange who landed in the south-west three years later, received little support from the gentry. Nor did his execution and the brutal suppression of his followers by Lord Chief Justice Jeffries during 'the Bloody Assizes' in the autumn arouse much sympathy among the propertied classes.

Once the rebellions were over, however, the differences between the king and Tory–Anglican opinion became apparent. James brought the stormy second session of parliament to an end after less than two weeks (9–20 November). By this time he had made known his intention to secure the repeal of the Test and Corporation Acts. With characteristic lack of political guile, he announced to parliament that the army raised to fight Monmouth would not be disbanded and that he had promoted Catholic officers in the army despite the Test Acts. Halifax had already been dismissed from the privy

[7] Jones, *Revolution of 1688*, p. 47.

[8] Quoted in Chandaman, *English Public Revenue*, p. 256.

[9] Peter Earle, *Monmouth's Rebels: the road to Sedgemoor 1685* (1977), especially pp. 196–212 for an excellent analysis of the rebels.

council when he opposed this, and significantly, the opposition to James's announcement in the Lords was led not only by the Whig earl of Devonshire, but by two other privy councillors, the earls of Nottingham and Bridgewater, and by Henry Compton, bishop of London. It is possible that James's announcement by itself is sufficient explanation for the political storm. But what undoubtedly intensified Tory (as well as Whig) opposition were events outside England. As in the crises of the late 1630s and early 1640s and between 1678 and 1681, events in Ireland, Scotland and Europe had a dramatic impact on what happened in England.

In Ireland, James's accession marked an acceleration of the policies of Catholicization which had been set in motion during Charles II's reign. James was not foolish enough to cut his links altogether with the powerful Protestant interests which controlled the Irish government in Dublin, and he did not replace the Protestant earl of Clarendon as lord lieutenant of Ireland until 1687. But he did give his support in Ireland to Richard Talbot, who had become earl of Tyrconnell in 1685 and whom Professor Roy Foster calls 'the champion of irredentist Catholic claims'. Tyrconnell began a campaign to purge the Irish army of Protestants. By September 1686, 40 per cent of officers and 67 per cent of the rank and file were Catholics and these percentages increased very rapidly thereafter. Tyrconnell, too, was able to pursue a policy of Catholicization in the Irish administration even before he replaced Clarendon in 1687.[10] Scotland, too, which James knew well after his temporary exile there during the Exclusion Crisis, seemed to English eyes to fit frighteningly into a general Catholicization trend in Britain, as James promoted Catholicism under the guise of toleration policies north of the border. That Catholicization inevitably meant absolutism was no doubt confirmed (if that were needed) by James's justification for issuing his Scottish Declaration of Indulgence by his 'Absolute power, which all our subjects are to obey without reserve'.[11]

In the mid-1680s the English also began to get news from Europe which brought home to them the horrors of Catholicism and had the effect of identifying James II's policies with Louis XIV's cruel campaign against French Huguenots. The Revocation of the Edict of Nantes in October 1685 produced a new flood of French refugees to England, bringing with them another batch of horror stories about the sufferings of Protestants at the hands of Catholics. In these circumstances, James's moderate Catholic aims were inevitably misunderstood. As with his father's Laudianism in the 1630s, what people *thought* James's plans were became more important than his actual intentions. His aim of securing limited toleration and political rights for Catholics was widely seen as the beginning of a policy of Catholic-inspired repression and *dragonnades*.

---

[10] R. F. Foster, *Modern Ireland 1600–1972* (1988), p. 140. See also Simms, 'The Restoration', in Moody et al., eds., *A New History of Ireland*, and J. Miller, 'The earl of Tyrconnell and James II's Irish policy 1685–88', *H.J.*, XX (1977).

[11] Quoted in W. A. Speck, *Reluctant Revolutionaries: Englishmen and the Revolution of 1688* (paperback edn., 1989), p. 17.

James's high hopes of mass conversions of Englishmen to Catholicism, which were crucial to the permanent success of his Catholicization policies, were consequently doomed to disappointment. This was specially serious because it was not enough for him simply to rely on promoting Catholics in the army, privy council and local government. The majority decision (by eleven judges out of twelve) in the *Godden* v. *Hales* case in June 1686 allowed him to do this by dispensing individuals from the Test Acts. But by 1688, despite a concentrated purge of the commission of the peace and lieutenancy, less than a quarter of JPs and deputy lieutenants were Catholics.[12] Consequently, James poured vast amounts of money and effort into a missionary campaign. Yet even the so-called 'closeting' tactic – James's programme of personal interviews with leading politicians – secured only one major conversion, that of the earl of Sunderland, and even that came very late, after the birth of James's son in June 1688. It is doubtful whether, given more time, James's missionary activity would have had more success. After Louis XIV's *dragonnades*, anti-Catholicism was more than ever deeply entrenched in England.

Throughout 1686 there were many signs of James's failure to secure the support of Anglican opinion. The most important was his public confrontation with Henry Compton, bishop of London, which originated in March 1686 when James issued some Directions to Preachers, ordering the clergy to confine their sermons to doctrines to be found in the catechism and to steer clear of provocative topics, like attacks on Rome. When the rector of a London parish, John Sharp of St Giles in the Fields, disobeyed in May, James ordered Compton to suspend Sharp from preaching. Compton's refusal resulted in James's decision to establish the court of ecclesiastical commission in July 1686, and its first act in September was to suspend Compton from his bishopric. It is not clear exactly when James finally decided to commit himself to a political alliance with the Protestant dissenters against the Church of England, a line-up which had had such disastrous consequences for his brother in the 1670s. During 1686 James made several individual orders to dissenters, including the Quaker Penn family, dispensing them from the penal legislation, and in November 1686 he established a Licensing Office where dissenters could buy certificates of dispensation. What finally decided James to abandon the Anglican alliance was possibly the failure of William Penn's mission to Holland to get the support of William of Orange and Mary for the repeal of the Test and Corporation Acts. William, although sympathetic to the cause of religious toleration, saw how politically unpopular it was in England and refused to be identified with it. Penn's return was followed closely by the dismissal of James's two principal Anglican ministers, the Hyde brothers, the earls of Clarendon and Rochester. Later in April 1687, the king began a long campaign to force Magdalen College, Oxford, the symbol of the Anglican educational monopoly, to accept a Catholic as its president. By this stage there could be no doubt that a new phase in the reign had begun.

---

[12] Miller, *Popery and Politics*, p. 219 and appendix 3; this excludes five English counties for which lists of JPs and deputy lieutenants do not exist.

On 4 April 1687, James announced the cornerstone of his new policy of appealing for the support of the dissenters: a Declaration of Indulgence which suspended all the penal laws, the Test and Corporation Acts. In the next few months, during which the king announced the dissolution of the parliament which had stood prorogued since November 1685, it became clear that James expected, as a quid pro quo for the Declaration of Indulgence, dissenter support for an intensified campaign to secure a parliament that would repeal the Test and Corporation Acts. How feasible were James's twin policies of allying with the dissenters and the campaign to pack parliament, which occupied this last phase of his reign? There seems no more reason why the former should have been any more successful than his brother's similar policy earlier. Danby's ecclesiastical census of 1676, though quantitatively inexact, was probably a fair reflection of the relatively small numbers of dissenters on which both Charles II and James II placed such reliance. More serious was the fact that the reaction of Protestant dissenters to James's appeal was not unanimously enthusiastic. Most were prepared to take advantage of the grant of toleration, despite their scruples about the constitutional propriety of an arbitrary suspension of parliamentary legislation. What many dissenters could not do was to trust James's motives. Were they not being used to further James's long-term aim of imposing intolerant Catholicism? Were Catholicism and toleration not, in any case, incompatible? Both doubts were voiced by Halifax, whose *Letter to a Dissenter* was published in the summer of 1687. The dissenters, he argued, were 'to be hugged now, only that you may be the better squeezed at another time'. 'This alliance between liberty and infallibility is bringing together the two most contrary things that are in the world. The Church of Rome doth not only dislike the allowing liberty, but by its principles it cannot do it.'[13] In this respect, too, James's credibility with dissenters, as with Anglicans, suffered from the comparison many made with Louis XIV's Revocation policy in France.

It is less certain that James's campaign to pack parliament was bound to fail. From the autumn of 1687 James and his advisers, notably Sunderland and Jeffreys, began systematically to build up a powerful electoral organization in many constituencies. In October three standard questions were put to all JPs to assess their reaction to the projected repeal of the Test and Corporation Acts, and on the basis of their replies new commissions of the peace were issued early in 1688: those JPs who had given unsatisfactory replies were ejected and replaced largely by dissenters. The most intensive electoral preparations were made in the boroughs under the direction of Robert Brent and Sir Nicholas Butler. The *quo warranto* campaign was renewed against recalcitrant boroughs and unreliable municipal officers were replaced. Ironically, Brent and Butler consciously imitated the tactics used successfully by the Whig exclusionists in the elections of 1679 and 1681, relying on the support of merchants, traders and craftsmen in the towns. After an exhaustive review of their efforts, Professor J. R. Jones concludes that the campaign to pack parliament may have been well conceived. James's alliance 'with the urban middle classes against the landowning aristocracy and gentry . . . with

---

[13] Quoted in Western, *Monarchy and Revolution*, p. 227.

time . . . could have resulted in the emergence of a synthetic ruling class to replace the traditional associates of the crown in government'.[14] One wonders whether the interests of the landowning and trading classes were as opposed as this analysis supposes. Also, would the urban groups to whom James appealed have been any more willing than the landowning aristocracy and gentry to swallow their anti-Catholicism and approve the repeal of the Test and Corporation Acts?

Since James's packed parliament never met, these doubts will never be resolved. What is certain is that by the end of 1687 the political nation – Whigs and Tories, Anglicans and Protestant dissenters, backed by public opinion 'out of doors' – were very suspicious of James's intentions. Two events in the first half of 1688 cemented the alliance of all leading Protestants against James II. By issuing a second Declaration of Indulgence on 27 April 1688, James hoped to drive a wedge between Anglicans and dissenters, when the Anglican clergy refused to read the declaration from the pulpits. However, Archbishop Sancroft and six bishops made it clear in a widely distributed petition that they refused to publish the declaration not 'from any want of due tenderness to Dissenters, in relation to whom they are willing to come to such a temper as shall be thought fit', but 'because that Declaration is founded upon such a dispensing power as hath often been declared illegal in Parliament'.[15] Anglicans and dissenters came together on the common ground of hostility to the king's use of the dispensing power. On 10 June, Protestants were given an even more powerful reason to unite, when Queen Mary gave birth to a son and so made possible an unlimited period of Catholic rule. Hatred of Rome proved to be a stronger force than the mutual dislike of Anglicans and dissenters. On 30 June the seven bishops who had signed the petition against the Declaration of Indulgence were acquitted of seditious libel; and seven leading Protestants, representing Whig and Tory opinion, Edward Russell, Henry Sidney, Lord Lumley, Bishop Compton, and the earls of Shrewsbury, Devonshire and Danby, wrote to William of Orange, pledging their support if he brought a force to England against James.

By his Catholic policies, James had stunted the loyalist reaction which had grown since the Exclusion Crisis and which had threatened to make England an absolutist state. Had he also brought the country to the verge of revolution?

It is difficult to reach a definitive answer to this question. On the one hand a detailed analysis of the answers of the country's governing classes to the three questions of October 1687 reveals the extent of hostility to James's policies; yet the vast majority were not willing to make an *open* declaration against his plans.[16] Even the famous letter

---

[14] Jones, *Revolution of 1688*, p. 11. For another view of the potential success of the campaign, see B. D. Henning, ed., *The History of Parliament: the Commons 1660–90* (3 vols., 1983), I, p. 42. For the opposite view, which I prefer, see P. E. Murrell, 'Bury St Edmunds and the campaign to pack parliament 1687–88', *B.I.H.R.*, LIV (1981).

[15] Browning, *English Historical Documents*, p. 84.

[16] J. Carswell, *The Descent on England* (1969), pp. 238–43; Jones, *Revolution of 1688*, pp. 166–7; Western, *Monarchy and Revolution*, pp. 211–12. See also J. Miller, *James II: a study in Kingship* (1978), pp. 178–9.

of 30 June was extremely vague about the purpose of William's invasion, beyond restraining James. Certainly there was no mention of James's deposition or exclusion. Nor were all the political nation willing to go even as far as the seven signatories of that letter. The earl of Nottingham represented a large body of conservative opinion which considered the letter 'high treason, in violation of the laws . . . and that allegiance which I owed to the sovereign and which I had confirmed by my solemn oath'.[17] Many hoped that James's policies would fail without radical opposition being necessary. Was it not likely that the new baby would die? There is very little evidence that many members of the political nation were willing to rebel against a king who was in a strong financial position and who had begun to remodel the army and navy.[18] In any case, most propertied Englishmen were too fearful of another civil war, too constrained by considerations of obedience and non-resistance to become rebels.

That is a possibility, but it is countered by the growing evidence of recent research that shows that the opposition to James II was not confined to the political elite by 1688, but received much popular and sometimes violent support from public opinion 'out of doors'.

Information

1688: a noble or popular revolt?

One of the most important developments in writing on the Glorious Revolution of 1688–9 has been to emphasize that what happened in the winter of 1688–9 was not a bloodless coup, a noble revolt. It is true that James's Catholic policies were met in 1688 by provincial risings in the north and midlands, led by nobles (see p. 355). But until recently popular demonstrations against James at that time have received relatively little attention. Anti-Catholic riots, including attacks on the property of prominent Catholics, spread in London and the provinces, as they had done in and around Colchester and the Stour valley in 1642 (see above, p. 178). Like the earlier riots, those of 1688 had elements of uncontrolled violence, but a clearer theme of the riots is of controlled, disciplined violence. Tim Harris, in an excellent survey of the riots up and down the country, calls them 'law- enforcement riots'.[19]

It is arguable that this popular activism fuelled the mood of panic that James exhibited in late 1688 and contributed greatly to his failure to withstand the invading forces of William of Orange.

---

[17] Quoted in Western, *Monarchy and Revolution*, p. 237.

[18] See ibid., pp. 121–4, 124ff, for the army and navy.

[19] Harris, *Revolution*, p. 301.

The intervention of William of Orange, 1688

Important as the widespread opposition to James II in England was in contributing to his downfall, it was matched by the intervention of William of Orange. Why did William of Orange invade England? The key to this question, and therefore to the question of why the 'Glorious Revolution' happened, is to be found in events that took place in Europe. The prime aim of William of Orange throughout his life was to oppose French expansion in Europe, which continued even after the Peace of Nijmegen in 1678. During the next six years French troops occupied territories beyond the northern and eastern frontiers of France, which she claimed were French by right. Strasbourg (October 1681) and Luxembourg (June 1684) were the most notable French conquests, which were ratified by the Truce of Ratisbon in August 1684. William's admiration for French culture was as great as his determination to halt and reverse these French gains. Yet for many years he was unable to organize an effective European coalition against France. Spain demonstrated her weakness in the brief war of 1683–4. The United Provinces was dominated by a republican peace party which saw William's plans as a threat to her desire for low taxes and trade with France. William was unable to prevent cuts being made in military expenditure in his own country. The emperor was distracted by a serious Turkish invasion, which in 1683 brought the Turks to the gates of Vienna. Though the siege was defeated, the Turks, encouraged secretly by Louis XIV, continued to occupy Emperor Leopold's troops in the Balkans. The England of Charles II was, of course, tied to France and incapable of an independent foreign policy.

After the Truce of Ratisbon, events in Europe began to change slowly in favour of William's plan to organize European cooperation against France. William's first success was in his own country, where events again illustrate the crucial impact made by the Revocation of the Edict of Nantes outside France. Since the connections between many Dutch merchants and French Huguenots were very close – some Dutch merchants had even become naturalized Frenchmen to further their trade – French atrocities against the Huguenots hit the business and family interests of many Amsterdam merchants. The Revocation had more effect than anything else in enabling William to obtain the support of the States of Holland and the City of Amsterdam and to secure the backing of the States General for war against France. Furthermore, in 1686 William organized the German states into the League of Augsburg, an anti-French coalition. Of more importance, in May 1687 the emperor's army won a crucial victory over the Turks at Mohacs, which ended the immediate threat of Turkish invasion and enabled the emperor to become an effective member of a grand coalition against France. The one power still necessary to strengthen the coalition was England. William never made clear his motives for invading England, but it is highly likely that his primary aim was to bring England out of her isolation and into the impending war against France. This is not to say that he was not also concerned to protect his wife's right of succession to the throne, which was threatened by the birth of James's son. But it is possible that this was subordinate to his major aim of gaining control of English foreign policy.

When did William decide to invade England?[20] Some historians have argued that William had been planning an invasion since the early 1680s. Certainly he had long been in touch with opposition leaders in England and had kept himself well informed about English opinion. In 1687 he sent two emissaries, Everard van Weede van Dijkvelt in the spring and Willem Zuylestein in August, who established an even firmer relationship between William and major political figures in England. There is, however, no evidence that he seriously considered armed intervention in England before the end of 1687. Nor is it likely that he did so, because the European situation was not conducive to such a step. It was not until early in 1688 that events in Europe enabled William to feel secure enough to consider an English invasion as a practical option for later in the year; and it was not until April 1688 that he told Edward Russell that this was what he intended. In June, Zuylestein was sent on a second mission to England, under the cover of bringing William's congratulations on the birth of James's son, to procure a letter of invitation from leading figures in England.

The final problem about William's intervention is to explain why the invasion was successful and why it culminated in the 'Glorious Revolution'. Neither of these was inevitable. The odds against the success of the invasion were great: in Europe, William risked exposing the United Provinces to a French attack in his absence; the practical problems associated with launching an invasion across the Channel caused many earlier (and later) efforts to be abandoned; and William's reception in England was far from certain. The problem of Dutch security was removed when the French in September committed themselves to a full-scale attack on the Palatinate. William overcame the logistical problems of the actual invasion by taking advantage of the pre-vailing winds which kept the English navy helplessly at anchor and helped his fleet sail westwards through the English Channel to land at Torbay on 5 November. Four days later he entered Exeter.

In the following weeks, William's moderate public declarations encouraged the defection to his side of Tory as well as Whig magnates in a remarkable illustration of the extent to which James's Catholic policies had united the Protestant nation against him. Sir Edward Seymour and his West Country rival, the marquis of Bath, openly declared for William soon after he landed, ensuring that his rear was secure as he began to march from Exeter on 21 November slowly towards London. As he did so, a series of provincial risings and demonstrations in his support occurred. Already on 15 November, Lord Delamere had secured control in Cheshire; a week later, on 21 and 22 November, the earls of Devonshire and Danby seized Nottingham and York respectively, and other provincial towns made declarations in William's favour.[21]

It is important that the widespread disaffection among Whigs and Tories with James's policies should not be played down. But it is far from certain that at this stage

---

[20] The most convincing answers are those put forward by S. B. Baxter, *William III* (1966), pp. 224–5, 229–33; Jones, *Revolution of 1688*, pp. 250–5; and Speck, *Reluctant Revolutionaries*, pp. 75–6.

[21] For the northern risings in 1688, see David H. Hosford, *Nottingham, Nobles and the North: aspects of the Revolution of 1688* (1976).

William and most of his supporters aimed to depose James II. There is no doubt that this was not in the minds of many powerful Tories and their supporters, including the Hyde brothers, Halifax and the earl of Nottingham, and most bishops, who were not prepared to abandon the king. It is true that they did very little to help James, and they were almost certainly prepared to see him compelled by the invasion to change his policies. But they were far too deeply attached to their principles of passive obedience and non-resistance to want to see James lose his throne. James, however, left this 'loyal opposition'[22] without a cause. On 23 November at Salisbury he appears to have lost his nerve. Instead of marching with his army to resist William's forces in the south-west, he ordered a retreat to London. At this point John Churchill (who became earl of Marlborough in 1689 and duke in 1702) defected to William. On 11 December, with William's army marching slowly through the southern counties towards the capital, James left London intending to go to France. He was captured and returned to London, but on 22 December he made his escape to the Continent. James's collapse of nerve ensured that when William reached London he had the support of all leading Whigs and Tories. His decision not to stay in England removed the final obstacle to the 'Glorious Revolution' and a change of monarch. It remains to be seen whether the 'Glorious Revolution' brought about any more fundamental changes in Church and State.

---

[22] Western, *Monarchy and Revolution*, p. 270.

PART 5

The reigns of William III
and Queen Anne,
1689–1714

Introduction

The most important historical problem that dominates the reigns of the later Stuarts is to assess the importance and significance of the Glorious Revolution. That problem will be addressed in the remaining chapters of this book. But first it is important to set out the main features of the political and religious context of the period in which the Glorious Revolution took place and when its long-term effects on the Church and State became apparent. This will be done first of all for the whole period from 1689 to 1714, and then for the reign of William III, 1689–1702.

The reigns of William III and Queen Anne are characterized by three important features: the development of party rivalries which cut deeply into English society in London and in the provinces, the establishment of parliament as a permanent part of the constitution, and the prevalence of extreme political instability. These features and the problems associated with them are the themes of Part 5 on Britain after the Glorious Revolution.

The predominance of party political rivalries. During the last thirty years the nature of political rivalries and the existence of political parties in this period have been hotly debated. There is now little doubt that conflict between Whig and Tory politicians and Whig and Tory principles played a large part in English politics from 1689 to 1714. However, much uncertainty still remains. To what extent was Whig–Tory rivalry after 1689 simply an extension of that which had developed during the Exclusion Crisis? In what ways did the Glorious Revolution affect the Whig and Tory parties and what they stood for? Given that the Whig–Tory division was an important one after 1689, did it threaten to undermine the foundations of the country's political structure? Was it the only, or the most important, division in English politics, or were court–country political alignments important? If they were, to what extent did the latter cut across or obliterate completely divisions on Whig–Tory lines? Perhaps the most intriguing question of all about the political history of this period is why did the Tories, who (as will be seen) were the strongest and most popular political group in England after the Glorious Revolution, suddenly collapse in 1714 and leave the way clear for the Whigs to dominate English political life for much of the Hanoverian age?

Parliament and the monarch: changes in the nature of the English State. By 1714, in contrast to 1688, parliament's place in the constitution was assured. By the death of Queen Anne, the English constitution had developed irrevocably in a different way from that of many other continental European absolutist states. It is not only the timing and reasons for this development that are in doubt, though these problems are important: when and why were the powers of the monarchy limited during the reigns of William III and Queen Anne? Did the Glorious Revolution play a crucial role in this process or was the impact of the long wars against France more crucial than the ideas and foresight of the 'revolutionaries' of 1688–9 in moulding the English constitution? Given that parliament's powers were greatly enhanced, can one exaggerate the extent to which the personal prerogative powers of the monarchy had been eroded by 1714? Is the growth of 'the cabinet system' in this period an indication of the diminution of royal authority, as is sometimes implied? Were the limitations on their power that William and Anne were forced to accept as effective as they were intended to be? To what extent were attempts to tie the monarch's hands counterbalanced by the growth during the war years of a large and efficient executive controlled by and at the disposal of the crown? The major aim of this part is to point the way to possible answers to all these questions.

Political instability. Arguably the greatest and most intractable problem about the last twenty-five years of Stuart England, though, is to explain why these were years of great political instability, in contrast to the relative peace and calm of political life in early Hanoverian Britain. This is a contrast that should not be exaggerated. As will be seen (p. 415), the political instability of Britain after the Glorious Revolution did not seriously threaten to crack the foundations of the country's political structure, as had happened in the 1640s. Moreover, Britain after 1714 was not by any means devoid of political controversies or Whig–Tory political rivalries. But these qualifications should not obscure the fact that the Glorious Revolution was followed by a prolonged period of political volatility. Specific reasons for this will be suggested later, but perhaps a general explanation for it will not be out of place here. The Glorious Revolution was not a blueprint for political stability. The Bill of Rights, like a large list of its seventeenth-century predecessors, including the Propositions of Newcastle 1646, the Heads of the Proposals 1647, the various versions of the Agreement of the People 1647–9, the Instrument of Government 1653, the Humble Petition and Advice 1657, and the 'Restoration Settlement' in the early 1660s, did not prove to be the 'settlement' which had been sought since the collapse of the Elizabethan constitution in 1640. The most dramatic change brought about by William III's accession in 1689 was to effect a revolution in English foreign policy, in which the Francophile policy of Charles II and the isolationism of his brother gave way to active and full-scale intervention by England in Europe against the might of France. These expensive wars against France (1689–97, 1702–13) in turn sparked off a revolution in public finance, since the existing system of parliamentary taxation and the hereditary revenues of the crown were insufficient to meet the massive financial burden which ensued. These twin revolutions in foreign policy and public finance necessitated frequent sessions of parliament to underwrite large grants of parliamentary taxation and eventually to provide a parliamentary guarantee for the repayment of loans made to the government. The consequent annual sessions from 1689 onwards were a breeding ground in which political rivalries could develop.

Parliaments had, of course, met frequently in Restoration England. In the twenty-one years after 1660, parliament only failed to meet twice, in 1672 and 1676. Of more importance, after 1714 there continued to be annual parliamentary sessions without producing the political instability of 1689–1714. However, the most startling contrast in the nature of political life during the reigns of William III and Queen Anne, and one which sets it apart from both the preceding and succeeding periods, is the frequency of general elections. From 1660 to 1688 there were only five; from 1689 to 1715 there were eleven. The Triennial Act of 1694 limited the life of individual parliaments to a maximum of three years. The drafters of the Septennial Act in 1716 rightly commented that this 'proved very grievous and burdensome, by occasioning . . . more violent and lasting heats and animosities among the subjects of the realm, than were ever known before the said clause was enacted'. Not only did the frequent general elections help to maintain the intense political excitement of the period, but they also ensured that the membership of the House of Commons constantly changed, so preventing the crown from building up a court party in the House. Just how important the Triennial Act was in contributing to the political instability of these years can be seen by the dramatic effect of its repeal and its substitution by the Septennial Act in 1716, which facilitated the growth of political stability during the age of Walpole.

The third vital ingredient making for political instability was the emergence of an electorate, growing both in numbers and in independence. This process had been in progress since at least the early seventeenth century, until by the reign of William III the electorate numbered at least 200,000 and by 1722 at least 330,000. As Geoffrey Holmes and William Speck have shown, this was a proportion of the total population (just 4.3 per cent) that was only slightly exceeded by those (4.7 per cent) enfranchised by the first Reform Act of 1832.[1] Of course, as historians of nineteenth-century England have shown, the independence of the electorate in the days of open balloting can be exaggerated. Tenants often found it difficult to disobey the wishes of their landlords. Yet the fact that bribery was common in late seventeenth- and early eighteenth-century elections is by itself an indication that voters could be influenced in the way they voted.[2] It does suggest that electors might also be persuaded to use their vote on grounds of principle. Indeed, there is every indication that the electorate from the 1690s onwards was not only growing in numbers but also becoming much better informed than ever before. In 1695 the Licensing Act was allowed to lapse and this marked the formal end of the censorship of the press by the State and Church, which in any case was becoming increasingly difficult to enforce. Nevertheless in 1695 the main restraint on the development of newspapers and political literature of all kinds

[1] W. A. Speck, *Tory and Whig: the struggle for the constituencies, 1701–15* (1970), pp. 16–17; G. Holmes, *The Electorate and the National Will in the First Age of Party* (1976), pp. 18–27. For a different view, see J. C. D. Clark, *English Society 1688–1832: ideology, social structure and political practice during the ancien regime* (1985), pp. 15–26.
[2] See G. L. Cherry, 'Influence of irregularities in contested elections upon election policy during the reign of William III', *J.M.H.*, XXVII (1955), pp. 109–24.

was removed. Political journalism flourished, and with it appeared a more volatile electorate than ever before.

Nevertheless, it is likely that the development after 1689 of annual parliaments, frequent parliamentary elections, and the growth in both numbers and independence of an electorate, merely provided the framework for political instability. Without the appearance of issues towards which the electorate, as well as its representatives, could have fundamentally different attitudes, it is hardly possible that political rivalries would have been as intense as they became. Significantly, the only period in Restoration England which compares with England after 1689 in this respect is the Exclusion Crisis of 1679–81; then too there were issues which divided the political nation. As will be seen, many of the same issues – commitment to the Protestant succession *against* a willingness to accept a Catholic monarch with limitations, a belief in the individual's right to resist a tyrannical monarch *against* an attachment to the divine right of kings and passive obedience, a willingness to extend religious toleration and political liberty to Protestant dissenters *against* total opposition to any infringement of the Anglican monopoly in Church and State – re-emerged after 1689. Moreover, events in England after the Glorious Revolution not only revived these old issues, but also provided new areas of political controversy. Above all, the long wars against Louis XIV after 1689, in which so many changes in England after the Glorious Revolution originated, forced English people for the first time to consider urgently and seriously the role their country should play in European affairs. William's determination to drag his new kingdom into the European struggle against Louis XIV eventually drove a great wedge into English society between those willing to participate with the European community to prevent Bourbon and Catholic hegemony of Europe, and those who stood fast by their instinctive xenophobia and isolationism. The war, with questions such as how it should be conducted and when it should be ended, provided the flashpoint for political rivalries that, when they became entangled with issues like the Protestant succession and union with Scotland, threatened to plunge England again into a civil war. Only when these issues, as well as the conditions in which they could thrive, were removed would political stability be possible.

12

The reign of William III, 1689–1702

Summary

The Glorious Revolution is the centrepiece of this chapter. After looking at the main features of politics in the reign of William III, the chapter gets to grips with the ongoing controversy both about its nature and the impact that the Glorious Revolution had on the country in the late seventeenth century and after.

The main purpose of the chapter is to provide enough information for you to develop your own views about the revolution's importance in shaping the future development of the country.

Politics in the reign of William III

Three main features of politics in the reign of William III need to be highlighted here. The first is the predominance of party political rivalries based on principles, not family and personal relationships. In work published between 1940 and 1956, Professor Robert Walcott attempted to establish a new view of the structure of politics from 1689 to 1714, asserting that the political connections were held together less by adherence to a shared set of principles than by family relationships and ties of interest. In reaching this conclusion, Professor Walcott was much influenced by the research of Lewis Namier, whose similar analysis of the structure of politics in the middle of the eighteenth century had already gained the status of historical orthodoxy. In extending Namier's analysis backwards into the late seventeenth and early eighteenth centuries, Walcott flew in the face of the accepted view of the politics of that period which had been arrived at and popularized between the two world wars, notably by Keith Feiling and G. M. Trevelyan. Feiling and Trevelyan believed that conflict between the Whig and Tory parties, though it was not the only one, was the prime feature of politics between 1689 and 1714. It was this belief that Walcott sought to prove wrong. 'The more one studies the party structure under William and Anne', he wrote in 1956, 'the less it resembles the two-party structure described by Trevelyan . . . and the more it seems to have in common with the structure of politics in the Age of Newcastle as explained to us by Namier.'[1] Walcott's version of politics after 1689 had a brief period of acceptance,[2] but in his Ford lectures in 1965 Professor J. H. Plumb launched a vitriolic attack on Walcott, followed two years later by Geoffrey Holmes who, in his *British Politics in the Age of Anne*, also came out firmly against what Professor Plumb had called Walcott's 'basically very unsound' book, *English Politics in the Early Eighteenth Century*, which 'has led to appalling confusion'. Other historians in a long list of learned articles pressed home this attack, and with great vigour and skill – if with too much viciousness and too little humanity. Walcott's opinions were blasted out of sight and the importance of party political divisions after 1689 reasserted.[3]

The second feature of Williamite politics is the fluidity of these party divisions. As will be seen, Walcott's critics have been much more successful in proving the overwhelming importance of party strife as a consistent feature of the politics of Queen Anne's reign than they have been with those of the preceding reign. The confused picture of politics in William's reign that remains is partly a result of the lack of the types of primary sources, especially division lists, that have been used to prove the importance of parties in Anne's reign. Only eight division lists have been found for William's reign; all of them date from 1696 and after, and only two of them supply the names of MPs who voted on both sides of the division. Partly also, surviving contemporary comments sometimes add to the confusion. Since it was common for contemporaries to denigrate political parties as factious, many politicians were unwilling to claim that they were party politicians. It might be true that 'party activity in the late seventeenth century was like sin, universally condemned and widely indulged',[4] but this was an attitude which makes extremely difficult the task of the historian who wants to recreate the actual structure of politics. What is worse, contemporaries frequently used a bewildering array of names to describe political groups in William's reign, not only 'Whigs' and 'Tories', but the 'Court', 'Country' and 'Church' parties, 'Patriots', 'Jacobites', 'Trimmers', 'Republicans' and 'Commonwealthmen'. If all this were not bad enough, those politicians who with a fair degree of certainty can be classified as Whigs and Tories at the end of William's

---

[1] R. Walcott, *English Politics in the Early Eighteenth Century* (1956), p. 160.

[2] See D. Rubini, *Court and Country 1688–1702* (1968), *passim*.

[3] See the Bibliographical note, pp. 529–30.

[4] E. L. Ellis, 'William III and the politicians' in G. Holmes, ed., *Britain after the Glorious Revolution 1689–1714* (1969), p. 119.

reign appear to hold different ideas and have different aims from those Whigs and Tories before and immediately after the Glorious Revolution. Looking at the political history of the 1690s, the historian is in danger of suffering from attacks of double vision. With one eye he sees Whigs and Tories; with the other he sees court and country MPs. Is it possible to provide the student of this period with a guide – a pair of spectacles – that will bring definition to the otherwise blurred picture of politics in the 1690s?

In one sense it is not, because politics in the 1690s were confused. Though there are signs of its early development, there was as yet nothing resembling modern party political organization. There were no party whips, no means of disciplining MPs to prevent them from crossing party lines. Late seventeenth-century MPs were subject to the tugs of other loyalties than party – to the crown and the court or to their neighbours and constituents. As a result, at times in the 1690s it is difficult to see any consistent party political alignment, and one begins to wonder if the word 'party' is a misleading term that ought to be abandoned in a seventeenth-century context. Certainly all comparisons with modern highly organized and permanent political parties ought to be rejected. With these qualifications some signposts can be suggested to guide the student through the confusion of politics in the 1690s. One is that Whig and Tory political groups, separated by important differences of principle as well as by competition for office and power, did exist and were a fundamental part of the political structure of William's reign. It would be wrong to go on from there to assume that all MPs were Whigs or Tories or that all Whigs and Tories were consistent Whigs and Tories. Politics in William's reign were much too fluid for either of these assumptions to be correct. Yet one can identify typical Whig and Tory attitudes to the main political issues of the 1690s. Those who were unreservedly committed to the Protestant succession were invariably Whigs, while Tories were much less certain about the legality and morality of cutting their ties with James II and his son. On the other hand, those who were staunch supporters of maintaining the monopoly of the Anglican Church were usually Tories, while Whigs were more willing to allow both religious toleration and political rights to Protestant dissenters. Commitment to the war against France, to an all-out war effort even if this meant an expensive land war in Europe, and to cooperation with fellow Europeans, were typical Whig responses to the war and foreign policy in the 1690s. Tories tended to view the war with much less enthusiasm, to demand a less expensive maritime strategy and an end to the war once English interests seemed to be no longer being served by it. As will be seen, there were three periods in William's reign when polarization along these Whig and Tory lines was especially marked, from 1689 to 1690, from 1694 to 1697, and from 1701 to 1702.

Another signpost to politics in William's reign is that conditions during the reign sometimes ensured that these Whig and Tory divisions, though never obliterated completely, were not as prominent as at other times. For one thing William III, like Queen Anne later, always used his influence to suppress party rivalry. As will be seen, he was determined to rule with ministers who were chosen regardless of party. Though he was not always successful (indeed, in the mid-1690s he had to appoint many more Whig ministers than he wanted), he did have one major success in ensuring that the future of the Church was relatively dormant as a political issue for most of his reign.

Anglican fears of the growth of dissent and heresy mounted, as will be seen, but when William appointed moderate churchmen as bishops and refused to allow Convocation to meet, militant Anglicanism was effectively suppressed as a political force. Nor for much of the 1690s was the royal succession the live political issue that it was to be after 1701. It is true that the Whigs were more content with a foreign, Calvinist king than the Tories, but the prospect of the succession on William's death of a firmly Anglican queen and then of her son, the duke of Gloucester, reconciled many Tories to the new regime. With the Church and the succession temporarily taken out of the political arena, conditions were therefore ripe for the recrudescence of older 'country' grievances that had appealed to most MPs throughout the seventeenth century: a dislike of high taxes to finance wars, maladministration and corruption in central government, and lavish grants to royal favourites. As in the 1620s, the 1660s and the 1670s, so in William's reign the House of Commons became the focus for country resentment and distrust at the growing power of royal government and its threatened incursions into provincial self-government. From 1690 to 1694 attempts to curb the power of the executive by means of treason, place and triennial legislation received the support of both 'country' Whigs and Tories. When the war was ended temporarily in 1697, the blurring of Whig–Tory party lines became even more marked, as MPs united to oppose the standing army which William III refused to demobilize. From 1697 to 1701, before the war against France was resumed, it is difficult to use Whig–Tory terminology to explain the great 'country' campaign to reduce the size of the standing army and to impose further limitations on the crown, which culminated in the Act of Settlement in 1701.

These alliances between 'country' Whigs and Tories, however, point to a third feature of politics in William III's reign: both Whigs and Tories were undergoing a major transformation, so that by the end of the reign both parties were in certain crucial respects different from their predecessors at the time of William's accession. The decisive political group that acted as a catalyst in this process was a small band of MPs associated with Paul Foley and Robert Harley. Despite having possibly as few as a dozen consistent supporters, Foley and Harley played a key role in the political configurations of the 1690s and indeed Harley continued to play a central and increasingly important role in politics right down to 1714. Immediately after the Glorious Revolution in 1689 and 1690, Foley, Harley and their associates were indistinguishable from other Whigs. In January 1690 they voted for the Sacheverell Clause which the Whigs wanted to include in a new Corporation Act and which became the touchstone of post-Glorious Revolution Whiggery. In the early and mid-1690s it becomes less easy to identify the Foley–Harley group as Whigs, especially since both men took a leading part in pressing 'country' demands against the crown and its Whig ministers. Also Harley began to reiterate a non-party philosophy which remained a consistent principle throughout his subsequent career. Yet not all his followers shared his scruples about party government, and even Harley from the mid-1690s onwards was driven by his attacks on the king's Whig ministers into a close alliance with Tory MPs. By the late 1690s the new alignment of 'country' Whigs, led by Foley and Harley, and the Tories was very close, so that by this date it becomes possible to see the outlines of a 'new' Tory party: a party which through Foley and Harley had adopted the erstwhile

Whig emphasis on distrust of the executive and on demands for limitations on the royal prerogative; a party which placed less emphasis than its pre-1689 predecessor on divine right and passive obedience; and a party which resented the heavy expense of the French war. Meanwhile the transition of the Foley–Harley group to the Tories allowed fundamental changes to be effected in the Whig party. The defection of the old 'country' Whigs paved the way for the prominence of a new generation of Whigs after 1690 (the Junto Whigs), whose views and attitudes were considerably different from those Whigs who had served their political apprenticeship before the Glorious Revolution. These 'new' Whigs were less fearful than their predecessors of a strong executive; men who sought to drop the traditional association of Whiggery with resistance and contractual monarchy (not completely successfully as will be seen), and men who were willing to support William III in effectively prosecuting the war. This transformation of the Whigs and Tories took a long time to complete (by itself it is another major reason for the confused political situation in the 1690s); but the process of creating a 'new Whig' and a 'new Tory' party had gone a long way by the last years of William's reign. As will be seen, conditions in those years, from 1700 to 1702, raised Whig and Tory party rivalry to a new pitch of tension, but it was a rivalry which undoubtedly had its antecedents in the 1690s. The character of the political parties which thrived during Queen Anne's war were moulded by the events which had taken place under the pressure of King William's war.

The Glorious Revolution, 1689–1690

Historiography

The Glorious Revolution in England: changing historians' views

There were three revolutions in Britain and Ireland in the late 1680s and early 1690s: in England, Scotland and Ireland. Those in Scotland and Ireland will be examined later.

The nature and impact of the revolution in England has been the cause of much historical controversy. There have been two major different views.

- A revisionist view which plays down the significance of the Glorious Revolution. It was, it is argued, merely a bloodless noble revolt, and any revolutionary aspects of it were countered by the Tory role in events. It is true that the crown changed hands by discussion and decisions in parliament. But that was the limit of the

> revolutionary nature of events in 1688–9. The Declaration of Rights, which was drafted when the monarchy changed hands, merely asserted ancient rights and liberties and did not make new ones. Furthermore, William and Mary's acceptance of the crown was not conditional on their agreement to the Declaration of Rights.

- A more recent, late twentieth and early twenty-first century view. The Glorious Revolution, it is argued, involved a large element of popular, sometimes violent, activity. It was not merely a bloodless 'noble revolt'. Some historians have argued that the Declaration of Rights did assert new limitations on the power of the crown, paving the way for a fundamental transformation of the English State from a personal to a limited, mixed monarchy.

In what follows it will be argued that the revisionist view of the events of 1688–9 and the Declaration of Rights is a strong one. As has been seen, there was a great deal of popular political activity and violence in 1688–9, but this and the events of 1688–9 did not have revolutionary effects. But it will also be argued that these events led inevitably to England's involvement in a major European war, and it was this that helped to bring about permanent and revolutionary changes in the nature of the English State. In other words, when evaluating the significance of the Glorious Revolution, it is of vital importance to define what one means by that label. The 'real' Glorious Revolution – the one that brought about dramatic and revolutionary changes – took place in and after 1689, crucially during the 1690s and early 1700s. Those changes did not take place during the fudged Glorious Revolution of 1688–9.

Even one of the most outspoken advocates of the view that the Glorious Revolution marked an episode in 'Britain's fight for liberty' concedes that the Declaration (later the Bill) of Rights was not a statement of sweeping, fundamental constitutional changes, and the Toleration Act was a much more limited measure than its title suggests.[5] Why were only limited constitutional and ecclesiastical changes effected in 1688–9?

Even if sweeping changes had been intended in 1689, it is extremely unlikely that William would have cooperated in bringing them about. He would have seen them as an unacceptable deviation from his major preoccupation with the European war and with his task of bringing England into it. However, it is clear that those people who in 1689 envisaged making major constitutional or ecclesiastical changes were swept aside.[6] Most, but not all, prominent politicians had only limited aims; they were determined to restore old liberties, not enact new ones. Like the parliamentary leaders of the Long Parliament who regarded Charles I and the Laudians as the revolutionaries (as they were), so the political nation in 1688 had united to resist what it considered to be the

---

[5] E. Vallance, *The Glorious Revolution: 1688 – Britain's Fight for Liberty* (2006), pp. 176–8, 306.

[6] These included the 'true Whigs', who felt that what happened in 1689 was a betrayal of Whig radical principles: M. Goldie, 'The roots of true Whiggism', *History of Political Thought*, 1 (1980).

revolutionary innovations of James II. But there the parallel with 1640 ends, as indeed the revolutionaries of 1688 were determined it should. The Civil War and its aftermath still roused deep feelings, and the events of the 1640s and 1650s were commonly used as ammunition in the political propaganda warfare of the 1690s. But conservative propertied Englishmen were united in their aim of preventing a recurrence of the violence and radicalism of the English Revolution. When the old republican and regicide Edmund Ludlow returned from exile in Switzerland in November 1689, no one in the House of Commons opposed a motion for his arrest or tried to prevent his return into exile. The prime instinct of most politicians and political groups in 1688–9 was to work for a restoration of political order as soon as possible, and not to waste time tackling theoretical, ideological questions. In any case, though united on the need to restore order, the political nation was deeply divided on many major questions. The winter of 1688–9 revealed that the Protestant unity of 1687–8 had only been temporary. Any chance that might have seemed to exist for altering the character of the constitutional and ecclesiastical structure in England was lost as the Convention disintegrated amid wrangling, animosity and bitterness that were rooted in the feuds of the past.

The succession

By far the most immediately important source of political division was the succession problem. In the winter of 1688–9 many different possible solutions were publicized and discussed in print as pamphlet after pamphlet streamed from the presses. Was the return of James a possibility if he would accept limitations on his power? Was the establishment of William as regent for James an acceptable compromise? If James was no longer king, should William or Mary rule alone or should they jointly be offered the crown? These questions presented the Tories with the greatest heart-searching. As the group most passionately wedded to divine right and passive obedience, they were faced with the problem of reconciling their beliefs with the acceptance of a new monarch while the divinely appointed king was still alive. It is this which accounts for the frantic efforts of the Tories to maintain James as king. Even after James fled from London on 11 December, a meeting of peers at the Guildhall revealed strong support for maintaining him as king among High Tories, led by the Hyde brothers, the earls of Rochester and Clarendon, and by Archbishop Sancroft and Bishop Turner of Ely.[7] What cut the ground from under the feet of these 'Tory loyalists', however, was James's refusal to stay in England and be a focus around which a king's party could organize. Even when James returned to London after his capture on 16 December, he showed that he was unwilling to play the kind of role his father had adopted in the eighteen months after the calling of the Long Parliament in November 1640. He soon found a second opportunity to escape on 22 December, thus effectively removing

---

[7] R. A. Beddard, 'The Guildhall declaration of 11 December 1688 and the counter revolution of the loyalists', *H.J.*, XI (1968), pp. 403–20; idem., 'The loyalist opposition in the Interregnum: a letter of Dr Francis Turner Bishop of Ely and the Restoration of 1688', *B.I.H.R.*, XL (1967).

the possibility of another civil war. From now on even the High Tories were forced to support William as the only guarantor of public order. On 24 December a meeting of sixty peers agreed to ask William to run the country and make arrangements to hold parliamentary elections. An assembly of MPs and the lord mayor, aldermen and common councilmen of London concurred, and circular letters ordering parliamentary elections to be held were sent out on 28 and 29 December.

Yet these decisions did not resolve the Tory dilemma. In fact, it was even more acute when the Convention met on 22 January 1689. If they were to remain faithful to their long-held principles, the only honourable course for Tories was to refuse to recognize any other monarch than James II. Yet only a handful of mainly clerical 'nonjurors' took that course: Archbishop Sancroft, five bishops and about 400 clergy later refused to swear an oath of loyalty to William and Mary and thereby abandoned all chance of holding public offices. This was clearly not an appealing prospect, but the alternative – accepting the new regime while retaining their belief in the legitimate succession – forced the Tories to rely on highly ingenious casuistry. The Tory dilemma was presented in its clearest form at the end of the debates in the Convention on 28 January when it was agreed

> That King James the Second, having endeavoured to subvert the constitution of the kingdom by breaking the original contract between king and people, and by the advice of Jesuits and other wicked persons having violated the fundamental laws and having withdrawn himself out of this kingdom, has abdicated the government and that the throne is thereby become vacant.

To a believer in the Tory political theory of hereditary right, a 'vacant' throne was an impossibility, and on 29 January the Tories in the House of Lords voted that the word be struck out of the resolution. When Rochester's motion for a regency was defeated in the Lords by fifty-one votes to forty-eight, some Tories, led by Danby, brought forward a new proposal which smacked of sheer desperation. Princess Mary was to be recognized as rightful queen on the grounds that James had 'deserted' the kingdom, that the baby son born in June 1688 was not James's son but had been smuggled into Queen Mary's bedchamber in a warming-pan, and that therefore Princess Mary was James's lawful hereditary heir.

The stream of Tory fairy tales was cut short temporarily by William of Orange. It was he who held the key to the immediate situation and who was able to dictate the course of events. On 3 February he made it clear that he would rule neither as a regent nor as a consort, and Mary, who was always the model of wifely subservience, agreed. Her sister, Anne, meanwhile disclaimed the right to succeed if Mary should die before William. English politicians, therefore, were faced with the stark choice of accepting William and Mary as king and queen with William as the dominant partner, or of taking the consequences of a prolonged interregnum and possible popular insurrection. On 6 February the House of Lords accepted the Commons' motion including 'abdication' and 'vacancy', and parliament agreed to offer the throne jointly to William and Mary. Desperately the Tories tried to justify what was in fact a serious contravention of their principles. To the warming-pan myth they also added the claim that the Glorious

Revolution had been divinely ordained and therefore could not have been resisted.[8] A prominent Tory political theorist, Edmund Bohun, tried to justify allegiance to William and Mary on the grounds that William had acquired the right to the throne in a 'just war'.[9] The most popular Tory theoretical justification for accepting the Glorious Revolution, however, was the one used to justify allegiance to the republican regime of the 1650s: that obedience was due to any government that ensured security and protection for society. As propounded by William Sherlock, Dean of St Paul's, many Tories gratefully accepted this notion and quietened their uneasy consciences by the tortuous argument that they obeyed William only as de facto king, but continued to recognize James as the de jure monarch.[10]

The Whigs, unlike the Tories, had no scruples of conscience about accepting William as king. Their views about the original contract between monarchs and their subjects and about the latters' right to resist tyrannical monarchs, which had been worked out during the Exclusion Crisis, were well suited to justify their role in 1688. On the face of it, therefore, the Whigs came out of the revolution in better shape than the Tories. In fact, this is only partly true. The equivocal attitude of the Tories to the new regime was a great political burden to them in the next few years. The fact that they were instrumental in ensuring that the oath of loyalty to William and Mary drafted in February 1689 did not describe the new king and queen as 'rightful and lawful' heirs was hardly likely to endear them to the new monarchs. And when that phrase was at last inserted in a new oath of loyalty in 1696, many Tory office-holders refused to take the oath voluntarily. Moreover, much later, at the end of Anne's reign, the ambiguous attitude of many Tories to the Protestant succession was, as will be seen, a major cause of the collapse of the Tory party. Yet the Whigs, too, were in a vulnerable position after the Glorious Revolution. The Whig association with doctrines of contract and resistance could easily be smeared as extremist, republican notions, a fact which was to prove extremely embarrassing to the Whigs in the future. Desperately, Whig politicians tried to play down the radical implications of their philosophy, but the Sacheverell case in 1710 showed the extent of their failure (see below, pp. 446–9). Nor was the position of the Whigs immediately after the Glorious Revolution as good as many of them hoped it would be. William was aware of the need to conciliate prominent politicians with the new regime. His first list of ministers must have been a great disappointment to Whig hopes. The Whig earl of Shrewsbury was appointed one of the secretaries of state, but the earl of Nottingham, a Tory 'loyalist' of 1688 and a very late convert to William's cause, was the other. In addition, such hated enemies of the Whigs as Danby and Halifax were given signs of royal favour, even though their offices, lord president and lord privy seal respectively, were only posts of dignity. Moreover, William put the key offices of lord treasurer and lord chancellor into commission so that no one could dominate

---

[8] G. Straka, 'The final phase of divine right theory in England, 1688–1702', *E.H.R.*, LXXVII (1962); J. P. Kenyon, *Revolution Principles: the politics of party, 1689–1720* (1977), p. 54.

[9] M. Goldie, 'Edward Bohun and *Ius Gentium*: the Revolution debate 1689–93', *H.J.*, XX (1977), pp. 569–86.

[10] C. F. Mullett, 'A case of allegiance: William Sherlock and the Revolution of 1688', *Huntingdon Library Quarterly*, X (1946–7).

them. Nothing could have better reflected William's desire to show that he commanded wide political support in England and his determination to assert the independent power of the crown.

The Declaration of Rights

It is this aim of the king, however, which some MPs were equally determined to prevent in 1689. Clearly some MPs, both Whigs and Tories, were unwilling to let pass this chance to limit the king's powers. 'Will you establish the crown and not secure yourselves?' asked the West Country Tory, Sir Edward Seymour, while the Whig William Sacheverell pointed out that 'all the world will laugh at us, if we make a half settlement'. Therefore on 29 January the House of Commons, agreeing with Lord Anthony Falkland's plea that 'before you fill the throne, I would have you resolve, what power you will give the king, and what not', set up a committee to formulate a list of the rights of the subject, both those existing and those to be brought about by legislation which William and Mary were to agree to before they accepted the throne.[11] The committee's report, which was ready by 2 February, contained a sweeping programme of constitutional changes, consisting of twenty-eight 'heads', including guarantees for the continuance of parliament, religious liberty for Protestants, and proposals for the reform of chancery and treason trials, and for judges to be appointed 'during good behaviour' with fixed salaries and not 'during the king's pleasure'.[12]

That there was a a desire amongst some in the Convention to limit the power of the crown can also be seen in the debates on William's request for a permanent financial settlement. When it was first discussed on 26 and 27 February 1689, voices from all parts of the political spectrum warned against granting either a large permanent revenue or a permanent revenue at all. The Tory Sir Thomas Clarges believed that 'we ought to be cautious of the Revenue, which is the life of the government, and consider the last two reigns'. 'Our greatest misery was, our giving it [the Revenue] to king James for life, and not from three years to three years, and so you may have often kissed his hands there', said Colonel John Birch.[13] With sentiments like these prevalent in the Convention, as in the early years of the Cavalier Parliament, progress towards a financial settlement was very slow. By 11 March all that was agreed, despite William's urgent requests, was that the crown's existing ordinary revenue could be collected until 24 June 1689, and on 20 March the old familiar figure of £1,200,000 was brought forward again as the crown's estimated ordinary expenditure. Apart from voting extraordinary parliamentary subsidies for the war, this was as far as the Convention went towards settling the king's permanent revenue. The completion of this task was

---

[11] R. J. Frankle, 'The formulation of the Declaration of Rights', *H.J.*, XVII (1974), pp. 266–7.

[12] This report is printed in Henry Horwitz, *Parliament, Policy and Politics in the Reign of William III* (1977), pp. 367–8.

[13] Quoted in E. A. Reitan, 'From revenue to civil list, 1689–1702: the Revolution Settlement and the "mixed and balanced" constitution', *H.J.*, XIII (1970), pp. 576–7; Clayton Roberts, 'Constitutional significance of the financial settlement of 1690', *H.J.*, XX (1977), p. 67.

left to William's second parliament, which in March 1690 granted the king the excise for life, but only allowed him the receipts from customs for four years. How serious a limitation on the independence of the crown this would have been in peacetime remains a matter of controversy[14] because its provisions were soon rendered out of date by the financial needs of war, which permanently ended the possibility of the financial independence of the English monarchy.

What is certain is that the members of the Convention failed to carry out the aims many of them had of putting severe limits on royal power by a Declaration of Rights.

Information

The Declaration of Rights, 1689

Only eleven of the twenty-eight 'heads' drawn up by the committee which reported on 2 February were included in the final version of the Declaration of Rights. All of those that required new legislation were rejected and the declaration retained only those 'heads' which were considered to reflect existing rights. Undoubtedly the most important of these were the declarations that

- the use of the suspending power
- the maintenance of a standing army in peacetime
- the raising of money without the consent of parliament were all illegal.

Many other statements in the declaration (for example, 'Election of Members of Parlyament ought to be free') were so vague as to be ineffective. Other clauses raised important questions of definition: for example, what was meant by 'excessive' bail, or 'cruell and unusuall' punishments.

This power of suspending laws was declared illegal, but with the qualification 'as it hath been assumed and exercised of late'.

Most important of all, those 'heads' in the report of 2 February that needed new legislation were rejected by the Convention. The declaration left untouched most of the personal powers of the monarchy to choose its own ministers, make its own policy (especially foreign policy) and influence opinion in parliament by means of elections, placemen and the general disposition of patronage.

---

[14] See the contrasting views of Reitan and Roberts (see note 13). The best balanced discussion is by J. Miller, *The Glorious Revolution* (1983), pp. 39–43.

Nor, contrary to legend, was the offer of the throne to William and Mary made conditional on their accepting even the castrated version of the Declaration of Rights. Though the declaration was read to them before they formally accepted the crown, neither William nor Mary gave any indication that they felt bound to adhere to its provisions.[15] There are many possible reasons for the limited nature of the constitutional settlement in 1689. Probably for some MPs William's known intention not to allow drastic inroads into the royal prerogative was important, and ambitious politicians took the hint. Certainly some Whigs in 1689 seemed less in favour of restricting the power of the crown than might have been expected, given the attitude of Whigs during the Exclusion Crisis, largely because they hoped that it would be Whig ministers who would dominate the new king's government. For most MPs, however, the most important consideration was the pressing need to fill the throne quickly and not to waste time in drafting and passing complicated constitutional legislation. The Declaration of Rights (enacted as the Bill of Rights in December 1689) was a conservative document.[16] Apart from bringing about a change of monarchs, it brought about no fundamental alterations in the constitution. These were to be brought about by the Glorious Revolution of the 1690s and early 1700s, not the Glorious Revolution of 1688–9.

The Church: comprehension or toleration?

The Glorious Revolution of 1688–9, like the Restoration, presented another opportunity to widen the membership of the Church of England and extend toleration to those Protestants outside the Church. As in 1660, the hopes of non-Anglicans were raised both by the expectation of some reward for their political role in the events of the immediate past and by the tolerationist views of the new king. Though a firm Calvinist, William had always appointed men to his service regardless of their personal religious convictions, whether Catholics or Jews.[17] On his arrival in England he had talks with prominent dissenters in which he dropped broad hints of his support for a comprehensive Church settlement. To emphasize the similarity with 1660, Richard Baxter was still active among the Presbyterian leadership, which felt itself in a strong enough position to put forward a plan that bishops should act in consultation with presbyters in diocesan affairs. Among prominent Anglicans, also, including high churchmen like the suspended Archbishop Sancroft, there was a strong feeling that the Protestant unity of 1688 should be made the basis for a more comprehensive Church and so permanently strengthen it against the Catholic threat. The leading lay

---

[15] Frankle, 'Formulation of the Declaration of Rights', p. 270.

[16] The Bill of Rights is printed in W. C. Costin and J. F. Watson, eds., *The Law and Working of the Constitution: documents 1660–1914* (2 vols., 2nd edn., 1961), 1, pp. 67–76. For a different view of the Declaration of Rights from mine, see L. G. Schwoerer, *The Declaration of Rights 1689* (1981) and H. Nenner, 'Constitutional uncertainty and the Declaration of Rights', in B. Malament, ed., *After the Reformation* (1980).

[17] S. B. Baxter, *William III* (1966), p. 186; J. I. Israel, 'William III and toleration', in P. P. Grell, J. I. Israel and N. Tyacke, eds., *From Persecution to Toleration* (1991).

exponent of this view was Nottingham, who at the end of February and early in March 1689 introduced a Comprehension Bill and a Toleration Bill into the House of Lords. These bills were very similar to those which had been projected in 1660. It was hoped that the terms of the Comprehension Bill would be flexible enough to enable most Protestant dissenters to enter the Anglican Church; and for the tiny minority who could not, the Toleration Bill granted a limited freedom of worship. However, during the next few months, despite the apparently favourable climate, the plans for a comprehensive Church collapsed, and of the two measures only the Toleration Bill became law (on 24 May 1689).

Why was yet another chance missed either to establish a more comprehensive Anglican Church or to extend religious toleration to Protestant dissenters? Few MPs were working for toleration in 1689; the major political thrust of those pressing for religious reform was directed towards achieving comprehension. Many Anglicans had opposed this in the past, because they feared that it would mean the beginning of the end of the Anglican monopoly in Church and State. Unfortunately, events early in 1689 seemed to confirm these fears. William played a big part in this. As a Calvinist, not only was he the object of Anglican suspicion about his intentions, but on 16 March he made an ill-advised speech in the House of Lords in favour of throwing open public offices to 'all protestants that are willing and able to serve'.[18] Ironically, within a few weeks of his accession William, in effect, was proposing the very thing – the repeal of the Test and Corporation Acts – that had united the political nation against his predecessor. Not surprisingly, Anglicans, whose consciences were already very tender because of the traumatic events of the last few months, reacted quickly to oppose the plan. On the evening of the king's speech, over 150 MPs met at the Devil's Tavern in Fleet Street to condemn William's overt attack on the Anglican monopoly. Events in Scotland may also have contributed to Anglican militancy in England, as the Scottish Presbyterians in the succeeding weeks seized power and abolished episcopacy north of the border yet again (see below, pp. 430–2). Moreover, early in April Richard Hampden, by introducing a Comprehension Bill which granted more generous concessions to dissenters, appeared to confirm that non-Anglicans would not be satisfied with Nottingham's proposals.

It is arguable that by this stage comprehension was already a lost cause. The deep repugnance felt for it by rank-and-file Anglican clergy and their provincial lay patrons would soon become apparent. But for the moment this was delayed, and for the rest of the year William and Nottingham kept the hopes of comprehension alive. William appears to have regretted his blunder of 16 March, and on 9 April, using a Whig privy councillor, William Harbord, as his spokesman, the king tried to make amends by stressing that he 'was altogether of the judgement of the Church of England', and indicating that he would listen favourably to a request for the summoning of Convocation

---

[18] William apparently made this speech on the advice of Richard Hampden: Horwitz, *Parliament, Policy and Politics*, p. 22.

to discuss the plans for comprehension.[19] For the next few months William attempted to conciliate churchmen by further pro-Anglican public statements and by encouraging Nottingham to secure the support of suspended nonjuring bishops for comprehension. Nottingham was also authorized to draft detailed plans for comprehension to be submitted to Convocation. Just how useless these political preparations were, was seen when Convocation met on 21 November. Convocation allowed the fanatical fears of the mass of the lower Anglican clergy to be unleashed. During its short session of three weeks, the lower house of Convocation would have no truck with any move that appeared to be a compromise with Protestant dissenters. Now that the threat of popery had diminished, the fragile Protestant unity of 1688 crumbled.

As a result only the Toleration Bill became law in 1689. It is possible to minimize the significance of the Toleration Act.[20] For the first time, all Protestants who took the oath of supremacy and allegiance and made a declaration against transubstantiation were legally allowed to worship. John Locke welcomed the Act, writing to a friend in the United Provinces that

> Toleration has now at last been established by law in our country. Not perhaps so wide in scope as might be wished for by you and those like you, who are true Christians and free from ambition or envy. Still, it is something to have progressed so far. I hope that, with these beginnings, the foundations have been laid of that liberty and peace, in which the church of Christ is one day to be established.[21]

Yet, as Locke implied, the scope of the Act was limited. It was, after all, something its drafters had never intended; what had been meant to be applied only to a minority, who would not join a more comprehensive Anglican Church, had to be enforced against all Protestant dissenters. It is not surprising, therefore, that it gave less than total satisfaction to the latter, who had hoped for much greater changes from the Glorious Revolution. Many Protestant dissenters were legally allowed to worship, but those who did so were liable to penalties of one kind or another. Some of these were minor, but no less irritating in denoting the dissenters' continued status as second-class citizens: for example, dissenter meeting-houses had to be registered with a bishop or at the Quarter Sessions, and dissenting services had to be conducted with the doors of the meeting-house wide open. More seriously, the Test Acts enforcing acceptance of the Anglican sacraments on all office-holders were maintained. Moreover, certain classes of Protestant, most notably those who denied the doctrine of the Trinity, were especially exempted from even the limited toleration allowed other Protestant dissenters. What is perhaps more surprising than the dissatisfaction with which dissenters viewed the Toleration Act is the fact that many Anglicans were unenthusiastic about it.

---

[19] Horwitz, *Parliament, Policy and Politics*, p. 25.

[20] See the editors' introduction, N. Tyacke, '"The Rise of Puritanism" and the legalising of dissent 1571–1719', and J. I. Israel, 'William III and toleration' in Grell et al., eds., *From Persecution to Toleration* for arguments that the Toleration Act was a landmark in the history of toleration.

[21] Quoted in Tyacke, 'The Rise of Puritanism' in ibid., p. 41.

Although on the face of it the religious settlement had left Anglican monopoly of public offices intact, the minimal encroachment on the Anglican monopoly of the Church allowed in 1689 was met with great alarm in many Anglican circles, especially outside the narrow episcopal group patronized by Nottingham and William. As will be seen, the next few years seemed to many rank-and-file Anglicans, clerical and lay, to justify their belief that dissent was a growing threat to the privileged position of the Church and this was to make 'the Church in danger' a potent political slogan (see pp. 405–8).

The only way William could smother the religious wrangling was to adjourn Convocation, which he did on 14 December 1689, and he did not allow it to meet again until 1701. A little over a month later, on 27 January 1690, William was driven to adjourn the Convention, and to dissolve it on 6 February. Perhaps if he had been more familiar with the history of English politics since the mid-seventeenth century, the new king might have found the bitterness of politics during the Convention, if not less irritating, more intelligible. Much of the political passion of the 1690s derived its strength from the past. One sign of this is the blossoming interest in the mid-century revolution. Clarendon's *History of the Rebellion*, completed by the 1670s, was not published until 1702–4. Clarendon's son, Rochester, emphasized in the preface that his purpose in printing it now was to buttress Tory propaganda, 'rather as an instruction to the present age than a reproach upon the Last'.[22] Rochester's opponents were not slow to use ammunition drawn from the past. A Whig edition of Edmund Ludlow's *Memoirs*, drastically bowdlerized to remove offending passages (probably by John Toland), first appeared in 1696.[23] Obviously the Whig and Tory caricatures presented by their opponents' propaganda – the Whigs as collaborators with and defenders of the regicide regimes of the 1650s, and the Tories as proponents of the type of absolutist pretensions Laud and Charles I were alleged to have held – were false. But the English Revolution and its aftermath contributed greatly to the bitterness of politics after the Glorious Revolution of 1688–9. Both Whigs and Tories felt that they had old scores to settle: the Tories for the sufferings of Anglicans and royalists from the effects of sequestrations and punitive taxation at the hands of the parliamentary and Cromwellian regimes in the 1640s and 1650s; the Whigs for the expulsion both of Puritan clergy from their livings in the 1660s and of Whigs and dissenters from municipal corporations in the 1680s.

In these circumstances, William's initiative in pressing for an Act of Indemnity was bound to fail. His message to the Convention on 25 March 1689, calling for an end to 'all controversies' over the 'disorders in the late times' fell on deaf ears.[24] Instead many Whigs seized every opportunity to take revenge on their Tory opponents. The Indemnity Bill was lost, some Whig hotheads even pressed for two of James II's judges to be hanged, and those who had served in Charles II's and James II's governments were attacked.

---

[22] Quoted in R. C. Richardson, *The Debate on the English Revolution Revisited* (1988), p. 36.

[23] Blair Worden, editorial introduction to *A Voyce from the Watch Tower*, Camden Soc., 4th ser., XXI (1978).

[24] Horwitz, *Parliament, Policy and Politics*, p. 29.

Halifax especially was singled out for his role in defeating exclusion in 1681, and early in 1690 he was driven from office. The Whig offensive culminated in January 1690 in the debates on the Corporation Bill, which was designed to restore the franchises forfeited or surrendered by boroughs in the previous two reigns. Some Whigs, including William Sacheverell, determined to make this an even severer anti-Tory measure by proposing that a clause be added making anyone who had helped in the forfeiture of a charter ineligible for office for seven years. The Sacheverell clause split the lower House and it was defeated on 10 January, after long and bitter debate, by ten votes.

William's subsequent decision to dissolve the Convention was the result of a deep disillusionment with English politics, especially with the Whigs. It is possible that he even considered abdicating – though surely never seriously? The time he was having to spend on domestic affairs negated the primary reason he had come to England: to expedite the war against France. To this was also now added the need to reconquer Ireland, which required his personal attention. But, if William thought that dissolution of the Convention would end the bitterness of English politics, he was disappointed. The subsequent elections during February and March 1690 were characterized by severe partisan rivalry. Both Whigs and Tories circulated 'blacklists' to persuade the electorate not to support the 150 MPs ('Jacobites') who had voted on 5 February 1689 against 'abdication' and 'vacancy', or for the 146 MPs ('Commonwealthmen') who had voted for the Sacheverell clause.[25] It is clear that by the spring of 1690 the Glorious Revolution of 1688–9 had made no greater impact on the pattern of politics than it had on the constitution.

A country at war, 1690–1697

King William's war

Information

The revolutionary impact of William's war

The fact that England was involved in a large-scale European war against France for much of the period from 1689 to the death of Queen Anne is the key to many developments in England (and, from 1707, Britain) during the last twenty years of the Stuart age. The most important effect of the Glorious Revolution was that it brought

---

[25] The Tory 'blacklist' is printed in A. Browning, *Thomas Osborne, Earl of Danby and Duke of Leeds* (3 vols., 1944–51), III, pp. 164–72.

to the English throne a man whose prime aims were centred, not in England, but in Europe. William III was first and foremost a European, interested in establishing the peace of the Continent by maintaining a balance of power between the two major European dynasties, the Habsburgs and the Bourbons. Since Louis XIV's France was the major threat to European peace, William was committed to curbing French power. Therefore, a major effect on England of William's accession was to force a radical realignment in her foreign policy away from the puppet-like dependence on France of Charles II and the isolationist pose adopted by James II.[26] William took England into a European war against France, as everyone at the time knew that he would, and in the process transformed his new kingdom into a major world power. The resulting pro-Habsburg, anti-Bourbon direction of British foreign policy was to last until the mid-eighteenth century; Britain's status as a great power endured even longer, until the mid-twentieth century.

Louis XIV's aims in Europe after 1688 are less easy to discern than William III's. The succession to the Spanish throne was certainly a principal concern of the French king at this time. Charles II, the Spanish king, was childless, had been an invalid since birth, and was likely to die at any time. Indeed, in 1688 Louis's agents at Madrid reported that Charles II's health was deteriorating rapidly. Louis XIV's claim to determine the Spanish succession on Charles's death was very strong. Louis was married to Charles II's elder sister, Maria Theresa, and therefore their son, the dauphin, was one of the chief claimants to the throne. The legality of this claim, however, was weakened by the fact that Maria Theresa had formally renounced her claims to the Spanish throne, so strengthening the case of two other claimants, Joseph Ferdinand, the electoral prince of Bavaria, and Emperor Leopold. The electoral prince of Bavaria's claim lay through his mother, Maria Antonia, the daughter of Charles II's younger sister, Margaret Theresa, and Emperor Leopold. Maria Antonia, however, had also renounced her claims to the Spanish throne. The Emperor Leopold therefore traced his claim to the Spanish throne through his mother, the younger sister of Philip IV.

Confusing though the competing claims are, the simple point is that each of the three claimants felt his case was the strongest and each employed lawyers who supported this conviction. In all probability, therefore, Louis's invasion of the Palatinate in the autumn of 1688 was intended as a preliminary to the determination of the Spanish succession. By a show of military strength, not a long war, Louis perhaps hoped to break up the German opposition to France which had resulted in the League of Augsburg, and thus to persuade the German states and the Emperor to negotiate a

---

[26] G. C. Gibbs, 'The revolution in foreign policy', in Holmes, ed., *Britain after the Glorious Revolution*, pp. 59–79.

settlement of the Spanish succession in the French interests.[27] If this was the case, Louis's aims backfired badly. Not only did the French invasion of the Palatinate allow William to invade England without the threat of French occupation of his homeland (as has been seen), but Charles II did not die; indeed, he lived for another twelve years. Moreover, the French encountered unexpected resistance from the German states, which meant that Louis's planned short campaign escalated into a nine-year major war. In February 1689 the Dutch formally declared war on France and in May the States General and Emperor Leopold signed the Grand Alliance against France, which was joined in the succeeding months by England, Spain, Savoy and many of the German states. France was diplomatically and militarily isolated. William's dream of a European coalition to curb French power was at last a reality.

Unfortunately for William, at the very moment of his diplomatic triumph he was distracted from what he considered to be his major task of organizing the Grand Alliance against France on the Continent, not only by the wrangling of politicians in the English Convention, but also by the outbreak of a revolution in Ireland.

Tim Harris usefully distinguishes two revolutions in Ireland in 1689–91. The first he describes as 'an attempted Catholic revolution'. This differed from the Glorious Revolution in England of 1688–9 in the scale of the violence involved and in the revolutionary intentions of the participants in it. The attempted Catholic counter-revolution was led by the so-called Patriot Parliament, which met in Dublin in May 1689. In a House of Commons of 224 members there were only six Protestants, and it proceeded to pass a stream of anti-English legislation, asserting Irish legislative and jurisdictional independence of England. Moreover, the Patriot Parliament repealed the Act of Settlement, restoring many of the estates confiscated from Catholic landowners since 1641. 'It boldly announced our national independence', wrote Wolfe Tone of the Patriot Parliament, 'in words which Molyneux shouted on to Swift, and Swift to Lucas, and Lucas to Flood, and Flood to Grattan redoubling the cry, Dungannon church rang and Ireland was again a nation.'

In the face of this Catholic nationalist explosion, Ulster Presbyterians had to arm themselves and many of them fled to Londonderry and Enniskillen, where they appealed to William for support. This was the occasion for a second revolution in Ireland, called by Harris a 'Williamite counter-revolution'. In many respects, William had little option but to lead it. In February 1689 James had left St Germain, and on 12 March he landed at Kinsale in south-west Ireland, where he was met by the earl of Tyrconnell, who held the country for him. William had to act to prevent Ireland from becoming a launching pad for a French invasion of England. In May he sent Colonel Percy Kirke with a force to relieve Londonderry, which had been under siege since 19 April 1689. This Kirke successfully did on 30 July, though amid accusations of his unwarranted delay from the besieged as thousands of them died from starvation and disease; and on

---

[27] See J. R. Jones, *The Revolution of 1688 in England* (1972), pp. 267–80 for a good analysis of Louis's intentions.

Claimants to the Spanish succession

Map 3 The Low Countries during the wars of William III and Queen Anne, 1689–1697 and 1702–1713

the same day a Protestant detachment from Enniskillen won a skirmish with James's forces at Newton Butler.

These victories brought only temporary relief and, in August, William sent to Ireland a larger force of 10,000 men under General Schomberg. Though a veteran of many European campaigns, Schomberg suffered the fate of many other generals sent to Ireland, though the subsequent disaster which hit his army was made more certain by the timing of the expedition and the lack of supplies. Heavy and persistent autumn rain, inadequate food and shelter, and proximity to the Irish bogs were the right conditions for the rapid spread of infectious diseases like typhus, which were common among seventeenth-century armies. Schomberg lost about half his army without firing a shot in battle. In retrospect the turning point in the English reconquest of Ireland was William's personal intervention and his victory at the battle of the Boyne on 1 July 1690, which was made possible, in part at least, by the best asset possessed by all prudent generals, numerical superiority over the enemy, though William's personal bravery during the battle is not to be denied. It was a turning point in retrospect only, however. William left Ireland in September, but it took over a year for his subordinates, Ginkel and Marlborough, to complete the conquest of Ireland. On 3 October 1691, Limerick surrendered, and at Limerick the lords justices of Ireland signed the treaty negotiated

Map 4 Western Europe during the wars of William III and Queen Anne, 1689–1697 and 1702–1713

by Ginkel and Patrick Sarsfield, James's general. Sarsfield and his Catholic colleagues won for their Irish co-religionists a fairly generous settlement: limited religious toleration (a return to the conditions of Charles II's reign), protection for the property of Catholic landowners, and freedom for the Irish army to go to France, all to be ratified by an Irish parliament. The Treaty of Limerick, though, was a worthless piece of paper. In 1690 and 1691 the English parliament overthrew it by repealing all the legislation of the Patriot Parliament and imposing an Anglican test on all office-holders and MPs. Catholics were driven from their estates and from politics. The Dublin Parliament which met in October 1692 was a Protestant one. As in England, Protestant unity crumbled once the immediate danger of Catholicism receded, and the Presbyterians, who had been crucial in securing the Glorious Revolution in Ireland, were abandoned to become second-class citizens. Williamite Ireland was ruled by a narrowly based Anglo-Irish landed class, supported by an established Church to which very few Irish people belonged. Ireland was again reduced to a colonial subservience, which was reinforced by subsequent enactments of the English parliament aimed at preventing Irish economic competition with English agriculture and industry, signalling the complete failure of Ireland's 'attempted Catholic revolution' and the success of the 'Williamite counter-revolution'.

If, as is likely, William considered the Irish campaign an irksome distraction from the major arena of the struggle against France, it did help him confirm many of his subjects in their view that the war was in England's interests. A responsible section of English opinion became more than ever convinced that the war was necessary to preserve the Glorious Revolution, to prevent the invasion of Ireland, Scotland and England, and the return of James II as a French puppet king. The Irish campaign pressed home the point that the war against France was necessary for English security, which was imperilled until Louis XIV recognized William's title as king of England. However, this fact did not always remain uppermost in the mind of some English MPs in the 1690s. As has been seen, English MPs had rarely shown (even in the 1620s) much enthusiasm for a land war in Europe, suspecting that a large proportion of the high taxes they were asked to pay was siphoned off into private (or royal) pockets or was wasted by maladministration. What also caused their enthusiasm for war to cool was that the war at sea, as well as on land, went badly.

The war at sea got off to a disastrous start. On 30 June 1690, off Beachy Head, an allied Dutch–English fleet of fifty-eight ships commanded by Admiral Torrington fought a French fleet of seventy-five ships. When so many sailing ships meet each other, clear-cut results are unlikely, but in this case all reports agreed that the allied fleet was dispersed in a decisive French victory. The order to engage the enemy, despite being outnumbered, came from Queen Mary and her advisers, notably Nottingham, in London (William was in Ireland), and Torrington was forced to obey against his better judgement. But it was the admiral who took the blame for the defeat. He was court-martialled at the end of the year, and though acquitted he was dismissed. With the army in Ireland, the defeat left England temporarily defenceless, but the French failed to take advantage. Farcically, given the frantic panic and fear of full-scale invasion in England, all that resulted was the bombardment of Teignmouth on 26 July by the French admiral, Tourville. But the defeat did stimulate another bout of re-organization of the English navy, the building of new men-of-war, a new shipyard at Plymouth and a dry dock at Portsmouth. The reorganization may have played some part in the allied navy's subsequent success in preventing the French navy from covering an invasion force across the Channel. In May 1692, with James II watching from the nearby cliffs, the French fleet was dispersed in the Bay of La Hogue by Admiral Russell, although one suspects that as in the case of the battle of Beachy Head, ill-advised civilian intervention had more influence on the outcome of the battle than the resources or naval organization of the two sides. This time it was Tourville who, vainly protesting, was ordered by Louis XIV to engage the enemy at all costs.

The allied conduct of the war at sea was no more immune from mammoth blunders. In 1693 a large convoy of around 400 Dutch and English merchant ships bound for the Levant was allowed to sail, grossly underprotected by only a handful of men-of-war, and Admiral Tourville's fleet had little trouble in destroying at least 100 of the convoy off the south coast of Portugal. This was perhaps the crucial event which forced William in 1694 to order Admiral Russell to take a fleet to the Mediterranean, where it stayed, based at Cadiz, until 1696. As well as being significant in pointing the way to the future British naval presence in the Mediterranean in the eighteenth century, this was the most successful naval decision of William's war. Russell's fleet in the Mediterranean hampered the French war effort in Italy and Spain and blockaded half of the French fleet in Toulon, preventing it from joining with Tourville's fleet based in Brest. In 1696, however, these advantages were lost, as Russell was withdrawn from the Mediterranean to forestall another invasion attempt across the Channel.

If anything, the land war appeared to go even worse for the allies than the war at sea, and to be more interminable. William's war in Flanders rivalled the English Civil War in its lack of an overall strategic pattern, with both armies manoeuvring and counter-manoeuvring with few apparent long-term aims. When the armies did, infrequently, meet in full-scale battles, William's army came off the worst. The battles of Steenkirk (August 1692) and Neerwinden (July 1693) were not decisive in the war, both sides suffered heavy casualties, but on both occasions William's losses were heavier than the French and his military reputation was adversely affected. The major difference between the English Civil War and William's war was the latter's lengthy sieges. No English towns had the military fortifications to withstand a lengthy siege like the towns in the Spanish Netherlands which were the battleground for much of William's war. In siege warfare the French proved superior, notably the French general Vauban, who successfully took a series of garrisons along the river Meuse, Mons (April 1691), Namur (June 1692), Huy (July 1693) and Charleroi (1694). William's only major success in the war was to recapture Namur in August 1695.

Like the mutual exchanges of pieces in a drawn game of chess, however, each capture and recapture of these towns brought victory in the war no nearer for either side. Why was the war so long-drawn-out and inconclusive? Partly, the answer lies in the fact that, like all wartime coalitions, the Grand Alliance was weakened by mutual suspicions and distrust. Both the imperial and Spanish courts felt a natural uneasiness at allying with the Protestant states of northern Europe, especially since they were, in effect, supporting a Protestant usurper against the rightful Catholic king of England. Although reassured by his theologians that this course was not sinful, Emperor Leopold remained sceptical, and from 1692 to 1696 engaged in secret negotiations with Louis XIV, during which the possibility of the succession of James II's son in England after the deaths of William and Mary was discussed.[28] Even if these differences had not existed, it is hardly likely that the council of allied ministers, which sat

---

[28] M. A. Thomson, 'Louis XIV and William III, 1689–97', in R. Hatton and J. S. Bromley, eds., *William III and Louis XIV: essays 1680–1720 by and for Mark A. Thomson* (1968), pp. 26–7.

throughout the war at The Hague, would have been any more effective than it was in agreeing on a sensible war strategy. Louis XIV, in contrast, reaped all the advantages of a unified command.

Opinions differ about the extent of William Ill's success in overcoming these difficulties.[29] Certainly his task was immense. Not only had he to keep a large coalition together, and act as principal general of the allied army, but he had to divide his time between London and the Continent. Not least of his difficulties was that of commuting between London and The Hague in conditions of great hardship and personal danger. In January 1691 after a voyage of four days the royal yacht became fogbound and lost somewhere off the Dutch coast. William then got into an open rowing boat for a journey which lasted for sixteen hours in freezing fog with loose ice floating in a sea infested with French privateers.[30] It is difficult to escape the conclusion that his success in overcoming his difficulties was greater in the diplomatic than in the military sphere. The Grand Alliance was his creation and that it kept together for as long as it did was largely due to his work. As a soldier he allowed the French to dictate the tactical pattern of the war of constant manoeuvring and sieges, and of avoiding conclusive battles. Seen in the context of seventeenth- and eighteenth-century warfare, however, perhaps this is too harsh a judgement on William's military abilities. Even a soldier of outstanding genius like Marlborough in the next war failed to break the pattern of long-drawn-out wars which characterized the seventeenth and eighteenth centuries in Europe. Like the Thirty Years War (1618–48), Anne's War (1702–13), the War of the Austrian Succession (1742–8), and the Seven Years War (1756–63), William's was a long war of attrition.

Such a war, of course, was not only long-drawn-out, it was also expensive. Financial exhaustion on both sides contributed greatly to the conclusion of peace. In addition, the overseas trade of Europe was disrupted by the war. The allies operated a partially successful naval blockade of French ports, and French attacks on English and Dutch shipping, of which the Smyrna convoy disaster was the biggest example, had a serious effect on the economy of both maritime powers. However, peace negotiations began long before the war made an impact on the European economy. Louis XIV had not wanted a long war, as has been seen, and almost from the start of the war he appeared anxious for peace: 1693, it has been said, 'witnessed what we should now call a peace offensive on the part of France'.[31] In the second half of that year, secret negotiations began between representatives of Louis XIV and William III, which were maintained intermittently throughout the war. William soon abandoned his initial hopes of reducing France to her frontiers of 1648 and 1659. Louis, however, found it harder to overcome his objections to recognizing William as king of England. But during the negotiations he eventually did so. When peace was finally concluded at Ryswick in September 1697, William's greatest gains were Louis's recognition of him as king of England and

---

[29] Contrast D. Ogg, *England in the Reigns of James II and William III* (1955), pp. 374–5, and S. Baxter's more favourable view in *William III*, especially pp. 288–364.

[30] Baxter, ibid., pp. 292–3.

[31] Thomson, 'Louis XIV and William III, 1689–97', pp. 27–8.

the French king's promise not to aid any of his enemies. Moreover, Louis abandoned the conquests he had made in the Spanish Netherlands and the Empire, though with the exception of Strasbourg. The Peace of Ryswyck, however, was not the basis for permanent European peace, simply because it ignored the Spanish succession problem. Immediately after the conclusion of the war, both Louis and William began to try to settle this by diplomatic means. Their failure was to produce another long period of war, the War of the Spanish Succession.

King William's war and politics: the transformation of the Whig and Tory parties, 1690–4

The effect of King William's war on English politics and on the constitution was no less decisive than its impact on English foreign policy.[32] As has been seen, the adjournment of Convocation at the end of 1689 effectively withdrew the church controversy from the political arena until Convocation met again in 1701. Moreover, Tory doubts about the legality of William's accession were partially satisfied in the 1690s by the ingenuity of political theorists and by the comforting prospect that the successors to the throne, if William and Mary died childless, were staunch Anglicans, James's elder daughter, Anne, and her son, the duke of Gloucester. The way was therefore cleared for the war in Europe to become the principal political issue in England during the 1690s. Although the misgivings of xenophobic Englishmen about the wisdom of continental involvement were never completely satisfied, opposition to William's war was never so strong as that which developed to Anne's war later. However, in the 1690s there was plenty of room for disagreement about the conduct and expense of the war. Controversy about the vast amounts of money that were poured into supporting a large army in Flanders, and allegations about corruption and maladministration in the running of the war were constant themes in the parliaments of wartime England.

It soon became clear that this controversy cut across the Whig–Tory political alignment that had persisted from the Exclusion Crisis to the dissolution of the Convention in 1690. Most notably in the meetings of the commission of public accounts, former Whig and Tory opponents discovered that they had a great deal in common. Paul Foley, Robert Harley and their Whig associates led the way in working with Tory MPs to attempt to curb the financial extravagance of the crown and to secure some parliamentary restraints on government expenditure. Moreover, as time went on, country Whigs and Tories united on a wider programme of attempting to check the power of the crown by securing many of the constitutional demands which had been put forward in February 1689 but which had been omitted from the Declaration of Rights, including frequent parliaments that were free of royally appointed placemen, and an independent judiciary. It must be strongly emphasized that the emergence of this new political alignment of country Whigs and Tories was

---

[32] For the effects of the war on the constitution, see pp. 465–75.

very gradual, and that it never developed the cohesion that later commentators have ascribed to it by describing it as 'the Country Party'. Nor is it strictly true that Robert Harley was the 'leader' of this political group. Certainly, until he first headed the ballot for membership of the commission of public accounts in 1694, he was a junior member of the commission, and even then he was only one of its leaders, along with the more experienced Foley and Sir Thomas Clarges.[33] These qualifications, however, should not be allowed to obscure the fact that under the pressure of war the old Whig and Tory parties disintegrated and a new pattern in English politics began to appear.

It would be wrong to exaggerate the sharpness of the break in the pattern of politics between the Convention Parliament and William's first parliament which assembled in March 1690. But after 1690 the clashes between Whigs and Tories, raking over the feuds of the Exclusion Crisis and its aftermath, which had characterized the Convention, are not so prominent. In May 1690, William succeeded in getting passed an Act of Grace, pardoning all but a handful for their activities before 1688, which he had failed to do in the Convention. The new political climate was due not so much to William's attempt to dampen party strife, as to the fact that the war had introduced into politics a completely new situation which produced new responses from politicians. At first, from the crown's point of view, these responses were favourable. In the first two parliamentary sessions (March to May 1690 and October 1690 to January 1691), grants expected to produce almost £4,600,000 were approved which only fell just short of what the government had asked for. It is possible that this can be accounted for by the fact that Danby, now lord privy seal, was once again busy using his old techniques of persuasion among MPs. But Danby's influence in post-revolution politics can be exaggerated. In the competition for the king's favour he was certainly overshadowed by Secretary Nottingham. Bishop Burnet was probably nearer the mark. 'The French fleet', he wrote, 'by lying so long on our coast . . . and the King's behaviour in Ireland, as well as King James's meanness, has made so wonderful a change in all men's minds with relation to them both.'[34] The battles of Beachy Head and the Boyne had made many people in England appreciate that the war in Europe was not simply one that concerned the Dutch.

However, William's satisfaction at the parliamentary generosity in the first two sessions was tempered by the passage in December 1690 of an Act establishing a commission of public accounts. This was one of the first major constitutional changes limiting the power of the crown that came about as a result of the Glorious Revolution of the 1690s and early 1700s. Its members were chosen by parliament and it was given a general brief to examine the state of the public finances. Although William was forced by his financial needs to give his assent, he may have hoped that the commission would have split the opposition: instead it gave his critics an institutional focal point from which to snipe at the power of the court.

---

[33] J. A. Downie, 'The commission of public accounts and the formation of the country party', *E.H.R.*, XCI (1976), pp. 33–51.

[34] Quoted in Horwitz, *Parliament, Policy and Politics*, pp. 62–3.

On the face of it, though, the disparate membership of the first commission did not make this a likely outcome. Its six Whig members, notably Sir Robert Rich and Paul Foley, who had all voted for the Sacheverell clause in 1690 and came from families with strong sympathies for dissenters, contrasted oddly with their fellow commissioners, like Sir Thomas Clarges and Sir Benjamin Newland, who were staunch Anglicans.

These differences did prevent the commission working effectively at first, but gradually they were overcome and the commission became a powerful political force. After working throughout the summer of 1691, the first fruit of the commission's work was seen early in November when it presented to parliament a report which was a sweeping indictment of waste in government expenditure. Cranfield and Weston in the early seventeenth century had come to similar conclusions, which were largely ignored by James I and Charles I. War, however, gave Foley and Clarges an advantage which early seventeenth-century lord treasurers had not possessed. The commissioners used their findings to persuade a Commons' select committee to recommend cuts in the official army and navy estimates for 1692, thereby initiating regular parliamentary scrutiny of proposed government wartime spending. From now on officials were frequently summoned by the commission or by select committees of the Commons to account for the way public money had been or was to be spent. Most important of all, from 1690 and 1691 onwards it became common practice for parliament to appropriate many grants of money to specific named uses. No longer was it possible for the king or his officials to sidetrack money voted for the war for any other purpose. The successive annual commissions which were appointed until 1697 played an important role in reducing considerably the financial independence of the crown and increasing parliament's control of public finance.

The maturing alliance between country Whigs and Tories, which developed in the commission of public accounts, also resulted in a revival of the 'country' programme, which had been pressed by many MPs in the reign of Charles II and which had been restated in the 'heads' of February 1689, the preliminary version of the Declaration of Rights. The third session of William's first parliament (October 1691 to February 1692) is notable for the strong support seen in the Commons for two 'country' measures aimed at limiting the crown's ability both to determine the outcome of treason trials and to remove judges at will. Bills to protect personal liberties in these ways passed the Commons in the winter of 1691–2 and the Judges' Bill, which would have brought about an independent and salaried judiciary, passed the House of Lords as well. It is an early indication of the profound change that was coming over post-revolution Whiggery and Toryism that, apart from the Foley–Harley group, prominent Whigs opposed both measures. It was with Tory support that these measures aimed at reducing the royal prerogative made such progress. As yet, however, in both these cases the new opponents of executive power had no more permanent success than their Whig predecessors of the 1670s and early 1680s. The Treason Trial Bill was defeated in the House of Lords, and in February 1692, William used his personal veto to kill the bill restricting his power of dismissing judges. It has been suggested that the king opposed the latter bill because he was not willing to accept judges' salaries as a permanent charge on the ordinary revenue of the crown. But surely there is more to it than this. Even though he had been appointing judges 'during good behaviour' as the bill proposed, his autocratic philosophy would not let him lightly accept from parliament a statutory restriction on the royal prerogative. William never lost fully his personal control of policy-making either abroad or in England. But the prolongation of the war did force the king to accept more limitations on his prerogative power, in addition to his loss of financial independence. During the next two years William was forced to trade some of his independence in choosing his ministers and control over the summoning and dissolution of parliament in return for grants of wartime revenue.

When William's first parliament met for its fourth session in November 1692, criticism of the conduct and expense of the war was fuelled by the failure to follow up the naval victory at La Hogue and the sequence of military defeats in Flanders, culminating in the loss of Namur and the disaster at Steenkirk. That dissatisfaction did not extend to opposition to the war itself is underlined by the fact that early in this session parliament approved war expenditure of just over £4 million, cutting the official estimates of what was necessary by only a token 5 per cent. Moreover, after the Christmas recess parliament resolved to raise the bulk of the sum needed by a land tax of four shillings in the pound. This agreement to a massive 20 per cent tax on their rental income was an impressive affirmation by the landed classes of their support for the war. But it is equally clear that the majority of MPs did not want to see their money poured into the Flemish theatre of the war, or even (as Nottingham urged) into a military invasion of France, to take advantage of the disarray of the French fleet after La Hogue. On the contrary, in the parliamentary debates in the winter of 1692–3 an alternative popular war strategy emerged, in which the emphasis was primarily naval not military: a reduction of the army and withdrawal of many of the land forces from Europe, to be replaced by a series of naval attacks on the French coastline and French shipping. The principal proponent of this strategy was the high Tory Rochester, who had recently been appointed to the privy council, and he had behind him much grass-roots support from already heavily taxed and conservative landed MPs. Among the bulk of provincial country gentlemen by the end of the seventeenth century it was a common (though arguably wrong) assumption that naval warfare was cheaper than expenditure on a large European army. Moreover, through a romantic haze many English MPs looked back to the naval victories of Elizabeth's day against the Spanish, and of Charles II's reign against the Dutch (conveniently forgetting the Medway debacle). As will be seen, this 'blue-water' strategy was to become a prominent part of Tory ideology throughout the wars against France (see below, pp. 424–30).

In the 1692–3 parliamentary session, dissatisfaction with the war produced mounting attacks on Admiral Russell, who was forced to resign, and on Secretary Nottingham. It also gave impetus to the campaign to secure legislation designed to curb the power of the crown. At the end of December 1692 a Place Bill, which excluded from the Commons all MPs who were elected after February 1693 and who were office-holders, passed the House of Commons and only failed in the Lords by a couple of votes. Significantly, this was a measure which had been a favourite Whig one in the reign of Charles II, but which was now pressed by Tory MPs and their country Whig allies. This alliance had even more success when a Triennial Bill passed both Houses, forcing William III to use his veto to kill the bill at the end of the parliamentary session on 14 March 1693.

By the spring of 1693, William's constant disillusionment with English politics had reached a new nadir. His ministers, Nottingham and Danby, had so far secured for him adequate war supplies, but the previous parliamentary session must have caused the king to wonder how much longer MPs would continue to finance a war strategy of which they were becoming intensely suspicious without major royal concessions such as triennial and place legislation. It was at this time that William, therefore, began to consider appointing new ministers who might be able to devise new means of financing the war and to provide more able leadership in parliament. This was the course of action urged by the earl of Sunderland, whose career is remarkable even in an age not short of examples of men of abundant political agility. The earl of Shaftesbury's survival despite changing regimes has been commented on, though perhaps his career is not as atypical as it seems at first sight. Danby's political career is also remarkable for its length, which even three impeachments could not curtail, but his power after 1689 was but a pale shadow of that which he had exercised in the 1670s. Sunderland, on the contrary, despite having committed himself fully to James II in the 1680s, returned to a position of influence in the counsels of William III, arguably greater than that he had held during the previous reign.

Nevertheless Sunderland at first had little success in persuading William to abandon his present ministers and appoint new ones. Partly, this is to be explained by William's personal dislike of the principal Whig contenders for office, Sir John Somers, Thomas Wharton, Charles Montague, Admiral Edward Russell and Sir John Trenchard. Wharton especially had a scandalous private life and a reputation for irreligion that was to alienate Anne perhaps even more than William. The king, too, found it difficult to overlook the connection of these ambitious young Whig politicians with republican ideas. 'He believed the Whigs loved him best,' William is reported to have said, 'but they did not love monarchy, and although the Tories did not like him so well as the others, yet as they were zealous for monarchy he thought they would serve his government best.'[35] Above all, William was reluctant to abandon both his resolve to appoint men regardless of party affiliations and his independence in choosing his own ministers. Early in 1693 he appointed Somers as lord keeper and Trenchard as secretary of state, but he adamantly refused to go further. Sunderland, however, schemed assiduously during the summer during William's usual absence on the Continent. Late in August he convened a meeting at his house at Althorp in Northamptonshire attended by Russell, Wharton, Montague and the earls of Shrewsbury and Devonshire, and when William returned to England late in October he was met by intensified pressure to accept Sunderland's advice. He reluctantly conceded that Nottingham's dismissal was

---

[35] Quoted in J. P. Kenyon, *The Stuarts* (Fontana paperback edn., 1966), p. 174.

the least that was necessary to secure parliamentary supply in the forthcoming session; Nottingham surrendered his seals of office to his fellow secretary, Trenchard, on 6 November, the day before parliament reassembled. The 1693–4 session, however, showed that more than this was needed to divert the parliamentary opposition from its programme of constitutional legislation. The Triennial, Treason Trial and Place Bills of previous sessions were all revived and the latter this time passed both Houses. In January 1694 William's veto was again used and this provoked the Commons to pass a motion that whoever had advised William to use the veto was 'an enemy to their Majesties and the kingdom'.

After these parliamentary setbacks, William at last heeded Sunderland's advice by making a succession of Whig appointments, Shrewsbury as secretary of state instead of Nottingham, Russell as sole admiral in March, and Montague as chancellor of the exchequer in April. Furthermore, four prominent Whig earls, Shrewsbury, Devonshire, Bedford and Newcastle, were promoted to dukedoms. (The Tory earl Danby was promoted duke of Leeds at the same time.) When William left for his subsequent summer visit to the Continent in May, Sidney, Lord Godolphin was excluded from Queen Mary's inner cabinet which was dominated by Whigs, and the king gave his permission for Shrewsbury, Trenchard and Somers to purge the customs and excise commissions and fill the vacancies with their supporters.

In favouring this group of young Whig politicians in these ways, William was strongly swayed by the fact that some of them had close links with the City and had proved to be extremely able in financial matters. With parliamentary grants for the war under increasing criticism on the grounds that they were being spent with Dutch rather than English interests in mind, William had every incentive to explore new means of financing the war. The result was the beginning of 'a financial revolution' that was to change the nature of the English constitution radically and permanently.

Information

The 'financial revolution' of 1693–1694

This was the achievement of 'the Whig Junto', the young Whig politicians now favoured by William III. Two of the many financial schemes they devised have become permanent features of British government finance:

- the National Debt, which had its origins in the Million Loan Act of January 1693
- the Bank of England, created by the Tonnage Act of April 1694.

> The constitutional significance of these measures will be explained in detail later (pp. 470–2). But it is worth pointing out two important points about them now:
>
> - These financial measures enabled the crown to borrow money on a scale never seen before, and thus enabled England under William III and Queen Anne to become a major European superpower alongside France for the first time.
> - This advantage was secured by the crown only by making huge constitutional concessions. In 1693–4 the king's debt had become a National Debt. Loans were now underwritten, not by a worthless royal promise of repayment, but by a parliamentary guarantee to do so. As a result, regular parliaments were necessary to service the National Debt (as they still are today) and this limitation on the crown's power of calling and dismissing parliaments at will was the constitutional price it was forced to pay for 'the financial revolution'.

The constitutional significance of these measures was lasting; their importance in the politics of William's reign is that they were essentially Whig creations in which Montague played a leading (if not a sole) role. Tory opposition, led by Rochester, Halifax and Nottingham (though not by Danby), condemned the new bank as 'fit only for republics',[36] but was not able to prevent the beginnings of a 'financial revolution' that brought immediate advantages to William III. Certainly the king felt it was more than coincidental that these Whig financial measures were succeeded by an improvement in the military situation, culminating in the recapture of Namur in August 1695. Moreover, events in 1693 and 1694 may have led him to doubt his original assessment that the new Whigs 'did not love monarchy'. Lack of evidence such as full accounts of parliamentary debates and personal letters and papers precludes certainty on this point, but (with the exception of Shrewsbury) all the new Whig ministers appear to have adopted towards the proposed constitutional legislation of 1693–4 an attitude which was at best ambiguous. Shrewsbury is the exception without doubt. When he became secretary of state in March 1694, he did so only on the understanding that William would withdraw his objection to a Triennial Bill. In the debates on a bill for annual parliaments in December 1693, Montague was unreservedly opposed and he rejected all medieval precedents in its favour. 'That of annual parliaments', said Montague, 'is as much an antiquated law as any – annual parliaments were never insisted upon – when perhaps it will not be in the king's power to dissolve. You are setting up a Senate of Venice.'[37] In the debates on the Triennial Bill a year later, when William, as he had promised, gave the bill his assent, the voices of the new Whig ministers apart from Shrewsbury were curiously silent.

---

[36] Quoted in Horwitz, *Parliament, Politics and Policy*, p. 131.
[37] Quoted in Kenyon, *Revolution Principles*, p. 43.

The year 1694 is significant in the history of Britain after the Glorious Revolution. In the development of the constitution, 1694 saw the introduction of the principle that parliament should in future underwrite government debts; consequently, annual parliaments were needed thereafter to maintain the monarchy's financial credit. If this was in any doubt, the Triennial Act was a further reminder that the pressure of war was forcing William to concede more of the crown's constitutional powers than ideally he would have liked. Henceforth parliaments were to meet once in every three years at least, no parliament was to last longer than three years, and the gap between the dissolution of a parliament and the issuance of writs for a new one ought not to be greater than three years.

But 1694 was also a significant year in the history of domestic politics as well as in the development of the constitution. The Triennial Act ensured that politics remained unstable until its repeal in 1716. It also saw 'the last stand made by any Whig leader [Shrewsbury] to secure major constitutional change on behalf of the independence of the legislature'.[38] As the 'new' Whigs dissociated themselves from their radical past, the alliance between Foley and Harley's 'old Whigs' and the Tories became increasingly close. The last years of William's war were to see this new pattern in English politics more evident than ever before.

War and politics: the rise of the Junto Whigs, 1695–1697

During the last years of William's war, political alignments at Westminster along Whig and Tory lines were much clearer than at any time since the Convention of 1689–90. Yet in one crucial respect the Whigs and Tories of the mid-1690s were different from their predecessors immediately before and after the Glorious Revolution. 'By an odd reverse', wrote Burnet, 'the Whigs, who were now employed, argued for the prerogative, while the Tories seemed zealous for public liberty.'[39] It would be a mistake to think that the Foley–Harley 'country' Whigs had been fully absorbed by the Tories and that their association with the 'new' Whigs was totally cut, but on many issues the 'country' Whigs had much in common with the Tories. The first few existing division lists for the reign of William III (for the 1695–6 and 1696–7 sessions of William's second parliament) suggest that by 1696 there had occurred 'the virtual completion of the process whereby a House of Commons divided into court and country parties, each with its Whig and Tory members, has been replaced by one in which Whig and Court on the one hand, and Tory and Country on the other, are synonymous terms'.[40]

Certainly the main characteristic of the leaders of the 'new' Whigs, Somers, Montague, Wharton and Russell, whom contemporaries began from the spring of 1695 to label derogatorily the 'Junto', was their desire to control the patronage and

---

[38] J. H. Plumb, *The Growth of Political Stability in England 1675–1725* (1967), p. 134.
[39] Quoted in B. W. Hill, *The Growth of Parliamentary Parties 1689–1742* (1976), p. 68.
[40] I. F. Burton, P. W. J. Riley and E. Rowlands, *Political Parties in the Reigns of William III and Anne: the evidence of division lists* (*B.I.H.R.*, Special Supplement, no. 7, 1968), p. 33.

government of the king. Their appetite for power was more apparent than their adherence to principle. It would be difficult to imagine any less likely inheritors of the Good Old Cause. By 1694 the Junto Whigs' unqualified support for the war and their rejection of anti-prerogative principles had been rewarded by appointment to government offices. The Junto Whigs, however, had not succeeded in their aim of totally dominating the king's government. They never did so: William was too determined to maintain his own control of his government to allow that to happen. However, during the next three years the combined value of the members of the Junto in providing money for the war forced William to allow them to increase their hold on his government. Unlike the 'Cabal' of Charles II's reign, the Junto of William III's reign was united enough (despite differences of personality and temperament) and organized enough to secure by 1697 'a qualified form of party government'.[41] Nevertheless, the years from 1695 to 1697, as well as revealing the reasons why the Junto were able to achieve this dominating position, also indicate why this dominance was never total and why, once the war ended, it was quickly lost.

The obstacles preventing the Junto Whigs from controlling the king's government in the mid-1690s were daunting. Not only was William's personal power still great, despite the development of a 'cabinet council' in the early years of the war, but the king also never overcame the repugnance and suspicion he felt for the members of the Junto. This partly accounts for Sunderland's close relationship with William at this time. In the king's eyes, Sunderland's greatest asset was that he was independent of the Junto, and so in a position to use the parliamentary skill and financial expertise of the Junto without allowing them a dominating position. In this respect Sunderland's role, acting in close collaboration with the king and independent of political groups in parliament, was that developed in Anne's reign by later royal 'managers', especially Godolphin, Marlborough and Harley (see below, pp. 416–20). Arguably an even greater obstacle faced by the Junto than Sunderland's influence at court was that their support in parliament and in the country was limited. It is a fact of supreme importance, for Anne's reign as well as William's, that until 1715 the 'new' Whigs were a minority party in English politics. Their main political stronghold was the House of Lords. In the lower House and in the country at large, they were less popular. In the 1690s they had in Montague and Wharton two superb parliamentary managers, but both had to face growing popular opposition to the royal policies with which the Junto Whigs had associated themselves. In the Commons, the influence of Montague and Wharton was rivalled by that of Foley and Harley, who voiced the growing indignation felt by the bulk of landed MPs at England's escalating involvement in a full-scale continental war, and its effects: soaring land taxes, the new power of the Bank of England and the 'monied interest', the persistent favour shown to William's Dutch favourites, and the growth of executive power.

In the last session of William's first parliament (January to May 1695), this popular opposition became more intense, partly because the danger of James II's return had

---

[41] Ellis, 'William III and the politicians', in Holmes, ed., *Britain After the Glorious Revolution*, p. 131.

apparently receded, but mainly because of the death of Queen Mary at the end of December 1694. Throughout their joint reigns, Mary's influence on her husband had been slight, but her mere presence as queen had reconciled many doubters to the new monarchy. Mary's death effectively removed any inhibitions many Tory MPs had felt about attacking the new regime. In January 1695, Nottingham for the first time since his dismissal mounted a full-scale parliamentary attack on the government's war strategy and on the 'evils' of the Bank of England. It is a significant indication of the Junto's weakness in the House of Commons that they were only successful when they allied with this 'country' opposition. In the spring of 1695, the commission of public accounts made a series of allegations of corruption against Henry Guy, a treasury secretary, and Sir John Trevor, the speaker of the House of Commons, who were accused of receiving bribes from the City of London and the East India Company. With Wharton's and Montague's encouragement, the attack widened to include Danby among its targets, and in April, for the third time in his career, articles of impeachment were drawn up against him. William III, like Charles II twice before, dissolved parliament to save Danby.

There is little evidence that the general election of October 1695 significantly improved the Junto Whigs' parliamentary position. In the first session of the new parliament (November 1695 to April 1696), Harley's influence was greater than ever; he received the highest number of votes of those elected to the 1696 commission of public accounts. The Junto was not able to prevent the government from coming under attack on many fronts, forcing William to grant many concessions. In order to divert demands for a parliamentary-nominated council of trade, in December 1695 William established his own council by royal order. After the Christmas recess, the king gave way with ill grace to a Commons' request that the grants of Irish land to Portland be stopped. 'I will find some other way of showing my favour to him', he said.[42] Also in January, William at last gave his assent to a Treason Trials Act. Most serious of all, from the Junto Whigs' point of view, Foley and Harley piloted through parliament in the spring of 1696 an Act establishing a Land Bank, which was set up as a direct competitor of the Bank of England. Indeed, the promoters of the Land Bank, in promising to raise over £2.5 million by subscription, appealed directly to the landed interest, because those who had subscribed to the Bank of England were specifically excluded from participating in the Land Bank scheme.

Why, then, did the fortunes of the Junto Whigs revive in the last eighteen months of the war? There were three major reasons. First, although William never totally lost his repugnance for the Junto lords or for party government, he was forced to recognize that only the Junto had an effective solution to the financial needs of the war. The Land Bank scheme was a total failure. It raised only a fraction of its promised £2 million subscription, and the Bank of England had to step in with a large loan, once more emphasizing the Whigs' financial value to William. Already during the winter of 1695–6, Montague had steered through parliament a scheme to introduce a reformed coinage. Furthermore, in the spring of 1697 the Bank of England again provided the

---

[42] Quoted in Horwitz, *Parliament, Policy and Politics*, p. 164.

solution to a severe liquidity crisis by another large loan. In return, in April 1697 an Act was passed incorporating the bank, allowing it to increase its capital stock by another £1 million, and giving it a monopoly of joint-stock banking until 1710. Secondly, not only did the Junto Whigs improve their position at court by their achievement of a Whig financial revolution, but for a brief period they found themselves in 1696 in an unusually popular position in the House of Commons. In February 1696 the revelation of a plot to assassinate the king gave the Whigs (as in 1679) an opportunity to discredit their opponents. The Tories of 1696, however, were in a much more vulnerable position than those of 1679. When in response to the assassination plot the Commons adopted a motion that all MPs should take an oath of loyalty to William as 'the rightful and lawful king', all the Tory doubts of 1689 were revived in an extreme form. About ninety MPs refused to take the oath and in the Lords nineteen peers, including Nottingham, refused to make a similar declaration. In April 1696 it was made compulsory for all office-holders to take the 'association' oath, and William gave his support for a full-scale purge of all non-subscribers from the lieutenancy and commission of the peace, and their replacement with Whig nominees. That the Junto Whigs were able to exploit to the full this fortunate turn of events points to a third reason for their success in 1696–7: the effective organization of their supporters both at Westminster and in the localities. Much of this organization was informal – private meetings of ministers to discuss parliamentary strategy and drum up support among individual MPs – and therefore is ill documented. Undoubtedly though these private meetings did take place, as well as the more formal meetings of Whig supporters before crucial parliamentary occasions at the Rose Tavern, near Covent Garden, which were common from the autumn of 1696 onwards.

The parliamentary session of October 1696 to April 1697 is one of the few examples of Whig ascendancy from 1690 to 1714. In November 1696 the Junto's control of the Commons secured majorities in favour of an attainder bill against Sir John Fenwick, who had been arrested in connection with the assassination plot, and the rejection of Fenwick's counter-accusations against Shrewsbury and Russell. Significantly, in this session also the political power of the Junto's opponents was undermined when the commission of public accounts was not continued in 1697. At the end of the session, William recognized the Whig ascendancy by promoting Somers to a barony and the lord chancellorship, Russell to the earldom of Orford, and Montague to be first lord of the treasury. The Junto held power and influence which they were not to attain again until another brief period in 1708–9. The end of the war was to show that they could not maintain their ascendancy in peacetime.

Peace and politics: the collapse of the Junto, 1697–1701

Even in the last phase of William's war, the Junto's political position in parliament and at court had not been secure. Their influence in the lower House was weakened considerably by the promotion of Somers and Russell to the House of Lords, where they joined Wharton, who had succeeded to his father's barony in February 1696. Sunderland's emergence at the same time from 'behind the curtain' to become lord chamberlain emphasized the continued power of their rival at court. It was, however, the end of the war which brought about the downfall of the Junto Whigs, who had risen to power as the party of war and a strong executive. The Treaty of Ryswick released a popular conservative reaction of pacifism and provincialism: a demand to end England's military involvement in Europe and to return power to the traditional rulers of provincial England. Like the county committees fifty years before, the Junto Whigs were considered to be the symbols of centralization and arbitrary rule, and were thus swept away. The years of peace culminated in their impeachment and the Act of Settlement, a statement of provincial resentment at the growth of executive power brought about by the war.

Increasingly during the war, William and his ministers had had to work hard to convince his English subjects that his European policy was in their interests, as well as those of the Dutch. On the whole these efforts had been successful; MPs complained but voted the necessary war supplies. In peacetime, however, after 1697 William's dual position seemed less advantageous to England. Peace made the king seem more alien and less necessary to English security and political stability. Unlike his English subjects, William realized that the Treaty of Ryswick did not provide a framework for permanent European peace, since it made no attempt to solve the problem of who was to succeed the ailing Charles II of Spain. In an effort to avert a major European war, William and Louis XIV in the three years after the Treaty of Ryswick tried to settle the claims of the three principal contenders for the Spanish throne by diplomatic means. Their efforts produced two secret Partition Treaties which 'to a twentieth-century student . . . look rather like a combination of the Great Powers to enforce a rudimentary system of collective security'.[43] The first Partition Treaty signed in October 1698 arranged for the bulk of the Spanish kingdom and Empire to go to Joseph Ferdinand, the electoral prince of Bavaria, for Naples, Sicily and Guipúzcoa to go to the dauphin, and for Milan to go to Archduke Charles. Not surprisingly, Archduke Charles's father, Emperor Leopold, refused to have anything to do with this arrangement. In any case a new treaty became necessary a few months later when Joseph Ferdinand died. As a result William, again without consulting parliament, concluded with Louis XIV a second Partition Treaty in March 1700, which granted all the Spanish possessions to Archduke Charles, leaving only Naples, Sicily, Guipúzcoa and Milan to the French claimant. During the partition negotiations, William felt that it was necessary to keep a large part of his army mobilized in order to strengthen his hand in the diplomatic manoeuvres, as well as to be ready for the war that would inevitably follow if the negotiations failed.

When the Partition Treaties were made public in England in the summer of 1700, they roused a storm of opposition. Before then, however, all that was generally known about William's policies was his intention to maintain the army at its wartime strength.

---

[43] M. A. Thomson, 'Self-determination and collective security as factors in English and French foreign policy, 1689–1718', in Hatton and Bromley, eds., *William III and Louis XIV*, p. 276.

It was therefore on the question of the standing army that the great gulf between William's European outlook and the insular pacifism of most of his subjects first became clear. 'There is a deadness and want of spirit in the nation universally', wrote Somers in the summer of 1698, 'so as not at all to be disposed to the thought of entering into a new war and that they seem to be tired out with taxes.'[44] It was not just high taxation that accounted for the anti-war sentiments of many after 1697, although the land tax, especially in the highly assessed southern and eastern counties, was greatly resented. Many people felt that the Treaty of Ryswick had removed the principal cause of England's quarrel with France: Louis XIV had recognized William as king of England. Moreover, the peace was seen as a marvellous opportunity to minimize all connections with the hated Dutch. To memories of three Anglo-Dutch wars over the previous fifty years and a long history of commercial rivalry were now added William's frequent visits to the Dutch republic and his apparent reliance on Dutch advisers. Like James I's favourites at the beginning of the century, William's Dutch entourage became the focus for an outbreak of escalating national xenophobia. In these circumstances it is debatable whether a concerted effort by William to explain that English interests were inextricably bound up with his efforts to secure European agreement about a Spanish succession would have made any headway. His failure to do this, or at least to inform his ministers of his activities, made harder than it might have been the Junto lords' task of defending in parliament his intention of keeping most of his army mobilized.

For all these reasons, many Whigs who had supported the Junto in the latter stages of the war joined with Tories in the attack on William's standing army in the last session of William's second parliament (December 1697 to July 1698) and the first session of his third parliament (December 1698 to May 1699). To a large extent Whig and Tory divisions are difficult to see in these sessions as the vast majority of MPs united, not only to oppose standing armies, but also to support the traditional 'country' pro-gramme of place legislation, enquiries into mismanagement of the war, and so on. Consequently, it has become fairly common for historians to write about this inter-war period as being dominated by a 'New Country Party' led by Robert Harley. Again, as in the early 1690s, this is an analysis which implies too much party organization and gives too much credit to Harley's manipulation of opinion. It is true that Harley was now no longer overshadowed by his colleagues; Foley, for example, was an ill man and died in 1699. But it seems likely that Harley did not need to manipulate MPs. There was already in parliament a *spontaneous* groundswell of opinion in favour of reducing taxation, and against English entanglement on the Continent and the inter-ference of foreigners in English government. Harley's achievement was to recognize the strength of this opinion in the country and to marshal it behind him with the principal aim of removing the Junto lords from office. Beyond that, Harley's aims are less clear-cut. Especially uncertain is the degree of his association with the high Tory leaders, Rochester, Nottingham and Seymour.[45] There is little evidence that at this

---

[44] Quoted in Horwitz, *Parliament, Policy and Politics*, p. 240.
[45] It is doubtful if Harley ought at any stage in his career to be classified as a Tory, let alone as the Tories' leader. See below, pp. 449–51. For a different view, see Hill, *Growth of Parliamentary Parties*, p. 85.

stage he wanted office for himself. In this respect he was still typical of most MPs in the seventeenth century, who were inherently distrustful of central government and who therefore favoured a negative programme of limiting the power of that government, with little attempt to recognize the practical problems of government, let alone produce constructive suggestions to overcome them. It was not until 1704 that Harley accepted the challenge of ministerial office.

Before parliament met in December 1697, for the first time after the conclusion of peace, the arguments against standing armies had been well rehearsed in pamphlet literature.[46] Standing armies were unnecessarily expensive. The navy was all that was needed for the security of an island nation. Above all, did English experience from the time of Cromwell to the reign of James II not teach that standing armies were the bulwark of absolutism? Significantly, the co-authors of the most famous anti-army pamphlet, *An Argument, Showing a Standing Army is Inconsistent with a Free Government*, John Trenchard and Walter Moyle, were 'old' Whigs who were steeped in republican theories. Their republicanism, however, was clothed in the respectable guise of admiration for ancient Rome and proved no obstacle to their association with more conservatively minded MPs. Even Harley gave Trenchard information to include in his influential pamphlet, *A Short History of Standing Armies*, published in November 1698.[47] The arguments did not fall on deaf ears. On 10 December 1697 the Commons passed a resolution that all forces raised since September 1680 should be disbanded, which would have effectively cut the size of the army in England to 8,000 men. In addition, the opposition pressed home its attacks on William's advisers. As a result Sunderland resigned at the end of December, and five bills for the resumption of all royal grants since 1660, introduced in the Commons in February 1698, were aimed directly at the king's Dutch favourites. The Junto, too, faced enormous political opposition. As yet, however, they survived. Although they had made no effort to protect Sunderland, they were too valuable to William to be sacrificed. This was emphasized in the way the Junto piloted the East India Bill through parliament in the last months of William's second parliament. The charter of the old East India Company was revoked and a new company established, which promised to lend the government £2 million at 8 per cent interest. This and the fact that the money was quickly raised reinforced William's natural inclination not to allow parliament to dictate who his ministers should be. It took two subsequent stormy sessions of a new parliament to force him to change his mind.

The general election of the summer of 1698 must have brought home to William the realization that the new parliament would not be any more amenable to Junto management than the old one. Many local elections were characterized by anti-court propaganda, and when parliament met in December 1698, William's renewed request for supply to maintain the army at its wartime level provoked a Commons' resolution

---

[46] See L. G. Schwoerer, *'No Standing Armies!' The antiarmy ideology in seventeenth-century England* (1974), especially ch. 8.
[47] Kenyon, *Revolution Principles*, p. 54.

that the army should be reduced to 7,000 men, and that these were to be not foreigners but 'natural born subjects of England'. Not surprisingly, William sank into another of his periodic depressions, caused by what he considered to be the unreasonable behaviour of English politicians. As in 1690 his letters home to his Dutch confidants imply that he was toying with thoughts of abdication. At least that is the obvious interpretation of his dark threats of taking 'resolutions of extremity' and 'steps that will amaze' parliament in December–January 1698–9. In January the Disbanding Bill, putting into effect the Commons' resolution to reduce the size of the army, passed both Houses. In the remainder of this parliamentary session (to 5 May 1699) and in the next (16 November 1699 to 11 April 1700), the Junto's position collapsed after a succession of ministerial defeats. The resignation of Orford (Russell) from the admiralty in May 1699 was preceded by the rapid parliamentary progress of a new Place Bill, a parliamentary inquiry into his administration of the navy, and a successful move to tack an amendment appointing a commission to investigate William's grants in Ireland on to a land tax bill. Before parliament met again in November, Montague resigned from the treasury. Somers remained in office and even rode out a parliamentary storm in December over allegations that he was partly responsible for the activities of Captain William Kidd, who had turned pirate after being sent to the Indian Ocean to protect East India Company merchants. But it became clear that Somers would not survive long, as a bill to resume all royal grants of Irish land since February 1688 made rapid progress in parliament, and the Commons, on 10 April 1700, resolved that the king should eject all foreigners from his councils. For William this was the last straw. He prorogued parliament on 11 April and later in the month Somers, who refused to resign, was dismissed from his office of lord chancellor.

Even now William delayed accepting the logic of the situation and appointing ministers from among those who commanded such wide support in parliament. What forced him to do so, however, was the uncertainty about the succession brought about by the death of the eleven-year-old duke of Gloucester at the end of July 1700. It therefore became very urgent that arrangements should be agreed for the succession in the likely eventuality that both William and Anne would die childless. When William returned from his usual summer visit to the Continent in October, he had meetings with Rochester, Godolphin and Harley of which no formal record survives but at which there is little doubt that William agreed to dissolve the existing parliament, appoint Tories to office and pass an Act establishing the succession and embodying further limitations on the power of the crown. Consequently, in December parliament was dissolved, Nottingham's nominee, Sir Charles Hedges, became secretary of state, Rochester was appointed lord lieutenant of Ireland, and Godolphin was promoted to first lord of the treasury.

When parliament met in February 1701, these new appointments were the only visible important changes from the last parliament. Harley's election to the speakership of the new House of Commons stressed that its preoccupations would be the same as those of its predecessor: peace and limitations on the power of the crown. The long-awaited death of King Charles II of Spain in November 1700, the publication of his will leaving his kingdoms and empire to Louis XIV's grandson, Philip of Anjou, and Louis XIV's public acceptance of the will in November, failed to change the prevailing mood of pacifism in England. Many, indeed, believed that the will provided a good guarantee of European peace and English security, since Charles II had left his throne to Philip of Anjou on the condition that the crowns of France and Spain would never be united. Moreover, the Partition Treaties had now been published and this served also to increase support in England for acceptance of Charles II's will. Not only did both Partition Treaties favour French traders in the Mediterranean by granting France Naples and Sicily, but the fact that they had been conducted in secrecy also precipitated a major parliamentary attack on the king's ministers, culminating in impeachment proceedings against Portland and the Junto lords, Somers, Orford and Montague (who had been created Baron Halifax in December 1700). The second major concern of the new parliament was to put into practice the agreement reached between William, Harley and the Tories in the previous autumn. The result was the Act of Settlement, which received the royal assent on 12 June.

Information

The Act of Settlement, 1701

The Act's main provisions were as follows:

- The successors to the throne after the deaths of William, Anne and any children they might have were to be Protestant and Hanoverian, in the shape of the progeny of James I's daughter, Elizabeth, the wife of the elector palatine, namely Sophia, electress of Hanover and her heirs, who were required 'to joyn in Communion with the Church of England as by Law established'.
- Office-holders were not to sit in parliament.
- All government matters should be transacted openly in the privy council.
- Judges should hold their offices during good behaviour and with fixed salaries.
- Monarchs after Anne's death should not leave the country without parliamentary consent.
- An English monarch of foreign descent should not take England into a war for the defence of lands that did not belong to the English crown.
- All foreigners were excluded from the privy council, office or place in parliament.

The only one of these that came into effect was the first one. The others were all repealed either before or after 1714.

Party issues redefined, 1701–1702

The last twelve months of William's reign witnessed a remarkable transformation in English politics. After the end of William's war, opinion in England had turned decisively and unanimously against the effects of war and involvement in Europe. The Whig and Tory alignment of English politics, which had existed during the latter stages of the war, became blurred and indistinct as the nation united in favour of peace and withdrawal from Europe. But during the course of 1701 this unanimity was shattered by the reappearance of controversies about the renewal of war, the succession to the throne, and the state of the Church; these formed the basis of Whig and Tory rivalries which were to last throughout the reign of Queen Anne.

War and the succession

The most important determinant of political change, as in the earlier part of the reign, was war. Dramatically, in the spring and summer of 1701 public opinion in England swung in favour of a renewed war against France. The pacifism seen in the first weeks of William's fourth parliament evaporated and within five months of its first meeting it voted large grants of money to finance the war (2 June) and agreed to support any alliances which William might make (12 June). This conversion was brought about almost entirely by the provocative actions of Louis XIV; as in 1685, decisions Louis made in Europe had a decisive and unforeseen impact on English opinion. As has been seen, many in England believed that Louis's acceptance of Charles II's will would not endanger England's security. Louis effectively destroyed that belief by persuading the French courts to recognize the right of the new Spanish king, Philip of Anjou, to succeed to the French throne if his elder brother should die, by forcibly taking over key towns in the Spanish Netherlands, and by announcing a series of embargoes on English trade with France and Spain. Fortunately, the difficult task of finding a convincing explanation for Louis's action is not one for students of English history.[48] What is certain is that they made clear, in a way William by himself could not do, that Louis's expansionist aims in Europe were a threat to English interests.

This point was hammered home in England by a sustained propaganda campaign outside parliament in favour of war, which culminated early in May in the presentation to parliament of the Kentish Petition and the *Legion Memorial*. The former was drafted at the Maidstone Quarter Sessions on 29 April; the latter, allegedly representing the views of 'many thousands of the good people of England', was the work of Daniel Defoe. At least two other counties, Warwickshire and Cheshire, also presented urgent demands that parliament support William against France. This campaign so suited the king that historians have been tempted to believe that William inspired it and that he employed Defoe's literary talents for the purpose. Unfortunately, the evidence to support the latter view is weak, though the connection between Defoe and the Junto is

---

[48] See Gibbs, 'The revolution in foreign policy', p. 71 for a suggested explanation.

better documented.[49] There is no reason to doubt that both the king and the Junto at least condoned, if they did not initiate, the popular war movement. Perhaps, though, historians, like many Tories in the House of Commons at the time, have been too anxious to see these events in terms of the manipulation of public opinion. In May a majority in the Commons voted the Kentish Petition 'scandalous insolent and seditious and tending to destroy the constitution of parliament', and condemned the petitioners as 'tools of the ministry'.[50] But perhaps this criticism misses the point. Provincial England, as well as the capital, was well provided with foreign news by the many newspapers which had appeared in the years after the lapse of the Licensing Act in 1695. 'By 1700 the reading of newspapers had become a settled habit in England', writes G. C. Gibbs, 'and . . . the habit was not confined to a ruling minority.'[51] It is possible that volatile public opinion responded as much to what was written in newspapers as to persuasion by the king or his Junto ministers. The same is possibly true of the majority of MPs. Although some Tories pressed ahead with the impeachment proceedings against the Junto lords, there was no strong parliamentary opposition to the war by the time parliament was prorogued in June 1701. Any who did still have doubts were silenced early in September when James II died, and Louis XIV made another, impolitic decision and publicly recognized James III as king of England. Consequently, the new MPs, elected in November, assembled at Westminster on the last day of the year temporarily united in favour of war. It was a Tory, Edward Seymour, who successfully moved that a clause be added to the Grand Alliance, which had been negotiated between England, the United Provinces and the emperor at the end of August, that the allies should continue the war until Louis XIV recognized the Protestant succession in England. In addition, the Grand Alliance sought to curtail French power first by securing the Spanish Netherlands as a barrier to protect the Dutch Republic, secondly by ejecting French troops from the Italian possessions of Spain and the Empire, and lastly by ensuring that the thrones of Spain and France remained permanently separate.

However, differences between Whigs and Tories about the war did not take long to develop, as Tory scepticism about continental wars soon reappeared. Significantly, William in the autumn of 1701 began to think in terms of a return to a Junto ministry which had proved so successful in obtaining finance for the war of the 1690s. This inclination must have been confirmed by new evidence of Tory uncertainty about the Protestant succession. Whereas the enthusiasm of Whigs for the war was based on their full commitment to a Protestant succession, many Tories at Westminster and in the provinces soon made it apparent that, despite all their protestations, their support of a Protestant succession, and therefore of a war designed to secure such a succession, was less than wholehearted. This became clear in the Tory reaction to the Abjuration Act, agreed on in February 1702, which obliged all office-holders, members of the

---

[49] Kenyon, *Revolution Principles*, p. 57.
[50] Quoted in Horwitz, *Parliament, Policy and Politics*, p. 289.
[51] Gibbs, 'The revolution in foreign policy', p. 73.

Houses of Lords and Commons, clergymen, dissenting ministers, teachers and lawyers to take an oath repudiating the Pretender. The oath caused the earl of Nottingham such an agony of indecision that he only took it after a delay of two months and not before he had been assured by the archbishop of York that 'you are left as much at liberty after you have taken this oath'.[52] Other MPs took the oath in a similar pragmatic spirit. 'The Jacks . . . should never be able to do any thing if they . . . did not take all the oaths that could be imposed', said a future MP for Southwark.[53] Among Tories outside the Westminster limelight there was even more resistance to the Abjuration oath, and this was reflected in an attempt in Anne's first parliament (1702–3) to provide a bill to extend by a year the time limit for taking the oath. Clearly many Tories had still not cut their ties with theories of divine right monarchy. This fact was of supreme importance in explaining why the Tories failed in the next reign to capitalize on the widespread support they enjoyed in the country on other issues. It also helps to explain why before the end of William's reign the war and the succession were joint issues on which Whig and Tory opinions polarized at opposite extremes.

The Church

To some extent Tory uneasiness about the long-term succession to the throne in the last months of William's reign was overcome by the knowledge that the immediate successor, at least, was an Anglican Stuart princess. However, even this prospect did little to alleviate Tory fears about the future of the Church of England; indeed, as will be seen, Anne's accession gave a new lease of life to militant Anglicanism. Already throughout the 1690s Tory landowners and the mass of parish clergy were becoming increasingly anxious about the state of the Church. At the end of 1696 these submerged fears broke the political surface with the appearance of a pamphlet written by Francis Atterbury, *A Letter to A Convocation Man*. A young Oxford don, nurtured in the heady atmosphere of Anglicanism and Stuart loyalism of Christ Church College, Atterbury was a natural propagandist for the High Church cause. *A Letter to a Convocation Man* reflected all the frustration of Anglicans who, with Convocation adjourned since 1689, had no political forum in which to ventilate their grievances, and who saw the hierarchy of the Church dominated by moderate bishops intent on keeping the Church out of politics. *A Letter* demanded that Convocation be recalled on the revolutionary ground that the summoning of Convocation was the clergy's legal right and not part of the royal prerogative. Despite being condemned by Archbishop Tenison and leading bishops, Atterbury's pamphlet was seized on avidly by parish clergy and by the high Tory Rochester. When Rochester became lord lieutenant of Ireland in December 1700, he made it a condition of his acceptance of office that William give in to the growing demands of the lower clergy and their secular High Church allies. Therefore

---

[52] Quoted in Henry Horwitz, *Revolution, Politicks: the career of Daniel Finch, 2nd earl of Nottingham 1647–1730* (1968), pp. 165–6.
[53] Quoted in G. Holmes, *British Politics in the Age of Anne* (1967), p. 88.

in February 1701 Convocation met for the first time since 1689, religion again became a prime political issue, and Tories rallied to the political slogan, 'the Church in danger'.

Why did militant Anglicanism reappear with such force in the last part of William's reign? Although the vast majority of Anglicans had supported the Glorious Revolution, they had done so with troubled consciences. For Anglicans, writes Dr Bennett, the clerical nonjurors 'were like a ghost of the past, confessors who stood in the ancient ways, devout, logical and insistent'.[54] Such consciences were, therefore, easily alarmed, especially when the Glorious Revolution seemed to have allowed the rapid growth of Protestant dissent. Although, as has been seen, the Toleration Act of 1689 hardly deserves its name, it did allow licensed worship to take place outside the Church of England. Between 1689 and 1710 what must have seemed in Anglican eyes an alarmingly high number (3,614) of meeting houses of various sorts were licensed. Dissenting academies were established.[55] Moreover, the Anglican Church's monopoly of state offices as well as its predominant religious role seemed threatened by the growing practice of occasional conformity. The Test and Corporation Acts remained in being, but were evaded by nonconformists, who attended Anglican services infrequently simply to receive from the magistrate a certificate of attendance in order to qualify for public office. In November 1697 the lord mayor of London, Sir Humphrey Edwin, twice worshipped at an afternoon service at a conventicle in his full regalia of office after attending an Anglican church in the morning. Incidents like this not surprisingly provoked a bitter response from Anglicans. After decades of persecution since the Restoration, relieved only by short-lived royal experiments in toleration, Protestant dissenters apparently seemed to be flourishing.

However, it remains an open question whether dissent was a real threat to the Anglican dominance in Church and State. Was dissent ever able to withstand the competition of the Church of England for the favours of the powerful landed and mercantile classes? Since membership of the Church of England was the passport to social acceptability and a political career, it is difficult to believe that it could. But again, as on many other occasions in history, what appeared to be the truth was more important than the truth itself. To many Anglicans the Church did appear to be in danger. High Church Tories felt worried and threatened as they contrasted the apparently flourishing condition of dissent with the material poverty of the Anglican Church, which had undergone no serious economic reform despite the urging of generations of Puritans from the 1560s to the 1650s, and which more recently had been heavily hit by wartime taxation. Moreover, the size of the Church's congregations as well as its income seemed to be threatened. During the 1690s, the Church came under severe attack from novel theological doctrines. In Chapter 14 it will be seen that in the late seventeenth century, with the development of science and scientific methods, there also emerged a rational attitude to religion (see below, pp. 477–80). One aspect of this

---

[54] G. V. Bennett, *The Tory Crisis in Church and State 1688–1730: the career of Francis Atterbury, bishop of Rochester* (1975), p. 10.
[55] Ibid., p. 13.

was the appearance in the 1690s of the Deists, whose basic philosophy was that all beliefs, including the belief in God, should be the product of reason. This was the theme of John Locke's *The Reasonableness of Christianity* (1695), in which, although he recognized the importance of revelation, reason was put forward as the prime source of Christian belief. Just what this concept could mean in the hands of a less careful writer than Locke was seen when John Toland published his *Christianity Not Mysterious* in 1696. 'Whereas Locke was content to show that Christianity is reasonable, Toland proved that nothing contrary to reason and nothing above it can be a part of Christian doctrine.' Toland's book, therefore, was an explicit attack on the teaching of divines in the past and on the leadership of the Church in the present. Church ministers, wrote Toland (echoing those radicals who had criticized all professional groups during the English Revolution), used 'scholastic jargon' 'to make plain things obscure'.[56] With the lapse of the Licensing Act in 1695, radical notions like these were now easier to publicize. Another major theological line of attack on the Anglican Church was directed against the doctrine of the Trinity. Unitarians and Socinians were able to spread their ideas with the collapse of press censorship. So too were a host of less sophisticated anticlerical authors. In vain the Blasphemy Act of 1697 tried to stem the tide of words which seemed to threaten to engulf the Church.

What made all this especially shocking to many ordinary clergymen and country gentlemen alike was that the upper ecclesiastical hierarchy, far from opposing some of these heterodox ideas, seemed to share them. In the years after the Restoration, a group of Anglican divines developed a philosophy which appeared very similar to that of the Deists. These Latitudinarian divines (so called by their critics) stressed the importance of reason in religion, and reacted sharply to the 'fanaticism' and 'enthusiasm' of the religious sects of the early and mid-seventeenth century. Both Archbishop Tillotson and his successor in 1695, Archbishop Tenison, adopted this view, and in addition they saw their prime purpose as being to make the Church more spiritually effective, its strength more dependent on a reformed inner vigour than on the support of the State. Tenison especially encouraged the foundation of voluntary societies like the Society for the Promotion of Christian Knowledge and the Society for the Propagation of the Gospel in the late 1690s. His view of the Church – a Low Church view – was clearly worlds apart from that of militant High Church Anglicans who harked back to an authoritarian alliance between Church and State.[57]

When Convocation met in February 1701 there was at last a platform for all these High Church fears to be publicized. So extraordinary and violent were the attacks directed against Archbishop Tenison and his episcopal colleagues that the session had to be adjourned. But the high Tory politicians took up Convocation's demands for action against heresy and for protection for the Church. Rochester and Nottingham had little difficulty in dragging religion into the political arena and using it as a party weapon against the Whigs. Sermon after sermon pressed home the myth of King

---

[56] Quoted in G. R. Cragg, *From Puritanism to the Age of Reason* (1950), pp. 141, 148.
[57] See pp. 475–80 for an analysis of opinion within the Church of England in this period.

Charles the Martyr, which enjoyed a resurgence in the 1690s. William Lancaster's sermon to the Commons on 30 January 1697 is typical of many:

> I know not but there may be men in the world, thus left to themselves, who instead of repenting of a most horrid murder and of shedding innocent blood, have themselves and their posterity justified the doing it, and advanced from the blood of one king, to maintain the lawfulness of resisting all kings.[58]

So the identification of dissent with Whiggery and Whiggery with republicanism, which had been used so effectively by Clarendonians in the 1660s, was revived as a party weapon against the Whigs in the 1690s and early 1700s. This was a formula that was to be used by the Tories against the Whigs with explosive effect in Anne's reign. But already when William III died on 8 March 1702 (from complications which developed after he had suffered a simple collar-bone fracture in a riding accident two weeks before), English political life was torn apart by bitter party rivalry.

---

[58] Quoted in Kenyon, *Revolution Principles*, p. 72.

13

The reign of Queen Anne, 1702–1714

Politics in the reign of Queen Anne

Summary

One of the most important historical problems of the reign of Queen Anne is to clarify how the crown coped with a new, emerging constitutional system, in which its powers were being gradually eroded. In doing this it found itself obliged to work with either the Whigs or the Tories if the queen's business was to be done. Queen Anne and her advisers (her 'managers', as they were known at the time) retained enough influence to try to exercise power independent of party. But it was an attempt which by and large failed. What is surprising is that for much of her reign Queen Anne chose to work with and appoint Whig ministers and not Tories, who seemingly had views on the Church and other matters that she would find compatible with hers. Why she did that and why at the end of the reign, at a time when the Tories' position seemed very strong, the Tories collapsed as an effective force in British politics for nearly a century are questions that help tie together the themes of this chapter.

If Whigs and Tories were to cooperate, wrote Lord Stawell on 3 May 1711, 'I shall conclude the lamb will lye down with the leopard.' Changing the metaphor, Lord Halifax believed it would be like 'mixing Oyl and Vinegar (very truly)'.[1] Unlike the

---

[1] Quoted in G. Holmes, *British Politics in the Reign of Queen Anne* (1st edn., 1967; revised edn. with new introduction, 1987), p. 49.

reign of William III, there is no doubt about the continuing predominance of party rivalries during the reign of Queen Anne. The evidence of division lists, tellers' names in divisions recorded in the *Commons Journals*, and the Proxy Book of peers, which lists the names of those colleagues who were entrusted with the proxy votes of absent peers, indicates that the vast majority of MPs from 1702 to 1714 followed a consistent Whig or Tory voting pattern. Nor did most MPs follow Whig or Tory party lines only on major issues of principle, but also on minor tactical issues – on the choice of speaker and the amendment to a South Sea Company Bill, as well as on the future of the Church. Moreover, party rivalry extended beyond 'parliament. To a certain extent, smart London society polarized into separate Whig and Tory social circles. For the upper elite, the Whig Kit-Cat Club and the Tory Society of Brothers became mutually exclusive dining and drinking clubs. Less grand and more popular, many of the coffee and chocolate houses, which proliferated in London at the turn of the century, developed a reputation as either Whig or Tory establishments, the Whigs frequenting the Cocoa Tree in Pall Mall and the St James's Coffee House, the Tories Ouzinda's Chocolate House in St James's Street and the Smyrna in Pall Mall. This political apartheid was sometimes carried to comically absurd limits: in 1713 the earl of Sunderland, arriving at the house of his Whig colleague, Lord Halifax, for a dinner party, went home when he realized that Robert Harley (now earl of Oxford), who was by this time more closely identified with the Tory party than ever before, was also invited.[2]

Not surprisingly, many of the increasing number of newspapers committed themselves to one of the two major political groups. Whig newspapers, like John Tutchin's *Observator* and *The Post Man*, and Tory papers, like *The Post Boy*, *Rehearsal* and the more sophisticated *Examiner* for which Jonathan Swift wrote in 1710–11, were well versed in the techniques of party propaganda. Some of the political journalism of the day had a literary polish – Addison, Steele and Defoe, as well as Swift, contributed regularly to newspapers and journals – but its satire could be scurrilous as well as subtle, sometimes provoking a violent reaction. John Tutchin was beaten up at least twice by a Tory mob, and in September 1707 he died after being viciously attacked in the street.[3] A few newspapers published only for a London audience; the best example is *The Daily Courant*, the first daily newspaper in Britain, which began publication on 11 March 1702. Many, however, circulated widely in the provinces. It was a manuscript newsletter, produced by an army of clerks under the direction of John Dyer, that was read most avidly by both metropolitan and provincial Tory squires and parsons. It is 'very common in these northern parts', wrote William Bowes from Durham in May 1705.[4] By 1712 an estimated 67,000 copies of all newspapers were sold each week, in addition to an unknown number that were given away. The size of the readership is difficult to calculate, because it is not known how many people read each individual newspaper, but if one assumes that every newspaper circulated among ten people, the conclusion is that by the end of

---

[2] Ibid., p. 21.
[3] Kenyon, *Revolution Principles*, p. 122.
[4] Quoted in Speck, *Tory and Whig*, p. 92.

Anne's reign newspapers were read by nearly three times the number of electors.[5] Moreover, like the 1640s, the two decades after the lapse of the Licensing Act in 1695 were a golden age for printed material of all kinds published for a wide audience. The vast numbers of printed sermons, pamphlets and ballads on political issues which were published in the early 1700s, in addition to newspapers and weekly journals, helped to carry party divisions beyond Westminster and London into provincial society and politics.

Popular participation in politics was as great during the reign of Queen Anne as it had been during the Exclusion Crisis and the Glorious Revolution. Nor is there any doubt that from 1701 to 1715 political elites were also greatly affected by 'the rage of party'. As in the early 1640s and during the Exclusion Crisis, the unity of vested interests which bound the landowning classes together was shattered by ideological divisions. In the sixteenth and seventeenth centuries, competition for places in the lieutenancy, on commissions of the peace and for lesser local government offices, was always intense. But now a political element was injected into this competition, as well as considerations of patronage and social prestige. Both political parties, as will be seen, aimed to use their influence over the central government to purge the lieutenancy and magistracy of their opponents. The consequent division in county society can be most clearly seen at election times. In most counties and boroughs, elections were fought on party lines: the 'Church' or 'Tory interest' versus the 'Whig interest'. If anything, this kind of grass-roots party competition intensified during the early 1700s as election followed election; there were seven general elections between 1701 and 1715. In many counties the role of election manager was filled by powerful landed magnates, like the Whig Lord Wharton, whose sphere of influence extended from Wiltshire through Buckinghamshire and Oxfordshire to Yorkshire and Cumberland and Westmorland, or Sir Edward Seymour, who helped to maintain the Tory dominance in the south-west. In many boroughs, where there was a longer, if intermittent, history of party organization which went back to the Exclusion Crisis, it is hardly an exaggeration to talk in terms of the development of party caucuses, which endeavoured to maintain their supporters in a state of readiness for parliamentary elections. It is clear that at the local constituency level the organization of parties was much more sophisticated than at Westminster. Many of the signs of party politics familiar to historians of the late nineteenth and twentieth centuries can be seen, including party agents, party propaganda literature and canvassing. Even party symbols appeared in various forms. In 1710 (for reasons which will become apparent) the portrait of Dr Henry Sacheverell was a popular Tory emblem, displayed on banners at party meetings and the hustings. This caused an enterprising entrepreneur to manufacture chamberpots with this Tory device inside on the bottom, without doubt to sell to anti-Sacheverell Whigs.[6] The serious point, of course, behind all this party swagger is that it presupposes that there was an electorate,

---

[5] Holmes, *British Politics*, p. 30.
[6] Speck, *Tory and Whig*, p. 42.

Figure 13.1(a) Two contrasting cartoons from 1709. (a) condemns Tories for supporting Catholicism and Jacobitism, trampling underfoot toleration, liberty and property, and putting England on the road to the poverty and absolutism of France (symbolized by the wooden shoes hanging at the back of the coach).

Source: © The Trustees of the British Museum. All rights reserved.

which was not only growing in numbers, but was open to the influence of party propaganda, whether serious or frivolous, and which could not be depended on to follow meekly and unthinkingly the lead given by its social superiors.

If the existence of political parties in the reign of Queen Anne is not in doubt, the historian of this period must nevertheless beware of taking much of contemporary party propaganda at its face value. As in more recent times, political propaganda created party 'images' that were mere caricatures of the real political parties. The early eighteenth century produced its equivalent of the modern stereotypes of the cloth-capped,

Figure 13.1(b) (b) is a Tory riposte equating low-Church Whiggery with Cromwell (in the coach) trampling on monarchy, episcopacy and liberty.
Source: © The Trustees of the British Museum. All rights reserved.

working-class Labour party worker and the tweed-suited, middle-class Conservative party stalwart. The typical Tory was seen as someone closely identified with the 'landed interest' and with the Church of England, who bemoaned his falling rental income and his excessive land tax demands, and who was therefore critical of England's involvement in expensive continental wars. The 'average' Tory was also a xenophobic English nationalist, with a dislike of all foreigners including the Hanoverians. So the Tory image included lingering loyalty to the Pretender and flirtation with Jacobitism. The typical Whig image created by contemporary propaganda, on the other hand, was identified with the 'monied interest', with City businessmen and merchants who were profiting from the revolution in public finance brought about by the war. The Bank of England became in Tory eyes the hated symbol of soaring Whig profits made from investment in government stock, war supplies and joint stock companies. So the 'average' Whig was as fully committed to the continental war as he was to the Hanoverians and to the cause of Protestant dissent. As will be seen, these party images contain a great deal of truth; but, like their modern counterparts, they are caricatures that obscure important features of contemporary politics.

First, there were no clear-cut religious and social-economic divisions between Whigs and Tories during the reign of Queen Anne. Although Whigs were more willing than Tories to allow concessions to Protestant dissenters, the vast majority of MPs of both parties were Anglicans. Similarly, the 'landed interest versus monied interest' picture is a reflection only of the hatred and envy felt by many Tories of those City financiers whose enhanced power and profits had been stimulated by the war. Not all Tories were landowners, nor all Whigs businessmen. Landowning Whigs were as common as Anglican Whigs; otherwise it would be difficult to substantiate a hypothesis of a Whig–Tory split within the upper reaches of landed society. Nor is it difficult to find Tories who had connections with City finance and trade. Even the Bank of England had Tory directors. To assume that the interests of the landowning and mercantile classes were completely separate is to ignore the fact that for landowners in the late seventeenth and early eighteenth centuries, as for their predecessors a century earlier, there was no significant barrier of social prejudice preventing them from extensive entrepreneurial activities outside their estates.

Secondly, it would be wrong to draw the conclusion from contemporary party propaganda that the political nation was divided into two numerically equal groups. Although in Anne's reign the number of uncommitted, independent MPs was probably smaller than at any other time during the seventeenth and eighteenth centuries, the prevailing opinion whether at Westminster or in the constituencies was Tory not Whig. This is reflected in the parliamentary history of Anne's reign. Although the Whigs maintained a stronghold in the House of Lords, never (apart from a brief period after the 1708 general election) did they represent majority opinion in the House of Commons. As in William's reign, the Whigs secured support from the crown because of their commitment to the war, but it was temporary. The Whigs' overwhelming defeat at the general election of 1710 emphasized that the Tories were much more representative than the Whigs of the views of the rulers of provincial England. Tory ideology had deep roots in rich historical soil. The Tory alliance with the Anglican Church had been secured by the traumatic events of the English Revolution, which for many had smeared dissent irrevocably with republicanism. Arguably the Tory attitude to expensive wars and continental entanglements had even longer historical roots, stretching back beyond the Anglo-Dutch wars in the late seventeenth century to Buckingham's and Charles I's wars in the 1620s, and perhaps even to the Elizabethan wars in the 1580s and 1590s. For propertied country gentlemen these European wars had driven home a clear, unpalatable lesson: that war necessitated not only high taxation, but a large extension of the tentacles of central government into their own local spheres of influence. This was one threat which was guaranteed to cause the provincial rulers of country society to join hands to resist. In this sense the Tory party of Queen Anne's reign was the inheritor of the 'country' tradition of the seventeenth century, and it attempted (only partially successfully) to prevent a massive increase in the fiscal and executive powers wielded by the later Stuart State. Moreover, not only did the Tories fail to establish completely their ideology of provincial autonomy, but on the death of Queen Anne they disappeared for generations as an effective political force. It will be a major aim of the following section to find an explanation for the stark contrast between, on the one hand, the apparently strong position of the Tory party during Anne's reign and, on the other hand, its practical ineffectiveness before 1714 and its eclipse (if not disappearance) as a major political force thereafter.

Finally, the ballyhoo created by the parties in the early 1700s should not lead one to assume either that the 'rage of party' was so serious that it threatened the foundations of the country's political structure or that all politicians in the reign of Queen Anne were either Whigs or Tories. The first assumption was one that was made by some historians who rightly challenged the Namierite, non-party analysis of politics in this period, but who mistakenly believed that by 1714 Whig–Tory rivalries brought the nation to the verge of a crisis of early 1640s proportions.[7] In fact, the knowledge of what had happened in the 1640s was one reason why most Whigs and Tories were not willing to press their disagreements to a point beyond which events got out of the control of the propertied classes. Professor Holmes has also argued that the changed social and economic conditions of the late seventeenth and early eighteenth centuries – stagnant or only slowly rising population levels, rapidly increasing agricultural productivity and rising standards of living – provided conditions which made it unlikely that there would be a serious threat to the social order from those outside the propertied classes.[8] Whig and Tory political rivalries in the reign of Queen Anne were intense but they did not threaten the established social and political order.

Moreover, an important minority of politicians succeeded in resisting the appeals of either party. This is true especially of Godolphin and Harley, and, to a more qualified extent, of Marlborough. They were queen's men, her 'managers' as contemporaries described them, not party politicians. All three had close personal ties with Queen Anne: Marlborough and Godolphin through Sarah Churchill, and Harley because of Abigail Masham's friendship with the queen. But, of more importance than the influence of these women at court in binding Godolphin, Marlborough and Harley to the queen was their common hatred of party politics. All three men were forced during Anne's reign to ally closely with Whig or Tory politicians, Marlborough and Godolphin from 1705 to 1710 with the Whigs, and Harley from 1710 to 1714 with the Tories, but they did so only after they had found it impossible to carry on the queen's government

---

[7] This is now recognized by Professor Holmes, who in 1981 conceded that 'the reality was less stark than we [W. A. Speck and himself] then depicted it': 'The achievement of political stability: the social context of politics from the 1680s to the age of Walpole', in J. Cannon, ed., *The Whig Ascendancy* (1981), p. 3. See also J. V. Beckett, 'Stability in politics and society 1680–1750', in C. Jones, ed., *Britain in the First Age of Party 1680–1750* (1987).

[8] Holmes, 'The achievement of political stability'.

without reference to party. Even then neither Godolphin, Marlborough nor Harley allowed themselves to be identified fully with the ideology of either Whig or Tory party. In this they were not alone in English politics. Some MPs continued to resist the appeal of party propaganda and to remain loyal to what they considered to be a national interest that was above narrow party advantage. During the reign of Queen Anne, party rivalries predominated in English politics, but the pattern of politics is inexplicable without reference also to the continuing personal influence of the monarch and to the role of the queen's managers and their supporters.

The failure of the 'managers', 1702–1708

Queen Anne and the 'managers'

It is a measure of the continuity in seventeenth-century life and institutions that the political world at the beginning of the eighteenth century, as it had done at the beginning of the seventeenth, revolved round the monarch. Queen Anne, like her predecessors, ruled as well as reigned. As has been seen, in certain important respects the powers of the monarchy had been curtailed largely under the pressure of wartime conditions, but these changes had not removed the crown from the centre point of politics and government. Therefore, in order to understand the political history of Anne's reign, one ought to make an effort to assess what kind of woman the new queen was. Anne's personality and even her intimate personal relationships are the concern not only of romantic novelists and playwrights, but of the historian. They had an important impact on the course of politics during her reign.

When Anne came to the throne she was thirty-seven. Since her marriage to Prince George of Denmark in 1683, she had been pregnant annually. As a result she had had twelve miscarriages and six babies, which had all died before she became queen. The psychological effects of such a terrifying maternal history were *perhaps* tempered by the normality of the pattern of regular child bearing suffered by seventeenth-century women and contemporary high infant mortality. (There can, of course, be no certainty that the frequency with which babies died made infant mortality easier to bear than nowadays.) Certainly, physically it had made Anne an ill and prematurely old woman by the time she became queen. She was also fat and continually plagued by gout and other circulatory complaints, and consequently she could not walk far unaided. All this, hardly surprisingly, limited her ability and effectiveness as ruler of the country, perhaps even more so than her reputed limited intellectual powers. Her physical deficiencies are easier to assess than her mental limitations; both inevitably led her to rely more than she might otherwise have done on her advisers and her friends.

The famous friendship of Anne and Sarah Churchill was intense, intimate and private, with its own language; Anne called Sarah and her husband John Churchill, earl (later duke) of Marlborough, 'Mr and Mrs Freeman', the queen and Prince George were 'Mr and Mrs Morley'. G. M. Trevelyan explained the passion that underlay the friendship by the contrasting temperaments of the two women: it was 'rooted in genuine human affection . . . Anne's mind was slow as a lowland river, Sarah's swift as a mountain torrent'.[9] Historians living in an age more influenced by the writings of Freud look for a more explicitly sexual element in the relationship, akin to that between James I and Carr and Villiers, and William III and Portland and Albemarle. Whatever its roots and its importance in Anne's private life, the public effects of Sarah's friendship with the queen were to facilitate Marlborough's promotion to captain-general of the English army, and to help Marlborough and Sidney, Lord Godolphin (whose son married Marlborough's eldest daughter) maintain the most powerful position in England under the queen during the first half of Anne's reign. That it was far from being the only or major explanation can be seen by the fact that Marlborough's and Godolphin's political power survived the breakdown of Sarah and Anne's friendship in 1707. Yet the two men clearly recognized that it was important to their career prospects, as they signified by their hatred of Abigail Hill, Lady Masham, who replaced Sarah as Anne's closest confidante. The result of Sarah and Anne's petty and bitchy quarrel was to allow Abigail Hill, the cousin of Robert Harley, to become the daily companion of the most powerful person in the country. Undoubtedly, later Whig historians exaggerated the dominating influence of Abigail over the queen, but it is undeniable that she did act as Harley's spokesman at court and helped her cousin's political career. The importance of bedchamber politics in Anne's reign can be overestimated, but it ought not to be discounted altogether. This is most forcibly illustrated by the blighted careers of those politicians whom Anne personally disliked, whether Tory or Whig. Her Hyde uncles, Rochester and Clarendon, were never accepted as part of her intimate circle of friends, and, though Rochester was appointed lord lieutenant of Ireland soon after her accession, Anne had no compunction in forcing his resignation within a few months. The most outstanding effect on a Whig politician of the queen's disfavour is that of Lord Wharton. Anne hated and distrusted all the 'five tyrannizing lords' of the Whig Junto, but of these she abhorred Wharton most of all. It is difficult to know to what extent Wharton deserved his outrageous anticlerical and sexually permissive reputation. It was widely believed that in 1681, as Danby alleged in the House of Lords years later, Wharton 'had pissed against a Communion table [and] done his other occasions in a pulpit' in Barrington parish church in Somerset.[10] What is certain is that Wharton made no secret of his atheist views. That alone, apart from his sexual adventures, was enough to ensure that he found no personal favour with a moral and devoutly Anglican queen, and also explains Anne's political antipathy to Wharton and his Junto colleagues.

---

[9] G. M. Trevelyan, *England in the Reign of Queen Anne* (3 vols., 1930–4), I, p. 167.

[10] John Carswell, *The Old Cause: three biographical studies in Whiggism* (1954), p. 59.

Historiography

Queen Anne: changing historians' views

For a long time Queen Anne was portrayed as a weak woman, lacking the abilities to make an effective ruler. This view was in part based on her debilitating physical condition and also on her alleged reliance on female friends and male advisers. Historians too were often scathing about Anne's intelligence (or lack of it).

More recently, however, historians have reassessed and rehabilitated Anne's capacity to rule. Portraying the new queen as a weak, ill woman, reliant on friends and advisers, one is in danger of assuming that Anne was a pawn in a male political world. However, though not by any means an Elizabeth I, Anne could stand up for herself in a man's world. Significantly, her husband, Prince George of Denmark, remained as subservient to her as had Queen Mary to William III. Perhaps this is not surprising: historians have had little good to say about Prince George's abilities – G. M. Trevelyan called him 'a kindly, negligible mortal', while, more recently, to Professor G. Holmes he was 'boneheaded'.[11] Anne, however, could subdue more domineering and able men than George; even Godolphin and Harley when at the peak of their political influence could never take Anne for granted. She could be as independent to the point of stubbornness, and as mean and petty, as could Elizabeth I. The heartless ways in which she dismissed Godolphin and Marlborough after many faithful years in her service indicate the calculating, iron quality in Anne's make-up. Her ill-health did give royal ministers more scope to assume control over details of policies than they were allowed by William III, but neither the cabinet council nor her ministers ever took major policy decisions without Anne's consent. Given her physical condition, her attention to the details of administration and her attendance at major meetings of the cabinet council and important debates in the House of Lords is remarkable. Without doubt the queen was the most important political character of the reign.

Anne was just as determined as her predecessor to maintain the independence of the crown and to stave off any more incursions into the royal prerogative. She was equally determined to appoint her ministers without reference to the demands of political parties. 'All I desire', she wrote to Godolphin in 1706,

---

[11] Trevelyan, *Anne*, I, p. 178, and Holmes, *British Politics*, p. 212.

is my liberty in encouraging and employing all those that concur faithfully in my service, whether they are called Whigs or Tories, not to be tied to one or the other. For if I should be so unfortunate as to fall into the hands of either, I shall not imagine myself, though I have the name of Queen, to be in reality but their slave, which, as it will be my personal ruin, so it will be the destroying of all government. For instead of putting an end to faction it will lay a lasting foundation of it.[12]

These were sentiments wholeheartedly shared by the three men who became Anne's closest political advisers during her reign, Godolphin, Marlborough and Harley. From 1702 until 1710, Godolphin as lord treasurer and Marlborough as captain-general were her chief ministers, the 'duumvirs'. Of the two, Godolphin was the more influential, not because he was more politically skilful (which is doubtful), but largely because Marlborough was frequently absent abroad on military campaigns. It was still as true as in the reign of Elizabeth I that the cardinal principle of political success was constant presence at court. Until 1710 Godolphin's predominant position among the queen's ministers was more secure and unchallenged than any royal minister since the Restoration, and perhaps only equalled by Robert Cecil and the duke of Buckingham in the earlier seventeenth century. In that sense he was the 'prime minister'. In the early years of the reign Godolphin's and Marlborough's ally in the House of Commons was Robert Harley, as speaker of the House from 1702 and then as secretary of state from 1704. As yet, however, Harley hardly played as important a part in the government as implied by those who described the three ministers as the 'triumvirate'. Indeed, from 1705 Harley began to drift away from the other two ministers until early in 1708 he resigned as secretary of state. Only in 1710 did he succeed to Godolphin's position as unrivalled 'prime minister' of the crown. Neither Godolphin from 1702 to 1710 nor Harley from 1710 to 1714, however, held anything like the position analagous to a modern prime minister; neither was the leader of the majority party in the House of Commons; their principal power base was instead the royal closet.[13]

Unfortunately, Godolphin lacked a politician's thick skin, which made him sensitive to criticism, especially that of High Church clerics. After the general election of 1705, Archbishop Sharp of York found Godolphin 'in great concern and very near weeping' after reading an attack on him in a pamphlet by James Drake, *The Memorial of the Church of England*.[14] Godolphin's chief merits in Anne's eyes were his administrative ability and his financial expertise. His career in public finance was long and distinguished. Much of Marlborough's success in the war against France was based on the work of Godolphin at the treasury, ably assisted by Henry Boyle as chancellor of the exchequer. Both Godolphin and Marlborough supported Anne at her accession in her resolve not to become the captive of any party and to concentrate on the prosecution of the war.

---

[12] Quoted in Trevelyan, *Anne*, I, pp. 175–6.
[13] See Holmes, *British Politics*, pp. 440–2 (Appendix c) on the use of the term 'prime minister' in this period.
[14] Bennett, *Atterbury*, p. 81.

It is true that Anne inclined to the Tories on her accession. The hated Whig Junto lords were stripped of their offices; Wharton even lost the lord lieutenancy of Buckinghamshire. The principal high Tory leaders replaced the Whigs in key offices: Nottingham as secretary of state, Rochester as lord lieutenant of Ireland, Seymour as comptroller of the household and Jersey as lord chamberlain. During the first general election of her reign in July 1702, the electorate followed the royal lead as usual and voted a Tory majority of about 133 in the House of Commons. Yet significantly, the non-party Godolphin was victorious in his tussle with Rochester for the lord treasurership in the first weeks of the reign. Clearly the appointment of high Tory ministers did not signify a surrender to single party government. What was intended was an alliance with the Tories, but with the latter very definitely as the junior partners.

Yet in the first phase of the new reign from 1702 to 1708, Anne, Marlborough and Godolphin were forced to abandon their ideal of non-party rule: the queen and her 'managers' surrendered surprisingly, given their Tory associations in 1702, to the Whigs. Within a very short space of time the high Tory ministers were forced to resign: Rochester in February 1703 and Seymour. Jersey and Nottingham in the spring of 1704. Godolphin was the first to realize the inevitability and the necessity of the appointment of Whig ministers for the sake of effctive government and he began to press for this from 1705. Marlborough was converted to the same view slightly later, but it was not until 1708 that Anne's resistance, ably supported by Harley, to party rule by the Whigs was overcome and she allowed the Junto lords to be appointed to important offices. Why were the queen and her managers from 1702 to 1708 driven, reluctantly and temporarily, to abandon their earnest attachment to non-party rule, and why did they turn to the Whigs and not to the Tories? The answer will be found in the following sections on the Church, the war, the succession and the union with Scotland. On these issues the English political world was deeply split into Whig and Tory camps. It was not very long before Anne and her managers realized that the Tory point of view on all these issues did not correspond with what they considered to be the national interest. To Anne's discomfiture, the hated, obnoxious Junto Whigs, not the Tories, came to be seen as the patriots.

The Church: occasional conformity

It hardly seemed likely at the beginning of the reign that Tory efforts to protect the Church of England would be a major reason why the new Anglican queen and her principal ministers would lose patience with Tory politicians. Most High Churchmen saw Anne's accession as the cause for a great deal of rejoicing. They hoped that the Church of England under an English, Anglican, Stuart princess would receive the support and protection of the crown against the growing tide of dissent and irreligion, which they felt it had not had under a foreign, Calvinist king. As a result, the High Church revival which had been gathering pace in the last years of William III's reign carried forward into the new reign with increased impetus. And Anne appeared in the early months of her reign to be willing to fill the role that the high Tories expected of her. She appointed leading high Tories as her ministers, and she allowed Secretary of State Nottingham and Lord Keeper Sir Nathan Wright to purge Whigs from the central and local administration. In her speech at the end of the old parliament on 25 May 1702, she inserted a passage suggested by Nottingham, which further fuelled Anglican aspirations. Her 'own principles', she said, 'must always keep her entirely firm to the interests of the Church of England and would incline her to countenance those who had the truest zeal to support it'.[15] To the delight of Anglicans, Anne even revived the practice of touching to heal the skin disease, scrofula, 'the Queen's evil', which had lapsed under William III. With a Tory majority being secured in the July general election, and Atterbury putting the finishing touches to his plans for an all-out attack on 'moderate' bishops, all seemed ripe for a massive High Church assault when parliament and Convocation met in the winter of 1702–3.

As might be expected, this High Church offensive focused on the issue of occasional conformity, whereby dissenters attended an Anglican church to qualify for public office and so evade the Test and Corporation Acts. To Anglicans, occasional conformity epitomized their fears about the apparent growth of dissent and its threat to the Church. It was denounced as 'a religious piece of hypocrisy as even no heathen government would have endured', 'the vizor mask of cozenage, knavery and hypocrisy; it is the spiritual tool to serve the turn of all wicked designs, mere party cant and fanatical jargon, the very sound whereof should be a warning piece to alarm every honest man to stand upon his guard, and look about him'.[16] These were the typically forthright and extravagant views of a Fellow of Magdalen College, Oxford, Dr Henry Sacheverell, who in the early years of Anne's reign began to replace Atterbury as the major mouthpiece of the High Church movement. As original thinkers there is really no comparison between Atterbury and Sacheverell. Prolific though he was as a writer and preacher, there is very little evidence that Sacheverell had any profound intellectual ability. His gifts lay in the propounding of ideas not in their formulation; he was the most prominent of a crop of brilliant, if detestable, Anglican preachers produced by Oxford University in the early eighteenth century. Like most self-appointed spokesmen of 'the silent majority' Sacheverell not only voiced the fears of many, but also in the process exaggerated them and so inflamed public opinion, sometimes to the point of violence. Yet whatever one thinks of his methods, they were certainly effective. His first major sermon was preached at Oxford in June 1702 and printed as *The Political Union: A Discourse Showing the Dependence of Government on Religion*. Its contents were commonplace Tory–Anglican pulpit propaganda, proclaiming the indivisibility of Church and State and the vile nature of dissenters. But its language was emotive and highly charged. 'Presbytery and republicanism go hand in hand', thundered Sacheverell. The dissenters are the enemies 'against whom every man that wishes [the Church's] welfare ought to hang out the bloody flag and banner of defiance'.[17] With this battle-cry, backwoods Tory Cavaliers

---

[15] Quoted in Trevelyan, *Anne*, I, p. 210.
[16] Quoted in Kenyon, *Revolution Principles*, pp. 92, 116.
[17] Quoted in ibid., p. 93.

came to parliament in October 1702 determined to make occasional conformity the major issue of the session. If they needed any further prompting, this was provided early in the new session when the Commons investigated a disputed election at Wilton in Wiltshire, revealing that the Whig mayor of Wilton had packed his corporation with nonconformist burgesses to secure the election of two Whig MPs. On 4 November, William Bromley and Arthur Annesley, the MPs for the two universities, introduced in the Commons the first punitive Occasional Conformity Bill. Anyone who qualified for office by receiving the Anglican sacrament and then attended a dissenter meeting was to be fined £100 on conviction and £5 for each subsequent day he continued in office. The Tory campaign to secure a ban on occasional conformity was maintained at a high pitch for three parliamentary sessions from November 1702 to December 1704. Why, despite the popular support it received in the country, in the Commons and from the pulpits, did it fail?

First of all, of course, the Whigs voted consistently against a measure which would have effectively deprived many of their supporters of the vote and of public office. Outvoted the Whigs might be in the Commons, but in the Upper House they were stronger, and there all three Occasional Conformity Bills were killed in January 1703, December 1703 and December 1704. However, Whig strength in the House of Lords does not by itself explain the defeat of the High Church cause. The Whigs in fact secured the powerful support of the queen's managers, of the majority of the bishops, and eventually of the queen herself. As far as Marlborough and Godolphin are concerned, it seems clear that their opposition to the Occasional Conformity Bill was rooted in the practical consideration that wartime was not a suitable period for the airing of controversial legislation. Like Pym and the middle group in the early 1640s, Marlborough and Godolphin were intent on defusing a potentially divisive political issue and concentrating on financing and organizing the war effort. As yet, however, the queen was in favour of an Occasional Conformity Bill, and therefore the opposition of the 'duumvirs' had to be covert. Both ministers voted for the measure in the House of Lords, but they allowed Robert Harley to use all his considerable political talents against it. This must have been a task which Speaker Harley found congenial. Although he had long since cut his close ties with his family's dissenting–Puritan–Whig background, he had no sympathy with the high Tory extremists. In addition, Harley was a master of the art of political wheeler-dealing and intrigue.

On 21 October 1702, Harley had his first secret meeting with Atterbury, which was followed by other clandestine conversations with other high Tories, including one in a rowing boat in the middle of the Thames with Dean George Hooper of Canterbury. Sometimes one feels that Harley revelled in secrecy for its own sake. At these meetings Atterbury got the impression that Harley was promising the backing of the queen and Godolphin for a complete programme of High Church reforms. Meanwhile, however, in the House of Lords amendments were added to the Commons' version of the Occasional Conformity Bill which limited its scope only to state officers, not municipal officials. The mangled bill was subsequently defeated. Not surprisingly, Atterbury was angry at Harley's trickery, and spurned his overtures in the next session in the winter of

1703. Instead Harley was forced to rely on a press campaign against the High Church and in this to use the talents of Daniel Defoe, who had published a witty parody of High Church propaganda, *The Shortest Way with Dissenters*, for which he was imprisoned in Newgate. Here Harley visited him and bought Defoe's pen for the service of the government. In December 1703, however, the second Occasional Conformity Bill was defeated in the House of Lords by only twelve votes. Therefore Harley, especially after he became secretary of state in May 1704, when he replaced Nottingham (who resigned because of the failure of the occasional conformity legislation) renewed his attempt to get Atterbury's support. This time he was successful. By securing the deanery of Carlisle for Atterbury and holding out the prospect of richer ecclesiastical prizes, Harley effectively undermined Atterbury's influence with the High Church rank and file.

Undoubtedly, the Whig numerical supremacy in the House of Lords and the political machinations of Harley and his superiors were largely responsible for the collapse of the anti-occasional conformity cause early in Anne's reign. Yet it is difficult to avoid the conclusion that the High Church leaders themselves contributed to their own defeat. Especially after the overthrow of the first two bills and the loss of office by their two principal leaders, Rochester and Nottingham, the high Tories adopted extremist tactics which lost them the support of many moderate Tories and of the queen. Soon after the start of the 1704–5 parliamentary session, a meeting of 150 Tories at the Fountain Tavern in the Strand, at the prompting of Bromley and Nottingham (though perhaps not of Rochester), adopted the irresponsible tactic of agreeing to tack an occasional conformity clause on to the Land Tax Bill for the coming year. In effect, they proclaimed that they were willing to refuse to grant money for the war if their demands regarding the Church were not met. This blatant disregard of the national interest in the pursuit of party political considerations was too much even for many Tories. Significantly, Henry St John turned against the high Tories and from this date began his turbulent and important political relationship with Robert Harley. Queen Anne, too, now turned against the high Tory leaders. It is tempting to believe that it was not just the constitutional radicalism of the proposed 'tack' that persuaded her to take this course. Despite the impression she made in the early months of her reign, Anne was not a High Church bigot from the same mould as Bromley and Seymour, who harked back nostalgically to the old union of Church and divinely appointed monarchy. Although a devout Anglican and anxious to further the interests of the Church of England, the new queen was astute enough to realize that the monarchy after the Glorious Revolution could no longer claim to rule by divine right. In 1710 she irritably dismissed references in a loyal address from the City of London to the divinity of her crown. 'Having thought about it often,' she told the duke of Shrewsbury, 'she could by no means like it, and thought it unfit to be given to anybody that she wished it might be left out.' By the winter of 1704 she withdrew her support for the High Church cause. The war effort must come first. 'Our enemies have no encouragement left but what arises from their hopes of our divisions', she told parliament at the opening of the new session. ''Tis therefore your concern not to give the least countenance to those hopes. I hope there will be no concentration among you but who shall most promote the public welfare.'[18] When the 'tack' was proposed in November 1704, the Tories split – 'tackers' and 'sneakers' were the labels coined by the newspapers – and the 'tack' was easily defeated. In the following month the third Occasional Conformity Bill was thrown out by the House of Lords.

By 1705 the High Church cause was in complete disarray, the high hopes of 1702 unfulfilled. In June the general election even produced Whig gains in the House of Commons (on one estimate, net Whig gains of sixty).[19] Moreover, when in December Rochester moved in the Lords that the Church was in danger, he was comprehensively defeated, and a motion was passed that 'whoever goes about to suggest that the Church is in danger under Her Majesty's administration, is an enemy to the Queen, the Church and the Kingdom'. As Sacheverell was to show in 1710, High Church sentiment was still there to be exploited. But for the time being it was a spent political force. To the dismay of the Whig Junto, however, the defeat of the High Church Tories brought them little nearer their ultimate political prize. By 1705 Godolphin and Marlborough supported the Junto's clamourings for office, but Anne held out stubbornly. It was only after much reluctance that she allowed the appointment of the Whig William, Earl Cowper as lord keeper of the great seal in October 1705 and of Sunderland as secretary of state in December 1706. In the summer of 1707 she delivered a slap to the face of the Junto by ignoring their demands for the appointment of two Whig divines to vacant bishoprics, Exeter and Chester, and instead offered them to Offspring Blackall and Sir William Dawes, Tory nominees of Archbishop Sharp.[20] The importance of the bishopric crisis of 1707 is its indication of Anne's resistance to Whig rule. Yet the pressure from the Whigs for office was growing; it was not just on the Church issue that they were proving to be more useful to the queen and her ministers than the Tories.

The war and the succession

If the Tory attitude to the Church played a part in driving the court and the royal managers unwillingly into the arms of the Whigs in the early part of the reign, so too did the reaction of many Tories to the war and to the prospect of Hanoverian succession to the throne. Anne's war against Louis XIV was partly to prevent French domination of Spanish Mediterranean and American trade; it was at least as strongly a war to safeguard the Protestant succession in England. The dramatic way in which English public opinion had swung sharply in favour of war against Louis XIV in 1701 has already been seen. Despite Dutch apprehensions, Anne's accession made no

---

[18] Quoted in Trevelyan, *Anne*, II, p. 12.

[19] H. L. Snyder, 'Party configurations in the early eighteenth-century House of Commons', *B.I.H.R.*, XLV (1972), p. 45.

[20] G. V. Bennett, 'Robert Harley, the Godolphin ministry and the bishopric crisis of 1707', *E.H.R.*, LXXXII (1967). Professor Kenyon wonders whether Offspring Blackall was a Tory divine before 1708, though he clearly was subsequently: Kenyon, *Revolution Principles*, pp. 119–20.

difference to England's commitment to the Grand Alliance concluded by William III in August 1701. As far as Anne was concerned, the lesson taught by her predecessor had been well learned: that English interests were inextricably involved in maintaining the balance of power in Europe against French domination. Anne's first act as queen was to declare to her privy council that her two principal aims were the reduction of the power of France and the maintenance of the Protestant succession. On the same day, parliament voted addresses calling for a vigorous prosecution of the war. This appearance of national unity on the war and the succession, however, was misleading. Soon a rift in English political life, familiar to students of William's reign, reappeared. The Whigs had no doubts about the desirability of a Protestant succession; they were therefore strongly and consistently in favour of the war. The Tories, on the other hand, as their attitude to the Regency Bill in 1705–6 illustrated, were much less firmly committed to the Protestant succession and therefore easily lost their early enthusiasm for the war. Consequently, as on the church issue, Anne and her ministers discovered that the Whig view of the war and the succession was more attractive than that of the Tories.

During the first half of the reign, the court faced unpalatable Tory opposition to its war policy. At first this manifested itself in Tory criticism of the ministry's strategic concentration on full-scale war in the Netherlands. The debate on war strategy began even before the formal declaration of war on 4 May 1702. It is clear from accounts that survive of discussions in the cabinet and privy council on 1 and 2 May that Rochester and Marlborough were engaged in a furious quarrel, partly over the lord treasurership, which Rochester, not without good reason given his financial experience in Charles II's and James II's reigns, felt ought to be his and not Godolphin's. However, the two men were also at odds over the type of war England should be involved in. Against Marlborough's project of a full-scale military expeditionary force to the Low Countries, Rochester developed all the arguments he had used in the 1690s against William III's similar war strategy: the stupidity of attacking the enemy at his strongest points in the fortress towns of the Low Countries, and the vast expense of continental warfare which was considered to be of little concern to this country. Instead Rochester tried to persuade his ministerial colleagues to adopt the 'blue-water' war strategy so popular in Tory country houses and with Tory backbench MPs. England, Rochester proposed, should act only as an auxiliary in the continental war and should concentrate her war effort against Spain's and France's colonies and shipping. As Rochester saw it, the 'blue-water' war strategy had at least three advantages over a continental strategy: it would hit France and Spain at the weakest places in their defences; a maritime colonial war was much cheaper than pouring money into supplying armies in Europe; and English interests were much more clearly identifiable in the New World than on the Continent of Europe.

That these were persuasive arguments to many MPs can be seen by the activities of the House of Commons in the first session of parliament in the winter of 1702–3. Instead of concentrating on the war, some MPs tried to revive the impeachment of 1701 against the Junto, and St John and Bromley brought allegations of corruption in the commission of public accounts against Paymaster-General Ranelagh and Halifax.

When it came to granting money for the war, the Commons showed the strong feeling in favour of Rochester's 'blue-water' ideas by voting twice as much money for the navy as for the army, and early in January 1703 the Tories tacked an anti-Dutch amendment on to a vote to increase the number of troops in the Low Countries; the government was to 'insist upon it with the States General that there be an immediate stop of all ports, and all letters, bills . . . trade and commerce with France and Spain'.[21] But was the 'blue-water' strategy a sensible one? The first reason to think it was not is that English expenditure on the army in this period was only marginally more than on the navy.[22] Moreover, not only would a 'blue-water' strategy have been as expensive as a continental war, but also it was based on the false assumption that colonies and colonial trade were as important to France as they were to England. It seems clear that the only way that the France of Louis XIV could have been defeated was militarily in Europe. Perhaps for these reasons Rochester received less support from his fellow Tory leaders, Nottingham, Bromley and Seymour, than he did from the Tory rank and file. He lost the cabinet tussle with Marlborough: Godolphin was appointed lord treasurer, England declared in favour of full-scale military intervention in Europe, and Rochester resigned as lord lieutenant of Ireland in February 1703.

In the early phase of Anne's war, the strategy of England and the allies changed, but in a way envisaged by William III rather than by Rochester. Before his death William realized that the chances of success of a claimant to the Spanish throne would be vastly improved by the claimant's presence in Spain along with allied troops. In 1702 an allied expedition to Cadiz, though abortive, was mounted with the intention of forcing Cadiz to submit to the Viennese Habsburgs as rightful rulers of Spain. This strategy was confirmed by the Methuen Treaties with Portugal in 1703. Portugal broke with France, and the allies agreed to proclaim Archduke Charles as king of Spain and to send him to Spain with a large army. The limited war aims of 1701 – the partition of the Spanish Empire – were transformed into securing the kingdom of Spain for Archduke Charles. This was the policy of 'No peace without Spain', which in the long run ensured that England would become a major Mediterranean power. More immediately it meant that the allies had committed themselves to a prolonged war south, as well as north, of the Pyrenees. The most notable feature of the War of the Spanish Succession is the contrast between Marlborough's and Eugene's victories north of the Pyrenees and the eventual failure of the allied forces in Spain.

At the outset, the war in northern Europe was not particularly successful for the forces of the Grand Alliance. The old deadlocked pattern of William III's war of sieges, manoeuvres and counter-manoeuvres round the fortress towns on the Meuse and the lower Rhine was resumed. It is true that in the first campaign of the war in the summer and autumn of 1702, Marlborough took all the major fortresses on the Meuse and lower Rhine except Bonn. But this threatened to be merely an episode in the familiar

---

[21] Quoted in Holmes, *British Politics*, p. 68.

[22] G. Holmes, 'Post-Revolution Britain and the historian', in Holmes, ed., *Britain after the Glorious Revolution*, p. 21.

story of the capture and recapture of these towns by allied and French troops. Nor were the allies any more united in 1702 than they had been during William's war. Emperor Leopold was still distracted by domestic problems, a Hungarian rebellion and the imminent prospect of invasion by the Turks. Moreover, in September 1702 Louis XIV persuaded the elector of Bavaria to join the war against the allies. Yet perhaps by 1706 – certainly by 1708 – the French had been effectively defeated in Italy and in north and central Europe. How can one account for the allied victory north of the Pyrenees? Much of the explanation can be seen in the military campaign which culminated in the battle of Blenheim on 2 August 1704: a combination of the military genius of Marlborough and Prince Eugene of Savoy and the financial support they received from the English treasury. Like Cromwell, Marlborough's success as a soldier stemmed from the fact that he did not obey the rules of conventional contemporary warfare. His diplomatic and military advisers recommended that he keep his forces engaged in the Low Countries; not only was it considered impractical to move large armies quickly over long distances, but Marlborough faced strong opposition, especially from the Dutch, against an alternative military strategy. Early in 1703, for example, Marlborough determined on a full-scale invasion of France, but he was forced by Dutch and English opposition to abandon his plans and concentrate instead on dislodging the French from more fortress towns in the Netherlands and on the lower Rhine, which he did successfully, capturing Bonn, Huy and Limbourg in the spring of 1703. When the French and Bavarians launched an offensive later in the year along the Danube, threatening to march on Vienna, Marlborough's plan to counter it could easily have suffered a similar fate. That it did not was partly due to Marlborough's daring military leadership. Under the cover of a limited campaign in the Moselle valley, Marlborough marched his army to Koblenz, and then on his own initiative began a rapid advance along the Rhine valley to Mainz and Heidelberg, and from there led his army south-east across Germany to the Danube, linking up at Mundelsheim with the forces of Prince Eugene of Savoy and Prince Lewis of Baden. Their joint forces then captured the fortress of Schellenberg near Donauworth on the Danube on 21 June, and on 2 August comprehensively defeated the Franco-Bavarian army at the battle of Blenheim. The French general, Tallard, was captured and condemned to the qualified blessing of a life as prisoner of war in Nottingham. Military historians rightly concentrate on Marborough's skill as a strategist and tactician. But it must not be forgotten that Marlborough's march deep into Europe with very long supply lines was not possible without massive financial support. A significant feature of the campaign, in fact, was that the allied troops were well supplied and paid: a tribute to the work of Lord Treasurer Godolphin and Chancellor of the Exchequer Boyle, who improved on the financial machinery erected during William's war. 'England', wrote G. M. Trevelyan, 'beat France with the purse as much as with the sword.' However, Marlborough's military skill is not to be underrated. Blenheim was a crucial victory, but it did not win the war. France was still strong both in Italy and in the Netherlands and, with Marlborough's resurrected scheme for an allied invasion of France in 1705 blocked by the Dutch and Austrians, the war seemed doomed to revert to its deadlocked pattern of conflict in the Netherlands.

In this context, Marlborough's two major victories in the Low Countries – at Ramilles on 12 May 1706 and at Oudenarde on 11 July 1708 – were specially significant, and are in startling contrast to William III's dismal military record in the same theatre of war. Finally, in explaining the defeat of the French in Europe, it would be an unforgiveable example of blinkered Anglocentric history not to record the military contribution of Prince Eugene of Savoy. Even a biographer considers him the junior military partner of Marlborough, but his victory at Turin in September 1706 delivered Italy from French control.[23]

In the early stages of the war in Spain, the allied forces also secured some major victories. The English fleets under Sir George Rooke and Sir Cloudesley Shovell, which had been sent to escort Archduke Charles to pursue his claim to be Charles III of Spain, captured Gibraltar on 23 July 1704, and on 13 August prevented the French Toulon fleet from retaking the base after a full-scale naval battle off Malaga. Moreover, the military invasion of Spain also began well. Charles and the English general, the earl of Peterborough, captured Barcelona on 3 October 1705, and subsequently many towns in eastern Spain, especially in Catalonia, rallied to support 'Charles III'. Just how much the allies owed these victories to their own military skill and how much to Catalan fervour against the hated Castilians is difficult to judge, but that Catalan nationalism was undoubtedly a major factor is illustrated by the fact that the allies were much more successful in eastern Spain than elsewhere. Allied forces under the earl of Galway invaded Spain from Portugal and on 27 June 1706 occupied Madrid, but they were not able to hold it for long and on 14 April 1707 they suffered a crushing defeat at the battle of Almanza. Just as Archduke Charles found himself unwittingly the leader of Catalan separatism, so Philip V became the focus of Castilian nationalism against the foreign invaders. Other defeats in Spain followed, including eventually the fall of Catalonia and its subjugation to Castilian Spain. Partly the explanation lies in the fact that the allied resources were dangerously overextended, in north-west Europe, in Italy and in Spain. But perhaps of more importance is the fact that the allied cause in Spain was wrecked on the rock of Castilian nationalism.

With the war in Europe apparently won and the war in Spain going very badly, it is not surprising that by the middle of the reign Tory disenchantment with England's involvement in a continental war increased. Certainly Tory country gentlemen joined, like everyone else, in the bouts of jingoistic fervour which greeted Marlborough's victories; Blenheim, it was said, 'being more for their 4s in the pound than ever yet they saw'. But sentiments like this were short-lived, and the crushing financial burden of the war, which was by now costing £4 million a year, especially the land tax of four shillings in the pound assessed on landed incomes, produced constant complaints and inspired a running parliamentary attack on the conduct of the war. By 1708 Whigs and Tories were moving further apart on the question of the war than ever before: it was now no longer differences over war strategy that divided the parties. Already by 1708 one can detect the beginning of the Tory desire for peace, which after 1708

---

[23] Derek McKay, *Prince Eugene of Savoy* (1977), pp. 246–7.

became a major area of contention between the parties, as will be seen. Without much question the unresolved doubts about the Protestant succession in the minds of many Tories contributed to their cooling enthusiasm for the war. In 1705–6 the debates on the Regency Bill forced Tories to confront this difficult problem again, and again it became clear that the attitude of many Tories to the major aim of the war, the maintenance of the Protestant succession, was, at best, lukewarm.

Ironically given the way it rebounded against the Tories, the origin of the Regency Bill was a Tory party manoeuvre to discredit the Whigs. In November 1705 the major Tory party leaders, Nottingham, Rochester, Buckingham, Anglesey and Jersey, put forward for debate in the House of Lords the proposition that Anne should invite the successor to the throne, Princess Sophia, to England, arguing that this was the only safeguard against a sudden Jacobite invasion. Although there was undoubtedly a need for provisions to be made for carrying on the government after Anne's death, since most of the initiators of this 'Hanover motion' (Nottingham alone excepted) were Jacobite sympathizers, their true aim must have been to put the Whigs in an impossible dilemma. If the Whigs were to support it, as they must have wanted to, they would alienate the queen, who was against the motion; if they opposed it, it would discredit them at the electoral court and among their own supporters. In order to avoid this embarrassing choice, the Junto leaders, especially Somers and Wharton, cleverly devised the Regency Bill, which laid down the form to be taken by the interim government which was to rule on Anne's death and before the arrival of the Hanoverian successor. There was to be a Regency Council of 'lords justices', consisting of seven principal officers of state and the nominees of Princess Sophia or her successor, and parliament was to meet immediately on Anne's death and to sit for six months. Since this was a measure of which Anne approved, the Junto turned the tables on the Tories. In addition, the Junto determined to use the opportunity not only to gain the queen's favour, but to repeal some of the limitations on the monarch's power established by the Act of Settlement in 1701, which were to come into effect on Anne's death. The clause which would have forced privy councillors to put their signatures to the advice they gave the monarch was repealed. Moreover, despite a furious battle in which some 'whimsical' Whigs supported the Tories, the Junto succeeded in amending the place clause of 1701 so that MPs appointed to an old office could remain in the Commons if they were re-elected at by-elections. The most satisfying aspect of the Regency Bill for the Junto, though, was probably the open opposition to the main provisions of the bill that came from many Tory MPs. The impression this left was that the Tories aimed, in the words of a contemporary, 'to destroy the succession'.[24]

All this by itself was enough to alienate the queen further from the Tories: it has been suggested that Nottingham's role in the affair permanently destroyed his chance of being reappointed to any office by Queen Anne.[25] However, in the parliamentary session of 1707–8 the Tories compounded their offence in the queen's eyes by

---

[24] Quoted in Holmes, *British Politics*, p. 91.
[25] Ibid., p. 200, n.

supporting openly for the first time an attack on the official war policy of 'No peace without Spain'. On 19 December 1707, Somers carried a motion supporting the policy in the House of Lords, but in the Commons early in 1708 there was a sustained bombardment by the Tories on the conduct of the war in Spain. More than ever now, Marlborough and Godolphin were driven to rely on Whig support. Anne continued her resistance to the Junto, but was finding it increasingly difficult to maintain it. Whig support for the royal policy regarding Scotland made it virtually impossible.

The union with Scotland

That the union of England and Scotland as one country, Great Britain, was accepted by both nations in 1707 is, on the face of it, very surprising. Whenever union had been mentioned in the previous century, whether by Englishmen or Scotsmen, there had been little support for it. As has been seen, James I's proposed scheme in 1606–7 to unite his two kingdoms was met with howls of derision in England. Like most military conquests, the Cromwellian union of the 1650s was resented by the mass of the population in Scotland, and when the English republic collapsed so too did the union. In the late seventeenth century, at least three tentative proposals for union were raised, in 1667, 1670 and 1689, but they found little support. Indeed, the racial antagonism and national animosity which had characterized the relations between England and Scotland during the Middle Ages appeared to have intensified during the seventeenth century. Englishmen do not appear to have changed the opinion of the Scots that they had expressed in the debates on James I's plan for a union, that the Scots were a barbaric race of savages. Scots' hatred of the English exploded in 1637 into a nationalist revolt. It has been seen that the Anglo-Scots alliance made in September 1643 was rendered ineffective as a military force by mutual distrust and religious differences. The Solemn League and Covenant was no longer operative after the battle of Marston Moor in July 1644; it had collapsed altogether by 1646, and in 1648 and 1650 Scots' armies invaded England. In 1689 the attempts in the previous twenty years by Lauderdale and James II to impose autocratic rule from England provoked the Scots to assert their political and ecclesiastical independence from England. It is, therefore, an intriguing historical problem, as well as an important one, to try to explain, first, why the Act of Union came about in 1707, a century after the failure of James I's union project and only eighteen years after the Glorious Revolution; and secondly, why the Union survived, despite a recurrence of Anglo-Scottish mistrust and hatred after 1707. Like many of the questions asked in this book, it is easier to formulate than to answer. It has been frequently emphasized that there are no single 'correct' answers to most historical problems. This is certainly true of the reasons for the making and for the success of the Act of Union.

The Glorious Revolution of 1689–90 in Scotland made the union with England seventeen or eighteen years later harder than ever to comprehend. Much more than in England do those events in Scotland deserve to be called a 'revolution'. In England, William's royal authority was only slightly diminished by the events of 1689–90; in

Scotland he was forced to accept the demands of one group of politicians for Scottish ecclesiastical and constitutional independence. Some English historians have the unfortunate habit of referring to the inhabitants of Scotland by the blanket term 'the Scots'. Yet in 1689 the Scots were no more united in their attitude to King James's downfall than they had been to events in England in the 1640s and 1650s. Whereas James had united the English against him, in Scotland he still had supporters, especially the episcopalians and (of more importance) many Highland chiefs. A web of motives determined Highland antipathy to William III: hatred of lowland Scotland; Catholic sentiment; dislike of the Campbells who, in the person of Archibald Campbell, tenth earl of Argyll, returned from exile on William's accession. William therefore had to rely, much more than in England, on one section, albeit the largest, of the Scottish political nation: the Presbyterian element, which was strongly entrenched in Lowland Scotland. Ominously for William, when the Scottish Convention met on 14 March 1689 it quickly became clear that Presbyterian opinion was highly organized. Presbyterian MPs began to plan their political tactics at pre-session meetings of what contemporaries called 'the Club' under the leadership of Sir James Montgomerie, who could count on the support of about 70 of the 125 Scottish MPs. Even historians of Scotland have been taken aback by the 'surprising degree of political sophistication which distinguished its (the Club's) aims, tactics and organization'.[26] The Club played a major part in the drafting of the Claim of Rights and the Articles of Grievances which the Scottish Convention sent south to be approved by William and Mary. These documents embodied much more sweeping demands than the English Declaration of Rights: the Act of Supremacy of 1669 was to be repealed, and episcopacy as well as the Lords of the Articles, the royally appointed ministers who had controlled political affairs in Scotland before the revolution, were to be abolished. Not surprisingly, William resisted these extreme demands for an independent Scottish Presbyterian Kirk and parliament, and in the first session of the Scottish Convention (March–August 1689) his commissioner, George, earl of Melville, blocked legislation designed to bring into effect the Club's programme. But events in 1689–90 indicated that William was not in a position to resist for long organized opposition in Scotland. He had come to England primarily to strengthen his armies in the war in Europe, not to divert troops to Scotland.

In the summer of 1689 a Highland uprising in support of King James emphasized just how reliant William was on Presbyterian support in Scotland. The clansmen won a notable victory at the battle of Killiecrankie on 27 July 1689, though their leader, John Graham of Claverhouse, Viscount Dundee, was killed. A month later the Highlanders were defeated at Dunkeld, and Fort William was founded as a means of trying to impose Lowland domination on the Highlands. Nothing could have made clearer the extent of William's dependence on Presbyterian support. Consequently, when the Scottish Convention reassembled on 15 April 1690 he soon accepted all the

---

[26] J. Halliday, 'The Club and the Revolution in Scotland 1689–90', *Scottish Historical Review*, XLV (1966), p. 147. See also I. B. Cowan, 'Church and State reformed? The revolution of 1688–89', in J. I. Israel, ed., *The Anglo-Dutch Moment: essays on the Glorious Revolution and its world impact* (1991).

Club's political and religious demands: the Act of Supremacy of 1669 was repealed on 25 April, and the Lords of the Articles and lay patronage in the Church were abolished on 8 May and 19 July respectively. Presbyterianism was re-established with a revived general assembly, and episcopalians were expelled from their livings. The Scottish Glorious Revolution established a Kirk and a parliament in Scotland more independent than ever of England and of the crown.

Nor did the course of William III's reign appear to further the prospect of Anglo-Scottish union. On the contrary, relations between the two countries deteriorated alarmingly, especially because of two incidents, the Glencoe Massacre and the establishment of the Company of Scotland.

Information

The Glencoe Massacre, 1692

It may be that the importance of the Glencoe Massacre as an indication of deteriorating Anglo-Scots relations can be exaggerated. It has, however, lost none of its force as a sign of the ferocity between the people of Highland and Lowland Scotland.

The massacre grew out of efforts to pacify the Highlands where Jacobite loyalty and anti-Campbell sentiment continued to be a major security threat. The king's adviser on Scottish affairs in London, Sir John Dalrymple of Stair,[27] initiated a scheme compelling all Highland chiefs to take an oath of allegiance to William by 1 January 1692. Although Alexander MacDonald of Glencoe took the oath only five days after the deadline, it was decided to punish him, and on 13 February MacDonald and nearly forty men, women and children of his clan were slaughtered by the Campbell regiments from Fort William. The responsibility for the massacre has never been determined. Though William and Dalrymple authorized the massacre, it is probable that the information that MacDonald had taken the oath was deliberately withheld from them by the privy council and by MacDonald's enemies in Lowland Scotland. Dalrymple and his agent, John Campbell, earl of Breadalbane, though, had no sympathy for or understanding of the Highlanders and saw MacDonald's reluctance to take the oath as a great opportunity to get rid of 'that set of thieves'. William, too, ensured that the affair contributed to rising tension between England and Scotland by his lenient treatment of those who had allowed the massacre to take place.

---

[27] Dalrymple is sometimes referred to as Stair. The student needs to beware of the confusion caused by some historians of Scotland who call people by their surname, while others use their place of residence.

Much more important in producing friction between England and Scotland was the Company of Scotland, which was established in 1695 to trade to Africa and the Indies and to found colonies in any part of those continents not under the sovereignty of a European ruler. Because it was founded with high hopes that it would contribute to Scotland's much-needed economic recovery, English opposition to the company was resented especially deeply in Scotland. Though English mercantile opinion was not totally hostile – a large part of the company's initial subscription came from London – the powerful East India Company immediately organized a campaign against this threat of Scottish competition. More seriously, from William's point of view, the Company of Scotland endangered his foreign policy, especially when the company, frustrated by English opposition to its proposed trade to the East, adopted the Darien colony scheme.

Information

The Darien colony scheme

This was proposed by a financial adventurer, William Patterson, to set up a colony on the Darien Isthmus in Central America, in the heart of the Spanish Empire. William took very seriously indeed the subsequent Spanish complaints at a time when he was anxious that Spain should be given no excuse for joining France in a war against England. He had no wish to begin a war with Spain in defence of a Scottish colony. He forbade English merchants from investing in the Company of Scotland and English colonists from supplying the Darien colony. He also persuaded merchants in Hamburg and Amsterdam against investing in the company. Though the economic rationale behind the Darien colony was sound – the establishment of a trade entrepôt between the East and Europe – its failure was perhaps inevitable even without English opposition. The hostility of the Spanish Empire and of the Central American climate had already proved too much for similar colonization schemes. Nevertheless it would have been difficult in the late 1690s to persuade any Scot that the collapse of the Darien scheme was not caused by anything other than English treachery.

The effect of all these events after 1689 on Scottish and on English opinion was noticeably different. In Scotland, coming as it did at a time of major economic crisis, when there had been five disastrous harvests of famine proportions from 1695 to 1699, when Scottish trade in Europe was disrupted by the effects of an English war, as well as by English navigation legislation which excluded Scotland from English colonial trade, the English attitude to the Darien scheme roused anti-English sentiment near to breaking point and encouraged open consideration of total political separation from England. In England, however, the effect of the growing hostility between the two countries was to convert at least one section of opinion, the crown and its ministers, to the idea of a closer union between England and Scotland. By the end of his reign William, who had long been in favour of the idea, persuaded Godolphin and Marlborough to support him in proposing in the English parliamentary sessions of 1699–1700 and 1702 a legislative union between England and Scotland. It is clear that it was just because Anglo-Scots' relations were deteriorating that the English government wanted a union of the two countries. Its major considerations were strategic: not only did the English rely on Scottish troops for their European armies, but in time of war the prospect of a Jacobite invasion from Scotland, a revival of the Auld Alliance between France and Scotland, and civil war in Scotland was intolerable. These were considerations that inevitably appealed not only to the crown and the 'duumvirs', but also to those other consistent supporters of the war against France and of the Protestant succession, the Whigs. Significantly, it was the high Tories who sabotaged both the proposals for a legislative union in 1700 and the negotiations of 1702–3. Their economic arguments were very similar to those of 1606. Sir Edward Seymour said he was opposed to union 'for this reason: that a woman being proposed to a neighbour of his in ye country for a wife, he said he would never marry her, for she was a beggar, and whoever married a beggar cou'd only exspect a louse for a portion'.[28] To the economic disparity between the two countries was now added high Tory repugnance at the prospect of union with a Presbyterian country. For Anne and her ministers and also increasingly the Whigs, however, by 1702 the needs of security in wartime seemed a more compelling argument for union than any misgivings about its possible effects on the English economy and Anglican Church.

In Scotland at the beginning of Anne's reign there was no sign of any pro-union sentiment. On the contrary, the new Scots parliament which was elected in 1703, free from the royal control of the Lords of the Articles, seemed set on a course of political separation from England. Though disunited on other things, most Scots seemed united in their hostility to England: on this, for example, a republican, Andrew Fletcher of Saltoun, could find common ground with a Jacobite, James Douglas, duke of Hamilton. In the 1703 session, James Douglas, earl of Queensberry, the Queen's commissioner, was powerless in the face of overwhelming support for a series of anti-English measures. The Act Anent Peace and War enacted that all foreign policy decisions after Anne's death would have to be approved by the Scottish parliament. The Wine Act and the Wool Act allowed trade from Scotland in these commodities with France despite the war embargoes in force in England, so making possible English trade with France via Scotland: in other words, allowing merchants to break the trade sanctions against France. Most serious of all, the Act of Security of the Kingdom threatened to bar the Hanoverians from the Scottish throne 'unless . . . there be such conditions for government settled and enacted as may secure the honour and sovereignty

---

[28] Quoted in Baxter, *William III*, p. 375.

of this crown and kingdom, the freedom, frequency and power of Parliaments, the religion, liberty and trade of the nation from English or any foreign influence'.[29] Although Anne gave her assent to the former measures, she cavilled at the latter, dismissed Queensberry and appointed in his stead the marquis of Tweeddale, the leader of a political group nicknamed the 'Squadrone Volante', the Flying Squad. Tweeddale, however, failed as badly as Queensberry in his attempt to get the Scottish parliament to guarantee its support for the Hanoverian succession, although he was not helped by Queensberry's defection to the opposition in 1704. The Act of Security again passed the Scottish parliament in the summer of 1704, and this time Godolphin, days before the news of Blenheim reached London and therefore faced by a threatening situation in Europe and the prospect of a collapse of government in Scotland, advised Anne to give her assent, which she did on 5 April 1704. The anti-English attitude of the Scottish parliament in 1703 and 1704 confirmed what English ministers already felt and what more English politicians were coming to realize: that the only alternative to the threat of an independent, Jacobite, Francophile Scotland on Anne's death was union. Therefore, after the passage of the Act of Security, the Whig Junto proposed to Godolphin that he support the Aliens Bill as an explicit threat to force the Scots to negotiate for a union. The Aliens Act, which became law in March 1705, threatened that, unless by 25 December 1705 the Scottish crown was settled as the English crown had been settled, the import of all Scottish staple products into England would be banned and all Scots would be treated in law as aliens and therefore all Scottish property in England would be endangered.

By early 1705, then, pressing considerations of national security had converted the English crown, its ministers and leading Whigs to the need for an immediate union with Scotland. At this late date, however, there was still no sign of any similar conversion of opinion in Scotland. Just as the Aliens Act was passed in England, the case of Captain Green in Scotland illustrated the depth of anti-English feeling there. Green's ship, the *Worcester*, had been impounded in Leith on a charge of piracy which was clearly false, as was appreciated by many at the time. Yet, under the pressure of anti-English hysteria in the wake of the Darien scheme, the charge was proceeded with, and Green and two of his crewmen were executed. Given this background, the events in the Scottish parliament which began on 28 June 1705 are remarkable. Within two months the royal ministers in Scotland, Argyll, the new queen's commissioner, Queensberry, now back in her government as lord privy seal despite his defection to the opposition earlier, and Seafield, the lord chancellor, had persuaded the Scottish parliament to approve the appointment of commissioners to negotiate for a union with England; even the choice of the commissioners was left to the queen. As a result the Scottish commissioners, as well as those from England, were strongly in favour of union. The negotiations were therefore relatively brief, and a draft treaty was ready by 22 July 1706. England and Scotland were to become one country, Great Britain; the Hanoverian succession was guaranteed; there was to be a common parliament in which the Scots would be

---

[29] A. Browning, ed., *English Historical Documents, VIII: 1660–1714* (1953) p. 678.

represented by sixteen peers and forty-five MPs (this was not a direct reflection of the Scottish population figures, but it was better than Scotland's contribution to crown revenues warranted); there was to be an economic union, free trade between the two countries with the same customs duties; in addition, the Scots secured the promise of a cash payment of £398,085 10s 0d – the 'Equivalent' – which was reckoned to be compensation for taking on a share of the English National Debt and was to be partly used to compensate those who had lost in the Darien scheme. The proposed union, then, was an economic and a parliamentary one, in addition to the already existing regal union. It was not the legal or ecclesiastical union which James I had wanted a century earlier. In fact, in November 1706 the Scottish parliament passed an Act 'for securing the Protestant Religion and Presbyterian Church Government within the Kingdom of Scotland', and this was incorporated into the draft treaty.

Early in 1707 the draft treaty, though attacked fiercely by the Tories, passed the English parliament to come into effect on 1 May. More surprisingly, in stormy debates from 2 October 1706 to 2 January 1707 the Scottish parliament had already approved the draft treaty, almost unchanged, thereby agreeing to legislate itself out of existence. What converted many Scottish politicians to vote for the union? Professor W. Ferguson has produced an elaborate hypothesis which seeks to explain this in terms of bribery.[30] Only a large-scale programme of bribes to Scottish politicians by English ministers can explain, he argues, the apparent sudden volte-face of the Scots in 1706–7. This charge has a long history, originating in Jacobite propaganda at the time and reflected in later popular ballads like Burns's

> We're bought and sold for English gold
> Such a parcel of rogues in a nation!

What Professor Ferguson has clearly shown is that Queen Anne and her ministers gave money to Scottish politicians. But he has not shown that payments were made on a systematic scale or that they were intended as anything other than rewards for services rendered in the past; nor has he proved that, even if they were intended as bribes, they influenced their recipients' political views. Earlier cases of attempted bribery in the seventeenth century (by Gondomar in the reign of James I and by Louis XIV in the 1670s) suggest that bribery was an ineffective way of doing this.

Perhaps asking the question of why many Scots supported the union in terms of a sudden conversion of Scots politicians in 1706–7 is taking too much for granted. How representative of Scots opinion were the popular demonstrations against the union

---

[30] W. Ferguson, 'The making of the Treaty of Union of 1707', *Scottish H.R.*, XLIII (1964), and *Scotland's Relations with England: a survey to 1707* (1977). For a more moderate view of the Act of Union from the Scottish point of view, see David Daiches, *Scotland and the Union* (1977); T. C. Smout, 'The road to Union', in Holmes, ed., *Britain after the Glorious Revolution*, and 'The Anglo-Scottish Union of 1707: I. The economic background', *Econ. H.R.*, 2nd ser., XVI (1963–4), pp. 455–67; and G. S. Pryde, *The Treaty of Union of Scotland and England 1707* (1950).

from 1705 to 1707? Were those who voted for the anti-English legislation of 1703 and 1704 in favour of a political separation? These are questions to which there can be no definite answer. However, there are strong grounds for believing that not all Scots, politicians and non-politicians alike, were against union with England before 1706–7. There were strong arguments expressed at the time in favour of union which must have had some effect. The most compelling pro-union argument from the Scottish point of view was the economic one. As has been seen, most contemporary commentators believed that the Scottish economy was plunging into a severe crisis, for which it could be argued that union with England offered a practical remedy. Since Scottish agriculture was chronically underdeveloped, the only prospect of rapid economic progress seemed to be in foreign trade and in allied industries. The long-term development of Scottish foreign trade in the course of the seventeenth century seemed to suggest that the best way of stimulating it was by closer economic union with England. During the previous century Scottish foreign trade had shifted from a concentration on France, north-west Europe and the Baltic to become more focused on England. Therefore, the removal of hostile English import tariffs would undoubtedly benefit the transborder trade in cattle, corn and grain. Moreover, although Scottish merchants had not been totally excluded by the navigation legislation from trade with the English colonies (they had done so legally via Whitehaven as well as by illegal direct trade), the removal of all barriers to trading with the English empire, especially in North America, was obviously an appealing prospect to Glasgow merchants, for example. Of course, not all Scottish merchants would have agreed with these supposed advantages of union. (Merchants, like everyone else, do not often conform to common, stereotyped behaviour and attitudes.) Those merchants trading to France, for example, would gain no advantage from a union with France's greatest rival. But it is probable that the prospect of union with a more prosperous and economically advanced country did as much in Scotland to popularize the cause of union as the converse argument helped to persuade many people in England against it.

Arguments in Scotland in favour of union were not confined to economic reasons. It was probable that the political outlook of Scotland as an independent country was as gloomy as its economic prospects. An independent Scotland would not necessarily have resulted in a Jacobite restoration, but it would have been highly likely. The most probable outcome of that would have been civil war – the Presbyterian Lowlands versus the Jacobite Highlands – accompanied by a Scottish commitment to invading England in support of 'James VIII's' claims to the English throne. Few who foresaw that could have looked forward with much enthusiasm to a recurrence of the insecurity of the mid-seventeenth century when Scotland had tied her fortunes to another pretender to the English crown. It could be argued (and indeed was by proponents of union like Defoe) that political stability as well as economic prosperity was more certain for Scotland if she was united with England. Moreover, the draft treaty gave ample protection not only for the Scottish law, but also for the Scottish Kirk, and so the opposition of Scottish Presbyterian ministers was partially quieted. (They could hardly be said to have been silenced altogether: Scottish Presbyterian ministers in the early eighteenth century were more vociferous than contemporary English Anglican clergy, if that is possible.) Some Scots may have also been persuaded to support union by other considerations, like the 'Equivalent', or the wise English decision to repeal the Aliens Act once the union debate began in Scotland. In the last resort, though, it is impossible to say why most Scottish MPs voted for union. Given the fact that few Scots left a record of their personal reasons for the way they acted in 1706–7, the best conclusion is perhaps to say that they were influenced by a variety of motives, considering their individual interests as well as those of their country. In the last resort the majority of Scots people, especially supporters of the Presbyterian Kirk, probably thought that the Act of Union was the best bargain they could make.

As everyone knows the Act of Union was made, it survived, and, though under attack, it is still in existence over three centuries later. Its permanence, however, was far from certain for a long time after 1707. At no time is this clearer than in the first years of the union when at times it seemed possible that the Act might be repealed. For the Scots, especially, the disadvantages of the union seemed easily to outweigh what they had gained from it. The loss of Scottish independence, the demise of the Scottish parliament, after its brief period of unrestricted power since 1689, had been hard enough to swallow in 1707. Moreover, the English in the last years of Anne's reign seemed intent on securing further concessions from Scotland. From 1708 to 1713 the British parliament embarked on a series of measures which seemed designed to undermine many of the advantages Scotland had gained. Their legal independence, which the Scots had jealously guarded in 1706–7, was invaded in 1708 when parliament adopted a Treason Bill which established one law of treason for both England and Scotland. Even the independence of the Kirk seemed to be the target of English MPs who, cock-a-hoop after the Sacheverell case (see below, pp. 444–9), in 1711 supported a House of Lords' decision in favour of an Edinburgh episcopalian minister, James Greenshield, in March 1712 passed a Toleration Act allowing greater freedom to episcopalians in Scotland, and in May 1712 restored lay patronage in the Kirk. Moreover, the introduction of an export duty on linen in 1711, an increased tax on salt in 1712 and a malt tax in 1713 (the latter in direct contravention of the terms of the Act of Union) highlighted the fact that the union had not brought Scotland the advantages its proponents had promised. Indeed, one economic historian considers that the major economic benefits of union for Scotland did not appear until the 1780s.[31] So strong was the feeling against union in Scotland by 1713 that in June there was a concerted effort at Westminster by Scottish MPs, supported by the Junto Whigs, to secure the repeal of the Act of Union.

It therefore becomes far from easy to explain the survival of the union. The continued English attachment to it is more explicable than the Scottish. Union meant the Protestant succession in Scotland and therefore protection for England against a French and Jacobite invasion from the north. It is difficult to believe that the Junto

---

[31] R. H. Campbell, 'The Anglo-Scottish Union of 1707. II. The economic consequences', *Econ. H.R.*, 2nd ser., XVI (1963–4), p. 468.

Whigs would have sacrificed that. Surely their support of the Scottish MPs in June 1713 was primarily a cynical political manoeuvre designed to embarrass Harley and the government. For the Scots the advantages of continuing the union were less obvious immediately after 1707. They still retained an independent Kirk and law and therefore a large measure of their national identity, but, as has been seen, the English seemed to be determined to whittle that away. Nor did many Scots see much sign of the promised economic advantages of union in the years immediately after 1707. It is likely that the union survived its difficult early years from the Scottish point of view for two major reasons. First, union was the lesser of two evils. It is true that more Scots than English were Jacobites, but many Scots realized the horrible consequences of a Jacobite Scotland in terms of civil war and war against England. Both the strength and weakness of the Jacobite cause in Scotland are most clearly illustrated by the reaction to the Jacobite invasions of 1708 and 1715. On both occasions a majority of Scots, in effect, rejected a Jacobite restoration in favour of the Hanoverian succession. Above all, though, the union continued because many Scots discovered that it is harder to dissolve any union than it is to enter it.

Anne's capitulation to the Junto

The main achievements of Anne, Marlborough and Godolphin in the first half of the reign were brought about in large measure with the support of the Whigs and in the face of the hostile attitude of the Tories. All three Occasional Conformity Bills were rejected by the Whig-dominated House of Lords, which helped temporarily to stifle High Church fanaticism. The Whigs and the monied interest contributed as much to Marlborough's victories as they had to William III's. Moreover, the two major pieces of legislation of the early part of the reign, the Regency Act and the Act of Union, were essentially Whig measures. Yet, despite this and much to their disgust, the Whigs had received little political reward by 1707 beyond the appointments of Cowper as lord keeper of the great seal in October 1705 and Sunderland as secretary of state in December 1706. 'If one looks round every part of the administration, the management of the fleet (etc.) . . .', wrote Sunderland with understandable, though only slight, exaggeration, 'they are all of a Piece, as much Tory, and as wrong, as if Ld. Rochester and Ld. Nottingham were at the head of every thing.'[32] Anne resisted the arguments of Godolphin and Marlborough and consistently blocked all attempts to force her to give offices to the Junto lords. Not without good reason the Junto blamed Robert Harley for Anne's obstinate stance. Harley's influence with the queen increased, especially as Abigail Masham replaced Sarah Churchill as Anne's closest confidante at court in 1707, and Harley frequently warned the queen of the dangers of single-party government. Therefore in the summer of 1707 the Junto planned a sweeping campaign for the coming winter parliamentary session to force Harley out of office, and to convince the queen that she could not govern without them.

---

[32] Quoted in Trevelyan, *Anne*, II, p. 385.

In the first aim they were helped by the revelation in January 1708 that Harley's secretary, Gregg, had leaked secrets to the French, and, although Harley was cleared of complicity, his reputation undoubtedly suffered. What weakened his position more seriously than the Gregg affair, however, was his failure to provide a convincing defence of the conduct of the war in parliament. Clearly by now Harley and St John were becoming less convinced of the need to continue the war and this was reflected in the Commons at the end of January 1708 when St John, who was supposedly presenting the ministry's defence of war, produced a document which showed that only a quarter of the troops voted for Spain had in fact been at the disastrous battle of Almanza. In the preceding weeks Harley (though one can rarely be certain with such a slippery character) appears to have been negotiating secretly with Tory politicians with a view to forming a ministry without Godolphin.[33] If this is true, then it is a political battle which Harley lost. Marlborough and Godolphin brought matters to a crisis by absenting themselves from a cabinet meeting on 8 February and threatening to resign. At the cabinet meeting, the moderate Whig peers, the duke of Somerset and earl of Pembroke, supported the 'duumvirs' by refusing to serve if Harley was retained. Even so Harley need not have resigned; he still had the queen's support and could have resumed his negotiations with the Tories for a reconstructed ministry. Three days later, however, he resigned. Was the decisive factor in his decision the threat of impeachment that the Junto, using Gregg's evidence, was aiming to bring against him? Certainly, impeachment was not to be taken lightly, and Harley may have wisely chosen temporary political retirement instead of impeachment and the death penalty.

Harley and St John, who also resigned, were replaced by junior Whigs, Henry Boyle as secretary of state, and Robert Walpole as secretary of war. It is a further illustration of Anne's independence that she held out against the Junto Whigs for a further nine months, despite heavy Whig gains in the general election of May 1708. In the autumn she resisted a Junto ultimatum that Prince George be replaced as lord admiral by the earl of Pembroke, and that the earl's two posts of lord president and lord lieutenant of Ireland should go to Somers and Wharton. Only when her beloved George died on 28 October did Anne's resolve finally weaken, and early in November the Junto lords finally received their long-hoped-for political reward.

The failure of the Whigs and Tories, 1708–1714

Godolphin and the downfall of the Whigs, 1708–1710

In 1708 the political fortunes of the Junto Whigs were apparently on the crest of a wave. Even their enemies conceded that Somers, Wharton, Halifax and Orford were a group of gifted individuals. Moreover, in the early years of Anne's reign they attracted

---

[33] G. Holmes and W. A. Speck, 'The fall of Harley in 1708 reconsidered', *E.H.R.*, LXXXI (1965), pp. 673–98.

the support of a rising generation of brilliant politicians. Unlike his father, the minister of James II and William III, Charles Spencer, third earl of Sunderland was a committed party politician, but he inherited some, if not all, of his father's political skill. More talented were Robert Walpole and Charles, Viscount Townshend, whose families dominated Norfolk politics in the early eighteenth century. Walpole owed his first step forward in his political career to the patronage of the earl of Orford, and this early help was repaid by Walpole's almost constant support of the Junto in Anne's reign. The circle of political friends established by Walpole in these years reads like a *Who's Who* of early Hanoverian politics, including William Cavendish, marquis of Hartington (later duke of Devonshire), James Stanhope and William Pulteney. With this kind of support the Junto became an even more formidable political force than in the previous reign. They were held together by a high degree of loyalty to each other and to the principles of the new Whiggery, which in 1708 had at last brought them political power. Furthermore, in the 1708 general election the Whigs secured a rare majority in the House of Commons, largely due to an abortive Jacobite invasion of Scotland, which had an effect on English politics very similar to the assassination plot of 1696. Yet, as a decade earlier, the Junto Lords were not able to hang on to power for long. Within less than two years of attaining office, all the members of the Junto and their allies, including Godolphin, had either been dismissed or had resigned, and the general election of 1710 was a crushing victory for the Tories. Why was the Junto's second period of ascendancy as brief as the first?

In 1708 the position of the Junto was not so strong or so secure as it seemed. The Whig majority in the House of Commons was an aberration from the normal pattern of English politics since the Glorious Revolution. Usually the only secure parliamentary base the Whigs could rely on was the House of Lords. Very quickly in the following months, as the Jacobite threat of 1708 receded, Whig support in the House of Commons began to be eroded. Especially it was undermined by the growing opposition in the country to two major aims which the Junto stressed after regaining office: to continue to pour men and money into the war until Louis XIV was totally defeated and demoralized, and to weaken the power of the Church of England. As will be seen, opposition to these intentions both inside and outside parliament was very strong. But it is likely that even more damaging to the Whig Lords was their failure to secure the unqualified support of Queen Anne. Undoubtedly, the ending of the passionate friendship of Anne and Sarah Churchill after 1707 played a part in this. From 1707 to 1710 the two women indulged in a series of semi-public bitchy quarrels, which ended in Sarah being dismissed from Anne's presence for ever and being stripped of her household offices. No longer was Sarah able to attempt to influence the queen in favour of the Whigs, and her replacement as Anne's confidante, Lady Masham, allowed her cousin, Robert Harley, to have a base at court to scheme against the Junto. Yet these bedchamber intrigues were probably not the most important reason why the Junto never became part of Anne's intimate circle. As has been stressed before, Anne's independence can be underestimated. Already she had strong reasons not to like the Junto. She was irritated by the way that they had sniped at her during the bishopric crisis in 1707, and had only given way reluctantly to their appointment to office. The very way that they had forced themselves into office made her dislike them even more. Moreover, to these reasons by 1709–10 was added the fact that Anne's enthusiasm for the war, like that of most of her subjects, was cooling rapidly. She also made it clear that she was sympathetic to the popular fury roused by the Whigs' attack on the Church of England. She therefore needed little persuasion to connive at Harley's machinations in 1710 to engineer the dismissal of Godolphin and his Junto allies.

'No peace without Spain'

One of the principal features uniting the Whigs and the Junto Lords remained their commitment to the war against France. Despite the fact that Louis XIV appeared to be anxious to make peace, the Junto made it clear that they were not willing to end the war. Louis made his first peace proposal in 1705, but it was not until the winter of 1708–9 that he began to offer concessions that met the main demands of the allies. In March and April 1709 at The Hague, Louis's diplomats, Pierre Rouillé and his foreign minister, Jean Baptiste Colbert, marquis de Torcy, volunteered to withdraw French claims in Spain, the Indies, the Low Countries and Italy. When Marlborough and Lord Townshend arrived at The Hague to negotiate for Britain, de Torcy even promised that Louis XIV would recognize the Protestant succession in Britain and take measures (falling short of direct expulsion) to persuade the Pretender to leave France. These generous concessions were repeated at peace negotiations at Gertruydenberg in March 1710.[34] However, for Townshend, acting on instructions from his Junto masters, even these sweeping promises by the French were not enough. He persuaded the Dutch to raise their demands, and the allied negotiators drew up forty preliminary articles which included the requirement not only that Louis should agree to Philip's withdrawal from Spain in favour of Archduke Charles, but that if this was not done within two months, Louis should join the allies in a war to secure his grandson's deposition. Louis's refusal of the preliminaries in May 1709, given such stiff terms, is not surprising. Clearly the Whigs were not willing to make peace on any terms. This was further illustrated at the end of the year when Townshend concluded the Barrier Treaty with the Dutch. So anxious were the Whigs to keep the Dutch in the war to pursue their war aim of 'No peace without Spain' that Townshend promised British help to secure many 'barrier towns' in the Spanish Netherlands for the Dutch, as well as allowing the Dutch commercial concessions in the trade to Spanish America after the war.

It is easier to explain why the Whigs were so insistent on continuing the war than it is to accept that they were wise to do so. Some of the arguments in favour of extending the war aims in 1703 still held good in 1708. If the French and Spanish thrones were both occupied by Bourbons, would the peace of Europe, or at the very least the Protestant succession in Britain, not be threatened by an over-mighty Bourbon superpower? Distrust of Louis's protestations that he had no intention of uniting the French

---

[34] M. A. Thomson, 'Louis XIV and the Grand Alliance, 1705–10', in Hatton and Bromley, eds., *William III and Louis XIV*, pp. 201–10.

and Spanish thrones, given the French king's past record, was perhaps natural. Also there were still powerful commercial arguments for protecting and extending Britain's influence in Spain and the Mediterranean. In 1708 Britain concluded a secret agreement with Archduke Charles to allow British merchants limited rights to trade with Spanish colonies. Moreover, in September 1708 the navy captured Port Mahon and so paved the way for a further extension of British naval and commercial presence in the Mediterranean. However, the difficulty arises of determining whether or not 'No peace without Spain' was a wise policy after the allied victories in Europe and defeats in Spain from 1704 to 1708. At what point did it become clear that the growth of Spanish nationalist support for Philip ensured that it was unreasonable to expect Louis XIV to be able to persuade Philip to give up Spain and impossible to force Spain to abandon Philip? Even the crushing allied defeat in Spain at the battle of Brihuega in December 1710 failed to shake the resolve of the Whigs (at least in public) that the war in Spain could still be won. On that point, at least, it is easier to sympathize with the Tory view that the war in Spain was now irretrievably lost.

In their bellicose attitude to the war, the Junto soon became increasingly isolated in British political life. However, it is important that a distinction should be made between responsible opponents of the war and the irresponsible attitude adopted by many country Tories. With the war apparently already won, some politicians, like Queen Anne and Robert Harley, sensibly were converted to the view that a serious diplomatic effort should be made to secure a satisfactory peace settlement. Harley's opinion was confirmed after his departure from office in February 1708 during his enforced retirement in Hertfordshire. There he came into close contact with the war-weariness prevalent among country Tories. Unlike Harley, however, country Tories appear to have thought very little about the terms of the proposed peace, but simply believed that a peace treaty should be secured as soon as possible. Many events in 1708 and 1709 confirmed a majority of Tories in the view that Britain should withdraw from the war without delay. The bad harvest of 1708 and the following severe winter of 1708–9 added for many landlords the prospect of falling rental income to the actual escalating taxation caused by the war. Not only this, rocketing grain prices brought the possibility of famine and mob violence. To Tories on their country estates the spectre of rural rebellion at their gates was more real than the diplomatic subtleties of peacemaking in Europe. Moreover, early in 1709 the endemic hatred of many Tories for all foreigners was fed by the xenophobic propaganda released by the Whig bill to naturalize all foreign Protestants. Though rooted in the commercial rivalry of the seventeenth century, English dislike of their Dutch allies by 1709 had progressed to an irrational stage. The earl of Shaftesbury neatly captured the fanaticism of anti-Dutch hatred current in England in the reign of Queen Anne: 'If you would discover a concealed Tory, speak but of the Dutch and you find him out by his passionate railing.'[35] All foreigners and foreign influences were subject to the same vilification,

---

[35] Quoted in A. D. MacLachlan, 'The road to peace, 1710–13', in Holmes, ed.. *Britain after the Glorious Revolution*, p. 199.

and the debate on the Bill for the Naturalization of Foreign Protestants produced examples of extreme racial prejudice which have become all too familiar in the recent history of Britain. If unrestricted immigration was allowed, wrote one pamphleteer in 1709, foreigners would 'have admission into places of trust and authority, which in process of time might endanger our ancient polity and government, and, by frequent intermarriages, go a great way to blot out and extinguish the English race'.[36] Bigoted sentiments like these were unaffected by the evidence of the technical expertise and commercial enterprise contributed by immigrants to the British economy in the late seventeenth and early eighteenth centuries (see below, pp. 490–1, 494). Instead the immigration of about 8,000 foreign Protestants from the Palatinate in the two months after the Naturalization Bill became law was seen by many Tories as the fulfilment of their prophecy that the country was in the process of being swamped by the poor of foreign countries. English insularity reached a peak, which complemented the already strong feeling that a European war was no longer being fought in the interests of Britain. The Barrier Treaty of December 1709 was further confirmation to the Tories that they were correct. Moreover, the Tories saw themselves as pouring not only money into a needless war, but men as well. Early in September 1709 came news of Marlborough's battle at Malplaquet on the border between France and the Spanish Netherlands, in which 20,000 allied soldiers and 15,000 Frenchmen were killed. This was war mortality on an unprecedented scale and the needless carnage at Malplaquet was a great encouragement to the growing anti-war sentiment. In this climate there were even those who began to play on the submerged fears of a standing army which had been so potent at the end of William's war. If the war continued, would the probable outcome not be the emergence of Marlborough as a second Oliver Cromwell? 'History', wrote a correspondent of Harley in 1708, 'furnishes many examples of men who from the command of less force have aspired to sovereignty. But I believe there is no instance that ever any man who had tasted of absolute power could ever retire to a private life and become a good subject.'[37] By 1710 all these sentiments coalesced into a great popular desire for peace. It is an axiom of British politics after 1689 that the Whigs were in the strongest position when war fever was at its height, and vice versa. Unfortunately for their political prospects, the Junto only succeeded in forcing themselves into office at a time when hostility to the war was overwhelming in the country, in parliament and at court.

The impeachment of Dr Sacheverell

Without doubt the national revulsion against the Junto's war policy, combined with Queen Anne's loss of enthusiasm for the war, would have caused the downfall of the Junto. After the next general election, which was due in 1711, the Whigs would certainly have faced a hostile majority in the House of Commons, and would have found it very

---

[36] Quoted in Holmes, *British Politics*, p. 69.
[37] Quoted in Trevelyan, *Anne*, II, p. 387.

difficult to convince Anne to retain them in office. However, the downfall of the Junto came about even sooner than it might otherwise have done because of their decision to impeach Dr Henry Sacheverell. In so doing they brought the Church back into the political arena. Ironically, it was the Junto who took the initiative in sparking off an explosion which within a few months destroyed their immediate political position and damaged the Whig party's long-term prospects of recovery. Politically defeated though the High Church cause had been in 1705, the grievances that fuelled that cause were still deeply felt in the country houses and rectories of provincial England. With the advent of the Junto to power, it was naturally feared that the power of the Church of England would suffer even more. Nor were these fears unfounded. Soon after Wharton arrived in Ireland as the newly appointed lord lieutenant, he announced his intention of repealing the sacramental test for public office. Not for the first time English apprehensions were roused by the fact that Ireland was apparently being used as a testing ground for policies that were to be later extended to England. Rumours spread that the Junto intended to repeal the Test Act, and these were apparently substantiated by a clause in the Act for the Naturalization of Foreign Protestants (1709), which legalized the acceptance of the sacrament in a nonconformist chapel as a condition of naturalization. Might this soon be made the only condition of entering public office?

Equally important, in 1708 and 1709 Tory High Churchmen found themselves and their most fundamental political theories under a sustained bombardment in the sermons and pamphlets of Whig clerics and propagandists. In Benjamin Hoadley the Whigs at last found a clergyman who was prepared to stand up against the ranks of voluble High Church priests, led by Atterbury and Sacheverell. In a series of sermons from 1705 to 1709, Hoadley launched an attack on one of the basic justifications for the doctrine of passive obedience, St Paul's assertion in Romans chapter 13, verse 1 that 'the powers that be are ordained of God . . . therefore let every soul be subject to the higher powers'. According to Hoadley's interpretation, St Paul had advocated only obedience to those rulers who 'answer the good end of their institution'. Resistance to those rulers who acted tyrannically, on the contrary, was permitted, indeed encouraged. 'There is nothing in nature, or in the Christian religion', said Hoadley, 'that can hinder people from redressing their grievances, and from answering the will of Almighty God, so far as to preserve and secure the happiness of public society.'[38] Without doubt the most influential lay exposition of Whig political philosophy was *Vox Populi Vox Dei: or True Maxims of Government*; it was published in 1709 and went through eight editions in its first twelve months. Its assertion that ultimate power lay with the people was worthy of Leveller pamphlets of the mid-seventeenth century, and it was suitably dismissive of assertions that the people had no right to resist rulers who ignore 'the eternal laws of God and Nature'.[39]

---

[38] Quoted in Kenyon, *Revolution Principles*, p. 117.

[39] Professor Kenyon thinks this was written by Thomas Harrison: ibid., pp. 123ff. See also J. P. Kenyon, 'The Revolution of 1688: resistance and contract', in N. McKendrick, ed., *Historical Perspectives: studies in English thought and society* (1974), pp. 62–4.

Given the character of early eighteenth-century Anglican clergy, one would not expect them to remain silent in the face of these attacks. Godolphin once wryly commented that 'a discreet churchman is as rare as a black swan'. Yet clearly some were more discreet than others. In 1708 and 1709 both Offspring Blackall (now clearly a High Church divine) and Atterbury delivered important sermons in defence of the doctrine of passive obedience as a counter-attack to Hoadley. However, these were calm and reasoned pieces of academic exposition when compared with the notorious sermon delivered by Dr Henry Sacheverell on 5 November 1709 in St Paul's cathedral before the Corporation of the City of London. Like Sacheverell's earlier sermons, *In Peril Among False Brethren*, which was printed in large numbers soon after it had been delivered, is not remarkable for its originality. A contemporary, William Fleetwood, said that it was generally considered to be 'a rhapsody of incoherent, ill-digested thoughts, dressed in the worst language that could be found',[40] a view echoed by many later historians. Dr Bennett condemns it as 'a mish-mash of other men's sermons and the preacher's own past performances'.[41] Many High Church clerics, including Sacheverell, had delivered sermons before denouncing the threat to the Church and State posed by the growth of dissent, and asserting the fundamental importance of 'the subject's obligation to an Absolute and Unconditional Obedience to the Supreme Power'. However, what set *In Peril* apart was the extreme and provocative language which Sacheverell used. Indeed, Atterbury, who knew from Sacheverell's past performances what to expect, had attempted to prevent his fellow Oxford divine from being invited to give the sermon. Offensive and inflammatory the sermon was, but this does not seem a compelling reason why the government should have decided to single out Sacheverell for impeachment. Wharton and Godolphin (though not, according to his later account, Somers) pressed their colleagues to prosecute Sacheverell. On 13 December 1709 the House of Commons voted at the instigation of the government that Sacheverell's sermon was a 'malicious, scandalous and seditious libel', and on the following day the fateful decision was taken to bring articles of impeachment against Sacheverell.

The fact that the trial of Dr Sacheverell eventually rebounded against the Whigs makes the problem of discovering why he was brought to trial even more important. Unfortunately, since those behind the impeachment left no records of their thoughts or private discussions, this cannot be resolved with any certainty. One possible solution is that Godolphin and the Junto were stung into retaliation by the vicious personal abuse directed against them by Sacheverell's sermon; Godolphin was sensitive to criticism and could not have missed the use of his nickname in the reference to the 'crafty insidiousness of such wily Volpones'. Nor could the lord treasurer and his Junto colleagues have relished Sacheverell's condemnation of them for allowing the growth of dissent and wilfully conniving at the destruction of the constitution. Yet it is clear that Sacheverell offended more than the personal honour of the Whig ministers; his

---

[40] Quoted in Kenyon, *Revolution Principles*, p. 130.
[41] Bennett, *Atterbury*, p. 110.

sermon was also a scathing attack on their political principles. As part of his defence of the doctrine of passive obedience, he had made a withering onslaught on the Whig belief that the Glorious Revolution had been brought about by resistance. Sacheverell, alleged the articles of impeachment against him, 'doth suggest and maintain that the necessary means used to bring about the said happy revolution were odious and unjustifiable . . . and that to impute resistance to the said revolution is to cast black and odious colours upon his late majesty [William III] and the said revolution'.[42] In short, Sacheverell was attacking not only the subject's right to resist a tyrannical ruler, but also the Glorious Revolution itself.

In impeaching Sacheverell, the Junto saw a golden opportunity to present their own view of the revolution and of their 'Revolution Principles', and to do so publicly in a parliamentary trial rather than more quietly in a court of law. They also, at the same time, saw the impeachment as a speedy, expeditious way of getting rid of a demagogue, whose scriptural exhortations to put on 'the whole armour of God' and to wrestle 'not only against the flesh and blood, but against principalities, against powers, against the rulers of the darkness of this world, against spiritual wickedness in high places' came oddly from the lips of a devout exponent of the doctrine of non-resistance. Moreover, it is likely that the queen's ministers also hoped to use the trial of Dr Sacheverell as a party weapon against the Tories, and so halt their opponents' apparently inevitable political resurgence. The Whig managers of the trial intended to use Sacheverell's extreme defence of passive obedience and his attack on the Glorious Revolution to illustrate that the loyalty of Tories to the queen and to the Protestant succession was suspect and that the logical conclusion of Sacheverell's argument was Jacobitism. Walpole, who played a major part in organizing the trial in 1710, proved very adept after Anne's death in insinuating that all Tories were secret Jacobites. Yet in 1710 this political stratagem flopped. The trial, which began on 27 February 1710 and was intended to wreck the Tory party, misfired and instead came very close to destroying permanently the Whig party's political fortunes.

Just how badly wrong the trial went for the Whigs can be seen by the massive popular demonstrations throughout the country, but especially in London, in favour of Sacheverell. These culminated on the night of 1–2 March in frightening mob violence in the capital, only surpassed in scale by the Gordon Riots in the later eighteenth century. In part this was allowed to happen because of a tactical error on the part of the managers of the trial. By giving way to the delaying tactics of Sacheverell's lawyers the trial was postponed until 27 February, giving ample time for the London clergy to whip up the passions of their congregations to fever pitch. This by itself, though, is not sufficient explanation for why the Church of England should have become the focus of vehement popular support. The fact is that Sacheverell in his ravings against dissenters struck a rich vein of popular paranoia and prejudice which had already been exposed by the growing disenchantment with the continuing war against France. It was fairly easy in

---

[42] Browning, *English Historical Documents*, p. 206.

London to identify wealthy dissenters with the 'monied interest', which, according to Tory propaganda, was prospering from the war. To many the magnificent large meeting houses and chapels being built in London were an obvious confirmation of the truth of Tory charges that the war was simply being prolonged to line the pockets of the 'monied interest'. Moreover, Sacheverell also appealed to the xenophobia which was so pervasive in early eighteenth-century London. Were not many of those profiting from the war not only dissenters but also foreigners – Dutchmen, Jews, Huguenots? Was not the Bank of England dominated by immigrant families? Sacheverell brought together many current threads of anxiety: that the Church was in danger from the growth of dissent, and that traditional society was being undermined by the 'monied interest' and obnoxious foreign influences. Deep-rooted though these feelings were, Professor G. Holmes has left little room for doubt that the Sacheverell riots were not spontaneous.[43] Many of the 'mobs' who took to the streets in 1710 were people with respectable occupations; they were not the very poor and unemployed. They attacked only selected targets, mainly the bigger dissenting meeting houses, and made every effort to prevent damage to surrounding property. Behind the Sacheverell rioters were Tory and Church leaders, who exploited the popular hysteria in order to embarrass the government, and in this aim they were totally successful.

Even more serious for the Whigs, though, than events on the streets of London was that at the trial itself; although Sacheverell was found guilty, the Whig managers found that there were difficulties in defining their justification of the revolution, their 'Revolution Principles', which was one of the main purposes of the trial. They argued that the resistance in 1688 had not been treasonable, since it had been in defence of the fundamental law: James II had been threatening to subvert the constitution and his deposition was therefore lawful. Although they played down the fully blown version of the arguments they had used in 1688–9 – that subjects had a right to resist rulers who broke the original contract between rulers and the people – they found themselves nevertheless open to the charge that they were advocating rebellion and democracy. Desperately, Walpole and the other prosecution speakers at the trial asserted that they were not advocating a wholesale freedom to resist, but only one limited to cases of exceptional emergency. However, many must have agreed with Bishop Hooper, who, while rejecting the doctrine of passive obedience, nevertheless denounced the Whigs in 1710. Although

> he allowed, indeed, of the necessity and legality of Resistance in some extraordinary cases . . . [he] was of opinion that this ought to be kept from the knowledge of the people, who are naturally too apt to resist. That the Revolution was not to be boasted of and made a precedent, but we ought to throw a mantle over it, and rather call it Vacancy or Abdication. And that the original compact were two very dangerous words; not to be mentioned without a great deal of caution.[44]

---

[43] G. Holmes, 'The Sacheverell riots', *P. & P.*, LXXII (1976), pp. 55–85.
[44] Quoted in Trevelyan, *Anne*, III, p. 54.

It is a measure of the extent to which the trial of Dr Sacheverell rebounded against its promoters that the Tory and Church mobs of 1710 came to be blamed on the Whigs' incitement to popular rebellion.

Sacheverell's conviction by a small majority of seventeen votes in the House of Lords (sixty-nine votes to fifty-two) and his mild punishment of three years' suspension from preaching was a hollow victory for Godolphin and the Junto. The downfall of their ministry was now certain, and the process began in April 1710 with the appointment as lord chamberlain of the duke of Shrewsbury, who stirred himself to one of his few, but dramatic, short bursts of political activity. During his long period of retirement in Italy ('I have often commented', he wrote excusing his stay in the heart of Catholic Europe, 'that there's nowhere in Europe a Protestant country favoured with a warm sun'), he had cut his ties with the Whigs, and was now closely associated with Harley in an attempt to bring about a mixed ministry. Harley knew very well that Whig support was needed to sustain the public credit, but he had also never abandoned his ideal of non-party government. His negotiations with the Junto during the summer on these lines may account for the surprising fact that, when Sunderland was dismissed in June and replaced by the Tory earl of Dartmouth, his Junto colleagues, normally so loyal, did not resign. However, after Godolphin's dismissal and the appointment of Harley as chancellor of the exchequer in August, it rapidly became clear that Harley's hopes of forming a joint Whig–Tory ministry were impossible. The Tory leaders insisted on the dissolution of parliament being brought forward to the autumn, and in September, facing the certain prospect of a massive Tory electoral victory, the Junto resigned en masse. Rochester and St John were appointed as lord president and secretary of state. As expected, the general election in October 1710 reflected the overwhelming support in the country for Sacheverell and for an immediate peace. In the new House of Commons, the Tories had an estimated majority of 151. From now on Harley had no choice but to rely, to a much greater extent than he would have liked, on the Tory party.

Harley and the downfall of the Tories, 1710–1714

During the last four years of Anne's reign, the political climate undoubtedly favoured the Tories. The outcry against the war and in favour of low taxation in the general election in October 1710 confirmed that the Whig cause was in tatters. 'It is as vain to hope [of] restoring that decayed interest as for a man of sixty to talk of entering on a new scene of life that is only proper for youth and vigour', wrote Swift shortly afterwards.[45] The dominance of Tory opinion in the country was translated into massive majorities in the House of Commons after the elections of 1710 and 1713. Moreover, in 1712 the Whigs were even ousted from their usual controlling position in the Upper House, when Anne (for reasons which will be seen) created twelve Tory peers. Yet

---

[45] Quoted in Kenyon, *Revolution Principles*, p. 155.

despite all this, the Tories never exercised the influence over royal government from 1710 to 1714 that the Junto Whigs did in the periods of their ascendancy, 1694–7 and 1708–10. Royal government during Anne's last years never became Tory government; not did the Tories achieve the kind of legislative changes that their political support in the country and in parliament led them to expect. Fully blown Tory statutes enacted in this period can literally be counted on one hand: the Land Property Qualification Act 1711, the Act to Build Fifty New Churches 1711, the Occasional Conformity Act 1711, the Repeal of the Protestant Naturalization Act 1712, and the Schism Act 1714. It is true that under Tory pressure the war against France was brought to an end, but it was not achieved as quickly as many Tories wanted, and one important element of the peace settlement – a Franco-British commercial treaty – was overthrown. Nor did the three ecclesiastical statutes amount to the fundamental reform and protection of the Church demanded by many high Tory clerics and laymen. If all this is surprising, what is even more so is that soon after Anne's death the Tory party became insignificant as a political force and continued in eclipse for much of the remainder of the eighteenth century. Prominent among the problems facing the student of the last era of the Stuart age, then, is that of attempting to provide an explanation for the limited political potency of the Tories after 1710.

The key to understanding why the Tories failed to achieve many of their aims from 1710 to 1714 is the role played in this period by Robert Harley. It is necessary again to stress that, despite Harley's close association with Tory politicians since the end of William's reign, it is a great mistake to classify him as a Tory. Like Marlborough and Godolphin before him, he was a 'manager', independent of party. Moreover, he was more successful than Marlborough and Godolphin in maintaining his independent position. They had capitulated to the Whig Junto before 1710 in a way that Harley never did to the Tory cohorts after 1710. Harley retained his position as 'prime minister' from August 1710 until within six days of Anne's death, and during that period he successfully blocked many of the extreme Tory measures advocated by politicians like Henry St John. If anyone has a claim to be the leader of the Tory party after 1710 it is not Harley, but St John. After his departure from office in 1708 he spent nearly three years in the political wilderness among the country gentlemen of Berkshire and this experience showed him the apparently strong support he could gain by becoming a thoroughgoing Tory. It is this, not the contrasting personalities of Harley and St John, that lies at the heart of their well-known quarrel, which dominated the politics of the last years of Anne's reign. It is true that it would be difficult to find two more contrasting individuals: Harley, the introvert who clothed his aims in secrecy and who revelled in political intrigue, and St John, the extrovert who disdained hard political graft and often acted on impulse. But, more importantly, both men represented fundamentally different approaches to contemporary politics. St John had no time for Harley's attempts to build bridges between the two political parties; given the chance he would have driven all Whigs from office and done his best to exterminate the Whig party. Both men, too, had different aims regarding the major political issues of the day. Their quarrel became an ideological conflict on the future of the Church, the making of the peace, and the settlement of the succession. Both men attracted Tory support and in the process Harley detached a significant body of moderate Tories from St John's leadership. Consequently, unlike the Whigs, the unity of the Tory party was shattered. From 1710 to 1714, therefore, the Tory party, apparently so powerful, was rendered musclebound.

The failure of the Anglican 'counter-revolution'

In 1710 it seemed that the hopes of High Church supporters, so often frustrated in the past, would at last soon be fulfilled. By the autumn of 1710 High Church leaders had secured for themselves key political positions. St John was secretary of state, Bromley was speaker of the House of Commons, and Atterbury, despite the opposition of Archbishop Tenison and many bishops, was prolocutor of Convocation. After Harley's refusal to lend his support, Atterbury broke with him and planned an Anglican 'counter-revolution': a programme of church reforms, the details of which would be worked out in Convocation and its committees, and which would be pushed in its final form through the House of Commons by Speaker Bromley.[46] Moreover, the High Church party proved adept at harnessing for their cause the High Church fervour roused by the trial of Dr Sacheverell. In the spring and summer of 1710 a flood of loyal Addresses to the Queen demanded protection for the Church of England against its enemies. In August 1710 an influential political periodical, the *Examiner*, was founded by St John and others, and it began to employ writers like Swift and Atterbury to spread the High Church message. Everything seemed set to make 1711 the great year of church reform.

However, as in the earlier part of the reign, the High Churchmen were opposed by a powerful political combination that included not only the Whigs and the moderate bishops, but also the queen and Robert Harley. Working behind the scenes, Harley set about his congenial task of manipulating opinion against St John and Atterbury. Moreover, the queen's distrust of the High Church campaign, which she saw caused intense political bitterness, was increased by her dislike of St John. Indeed, the new secretary's well-known Deist views and scandalous private life hardly suited him as a leading spokesman of the High Church cause. Consequently, despite all the hard work of Atterbury during the winter of 1710–11 in producing many detailed proposals to revive the powers of the ecclesiastical courts, to increase the powers of bishops and to establish new parishes, the achievement of the High Church campaign was slight. The Act of February 1711 to establish fifty new churches was meant to be the first of many statutes to promote the Church of England. Not only did this Act have a limited effect (only twelve new churches were built during the next twenty years), but Atterbury, Bromley and St John found it difficult to use their undoubted political strength to force the queen and Harley to agree to support High Church measures. In the next few

---

[46] G. V. Bennett, 'The Convocation of 1710: an Anglican attempt at counter-revolution', in G. J. Cumings and D. Baker, eds., *Studies in Church History*, VII (1971).

months they managed to secure precious few concessions from the court. Only after St John threatened to resign in August 1711, when the peace negotiations were at a critical stage, did Anne agree to send an open letter to Archbishop Tenison pledging her general support for Atterbury's 'counter-revolution'. She also appointed Bishop Robinson of Bristol as lord privy seal. But, if the High Churchmen saw this as auguring a revival of the secular power of the clergy as in the days of Archbishop Laud, they were to be disappointed. In the remaining part of Anne's reign, only two more High Church measures became law: the Occasional Conformity Act of December 1711 and the Schism Act of 1714. The first was the successful culmination of a long campaign, but it was rarely enforced in practice. The second Act was potentially disastrous for opponents of the Church of England; it aimed to suppress the many dissenting schools and colleges established in recent years by imposing severe penalties on those who taught without a licence from a bishop. Fortunately, however, for the cause of nonconformity, the Schism Act was made inoperative by Anne's death. Moreover, significantly, both the Occasional Conformity Act and the Schism Act were not a direct outcome of High Church pressure, but were brought about because of disputes over the two issues which came to overshadow that of the Church in the last four years of Anne's reign, the making of peace and the succession.

The Peace of Utrecht

The years from 1710 to 1714 were remarkable for another distasteful display of isolationism in England, reflecting a deep desire for the withdrawal of the country from European affairs and from all contact with 'harmful' foreign influences. As the reaction to the Sacheverell trial had shown, these sentiments were part and parcel of the High Church hatred of dissent. Heretics and dissenters were seen as 'the importers of foreign vices'. But not just dissenters, Whigs and the 'monied interest' too were commonly lumped together with foreigners as the butts of a campaign against un-English activities. 'I scarce ever know a foreigner settl'd in England', wrote Atterbury, 'but became a Whig in a little time after his mixing with us.' Sir John Packington's main reason for wanting to end the war was 'to prevent the beggaring of the nation, and to prevent moneyed and military men becoming lords of us who have lands'.[47]

So powerful were these sentiments that at the beginning of the new parliament in November 1710 there developed an influential Tory pressure group to agitate for an end to the war and for measures to protect the 'landed interest' and the Church of England. The October Club began as a kind of beer-drinking society of provincial squires, but it developed into a serious political organization with a large and growing membership. It had reached about 150 MPs by April 1711, with regular weekly meetings at the Bell Tavern in King Street, Westminster, and with the experienced leadership of Sir Thomas Hanmer and Sir John Packington. Clearly this was a ginger group that the ministry could not ignore, and Harley threw his weight behind an October

---

[47] Quoted in Holmes, *British Politics*, p. 67, and Trevelyan, *Anne*, III, p. 107.

Club bill introduced in December 1710, imposing qualifications of incomes of £600 p.a. on all MPs for country seats and £300 p.a. on all borough MPs. Similar bills had failed in 1696, 1697 and 1702, but with Harley's support the October Club bill became law in February 1711. It is true that this Property Qualification Act was a watered-down version of the Act hoped for by extreme Tories, who would have liked to see it extended to the university and Scottish constitutencies, with its property qualifications restricted much more explicitly to income from land. Most of those who voted for the bill, however, intended that it should sweep Whig financiers, merchants and lawyers – the 'monied interest' and its hangers-on – out of parliament. The October Club also succeeded in 1712 in securing the repeal of the hated Protestant Naturalization Act passed in 1709, and the Club conducted a vigorous campaign against the war. In the process in January 1712 it brought about the expulsion from the Commons and imprisonment in the Tower of Robert Walpole on charges of corruption when he was secretary of war. Its most eminent victim was Marlborough, who was dismissed as captain-general at the end of December 1711.

Tory xenophobia and anti-war feeling voiced by St John and the October Club was not a major embarrassment to Harley. On the contrary, as has been seen, Harley had been unenthusiastic about the war since 1708, and immediately after entering office in 1710 he and Shrewsbury sent the earl of Jersey to France to begin secret peace negotiations. Subsequent events had confirmed Harley in his desire to end the war and to take the peace negotiations more seriously. The final allied evacuation of Madrid in November and the defeat of Stanhope's army at Brihuega in December 1710 convinced Harley and others that the war in Spain was irretrievably lost. Four months later any lingering doubts Harley may have had about abandoning the policy of 'No peace without Spain' must have vanished when Emperor Joseph died without a son, making it likely that his brother Charles would become not only king of Spain and the Spanish Empire, but also Holy Roman Emperor. There was now no point in pursuing a war to defeat a Bourbon superpower only to erect a Habsburg superpower in its place. There was thus a great deal of common ground between Harley and St John in their pursuit of peace. The main difference between them was not on the need for a peace settlement, but on its timing and its terms.

Harley rightly considered St John's pressure for an immediate peace irresponsible, totally ignoring the opinion of Britain's allies and the government's creditors. As far as the allies were concerned, it was only a few months since British ministers had been advocating all-out war and persuading them to turn down Louis XIV's generous peace terms. Clearly there was a need to try to persuade the allies to accept the sudden change of tack in British policy. This was difficult enough without St John openly displaying his willingness to make peace without any consideration of the interests of the Dutch. For this reason St John was excluded from the peace negotiations until April 1711 and even then Harley ensured that the energetic secretary did not dictate the course of Britain's diplomacy with the French. Furthermore, Harley attempted to win support in the City by his South Sea Company scheme, which he announced on 1 May 1711. The City had been shaken by the Tory electoral victory in 1710, and the talk of an immediate peace brought the threat that the government's major creditors, the Bank of England and the East India Company, might withhold further loans. The prime purpose of the new South Sea Company was to act as an alternative source of extra government loans to deal with the problem of the floating debt. The South Sea Company was to trade in South and Central America, which after the peace, it was hoped, would be thrown wide open to British investment. These commercial expectations proved unfounded and the company collapsed amid great scandal in 1720. But at the time the South Sea Company scheme fulfilled Harley's immediate purposes. Government creditors bought South Sea Company stock, and Tory support in the City was attracted by the prospect of supporting a rival to the Whig-dominated Bank of England.

Harley's approach to peacemaking was too circuitous for the zealots of the October Club, who wanted the ministry to follow a direct route to a peace settlement. Consequently, relations between Harley and St John, which were anyway becoming strained by their different attitudes to the future of the Church, were also soured by Harley's circumspect approach to peacemaking. St John, in any case, was already angry at Harley's hesitation before appointing him to office in September 1710, and early in 1711 there occurred the first open quarrel between the two ministers over St John's proposal for an expedition to capture Quebec. Later in the year ill-feeling between them increased, when St John learned that he had been kept out of the early phase of the peace negotiation. He remained frustrated as Harley kept a firm grasp on the course of events. Even when Harley was absent from parliament for two months, after he had been seriously wounded on 8 March 1711 by the knife of a French spy, Guiscard, whom he had been interrogating, St John was not able to usurp Harley's predominant position. Soon after Harley recovered his health, at the end of May 1711, he was created earl of Oxford, and promoted to lord treasurer, so receiving the public seal on his political supremacy. If any further sign was needed, it appeared in June 1712 when St John, to his chagrin, was created a mere viscount – Viscount Bolingbroke.

Bolingbroke may have failed to influence the peace negotiations as he would have liked, but that made it no easier for the Whigs and Britain's allies to stomach the preliminary peace articles agreed on by the British and French in the summer of 1711. To the disgust of the Whigs, Spain was to be abandoned to Philip V, and Britain broke her promise not to make a separate peace. It is true that the French accepted the principle of a Dutch barrier in the Netherlands, but this was not to be anything like as extensive as that agreed in 1709. Moreover, the allies fumed as they saw Britain secure for herself extensive concessions from the French: recognition of the Hanoverian succession, a thirty-year monopoly (the *asiento*) of British trade to Spanish America, trade rights in Spain, and British possession of Gibraltar and Minorca in the Mediterranean, St Kitts in the Caribbean, and Acadia (Nova Scotia), Newfoundland and Hudson Bay in North America. When these articles were published in September 1711, they were denounced predictably and rightly by the Whigs and allies alike as a sell-out. In Britain the opinion of one ally especially was noted with some alarm. Elector George of Hanover, son of Princess Sophia, who had been nominated as Anne's successor by the Act of

Settlement of 1701, made no secret of his anger at those in Britain who were responsible for the peace. As a result, at the end of 1711 one can detect the first signs among Tories of uneasiness about the wisdom of supporting the government's peace policy. A record of opposition to the war would hardly be a recommendation for political promotion under a Hanoverian monarch. But there was also a more disinterested consideration which led other people than the Whigs to wonder if peace was such a good idea: might not the end of the war allow France and Spain to support a Jacobite restoration?

One of the first Tory converts to opposition to the peace was Nottingham. In November 1711 he moved into an open alliance with the Whigs, who in return cynically agreed to support an Occasional Conformity Bill similar to those they had successfully fought against earlier in the reign. Their reward for this unprincipled behaviour was only a temporary one: on 7 December, with Nottingham's support, the Whigs secured a vote in the House of Lords by a majority of one condemning the peace 'without Spain'. In the long run, however, although the Occasional Conformity Bill became law, the opposition to the peace failed. Harley persuaded Anne to create twelve Tory peers and their votes in the Upper House reversed the Whig motion of 7 December. Moreover, in the winter of 1711–12 Harley and St John mounted an effective propaganda campaign designed to overcome British scruples about making a dishonourable peace. Foremost in their literary armoury was Swift's pamphlet *The Conduct of the Allies*, which was a violent attack on the Dutch, developing the Tory legend that the war had been prolonged to safeguard the particular interests of the allies, not of Britain, and therefore arguing that Britain ought to have no compunction about double-crossing her erstwhile allies. As a result Harley marshalled majority opinion in parliament behind him against the Whigs and a small band of 'Hanoverian Tories', who in the spring of 1712 organized themselves into the March Club. A series of votes in parliament from December 1711 to June 1712 condemned the Dutch and endorsed the government's peace policy. The House of Commons even approved the 'restraining orders', ordering Ormonde, Marlborough's successor, not to make contact with the enemy, a decision which denied Prince Eugene British military support and undoubtedly contributed to the Austrian army's defeat at Denain in July. The events of the spring and summer of 1712 showed that a majority in Britain were willing to sweep aside all considerations of national honour and Britain's international obligations in the pursuit of peace.

Given its discreditable preliminaries, one of the most surprising things about the peace settlement agreed in March and April 1713 at Utrecht by Britain, France and the Dutch (peace between France and the Empire was made a year later by the treaties of Rastadt and Baden) is that it proved to be 'one of the great European peaces',[48] establishing an international framework which lasted for a hundred years. That it did so was due to two general aspects of the peace settlement. First, the Utrecht treaties did not neglect the interest of Britain's allies. As William III had foreseen, a fundamental

---

[48] Thomson, 'Self-determination and collective security as factors in English and French foreign policy, 1689–1718', in Hatton and Bromley, eds., *William III and Louis XIV*, p. 283.

condition of European peace was the partition of the Spanish Empire. Britain took the concessions in the Mediterranean and South America already agreed by the preliminary articles, along with the ex-French possessions of St Kitts, Nova Scotia, Newfoundland and territories in Hudson Bay. France also formally agreed to recognize the Protestant succession in Britain established by the Act of Settlement. The emperor, though not represented at Utrecht, received massive chunks of the Spanish Empire in the Netherlands and Italy (Milan, Naples and Sardinia), and the duke of Savoy was given Sicily. The Dutch did take part in the negotiations: that they did so was partly a measure of Oxford's success in curbing Bolingbroke's anti-Dutch outbursts, but after the allied defeat at Denain the Dutch really had no alternative. Reluctant peacemakers they may have been, but at Utrecht they gained many of the barrier towns in the Netherlands which had always been their principal goal. The second merit of the Utrecht peace was its recognition of the limitations of what a peace treaty could achieve. The war had shown that Philip V could not be forced off the Spanish throne, and this was accepted in 1713. The Catalans were abandoned and Philip V's possession of the Spanish throne and Spanish possessions in South America was recognized. Of course, the peace of Utrecht did not provide a solution to all outstanding international problems. Its provision to prevent the future union of the Spanish and French thrones was very insecure indeed. In 1711 and 1712 three of the principal heirs of Louis XIV to the French throne died, the dauphin, the dauphin's eldest son the duke of Burgundy, and Burgundy's eldest son the duke of Brittany. As a result only a sickly two-year-old infant, Burgundy's younger son Louis, stood between Philip V and succession to the French throne. The only guarantee the Utrecht peacemakers could devise against that probability was Philip's renunciation of the French succession. Since this was hardly a promise that Philip could be relied on to keep, the peace of Utrecht cannot be given the credit for preventing the union of France and Spain. That came about instead by the fortunate fact that Louis XIV's heir did not die, but ruled France as Louis XV for nearly sixty years (1715–74). As far as Britain was concerned, too, the peace of Utrecht still left her without the emperor's recognition of the Protestant succession. Unfortunately, history does not provide tidy solutions. Much was settled in 1713, but much still remained to be decided by the diplomats who made the Quadruple Alliance in 1718.[49]

A Jacobite restoration or Hanoverian succession?

With peace concluded, political life in Britain came to be dominated by the question of who would succeed to the throne on Anne's death. This became increasingly urgent as the queen's health rapidly and visibly deteriorated; and in December 1713 she became seriously ill. Although she later recovered, the succession question was now again at the centre of the political world. The Whigs were totally united behind the provisions of the Act of Settlement of 1701 and the succession of Princess Sophia and,

---

[49] For the Quadruple Alliance, see G. C. Gibbs, 'Parliament and the treaty of Quadruple Alliance', in Hatton and Bromley, eds., *William III and Louis XIV*, pp. 287–305.

after her, of her son, George Lewis, elector of Hanover. The Tories, in contrast, were in disarray: only a minority had firm views about the succession. It is impossible to know how many were Jacobites like Richard Cresswell, the Tory MP for Bridgnorth, who after the Tory electoral victory of 1710 openly drank the Pretender's health at Bath. Undoubtedly, however, Jacobites were few in number in England where (as in Scotland) the propensity of people to voice Jacobite sentiments depended very much on the amount of alcohol they had consumed. When sober there were more Hanoverian than Jacobite Tories. Indeed in 1713–14 it is likely that the supporters of the March Club increased in numbers. In June 1713 during the debates on the Anglo-French commercial treaty negotiated by Bolingbroke, it became clear that some Tories opposed it because they distrusted Bolingbroke's motives in drawing closer to France. It is true that this was not the only reason for the defection of the eighty Tories who helped to destroy the treaty. Like Bolingbroke's commercial treaties with Spain in 1713, the French treaty was badly drafted and presented (this was the work of Matthew Prior). It also excepted woollen manufacturers from its reduction of mutual tariffs, and therefore brought on itself the wrath of clothier vested interests, Tory as well as Whig.[50] Yet the treaty became identified in the minds of some Tories with the one occasion, in August 1712, when Bolingbroke had escaped from Oxford's restraint and had allowed himself to be seen in Paris in public with the Pretender.

The debates on the French commercial treaty showed that the ranks of the October Club were split, and that Sir Thomas Hanmer had emerged as the influential spokesman of a group of Hanoverian Tories. In April 1714 nearly a quarter of the 340 Tory MPs voted in favour of a motion that the Protestant succession was in danger. By 1713–14, then, there were fewer Jacobite Tories than Hanoverian Tories, but it is likely that the biggest group of Tories by far were those who were still undecided about their attitude to the succession. The chronic inability of many Tories to commit themselves to the Protestant succession has already been seen. Their unwillingness to abandon the principle of hereditary succession had thrown many into long periods of tortuous indecision in 1701–2 when faced with the Abjuration Oath. To this was now added the more immediate consideration that the Hanoverians, who were Lutherans, foreigners and deeply involved in European affairs, were representative of everything most Tories hated deeply. Moreover, it did not take much imagination to foresee the plight of those Tories who had voted for the 'restraining order' after the arrival in England of Elector George, who had fought alongside Prince Eugene at Denain.

With the country teetering on the edge of civil war and with the Tories split and uncertain about the succession, the crying need was for clear leadership. They needed

---

[50] The extent to which Tories were Jacobites in the early eighteenth century has been debated with some vigour. For the view that the Tories were Jacobites, see E. G. Cruickshanks, *Political Untouchables: the Tories and the '45* (1979). For a different view, see L. Colley, *In Defiance of Oligarchy: the Tory Party 1714–60* (1982). For Tory divisions on the Anglo-French commercial treaty, see D. C. Coleman, 'Politics and economics in the age of Anne; the case of the Anglo-French trade treaty of 1713', in D. C. Coleman and A. H. John, eds., *Trade, Government and Economy in Pre-Industrial England* (1976).

someone at the centre to give them unequivocal guidance. The Tories were still very strongly represented in the country. The general election of August–September 1713 produced a House of Commons of about 363 Tory MPs and only 180 Whigs.[51] Yet this Tory majority never received the leadership it needed. Part of the explanation for this is that from the spring of 1713 onwards the quarrel between Oxford and Bolingbroke, which had smouldered fitfully since 1710, exploded into an open and bitter rivalry. With peace concluded, all common ground between the two ministers was gone. After the end of Anne's fourth parliament in July 1713, Bolingbroke and his allies, especially Lord Harcourt and Atterbury (now promoted to the bishopric of Rochester), tried to force Oxford to appoint Tory ministers and pursue Tory policies. As usual, Oxford emerged triumphantly from a prolonged bout of political in-fighting, and in August he appointed Bolingbroke's political enemies to key posts. Especially galling to Bolingbroke was the announcement that Bromley and Hanmer, both Hanoverian Tories, were to be respectively secretary of state and speaker of the new House of Commons. Oxford's victory, however, was not conclusive; on the contrary, it intensified the bitterness of the struggle between the two men in the last twelve months of the reign. Unfortunately for the Tory party, at this crucial time it was left adrift because the energies of Bolingbroke and Oxford were channelled into political rivalry, not leadership.

The attitudes to the succession problem of Bolingbroke and Oxford are very difficult to determine with any certainty. In the winter of 1713–14 both were in contact with the Pretender through a French agent, the Abbé Gaultier. However, this is by no means evidence that either of them was a committed Jacobite; this form of insurance against the possibility, however remote, of a change of regime was very common in the early eighteenth century, no less than in the fifteenth and sixteenth centuries. Not surprisingly, neither minister left a record of his private hopes regarding the succession, but all the indications are that Bolingbroke before March 1714 was much more prepared than Oxford to envisage the prospect of a Jacobite restoration. His visit to the Pretender in August 1712 in Paris has already been noted. He also maintained close connections with Jacobites in Britain, and made no attempt to curry favour with the Hanoverian court. In March 1714, however, he received the news (as did Oxford and Anne) that the Pretender refused under any circumstances to change his religion. This caused Bolingbroke to abandon during Anne's lifetime the prospect of a Jacobite restoration, and, with a Hanoverian succession almost certain, he began to look for a political strategy that would protect himself and the Tory party against the disfavour of Queen Sophia or King George. This he found in the scheme of uniting the Tories behind his leadership on the one issue on which the Tories were at one, the Church. At the same time, he would continue to undermine Oxford's position at court. Having secured an unassailable supremacy in parliament and at court, he would then be able to purge his opponents (Harleyites, Hanoverian Tories, and Whigs alike) from every

---

[51] E. G. Cruickshanks, 'The Tories and the succession to the Crown in the 1714 parliament', *B.I.H.R.*, XLVI (1973), p. 176.

public office of note, so that when the Hanoverians arrived they would have no alternative but to accept the fait accompli of the Tory dominance of public life.

Put like that it can be seen that this was an ambitious strategy, and at first it went well. At court Bolingbroke's influence rose at Oxford's expense. Partly by assigning some of the projected profits from the trade with Central and South America to Lady Masham, Bolinbroke weaned Anne's confidante from Oxford's patronage. In addition, Oxford's close relationship with the queen, which had survived his absence from office from 1708 to 1710, ended in the autumn of 1713. The cause seems slight; in September, Oxford asked that his son Edward, newly married to Lady Henrietta Holles, be made duke of Newcastle. The queen became convinced that Oxford was pursuing family ambition at the expense of all else, and Oxford's influence with her was gone. Moreover, Bolingbroke, with the cooperation of Atterbury, piloted the Schism Bill through parliament, and must have been satisfied with the support that the bill received from Hanoverian Tories like Hanmer and the earl of Anglesey (though not from Nottingham). Defoe concluded that the Schism Bill was 'the mine to blow up the white Staff'.[52] Not only were the Tories temporarily reunited against the hated dissenter schools, but Oxford's dislike of the measure put him in a very difficult position.

In the end, however, Bolingbroke's plans failed for three main reasons. First, he did not reunite the Tory party on any other issue than that of the Church. The Hanoverian Tories especially remained suspicious of him and not without good reason. Bolingbroke may not have been a Jacobite in the last months of Anne's reign, but he appeared to be one. Secondly, he was never accepted into the inner circle of Anne's court. Anne maintained her personal grudge against Bolingbroke, as against others, with great tenacity. Even when the queen dismissed Oxford, she refused to promote Bolingbroke to the lord treasurership. Finally, the major obstacle to Bolingbroke's scheme was Oxford's tenacity in hanging on to office. The lord treasurer held on until 27 July 1714, giving Bolingbroke too little time to profit by his dismissal before Anne died.

During the period from the autumn of 1713 until Anne's death, Oxford was the major block to Bolingbroke's ambitions to unite the Tory party, but he failed himself to provide the guidance the leaderless Tories needed. Judging by his actions, he was never anything other than a committed Hanoverian; in the spring of 1714 he even supported a Whig move to announce a reward for the capture of the Pretender if he should land in Britain. Oxford could have been the man to persuade uncommitted Tories to swell the ranks of the Hanoverian Tories. Unfortunately, however, in the winter of 1713–14 Oxford appears to have undergone a traumatic personal crisis, perhaps brought on by the death of his daughter or by the loss of the queen's favour. Whatever the reasons, outwardly he appeared apathetic and unassertive. He began to drink heavily and this adversely affected his work and his political influence. In the spring of 1714 he recovered slightly, but clearly all his diminishing energy was concentrated on the one aim of keeping himself in and keeping his rival out of office. Oxford was even less fitted in 1714 than in 1710 to be a leader of the Tory party.

---

[52] Quoted in Bennett, *Atterbury*, p. 177.

When Anne dismissed Oxford on 27 July, though she was very ill, she was still the key political figure she had been throughout her reign. It is as difficult to know what her hopes about the immediate future were as it is to ascertain those of Bolingbroke and Oxford. It is clear that she did not want Bolingbroke as her prime minister, and royal disfavour, as others had found before, was a deadly blight to a political career. What is less clear is whether or not Anne was in favour of a Jacobite restoration. It is true that she suffered bouts of conscience about usurping her half-brother's hereditary rights in 1702, and she disliked the Hanoverians as vehemently as any Tory. But, though suspicions remain, it is unlikely that after March 1714 she could contemplate a Jacobite restoration seriously.[53] On 30 July, in any case, she fell into a coma and matters at last were taken out of her hands. On the initiative of Lord Chancellor Harcourt and the privy council, Shrewsbury was appointed lord treasurer, making the Hanoverian succession certain. When Anne died on 1 August the Act of Settlement came into operation, and the Regency Council governed until the arrival of George I (his mother had died in June). So despite all the fears, the Stuart age ended, as it had begun, with the peaceful succession of a new dynasty.

The eclipse of the Tory party

The Tory party faced the end of the Stuart age in disarray, and on the accession of George I all their fears were confirmed. The Junto Whigs and their acolytes were appointed by the new king to every key public office. Moreover, this was the beginning of a long Whig supremacy in eighteenth-century British politics. Why did the Tories not recover in 1714 from this temporary setback, as they had done in 1689, 1697 and 1710, and as the Whigs had done in 1695 and in 1708? It is true that Bolingbroke and Oxford were under a cloud, and that the older generation of Tory leaders was either dead (Rochester died in 1711 and Danby in 1712) or no longer acceptable to the Tory rank and file (Nottingham had opposed the peace in 1711 and the Schism Act in 1714). But the Tories did not lack young and able leaders, like Hanmer and Bromley. They still had a natural majority in the country. What is more, the arrival of a foreign king presented them with the possibility, as in 1689, of rebuilding Tory unity by emphasizing the danger to the Church of England from a dissenter monarch, and by appealing to the traditional Tory hostility to the undue influence of foreign favourites and to involvement in Europe in the interests of the elector of Hanover but at British expense. Nevertheless the fortunes of the Tory party did not revive in the early years of George I's reign as they had in those of William III's reign. Why did 1714 mark the eclipse of the Tory party's influence for much of the eighteenth century?[54]

---

[53] Edward Gregg, 'Was Queen Anne a Jacobite?', *History*, LVII (1972), pp. 358–75.

[54] Recent work on eighteenth-century politics emphasizes that the Tory party, although eclipsed by the Whigs, did not disintegrate and disappear altogether soon after 1714, as was once thought. See the books by Cruickshanks and Colley cited in note 50 above.

This is a difficult question and it is fortunate that part of the answer to it lies beyond the scope of this book. Some contributory factors derived wholly from the period after 1714, most notably the Septennial Act of 1716. Typically, the new Whigs of the early eighteenth century do not seem to have had any compunction about introducing a measure designed to increase executive influence. By extending the life of individual parliaments to seven years, the Septennial Act greatly increased the scope of government patronage, which the Whigs quickly used to their own advantage. Moreover, the Whigs did not have to face a general election during a period of internal divisions in 1717 and 1720. The Tory party did not disappear, but the Septennial Act made it very difficult for it to present a serious challenge to Whig supremacy. Thus 1716 is a more fitting conclusion to the political history of the Stuart age than 1714. Nevertheless some possible causes of the Tory eclipse are visible before 1714. One is the vastly superior leadership and organization of the Whig party, which since 1689 had enabled the Whigs to overcome the drawback of being a minority party. By 1714 the Whigs were arguably more united than they had ever been before in defence of the Protestant succession and of their 'Revolution Principles'. Moreover, in Stanhope, Townshend, Pulteney and Walpole they had a group of high-flying leaders to replace the now ageing Junto (most of whom died in 1715–16). Because of developments before 1714 the Whigs were thus well placed and capable of taking advantage of their supremacy in 1714. In the first few months after Anne's death, they carried out a ruthless purge of their political opponents from public office on a scale never before attempted. Moreover, the general election of 1715 followed the formula established in earlier elections: the Whigs, because they had the open backing of the crown, secured the electorate's majority support. The Whig political advance of 1714–15 was made easier by the fact that only Nottingham of the major Tory leaders could be persuaded to accept office. Hanmer and Bromley were offered government posts by George I, but turned them down. Did they do so because the history of politics in the previous reign had shown that party unity could be an effective way to secure office? It is possible that they hoped to emulate the Whig Junto in 1708 and, after another general election, force the king to offer them more important ministerial positions. Whatever the reasons, their decision helped the Whigs to secure a firm grip on royal government. Do the technical organizational limitations of the Tories, though, provide a complete explanation for their failure to recover? It had not prevented Tory revival before.

A more cogent reason for the Tory collapse after 1714 can also be seen before Anne's death: the ambiguous attitude of many Tories to the Protestant succession. As has been seen, the failure of many Tories to come to terms with their conscientious objections to the Glorious Revolution had caused them endless trouble before 1714. It was still their Achilles heel on Anne's death: it laid them wide open to charges that they were disloyal to the new king. Moreover, Whig allegations that Tory fence sitting on the question of the succession was merely a cover for Jacobite loyalties were made more plausible by Bolingbroke's flight at the end of March 1715 to the Pretender's court. As a result during the Jacobite rebellion of 1715, though the vast majority of Tories rallied to George I, Walpole was able to find enough evidence of Tory sympathy for the Pretender to make his smear campaign against all Tories an enormous success. He employed the same tactics again in 1717, 1718, 1719 and 1723, when Jacobite invasions were feared. Certainly this was a major factor in the Tories' downfall. 'Toryism and Jacobitism' became as powerful a political cliché in the early eighteenth century as was 'dissent and sedition' in the reign of Charles II.

PART 6

Later Stuart England: change and continuity

14

Change

Summary

Arguably the reigns of the later Stuarts saw the beginnings of changes to Britain that were greater than any that had occurred before and were not matched in importance until the effects of the Industrial Revolution began to be felt from the eighteenth century onwards.

This chapter looks at these major changes and assesses their scale and importance:

- constitutional changes
- religious and intellectual changes
- economic and social changes.

The long-term effects of the Glorious Revolution: war and constitutional changes

In 1640–1 the Elizabethan constitution collapsed. Subsequently, during the English Revolution and the reigns of the later Stuarts, there was a search for a new constitutional 'settlement'. In the early years of the eighteenth century, many people believed that this search had been successful in 1688–9 when, it was thought, the architects of the Glorious Revolution had erected a constitution in which the three elements in it – king, Lords and Commons – balanced and limited each other, producing conditions of political stability and constitutional harmony. 'Herein indeed consists the true excellence of the English government', wrote Sir William Blackstone in the middle of the century,

> that all parts of it form a mutual check upon each other. In the legislature, the people are a check upon the nobility, and the nobility a check upon the people; by the mutual privilege of rejecting what the other has resolved: while the king is a check upon both, which preserves the executive power from encroachments. And this very executive power is again checked and kept within due bounds by the two houses . . . Thus every branch of our civil polity supports and is supported, regulates and is regulated, by the rest . . . Like three distinct powers in mechanics, they jointly impel the machine of government in a direction different from what either, acting by itself, would have done; but at the same time in a direction partaking of each, and formed out of all; a direction which constitutes the true line of the liberty and happiness of the community.[1]

However, the constitutional changes of the late seventeenth and early eighteenth centuries were not so straightforward or so complete as Blackstone and 'a prolific school of constitutional mythologists' in the latter century maintained.[2] It has already been seen that the Glorious Revolution of 1688–9, like the English Revolution and the 'Restoration Settlement', effected few permanent statutory changes in the constitution or in the crown's financial and administrative system. In 1689 the English government was as ill-equipped to finance a major war as all previous governments in the later sixteenth and early seventeenth centuries. All attempts before 1660 to remedy this had failed: as has been seen, in peacetime there was no general desire to reform the king's government, and in wartime (the 1590s, 1620s, 1640s and 1650s) attempts to create an efficient central executive invariably produced intense opposition (notably the Petition of Right in 1628 and the 'second civil war' in 1648) which ensured that such measures were not permanent.

Therefore, in 1689 one of the major constitutional problems of the Stuart age remained: to establish a reformed, strengthened central government without provoking fierce resistance based on fears that such reforms would lead to the decline of parliament and the establishment of absolutist government in England. If this was to be solved, there would have to be both a major readjustment and a clearer definition of the respective powers of the crown and of parliament. In many contemporary European countries, the solution had been found in the establishment of strong, authoritarian monarchies and a reduction in the powers of representative assemblies. As has been seen, the restoration of Charles II in 1660 made this a possible outcome in England

---

[1] Blackstone, *Commentaries on the Laws of England*, quoted in E. N. Williams, *The Eighteenth-Century Constitution 1688–1815* (1970), pp. 74–5.

[2] Mark A. Thomson, *A Constitutional History of England, IV: 1642–1801* (1938), p. 353.

also; that the English monarchy before 1688 did not become as strong as that in France was ensured mainly by the opposition roused by Charles II's and James II's quixotic decisions to follow Catholic policies. After 1689 the English crown could perhaps still have made itself politically independent of parliament; that it did not do so is to be explained only in the most indirect way by the long-term effects of the Glorious Revolution of 1688–9 but rather by the effects of what I have called above the Glorious Revolution of the 1690s and early 1700s. One immediate result of the invasion of William of Orange and his accession as king was to involve England in a long and expensive war against France, which lasted (apart from 1697 to 1701) from 1689 to 1713. Because of the unprecedented scale and cost of this war, the familiar problem faced by Tudor and Stuart rulers emerged in a more pressing form than ever before: how to finance a war with an antiquated system of public finance and with the likelihood that excessive demands for money would be met with hostility by parliament and most influential opinion in the country.

The Glorious Revolution of the 1690s and early 1700s and the wars of William III and Queen Anne's reigns proved to be a major catalyst of constitutional change. They had as great an impact on the long-term development of the British constitution as it has been seen that they had on the short-term pattern of English politics. During the 1690s and early 1700s, for the first time practical solutions were discovered for one of the major constitutional problems of the Stuart age. The development of a powerful central executive and the 'financial revolution', which took place as responses to the demands of the wars against France, aroused enormous mistrust in the country, but, unlike previous occasions, local opposition did not prevent such administrative and financial changes from becoming permanent. The explanation lies mainly in the fact that they were accompanied by a shift in the respective roles and powers of the crown and of parliament which helped to reconcile the political nation to them. These changes by no means represented a perfect constitutional settlement by 1714, as will be seen (see below, pp. 510–11). Nevertheless, by 1714 under the pressures of war the British constitution had diverged permanently from the drift elsewhere in Europe towards greater authoritarianism and centralization.

War and the king's government

All statutory attempts to curb the powers of the Stuarts had only limited or temporary success. The parliamentary leaders in the 1640s were themselves well aware that the legislation of 1641 was not an effective means of restricting Charles I. Moreover, the constitutional legislation passed in and after 1689 was more important in the context of contemporary politics than in the long-term development of the British constitution. The most successful statutory attempt to limit the crown's power after 1689 was the Triennial Act, which limited the crown's prerogative freedom to summon and dismiss parliaments at will, but the Bill of Rights (1689) and the Act of Settlement (1701) enacted only partial limitations on the powers of the monarchy. The Bill of Rights declared that extra-parliamentary taxation was illegal and that standing armies in peacetime had to be approved by parliament; it also abolished the powers exercised by James II of suspending parliamentary statutes and prohibited Catholics from succeeding to the throne. The Act of Settlement did not come into effect until Queen Anne's death, and before then its most important restrictions had been repealed. But when the Act did become effective in 1714, it guaranteed the independence of the judiciary by making permanent the tenure of office by judges, as well as preventing George I both from declaring war in defence of Hanover without parliamentary approval and from granting his countrymen offices or places in the privy council. All these were important, but they represented meagre statutory limitations on the powers of later Stuart and Hanoverian monarchs. Moreover, in certain respects these powers had grown since the days of James I and Charles I.

First, the later Stuarts had a bureaucracy that was bigger and more efficient than that possessed by their predecessors. Partly this was a reflection of the intellectual interests of some of the servants of the later Stuarts, like Samuel Pepys and William Blathwayt, who were friends of William Petty, the exponent of 'political arithmetic'. An expanded civil service was necessary, in their view, to collect statistics on which rational government decisions could be based (see below, pp. 485–6). However, far more important in causing the expansion of the king's government were the wars of the late seventeenth and early eighteenth centuries. Before 1689 this can be seen most clearly in the emergence of the treasury as a financial department, challenging (although not supplanting) the exchequer's role as the central institution of public finance. In this process the key date is 1667, significantly at the end of the second Dutch war, which had highlighted the need for financial reorganization. In May 1667, Charles II, with the Cromwellian practice of 'government by committees' in mind, appointed a treasury commission, which (under the influence of its secretary, Sir George Downing) began systematic record keeping 'as part of a deliberate campaign to exercise close control of revenue and expenditure'. By a series of privy council orders in 1668 the treasury secured its independence of the secretaries and of the privy council.[3] Later treasury officials, especially the earl of Rochester and the treasury commissioners of 1679 to 1684, ensured the permanence of these reforms, with the result that 'between 1660 and 1702 the Treasury office grew from something approaching the personal retinue of a magnate into a professional body of civil servants'.[4] Soon the treasury exercised control over the administration of the customs and excise and other revenues. Before 1689 also professional administrative methods were introduced into naval and military organization, most notably due to the work of Samuel Pepys as secretary to the admiralty 1673–9 and 1684–8, and of William Blathwayt as secretary at war from 1683.[5]

---

[3] Henry Roseveare, *The Treasury 1660–1870: the foundations of control* (1973), pp. 20, 31.

[4] S. Baxter, *The Development of the Treasury 1660–1702* (1957), p. 10.

[5] For administrative development before 1689, see Howard Tomlinson, 'Financial and administrative developments in England, 1660–88', in J. R. Jones, ed., *The Restored Monarchy 1660–88* (1979), pp. 94–117.

However, the most rapid growth in the king's government took place after 1689. During the wars against France, although by no means all traditional royal administrative methods were changed (see below, pp. 510–11), there was arguably a 'revolution in government' that made more impact on the structure of government administration than anything that happened in the 1530s.[6] The major changes did not take place in the older parts of the king's government; indeed, the number of offices at the royal court declined during the Stuart age, from 1,480 during the reign of Charles I to under 1,000 in the reign of George I. In 1713 the principal secretaries' office had only four under-secretaries and eight clerks. The total numbers employed in administrative departments like the admiralty and the navy office only rose from 147 in 1692 to 211 in 1716. The diplomatic service increased from 80 representatives in William III's reign to 136 in Queen Anne's. But the expansion of the army and navy raised to fight William III's and Anne's wars necessitated a bureaucratic explosion, especially in the financial departments of State. Over 40,000 were employed in the navy during these wars and the size of the army jumped from 10,000 troops in 1689 to an average of 76,404 in the war of 1689–97 and 92,708 in the war of 1702–13.[7] The number of bureaucrats employed in the royal financial departments (customs, excise, salt, stamps, post office, the treasury and the exchequer) rose from 2,524 in 1690 to 5,947 in 1716 and this figure did not include a large pool of part-time officials.[8] An indication of the size of this pool can be gained by the fact that in 1718 there were about 1,000 part-time customs officials (as against 561 full-time officials) working in London alone. It is therefore impossible to be precise about the size of the later Stuart government bureaucracy, but there is little reason to doubt Professor Holmes's estimate that by the 1720s there were about 12,000 permanent bureaucrats employed in government service, which represented a tenfold expansion in the civil service since the reign of Charles I and during the English republic.[9] Although this expansion was not as great as that which took place in contemporary France, the bureaucracy available to William III and Queen Anne was similar in kind to that employed by Louis XIV, a point emphasized by the admiration felt by the new breed of English civil servants, like Pepys and Blathwayt, for the authority and efficiency of French central government. Very slowly, in great contrast to the situation at the start of the Stuart age, there had appeared the outlines of a non-political civil service in Britain by the early eighteenth century.

The second great change that strengthened the king's government since the early seventeenth century was an improvement in the crown's finances. This is strikingly

---

[6] J. Brewer, *The Sinews of Power: war, money and the English state, 1688–1783* (1989), ch. 3; G. Holmes, *Augustan England: professions, state and society, 1680–1730* (1982), chs. 8 and 9; J. H. Plumb, *The Growth of Political Stability 1675–1725* (1967), pp. 11–12.

[7] Plumb, *Growth*, pp. 116, 123, 119–20; Brewer, *Sinews*, pp. 30, 66.

[8] Brewer, *Sinews*, p. 66.

[9] Holmes, *Augustan England*, p. 244; G. E. Aylmer, *The King's Servants: the civil service of Charles I 1625–42* (1961) and *The State's Servants: the civil service of the English Republic 1649–60* (1973).

illustrated by the contrast between the inability of Charles I to pay even for the limited wars of the 1620s and the achievement of the government of William III and Queen Anne in financing two full-scale European wars. They were enabled to do so because after 1689, using precedents established since the mid-seventeenth century, all three major sources of royal revenue – the crown's hereditary income, taxation and borrowing – were transformed. By the Restoration the only major element left of the traditional hereditary revenues of the crown was that from customs duties. Income from crown estates was already small before 1640, and the crown's revenue from wardships and purveyance, abolished with feudal tenures in 1646, was not restored in 1660. However, from the early 1670s customs duties which reached the crown rose rapidly, as a result of the expansion of overseas trade in this period and the decision to revert (as in the 1640s and 1650s) to direct collection of the customs. Between 1688 and 1702, 22.7 per cent of the crown's income came from customs duties.[10]

Before 1640 the burden of taxation in England had been the least onerous in the whole of Europe. Under-assessment for direct parliamentary taxation had reached ludicrous proportions, and, unlike France, there was little indirect taxation. Moreover, it was still theoretically considered that parliamentary taxation ought to be levied only on extraordinary occasions, when the king could not 'live of his own'. The parliamentary regimes of the 1640s, followed by the royalist council of war, inaugurated, however, the first attempts at a new taxation system in England. Weekly and monthly assessments from 1643 onwards were much more effective direct taxes than traditional parliamentary subsidies, and the excise, also introduced in 1643, was the first comprehensive purchase tax in England, levied on a wide range of commodities. Both were retained by Restoration governments. Moreover, from 1683 excise duties were collected directly by government officials, not tax farmers; and in the 1690s the land tax was revised on the same principles as assessments, to become the main source of direct taxation in late Stuart England. As in the case of the assessment, the yield of each land tax was decided on before it was levied and the sum then apportioned among the counties. Between 1688 and 1702, 23.2 per cent of the crown's revenue came from the excise and 32.5 per cent from land taxes. The traditional concept that the king should 'live of his own' was now abandoned, and for the first time taxation was accepted as a *normal* part of the crown's revenue. As a result the crown's revenue from taxes increased dramatically after 1689, as did the tax burden borne by English people. By the early eighteenth century, the English paid twice as much in taxation as did the French (17.6 livres per head per annum as against 8.1 livres in France); while the crown's income from taxation in the 1690s averaged £3.64 million a year, about double the income from taxation received by Charles II and James II before 1689.[11]

Easily as dramatic as the massive increase in the scale and sophistication of direct and indirect taxation in the late seventeenth and early eighteenth centuries was 'the

---

[10] The percentages in this paragraph are from the figures of Sir John Sinclair abstracted in Charles Wilson, *England's Apprenticeship 1603–1763* (1965), p. 217.

[11] Brewer, *Sinews*, p. 89.

financial revolution' in public borrowing that accompanied it.[12] Like governments at any time, the income of Stuart governments always fell short of their expenditure, and the gap had to be filled by short- and long-term borrowing. In the early seventeenth century this was done largely by James I and Charles I borrowing money in much the same way as private individuals, using their own assets as security. This is why the early Stuarts found investors increasingly unwilling to lend money to them and why they (and the parliamentarians in the 1640s) had to resort to forced loans. However, in the 1660s there emerged the beginnings of a new system of public credit. As has been seen, the additional aid levied by parliament in 1665 was devised by Sir George Downing and supported by Charles II. In order to persuade investors to advance money to the government, the tax was appropriated to a specific use (the second Dutch war) and creditors were to be repaid in rotation: those who had lent first were to be repaid first. Moreover, they received treasury orders promising repayment, and these orders were legally negotiable. Although these innovations received a setback in 1672 when the crown defaulted on interest payments to its creditors, they 'were to become the standard devices of "the financial revolution"'.[13] After 1689 the crown's need for loans was greater than ever before: between 1688 and 1702 the gap between royal income and expenditure was about £11.3 million. Among the many projects devised to meet this unprecedented deficit, two were ultimately successful. In January 1693 parliament authorized William III to borrow £1 million; the creditors were to be repaid by annuities and these were funded by new parliamentary excise duties. The second project, the foundation of the Bank of England, is more complicated, but the principles employed were similar to those used in 1693: the 8 per cent interest on a loan of £1,200,000 was to be repaid by specific duties allocated by parliament, and in return the subscribers were incorporated as a bank and given power to borrow more money on the security of parliamentary taxation. The effect of these measures of 1693 and 1694, as had been the intention of Downing in 1665, was to ensure that royal debts were underwritten not by the crown but by parliament. The king's debt became the National Debt. This system took a long time to become established; other projects like the Million Lottery of 1694, a national sweepstake, were tried but failed. Gradually parliamentary guarantees were established as the basis of public credit, with the result that investors were now more willing than ever before to lend money to the government. Between 1697 and 1720 the unredeemed public debt rose from £16.7 million to over £50 million.[14] Consequently, as well as enjoying a predictable income from taxation, William III and Queen Anne were able to borrow money on a more extensive scale than any other monarch in English history.

By 1714 the implications of these changes in the royal government in the late seventeenth and early eighteenth centuries were far-reaching for the prestige of the

---

[12] P. G. M. Dickson, *The Financial Revolution in England: a study in the development of public credit 1688–1756* (1967). See also H. Roseveare, *The Financial Revolution 1660–1760* (1991).

[13] Roseveare, *The Treasury*, p. 25, see pp. 255–6.

[14] Brewer, *Sinews*, p. 114.

British monarchy. English governments after 1559, wrote J. P. Cooper, were 'more than ever limited to a basically defensive [foreign] policy, however much their subjects hankered after past glories'.[15] This remained true until 1689: the only possible exception is the Cromwellian Protectorate, which carved out for itself a respectable international reputation, which Stuart monarchs before 1689 did not have. James I did not possess the financial resources to enable him to be the powerful figure in European diplomacy he would have liked to be; Charles I and James II (with the exception of the former's brief excursions into wars against France and Spain) followed isolationist policies; and Charles II seemed to many at the time to be little more than a puppet of Louis XIV. William III and Queen Anne, however, were able to take a leading role in European affairs. Moreover, by 1714 England and Scotland were united as Great Britain, and the country's overseas possessions were expanding rapidly. In great contrast to the period before 1689 (and certainly before 1640), the British monarch was the head of a country which was a major European and imperial power.

War and parliament

Growing local resentment and mistrust at the development of a strong central executive in the late seventeenth and early eighteenth centuries, leading to attacks on alleged maladministration and corruption in government and attempts to protect parliament from royal interference, were not unexpected. By the 1690s 'country' mistrust of central government had a long history stretching back for at least a century. In the reigns of the later Stuarts, fears about the future of parliament were as strong among some MPs as they had been in the reigns of James I and Charles I. However, after 1689 they had less foundation than earlier. By 1714 royal government in Britain was as strong as many continental governments, but it was far less free to indulge in policies of centralization and authoritarian rule. Accompanying the financial revolution that gave the crown the ability to take a leading role in European affairs that had not been possible for much of the sixteenth and seventeenth centuries were crucial changes in the constitutional relationship between crown and parliament. These assured parliament of a permanent place in the constitution, which had been the aim of many MPs throughout the Stuart age. Of even greater importance, they gave parliament the ability to control the activities of the royal government to an extent that had never been seen before.

This came about in two major ways. First, the crown's dependence on parliamentary taxation for wartime expenditure forced it to concede that the land tax should be administered largely by the people who paid it and that parliament should exercise overriding control over the way the money was spent. From the 1690s, the assessment and collection of the land tax was carried out by men who lived in the localities, not by bureaucrats foisted on the country by the central government. 'Land Tax administration

---

[15] J. P. Cooper, 'The fall of the Stuart monarchy,' in Cooper, ed., *The New Cambridge Modern History, IV: 1609–1648/59* (1970), p. 531.

underlined local social patterns.'[16] Of even more importance, the parliamentary classes won the right to subject the operations of all the crown's finances (not just the land tax revenue) to the closest surveillance. During the period before 1714, the principle of parliamentary appropriation of supply and parliamentary audit of the royal finances became established. Parliament in effect became responsible for the maintenance of the armed forces, and annual sessions were therefore necessary in order to grant the bulk of the money for this purpose. This provided more certainty of annual parliamentary sessions in wartime than in peacetime. A second constitutional effect of 'the financial revolution' was therefore more crucial. By perpetuating royal debts (now the National Debt) on a parliamentary basis, 'the financial revolution' ensured that, even in peacetime, annual sessions of parliament would be necessary to provide a constant guarantee of public creditworthiness. Parliaments were now indispensable to the financial viability of the king's government and annual sessions of parliament were assured. In 1698 this dependence was underlined when MPs felt that the grant to the monarch of a regular income of £700,000 p.a. for life (the civil list) would not undermine it.[17]

The king's government by the end of the Stuart age was financially stronger than ever before, but in a position that ensured that it was heavily dependent on parliament. Before 1714 this is most clearly shown in the slow but certain erosion of the royal prerogative. By 1714 the royal prerogative was limited in two main ways; neither was openly admitted by anyone, least of all by William III and Queen Anne, but both became practical limitations on royal power. The last two Stuarts were not as free as their predecessors to choose their own ministers or to determine their own foreign policies. As has been seen, William III and Queen Anne, in order to get their business through parliament, at times had to accept as ministers men whom they detested. Later Stuart parliaments gained some voice in the choice of royal ministers, a vital erosion of the crown's prerogative which Pym and the parliamentary leadership in the 1640s had completely failed to achieve. Moreover, William III and Queen Anne were also forced to consult parliament to a much greater extent than ever before in the making of foreign policy.

The transformation was highlighted in 1700–1. Until 1700 William III had conducted his own foreign policy without reference to opinion in England. The war against France in the 1690s is rightly known as 'William's war'. Even his English ministers were not told about the negotiations resulting in the Partition Treaty of 1698; parliament did not learn of them until 1700. However, in order to persuade parliament to accept the need for renewed war against France, in 1701 William III entered into a close dialogue with parliament about foreign affairs. 'What William had been forced to concede, Anne was unable to refuse', writes G. C. Gibbs; it 'became usual for ministers and others to expound foreign policy in Parliament and to lay treaties

---

[16] Colin Brooks, 'Public finance and political stability: the administration of the land tax, 1688–1720', *H.J.*, XVII (1974), p. 291.

[17] E. A. Reitan, 'The Civil List in eighteenth-century British politics: parliamentary supremacy versus the independence of the crown', *H.J.*, IX (1966), especially pp. 318, n. 2, and 319.

and papers before Parliament, either at its request or upon the initiative of the Crown.'[18]

Religious and intellectual changes

The Stuart age witnessed a search for a religious 'settlement' that lasted as long and was as difficult as the quest for a new constitutional relationship between crown and parliament. After 1660 the problems involved in reaching a religious settlement were more numerous than in the early seventeenth century, when there had been a large measure of agreement among most Protestants both about the form the Church should take and its relation to the State: its theology should be Calvinist predestinarianism; it should be governed by bishops; it should work in close cooperation with the State; and it should be the only Church allowed to exist. Religious toleration, it was felt, would inevitably upset the traditional hierarchical political and social order. However, developments during the 1640s and 1650s shattered the Protestant unity which had prevailed before 1640. During the revolutionary decades many varied forms of Protestantism emerged – Presbyterians, Independents, Congregationalists, Ranters, Quakers – and, although attempts were made after the Restoration to suppress these as effectively as Elizabeth I had crushed Presbyterians and separatists in the 1580s and 1590s, many of the sects survived. From this point onwards, only their common hatred of Catholicism could bring English Protestants together, as in 1688, and then only temporarily. Theological diversity now prevailed: Calvinist predestinarianism was no longer the common theology of English Protestants. Dissenters – those who refused to conform to the Church of England as it was established in the 1660s – became a permanent feature of English life. As a result, from 1660 onwards the search for a religious settlement became more difficult than ever before.

After 1660 the established Church was presented with two major, novel problems. First, if it was now only one among many other Protestant churches, ought the Church of England to maintain its close alliance with the State and to continue to play a major political role? Secondly, could the Church of England come to terms with Protestant dissenters, either by agreeing to accommodate them within a broad established Church or by granting them the right to exist outside the Church? Moreover, in addition to these intractable questions of Church–State relations, and of religious comprehension or toleration, the restored Church of England also faced a new set of problems which emerged from changes in the intellectual climate of the period. Many of these changes were brought about, in part, by the spread of the new experimental science, as will be seen. Despite the pleas of scientists to the contrary, the spread of the new science led some people to question traditional Christian beliefs. Not only was the Church of England now faced with the competition of Protestant dissent, but also

---

[18] G. C. Gibbs, 'The revolution in foreign policy', in G. Holmes, ed., *Britain after the Glorious Revolution 1689–1714* (1969), p. 72. See also Thomson, *Constitutional History*, pp. 231–3.

many churchmen feared that the Church was in danger of being overwhelmed by a growing tide of irreligion and atheism, as society became more secularized.

This section outlines some of the major responses of intellectual and religious opinion to these new problems in later Stuart England. As might be expected, the responses were diverse. However, in the period from 1660 to 1714 there developed, though not without intense opposition, the view that the Anglican Church was not (and never had been) independent of the State and ought to be subordinate to it, and that its major function ought to be pastoral rather than political. Furthermore, there emerged, again slowly and fitfully and in the face of much hostility, a conviction that Protestant dissenters ought to be tolerated and given freedom to worship. Finally, both these views were part of the response of some enlightened churchmen to the fact that later Stuart England appeared to be a period of diminished religious fervour, and that the Church had to concentrate on its missionary role and religion had to be defended on rational grounds. In the late seventeenth and early eighteenth centuries the vogue for rationalism in religion was part of a new rational approach to all current problems, in government and society as well as in the Church. Certainties founded on faith or on the writings of the 'ancients' were called into question. It came to be believed that by the application of reason – by basing arguments on facts discovered by observation and by personal experience, a method successfully adopted in the new sciences – there were no limits to the improvements that could be brought about in society and its institutions. With hindsight, to the late Stuart period can be traced the beginnings of a modern intellectual outlook: religious toleration, modern experimental science and a belief in mankind's capacity for infinite progress.

Anglicanism and dissent

Anglicanism

Since most English Protestants before 1640 were members of the Church of England, 'Anglican' is not a very helpful term to use in analysing religious opinion in that period. However, after 1640 'Anglican' denotes a separate group within the broad spectrum of English Protestantism. 'Anglicans' during the 1640s and 1650s were those who remained faithful to the Church as it had been established in 1559 and which had been abolished by parliamentary legislation in the 1640s. Recent scholarship on the 1640s and 1650s indicates how deeply rooted this Church was in popular culture by this time. The revolutionary religious changes decreed at Westminster in the 1640s seem to have left parochial life in many English towns and villages relatively untouched. Nearly three-quarters of church ministers kept their livings throughout the 1640s and 1650s.[19] And, although it is difficult to quantify religious allegiances among the mass of the people in this period (as at other times), John Morrill's estimate that

---

[19] I. M. Green, 'The persecution of "scandalous" and "malignant" parish clergy during the English Civil War', *E.H.R.*, XCIV (1979).

only 5 per cent of English people attended religious assemblies other than those in parish churches between 1643 and 1656 indicates the likely scale of popular Anglicanism among their congregations.[20] Only a small number of ministers were ejected from their livings; many of these found refuge in the country houses of sympathetic landowners, where they exercised the traditional forms of worship laid out in the Book of Common Prayer.[21] Though few in number, their experiences were important for the future because they did much to re-forge relationships between bishops and some lay people which had been broken in the Laudian days of the 1630s. In 1660 these experiences mingled with the resentment of royalist landowners who had suffered for their loyalty to the monarch in a short, sharp outburst of revenge against those who had collaborated with the revolutionary regimes. As has been seen, even before the ecclesiastical legislation of the early 1660s was passed, Anglican patrons ejected clergymen installed since 1640 from livings under their control and replaced them by their own nominees. The Church of England was restored on a wave of Anglican loyalism which neither Charles II nor Clarendon could resist (see above, pp. 299–305).

From 1660 to 1688 there was a remarkable degree of unanimity among the ecclesiastical hierarchy (including both archbishops of Canterbury, Sheldon, from 1660 to 1671, and Sancroft, from 1671 to 1691), rank-and-file clergymen and their lay supporters about what should be the role of the restored Church. Among the characteristics of mainstream Anglicanism during the reigns of Charles II and James II three features stand out. First, most Anglicans emphasized that the restored Church of England should play a major political role. The Church was believed to be independent of the State, but it should work in close alliance with it. Although, as has been seen, both Charles II (apart from brief periods especially from 1681 to 1685) and James II refused to accept this alliance, nevertheless churchmen continued to offer that, in return for the crown's support against its rivals, the Church of England would provide a major support for royal authority by proclaiming the ideology of non-resistance from its pulpits. Secondly, many Anglicans in Restoration England believed that the Church should be narrowly defined and that no concessions should be made to those Protestants who could not accept the Anglican sacraments and prayer book. They opposed both the comprehension of dissenters within the Church and the toleration of dissenters outside the Church. 'Indulgence to dissenting zealots', wrote an Anglican apologist in 1669, 'does but expose the State to the perpetual squabble and wars of religion.'[22] Increasingly, this intolerant attitude to dissent became the hallmark of Toryism and anti-exclusion in the conflicts that marked Restoration politics (see pp. 303–5). Thirdly, a sustained effort was made in this period to reinforce the authority of the restored Church by the writings of the Fathers of the early Church. Restoration Anglican

---

[20] J. Morrill, 'The Church in England 1642–49', in J. Morrill, ed., *Reactions to the English Civil War 1642–49* (1982), p. 90 and *passim*; J. Spurr, *The Restoration Church of England 1646–89* (1991), ch. 1.

[21] R. S. Bosher, *The Making of the Restoration Settlement: the influence of the Laudians 1649–62* (1951).

[22] S. Parker, *A Discourse of Ecclesiastical Polity*, quoted in G. R. Cragg, *From Puritanism to the Age of Reason* (1950), p. 202.

scholars, especially at Oxford University, continued the patristic studies of early seventeenth-century divines. The high level of ecclesiastical scholarship which was maintained in the seventeenth century was the product not only of the love of research for its own sake, but also of a concern to buttress the authority of the Church of England.[23]

Not all Anglicans after the Restoration shared these conservative, militant opinions of the majority. The origins of an alternative Anglican view of the Church can be traced to a group of scholars at Cambridge University, the so-called 'Cambridge Platonists', including Ralph Cudworth, Henry More, Benjamin Whichcote and John Smith. These teachers were a major influence on a younger generation of men, many of whom began a career in the Church of England after the Restoration and who became known by their enemies as 'Latitudinarians', including John Tillotson, the future archbishop of Canterbury, Isaac Barrow and Simon Patrick.[24] Like Arminianism and other 'isms', 'Latitudinarianism' is a loose term that obscures differences as well as reveals similarities among individuals. Professor Sykes, for example, points to affinities between Sheldon's outlook and that of the Latitudinarians, who were staunch episcopalians, and men who before 1688 emphasized the importance of non-resistance as strongly as other Anglicans.[25] However, there were certain ideas which set the Latitudinarians apart from other Anglicans. First, they reacted against the development and manifestations of Calvinist predestinarianism during the 1640s and 1650s. In their circles the 'enthusiasm' of the sects became a derogatory word. By 'enthusiasm' they meant the emphasis placed by many sects on the importance of individuals being guided by an 'inner light', a philosophy which had been carried to extremes by sects like the Quakers and Ranters in the 1650s. The Latitudinarians rejected 'enthusiasm' and Calvinist predestinarianism, and placed much less importance in their religious thought on theological questions and dogmas. This negative response to the English Revolution led the Latitudinarians to make a more constructive contribution to religious thought, since they went on to argue that revelation and faith were much less important as the basis of Christian belief than rational argument. Since many Latitudinarian divines were associated with scientists and were members of the Royal Society, it is tempting to see their emphasis on producing a rational defence of religion as a product of their interest in the new science.[26] Just as scientists in expounding their discoveries placed less emphasis on ancient authorities, so Latitudinarians (unlike other Anglicans) showed little respect for the authority of the Fathers. Instead they defended religion rationally and coolly; their sermons were not cluttered with references to ancient authorities, nor were they the rousing, passionate sermons delivered by High Church divines, like Atterbury and Sacheverell. Furthermore, unlike many Anglicans, Latitudinarians

---

[23] N. Sykes, *From Sheldon to Secker: aspects of English Church history 1660–1768* (1959), ch. 4.

[24] The best introduction to the Cambridge Platonists and the Latitudinarians is Cragg, *From Puritanism to the Age of Reason*, pp. 37–86.

[25] Sykes, *From Sheldon to Secker*, p. 146.

[26] B. Schapiro, 'Science, politics and religion', *P. & P.*, LXVI (1975), pp. 133–8.

wanted to broaden the Church to include many Protestant dissenters. 'Certainly in our English Church', wrote Cudworth in 1674, 'just as in Noah's Ark were all sorts of animals (if I may so express it), are all kinds of Protestants: Calvinists, Remonstrants, and I believe even Socinians all dwelling here, united with no apparent discord in one and the same communion.'[27] In this spirit Latitudinarians like William Lloyd, bishop of St Asaph associated with William Penn and other dissenters. Protestants, they believed, ought to form a united front against Catholicism, immorality and disbelief, which it was felt were growing in strength. English ecumenical Protestantism would be the first step on the road to a reunification of European Protestantism in order to wage more effectively the continuing war against Antichrist.[28] As has been seen, this more tolerant attitude to Protestant dissenters was shared by those Anglican magistrates who were less than enthusiastic about enforcing the intolerant Clarendon Code and who became identified with Whiggery and with exclusion in the political conflicts of Charles II's reign (see pp. 303–5).

The Glorious Revolution of 1688–9 had two major effects on the division within the Church of England which appeared in Restoration England between the High Church majority and the dissenting Low Church Latitudinarians. First, High Church Anglicanism lost the leadership of the Church it had held since 1660. Because Archbishop Sancroft and other church leaders refused to accept the revolution, they and other nonjurors were deprived of their posts in the Church. Latitudinarian divines were appointed to key offices in the church hierarchy in their place: Tillotson as archbishop of Canterbury (1691–4), Thomas Tenison as archbishop of Canterbury (1695–1715), Edward Stillingfleet as bishop of Worcester (1689), Simon Patrick as bishop of Chichester (1689) and bishop of Ely (1691), William Lloyd as bishop of Worcester (1699), and Gilbert Burnet as bishop of Salisbury (1689). Therefore from now on High Anglicanism became a movement centred in the rank and file of the clergy and among their lay patrons. The second effect of the events of 1688–9 was to widen the gap between the two groups. After 1689 High Church Anglicans were more than ever determined to protect the Church of England against its rivals. The different attitudes of High and Low Church Anglicans to Protestant dissenters became increasingly obvious in the bitter political debates of the reigns of William III and Queen Anne (see above, pp. 374–8, 405–8, 420–4, 444–9, 451–2). Moreover, High Anglicans found it much more difficult than Low Churchmen to accept the Glorious Revolution of 1688–9. Despite their earlier attachment to the ideology of passive obedience, Latitudinarians persuaded themselves that they could support William III, on the grounds that James's departure and William's accession were part of God's providential plan. Bishop Lloyd even preached a sermon before the queen on 30 January 1691 declaring that 'the marks of God's hand were so visible in it (the Glorious Revolution), at first, and are so daily more and more; that he is blind that

---

[27] Quoted in Sykes, *From Sheldon to Secker*, p. 146.
[28] See M. C. Jacob, *The Newtonians and the English Revolution 1689–1720* (1976), ch. 3 for the strand of millenarianism in Latitudinarian thought.

doth not see them'.[29] Tenison undoubtedly would not have been so forthright in public as he was round the earl of Clarendon's dinner table early in 1691, but his off-the-cuff remark captures the attitude of many Latitudinarians to the Glorious Revolution: 'after dinner', noted Clarendon in his diary,

> we fell upon the subject of the times, and concerning the Bishops who were to be deprived. Dr Tenison owned there had been irregularities in our settlement: that it was wished things had been otherwise, but we were now to make the best of it, and to join in the support of this government, as it was, for fear of worse.[30]

Clearly with such men in control a redefinition of the role of the Church in the years after 1689 was as inevitable as was the opposition it encountered from High Churchmen. Latitudinarian bishops continued to work for a comprehensive Church after 1689. They also wanted to strengthen the Church, not like the High Churchmen by seeking the support of the State, but by making the Church more spiritually effective. Only by stamping out pluralism and absenteeism and by missionary activity could the Church be made strong, believed bishops like Tenison. When he became archbishop of Canterbury he patronized societies to undertake this work, including the Society for the Promotion of Christian Knowledge and the Society for the Propagation of the Gospel. The Word too was to be spread to the colonies and all parts of the world. 'Others also,' said Samuel Bradford, a Boyle lecturer in 1699, 'especially the bodies and societies of men, which have commerce with the gentile world, might contrive methods for propagating their religion with their trade.'[31]

However, the Latitudinarian ideal of a comprehensive Church was never realized, as has been seen. As a result some Anglicans came to accept yet another view of the Church of England's place in society: as only one among other Protestant churches that were allowed to exist. Clearly this was a view, demoting the status of the Church, the authority of the bishops and its functions, that many High Church Anglicans would not accept, as the support for the Occasional Conformity Act (1711) and the Schism Act (1714) proved. But in 1714 the Latitudinarian supremacy in the Church was confirmed and the High Church party's eclipse made permanent. Only three years later, Bishop Hoadley of Bangor delivered a sermon that took the Latitudinarian view of the Church to its extreme conclusion. Christ, he said, 'left behind him no visible human authority, no Vice-regents, who can be said properly to supply his place; no Interpreters upon whom his subjects are absolutely to depend; no Judges over the consciences or religion of his people'. Private religious beliefs were all important; there ought to be freedom 'in affairs of conscience and external salvation'.[32] As the storm

---

[29] Quoted in Jacob, *The Newtonians*, p. 97.
[30] Quoted in ibid., pp. 92–3.
[31] Quoted in ibid., p. 167. See p. 468 for the Boyle lectures.
[32] Quoted in G. V. Bennett, *The Tory Crisis in Church and State 1688–1730: the career of Francis Atterbury, Bishop of Rochester* (1975), pp. 214–15.

roused by the sermon showed, not everyone agreed with Hoadley's view of the limited role of the Church of England and of the necessity for religious toleration. But in 1717 Convocation, the voice of intolerant High Church Anglicanism, was suspended, and it did not meet again (apart from a brief session in 1741) until 1855. Moreover, in 1719 both the Occasional Conformity and Schism Acts were repealed.

Dissent

> These kind of vermin swarm like caterpillars
> And hold conventicles in barns and cellars,
> Some preach (or prate) in woods, in fields, in stables,
> In hollow trees, in tubs, on tops of tables.[33]

So wrote John Taylor, 'the water poet', in 1641, and in the next two decades, as has been seen, many different religious sects proliferated, especially under Cromwell's tolerant regime. After the Restoration, especially in the 1660s and early 1670s and from 1681 to 1686, a determined campaign was mounted to suppress those sects that would not conform to the restored Church of England. Quakers and Baptists suffered especially because of their refusal to take the oath of allegiance. Quakers also refused to compromise like some other sects by attending church occasionally or by hiding their beliefs: Quakers carried on the evangelical tradition of pre-Civil War Puritanism and therefore made their nonconformity obvious. Above all, Quakers refused to acknowledge their social superiors by raising their hats or by respectful speech, subversive behaviour which made it difficult for many to forget their radical antecedents in the 1650s. All dissenting groups suffered after the Restoration, but the Quakers bore the brunt of the malice of militant intolerant Anglicanism; many more than 15,000 Quakers are estimated to have been fined, imprisoned or transported between 1660 and 1685.[34]

How did Protestant dissent survive the 'period of the great persecution' from 1660 to 1688? As other authoritarian regimes have found before and since, dissident minority groups flourish under conditions of oppression. For some dissenting sects the 'period of the great persecution' was one of great spiritual enrichment, producing classics like William Penn's *No Cross, No Crown*, and John Bunyan's *Pilgrim's Progress*, both of which were begun in prison. Some sects battled against persecution by missionary work; by the end of the Stuart age the greatest missionaries, the Quakers, were the only dissenting sect to have meetings in every English county.[35] Later nonconformity owed an incalculable debt to the spiritual strength and vigour of early dissenters. In some areas, however, dissent flourished primarily because of the failure of the Church of England to provide enough churches and vicars. Mostly these were areas where the Church

---

[33] Quoted in M. R. Watts, *The Dissenters from the Reformation to the French Revolution* (1978), p. 80.

[34] W. C. Braithwate, *The Second Period of Quakerism* (2nd edn., 1961), p. 115.

[35] Watts, *Dissenters*, p. 285.

had always been weakest, in forest, pastoral and fenland areas, for example, where parishes were large and communities scattered, and where there was a long tradition of opposition or apathy to the Church. Although the Church had made some attempts to fill these gaps in large parishes by building 'chapels of ease', these were often poorly endowed and there were not enough of them. In these areas dissent grew by default. The Yorkshire parish of Halifax, for example, covered 124 square miles in which there was only one parish church and twelve chapels of ease. Clearly this was a situation to be relished by an energetic Presbyterian minister like Oliver Heywood, even though he had been ejected from his living in 1662; when he died in 1702 there were seven Presbyterian meetings in the parish, with congregations of over 2,000 members.[36] Perhaps, however, the major factor in the survival of dissent during the reigns of Charles II and James II was the failure of some magistrates to execute the penal laws in full measure. Some were dissenters themselves, especially in towns, but most were Anglicans. It is possible that some Anglican magistrates were swayed by the intellectual arguments for toleration that began to appear in print after the Restoration: persecution is bound to be ineffective, since people can only be forced into *outward* conformity not *inner* belief; religious toleration is compatible with political stability, as in the case of the United Provinces; religious intolerance has disastrous economic side-effects, since it discourages the immigration of skilled Protestant workers.[37] But probably many Anglican magistrates were inclined to turn a blind eye to dissenters (and juries to acquit them) because most of the dissenters they knew were clearly not the seditious subversives they were often portrayed as being. Some dissenters, especially Presbyterians, attended parish churches, as well as their own meetings. Most were sober, respectable members of society. Moreover, from the early 1670s onwards the political cliché that dissent equalled sedition lost its appeal. Catholics not Protestants came to be seen as the greatest danger and Anglican magistrates were consequently less inclined to bring dissenters before the courts.

Dissent, then, survived the 'great period of persecution' and, limited though it was, the Toleration Act ensured that dissent would be a permanent feature of English society. However, the failure either to make it possible for dissenters to become members of the Church of England or to repeal the Test and Corporation Acts ensured that dissenters were deprived of their civil and political rights and were second-class citizens. So the great apartheid in English society between 'church' and 'chapel' was perpetuated, and this came about largely because of Anglican fears, especially after 1689, that dissent was growing at such a pace that it threatened to overwhelm the Church of England. How accurate was this Anglican image of Protestant dissent in the late seventeenth and early eighteenth centuries? As in the case of the popular view of Catholicism, there was an alarming discrepancy between reality and what many people believed. Dissenters were never more than a tiny fraction of the total population. Quantification is difficult obviously; too much reliance cannot be placed on Danby's religious census

---

[36] Ibid., p. 280.

[37] For the intellectual case for toleration, see Cragg, *From Puritanism to the Age of Reason*, pp. 190–224.

of 1676, but it estimated that the total dissenting population was 4.39 per cent (see above, p. 304). Dr Watts's analysis of the survey of dissenters made between 1715 and 1718 by the Committee of Three Denominations (Presbyterians, Congregationalists and Baptists) is the most complete available. It was estimated then that dissenters made up only 6.21 per cent of the total population of England and 5.74 per cent of the Welsh population. In England, Presbyterians were the most numerous (3.3 per cent), followed by Independents (1.1 per cent), Particular Baptists (0.74 per cent), Quakers (0.73 per cent) and General Baptists (0.35 per cent). In Wales there were more Independents (2.47 per cent) than Presbyterians (1.96 per cent) and Particular Baptists (0.31 per cent).[38] In 1704 the Kent General Baptist Association lamented 'the great decay, sinking and languishing' of the churches there, an assessment confirmed for the whole country by visitation records.[39] Moreover, the social and political stigma of dissent contributed to the falling off in the support of the landowning classes. Gentry patronage, which had been so important to Puritanism before 1640 and, to a lesser extent, to dissent during the 'great period of persecution', all but disappeared after 1689. It is less easy to be certain that dissent also lost much of its earlier spiritual vigour. However, it is possible that, as many dissenters, excluded as they were from politics and polite society, channelled their energies into trade and industry, so their spiritual zeal was sapped. The later history of the Quakers suggests that concentration on banking, brewing and iron production is incompatible with the maintenance of a thrusting, evangelical religion.

A more certain difference between reality and the Anglican image of rampant, organized dissent threatening the Church of England is the fact that dissenters were far from united. 'Dissent' can be as misleading a term as 'Puritanism' in that it encompasses individuals and groups of many varied beliefs. Efforts to unite dissenters, most notably Baxter's voluntary 'associations' in the 1650s and the Common fund and 'Happy Union' between Congregationalists and Independents in 1690 and 1691, met with only limited success. The differences between the denominations are reflected most clearly in the theological diversity among dissenters. The pre-1640 dominance of Calvinist predestinarianism was gone, though Congregationalists and Particular Baptists remained faithful to it. The General Baptists were the first sect to reject it in favour of a free will theology, followed after 1660 by many Presbyterians. The diversity of dissent provides another dimension to the splintered nature of Protestantism in England after 1640 both inside and outside the Church of England, in great contrast to the situation in the early seventeenth century. All Protestants, however, were united in their common concern at an apparent loss of support. It was not just Anglicans who felt that their Church was 'in danger'. Increasingly in the late seventeenth and early eighteenth centuries, irreligion came to be seen as constituting as great a threat to Protestantism as Catholicism.[40]

---

[38] Watts, *Dissenters*, p. 270.
[39] Ibid., pp. 385–6.
[40] J. A. I. Champion, *The Pillars of Statecraft Shaken: The Church of England and its enemies 1660–1730* (1992).

Science and rationalism

Inevitably Isaac Newton towers over the history of science in late Stuart England. Newton's genius was recognized during his lifetime: in 1669 the Lucasian Professor of Mathematics at Cambridge, Isaac Barrow, resigned his chair to allow Newton, his student, to be appointed in his place. His reputation still stands high for his work on the composition of light, published in *Opticks* (1704), and above all for his discoveries in mathematics and astronomy, which he presented in 1687 in the *Principia*. 'With the work of Isaac Newton', writes Professor A. R. Hall, 'the scientific revolution reached its climax as far as the physical sciences are concerned.' While recognizing the validity of that generalization, some of Newton's contemporaries deserve being rescued from unwarranted obscurity. These include Robert Boyle, and Robert Hooke, whose *Micrographia* (1665) illustrates his wide-ranging interests in astronomy, optics, microscopy and physiology, as well as John Ray and Nehemiah Grew, whose systematic classification of animals and plants respectively laid the foundations of modern biology.[41]

In all these ways and more, English scientists continued to make a major contribution to the European scientific movement as they had done before 1640. However, after 1640 several aspects of the new science are noticeably different from the previous period. For one thing the interest in science spread outside a narrow circle of scientists to a much greater extent than before. John Aubrey thought that 'the searching into Naturall knowledge began but since or about the death of King Charles the first'.[42] Although this minimizes the importance of sixteenth- and early seventeenth-century scientists, it points to the great importance of the 1640s and 1650s in the history of science and its acceptance by intellectual society which has been well documented by Dr Charles Webster.[43] He has shown that at both Oxford and Cambridge the initial disruption caused by the Civil War was quickly overcome, and, although the university statutes reflecting the conventional preoccupation with scholastic studies remained unchanged, there was enormous academic interest in all aspects of experimental philosophy. The major difference between the universities was the emphasis by academics at Cambridge (where John Ray was especially influential) on the biological sciences, while scientists at Oxford concentrated on the physical sciences. During the 1650s, scientific clubs developed, at which scientists met to discuss and disseminate new scientific ideas. The most famous of these is the Oxford Experimental Philosophy Club, which met in the lodgings of John Wilkins, warden of Wadham college. Other formal and informal meetings of scientists were also held in Oxford, Cambridge and London. Because these meetings were not well recorded, historians of science have found it difficult to establish the connection between them and the Royal Society. Clearly, though, there was a great deal of overlap between the membership of all these societies. The

---

[41] A. R. Hall, *The Scientific Revolution 1500–1800* (2nd edn., 1962), p. 244. Newton's work on the composition of light was published in earlier papers in 1672 and 1675. The best starting point for the study of Restoration science and scientists is M. Hunter, *Science and Society in Restoration England* (1981).

[42] Quoted in Michael Hunter, *John Aubrey and the Realm of Learning* (1975), p. 42.

[43] Charles Webster, *The Great Instauration: science, medicine and reform 1626–60* (1975), especially pp. 129–78.

formal beginnings of the Royal Society can be traced to November 1660, when a group of scientists meeting at Gresham College resolved to institute regular weekly meetings with John Wilkins as chairman. One and a half years later, the Society received a charter from Charles II.

The Society's royal charter in 1662 and its wide membership drawn from the landed and professional classes illustrate the new influential standing of science in fashionable society in Restoration England. One of the aims of the Royal Society's journal, *Philosophical Transactions*, begun in 1665 and edited by Henry Oldenburg, was to publicize scientific discoveries and to attract the support of the leisured classes. All this need not imply that the discoveries of Newton, Boyle, Hooke and the rest were well understood by those 'virtuosi' who took a fashionable interest in science, nor that these virtuosi in their own activities followed the Baconian ideal any more closely than did those in the early seventeenth century. John Aubrey's scientific work was 'haphazard and unsystematic'. His *Naturall Historie of Wiltshire*, he wrote, was a collection of 'the Observations of my frequent Road between South and North Wilts; that is between Broad-Chalke and Eston-Piers. If I had had then leisure, I would willingly have searched the Naturals of the whole County.'[44] Such an approach was miles away from the rigorously systematic, descriptive science of Ray and Grew.

Yet if the virtuosi did not fully understand or contribute much to the new science, they and many of their literate contemporaries did grasp the general principles and methods practised by the natural philosophers and they absorbed them into the intellectual mainstream of post-Restoration England. First, it came to be believed that the best way to approach a problem was to clear one's mind of presumptions based on what one had read in books; instead accepted 'truths' were to be treated with suspicion until they had been tested by personal observation and by collection of data. Secondly, in constructing explanations of observed phenomena, emphasis ought to be placed on mechanical rather than on occult causes. As will be stressed later, there was no clear break between science and magic in late Stuart England, but scientists were beginning (at least) to doubt magical explanations, as magic gradually lost the intellectual respectability it had had in the sixteenth and early seventeenth centuries. Finally, it was believed that these techniques of rational enquiry opened up the possibility of infinite progress in all fields. These were principles which amounted to a significant change in the intellectual climate of England in the late seventeenth and early eighteenth centuries.

One of the manifestations of this change has already been seen: the growth of Latitudinarianism within the Church of England. Another was the willingness of a few thinkers to apply the principles of rationalism to religion much more severely than the Latitudinarian divines by extending them into attacks on the Church and even in some cases on Christianity itself. Most scientists were concerned to reconcile their philosophy with religion. Nehemiah Grew argued that the two did not conflict, even though

---

[44] Quoted in Hunter, *Aubrey*, p. 132.

Philosophy teaches that to be done by Nature; which Religion, and the Sacred Scriptures, teach us to be done by God: no more than to say, That the Ballance of a Watch is moved by the next Wheel, is to deny that Wheel, and the rest, to be moved by the Spring; and that both the Spring, and all the other Parts, are caused to move together by the Maker of them. So God may be truly the Cause of This Effect, although a Thousand other Causes should be supposed to intervene: For all Nature is as one Great Engine, made by, and held in His Hand.[45]

In July 1691 Robert Boyle endowed a series of lectures to be given eight times a year 'for proving the Christian Religion against notorious infidels viz. Atheists, Theists, Pagans, Jews, and Mahometans'.[46] As Boyle realized, scientists were in a vulnerable position, since the intellectual methodology of the new science could be used to undermine the Church and Christianity. This is illustrated after the lapse of the Licensing Act in 1695 by the appearance of works by writers, like John Toland (see above, p. 407), who mounted an attack on organized Christianity. Most had in common both a hatred of the clergy and a desire to discard (or at least demote in importance) anything in religion that could not be explained by reason, especially 'revelation' and miracles. However, these writers were probably not as united or as organized as the hysterical reaction of churchmen to them might imply. It is difficult to put them into categories: 'Deists' and 'freethinkers' are perhaps the vaguest and therefore the best, since there were wide differences among them. Some, but not all, rejected the doctrine of the Trinity, and attacked the belief in the resurrection, for example. Perhaps orthodox divines exaggerated their importance, but the 'freethinkers', no less than the Latitudinarians, were products of the new rationalist intellectual climate.

Perhaps it is not being unduly schematic to see in this light, finally, the philosophy of John Locke and the attitude to government of men like Sir William Petty, John Graunt and Gregory King. Locke, wrote Dr J. W. Gough, 'did not attempt to carry conviction by multiplying quotations from authorities: he sought rather to demonstrate every point by considering it rationally, without reference to what his predecessors had said'.[47] On a different level, Petty sought to apply the same principles to the problems of government. 'The method I take', he explained in his *Political Arithmetick*

is not very usual; for instead of using only comparative and superlative Words, and intellectual Argument, I have taken the course (as a Specimen of the Political Arithmetick I have longer aimed at) to express myself in Terms of *Number, Weight* or *Measure*; to use only Arguments of Sense, and to consider only such Causes, as have visible Foundations in Nature.[48]

---

[45] Quoted in Hall, *Scientific Revolution*, p. 291.
[46] Quoted in Jacob, *The Newtonians*, p. 144. See ibid., chs. 4 and 5 for a discussion of the Boyle lectures.
[47] J. W. Gough, ed., *The Second Treatise of Civil Government, and a Letter Concerning Toleration by John Locke* (1946), p. xi.
[48] Quoted in C. Hull, ed., *The Economic Writings of Sir William Petty* (2 vols., 1899), I, p. lxv.

Here is an early statement of the potent belief that statistics ('political arithmetic') is the key to understanding the problems of society and the economy. John Graunt's *Observations on the London Bills of Mortality* (1662) and Gregory King's *Natural and Political Observations* (completed in 1696), statistical analyses of the population and wealth of the country, were important products of this intellectual optimism. Petty, Graunt and King are undoubtedly lesser figures than Newton and Locke, but they are equally representative of the transformation that was coming over English intellectual life in the late seventeenth and early eighteenth centuries.

Economic and social changes

Contemporaries had little doubt that political crisis and civil war during the 1640s were largely to blame for 'the decay of trade'. 'The first and principal reason of the decay of trade hath been the late intestine and unhappy wars of this nation', declared Thomas Violet unequivocally in 1650.

> Before the breaking out thereof, the trade of England was both free and flourishing at home and abroad. But immediately after by reason of obstructions both at home and abroad it began to fall into a consumption, under which it hath languished ever since.[49]

More melodramatically, but to similar effect, some London petitioners in January 1648 bewailed the economic ill-effects of political developments:

> Oh that the cravings of our Stomacks could be heard by the Parliament and the City! Oh that the Tears of our poor famishing Babes were botled . . . Oh ye great men of England, will not (think you) the righteous God behold our Application, doth not he take notice that you devour us as if our Flesh were bread? . . . Its your Taxes, Customs, and Excize, that compells the Countrey to raise the price of food, and to buy nothing from us but meer absolute necessaries.[50]

It is difficult to say what truth there is in these comments. The disruptive effects of the Civil War and its aftermath on the English economy are only relatively recently beginning to be studied.[51] However, although dislocation appears to have been great, it was only temporary and the economy quickly recovered. The middle of the seventeenth century is a valid dividing line in the development of the English economy. It marks the end of

---

[49] Thirsk and Cooper, pp. 57–8.

[50] D. M. Wolfe, ed., *Leveller Manifestoes of the Puritan Revolution* (1968), pp. 275–6.

[51] C. Carlton, *Going to the Wars: the experience of the British Civil Wars 1638–51* (1992); D. Pennington, 'The war and the people', in Morrill, ed., *Reactions to the English Civil War*; I. Roy, 'England turned Germany? The aftermath of the civil war in its European context', *T.R.H.S.*, 5th ser., XXVIII (1978), pp. 127–44; I. Roy, 'The English Civil War and English society', in B. Bond and I. Roy, eds., *War and Society* (1977); J. Broad, 'Gentry finances and the Civil War – the case of the Buckinghamshire Verneys', *Econ. H.R.*, 2nd ser., XXXII (1979), pp. 183–200.

a long period of population expansion and price inflation, and the beginning of an era of much greater economic growth than in the previous century. By the end of the Stuart age, the economy of England was much more soundly and broadly based than it had been at its start.

Economic changes

Agriculture

In the late seventeenth and early eighteenth centuries, there was a marked increase in the output of English farms at a time when agriculture was possibly employing a declining share of the national workforce. It is a mistake to describe changes in agriculture in terms of rapid and sudden surges forward. Alterations in farming practice and techniques are by their very nature bound to be slow and gradual. Yet in the period after 1650 more farmers than ever took up many of the improvements pioneered in the late sixteenth and early seventeenth centuries. The cultivation of coleseed and turnips and the practice of floating watermeadows spread in many areas of the south and west of England, and everywhere more land was cleared, drained and brought into cultivation. Moreover, many new farming improvements were introduced in the late seventeenth century that for a long time were thought by historians to have been innovations of eighteenth-century 'pioneers', especially Thomas Coke of Holkham, Viscount 'Turnip' Townshend, Jethro Tull, Arthur Young and Robert Bakewell. With the possible exception of the last named and his experiments in animal breeding, the roles of these five men in the history of English agriculture have been reduced from that of pioneers to popularizers. As has been seen, turnips were grown as a field crop in the early seventeenth century, and by the reign of Queen Anne, Defoe recorded that they were to be found 'over most of the east and south parts of England'.[52] Probably more important both as fodder crops and in influencing husbandry practice in arable areas, however, were new artificial grasses like clover, lucerne and sainfoin, which came to England from the United Provinces (sometimes brought by Dutch merchants) in the late seventeenth century. The new grasses could be sown instead of a fallow year, they fixed nitrogen in the soil, and they made possible convertible ('alternate' or 'up-and-down') husbandry on most arable farms. They therefore allowed more animals to be kept, and consequently, by heavier manuring, increased grain yields. The most spectacular application of these principles was in the so-called 'Norfolk' crop rotation of turnips, barley, clover and wheat, which was in use on the Norfolk estates of the Walpole family in 1673, well before Coke of Holkham popularized it in the eighteenth century.[53] It quickly spread to other light soil areas in East Anglia and

---

[52] Quoted in E. L. Jones, 'Agriculture and economic growth in England 1660–1750: agricultural change', in E. L. Jones, ed., *Agriculture and Economic Growth in England 1650–1815* (1967), p. 154.

[53] J. H. Plumb, 'Sir Robert Walpole and Norfolk husbandry', *Econ. H.R.*, 2nd ser., V (1952), pp. 86–9; R. A. C. Parker, 'Coke of Norfolk and the agrarian revolution', *Econ. H.R.*, 2nd ser., VIII (1955–6), pp. 156–66.

in western England, transforming once barren heaths into rich grain and sheep farmland.

Although the late seventeenth and early eighteenth centuries provided a period of fairly sustained farming progress in the adoption of new crops and techniques, it is not easy to explain why this should have been the case. It is true that the intellectual climate favoured innovation in all spheres of life. Soon after its foundation the Royal Society turned its attention to farming problems, and in 1664 it appointed a 'georgical' committee whose prime aim was 'the composing of a good history of agriculture and gardening in order to improve the practice thereof'. In the best Baconian tradition, questionnaires were distributed to collect detailed information about regional farming practices, 'whereby it may be known what is practised already and every place be enriched with the aids that are found in any place'.[54] However, as in other cases, there proved to be a wide gap between the aspirations and achievements of Restoration scientists in pure science and the practical applications of these principles. The survey of the 'georgical' committee was limited to six counties, and the only farming improvement the committee can be credited with is the planting of potatoes as a field crop, especially in Lancashire, where, however, it may well in fact have developed because of the proximity to Ireland, already the home of extensive potato cultivation. But the influence of the Royal Society in turning the attentions of some great landowners to farming cannot be discounted. Nor can the farming treatises written in this period, like Sir Richard Weston's *Discourse of Husbandrie used in Brabant and Flanders* 1645, Walter Blith's *The English Improver* 1649, John Worlidge's *Systema Agriculturae* 1669 (which advocated a seed drill long before Jethro Tull took out a patent for one in 1701), and John Houghton's agricultural newsletter, *A Collection of Letters for the Improvement of Husbandry and Trade*, which appeared regularly from 1681 to 1683 and from 1691 to 1703. It is impossible to estimate with any certainty how many people read these and how influential they were, but there is little doubt that they had more impact on landlords than on farmers; as a result, some great landowners began to take a more active interest in farming and to encourage their tenants to adopt the new husbandry by inserting improvement clauses in their leases and by giving them security of tenure. Few great landlords as yet, though, took up farming themselves as a fashionable hobby by developing model farms as some did in the eighteenth century.

Farmers were probably more responsive to market forces than anything else. There is a clear connection, for example, between the adoption of advanced farming practices in parts of Norfolk and Suffolk and the demand for food and industrial raw materials generated by the growing towns of Norwich and London and by the Dutch brewing and distilling industries. For most farmers, however, the food market appeared unattractive. Generalizations about price movements in this period must be treated with as much caution as those in the sixteenth and early seventeenth centuries, and short-term fluctuations and regional variations are less well established than is the long-term trend in food prices, which in the late seventeenth and early eighteenth

---

[54] Thirsk and Cooper, p. 150.

centuries levelled off after the 'price revolution' from the early sixteenth century onwards. Wool and grain prices especially appear to have been very sluggish; grain prices were low from 1675 to 1691, rose only slightly from 1691 to 1700 (a period of bad harvests), and then fell again.[55] Rising prices are so often associated with economic innovation and enterprise (whether in the thirteenth century or in the sixteenth) that it might seem logical to equate conditions of falling prices with economic stagnation and decline, but this is a false assumption. Falling or stagnant prices can be as powerful an incentive to farmers (or indeed manufacturers) to innovate, to seek to increase output and to cut costs, as rising prices. Falling food prices may have been the mainspring of the remarkable development of English agriculture in the period after 1650. Agricultural innovation was seen by many farmers as the only practical way to escape from the spiral of falling food prices and farm profits.

What were the effects of the adoption of new crops and techniques by English farmers in the late seventeenth and early eighteenth centuries? First, it accelerated the trend towards regional specialization that was already under way in the earlier period, producing great diversity of English farming practice even within relatively limited areas. A general farming pattern, however, can be seen emerging in the late seventeenth and early eighteenth centuries, based on the differences between the lighter soil and heavier soil areas. The light soil regions (sandy and heath lands, especially in Norfolk and Suffolk in the east, the chalklands of the Cotswolds in Oxfordshire and Wiltshire in the west, and the downlands of Kent and Sussex in the south) were well suited to growing the new fodder crops, and so developed mixed sheep–corn husbandry. The heavy soil areas (especially the cold, ill-drained clay vales of the midland counties), on the other hand, were not suited to the new husbandry. Here grain farmers came to terms with the competition of the more favoured areas by gradually converting to pasture farming. Leicestershire, Northamptonshire and parts of Lincolnshire were slowly transformed from grain to grazing counties, producing sheep for mutton and wool and cattle for fattening and for specialized dairying. Other farmers elsewhere, too, came to concentrate on specific crops that were suited to the soil, climatic and marketing conditions of their areas, as the market gardeners of the Thames Valley were already doing by the mid-seventeenth century. In the later period originated the fame of the Vale of Evesham and Kent as apple and cherry producers, and of Kent, Sussex, Herefordshire and Worcestershire as hop-growing counties.

A second result of the adoption of new husbandry practices was an increase in the output of English agriculture after 1650. This is impossible to prove quantitatively: farm records before 1714 are practically non-existent. One therefore has to rely on qualitative evidence. For the first time England in the late seventeenth century became a grain-exporter: rising from only 2,000 quarters p.a. in the 1660s, English grain exports reached over 300,000 quarters p.a. between 1675 and 1677, and continued to

---

[55] A. H. John, 'The course of agricultural change 1660–1760', in L. S. Pressnell, ed., *Studies in the Industrial Revolution* (1972), and idem., 'Agricultural productivity and economic growth in England 1700–60', in Jones, ed., *Agriculture and Economic Growth*, pp. 172–93.

rise until about the mid-eighteenth century.[56] No doubt this was partly as a result of the government bounties on the export of grain begun in 1670 and 1672, but it was also a reflection of the improved performance of English farmers. Probate inventories provide evidence to support this view. Oxfordshire, Leicestershire and Yorkshire farmers in the late seventeenth and early eighteenth centuries all possessed more animals when they died than did their predecessors. There is more conclusive evidence from the surviving records of individual farmers for the period in the decades after 1714, but one can assume with reasonable certainty that the growth in agricultural output began well before the death of Queen Anne.

Mining, manufacturing and inland trade

In contrast to the earlier period, mining and manufacturing in England, like agriculture, underwent a period of expansion and growth. Lacking much quantitative proof for this assertion, again one has to rely on other kinds of evidence: the diversification of English textile manufacturing, the development of more coalfields and production of more bar iron, the proliferation and technological advance of other industries apart from textiles, and improvements that were made in the means of internal trade.

In the century before 1650 the English woollen cloth industry was in a state of chronic dislocation as woollen broadcloth manufacturing, centred in Gloucestershire, Wiltshire, Essex and Kent, declined because of a falling-off in European demand, and the worsted new draperies took time to become established. In the late seventeenth and early eighteenth centuries, this painful period of readjustment was largely over. Many diverse branches of cloth manufacturing flourished. Moreover, the range of textiles produced was extended by the expansion of non-woollen textile industries. After 1650 the 'new draperies' were dominant in the English woollen cloth industry; but, apart from all being organized under the domestic system of production and all using some long-staple wool, the term 'new draperies' covers a wide range of products. Three types of new draperies especially expanded in the seventeenth and early eighteenth centuries: the coloured 'medley' cloths produced in an area stretching from Frome to Bradford-on-Avon, Norfolk 'stuffs' largely marketed through Norwich, and Devon serges (a mixture of long wool from Ireland and short wool from Spain) exported from Exeter, which in 1700 sent out about one-quarter of England's total cloth exports. Almost as significant in this period was the rapid development of non-woollen textiles: silk largely produced in Spitalfield in London by French Huguenot refugees; linen manufactured mainly in Lancashire, with a wide range of sub-branches, 'cottons' and 'fustians', made from mixtures of cotton and linen, and ribbons and tapes made on the newly introduced Dutch looms; and stocking knitting, which developed rapidly after 1650 in Leicestershire and Northamptonshire using the stocking knitting

---

[56] M. Turner, 'Agricultural productivity in England in the eighteenth century', *Econ. H.R.*, 2nd ser., (1982); M. Overton and M. Turner, 'Agricultural productivity in eighteenth-century England: debate', ibid., XXXVII (1984); R. V. Jackson, 'Growth and deceleration in English agriculture 1660–1790', ibid., XXXVIII (1985).

frame, invented by William Lee in the 1590s and now belatedly taken up to replace hand knitting. The national pattern of textile manufacturing itself is diverse, but local studies reveal an even greater detailed variety. In the parishes in and around Wigan in the early eighteenth century, occupations were noted not simply as 'weavers' but 'linen weavers', 'fustian weavers' or 'plod weavers'.[57] This diversification and expansion of textile manufacturing did not proceed without obstacles, the greatest being the rising imports of Indian cotton and calico textiles; in 1684 those amounted to 1.74 million pieces.[58] Pressure from native woollen manufacturers succeeded in gaining high import tariffs on Indian textiles in 1701 and 1721, but these were probably not so effective as the measures taken in the English parliament to prevent the development of an Irish cloth industry. An Act passed in the parliamentary session of 1698–9 forbade the export of cloth from Ireland and encouraged instead the export of Irish wool, which was needed for the Devon serge industry.

By the end of the seventeenth century, the cloth industry was probably becoming less important in relation to other manufactures in England than it had been at the beginning. In the early 1660s, woollen cloth made up 74 per cent of the total value of the exports of all goods of English origin; by 1700 the percentage had fallen to 69 per cent, and the figure fell more rapidly thereafter.[59] This was largely a reflection of the rapid progress made in this period by mining, the primary metal industries (the smelting of tin, copper, lead and iron), and by a wide range of secondary industries. Coal output figures are as notoriously difficult to calculate for this period as for the earlier period. There is, though, little doubt about the fact (if not the scale) of growing coal output after 1650. The major coalfield in the north-east expanded from the Tyne to the Wear and up the Northumberland coast. Moreover, from the mid-seventeenth century coal production was boosted by the introduction of railed wagonways from the coalfields to the coast. This period also saw the exploitation for the first time on a major scale of the Welsh and Cumberland coalfields, as well as the rapid development of the south-west Lancashire coalfield. In the early eighteenth century, production was facilitated by the introduction of steam pumping engines which enabled deeper mines to be worked. These were the invention not of pure scientists, but of practical men faced with the day-to-day problem of waterlogged mines. It was not solved easily. Thomas Savery's contraption, which he invented in 1698 to drain Cornish tin and copper mines, is more correctly called an atmospheric engine, because it used atmospheric pressure to raise the water out of the mines and steam pressure was then applied to force the water out. Early versions of it were Heath Robinson type machines which frequently blew up, causing many accidents. Thomas Newcomen's improved version introduced in 1708 was more successful. Although it was not until the late eighteenth century that the principle could be adapted to steam-powered machinery,

---

[57] J. Langton, 'Industry and towns 1500–1730', in R. A. Dodgson and R. A. Butlin, eds., *An Historical Geography of England and Wales* (1978), p. 175.

[58] D. C. Coleman, *The Economy of England 1450–1750* (1977), p. 162.

[59] Ibid., p. 139. These figures do not include re-exports, for which see pp. 494–8.

in its limited form as a pumping machine Newcomen's invention was used in many large mines by 1730 with successful results.

Rising coal output was closely linked with the expansion of the smelting of lead, copper and tin. Largely because of the introduction of an improved reverberatory furnace after 1650, coal was increasingly used to smelt non-ferrous metals. Since the furnaces used more coal fuel than metal ore, the logical development was to locate these industries on coalfields and so save transport costs. Although this was done to a limited extent before 1714 by shipping Cornish copper to South Wales, laying the basis for the development of metal industries (especially tinplate) there from the 1720s onwards, for the moment most smelting was done near the ore mines: lead in Derbyshire and north Wales, tin in Cornwall, and copper in Cornwall, Wales and the Lake District. Since it proved difficult to use coal to smelt iron ore, the production of bar iron has a divergent history from that of the non-ferrous metals. However, it is now certain that the iron industry's reliance on charcoal fuel did not hold it back. The discovery that there was no national timber fuel shortage in this later period (as before 1650) has explained what was hitherto a major mystery of the industrial history of this period. In the early 1700s a Bristol ironmaster, Abraham Darby, invented a method of using coal (coke) to smelt iron ore, which he developed in 1709–10, when he established his famous ironworks at Coalbrookdale in Shropshire. The puzzle was that few other ironmasters adopted Darby's invention until fifty or sixty years later. Earlier historians explained this by maintaining both that Darby tried to keep the invention secret within his closed circle of Quaker friends, and that his method was not perfect. Both these explanations, even if true, must now be regarded as secondary. The primary reason for the minor contemporary impact of Darby's invention is that there was no compelling need in the iron industry for it. Although there were occasional local timber shortages, generally ironmasters practised a sensible policy of timber cropping and replacement of trees. The move of the centre of the industry from the Weald to Wales, the Forest of Dean and south Yorkshire was caused not by abundant supplies of fuel in the new areas, but by a better class of ore and proximity to the secondary metal industries of the west Midlands. Although the English industry never produced enough bar iron to allow the cessation of Swedish imports, the output of the native industry continued to expand.[60]

Turning away from textiles, mining and the primary metal industries, the range of English manufacturing after 1650 defies a brief description. Three features of it stand out in contrast to the period before 1650. First, a much wider range of commodities was now produced, most notably refined sugar and tobacco, a result of the development of the colonial trades (see pp. 494–6). Old manufactures like brewing (especially in London) and pottery making in north Staffordshire expanded. Secondly, more

---

[60] G. Hammersley, 'The charcoal iron industry and its fuel 1560–1750', *Econ. H.R.*, 2nd ser., XXVI (1973), pp. 593–613; M. W. Flinn, 'The growth of the English iron industry 1660–1760', *Econ. H.R.*, 2nd ser., XI (1958), pp. 144–53; T. Brinley, 'Was there an energy crisis in Great Britain in the seventeenth century?', *Explorations in Economic History*, XXIII (1986), pp. 124–52.

manufacturing industries came to be located on coalfields, like glass and salt on the Tyne. The best example of the integration of different manufactures in this period is on the west Midlands coalfield. Behind the industry of that region producing small hardwares, like nails, axes and agricultural implements, lay a multitude of industrial processes located in or near the same area: coal mining to produce the fuel for the metalworkers' smithies, the production of bar iron, and the manufacture of narrow iron rods in water-powered slitting mills. Each part of this industrial chain was typically a small manufacturing unit, but the ultimate control of the industry often lay with the owners of the slitting mills who put out the rods of iron to the metalworkers. By the late seventeenth century, industry was densely concentrated in the Wolverhampton–Birmingham area, where between 1660 and 1710 34 per cent of all those people for whom probate inventories survive were metalworkers.[61] Thirdly, there were improvements not only in the range and output of manufacturing after 1650, but also in the quality of goods produced, largely due to improved technology. Finer silk, paper and glass, for example, were all produced in the late seventeenth century than ever before, and often the improved technology was brought by immigrants, enabling English industry to narrow the gap between it and hitherto more technologically advanced countries like the United Provinces.

The impression of manufacturing expansion after 1650 is confirmed by the mounting evidence of improvements in the means of internal trade even before the turnpike and canal revolutions of the eighteenth century: river and harbour improvements, the introduction of more frequent carrier services, stagecoaches and newspaper advertising.[62] These developments, of course, were a cause as well as a reflection of the developing economy. What else contributed to the industrial progress made in the late seventeenth and early eighteenth centuries? Although banking originated in the second half of the seventeenth century, its commercial influence was as yet slight compared to its importance in supplying the needs of public finance. The few private banks that developed (mainly as offshoots of the work of goldsmiths and scriveners) were in London: in the 1690s there were about forty, but the numbers fell in the early years of the eighteenth century. There were no private banks outside London before 1714; the first one was established in Bristol in 1716, but there were only about twelve country banks in 1750.[63] Most businesses were small in this period and did not need sophisticated banking facilities. Manufacturers overcame short-term financial crises by borrowing money from members of their family and from friends, and they expanded their businesses by 'ploughing back' profits, rather than by relying on investment from outside sources. Banking (and also joint-stock organization) was only of peripheral importance in English industrial development before the late eighteenth century.

---

[61] Langton, 'Industries and towns', p. 180.

[62] J. A. Chartres, *Internal Trade in England 1500–1700* (1977).

[63] D. M. Joslin, 'London private bankers 1720–86', *Econ. H.R.*, 2nd ser., VII (1954), repr. in E. M. Carus-Wilson, ed., *Essays in Economic History* (1962), II, pp. 340–59; L. S. Pressnell, *Country Banking in the Industrial Revolution* (1956).

More significant in the late seventeenth and early eighteenth centuries were the important roles played by dissenters and aliens. Some have sought to explain the economic success of dissenters in terms of 'the Protestant ethic' which allegedly encourages a capitalist outlook. However, a simpler explanation may be that dissenters were political and social outcasts. As such, few were able to follow a political career or were influenced by the conservative curricula of the universities. Schooled in dissenting academies, they learned useful skills like mathematics, accountancy and foreign languages, and found an outlet for their talents in trade and industry. Above all, because they were dissident, minority groups they stuck together, intermarried, lent money to each other in times of trouble, and passed business on to each other. Impressive networks of business relationships developed among dissenting families, but they did so because dissenters were victimized groups not because they were Protestants. The same is true to a certain extent in explaining the economic success of aliens in England. Especially important in this period were the Huguenots, whose technical skills made as great an impact on industries like silk, paper and glass as did the earlier wave of religious immigrants from the Low Countries on the woollen cloth industry. Because of the unknown extent of evasion, one cannot be as certain about the beneficial effects of government protection of industries, but the total ban on the import of French goods imposed in 1678 (which was later replaced by high import duties) was probably a help to infant industries like the manufacture of fine paper. Probably, however, the main determinant of economic progress in this period was the rising demand for manufactured goods in expanding overseas and domestic markets. This assertion is based on assumptions about the development of English colonies and colonial trade and about a general rise in the standard of living in and the growing urbanization of later Stuart society. These assumptions will be dealt with in the following sections.

Commerce and colonization

In the 1730s Viscount Bolingbroke coined the term 'commercial revolution' to describe the changes in Britain's overseas trade since the mid-seventeenth century, and this term has now become firmly established in the historiography of this period.[64] The importance of overseas trade has perhaps been exaggerated at the expense of internal trade and the domestic market, largely because the primary sources for studying the latter are sparser than overseas trade records. Nevertheless, economic historians are more justified in using 'revolution' in connection with changes in late seventeenth- and early eighteenth-century overseas trade than they are in the context of many other economic and social developments. In the late seventeenth century, the nature of English overseas trade was transformed: commodities that had been traded in only negligible amounts before 1650 leaped to importance; English trade to Europe was overshadowed by that to the Caribbean, North America, West Africa and the Far

---

[64] Plumb, *Growth*, p. 3; R. Davis, *A Commercial Revolution: English overseas trade in the seventeenth and eighteenth centuries* (Historical Association pamphlet, 1969); idem., *English Overseas Trade 1500–1700* (1973).

East; English provincial ports grew to challenge (although not by any means to over-throw) London's grip on the country's overseas trade; the English mercantile marine increased in size; and there developed new associated credit and insurance services. In short, in this period England (after 1707, Britain) emerged as a major imperial and commercial power, supreme over the Dutch, and with France as her only serious competitor for the major share of world trade.

Before 1650 English overseas trade had largely consisted of the exchange of woollen cloth for other manufactures, wine and foodstuffs, including grain. In 1714 cloth was still exported – in 1699–1701 it made up 47 per cent of England's total exports – but its importance was challenged by the re-export of commodities of American and Indian origin – in 1699–1701 tobacco, sugar and Indian calicoes amounted to 30 per cent of England's total exports.[65] An increasing percentage of these goods was retained for sale in England, but not as much as was re-exported to Europe. The demand for sugar and tobacco (and later for tea, coffee and chocolate) in Europe is explicable only by the transformation of the status of these commodities from luxuries to necessities in a very short space of time. Other changes in the type of goods traded in by 1714 were less dramatic than the meteoric rise of re-export goods: for example, England became a grain exporter not importer, and there was an increase in the export of English manufactured goods.

The transformation of the commodity structure of England's overseas trade was brought about by the establishment and development of Atlantic colonies and by trading ventures to Africa and the Far East. Unlike the period before 1650, these now made a definite impact on the nature of English overseas trade. However, it must not be assumed that the volume of English trade to Europe proportionately decreased. The import of flax, hemp, iron and timber from the Baltic, Scandinavia and Russia to London and east coast ports grew very fast. So too did trade to southern Europe, importing wine (from Spain and Portugal), fine wool, iron, dyestuffs and fruit, in exchange for cloth, grain and fish (from Newfoundland). This branch of English foreign trade became even more lucrative after the conclusion of the Methuen treaties in 1703. Moreover, most of the re-exports (two-thirds by the end of the seventeenth century) were sent to northern Europe. However, important as was the English trade to Europe, it has rightly received less attention than the growth of the new Atlantic, African and Far Eastern trades, by which English merchants at last freed themselves from the straitjacket of trade to Europe. The volume of the trade of the East India Company increased enormously in the late seventeenth century. Whereas between 1600 and 1640 the total value of East India Company exports only twice exceeded £100,000 p.a., in the 1680s it sometimes reached over £600,000 p.a., and in 1700–1 a peak of £703,497 was achieved.[66] East India Company imports of calicoes and

---

[65] R. Davis, 'English foreign trade 1660–1700', *Econ. H.R.*, 2nd ser., VII (1954), repr. in Carus-Wilson, ed., *Essays*, p. 258.

[66] K. N. Chaudhuri, 'Treasure and trade balances: the East India Company's export trade, 1660–1720', *Econ. H.R.*, 2nd ser., XXI (1968), p. 482.

(increasingly) tea emphasized that by the late seventeenth century English merchants in the Far East were concentrating on the Indian subcontinent and trade to China, not on the Indonesian islands. The company secured Bombay as its major base as part of Charles II's marriage settlement in 1661, but as yet it was not forced (as it was later in the eighteenth century) to do more than establish trading posts in the East. Across the Atlantic the English empire developed much more quickly. Although between 1660 and 1714 only four new colonies were established – New York and New Jersey in 1664, the Carolinas in 1670, and Pennsylvania in 1681 – the populations of these and of the settlements already established after 1607 grew rapidly in this period. In 1640 the free population of English colonies in America and the Caribbean was about 48,000; by 1700 it had risen nearly tenfold to about 440,000.[67] This had come about by natural population increase and also by immigration from Britain and Europe. European immigrants were a mixed bunch with varied motives, but included three types of religious migrants: Quakers who went to Pennsylvania in the 1680s, Huguenots to South Carolina in the same period, and refugees from the Rhine Palatinate to New York in 1708–9.

In addition to their free inhabitants, the American colonies included another new major element in the late seventeenth century: in 1640 there were no slaves in the English colonies, but by 1700 there were about 118,000, mainly in the Caribbean colonies of Jamaica, Barbados and the islands of the Lesser Antilles.[68] By about 1660, Barbados, Antigua, St Christopher and Montserrat were already experiencing severe problems of labour shortage. The indentured labour system, which continued to attract British migrants to the mainland colonies which had ample supplies of land to offer, could not be operated any longer in the small island colonies. The trade in slaves from West Africa, carried on at first mainly by the Dutch and then increasingly by the English merchants of the Company of Royal Adventurers to Africa, became the solution to the Caribbean labour problem. Within about forty years, from 1660 to 1700, the sugar plantation economy developed in the West Indies based on black slave labour. Whether or not the slave trade was profitable remains controversial (the indications are that it was not), but there is little doubt that by 1714 it had become a major axis of England's new overseas trading pattern. The Atlantic colonies produced sugar and tobacco for import to England and for re-export, and they provided an expanding market for English manufactured goods.

Three other major aspects of the 'commercial revolution' need emphasizing. First, partly as a result of the 'revolution', London's relative importance declined in relation to that of the provincial ports. It is true that London remained far and away the biggest city in the country. Between 1650 and 1700 its population grew from 400,000 to 475,000, and especially after the Great Fire the westward expansion of the City continued in a period of furious property development. However, in this period London's rate of expansion (18.75 per cent) was much slower than in the previous fifty years when its growth rate was 100 per cent. Moreover, in the late seventeenth

---

[67] R. Davis, *The Rise of the Atlantic Economies* (1973), p. 126.
[68] Ibid.

century some provincial ports probably grew at a faster rate. It is difficult to be certain because population statistics of provincial towns are notoriously inexact. Certainly Liverpool grew more rapidly: its population increased by over 50 per cent between 1700 (5,145) and 1710 (8,168). This is also probably true of Glasgow and Whitehaven, the latter developed by the Lowthers, who exported coal from the mines on their estates from Whitehaven and then subsequently branched out into the tobacco trade to Virginia. Sugar and tobacco and the associated refining industries were the basis of the new prosperity of these western ports. Bristol also shared in the Atlantic trades and was an outlet for the products of the west Midlands metal industries brought down the Severn. Exeter grew, mainly as an exporter of serges to Europe. Some east coast ports expanded rapidly, especially Hull and Newcastle: the latter's population grew from about 12,000 in the 1600s to 16,000 in 1700.[69] Secondly, in the late seventeenth century the size of England's mercantile marine grew considerably. Professor R. Davis estimated that the total tonnage of English merchant shipping rose from 115,000 tons in 1629 to 340,000 tons in 1686 and then levelled off to 323,000 tons in 1702. The new trades were in bulky commodities of sugar and tobacco from the American and West Indian colonies and of timber from Norway and the Baltic. Partly the growing tonnage of ships was supplied by prizes captured in the three Anglo-Dutch wars of the seventeenth century. Professor Davis estimated that in these wars English seamen captured between 2,023 and 2,723 Dutch ships and only lost at the most 500 ships. But the growing demand for ships came increasingly to be supplied by English shipyards, which slowly adopted the successful techniques of their Dutch rivals.[70] Thirdly, the growth of longer trade routes and a more diversified trading pattern stimulated the growth of marine insurance and credit facilities in London. Often these were merely adaptations of practices long used in Amsterdam, but increasingly London insurance underwriters, who met at Edward Lloyd's coffee house in the City, captured business from their Amsterdam rivals, as did London exchange brokers, who operated a sophisticated system of bills of exchange by which merchants settled their international debts.

Perhaps the biggest contrast of all between English overseas trade before and after 1650 is that in the later period one can be reasonably certain that the total value of English foreign trade grew. Quantitative estimates (again by Davis) are not totally reliable, especially those for the late seventeenth century, but even after 1697 when customs records became more abundant the figures are questionable because of the unknown extent of smuggling. Nevertheless Davis's estimates would have to be very wrong to undermine the validity of the trend of trade expansion.[71]

---

[69] P. Corfield, 'Urban development in England and Wales in the sixteenth and seventeenth centuries', in D. C. Coleman and A. H. John, eds., *Trade, Government and Economy in Pre-Industrial England* (1976), pp. 240–1.

[70] R. Davis, *The Rise of the English Shipping Industry in the Seventeenth and Eighteenth Centuries* (1962), especially pp. 15 and 51.

[71] R. Davis, 'English foreign trade 1660–1700', p. 267; idem., 'English foreign trade 1700–74', *Econ. H.R.*, 2nd ser., XV (1962), pp. 300–3. D. W. Jones, *War and the English Economy: the age of William III and Marlborough* (1988), pp. 312–14 argues that Davis's figures need to be adjusted downwards substantially, because the inclusion of both exports and re-exports amounts to double counting. Jones estimates that the growth of exports from 1660 to 1701 amounted to between £1.2 million and £1.3 million, and not £2.3 million.

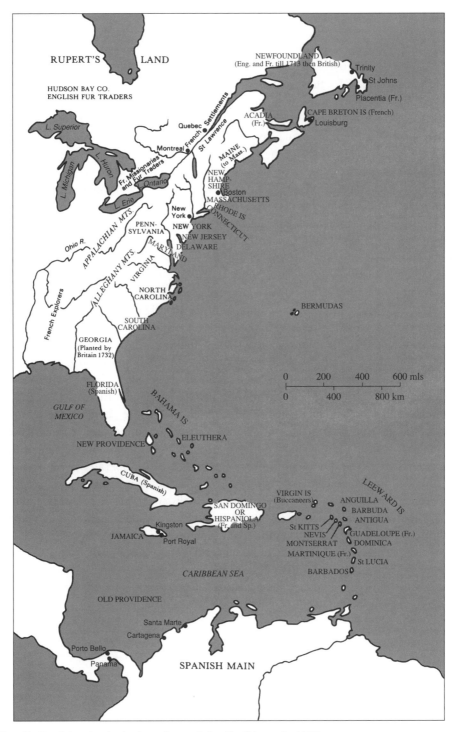

Map 5 English colonies in America and the Caribbean in 1700

Imports and exports, 1663–1724

Period	Total imports	Total exports
1663–1669	£4,400,000	£4,100,000
1699–1701	£5,849,000	£6,419,000
1722–1724	£6,758,000	£7,756,000

It is also true that there are uncertainties other than the statistical one. Did government protective legislation (the Navigation Acts, 1650, 1651 and 1660, and the Staple Act, 1663) play a major part in the trade expansion? Did the wars of the late seventeenth and early eighteenth centuries have a disruptive effect on English trade or were they a boon in supplying captured enemy ships and stimulating technical progress in English shipbuilding? Both questions have produced varying answers from historians.[72] What is certain is that the period of English neutrality from 1674 to 1689, when the Dutch remained at war with France, was a vital one in the progress of English overseas trade. This is probably the point at which English merchants overtook the Dutch in the colonial slave trade and the European carrying trade. Moreover, the English victory was a permanent one. By 1714, unlike 1650, London not Amsterdam was well on the way to becoming the centre of the commercial world.

Social changes

In describing the social structure of late Stuart England, students need to consider two problems. The first is how much reliance can be placed on Gregory King's 'Scheme of the Income and Expense of the Several Families of England . . . for the Year 1688', which he calculated in 1695–6. King was one of the foremost 'political arithmeticians' of his day, and his table neatly categorizing social groups and calculating incomes and expenditures *seems* to be an ideal description of the social structure of late Stuart England. Unfortunately, long-held doubts about the reliability of King's work on the social structure of contemporary England have now been systematically confirmed by Professor G. Holmes. He has shown that King did much less research on this aspect of his work than on demography and national income and wealth, which were more directly connected with his prime aim of providing the government with a statistical basis for levying taxation. Moreover, 'guesswork abounds in King's enumeration', especially of incomes, which are gross underestimates. Above all, King, by basing his estimates on the year 1688, ignored many of the important changes taking place in society at this time.[73] Not only is King's work now known not to be the reliable guide it

---

[72] Jones, *War and the English Economy* is a detailed guide to these questions.
[73] G. Holmes, 'Gregory King and the social structure of pre-industrial England', *T.R.H.S.*, 5th ser., XXVII (1977), pp. 41–68; P. H. Lindert and J. G. Williamson, 'Britain's social tables revised 1688–1867', *Explorations in Economic History*, XIX (1982).

was once thought to be, but work on the social history of late Stuart England has also called into question some long-held orthodox views about this period, without as yet producing any new ones to put in their place.[74] Perhaps this debate, which still has a long way to go, will eventually produce the kind of local studies that were stimulated by the 'storm over the gentry' about the earlier period. Only then will it be possible to put forward generalizations with more certainty than at present.

However, it is certain that the economic climate of late Stuart England was significantly different from that preceding it. The mid-seventeenth century marked the end of a fairly long period of price and population expansion throughout Europe. As with prices, lack of sources (in this case, population censuses) makes it impossible to produce exact population figures. Yet, regional variations notwithstanding, it is possible that the population of England and Wales fell during the late seventeenth century from 5.281 million in the 1650s to 5.058 million in 1701; and that it rose only slowly in the early eighteenth century, reaching just 5.576 million by 1741 (according to the Cambridge Group's estimates).[75] Taken together these economic, price and demographic trends represent a changed context in which to consider the standards of living of people in late Stuart England. The transition to an era of relatively stagnant prices and population has often been associated with the development of a more stable social structure than in early Stuart England. But it is likely that this assumption is as misguided as that which equates falling prices with a stagnant economy. In the late seventeenth and early eighteenth centuries, the beginnings of three major changes in the social structure of England can be detected: the growth in the size of estates and of farms as large landowners and farmers proved more able than smaller ones to withstand the economic problems of the period; a rise in the numbers and standard of living of wage-earners; and an increase in the size of towns and therefore the growth in importance of urban social groups.

In the present state of knowledge, the first of these generalizations must be considered to be the most tentative. This was not so until quite recently, when there seemed little reason to doubt Professor H. J. Habakkuk's argument that 'the general drift of property in the sixty years after 1690 was in favour of the large estate and the great lord . . . the same period saw an appreciable diminution of the area owned by small squires and the landed gentry'.[76] This hypothesis has appealing arguments in its support, especially the development of two legal devices since the mid-seventeenth century which seemed to protect large estates from being broken up and to enable them to get even bigger. In the late sixteenth and early seventeenth centuries, landlords

---

[74] For the debate on Professors Habakkuk's and Mingay's view of the social structure of late seventeenth- and early eighteenth-century England in H. J. Habbakuk, 'English landownership 1680–1740', *Econ. H.R.*, 1st ser., X (1939–40) and G. E. Mingay, *English Landed Society in the Eighteenth Century* (1963), see J. V. Beckett, 'English landownership in the later seventeenth and early eighteenth centuries: the debate and the problems', *Econ. H.R.*, 2nd ser., XXX (1977), C. G. A. Clay, *Economic Expansion and Social Change in England 1500–1700* (2 vols., 1984), Vol. 1, pp. 158–64, and B. Coward, *Social Change and Continuity in Early Modern England 1550–1750* (1988), pp. 46–48.

[75] E. A. Wrigley and R. S. Schofield, *The Population History of England 1541–1871: a reconstruction* (1981).

[76] Habakkuk, 'English landownership', pp. 2, 4.

found it difficult to ensure that on their deaths their estates would descend intact to their heirs. Estates disintegrated because deathbed settlements were not upheld in law. A legal solution was eventually found in the form of the strict settlement. This was an agreement made each generation between the head of the family and his heir, by which both agreed to become life tenants of the estates, therefore forgoing the right to alienate any portion of the estates for any period longer than their own lives. This agreement was guaranteed by the appointment of trustees whose duty was to look after the future interests of any unborn children (legally known as 'the contingent remainders'). Landlords also now seemed able to borrow money without the risk which was attached to mortgaging property in the early seventeenth century. With the development of the legal principle of equity of redemption in the late seventeenth century, mortgagees who forfeited on mortgage repayments were given time by the law courts to redeem their property and creditors were prevented from foreclosing on their property as they had done in the early seventeenth century. Because these devices were thought to enable landlords to keep their estates together and to borrow money more easily and safely so that they could purchase more land, it was argued that they were in a good position to secure favourable marriages with wealthy heiresses, as well as to secure lucrative government offices. However, attractive as these explanations are, their validity is now doubtful. Professor Habakkuk may have exaggerated the extent to which the strict settlement was employed: it was not used by landlords in other areas as much as it was by those in Northamptonshire and Bedfordshire, the area he studied. Nor do many landlords appear to have used the improved mortgage facilities to purchase more land. Moreover, even an apparently good marriage could lead to financial difficulties, especially if the offspring were daughters who had to be provided with expensive dowries. Opportunities to acquire government offices, even in the expanding civil service of the later Stuarts, were also open only to a few.

Until there are more local studies, uncertainty will remain and the Habakkuk model must be considered on trial. However, although legal explanations for the growth of large estates are dubious, there are reasons for thinking that in the century after 1640 economic conditions for landlords and for farmers were more difficult than in the preceding century, and that as a result many small landlords and farmers may have found themselves in difficulties from which they could escape only by selling out to their wealthier neighbours. In what ways was the economic climate hostile to small landowners and farmers in late Stuart England? Undoubtedly the situation became worse in and after the 1690s, but some of their difficulties originated earlier. The English Revolution brought about no large-scale redistribution of land in favour of 'new' men associated with the parliamentarian and republican regimes and drawn from outside the traditional ruling classes, as was once thought.[77] Yet rents fell throughout

---

[77] Joan Thirsk, 'The sale of royalist lands during the Interregnum', *Econ. H.R.*, 2nd ser., V (1952–3), pp. 188–207; idem., 'The Restoration land settlement', *J.M.H.*, XXVI (1954), pp. 315–28; H. J. Habakkuk, 'Landowners and the civil war', *Econ. H.R.*, 2nd ser., XVIII (1965), pp. 130–51; idem., 'Public finance and the sale of confiscated lands during the Interregnum', *Econ. H.R.*, 2nd ser., XV (1962), pp. 71–87; idem., 'The land settlement at the Restoration of Charles II', *T.R.H.S.*, 5th ser., XXVIII (1978), pp. 201–21.

the civil war,[78] and taxation was maintained at a high level throughout the war and afterwards. For royalist landowners, of course, the situation was worse, since they had to borrow money to pay composition fines in order to recover their sequestered estates, and in 1651 and 1652, 780 hard-line royalist 'delinquents' had their estates confiscated and sold by the Trustees of the Commonwealth. Although confiscated estates were restored in 1660 (along with crown and Church lands), no compensation was given to those who had sold lands to pay fines or who had incurred heavy debts in the process of repurchasing their lost estates. More seriously, after the Restoration many landlords apparently found it difficult to maintain their rental incomes. 'That rents decay every landlord feels, the reasons and remedies are not so well understood', wrote Sir William Coventry in 1670. Unfortunately, one is reliant on obviously biased views like this, but they were generally held during the reigns of Charles II and James II.[79] After 1690, however, the fall in rents is better demonstrated, and some landlords, especially in years of bad harvests, like 1693–1700 and 1709–10, even had to allow tenants to accumulate arrears of rents.[80] The rent problem facing landlords was a reflection of the difficulties of farmers in the period of generally sluggish prices for many agricultural products. Many landlords and farmers had to contend with stagnant or falling rents and prices in late Stuart England. In addition, landowners (whether landlords or farmers) from the 1690s onwards were burdened with an extra charge, the land tax. It is true that this tax was assessed at different rates throughout the country and that in some northern and western counties like Cumberland and Westmorland the rate was very light.[81] However, throughout most southern and eastern counties of England this was not the case, and it was levied at the full rate of four shillings in the pound throughout the war years. On the Coke estates in Norfolk between 1708 and 1710, over 17 per cent of the gross rental was paid in taxes.[82] Not surprisingly, many landowners resented their country's involvement in a war that hit them so severely.

The smaller the resources of the landlord or farmer, the less able was he to cope with this situation of increasing expenditure and falling incomes. Small landlords could not afford to meet high tax bills, nor afford to allow their tenants' arrears of rent to accumulate for two or three years, as did some great landlords. Neither were they able to recoup their fortunes by other means – by borrowing or by investing in government stocks. Notwithstanding the possible drawbacks, it was large landlords who made the most advantageous marriages. By Sir Thomas Grosvenor's marriage in 1677 to a twelve-year-old bride, Mary Davies, the daughter of a London merchant, his family eventually inherited a large part of the present West End from Oxford Street to Vauxhall and Chelsea, including Grosvenor Square, Park Lane and Victoria. Similarly, it was mainly larger farmers who had the capital to invest in farming

---

[78] Broad, 'Gentry finances in the civil war', pp. 183–200.
[79] Thirsk and Cooper, p. 79. See ibid., pp. 68–88 for other contemporary comments on this theme.
[80] Mingay, *English Landed Society*, pp. 54–5.
[81] Beckett, 'English landownership', pp. 573–4.
[82] Mingay, *English Landed Society*, p. 82.

improvements, which it has been seen was a way of escaping from the spiral of falling farm prices and profits. Many small farmers must have found it difficult to continue. Clearly, the decline of small farmers in England was a slow, gradual process. Some, like those in Chippenham in Cambridgeshire, disappeared in the early seventeenth century.[83] Others, especially those in market gardening, fruit growing, dairying and meat production, survived into the late seventeenth and early eighteenth centuries. But for many, especially grain farmers, it is likely that the period from about 1640 to 1760 was critical and that the trend towards larger farms accelerated.[84]

It is possible to come to a more optimistic conclusion about the standards of living of wage-earners in late Stuart England than in the previous period. One must beware of overstating the argument. Gregory King's figures illustrate the extent of poverty in the lower levels of society. It is also true that wage rates in some areas of the country remained as depressed in this period as in the early seventeenth century. This was so in areas like Suffolk and Essex, where there were few sources of employment other than farming and no alternative sources of income as waste and commonland rapidly disappeared. However, in those areas close to or in towns, labourers could command higher wages: for example, in London or in the industrial villages of the west Midlands small hardware industry or Sheffield cutlery trade. Unfortunately, the statistical basis for the argument that there was a general rise in real wages after 1650 is shaky.[85] However, the generally stagnant population level in England probably produced a slackening supply of labour and possibly a rise in money wages. Moreover, the fall in food prices supports the view that there was a rise also in real wages. As in generalizing about the fortunes of landlords and farmers, one has to litter one's remarks with 'perhaps' and 'maybe': one cannot be certain. There is, though, one final confirmatory indication of rising living standards of labourers in the late seventeenth and early eighteenth centuries: the change in popular consumption patterns. Again this is a highly tentative suggestion, but from the mid-seventeenth century there appears to have been, especially in southern England, a switch in cereal consumption from barley and rye bread to wheat bread, and a greater amount of meat being eaten. Also in the late seventeenth and early eighteenth centuries many people began to eat, wear and use many of the new products of the colonial and Far Eastern trades and expanding English manufacturing industries. Increasingly, many goods such as sugar, tobacco and Indian textiles were retained and sold in Britain instead of being re-exported. This is well documented for the mid-Hanoverian period: by 1750, for example, 90 per cent of imported sugar was sold in England.[86] Less is known about the amount of goods both produced and consumed in England, but the proliferation of consumer industries in late Stuart England suggests that there was an expanding domestic market and perhaps

---

[83] Margaret Spufford, *Contrasting Communities: English villagers in the sixteenth and seventeenth centuries* (1974), p. 91.

[84] J. Thirsk, 'Seventeenth-century agriculture and social change' in J. Thirsk, ed., *Land, Church and People* (1970).

[85] Professor Coleman's table estimating the rise in real wages is the best effort to make the most of the slight statistical evidence: *Economy of England*, p. 102.

[86] Ibid., p. 118.

the growth of a 'consumer society', served by an improved transport network and the development of retail shops.[87] The importance of these developments by 1714 should not be exaggerated, but it is certain that by this period far more people had more money to spend on non-essential items than at the beginning of the Stuart age.

The hypothesis of a growing domestic demand for food and manufactured goods, whether imported or produced in England, is compatible with two final new features of late Stuart society: the growth of non-landed elites and of towns. The later seventeenth century saw a rapid growth in the number and status of merchants and professional people. The latter included not only clerics, lawyers and doctors, but also civil servants and groups like schoolteachers, architects, surveyors, land agents and estate stewards, who were beginning 'to take on an embryonic professional identity'.[88] The same period was also one in which the populations of provincial towns grew faster than in the previous century, and faster than the total population of the country. The expansion of London and provincial ports, feeding on the growing trades to the colonies, the East and Europe has already been seen. The populations of others also grew, partly as a result of the industrial progress of the late seventeenth century, like Manchester and Salford (about 10,000–12,000 in 1700), Nottingham (about 7,000 in 1700), Leicester (about 6,000 in 1712), Birmingham (between 5,000 and 7,000 in 1700), and Leeds (about 5,000–6,000 in 1700). Others, like Chatham and Portsmouth (both with over 5,000 inhabitants in 1700), grew partly because of the demand for ships for war and peaceful uses. Finally, although their days of spectacular development lay in the future, by 1714 the growth of spa towns was noticeable: in 1660 the biggest, Bath, had a population of about 1,100.[89]

The quantitative growth of towns in late Stuart England may also have been complemented by a qualitative change that Peter Borsay has called 'an urban renaissance': the emergence of 'a far more acute urban culture and consciousness, sharply defined from that of rural society'. Dr Corfield, too, emphasizes the importance for the future of these changes in urban society: 'from about the 1670s onwards (or perhaps earlier),' she writes, 'something of the configuration of modern urban England began to emerge at least in outline'.[90] Perhaps the same can be said about the structure of modern landed society: a three-tiered structure composed of large landlords, big tenant farmers and a mass of landless labourers, instead of the two-tiered rural society of landlord and small, independent farmers which persisted in Ireland, and in parts of Scotland and Europe.

---

[87] The key articles on the growth of a consumer society are by N. McKendrick, 'The birth of a consumer society' and 'The consumer revolution in eighteenth-century England', in N. McKendrick et al., eds., *The Birth of a Consumer Society* (1982).

[88] Holmes, *Augustan England*, p. 21. This book is the essential starting point for the study of this group.

[89] C. W. Chalklin, *The Provincial Towns of Georgian England: a study of the building process 1740–1820* (1974), pp. 21–4.

[90] P. Borsay, 'The English urban renaissance: the development of provincial urban culture c.1680–c.1760', *Social History*, V (1977); 'Culture, status and the English urban landscape', *History*, LXVII (1982); *The English Urban Renaissance: culture and society in the provincial town 1660–1770* (1989). For a critique of Borsay and Borsay's reply, see A. MacInnes and P. Borsay, 'Leisure town or urban renaissance?', *P. & P.*, CXXVI (1990). Corfield, 'Urban development', p. 229.

Map 6a England *c*.1603: county boundaries and towns with over 5,000 inhabitants

Map 6b England *c.*1714: county boundaries and towns with over 5,000 inhabitants

15

Continuity: 1714 – the end of the Middle Ages?

Summary

It is undeniable that great changes took place in England during the reigns of the Stuarts, and one might be forgiven for taking these changes together as evidence that at some point during that period there occurred the 'beginnings of modern England' and 'the end of the Middle Ages'.

- In 1714 was the country not poised on the brink of transition from an agrarian to an industrialized society?

- Did 1714 not mark the dawn of 'the Age of Reason'?

- Had the seventeenth century of revolution not laid the basis for constitutional monarchy and political stability?

However, concentration on historical change is not without its dangers. Not only do elements of continuity sometimes become obscured in the process, but also historians are tempted to highlight 'modern' developments that they know became influential later, but which were not all that significant at the time. It is likely that few people in 1714 would have been aware of any of these notions. The importance of the changes that took place during the Stuart age ought not to be minimized, but they need to be seen in their proper historical context. The essential continuity of life in Stuart England is often overlooked.

Britain's transformation in the late eighteenth and nineteenth centuries into a predominantly industrial, urban society is inexplicable without reference to the remarkable economic progress made in the seventeenth and early eighteenth centuries, especially in the latter part of that period. At least part of the answer to the hotly debated question of why Britain became the 'first industrial nation' lies in the achievement by the British economy by the early eighteenth century of more diverse and expanding manufacturing, trade and agricultural sectors compared with her backward nature a century earlier.[1] The progress in overseas trade and in agriculture is especially significant in laying the foundation for Britain's later industrialization. The development of the colonies created a market and a source of raw materials for British industry. Moreover, some of the capital generated by overseas trade was invested in British manufacturing. Agricultural progress contributed to the expansion of Britain's industrial sector in at least three major ways. Increasing agricultural productivity enabled an expanding industrial and urban population to exist. Low prices for agricultural produce meant that the costs of many industrial raw materials (wool for cloth, barley for brewing, and so on) were kept low. Finally, low agricultural prices allowed people to spend more on non-food items, and so possibly helped to create an enlarged domestic market for the products of British industry.[2]

In 1714, however, Britain's transformation into an 'industrial nation' was a long way in the future. The basic social and economic framework of the country remained very much as it had been in 1603. Tarnished though Gregory King's reputation now is, no one has questioned his conclusion about the unequal distribution of wealth and the extensive nature of poverty in the England of his day. King believed that over half the total population in 1688 were 'decreasing the wealth of the kingdom', by which he meant that they spent each year more than they earned, and were dependent on charity or poor relief. Since poverty is not an easily definable concept, King's attempt to assess the scale of poverty in late Stuart England is bound to be arbitrary. However, whatever the statistical accuracy of King's conclusion, there is little doubt about the massive scale of poverty in the late seventeenth century or that it was a constant feature of English society during the Stuart age. Indeed, many of the generalizations made in the first part of this book about English society in the early seventeenth century remained true down to 1714 and in some cases beyond: for example, geographical mobility was common and the average expectation of life remained in the thirties well into the eighteenth century. There is little evidence to sustain the idealized vision of life in pre-industrial England held by the romantic poets writing in the early stages of the country's industrialization.

---

[1] M. W. Flinn, *The Origins of the Industrial Revolution* (1966) and R. M. Hartwell, ed., *The Causes of the Industrial Revolution in England* (1967) are good introductions to this controversy.

[2] Jones, ed., *Agriculture and Economic Growth*, especially the editor's introduction. See also the articles by N. McKendrick cited in chapter 14, note 87.

A time there was 'ere England's grief began,
When every rood of ground maintained its man.
For him light labour spread her wholesome store,
Just gave what life required and gave no more.

So wrote Oliver Goldsmith in *The Deserted Village*, with scant historical justification. For most people, life at the end of the Stuart age was a grim struggle for sustenance and survival. Prosperity still rose or fell with a good or bad harvest. England in 1714 still had a predominantly agrarian economy and therefore the state of the harvest affected the standards of living not only of landowners, farmers and farm labourers, but also of those not directly connected with agriculture. Industry in 1714 was still intimately linked with agriculture, both for its raw materials and for its organization of industrial production. Most industries remained labour-intensive and most were organized on the domestic system. Large-scale units of production with fixed capital plant, with the exception of a few shipyards and coalmines, were rare. In 1714 the factory age lay at least sixty years in the future. Despite the economic progress between 1603 and 1714, the English economy remained pre-industrialized.[3]

The beginnings of religious toleration in England and 'modern' attitudes to science and progress are undeniably to be found in the period after 1640. More and more, explanations for phenomena were couched in natural rather than supernatural terms. Yet it would be the greatest exaggeration to suggest that these trends were the only ones apparent, let alone the dominant ones, in 1714. On the death of Queen Anne, only a minority were reconciled to the fact that the search for a religious settlement which had gone on since 1640 should end in toleration for groups outside the Church of England. Most people probably realized that the cause of 'comprehension' was lost, but few were willing to accept 'toleration'. This is especially true of the general attitude of many to Protestant dissenters. The intolerant legislation passed in the last years of the reign of Queen Anne, the Occasional Conformity Act (1711) and the Schism Act (1714), was very popular among the bulk of the political nation. In another way, too, the search for a religious settlement was unresolved in 1714. Since at least the 1580s prominent Protestants, laymen and clerics, had been concerned to remedy 'the economic problems of the Church'. By 1714 their achievement was slight.[4] The last Stuart monarch, like the first, set an example of reform. Queen Anne assigned all the crown's revenue from the first fruits and tenths of ecclesiastical benefices to a fund, Queen Anne's Bounty, to augment the salaries of poorly endowed ministers. But little was done to follow the royal example. Few new churches were built in the areas where

---

[3] The idea that in the late seventeenth and early eighteenth centuries there took place a process of 'proto-industrialization' that laid the basis for later industrialization has been rightly criticized by D. C. Coleman: 'Proto-industrialization: a concept too many', *Econ. H.R.*, 2nd ser., XXXVI (1983). More recent writing on the Industrial Revolution had emphasized the continuity with earlier developments: D. Cannadine, 'The past and the present in the English Revolution 1880–1980', *P. & P.*, CIII (1984).

[4] See N. Sykes, *Church and State in England in the Eighteenth Century* (1934), ch. 8 for the state of the eighteenth-century Church.

they were needed. The Church after 1660 was as riddled with poor livings and pluralism as its predecessor. All efforts during the Stuart age to remove the most obvious single cause of this state of affairs failed: tithes remained in the hands of laymen, who considered them part of their property and refused to abandon them.

The development of science and rationalism in the seventeenth and early eighteenth centuries was not a straightforward one of the inevitable and gradual victory of modern, rational ideas over medieval superstition. The philosophy of the new science was by no means universally accepted in late seventeenth- and early eighteenth-century England. Its reputation in the eyes of some was tarnished by its association with radicalism in the 1650s and the apparent growth of irreligion in Restoration England. Meric Casaubon in the 1660s led an attack on the new science for undermining ancient learning and paving the way for the growth of atheism.[5] The battle between the 'ancients and moderns' in intellectual circles was far from over. Moreover, opposition to science came not only from intellectuals. In popular circles, science was criticized because most of the ex-aggerated claims made for the new experimental philosophy seemed to be empty ones. As has been seen, science made little contribution to technological advance and its general practical application was slight. This lay at the root of the sceptical attitude towards science which was reflected in Jonathan Swift's satirical description in *Gulliver's Travels* of the bizarre, useless experiments conducted by members of the Grand Academy of Lagado.

Not only did the new science not sweep all before it in the late seventeenth and early eighteenth centuries, but that period does not mark any clear break between science and magic. John Aubrey extended as much credibility to magical as to mechanical explanations. Moreover, occult interests were not confined to fellow travellers of the new science. The discovery that Isaac Newton's interest in alchemy and other occult notions co-existed with, and lasted longer than, his work on the *Principia* is a startling reminder that rationalism and mysticism were not yet seen to be incompatible by everyone, even by those deeply involved in the new science.[6] Moreover, even if some were beginning to express doubts about magic and alchemy in intellectual circles, at the popular level it may be that belief in magic was just as strong and prevalent as in the earlier period. Witchcraft prosecutions declined, but popular beliefs remained as distinct as ever from intellectual trends. There was still much about life in late Stuart England that was 'irrational' as well as intolerant.

The fact that the Stuart age was an important period of constitutional change can lead to two misleading assumptions: that the constitution inherited by the Hanoverians in 1714 was completely different from the ancient constitution, and that by 1714 the long search for a constitutional settlement had been successful. Late Stuart monarchs still ruled as well as reigned. Government in 1714 was still largely personal govern-ment by the monarch. William III and Queen Anne (and George I) retained a firm grasp on the process by which government decisions were made. The royal court remained the centre of politics. Ministers might have to secure support in parliament

[5] R. F. Jones, *Ancients and Moderns: a study of the rise of the scientific movement in seventeenth-century England* (2nd edn., 1961), pp. 241–4.
[6] F. E. Manuel, *A Portrait of Isaac Newton* (1968).

for their measures, but their main concern was to retain royal favour; when they lost that, their political fortunes inevitably collapsed. The personal inclinations and friendships of the monarch were still of major political importance. Nor was the immense personal power of the monarch eroded by the appearance of the cabinet.[7] This body first appeared in the early 1690s to provide continuous day-to-day control of wartime administration during William III's frequent absences on the Continent. From about 1695 the cabinet met regularly, even when the king was in England. During Anne's reign these weekly cabinet meetings continued with the queen present, and there were also twice-weekly meetings without her, known as meetings of the 'lords of the committee'. All this, though, did not necessarily mean a diminution of royal power and influence. Both William III and Queen Anne controlled the day-to-day business of government and all decisions of the cabinet had to be approved by them. Nor were all the important decisions of government made in cabinet; they continued to be made either in smaller committees or in informal consultations between monarch and ministers. Moreover, the changes in the royal administration, like those in the way policies were made, can also be exaggerated. The 'king's government' may have grown in size and efficiency under the last two Stuarts, but many aspects of it remained unreformed. Sinecures, outdated procedures, maladministration and corruption persisted, especially in old departments like the exchequer. Here efforts both to introduce salaries for officials and to end the system of life tenures for office-holders had even less success than the pathetically limited achievement in some of the newer departments. Vested interests proved too strong and the importance of offices as a source of patronage too great to allow efforts at reform to succeed. Consequently, 'economical' reform of the administration was postponed until the eighteenth and nineteenth centuries.[8]

When in the 1640s people had talked about 'settlement', they had meant a constitutional arrangement that would guarantee political stability and that the central government would rule in accordance with the wishes of the traditional rulers of the county communities. Clearly none of the regimes, parliamentary, republican or royalist, between 1640 and 1714 fully corresponded to that view of 'settlement'. Indeed, the last twenty-five years of the Stuart period saw an intensification of political conflict as the nation split on many important issues. Differences about the Church, the war and the succession were not the sole obstacles to political stability: when those issues cooled in the years after 1714, a fundamental constitutional problem still remained. As has been seen, both the royal government and parliament emerged in 1714 with enhanced powers, with the crown heavily dependent on parliament. But no system had been devised of establishing a working harmonious relationship between the two. As a result in 1714 the prospect of political stability seemed remote; there were few signs as yet of the way in which a practical solution to that problem would be found. That achievement was Walpole's in the 1720s, not that of the politicians of the Stuart age.

---

[7] J. Carter, 'Cabinet records for the reign of William III', *E.H.R.*, LXXVIII (1963); J. H. Plumb, 'The organisation of the cabinet in the reign of Queen Anne', *T.R.H.S.*, 5th ser., VII (1957).

[8] See Brewer, *Sinews*, pp. 70–9 for a balanced discussion, which stresses both the extent of corruption in British government and its limited extent compared with that in European administrations.

Bibliographical note

1. General works covering the whole period 1603–1714

The following three general historical surveys cover all or most of this period: M. Kishlansky, *A Monarchy Transformed: Britain 1603–1714* (1996); D. L. Smith, *A History of the Modern British Isles 1603–1707: the double crown* (1998), and J. Morrill, ed., *The Oxford Illustrated History of Tudor and Stuart Britain* (1996).

There are many general books on *the economic history of Stuart England*. D. C. Coleman, *The Economy of England 1450–1750* (1977) and B. A. Holderness, *Pre-industrial England: economy and society 1500–1750* (1977) are the best straightforward introductions, while C. Wilson, *England's Apprenticeship 1603–1763* (1965; 2nd edn., 1985) and C. G. A. Clay, *Economic Expansion and Social Change 1500–1700* (2 vols., 1984) are more detailed. Christopher Hill, *Reformation to Industrial Revolution: a social and economic history of Britain 1530–1780* (1967) offers a brilliant, yet controversial, interpretation. In the Macmillan Studies in Economic and Social History pamphlet series (commissioned by the Economic History Society), students are well provided with excellent brief introductions, with annotated bibliographies, to many aspects of the economic history of Stuart England: Ralph Davis, *English Overseas Trade 1500–1700* (1973), D. C. Coleman, *Industry in Tudor and Stuart England* (1975), J. A. Chartres, *Internal Trade in England 1500–1700* (1977), J. Thirsk, *England's Agricultural Regions and Agrarian History 1500–1750* (1987), and L. A. Clarkson, *Proto-industrialization: the first phase of industrialization?* (1985).

Social history has seen the publication of more lively and exciting writings than economic history in recent years. For guides to work published largely in the 1970s and 1980s, see Keith Wrightson, *English Society 1580–1680* (1982) and J. A. Sharpe, *Early Modern England: a social history 1550–1760* (1987), which are splendid syntheses of much exciting work on seventeenth-century social history; while B. Coward, *Social Change and Continuity in Early Modern England 1550–1750* (1988) is a briefer guide to this aspect. There are fewer pamphlets in the Macmillan Studies in Economic and Social History on social than on economic history, but R. Porter, *Disease, Medicine and Society in England 1550–1860* (1987) is very useful, as is R. A. Houston, *The Population History of Britain and Ireland 1500–1750* (1991; 2nd edn., 1995). The latter is especially welcome because it is a more accessible guide to the important work of the Cambridge

Group for the History of Population and Social Structure than is E. A. Wrigley and R. S. Schofield, *The Population History of England 1541–1871: a reconstruction* (1981). D. Hey, *An English Rural Community: Myddle under the Tudors and Stuarts* (1974), M. Spufford, *Contrasting Communities: English villagers in the sixteenth and seventeenth centuries* (2nd edn., 1979); and two books by D. Levine and K. Wrightson, *Poverty and Piety in an English Village: Terling 1525–1700* (1979) and *The Making of an Industrial Society: Whickham 1560–1765* (1991) are valuable local studies of English society.

The following are a selection of path-making monographs on Stuart social history, written before the early 1990s. R. Houlbrooke, *The English Family 1450–1750* (1984) is a major challenge to the thesis about relationships within families excitingly (but probably wrongly) supported by L. Stone in his *Family, Sex and Marriage in England, 1500–1800* (1977). M. Macdonald, *Mystical Bedlam: madness, anxiety and healing in seventeenth-century England* (1981), P. Slack, *The Impact of Plague in Tudor and Stuart England* (1985), and J. Walter and R. Schofield, eds., *Famine, Disease and the Social Order in Early Modern Society* (1989) shed much light on the mentalities of ordinary men and women in a country beset by frequent crises, although the best book on this topic is still K. Thomas, *Religion and the Decline of Magic* (1971). P. Slack, *Poverty and Policy in Tudor and Stuart England* (1988) and R. B. Outhwaite, *Dearth, Public Policy and Social Disturbance in England, 1550–1800* (2nd edn., 1995) are good introductions to contemporary poverty problems and attempts made to deal with them. On the 'lower sort' in English society, see. L. Beier, *Masterless Men: the vagrancy problem in Britain 1560–1640* (1985) and A. Kussmaul, *Servants in Husbandry in Early Modern England* (1981); while on 'the better sort', easily the best introduction is F. Heal and C. Holmes, *The Gentry in England and Wales, 1500–1700* (1994), which also includes the aristocracy.

For good introductions to *the roles of women throughout the Stuart period*, see M. Prior, ed., *Women in English Society 1500–1800* (1985), A. L. Erickson, *Women and Property in Early Modern England* (1993), J. Kermode and G. Walker, eds., *Women, Crime and the Courts in Early Modern England* (1994), A. Laurence, *Women in England 1500–1760: a social history* (1994) and A. Fletcher, *Gender, Sex and Subordination in England 1500–1800* (1995).

On *urban history* P. Clark and P. Slack, eds., *English Towns in Transition 1500–1700* (1976) and P. Clark, *The Transformation of English Provincial Towns 1600–1800* (1984) are useful general surveys. Good guides to further reading are P. Corfield, 'Urban development in England and Wales in the sixteenth and seventeenth centuries' and J. Barry, 'Introduction' in J. Barry, ed., *The Tudor and Stuart Town: a reader in English urban history 1530–1688* (1990). The best introductions to Stuart London are A. L. Beier and R. Finlay, eds., *The Making of the Metropolis: London 1500–1700* (1985) and V. Pearl, 'Change and stability in seventeenth-century London', in Barry, ed., *The Tudor and Stuart Town*.

Many books and articles on social history published from the early 1990s onwards are more difficult to categorise under a simple 'social history' heading; many are better described as 'socio-political history'. A major influence in bringing about this welcome historiographical trend are two articles by P. Collinson: 'The monarchical republic of Queen Elizabeth I' and 'De republica anglorum: or, history with the politics put back', both published in Collinson's *Elizabethan Essays* (1994). The main books that have

taken forward the interconnections between the history of society and politics are
M. Braddick, *State Formation and Social Change in Early Modern England c.1550–1700*
(2000), S. Hindle, *The State and Social Change in Early Modern England c.1550–1640* (2000),
and many of the essays in P. Griffiths, A. Fox and S. Hindle, eds., *The Experience of
Authority in Early Modern England* (1996), T. Harris, ed., *The Politics of the Excluded
c.1500–1800* (2001) and M. J. Braddick and J. Walter, eds., *Negotiating Power in Early
Modern Society: order, hierarchy and subordination in Britain and Ireland* (2001). All of these
are crucial in reshaping our views of the nature of the English State and of how the
authority of the crown was perceived and its decrees were received and moderated by
those once thought to been excluded from the political process. Also important in
revising long-held views of the composition of 'the political nation' is a raft of books
and articles that demonstrate how ordinary men and women participated in political
debates to a much greater extent than was once thought. Most of these are listed in
the chronological sections that follow. I. Atherton, 'The press and public opinion,' in
B. Coward, ed., *A Companion to Stuart Britain* (paperback edn., 2009) is the only brief
guide to the subject that covers the whole period of Stuart Britain.

A dominating historiographical trend in Stuart history is *the importance of 'The British
Problem'* – the task of putting the history of England within the wider context of the
composite kingdom of Wales, Ireland and Scotland of which it was an important part.
This is, of course, a major challenge and one not without its problems, for which see
T. Claydon, 'Problems with the British problem', *Parliamentary History*, 16 (1997). The
value of this 'British' approach is given more emphasis than its problems in S. Barber
and S. Ellis, eds., *Conquest and Union: fashioning a British state* (1995); A. Grant and
K. Stringer, eds., *Uniting the Kingdom? The making of British history* (1995); B. Bradshaw and
J. Morrill, eds., *The British Problem c.1534–1707: state formation in the Atlantic archipelago*
(1996); G. Burgess, ed., *The New British History: founding a modern state* (1999); S. J. Connolly,
ed., *Kingdoms United? Great Britain and Ireland since 1500: integration and diversity* (1999);
A. I. Macinnes and J. Ohlmeyer, eds., *The Stuart Kingdoms in the Seventeenth Century:
awkward neighbours* (2002). For those who want to investigate the history of Ireland,
Scotland and Wales as a preparation for attempting to write a more integrated
'British' history of this period, see, for Ireland, T. W. Moody, F. X. Martin and
F. J. Byrne, eds., *A New History of Ireland, III: Early Modern Ireland 1534–1691* (1976) and
the relevant chapters in R. F. Foster, *Modern Ireland 1600–1972* (1988); for Scotland,
M. Lynch, *Scotland: a new history* (1991), J. Wormald, *Court, Kirk and Community in Scotland
1460–1625* (1981), R. Mitchinson, *Lordship to Patronage: Scotland 1603–1745* (1983), and
K. Brown, *Kingdom or Province? Scotland and the regnal union 1603–1715* (1992); and, for
Wales, G. Williams, *Recovery, Recognition and Reformation c.1415–1642* (1987), G. H. Jenkins,
The Foundation of Modern Wales: Wales 1642–1780 (1987), P. Jenkins, *A History of Modern
Wales 1536–1990* (1992), and J. Gwynfor Jones, *Early Modern Wales c.1525–1640* (1994).

On the *history of central government*, D. L. Smith's *The Stuart Parliaments 1603–89*
(1999) has filled a gaping historiographical hole in this area of Stuart history.
G. E. Aylmer's trilogy is an important source of reference for officials of the State and
crown: Gerald Aylmer, *The King's Servants: the civil service of Charles I, 1625–1642* (1961),

The State's Servants: the civil service of the English Republic, 1649–1660 (1973) and *The Crown's Servants: government and civil service under Charles II, 1660–1685* (2002). The arcane world of public finance in this period is elucidated clearly by M. J. Braddick, *Parliamentary Taxation in Seventeenth-Century England: local administration and response* (1994) and *The Nerves of State: taxation and the financing of the English State 1558–1714* (1996). Much work has shown the importance of the royal court as a 'point of contact' between the crown and its subjects, as is seen in R. M. Smuts, *The Stuart Court and Europe: essays in politics and political culture* (1996), E. Cruickshanks, ed., *The Stuart Courts* (2000) and J. Adamson, *The Princely Courts of Europe: ritual, politics and culture under the ancien regime 1500–1750* (1999), all of which build on D. Starkey, ed., *The English Court from the Wars of the Roses to the Civil War* (1987).

Easily the best guide to *Stuart local government* is A. Fletcher, *Reform in the Provinces: the government of Stuart England* (1986). The best brief introductions to foreign policy in Stuart England are G. M. D. Howat, *Stuart and Cromwellian Foreign Policy* (1974), J. R. Jones, *Britain and Europe in the Seventeenth Century* (1966), J. R. Jones, *Britain and the Wider World 1649–1815* (1980), and J. Black, *A System of Ambition? British foreign policy 1660–1793* (1992).

The history of political ideas has undergone a quiet revolution following the recommendation of specialists in English literature that students in their research on contemporary thought take 'a linguistic turn' by looking at ephemeral sources such as ballads, satirical verses and 'libels', as well as visual material like paintings and woodcuts, descriptions of ritual ceremonies and so on. The authors of three recent articles surveying the history of political thought in the Stuart age demonstrate the value of this relatively new approach: M. Smuts, 'Political thought in early Stuart Britain', Colin Davis, 'Political thought during the English Revolution' and Justin Champion, 'Political thinking between Restoration and Hanoverian succession', in Coward, ed., *Companion to Stuart Britain*. J. Burns and M. Goldie, eds., *The Cambridge History of Political Thought 1450–1700* (1990) and G. Burgess, *British Political Thought 1500–1640* (2009) take a more traditional approach.

There is no detailed survey of the *Stuart Church*, but S. Doran and C. Durston, *Princes, Pastors and People: the Church and religion in England 1529–1689* (1991) is a good introductory survey. J. Spurr, *The Post-Reformation: religion, society and politics in Britain 1603–1714* (2006) is more detailed. Spurr also, in *English Puritanism 1603–89* (1998), has made a heroic effort to get to grips with a slippery group within the Church. The major religious groups outside the Church of England are dealt with splendidly in J. Bossy, *The English Catholic Community 1570–1850* (1975), A. Dures, *English Catholicism 1558–1642* (1983) and M. R. Watts, *The Dissenters from the Reformation to the French Revolution* (1978). The *history of witchcraft* in this period continues to attract much interest. The most recent detailed book on the subject is J. Sharpe, *Instruments of Darkness: witchcraft in England 1550–1750* (1996). On the *history of science*, a good starting point is the editors' introduction in D. C. Lindberg and R. S. Westman, eds., *Reappraising the Scientific Revolution* (1990); while R. S. Westfall, *The Construction of Modern Science* (1977), A. R. Hall, *The Revolution in Science* (1983) and H. Kearney, *Science and Change* (1971) are solid survey books. The most exciting book on this topic for this period is C. Webster, *The Great Instauration: science, medicine and reform 1626–60* (1975). K. Thomas, *Religion and the Decline of Magic* (1971), amongst my ten best best books on early modern English history, succeeds in revealing many ideas held by ordinary people, as opposed to a tiny circle of intellectuals – a task which, before his book appeared, had seemed impossible.

There are many collections of essays on various aspects of the history of Stuart England, including those by the most prolific historian of the period, Christopher Hill, *Puritanism and Revolution* (1958), *Change and Continuity in Seventeenth-Century England* (1974) and *The Collected Essays of Christopher Hill*, (3 vols., 1985 and 1986). J. H. Hexter, *Reappraisals in History* (1961) are essays written from a very different point of view than Hill's. The following collections contain mainly essays on economic and social history: E. Carus-Wilson, ed., *Essays on Economic History* (3 vols., 1954, 1962), F. J. Fisher, ed., *Essays in the Economic and Social History of Tudor and Stuart England* (1961), C. W. Chalklin and M. A. Havinden, eds., *Rural Change and Urban Growth 1500–1800* (1974), A. H. John and D. C. Coleman, eds., *Trade, Government and Economy in Pre-industrial England* (1976), J. Walter and R. S. Schofield, eds., *Famine, Disease and the Social Order in Early Modern Society* (1989) and J. Chartres and D. Hey, eds., *English Rural Society 1500–1800* (1990). B. Coward, ed. *A Companion to Stuart Britain* (2003) has essays by 25 leading historians who were all given a brief to survey the present state of play in their respective fields of expertise in Stuart history; while J. Wormald, ed., *The Seventeenth Century* (2008) has essays by seven leading historians of the period covering the Stuart period chronologically.

B. Coward and P. Gaunt, eds., *English Historical Documents 1603–60* (2010) is an edited selection of 614 documents from this period. Two volumes in the Cambridge series, J. P. Kenyon, ed., *The Stuart Constitution 1603–88* (2nd edn., 1986) and E. N. Williams, ed., *The Eighteenth Century Constitution 1688–1815* (1960) illustrate constitutional history; J. Thirsk and J. P. Cooper, eds., *Seventeenth-century Economic Documents* (1972) is a very comprehensive selection of economic and social history documents, and D. Wooton, ed., *Divine Right and Democracy: an anthology of political writing in Stuart England* (1986) includes many important documents on political ideas. W. B. Stephens, *Sources for Local History* (1973) and W. G. Hoskins, *Local History in England* (2nd edn., 1972) are good guides to the types of primary source available and to their value and limitations.

2. Early Stuart England, 1603–1640

S. R. Gardiner's massive *The History of England 1603–42* (10 vols., 1883–4) was the product of the 'Whig' school of historians, whose work was based on unfounded assumptions about the inevitability of English constitutional progress. That apart, however, Gardiner's classic account is still the best full narrative of the political history of this period. Before reading Gardiner, though, most students will want books that are briefer than Gardiner and that reflect modern historiographical trends. There are two good ones: D. Hirst, *Authority and Conflict: England 1603–58* (1986), now revised as

England in Conflict 1603–1660: kingdom, community, commonwealth (1991) and A. Woolrych's indispensable *Britain in Revolution 1625–1660* (2002). R. Lockyer, *The Early Stuarts: a political history of England 1603–42* (1989) is a splendidly detailed treatment of the politics of the period. The later chapters of A. G. R. Smith, *The Emergence of a Nation State: the commonwealth of England 1529–1660* (1984) provide a very accessible introduction to early seventeenth-century England, together with a useful compendium of information. Though now a little dated, J. P. Cooper, 'The fall of the Stuart monarchy', in J. P. Cooper, ed., *The New Cambridge Modern History, IV: The Decline of Spain and the Thirty Years War, 1609–48/59* (1970) and C. Russell, *The Crisis of Parliaments: English history 1509–1660* (1971) are full of useful ideas.

Since this period is in the process of fundamental historical reinterpretation, it is fortunate that there are three good guides to recent writing and research on it: H. Tomlinson, ed., *Before the English Civil War* (1983), R. Cust and A. Hughes, eds., *Conflict in Early Stuart England: studies in religion and politics 1603–42* (1989), and A. Hughes, *The Causes of the English Civil War* (1991). B. Coward, 'Was there an English Revolution in the middle of the seventeenth century?', in C. Jones, M. Newitt and S. Roberts, eds., *Politics and People in Revolutionary England* (1986) and G. Burgess, 'On revisionism: an analiyis of early Stuart historiography in the 1970s and 1980s', *H.J.*, 33 (1990) also survey recent historiographical trends, although in quite different ways. Many of the essays in two volumes in the excellent Macmillan Problems in Focus series, A. G. R. Smith, ed., *The Reign of James VI and I* (1973) and C. Russell, ed., *The Origins of the English Civil War* (1973) are also very useful.

The book that from the 1970s did most to stimulate a radical reinterpretation of early Stuart politics, commonly labelled 'revisionism', is C. Russell, *Parliaments and English Politics, 1621–29* (1979). Other key revisionist writings are G. R. Elton, 'Tudor government: points of contact: parliament', *T.R.H.S.*, 5th ser., XXIV (1974); G. R. Elton, 'Parliament under the Tudors: its functions and fortunes', *H.J.*, XXII (1979); and C. Russell, 'Perspectives in parliamentary history, 1604–29', *History*, LXI (1976). Russell's revisionist stress on consensus and the absence of serious ideological divisions in the 1620s is supported in the editor's introduction in K. Sharpe, ed., *Faction and Parliament: essays in early Stuart history* (1978; paperback edn., 1985) and is taken even further in K. Sharpe's work on the 1630s, *The Personal Rule of Charles I* (1992) and 'The personal rule of Charles I', in Tomlinson, ed., *Before the English Civil War* (above).

Recently, however, there has been a sustained onslaught on revisionism. The following are a few of many important works that are critical of Russell's interpretation of the 1620s: T. K. Rabb and D. Hirst, 'Revisionism revised: two perspectives on early Stuart parliamentary history' and C. Hill, 'Parliament and people in seventeenth-century England', *P. & P.*, XCII (1981). The best critique of revisionism in my view remains the editorial introduction to Cust and Hughes, *Conflict* (above).

Without any doubt the 'revisionist–counter revisionist' debate has created light as well as heat, stressing the ways that revisionists underplayed the extent of political conflict in early Stuart England. So, too, has a long-running recent controversy about the relationship between the localities and the nation in early Stuart England. A. Everitt's writings published in the 1960s (see section 3 below) had a seminal influence on this debate and led to the publication of many 'county community' studies to add to older ones like W. B. Willcox, *Gloucestershire: a study in local government, 1590–1640* (1940), J. Hurstfield, 'County government, 1530–1660' in *Victoria County History of Wiltshire*, V (1957), and T. G. Barnes, *Somerset 1625–40: a county government during 'the personal rule'* (1961). These include M. E. James, *Family, Lineage and Civil Society: a study of the society, politics, and mentality in the Durham region 1500–1640* (1974), A. Fletcher, *A County Community in Peace and War: Sussex 1600–60* (1975) and P. Clark, *English Provincial Society from the Reformation to the Revolution* [Kent] (1977). Although it ends in 1603, A. Hassell Smith, *County and Court: government and politics in Norfolk 1558–1603* (1974) contains important conclusions that are still relevant about county society in the early seventeenth century. The political history of early Stuart London has not been as well studied as that of provincial England, but the early chapters of V. Pearl, *London and the Outbreak of the Puritan Revolution 1625–43* (1961) and R. Ashton, *The Crown and the Money Market* (1960) and *The City and the Court 1603–43* (1979) help to fill the gap.

Everitt's 'county community' approach has been challenged recently, most notably by C. Holmes, 'The county community in Stuart historiography', *Journal of British Studies*, XIX (1980) and by A. Hughes, *Politics, Society and Civil War: Warwickshire 1620–60* (1987) and in her 'Warwickshire on the eve of the Civil War: a county community?', *Midland History*, VII (1982). Out of the debate has emerged a more sophisticated interpretation of local–central relations than hitherto, for which see V. Morgan, 'The cartographic image of the country in early modern England', *T.R.H.S.*, 5th ser., XXIX (1979), R. Cust and P. Lake, 'Richard Grosvenor and the rhetoric of magistracy', *B.I.H.R.*, LIV (1981), A. Fletcher, 'National and local awareness', in Tomlinson, ed., *Before the English Civil War*; K. Sharpe, 'Crown, parliament and locality: government and communication in early Stuart England', *E.H.R.*, CI (1986) and R. Cust, 'News and politics in early seventeenth-century England', *P. & P.*, CXII (1986).

On the religious history of the period there are good collections of essays edited by F. Heal and R. O'Day, *Continuity and Change: personnel and administration of the Church of England 1500–1642* (1976) and *Church and Society in England: Henry VIII to James I* (1977) and a general survey by C. Cross, *Church and People 1450–1660: the triumph of the laity in the English Church* (1976), which has a good bibliography. C. Hill, *Economic Problems of the Church from Archbishop Whitgift to the Long Parliament* (1956) is the basic book on what needed reforming in the Church and why little reform was achieved. Without doubt the most stimulating recent work on religious history in this period has been done by P. Collinson, N. Tyacke and P. Lake. Of Collinson's many works, two are indispensable: *The Religion of Protestants: the Church in English society 1559–1625* (1982) and a collection of his essays, *Godly People* (1983). N. Tyacke's most influential works are 'Puritanism, Arminianism and counter-revolution', in C. Russell, ed., *The Origins of the English Civil War* (1973) and *Anti-Calvinists: the rise of English Arminianism c.1590–1640* (1987); while 'Calvinism and the English Church', *P. & P.*, CXIV (1987) is a good starting point for the views of P. Lake. Tyacke's views of changes in the Church in the early seventeenth century have been criticized by P. White, 'The rise of Arminianism reconsidered', *P. & P.*, CI (1983) and in *Predestination, Policy and Polemic* (1992), by K. Sharpe, 'Archbishop Laud', *History Today*, XXXIII (1983) and by G. Bernard, 'The Church of England *c*.1529–1642', *History*, LXXV (1990). The ensuing lively debate has been conducted largely in the pages of *P. & P.* with contributions (in addition to the ones mentioned above) by W. Lamont (vol. CVII, 1985) and Tyacke and White (vol. CXV, 1987). Recent books by A. Walsham, *Providence in Early Modern England* (1999), C. Durston and J. Eales, eds., *The Culture of English Puritanism 1560–1700* (1996) and K. Fincham and N. Tyacke, *Altars Restored: the changing face of English religious worship 1547–1700* (2007) show that religious divisions were a serious destabilizing force in early Stuart England.

So also, in the view of many historians, were different views about the nature of the constitution. That such differences were very significant, however, has been disputed by G. Burgess in two major books: *Politics and the Ancient Constitution* (1992) and *Absolute Monarchy and the Stuart Constitution* (1996). These were written in response to J. P. Sommerville, *Politics and Ideology in England 1603–40* (1986; 2nd edn. titled *Royalists and Patriots: politics and ideology in England 1603–40*, 1999) that challenged the idea that there was 'a constitutional consensus' in early Stuart England. Much recent writing tends to support Sommerville's and not Burgess's thesis. Many recent books and articles provide evidence of constitutional divisions in early Stuart England, encouraging the application of the label 'principled opposition' to many of those who opposed the royal court in this period. Work by literary scholars has encouraged this trend. Writings by M. Peltonen, *Classical Humanism and Republicanism in English Political Thought 1570–1640* (1995); and D. Norbrook, 'Lucan, Thomas May, and the creation of a republican literary culture' and M. Smuts, 'Court-centred politics and the uses of Roman historians *c*.1590–1630' in K. Sharpe and P. Lake, eds., *Culture and Politics in Early Stuart England* (1993), have shown how familiar many people were with republican and humanist ideas at this time. In the light of all this work, it is not surprising to find in specialized monographs evidence of principled opposition to the royal court in the 1620s and 1630s. Some of the most important of these are R. Cust, *The Forced Loan and English Politics 1626–28* (1987); T. Cogswell, *The Blessed Revolution: English politics and the coming of war 1621–24* (1989); and L. Reeve, *Charles I and the Road to Personal Rule* (1989). Alternative interpretations of the 1630s to Sharpe's can be found in M. Butler, *Theatre and Crisis 1632–42* (1984), Hughes, *Warwickshire* (above), T. Cogswell, *Home Divisions: aristocracy, the State and provincial conflict* (1998), W. Hunt, *The Puritan Moment: the coming of revolution in an English county* [Essex] (1983) and C. Hibbard, *Charles I and the Popish Plot* (1983).

Many books and articles also emphasize the proliferation of 'the public sphere' as it becomes clear that many people once thought to be outside 'the political nation' were informed about and took part in contemporary political and religious debates in early Stuart England. Some of the most important of these are A. Bellamy, ' "Rayling rymes and vaunting verse": libellous politics in early Stuart England 1603–28' in Sharpe and Lake, eds., *Culture and Politics*, 'A poem on the archbishop's hearse: puritans, libels and sedition after the Hampton Court conference', *J.B.S.*, 24 (1995), and *The Politics of*

Court Scandal in Early Modern England: news culture and the Overbury affair, 1603–60 (2002); T. Cogswell, 'Underground verse and the transformation of early Stuart political culture', in S. D. Amussen and M. A. Kishlansky, eds., *Political Culture and Cultural Politics in Early Modern England* (1995), P. Croft, 'The reputation of Robert Cecil: libels, political opinion and popular awareness in the early seventeenth century', *T.R.H.S.*, 6th ser., 1 (1991), and 'Libels, popular literacy and public opinion in early modern England', *Historical Research*, 68, 1995; P. Griffiths, 'Secrecy and authority in late sixteenth- and early seventeenth-century London', *H.J.*, 40 (1997); A. Fox, 'Rumours, news and popular political opinion in Elizabethan and early Stuart London', *H.J.*, 40 (1997); P. Lake, *The Boxmaker's Revenge: 'orthodoxy', 'heterodoxy' and the politics of the parish in early Stuart London* (2001) and P. Lake and M. Questier, *The Antichrist's Lewd Hat: Protestants, Papists and plays in post-Reformation England* (2002).

Not surprisingly, writings on early Stuart England have been greatly influenced by 'new British history'. Books that contribute towards a better understanding of the interconnections between England, Ireland and Scotland in this period include T. W. Moody et al., eds., *A New History of Ireland* (section 1), B. Galloway, *The Union of England and Scotland 1603–8* (1986), D. Stevenson, *The Scottish Revolution 1637–44: the triumph of the Covenanters* (1979), M. Lee, *The Road to Revolution: Scotland under Charles I, 1625–37* (1985), P. Donald, *An Uncounselled King: Charles I and the Scottish troubles 1637–41* (1990) and A. McInnes, *Charles I and the Making of the Covenanting Movement 1625–41* (1991). All these illustrate the ways in which the 'british problem' was a major source of instability in this period.

What was happening at the centre of politics has not been neglected. Great strides forward have recently been made in our understanding of the early Stuart court and the political role of patronage, as well as in the interrelationship of politics and culture in this period. On the former topic, the essays by N. Cuddy and K. Sharpe in Starkey, ed., *The Court from the Wars of the Roses to the Civil War* (section 1), L. Peck, *Patronage and Corruption in Early Stuart England* (1990) and L. Peck, ed., *The Mental World of the Jacobean Court* (1991) are crucial. On the latter there are important contributions by K. Sharpe, *Criticism and Compliment: the politics of literature in the England of Charles I* (1987), R. M. Smuts, *Court Culture and the Origins of a Royalist Tradition in Early Stuart England* (1987), D. Norbrook, *Poetry and Politics in the English Renaissance* (1984) and Butler, *Theatre and Crisis*. There are also good studies of those who advised the kings. The best studies of some of their subjects include two complementary studies of Cranfield by R. H. Tawney, *Business and Politics under James I: Lionel Cranfield as merchant and minister* (1958) and M. Prestwich, *Cranfield: politics and profits under the early Stuarts* (1976); R. Lockyer, *Buckingham* (1981); H. R. Trevor-Roper, *Archbishop Laud* (2nd edn., 1962); C. Carlton, *Archbishop William Laud* (1987); C. V. Wedgwood's revised version of her 1935 study, *Thomas Wentworth, First Earl of Strafford* (1961); M. J. Havran, *Caroline Courtier: the life of Lord Cottington* (1973); P. E. Kopperman, *Sir Robert Heath 1575–1649* (1989); L. Peck, *Northampton: patronage and policy at the court of James I* (1982); and N. Lossky, *Lancelot Andrewes: the preacher 1555–1626* (1991).

There is no good detailed biography of the first Stuart monarch. D. H. Willson, *James VI and I* (paperback edn., 1961) is in need of revision on the lines pioneered by

J. Wormald, 'James VI and I: two kings or one?', *History*, LXVIII (1983). This is achieved briefly in the introductory biographies of James VI and I by S. J. Houston (2nd edn., 1995), R. Lockyer (1998) and C. Durston (1993). These succeeed in rehabilitating James's reputation from the 'wisest fool in Christendom' label pinned on him for such a long time. But there are now signs that this has gone too far. The following suggest that James's ecclesiastical legacy to his son in Scotland was very bad: N. Canny, 'Irish, Scottish and Welsh perspectives'; J. Goodare, 'The Scottish parliament of 1621', *H.J.*, 38 (1995); J. D. Ford, 'Conformity in conscience: the structure of the Perth Articles debate in Scotland, 1618–38', *J. Eccl. H.*, 46 (1995); T. Webster, 'Religion in early Stuart Britain', in Coward, ed., *Companion to Stuart Britain* (section 1); A. R. MacDonald, *The Jacobean Kirk 1576–1625: sovereignty, polity and liturgy* (1998). P. McCullogh's study of court sermons, *Sermons at Court* (1998), is also critical of James's ecclesiastical policies south of the border after 1618, when the king's drift closer to anti-Calvinist divines caused political tensions during his last years. James's contribution to the rising political tension in England is brought out in T. Cogswell, 'Phaeton's chariot: the parliament-men and the continental crisis in 1621', in J. P. Merritt, ed., *The Political World of Thomas Wentworth, Earl of Strafford, 1621–1641* (1996). These changing trends in historians' views of James VI and I are usefully brought together in R. Houlbrooke's essay, 'James's reputation 1625–2005', in his edited collection of essays, *James VI and I: ideas, authority and government* (2006).

There are good biographies of Charles I by C. Carlton (1983), P. Gregg (1981), C. Durston (1998) and M. Young (1997). All are very critical of Charles's abilities as an early modern monarch and load a lot of blame for the troubles he faced by 1640 on his shoulders. Attempts have been made to question that view, notably by K. Sharpe, 'Private conscience and public duty in the writings of Charles I', *H.J.*, 40 (1997) and Mark Kishlansky, 'A case of mistaken identity', *P. & P.*, 189 (2005). These, in turn, have been objected to, notably by C. Holmes in a critique of Kishlansky in *P. & P.*, 205 (2009). Students fortunately now have an excellent guide to debates like this about Charles I in a splendid authoritative biography by R. Cust, *Charles: a political life* (2005), which is fair-minded in emphasizing that Charles was not without strengths as a king, but which in the end comes down on the side of the king's detractors.

Many of the best introductory books on aspects of the economic history of early seventeenth-century England have been mentioned already. Others which deal specifically with this period are R. B. Outhwaite, *Inflation in Tudor and early Stuart England* (2nd edn., 1982) and J. Thirsk, ed., *The Agrarian History of England and Wales, IV: 1500–1640* (1967). One ought not to be put off by the size of the latter; it has many excellent essays, some of which (by P. J. Bowden, J. Thirsk, J. Chartres and M. Barley) have been published separately by Cambridge University Press (1990). E. Kerridge, *The Agricultural Revolution* (1967) contains a mass of information about agrarian history, but its thesis of rapid agricultural progress in the seventeenth century is suspect. D. Palliser's optimistic view in 'Tawney's century: brave new world or Malthusian trap?', *Econ. H.R.*, XXXIX (1982) is persuasive, but has not remained unchallenged.

Since 1941 historical writing on the social history of England before 1640 has been dominated by the controversy over the economic fortunes of the landowning classes.

Though the 'storm over the gentry' is now over, the contributions to it still make compelling reading. Good guides to it can be found in L. Stone, ed., *Social Change and Revolution in England 1540–1640* (1965) and R. C. Richardson, *The Debate on the English Revolution Revisited* (1988).

A good way of getting to understand the early seventeenth century is to read some contemporary material. Major constitutional documents specifically on the early seventeenth century are to be found in the first sections of Coward and Gaunt, eds., *English Historical Documents, 1603–1660* (section 1), J. Tanner, ed., *Constitutional Documents of the Reign of James I, 1603–25* (1960) and S. R. Gardiner, ed., *Constitutional Documents of the Puritan Revolution, 1625–60* (3rd edn., 1906). See also Kenyon, *The Stuart Constitution* and Thirsk and Cooper, *Seventeenth-Century Economic Documents* listed in section 1 above. The following may stand as examples of the many available printed primary sources illustrating this period: W. Notestein, ed., *The House of Commons 1604–10* (1971); J. F. Keeler and P. L. Hughes, eds., *Stuart Royal Proclamations of James I* (1973); J. L. Larkin, ed., *Stuart Royal Proclamations: II. Royal Proclamations of King Charles 1625–46* (1982); M. F. Keeler et al., eds., *Proceedings in Parliament 1628* (6 vols., 1977–83); F. J. Fisher, ed., *The State of England, 1600, by Thomas Wilson*, Camden Miscellany, XVI (1936); J. P. Cooper, ed., *The Wentworth Papers 1597–1628*, Camden Soc., 4th ser., XII (1973).

3. The English Revolution, 1640–1660

S. R. Gardiner again provides the best full narrative history of this period in his *The History of the Great Civil War* (4 vols., 1893) and *The History of the Commonwealth and Protectorate* (4 vols., 1903). Gardiner's work, which was reprinted by Windrush in 1987, was completed after his death by C. H. Firth, *The Last Years of the Protectorate* (2 vols., 1910) and G. Davies, *The Restoration of Charles II* (1955). In the same category of narrative history, but totally lacking in any kind of thematic content or explanations of why events occurred, is C. V. Wedgwood's unfinished trilogy, *The King's Peace 1637–41* (1955) and *The King's War 1641–47* (1958). For hard-pressed students these will not be the best starting points for the history of these two decades. These are to be found in I. Roots, *The Great Rebellion 1640–60* (1966) and G. E. Aylmer, *Rebellion or Revolution? England 1640–60* (1986), as well as in the more up-to-date and detailed surveys by M. Braddick, *God's Fury, England's Fire: a new history of the English Civil Wars* (2008), I. Gentles, *The English Revolution and the Wars in the Three Kingdoms 1638–52* (2007), chapters 6–14 of Woolrych, *Britain in Revolution* (section 2) and D. Scott, *Politics and War in the Three Stuart Kingdoms 1637–49* (2004). The second part of R. Ashton, *The English Civil War: conservatism and revolution 1603–49* (1976) is a detailed account of the 1640s that (as its subtitle indicates) reflects the late 1970s fashion for emphasizing conservatism in the English Revolution. So too does J. Morrill, *The Revolt of the Provinces: conservatives and radicals in the English Civil War, 1630–50* (1976; revised edn., 1980), but Morrill's is a much more exciting interpretation of the militant conservatism and neutralism of the 1640s than Ashton's. D. Underdown, *Pride's Purge: politics during the English Revolution* (1971) brilliantly reconstructs the interaction of events in the localities and at Westminster.

Good collections of essays on this period are to be found in R. Cust and A. Hughes, eds., *The English Civil War* (1997), P. Gaunt, ed., *The English Civil War* (2002), J. Adamson, ed., *The English Civil War* (2009), C. Russell, ed., *The Origins* (listed in section 2) and its companion volumes in the Macmillan Problems in Focus series, J. Morrill, ed., *Reactions to the English Civil War* (1982) and G. E. Aylmer, ed., *The Interregnum: the quest for settlement 1646–60* (1972). R. H. Parry, ed., *The English Civil War and After, 1642–58* (1972), B. Manning, ed., *Politics, Religion and the English Civil War* (1973), R. C. Richardson et al., eds., *Freedom and the English Revolution* (1986), C. Jones et al., eds., *Politics and People in Revolutionary England* (1986), J. Morrill, ed., *The Impact of the English Civil War* (1991) and J. Morrill, ed., *Revolution and Restoration: England in the 1650s* (1992) also contain useful essays.

Many major and minor personalities who flourished in this period have attracted biographers. I have picked out the following, which I have enjoyed and are valuable in illustrating aspects of the period. C. Russell, 'The parliamentary career of John Pym, 1621–29', in P. Clark, A. G. R. Smith and N. Tyacke, eds., *The English Commonwealth 1547–1640* (1979) is most illuminating on one of the key figures of the early 1640s. P. Thomas, *Sir John Berkenhead 1617–79: a royalist career in politics and polemics* (1969) is an important account of a royalist journalist, and is valuable for the study of propaganda and the early development of English newspapers. M. Ashley, *John Wildman: plotter and postmaster* (1947) and P. Gregg, *Free-born John: a biography of John Lilburne* (1961) are interesting studies of two Leveller leaders. Ruth Spalding, *The Improbable Puritan: a life of Bulstrode Whitelocke 1605–75* (1975) has important information about a political personality who survived all changes in regime in the 1640s and 1650s and whose diary and memoirs are major sources of information about this period (see below). There are also useful biographies by N. Matthews, *William Sheppard: Cromwell's law reformer* (1984), V. Rowe, *Sir Henry Vane the Younger* (1970), J. Scott, *Algernon Sidney and the English revolution 1623–77* (1988) and A. Hopper, *'Black Tom': Sir Thomas Fairfax and the English Revolution* (2007). The preponderance of biographies of parliamentarians reflects the relative neglect by historians of royalists and royalism. This is now being addressed. See, for example, the essays in J. McElligott and D. L. Smith, eds., *Royalists and Royalism during the English Civil War* (2007).

In recent years much work has been done from a local perspective. Local histories of this period are far from new. R. C. Richardson, *The Debate on the English Revolution Revisited* (1988), pp. 133–6, gives examples of many such studies written between the seventeenth century and the 1930s. However, Alan Everitt's writings in the 1960s marked a new departure in the local history approach to the English Revolution, especially his *Suffolk and the Great Rebellion* (Suffolk Record Society, III, 1961), *The Community of Kent and the Great Rebellion, 1640–60* (1966), 'The county community', in E. W. Ives, ed., *The English Revolution 1600–60* (1968) and *The Local Community and the Great Rebellion* (Historical Association pamphlet, 1969). With the conviction that England was divided into semi-autonomous counties, Professor Everitt proceeded to recreate the political and social structure of the 'county communities' of Suffolk, Kent, Leicestershire and Northamptonshire. Under his influence others set about writing similar studies of other counties and towns. To those county studies mentioned in the previous section one might add the urban studies by A. M. Johnson, 'Politics in Chester during the civil wars and Interregnum', in P. Clark and P. Slack, eds., *Crisis and Order in English Towns, 1500–1700* (1972) and R. Howell, *Newcastle-upon-Tyne and the Puritan Revolution* (1967). Recently there has been a significant deviation from the Everitt emphasis on the county community–Westminster dichotomy. Studies have appeared that stress the interaction between local and national politics. This is true of J. S. Morrill, *Cheshire 1630–60: county government and society during 'the English Revolution'* (1974), D. Underdown, *Somerset during the Civil War and Interregnum* (1973), and especially Hughes, *Warwickshire* (section 2), and C. Holmes, *The Eastern Association in the English Civil War* (1975). The latter is a brilliant study which bridges both the local–national divide as well as that which often separates military from political history.

In addition to Richardson, good starting points for one of the most contentious historical problems of this period are Hughes, *The Causes of the English Civil War* (section 2) and C. Russell, *The Causes of the English Civil War* (1990). L. Stone, *The Causes of the English Revolution* (1972), like most things that Stone writes, is readable and interesting, but its overall thesis needs to be treated with caution. Both Hughes and Russell stress the importance of seeing the origins of the English Revolution in a British context. On this, the most important works to date are C. Russell's big book, *The Fall of the British Monarchy* (1991) and his more accessible articles, 'The British problem and the English Civil War', *H.J.*, LXXII (1987) and 'The British background to the Irish Rebellion of 1641', *Historical Research*, LXI (1988), together with D. Stevenson, *Scottish Covenanters and Irish Confederates* (1981) and *The Scottish Revolution 1637–44* (1973), and J. Morrill, ed., *The Scottish National Covenant in its British Context 1638–51* (1990). See also Scott, *Politics and War in the Three Stuart Kingdoms*. The titles of recent books reflect the strong influence of 'new British history' on the history of the English Revolution: J. Morrill, 'The war(s) of the three kingdoms' in Burgess, ed., *New British History* (section 1); P. Gaunt, *The British Civil Wars, 1637–51* (1997); J. Young, *Celtic Dimensions of the British Civil Wars* (1997); M. Bennett, *The Civil Wars in Britain and Ireland, 1638–51* (1997); J. S. Wheeler, *The Irish and British Wars, 1637–54: triumph, tragedy and failure* (2002). However, John Adamson's critique of this approach, while not denying its value, is worth some attention: J. Adamson, 'The English context of the British Civil Wars', *History Today*, 48 (1998), as is E. Shagan's argument in 'Constructing discord: ideology, propaganda and English reponses to the Irish Rebellion', *J.B.S.*, 36 (1997).

Crucial for understanding another 'context' of the Civil War is J. Morrill, 'The religious context of the English Civil War', *T.R.H.S.*, 5th ser., XXXIV (1984). The best starting points for the religious history of England from 1642 to 1660 are J. Morrill, 'The Church in England 1642–9' in Morrill, *Reactions*, and C. Cross, 'The Church in England 1646–60', in Aylmer, ed., *Interregnum*. As in other respects, in recent years radical religious and other groups have received less attention than hitherto.

A good example of this trend is the treatment of the Ranters in J. C. Davis, *Fear, Myth and History: the Ranters and historians* (1986). But good starting books for the extensive literature on some of these are G. Aylmer, ed., *The Levellers and the English Revolution* (1975), C. Hill, *The World Turned Upside Down* (1972), B. Reay and L. McGregor, eds., *Radical Religion in the English Revolution* (1984) and F. Dow, *Radicalism in the English Revolution* (1985).

J. Adamson (not without controversy) has introduced another 'context' in which to set the English Civil War. He has emphasized the role of Viscount Saye and Sele and the peerage in 'The baronial context of the English Civil War', *T.R.H.S.*, 5th ser., XXIX (1990), 'Politics and the nobility in Civil-War England', *H.J.*, XXXIV (1991) and other articles, which have been savagely attacked by M. Kishlansky in 'Saye what?', *H.J.*, XXXIII (1990) and 'Saye no more', *J.B.S.*, XXX (1991). More recently, he has written a big book on the role of the nobility, *The Noble Revolt: the overthrow of Charles I* (2007), covering the period from 1640 to 1642, and a sequel is promised.

Equally interesting as the work on the British, religious and baronial 'contexts' behind allegiances in the Civil War is D. Underdown's fascinating hypothesis about religious–cultural divisions in this period, *Revel, Riot and Rebellion: popular politics and culture in England 1603–60* (1985). For a critical appraisal of it, see J. Morrill's article in *J.B.S.*, XXVI (1987). One of the best analyses of allegiance in the English Civil War is M. Stoyle, *Loyalty and Locality: popular allegiance in Devon during the English Civil War* (1994).

R. Hutton, *The Royalist War Effort* (1982), together with I. Roy, 'The royalist council of war, 1642–6', *B.I.H.R.*, XXXV (1962) go some way towards counterbalancing the attention given to the parliamentary side in the 1640s; while C. Carlton, *Going to the Wars: the experience of the British Civil Wars 1638–51* (1992), together with I. Roy, 'The English Civil War and English society', in I. Roy and B. Bond, eds., *War and Society: a yearbook of military history* (1975), I. Roy, 'England turned Germany?', *T.R.H.S.*, 5th ser., XXVIII (1978), J. Broad, 'Gentry finances and the Civil War – the case of the Buckinghamshire Verneys', *Econ. H.R.*, 2nd ser., XXXII (1979) and D. Pennington, 'The war and the people', in Morrill, *Reactions*, are essential reading for those wanting to evaluate the impact of the Civil War largely on civilians. B. Donagan, *War in England 1642–9* (2009) examines the experiences of soldiers during the war. On the war, see M. Wanklyn and F. Jones, *A Military History of the English Civil War 1642–46: strategy and tactics* (2005).

Recent writing on the history of the early 1640s stresses the revolutionary aims of the king's opponents and the revolutionary drift of events, in contrast to the earlier emphasis by historians on conservatism. For this see especially D. Cressy, *England on the Edge: crisis and revolution 1640–42* (2006) and articles by D. Wootton in Cust and Hughes, *The English Civil War*, and D. Como in *P. & P.*, 196 (2007). On the early 1640s, Russell's *Fall of the British Monarchy* complements but has not replaced A. Fletcher's detailed study, *The Outbreak of the English Civil War 1640–43* (1981). An even older book, J. Hexter, *The Reign of King Pym* (1941) is still useful on the political divisions among parliamentarians during the early part of the Civil War. Also useful are Hexter's 'The problem of the Presbyterian-Independent', *American H.R.*, XLIV (1938), reprinted in his *Reappraisals in History* (1961), and V. Pearl, 'The "Royal Independents" in the English Civil War', *T.R.H.S.*, 5th ser., XVIII (1968). The best books that clarify the complicated army–parliamentary politics of the later 1640s are A. Woolrych, *Soldiers and Statesmen: the general council of the army and its debates 1647–8* (1987) and I. Gentles, *The New Model Army* (1991), which both take a different line from M. Kishlansky, *The Rise of the New Model Army* (1979). There is a useful summary by Gentles of the role of the New Model Army in 'The politics of Fairfax's army, 1645–49', in Adamson, *English Civil War*. The following have different views about the motives of the regicides and the prospect of a last-ditch settlement with Charles I: D. Norbrook, *Writing the English Republic: Poetry, Rhetoric and Politics 1627–60* (1997) and S. Kelsey in his articles in *H.J.*, 45 (2002) and *E.H.R.*, 118 (2003). See also the essays in J. Peacey, ed., *The Regicides and the Execution of Charles I* (2001).

On political theory rather than political practice in the 1640s, there are A. Sharp, *Political Ideas of the English Civil War 1641–49: a collection of representative texts with a commentary* (1983) and J. S. Sanderson, *'But the People's Creatures': the philosophical basis of the English Civil War* (1989).

There are three excellent brief introductions to the history of the 1650s: T. Barnard, *The English Republic* (1982), A. Woolrych, *England Without a King* (Lancaster pamphlets, 1983) and R. Hutton, *The British Republic 1649–60* (1990). These should be treated only as introductory books, since they do not reflect recent work done on the 1650s. On the early 1650s, B. Worden, *The Rump Parliament 1648–53* (1974) needs to be read alongside S. Kelsey, *Inventing a Republic: the political culture of the English Commonwealth* (1997). A. Woolrych, *Commonwealth to Protectorate* (1982; paperback edn., 1986) is still the definitive work on the establishment of the Cromwellian Protectorate, but research on the Protectorate has moved on very quickly. Many new views of the regime are reflected in B. Coward, *The Cromwellian Protectorate* (2002), as well as in P. Little and D. L. Smith, *Parliaments and Politics during the Cromwellian Protectorate* (2007) and the essays in P. Little, ed., *The Cromwellian Protectorate* (2007). C. Durston's study of *Cromwell's Major-Generals: godly government during the English Revolution* (2001) is authoritative.

Not surprisingly, Oliver Cromwell has attracted the most attention. Of older books on him, the ones that seem to me to convey the essence of Cromwell's character and aims best are S. R. Gardiner, *Oliver Cromwell* (1909), C. H. Firth, *Oliver Cromwell and the rule of the Puritans* (1900), R. S. Paul, *The Lord Protector* (1955) and C. Hill, *God's Englishman* (1970). A. Fraser, *Cromwell, Our Chief of Men* (1973) is a mine of information about the man, and no Cromwell enthusiast should be without P. Gaunt, *The Cromwellian Gazeteer* (1987). There are three recent studies of Cromwell by B. Coward (1991), P. Gaunt (1996) and C. Davis (2000). See also D. Smith, *Oliver Cromwell: politics and religion in the English Revolution 1640–58, documents and commentary* (1991); and J. Morrill, ed., *Oliver Cromwell and the English Revolution* (1990), which reflect the state of studies of Oliver Cromwell by the early 1990s. During the last few years these studies have moved along rapidly and are reflected currently in the essays in P. Little, ed., *Oliver Cromwell: new perspectives* (2009). The subtitle is very apt. Contemporary images of Cromwell in paintings, woodcuts, poems and satirical verses are brought togther in L. L. Knoppers, *Constructing Cromwell: ceremony, portrait and print 1645–61* (2000).

The best introduction to the impact of the Cromwellian regime on Ireland and Scotland is D. Stevenson, 'Cromwell, Scotland and Ireland', in Morrill, *Oliver Cromwell and the English Revolution*, which has a useful bibliography. The standard works on Scotland and Ireland in the 1650s are T. C. Barnard, *Cromwellian Ireland 1649–60* (1975) and F. D. Dow, *Cromwellian Scotland 1651–60* (1979).

The impact of the Cromwellian regime on provincial England has not been extensively studied, but there are good studies of some English localities in the 1650s by A. Coleby, *Central Government and the Localities: Hampshire 1649–89* (1987) and S. Roberts, *Recovery and Restoration in an English County: Devon local administration 1646–70* (1986), in addition to the local studies by Fletcher (section 1), and Everitt, Morrill and Hughes listed above. The most stimulating in my view is P. D. Halliday, *Dismembering the Body Politic: partisan politics in English towns 1650–1720* (1996).

The best balanced survey of Cromwellian foreign policy is R. Crabtree, 'The idea of a Protestant foreign policy', in I. Roots, ed., *Cromwell: a profile* (1973). For a much more lively and idiosyncratic approach, see S. Pincus, *Puritans and Patriotism: ideology and the making of foreign policy 1650–68* (1996).

J. Collins, 'The Church settlement of Oliver Cromwell', *History*, 87 (2002) is valuable but the writings of C. Durston are more authoritative on the impact of the Cromwelliam Church settlement. See especially his 'Puritan rule and the failure of cultural revolution', in C. Durston and J. Eales, eds., *The Culture of Puritanism* (1996).

Good guides to the tangled events of the late 1650s are R. E. Mayers, *1659: the crisis of the Commonwealth* (2004), A. Woolrych, 'Introduction', in *The Complete Prose Works of John Milton: VII (1659–60)* (1980), pp. 4–228, A. Woolrych, 'The Good Old Cause and the fall of the Protectorate', *H.J.*, XIII (1957), A. Woolrych, 'Last quests for settlement 1657–60', in Aylmer, *Interregnum*, B. Reay, *The Quakers and the English Revolution* (1975) and R. Hutton, *The Restoration: a political and religious history of England and Wales 1658–67* (1985).

Those tired of navigating through the morass of conflicting views held by professional historians about the English Revolution might find it refreshing to look at printed contemporary source material, which is abundant for this period. Here is a selection: S. R. Gardiner, ed., *Constitutional Documents of the Puritan Revolution 1625–60* (3rd edn., 1906); A. S. P. Woodhouse, ed., *Puritanism and Liberty, being the Army Debates 1647–9* (3rd edn., 1986; reissued with new preface, 1992); W. D. Macray, ed., *Clarendon's History of the Rebellion* (6 vols., 1888; repr. 1958); B. Whitelocke, *Memorials of the English Affairs* (2 vols., 1853); W. Coates, ed., *The Journal of Sir Simonds D'Ewes* (1942); L. Hutchinson, *The Life of Colonel Hutchinson* (1974); Richard Baxter, *Autobiography* (N. H. Keeble, ed., 1974); N. H. Keeble, ed., *Calendar and Correspondence of Richard Baxter* (2 vols., 1991); D. H. Pennington and I. Roots, eds., *The Committee at Stafford 1643–5* (1957); D. M. Wolfe, ed., *Leveller Manifestoes of the Puritan Revolution* (1968); W. Haller, ed.,

Tracts on Liberty in the Puritan Revolution (3 vols., 1934); I. Roots, ed., *Speeches of Oliver Cromwell* (1989) and C. Hill, ed., *Winstanley: The Law of Freedom and other writings* (1973).

4. Later Stuart England, 1660–1714

There are four brief and clear introductions to the history of Restoration England before the Glorious Revolution: R. M. Bliss, *Restoration Government: politics and government 1660–88* (Lancaster pamphlets, 1985); K. H. D. Haley, *Politics in the Reign of Charles II* (1985); J. Miller, *Restoration England: the reign of Charles II* (1985); and P. Seaward, *The Restoration, 1660–88* (1991); while J. R. Jones, ed., *The Restored Monarchy 1660–88* (1979) is a collection of useful essays on this period. All these, including a single-volume survey of this period by J. R. Jones, *Country and Court: England 1658–1714* (1978), are old-fashioned in their interpretation of events but set out clearly a chronological framwework. Two books by T. Harris – although somewhat repetitive – reflect the most recent trends in the history of later Stuart Britain: *Restoration: Charles II and his kingdoms* 1660–1685 (2005) and *Revolution: the great crisis of the British monarchy 1685–1720* (2006). Other general books on this period are W. A. Prest, *Albion Ascendant: English history 1660–1815* (1998) and A. Marshall, *The Age of Faction: court politics 1660–1702* (1999).

On the Restoration 'Settlement' and its aftermath, the key books are Hutton, *The Restoration* (section 3); D. T. Witcombe, *Charles II and the Cavalier House of Commons, 1663–74* (1966) and P. Seaward, *The Cavalier Parliament and the Reconstruction of the Old Regime 1661–67* (1989). C. D. Chandaman, *The English Public Revenue 1660–88* (1975) has done much to challenge older views about royal government in this period; while J. Miller, *Popery and Politics in England 1660–88* (1973) and *After the Civil Wars: English politics and government in the reign of Charles II* (2000) are indispensable in showing the continued importance of religion in politics after 1660. The classic account of the Exclusion Crisis is J. R. Jones, *The First Whigs: the politics of the Exclusion Crisis 1678–83* (1961). But its conclusions need to be revised in the light of recent work, especially by M. Knights, *Politics and Opinion in Crisis 1678–81* (1994) and *Representation and Misrepresentation in Later Stuart Britain: partisanship and political culture* (2005). See also M. Goldie's introduction to *Roger Morrice and the Puritan Whigs: the Entring Book of Roger Morrice 1677–91, vol. 1* (2007) for a detailed analysis of the current state of research on this period. What has not been revised is the explosion of popular political and religious debate that accompanied the crisis of the late 1670s and early 1680s. Two articles from many demonstrate the political importance of 'the public sphere' in this period: J. Miller, 'Public opinion in the reign of Charles II', *History*, 80 (1995); S. Pincus, ' "Coffee politicians does create": coffee houses and Restoration political culture', *J.M.H.*, 67 (1995).

Studies of Restoration politics from a local perspective also demonstrate the way in which political divisions of the period were rooted in the conflicts of the early part of the century. There are good local studies of Restoration Hampshire by Coleby, of Restoration Devon by Roberts and Restoration provincial towns by Halliday (see section 3) and an exciting book by P. Jenkins, *The Making of a Ruling Class: the Glamorgan gentry 1640–1790* (1983), as well as articles on Restoration Herefordshire by N. E. Key and on Restoration Bristol by J. Barry in T. Harris, M. Goldie and P. Seaward, eds., *The Politics of Religion in Restoration England* (1990). The best study of urban politics in Restoration England is T. Harris, *London Crowds in the Reign of Charles II: propaganda and politics from the Restoration to the Exclusion Crisis* (1987). J. R. Western, *Monarchy and Revolution: the English State in the 1680s* (1972) is the most useful book on the political history of the period just before the Glorious Revolution.

J. Miller, *The Glorious Revolution* (1983) and J. R. Jones, *The Revolution of 1688 in England* (1972) are good introductions to this important episode in the history of later Stuart England. More detailed studies of the revolution can be found in E. Vallance, *The Glorious Revolution 1688: Britain's fight for liberty* (2009) and S. Pincus, *The First Modern Revolution* (2009). The tercentenary celebrations of it in 1988–89 produced a huge crop of books and articles, of which W. A. Speck, *Reluctant Revolutionaries: Englishmen and the Revolution of 1688* (1988; paperback edn., 1989) is the clearest account and discussion of the implications of what happened in 1688–9. More detailed analyses of the significance and consequences of the Glorious Revolution are to be found in collections of essays that originated in conferences organized to commemorate that event: J. I. Israel, ed., *The Anglo-Dutch Moment: essays on the Glorious Revolution and its world impact* (1991); O. P. Grell, J. I. Israel and N. Tyacke, eds., *From Persecution to Toleration* (1991); R. Beddard, ed., *The Revolutions of 1688* (1991); J. R. Jones, ed., *Liberty Secured? Britain before and after 1688* (1992) and E. Cruickshanks, ed., *By Liberty or Default? The Revolution of 1688–89* (1989). J. Brewer, *Sinews of Power: war, money and the English State 1688–1783* (1989) examines some of the momentous consequences that occurred in Britain after the Glorious Revolution.

The major stimulus to much of the historical revision that has taken place since the 1950s about politics after the Glorious Revolution was the attempt by R. Walcott, in his *English Politics in the Early Eighteenth Century* (1956) to argue that political parties were not important and that the political structure of the period was like that outlined by Lewis Namier in his study of England in the middle of the eighteenth century. This provoked a reaction in the form of a legion of articles showing that political parties existed in this period (for a bibliography, see H. Horwitz, 'Parties, connections and parliamentary politics, 1689–1714: review and revisions', *J.B.S.*, VI (1966–7)). It also prompted important books about the political history of England in the reigns of William III and Queen Anne: J. H. Plumb, *The Growth of Political Stability in England 1675–1725* (1967), G. Holmes, *British Politics in the Age of Anne* (1967), W. A. Speck, *Tory and Whig: the struggle for the constituencies, 1701–15* (1970), and H. Horwitz, *Parliament, Policy and Politics in the Reign of William III* (1977). All these, together with J. P. Kenyon, *Revolution Principles: the politics of party 1689–1720* (1977), are stimulating guides to the complicated politics of this period. For recent writing on the 1690s, see C. Rose, *England in the 1690s: revolution, religion and war* (1999), and on the last part of the Stuart age, see W. A. Speck, *The Birth of a Nation 1700–1710* (1994). Good brief guides to recent shifts of historical opinion on party politics and on the seriousness of the political instability of this period can be found in G. Holmes, 'The achievement of political stability: the social context of politics from the 1680s to the age of Walpole', in J. Cannon, ed., *The Whig Ascendancy* (1981), G. Holmes's introduction to the 1987 reprinted edition of his *British Politics in the Age of Anne*; J. V. Beckett, 'Stability in politics and society 1680–1750', in C. Jones, ed., *Britain in the First Age of Party 1680–1750* (1987) and J. Black, 'An age of political stability?', in J. Black, ed., *Britain in the Age of Walpole* (1984). The latter is also a good starting point for tackling the questions of to what extent and why the party divisions and political volatility of the reigns of William III and Queen Anne disappeared in the period after 1714.

Students may like to study the history of late Stuart England by reading biographies of some major politicians. There are biographies of Charles II: by A Fraser, *King Charles II* (1979), J. R. Jones, *Charles II: a royal politician* (1990), R. Hutton, *Charles II: king of England, Scotland and Ireland* (1991), J. Miller, *Charles II: a biography* (1991), and A. Keay, *The Magnificent Monarch: Charles II and the ceremonies of power* (2008). J. Miller, *James II: a study in kingship* (1978) has many new insights into the history of England between 1660 and 1689. The standard biographies of the last two Stuart monarchs are S. B. Baxter, *William III* (1966) and E. Gregg, *Queen Anne* (1980). The studies of the subjects of these Stuart monarchs that I found most readable and/or useful are A. Browning, *Thomas Osborne, Earl of Danby* (3 vols., 1944–51), J. P. Kenyon, *Robert Spencer, Earl of Sunderland* (1958), K. H. D. Haley, *The First Earl of Shaftesbury* (1968), H. Horwitz, *Revolution Politics: the career of the second earl of Nottingham* (1968), G. V. Bennett, *The Tory Crisis in Church and State: 1688–1730: the career of Francis Atterbury, bishop of Rochester* (1975), and F. Harris, *A Passion for Government: the life of Sarah, duchess of Marlborough* (1991).

General books that cover this period of the history of Ireland and Scotland are listed in section 1. To these might be added here D. Dickson, *New Foundations: Ireland 1660–1800* (1987), J. Wormald, ed., *Scotland Revisited* (1991), I. B. Cowan, 'Church and State reformed? The revolution of 1688–9' and D. Hayton, 'The Williamite Revolution in Ireland 1688–91' in Israel, ed., *The Anglo-Dutch Moment*.

On foreign policy, the Church and dissent, and the economic, social and intellectual history of late Stuart England, there are useful introductory books listed in section 1. In addition, K. Feiling, *British Foreign Policy 1660–72* (1957) and especially the essays in J. S. Bromley and R. Hatton, eds., *William III and Louis XIV: essays by and for Mark A. Thomson* (1968) are invaluable. J. Spurr, *The Restoration Church of England 1646–89* (1991) splendidly filled a big historiographical hole to become the standard work on that subject. Older studies, though, are still useful, including N. Sykes, *From Sheldon to Secker: aspects of English Church history 1660–1768* (1959), R. S. Bosher, *The Making of the Restoration Settlement: the influence of the Laudians 1649–62* (1951), and I. M. Green, *The Re-establishment of the Church of England 1660–63* (1978). The best introductory book on dissent in this period is Watts, *The Dissenters* (see section 1), but older books like G. R. Cragg, *Puritanism in the Period of the Great Persecution* (1957) have much to offer. Most of the general books on economic aspects mentioned in section 1 also deal with this period. R. Davis, *A Commercial Revolution: English overseas trade in the seventeenth and eighteenth centuries* (Historical Association pamphlet, 1969) concentrates on the period after 1660, as does E. L. Jones, ed., *Agriculture and Economic Growth in England 1650–1815* (1967). The basic book on topics like agriculture, prices, internal trade and land-ownership is J. Thirsk, ed., *The Agrarian History of England and Wales, vol. V 1640–1760* (1985). Books that cover later Stuart intellectual and social history have also been listed in section 1. Of those books that deal only with this later period, the following have particularly exciting conclusions: P. Borsay, *The English Urban Renaissance: culture and society in the provincial town 1660–1760* (1989), P. Earle, *The Making of the English Middle Classes: business, society and family life in London 1660–1730* (1989; paperback edn., 1991), J. Plumb, 'The commercialization of leisure', N. McKendrick, 'The birth of a consumer society' and 'The consumer society in eighteenth-century England', in N. McKendrick et al., eds., *The Birth of a Consumer Society* (1982), and M. Hunter, *Science and Society in Restoration England* (1981).

A. Browning, ed., *English Historical Documents, VIII: 1660–1714* (1953) and W. C. Costin and J. Steven Watson, eds., *The Law and Working of the Constitution: Documents 1660–1914, I: 1660–1783* (2nd edn., 1961) are useful supplements to Kenyon, *Stuart Constitution* and Williams, *The Eighteenth Century Constitution* listed in section 1. Those who persevere will find that dipping into the following collections of parliamentary debates will enrich their understanding of the period: A. Grey, *Debates of the House of Commons from . . . 1667–1694* (10 vols., 1763); C. Robbins, ed., *The Diary of John Milward* (1938); B. D. Henning, ed., *The Parliamentary Diary of Sir Edward Dering 1670–73* (1940); and H. Horwitz, ed., *The Parliamentary Diary of Narcissus Luttrell, 1691–93* (1972). Easier to read and more obviously appealing are personal diaries of contemporaries, such as Samuel Pepys's *Diary* (R. C. Latham and W. Matthews, eds., 11 vols., 1970–83), John Evelyn's *Diary* (E. S. de Beer, ed., 6 vols., 1955), M. Hunter and A. Gregory, eds., *An Astrological Diary of the Seventeenth Century: Samuel Jeake of Rye 1652–99* (1987), the earl of Ailesbury's *Memoirs* (edited by W. E. Buckley for the Roxburgh Club, 2 vols., 1890) and Bishop G. Burnet, *History of His Own Time* (abridged by Thomas Stackhouse, intro. by D. Allen, 1986).

After all that, you may still want to find other books and articles, especially if you are doing a dissertation or extended essay. Guides to further reading can be found in the writings in the footnotes of this book, the bibliographies in the books listed here, and standard bibliographies, especially Godfrey Davies and Mary F. Keeler, eds., *Bibliography of British History: Stuart Period 1603–1714* (1970) and J. Morrill, *Seventeenth Century Britain* (1980). Also useful are W. L. Sachse, ed., *Bibliographical Handbooks: Restoration England 1660–89* (1976), G. R. Elton, *Modern Historians on British History 1485–1945* (1970), and the *Annual Bulletin of Historical Literature* (published for the Historical Association), which has review articles on the most important historical works published each year on the Stuart period. The most comprehensive source is 'The Bibliography of British and Irish History (BBIH)', which can be accessed via the subscription-only Royal Historical website: **www.royalhistoricalsociety.org**.

Appendix: Timeline

1603

March	Death of Queen Elizabeth and accession of James VI of Scotland as James I of England. Surrender of earl of Tyrone and end of Irish Rebellion
April	Millenary Petition presented to James VI on his way south to London
May	Robert Cecil created Lord Cecil of Essendon

Plague in London killed 22.6 per cent of the population

Revelations of the Main and Bye Plots (Sir Walter Raleigh sent to Tower for alleged part in the Main Plot to put Arabella Stuart on the throne)

1604

January	Hampton Court Conference
February	Death of Archbishop Whitgift
March	First session of James's first parliament (to July): union of England and Scotland proposed; Buckinghamshire election dispute; 'Form of Apology and Satisfaction'
July	Royal proclamation demanding conformity to forthcoming new church canons by November
August	Treaty of London ended war with Spain
September	New canons issued defining the nature of the Church of England
October	Royal proclamation declaring James 'King of Great Britain'
November	Proposed issue of Union currency
December	Consecration of Richard Bancroft as archbishop of Canterbury. Campaign to deprive church ministers for non-subscription to new canons began

Great Farm of customs (leasing by crown to syndicates of merchants of the collection of customs dues) began

James published his *Counterblast to Tobacco*

1605

February	James inaugurated campaign against recusants (Catholics who refused to conform to the English Church)
April	Robert Cecil created earl of Salisbury
Spring	Petitions from various counties protesting at Bancroft's and James's expulsion of church ministers
November	Gunpowder Plot discovered. Second session of James's first parliament (to May 1606): measures passed against recusants

1606

April	Royal proclamation that all British ships carry a new Union flag
November	Third parliamentary session of James's first parliament (to July 1607): debates on proposed union of England and Scotland

Bate case ended with important judgment allowing the king to levy impositions by his prerogative right

1607

May	Midlands Rising against enclosures
July	End of third session of James's first parliament
September	Flight of earl of Tyrone from Ireland

Robert Carr, James's Scottish favourite, knighted. Francis Bacon appointed solicitor-general

Establishment of first permanent English colony in America at Jamestown, Virginia

Publication of John Cowell's *The Interpreter* and John Norden's *The Surveyor's Dialogue*

1608

April	Death of Lord Treasurer Thomas Sackville, earl of Dorset
May	Appointment of Robert Cecil, earl of Salisbury, as lord treasurer, who ordered survey of all crown lands
July	Salisbury issued new Book of Rates as a result of the decision in Bate case (1606)
November	Public declaration by the king that he would curtail his gifts of land

Appointment of commissioners to supervise the plantation (colonization) of Ulster

1609

March	Twelve-year truce between Spain and the United Provinces
May	James agreed not to alienate (sell or grant away) any crown lands

1610

February	Fourth session of James's first parliament (to July): debates on impositions and the Great Contract
April	Death in Rome of Robert Parsons, English Jesuit
May	Assassination of Henri IV of France
July	Imprisonment of Arabella Stuart for marrying William Seymour, earl of Hertford
October	Fifth session of James's first parliament (to December): collapse of the Great Contract
November	Death of Richard Bancroft, archbishop of Canterbury

1611

March	Robert Carr created Viscount Rochester
May	Creation of baronetcies for sale at £1,095 each

Publication of the Authorized Version of the Bible

George Abbot appointed archbishop of Canterbury

1612

May	Death of earl of Salisbury (treasurership put into commission); marriage contract between Princess Elizabeth and Elector Palatine Frederick
November	Death of Prince Henry

1613

February	Marriage of Princess Elizabeth and Elector Palatine Frederick
May	Don Diego Sarmiento de Acuna (later count of Gondomar) arrived in England as Spanish ambassador
September	James I approved the divorce of Lady Frances Howard and the earl of Essex. Death in the Tower of Sir Thomas Overbury, an opponent of the divorce

November   Robert Carr created earl of Somerset

December   Somerset married Lady Frances Howard

Sir Edward Coke appointed chief justice of the King's Bench, and Sir Francis Bacon appointed attorney-general

1614

March   Ralph Winwood appointed secretary of state

April   Addled Parliament met (to June): clashes over impositions

July   Thomas Howard, Lord Suffolk, appointed lord treasurer; and Somerset appointed lord chancellor

December   Cockayne Project began when Company of Merchant Adventurers' monopoly of the cloth trade suspended

Publication of John Napier's *Descriptio* (on logarithms)

1615

May   Commission established ostensibly to prevent further building in London

September   Death of Lady Arabella Stuart

October   Arrest of earl and countess of Somerset, accused of Overbury's murder (see 1613)

Lionel Cranfield appointed surveyor-general of the customs

Sales of peerages began

1616

March   Release of Sir Walter Raleigh from the Tower (see 1603) to allow him to lead an expedition to Guiana

July   Trial and conviction of the earl and countess of Somerset for Overbury's murder

August   George Villiers made a viscount and master of the royal horse

November   Dismissal of Sir Edward Coke as lord chief justice of the King's Bench over the case of commendans. Replaced by Sir Henry Montague, Viscount Brackley (nicknamed by legal rivals 'break-law')

1617

January   Villiers created earl of Buckingham

May   James I's visit to Scotland (to August)

September   Sir Edward Coke re-admitted to the privy council

Restoration of the charter of the Company of Merchant Adventurers and end of the Cockayne Project

1618

January   Sir Francis Bacon became lord chancellor; Buckingham created a marquis

May   James I's Declaration of Sports published

July   Dismissal of Lord Treasurer Suffolk after trial for financial corruption

August   Invasion of Bohemia by the emperor's army in retaliation for the establishment of a Protestant government in Prague in May: the beginning of the Thirty Years War. The Five Articles of Perth were accepted in Scotland

October   Execution of Raleigh on return from Guiana for alleged part in 1603 Main Plot

Beginning of Cranfield's campaign of expenditure cuts in the royal household and navy

1619

January   Cranfield became master of the court of wards; Buckingham appointed lord high admiral

February   Dismissal of Sir Thomas Lake, a client of Suffolk, after a scandal involving Lord and Lady Roos

March   Death of Queen Anne

May   The king's delegate backed the anti-Arminians at the Synod of Dort

September   Elector Palatine Frederick accepted offer of throne of Bohemia

William Harvey announced his discovery of the circulation of the blood in the body

1620

August   The Palatinate invaded by Imperial troops

October   King Frederick of Bohemia expelled from his kingdom after the battle of the White Mountain

December   Pilgrim Fathers established a colony at Plymouth, New England

1621

January   Meeting of first session of James's third parliament (to June): debates on monopolies; impeachment of Bacon

May	Savage punishment by parliament of Floyd, a Catholic, who had allegedly denied the Elector Palatine's right to the Bohemian throne
June	Arrest of Sir Edward Sandys and the earls of Oxford and Southampton for opposition in parliament
July	Royal proclamation cancelling 18 monopolies and promising to review 17 others
November	Meeting of second session of James's third parliament (to December): the Commons' Protestation

End of the 12-year Truce of Antwerp

Cranfield created lord treasurer and earl of Middlesex

Trade depression to 1623

1622

March	Massacre of Jamestown settlers by Indians

1623

February	The Amboyna Massacre of agents of the English East India Company by the Dutch in the Spice Islands (news reached England in May 1624)
March	Visit of Prince Charles and Buckingham to Madrid (to October)
May	Buckingham created a duke
June	Elector Palatine Frederick expelled from the Palatinate by Imperial troops
October	Popular welcome for Prince Charles and Buckingham on return from Madrid

1624

February	James's fourth and last parliament (to May): pressure for war; Monopolies Act; impeachment of Cranfield
June	Collapse of the Virginia Company
November	Anglo-French treaty providing for the marriage of Prince Charles and Henrietta Maria, the suspension of recusancy laws in England and English help for the French against the La Rochelle Huguenots

Foundation of the first English colony in the Caribbean at St Kitts by Captain Thomas Warner

1625

January	Disaster hit Mansfield's expedition before it reached the Palatinate
March	Death of James I and accession of Charles I
May	Marriage by proxy of Charles I and Henrietta Maria (they first met at Dover in June)
June	Meeting of first session of Charles's first parliament (to July): attack on Arminians; grant of two subsidies and of tonnage and poundage for one year
July	Richard Montague, author of the pro-Arminian *A New Gag*, made Charles's chaplain
August	Meeting of second session of Charles's first parliament at Oxford: attacks made on Buckingham
September	Failure of Buckingham's Cadiz expedition (disgraced fleet returned home in November)
October	Charles proposed Act of Revocation, revoking all crown gifts of royal and Kirk property in Scotland made since 1540

1626

February	Attempt at a conference at York House to defuse the religious controversy over Arminianism failed. Buckingham supported the Arminians
Summer	Charles and Henrietta Maria quarrelled frequently in public
June	Dissolution of Charles's second parliament
September	A forced loan (to raise the equivalent of five subsidies) ordered to pay for the war against Spain; Lord Chief Justice Carew dismissed because the judges refused to endorse the legality of the forced loan

1627

England declared war on France

October	Humiliating defeat of Buckingham's expeditionary force to aid the French Huguenots on the Isle of Ré off La Rochelle; Archbishop Abbot suspended for refusing to license Robert Sibthorpe's sermon defending the forced loan
November	The judges in the Court of King's Bench upheld the right of the king to imprison without trial five forced loan refusers ('the Five Knights'). The king subsequently altered the record of the judgment to make it appear that the judges had upheld the king's *general* right to imprison without trial

1628

March	Charles's third parliament met
June	Charles I accepted the Petition of Right, condemning extra-parliamentary taxation, arbitrary imprisonment, billeting of troops and martial law. Parliament adjourned
July	William Laud appointed bishop of London; Roger Mainwaring, a divine impeached by parliament, was pardoned by Charles I; John Lambe, a friend of Buckingham, was murdered in a London street by a mob
August	Assassination of Buckingham by John Felton; Richard Montague, author of the Arminian pamphlet, *A New Gag* (1624), consecrated bishop of Chichester
December	Thomas Wentworth appointed president of the council of the north

1629

January	Second session of Charles's third parliament began
March	Speaker Finch prevented from adjourning the Commons until three resolutions were passed against extra-parliamentary tonnage and poundage and religious innovations. The king dissolved parliament
April	Peace made with France by the Treaty of Suza

Lord Treasurer Weston began a campaign to reform the navy, ordnance and royal household (to 1632)

1630

May	Birth of Prince Charles (the future Charles II), the consequence of the new, closer relationship between Charles and Henrietta Maria after the death of Buckingham
June	The governor of the Massachusetts Bay Company (formed in 1629) landed with 4 ships and 400 settlers at Salem, Massachusetts
August	The exchequer judges confirmed the king's right to fine landowners worth £40 per annum or more who had not received a knighthood
November	Peace made with Spain by the Treaty of Madrid

1631

January	Successive bad harvests in 1629 and 1630, soaring food prices and food riots prompted the privy council to issue Books of Orders

1632

January	Wentworth appointed lord deputy of Ireland
November	Sir John Eliot died in the Tower (he had been there since 1629 for his part in the events of 2 March 1629)

A new English colony, Maryland, founded by Lord Baltimore

1633

Charles visited Scotland (he was crowned there in June) and decided to introduce an English Prayer Book in Scotland

February	William Prynne sent to the Tower for writing *Histromastix*, condemning stage-plays (his ears were cut off as a punishment in May 1634); abolition of the Feoffees of Impropriations, established in 1625 to buy impropriated tithes and use them to employ Puritan lecturers
August	Death of Archbishop Abbot; replaced as archbishop of Canterbury by Laud; republication of the 1618 Declaration of Sports
October	Birth of Prince James (the future James II)

1634

September	Sir Robert Heath, chief justice of the common pleas, dismissed for his opposition to Laudianism
October	First ship money writs issued to maritime counties

Restoration of the monopoly of the Company of Merchant Adventurers

1635

March	Death of Lord Treasurer Weston
May	Commission on depopulation established to raise money by selling licences confirming illegal enclosures
June	Ship money levied on the whole country (annual ship money writs were issued from now until 1639); revival of the forest courts to raise money by fines
December	Judges declared that ship money was legal

New ecclesiastical canons (based on the English canons of 1604) issued in Scotland

1636

March	William Juxon, bishop of London, appointed lord treasurer

1637

June	Prynne, Bastwick and Burton were branded and had their ears cut off for publishing anti-episcopal pamphlets
July	Riots in St Giles's Church, Edinburgh, against the English prayer book
November	Petitioning movement in Scotland against the new prayer book; elections to a Scottish National Assembly; trial of John Hampden for refusing to pay ship money began in the exchequer court (the final judgment against Hampden was given by a majority 7 : 5 vote in June 1638)

1638

February	The Scottish National Assembly drew up a National Covenant abolishing the Book of Common Prayer
November	The Scottish Assembly abolished bishops, which provoked military action by the English against the Scots (the first Bishops' War)

1639

June	The first Anglo-Scottish Bishops' War ended by the Truce of Berwick
September	Wentworth returned from Ireland to London and advised the recall of parliament in England

1640

January	Wentworth created earl of Strafford and lord lieutenant of Ireland
April	Charles I's fourth parliament (the Short Parliament) met
May	Short Parliament dissolved

New ecclesiastical canons issued by Convocation

August	Second Anglo-Scottish Bishops' War began. Scottish troops occupied Newcastle; Scottish conservative nobles signed the Cumbernauld Bond against the Covenanters
October	English troops defeated in second Bishops' War, which was ended by the Treaty of Ripon
November	First meeting of Charles I's fifth parliament (the Long Parliament): attacks on the ship money judges and monopolists; impeachment proceedings began against Strafford and Laud; new ecclesiastical canons condemned
December	London Root and Branch Petition against bishops presented to parliament

1641

January   Kent petition against bishops presented to parliament

February   Pro-bishop petitions received by parliament, including Sir Thomas Aston's *Remonstrance against Presbytery*; Triennial Act passed

March   Trial of Strafford for treason began in the House of Lords

April   Failure of the prosecution to prove their case in Strafford's trial; discussion of the 'bridge appointments' of leading parliamentarians to great offices of state in return for saving Strafford's life

May   Act against dissolving the Long Parliament without its own consent passed; news of an army plot was followed by parliamentary agreement on a Protestation Oath against popery; Strafford was executed after an Act of Attainder was passed against him; in the House of Commons Sir Edward Dering presented a Root and Branch Bill, proposing the abolition of bishops

June   Tonnage and Poundage Act passed; House of Lords rejected a bill excluding bishops from parliament; the king announced his intention to visit Scotland; the Ten Propositions agreed by parliament as a basis for negotiations with the king

July   Acts passed abolishing the Courts of star chamber and high commission

August   Act abolishing ship money passed; Charles left on his Scottish visit

September   Charles made concessions to the Scottish Covenanters; end of first session of the Long Parliament

October   Allegations of a royalist plot ('the Incident') against the Covenanters; beginning of second session of Long Parliament; outbreak of rebellion in Ireland

November   Commons agreed an Additional Instruction to be sent to parliamentary commissioners in Scotland, demanding parliamentary appointment of the king's main officials in return for parliamentary support for an English army in Ireland; Grand Remonstrance passed in the Commons by 159 to 148 votes; Charles I returned to London to a warm welcome from the City

December   Militia Bill introduced in the Commons; the ruling oligarchic clique in London was defeated in City elections; 13 bishops who had been prevented by mobs from entering parliament demanded that parliamentary proceedings in their absence be declared null and void, for which they were impeached by parliament

1642

January	Charles I failed to arrest five members of the Commons and one member of the lords; the king left London; petitioning campaign against bishops
February	Act excluding bishops from parliament passed; Henrietta Maria left England to seek foreign help for her husband
March	Parliament issued the Militia Ordinance without the king's assent; Act of £400,000 passed
April	Charles prevented from seizing the ammunition stored in the garrison at Hull
June	Parliament agreed the Nineteen Propositions as a basis for negotiations with the king; royal commissions of array issued to challenge the orders given by parliament to raise troops under its Militia Ordinance
July	Lord Strange forcibly prevented by parliamentary supporters from seizing the ammunition stored in Manchester, the first significant armed conflict of 1642
August	The king raised his standard at Nottingham, the official start of the Civil War
September	Parliamentary ordinance closing theatres passed
October	The first major battle of the Civil War at Edgehill ended in a draw
November	A group of Staffordshire gentry decided to raise 'a third force' to insulate their county from the war; the king's march on London was halted by London trained bands at Turnham Green
December	Parliament agreed to begin peace negotiations with the king; demilitarization 'treaty' agreed by some Cheshire gentry at Bunbury; parliamentary Eastern Association established

1643

February	'Treaty' negotiations between the king and parliamentary commissioners began at Oxford; Henrietta Maria returned from the Continent with men and money and joined the earl of Newcastle's army at York; parliament passed the weekly assessment ordinance
April	Collapse of the Oxford 'treaty' negotiations
May	Parliamentary compulsory loans ordinance passed
Spring–summer	Royalist military successes by the earl of Newcastle's army in the north-east (victories in Yorkshire and Lincolnshire) and by the armies of Sir Ralph Hopton, Prince Maurice and Prince Rupert in the south-west (victories at Roundway Down and Bristol in July)

July	Parliamentary excise ordinance passed; Westminster Assembly of Divines began to discuss a new Church settlement
August	Parliamentary impressment ordinance legalizing conscription passed; a parliamentary ordinance passed allowing the earl of Manchester to raise an Eastern Association army by conscription; parliament–Scottish alliance (the Solemn League and Covenant) agreed in Scotland
September	Charles made the Cessation Treaty with the Irish; Solemn League and Covenant ratified in England
December	Death of John Pym

1644

January	Royalist 'parliament' met at Oxford; Scottish army entered England to join its parliamentary allies; disagreements between religious Presbyterian and religious Independents in the Westminster Assembly were highlighted by publication of the Independents' *An Apologeticall Narration*
February	Duke of Montrose appointed lieutenant general of the royalist forces in Scotland
June	Scottish and parliamentary armies besieged York; first signs of religious disagreements between English and Scottish allies
July	Defeat of the royalist armies (led by the earl of Newcastle and Prince Rupert) by the combined Scottish and parliamentary forces at Marston Moor, Yorkshire
August	Defeat of the parliamentary army led by the earl of Essex at Lostwithiel, Cornwall
September	Montrose and Antrim defeated a Covenanter army at Tippermuir in Scotland
October	Indecisiveness of the earl of Manchester and the parliamentary forces at and after the battle of Newbury led to a public quarrel between Manchester and his second-in-command, Oliver Cromwell
November	Charges and counter-charges brought against each other by Manchester (and the Political Presbyterians) and Cromwell (and the Political Independents) in parliament
December	The earl of Essex, the Political Presbyterians and the Scots considered re-opening negotiations with the king; a Self-Denying Ordinance proposed

1645

January	Parliament approved the Westminster Assembly's recommendations that the Book of Common Prayer be replaced by the Directory of Public Worship; Royalist–parliamentary 'treaty' negotiations began at Uxbridge (they collapsed in February); execution of Laud
February	New Model Ordinance passed by parliament
April	Self-Denying Ordinance passed by parliament
June	Parliamentary victories at the battle of Naseby and . . .
July	. . . at the battle of Langport
August	Parliamentary ordinance establishing a national Presbyterian Church passed (further ordinances passed in March and June 1646)
September	Bristol surrendered to the New Model Army; royalist defeat at Rowton Heath in Cheshire; Montrose defeated at Philiphaugh in Scotland; the king ordered Prince Charles to leave for France

1646

February	Parliament passed an ordinance abolishing the court of wards and liveries
March	Surrender of Hopton's royalist forces to the New Model Army
May	The king left Oxford to surrender to the Scots at Newark (Notts.)
June	The surrender of Oxford, the royalist HQ during the war, marked the end of the Civil War
July	Increasing number of army mutinies over lack of pay and indemnity against prosecution; parliament approved the Propositions of Newcastle as a basis for negotiations with the king
September	Death of the earl of Essex
October	Parliamentary ordinance abolishing bishops passed

1647

February	Parliament proposed to reduce the New Model Army in size
March	Parliament condemned an army petition for redress of its grievances as treasonable
March–April	Negotiations between the New Model Army and parliamentary commissioners at Saffron Walden (Essex)

May	Commons voted to disband the New Model Army with only eight weeks' arrears of wages paid
June	New Model Army soldiers led by Cornet Joyce seized the king from his parliamentary guards at Holmby House (Northants.) and took him to the army's HQ at Newmarket; Oliver Cromwell joined the army there; the army issued *A Solemn Engagement* and *A Declaration of the Army*, making political demands and impeaching eleven MPs
July	The army moved to Reading: *The Heads of the Proposals* debated there in the army council, now with representatives (agitators) of the rank and file present, and negotiations with the king began; the Political Presbyterians' attempted counter-revolution in London
August	*The Heads of the Proposals* were published and the New Model Army occupied London
October	Agitators with Leveller links appeared in five cavalry regiments; *The Case of the Armie Truly Stated* and *The First Agreement of the People* published; the Putney Debates in the army council began
November	The king escaped from Hampton Court to Whitehall; the army met at three separate rendezvous and an army mutiny at Ware (Herts.) was crushed
December	Charles I made an alliance (the Engagement) with the Scots and rejected parliamentary peace proposals (the Four Bills); Christmas Day revolt in Canterbury (Kent) against Presbyterianism

1648

January	The Vote of No Addresses passed by parliament
March	Revolt in Pembrokeshire (south Wales) against the New Model Army
April	Windsor prayer meeting of the army council, after which Cromwell left to suppress the rebellion in south Wales
May	Rising against the New Model Army in Kent and in the navy and . . .
June	. . . in Essex
July	The Scottish army, led by the duke of Hamilton, invaded England; the south Wales rebels surrendered at Pembroke
August	Defeat of the Scottish army at Preston by Cromwell, and of the Essex and Kent rebels at Colchester by Fairfax; the Vote of No Addresses was revoked
September	Parliamentary negotiations with the king began at Newport (Isle of Wight)
November	*The Remonstrance of the Army* issued

December The New Model Army's second occupation of London; the Commons voted to continue the Newport negotiations with the king; Pride's purge of parliament; the Levellers' second *Agreement of the People* published

1649

January Parliamentary ordinance for the trial of the king passed; the trial and execution of the king; the Officers' *Agreement of the People* published; the duke of Ormonde's agreement with the Confederate Catholics in Ireland

February John Lilburne's *Englands New Chains Discovered* published (second part published in March); arrest of the Leveller leaders; parliamentary resolutions to abolish monarchy and the House of Lords passed (Acts to this effect passed in March)

April Digger communities established in Surrey; sales of estates of the crown and of dean and chapters of cathedrals began

May Act declaring England a republic ('the Commonwealth') passed by the Rump Parliament; army mutinies suppressed by Fairfax and Cromwell at Burford (Oxfordshire) and elsewhere

August English expeditionary force under Cromwell set off to suppress the Irish rebellion

September Parliamentary press censorship ordinance passed; the New Model Army's victory and massacre at Drogheda and at . . .

October . . . Wexford in Ireland

1650

January Engagement Oath of loyalty to the new republic ordered to be taken by all adult males

February Act for the Propagation of the Gospel in Wales passed

May Act decreeing the death penalty for adultery passed

June A weekly government newspaper, *Mercurius Politicus*, edited by Marchamont Needham, launched; Cromwell on his return from Ireland was appointed commander of an expeditionary force against the Scots and Charles II

August Blasphemy Act against religious nonconformity passed

September Cromwell's victory over the Scots at Dunbar. Act repealing all laws compelling attendance at the national Church was passed

1651

July	Act for the sale of lands of principal royalist supporters passed (further Acts passed in July and August 1652)
September	Cromwell's victory over Charles II at Worcester; Charles II began his exile on the Continent (until 1660)
October	Navigation Act passed

1652

January	Hale Commission began to produce proposals for the reform of the law
May	First Anglo-Dutch war of the seventeenth century began; naval battle of the Dunes
August	Settlement of Ireland Act passed
September	Admiral Blake's victory over the Dutch in the Channel
November	Dutch naval victory over the English off Dungeness

1653

February	Anglo-Dutch naval battle off Portland
April	Cromwell forcibly dissolved the Rump Parliament; new council of state appointed
July	Opening of Barebones Parliament, an assembly of representatives of England, Wales, Scotland and Ireland, nominated by the council and the army; purges of the commissions of the peace began; English naval victory over the Dutch at the battle of Texel
August	Barebones Parliament voted to abolish the court of chancery; acts to legalize civil marriages and to register births, marriages and deaths passed
November	Barebones Parliament voted to abolish lay patronage of church livings
December	A motion to abolish tithes narrowly defeated in Barebones Parliament; vote in Barebones Parliament to resign its power to the army; dissident minority ejected by the army; Cromwell accepted the Instrument of Government and was installed as Lord Protector

1654

January	Oath of Engagement abolished
March	Protector and council issued the triers ordinance
April	Anglo-Dutch war ended by the Treaty of Westminster; Protector and council issued ordinance for the union of England and Scotland

August	Protector and council issued the ejectors and chancery reform ordinances
September	Beginning of the first Protectorate Parliament: MPs forced to sign a 'Recognition', recognizing the Instrument of Government or resign; attacks on the army; attempts to restrict religious freedom
November	Imprisonment of George Cony for refusing to pay customs duties
December	The Western Design expeditionary force set off for the Caribbean

1655

January	Cromwell dissolved the first Protectorate Parliament
March	Penruddock's royalist rising suppressed
April	Defeat of the Western Design expeditionary force at San Domingo in the Caribbean
May	Cromwell and the council ordered the imprisonment of George Cony's lawyers; Western Design expeditionary force captured Jamaica
June	Resignation of Lord Chief Justice Rolle
July	News of the defeat of the Western Design reached London
August	Appointment of the major-generals
October	Revised 'moral order' instructions given to the major-generals, who began their work in the localities; Anglo-French defensive treaty made and war with Spain began
December	Cromwell allowed the readmission of the Jews to England

1656

| September | Opening of the second Protectorate Parliament after the exclusion of over 100 MPs by the Protectorate council. English capture of Spanish treasure fleet off Cadiz |
| October | James Nayler, a Quaker, arrested and charged with 'horrid blasphemy' |

1657

January	Cromwell decided to abandon the Instrument of Government and the major-generals
February	Cromwell put the case for this to a meeting of hostile army officers
March	The Humble Petition and Advice was presented to Cromwell; offensive Anglo-French alliance signed
April	Defeat of the Spanish navy by Blake at Santa Cruz in the Canaries

May	Cromwell accepted the Humble Petition and Advice but refused the associated offer of the crown
June	Cromwell was installed for a second time as Protector; end of the first session of the second Protectorate Parliament
August	Death of Admiral Blake
September	Capture of Mardyke from the Spanish
November	Henry Cromwell appointed Lord President of Ireland

1658

January	Beginning of second session of the second Protectorate Parliament: republican attacks on the new constitution
February	Cromwell dissolved the second Protectorate Parliament
June	Anglo-French victory over Spain at the battle of the Dunes, followed by the surrender of Dunkirk to the English
September	Death of Oliver Cromwell, succeeded by Richard Cromwell as Lord Protector

1659

January	Meeting of the third Protectorate Parliament: attacks on the army and attempts to restrict religious freedom
April	Dissolution of the third Protectorate Parliament
May	Recall of the Rump Parliament: attacks by civilian republicans on the army
August	Defeat of a royalist rising in Cheshire led by Sir George Booth
October	The army expelled the Rump and established a committee of safety headed by Charles Fleetwood
December	Fleetwood resigned and recalled the Rump Parliament

1660

January	General George Monck and the English army in Scotland, having declared for the Rump Parliament, marched southwards
February	Monck reached London and allowed the MPs excluded from parliament by the army in 1648 to return
March	The Rump Parliament (what remained of the Long Parliament that had first met in November 1640) declared itself dissolved, and ordered new elections

April	Declaration of Breda issued by Charles II; meeting of the Convention Parliament (to December): resolution in favour of government by king, Lords and Commons; inadequate financial settlement made; no religious settlement made; feudal tenures remained abolished; excise tax continued; Act for Confirmation of Judicial Proceedings; Act of Indemnity; Navigation Act
May	Return and restoration of Charles II
October	Worcester House conference on a religious settlement

1661

January	Bodies of Oliver Cromwell, Bradshaw and Ireton exhumed and hung on the gallows at Tyburn; Venner's Rising
April–July	Savoy House conference on a religious settlement
May	First session of Cavalier Parliament (to July): bishops restored to House of Lords; Solemn League and Covenant ordered to be burned; Militia Act; Act condemning parliament's claim to legislate without the king; Act against tumultuous petitioning; Corporation Act
November	Second session of the Cavalier Parliament (to May 1662): Act for censorship of the press; Quaker Act

1662

April	Prayer Book revised by convocation accepted by parliament
May	Hearth tax established; Uniformity Act
December	Charles II's first Declaration of Indulgence

1663

| February | Third session of Cavalier Parliament (to July): Staple Act |
| April | Charles II withdrew the Declaration of Indulgence |

1664

| March | New Amsterdam (New York) granted to James, duke of York by Charles II; fourth session of Cavalier Parliament (to May) |
| November | Fifth session of Cavalier Parliament (to March 1665): Triennial Act; Conventicle Act |

1665

February	Parliamentary grant of £2.5 million for the Dutch war to be raised by assessments: start of second Anglo-Dutch war
June	Anglo-Dutch naval battle off Lowestoft
August	English attack on Dutch fleet in the neutral port of Bergen
October	Sixth session of Cavalier Parliament: further parliamentary grant of £1.25 million for the Dutch war; Downing's proposal for appropriating the grant to pay the crown's creditors accepted; Five Mile Act

Great Plague in London

1666

France and Denmark joined the war against England

April	Defection from the war of England's ally, bishop of Munster
June	Anglo-Dutch Four Days' Battle in the Channel
July	Anglo-Dutch St James's Day Battle in the mouth of the Thames
September	Seventh session of Cavalier Parliament (to February 1667): further wartime grant by parliament of £1.8 million; Commons' attacks on royal naval officials; Great Fire of London

1667

January	Supply Bill passed appointing a parliamentary commission to examine the public accounts
May	French General Turenne overran the Spanish Netherlands; death of Lord Treasurer Southampton, who was replaced by a treasury commission that began a retrenchment campaign
June	Dutch naval victory in the Medway
July	Anglo-Dutch war ended by Treaty of Breda
October	Eighth session of Cavalier Parliament (to December); Clarendon fled to France to escape impeachment by parliament

1668

January	Triple Alliance between England, United Provinces and Sweden
February	Ninth session of Cavalier Parliament (to May): parliamentary criticism of maladministration during the Dutch war; opposition to Charles II's pro-toleration tendencies
August	Louis XIV sent Charles Albert de Croissy as ambassador to London to propose an alliance with England

1669

October   Tenth session of Cavalier Parliament (to December): Act of Supremacy bringing Scottish Church under English control

Isaac Newton appointed professor of mathematics at Cambridge University when his tutor, Isaac Barrow, resigned

1670

February   Eleventh session of Cavalier Parliament (to April): second Conventicle Act; massive increase in parliamentary grant of money

May   Secret Treaty of Dover signed

October   Twelfth session of Cavalier Parliament (to April 1671)

December   Public Treaty of Dover signed

1671

September   Crown resumed direct administration of the customs

1672

First year without a parliamentary session since the Restoration

January   Stop of the Exchequer (Charles II suspended for a year most repayments of the capital of loans to government creditors)

March   Second Declaration of Indulgence issued; start of third Anglo-Dutch war; English navy failed in its attack on the Dutch Smyrna fleet

May   Anglo-Dutch naval battle off Southwold Bay

June   French armies under Turenne and Condé occupied Utrecht, precipitating the downfall of the de Witts and the appointment of William of Orange as Stadhouder of the United Provinces

1673

February   Thirteenth session of Cavalier Parliament (to March); parliamentary grants of £1,126,000; attacks on Declaration of Indulgence; Bill for Relief of Protestant Dissenters; Peter du Moulin's *England's Appeal from the Private Cabal at Whitehall to the Great Council of the Nation* published

March   Cancellation of Declaration of Indulgence; new Test Act

Easter   James, duke of York failed to take the Anglican sacraments

June	Clifford and James, duke of York resigned under terms of Test Act; Clifford replaced as lord treasurer by Sir Thomas Osborne (created earl of Danby in June)
September	James, duke of York married Mary of Modena; Shaftesbury dismissed from office of lord chancellor (and later in May 1674 expelled from privy council and lord lieutenancy of Dorset)

1674

January	Fourteenth session of Cavalier Parliament (to February): new Test Act proposed; proposals to place limitations on the power of future Catholic monarchs; attacks on Lauderdale, Buckingham and Arlington
February	End of third Anglo-Dutch war by Treaty of Westminster
Autumn	Danby's conferences with bishops, devising Anglican policies

1675

February	Privy council order to enforce all measures designed to preserve the monopoly of the Church
April	Meeting of fifteenth session of Cavalier Parliament (to June): Test Bill introduced in Lords by Danby; parliamentary attacks on Lauderdale and Danby; Place Bill proposed
August	Charles II's secret subsidy agreement with Louis XIV
October	Sixteenth session of Cavalier Parliament (to November): grant of only £300,000; appropriation clause tacked on to the Supply Bill

1676

February	Charles II made another subsidy agreement with Louis XIV

Danby's ecclesiastical census

1677

February	Seventeenth session of Cavalier Parliament (to May): Shaftesbury, Buckingham, Salisbury and Wharton imprisoned by Lords for claiming that parliament was dissolved; generous financial grants promised; defeat of attempt to tack appropriation clause on to Supply Bill; Danby supported a programme of limitations on a Catholic monarch
Spring	France invaded Flanders
October	Betrothal of James's elder daughter, Mary, and William of Orange

1678

January	Eighteenth session of Cavalier Parliament (to May): intensified distrust of the court; grant of an inadequate poll tax; Commons grant of £200,000 to disband the English army after news of a Franco-Dutch truce reached London
May	Nineteenth session of Cavalier Parliament (to July)
July	Treaty of Nijmegen between the French and Dutch
August	First allegations by Titus Oates and Israel Tonge of a Popish Plot (followed by further allegations in next weeks)
October	Twentieth session of Cavalier Parliament (to December): parliamentary condemnation of Popish Plot; Charles issued anti-Catholic proclamations and agreed to a new Test Act. Murder of Sir Edmund Berry Godfrey JP followed by a wave of anti-Catholic hysteria
November–December	Duke of York's ex-secretary, Edward Coleman, and three others executed for taking part in the Popish Plot (and further 35 executed between now and 1681)
December	Ralph Montagu's revelations in Commons of Danby's secret subsidy negotiations with Louis XIV

1679

January	Dissolution of Cavalier Parliament
March	First Exclusion Parliament met (to May): impeachment of Danby; moves to disband the English army; Habeas Corpus Amendment Act; impeachment of James, duke of York discussed; first Exclusion Bill read twice in Commons
April	Coleman's correspondence with Rome made public; Charles II appointed opponents of the court, including Shaftesbury, to the privy council
June	Defeat of Scottish Covenanters' rebellion at Bothwell Bridge
August	Serious illness of Charles II
November	Pope-burning demonstrations in London (and in November 1680)

1680

October	Second Exclusion Parliament met (to January 1681); Exclusion Bill passed the Commons, defeated in Lords in November

1681

March	Third Exclusion Parliament met at Oxford: Exclusion Bill passed both Lords and Commons before the dissolution
July	Imprisonment of Shaftesbury on a charge of treason
October	French troops occupied Strasbourg
November	Acquittal of Shaftesbury
1681–4	'Tory reaction': purges of Whigs from commissions of peace and town corporations by *quo warranto* campaign; increase in royal revenue from customs duties

1682

Autumn	Monmouth toured north-west England seeking support
November	Shaftesbury fled to Holland

1683

Rye House Plot. Execution of William, Lord Russell and Algernon Sydney for their part in the plot

1684

Despite the Triennial Act, Charles failed to summon a new parliament; Danby released from the Tower; James, duke of York restored to the privy council

June	French troops occupied Luxembourg
August	Truce of Ratisbon ratified French conquests in Europe

1685

February	Death of Charles II; accession of James II
May	First session of James's first parliament (to July): generous financial grants
Summer	Rebellions of Argyll and Monmouth
July	Defeat of Monmouth at battle of Sedgemoor, followed by the 'Bloody Assizes' of Lord Chief Justice Jeffries
October	Revocation of Edict of Nantes, followed by Louis XIV's *dragonnades* against Huguenots and flight of latter to England
November	Second session of James's first parliament lasted only two weeks. (Dissolution announced in 1687.) Dismissal of Halifax from privy council

1686

March	James II's Direction to Preachers suppressing anti-Catholic sermons
May	John Sharp, rector of St Giles in the Field, disobeyed James's Directions and Bishop Compton of London refused to suspend him
June	Decision in *Godden* v. *Hales* case allowed James II to dispense individuals from the Test Acts
July	James II established the Court of Ecclesiastical Commission
September	The Court of Ecclesiastical Commission suspended Compton from his bishopric
November	James II established a Licensing Office to sell to dissenters certificates of dispensation from penal legislation
1686–8	Purges of commissions of the peace and lieutenancies; royal 'closeting' and missionary campaigns to secure Catholic converts

1687

Dismissal of the Hyde brothers, the earls of Clarendon and Rochester

April	James's campaign to force Magdalen College, Oxford to appoint a Catholic as its president; James's first Declaration of Indulgence
Summer	Halifax's *Letter to a Dissenter* warning dissenters against allying with the king
Autumn	James II, Sunderland and Jefferies began a campaign to try to secure a parliament that would repeal the Test and Corporation Acts
October	Three questions put to JPs to assess their reactions to the projected repeal of the Test and Corporation Acts

1688

Early in the year, William of Orange decided to invade England

April	James's second Declaration of Indulgence; Archbishop Sancroft and six bishops refused to publish the declaration in their churches
June	Birth of James, son of James II and Mary of Modena; Sunderland's conversion to Catholicism; acquittal of Archbishop Sancroft and the six bishops; seven leading Whigs and Tories invited William of Orange to invade England
November	William of Orange landed at Torbay and occupied Exeter; provincial risings in his support in Cheshire, Nottingham and York; James lost his nerve at Salisbury and returned to London

| December | High Tory peers supported James in their Guildhall Declaration; James fled to France; an assembly of ex-MPs and London citizens issued writs for a new parliament |

1689

January	Meeting of the Convention Parliament (to January): vote in Commons that the throne was 'vacant' overturned in the Lords but later accepted; motion in Lords for a regency defeated by 51 to 48 votes; parliamentary vote to offer throne to William and Mary; Toleration Act
February	Declaration of Rights read to William and Mary in the Banqueting Hall; coronation of William III and Mary II; about 400 nonjurors refused to swear an oath of allegiance to William III and Mary II; the Dutch declared war on France
March	James II landed at Kinsale in south-west Ireland; Scottish Convention Parliament met (to April): Claim of Right and Articles of Grievances sent to William III
May	States General and Emperor Leopold signed the Grand Alliance against France (later joined by England, Spain, Savoy and many German states); Irish 'Patriot Parliament' in Dublin passed anti-English legislation
July	Colonel Kirke relieved siege of Londonderry; Jacobite Scots won victory at Killiecrankie
August	William III sent an army under General Schomberg to Ireland against James II; defeat of Jacobite Scots at Dunkeld
November	Return of Edmund Ludlow from exile in Switzerland; convocation met and demanded anti-dissenter measures
December	Adjournment of convocation (did not meet again until 1701); Declaration of Rights enacted as the Bill of Rights

1690

March	First session of William's first parliament (to May); grant of excise to crown for life, and customs receipts for four years
April	Second session of Scottish Convention Parliament: William III accepted Scottish demands re-establishing Presbyterianism in Scotland
June	French victory over English and Dutch allied fleet off Beachy Head; Admiral Torrington court-martialled
July	William III's victory over James II at the battle of the Boyne

October	Second session of William's first parliament (to January 1691): parliamentary grants of £4.6 million.
December	Act establishing Commission of Public Accounts.

1691

April	The French took Mons
October	Third session of William's first parliament (to February 1692); opposition to royal control of the judiciary. William III's generals took Limerick

1692

February	The Glencoe Massacre
May	Defeat of the French fleet in the Bay of La Hogue
June	The French army took Namur
August	Drawn battle at Steenkirk
October	Protestant-dominated Irish parliament met after a vigorous anti-Catholic campaign since 1690
November	Fourth session of William's first parliament (to March 1693): criticism of the conduct of the war; demand for a 'blue-water' war strategy and for a Place Bill and Triennial Bill; parliamentary approval of war expenditure of over £4 million and for a 20 per cent land tax

1693

July	Drawn battle at Neerwinden; French army took Huy
November	Fifth session of William's first parliament (to April 1694): Triennial and Place Bills vetoed by William III. Resignation of earl of Nottingham as secretary of state

1694

March	William III appointed Whig ministers, Shrewsbury as secretary of state and Edward Russell as lord high admiral and . . .
April	. . . Charles Montague as chancellor of the exchequer; Bank of England created against Tory opposition
November	Sixth session of William's first parliament (to May 1695): Tory attacks on Whig finance and the continental war; Triennial Act
December	Death of Queen Mary

1695

Lapse of Licensing Act; publication of John Locke's *The Reasonableness of Christianity*

August	William III recaptured Namur from the French
November	First session of William III's second parliament (to April 1696): more Tory attacks on Whig finance; Tory Land Bank established and failed

1696

Whig edition (by John Toland) of Ludlow's *Memoirs* published; Francis Atterbury's *A Letter to a Convocation Man* demanded the recall of convocation; John Toland's *Christianity Not Mysterious* published

February	Revelation of a plot to assassinate William III, followed by refusal of about 90 Tory MPs to swear an oath of loyalty to William III
October	Second session of William's second parliament (to April 1697): brief period of Whig ascendancy in the Commons

1697

September	Treaty of Ryswyck temporarily ended the French war
December	Last session of William's second parliament (to July 1698): attacks on a standing army and William III's Dutch favourites. Resignation of Sunderland

1698

October	First Partition Treaty
December	First session of William's third parliament (to May 1699): more attacks on a standing army and placemen

1699

November	Second session of William's third parliament (to April 1700): attacks on the Whig Junto; discussion of union of England and Scotland

1700

March	Second Partition Treaty
July	Death of the 11-year-old duke of Gloucester, heir to the throne and last surviving child of Princess Anne
November	Death of Charles II of Spain
December	Rochester appointed lord lieutenant of Ireland and Godolphin as first lord of the treasury

1701

February	Meeting of William's fourth parliament (to June): Act of Settlement; conversion of many MPs to the renewal of the war. Meeting of convocation for the first time since 1689
May	Kent petition and Daniel Defoe's *Legion Memorial* in favour of war
September	Death of James II; recognition of his son as James III by Louis XIV
December	Meeting of William's last parliament (to May 1702): Abjuration Oath against the Pretender passed

1702

March	Death of William III; accession of Queen Anne; Godolphin appointed lord treasurer; publication of *The Daily Courant*, England's first daily newspaper
May	Britain, the United Provinces and Austria declared war on France
June	Dr Henry Sacheverell's sermon *The Political Union* printed
October	Start of Anne's first parliament (to February 1703): Tory demands for an Occasional Conformity Bill and a 'blue-water' war strategy; further discussions of union of England and Scotland

Daniel Defoe's *The Shortest Way With Dissenters* published. Clarendon's *History of the Rebellion* published between now and 1704

1703

February	Rochester resigned as lord lieutenant of Ireland
November	Second session of Anne's first parliament began (to April 1704): Tory demands for an Occasional Conformity Bill again frustrated

Meeting of new Scottish parliament: anti-English measures passed (Act Anent Peace and War; Wine Act; Wool Act; Act of Security). Methuen treaties with Portugal signed

1704

May	Sir Robert Harley appointed secretary of state in place of Nottingham
July	Capture of Gibraltar by the English
August	Allied forces under Marlborough defeated the French and Bavarians at Blenheim on the Danube; English naval victory off Malaga
October	Last session of Anne's first parliament (to March 1705): continued Tory demands for an Occasional Conformity Act and complaints at the high cost of the war

1705

February	Aliens Act passed by the English parliament threatening to treat Scots in England as aliens unless the Scottish parliament agreed to the Hanoverian succession
June	New session of the Scottish parliament: commissioners appointed to begin negotiations with the English for a union
October	William, Earl Cowper appointed lord keeper of the great seal; start of first session of Anne's second parliament (to March 1706)

1706

January	Regency Act passed
April	Negotiations for union of England and Scotland made progress
May	Marlborough's victory at Ramilles
July	Treaty of union of England and Scotland drafted
December	Sunderland appointed secretary of state; start of second session of Anne's second parliament (to April 1707)

1707

January	Scottish parliament approved the draft union treaty
March	Act of Union of England and Scotland as Great Britain ratified
October	Last session of Anne's second parliament began (to April 1708): Tory attacks on royal policy of 'no peace without Spain'

1708

February	Resignation of Harley as secretary of state; replaced by Henry Boyle, a Whig. (Another Whig, Robert Walpole, replaced Henry St John as secretary at war)
May	Heavy Whig gains in general elections
July	Marlborough's victory over the French at Oudenarde
October	Death of Queen Anne's husband, Prince George of Denmark
November	Appointment of Whig Junto lords to key offices; start of first session of Anne's third parliament

1709

March	Treason Act passed; Naturalization of Foreign Protestants Act
August	Marlborough's victory over the French at Malplaquet

| November | Dr Henry Sacheverell's sermon *In Peril Among False Bretheren* in St Paul's Cathedral; start of last session of Anne's third parliament (to April 1710) |
| December | Commons voted Sacheverell's sermon libellous and Sacheverell was impeached |

1710

March	Riots in London in favour of Sacheverell. Sacheverell found guilty but given only a light sentence
April	Appointment of Charles Talbot, earl of Shrewsbury as lord chamberlain
June	Whig secretary of state Sunderland replaced by a Tory, the earl of Dartmouth
August	Dismissal of Godolphin as lord treasurer; Harley appointed chancellor of the exchequer; Tory periodical, *The Examiner*, founded; peace negotiations with France began
September	The remaining Junto lords resigned; Rochester appointed as lord president and Henry St John as secretary of state
October	Massive Tory majority at general election
November	Beginning of first session of Anne's fourth parliament (to June 1711)
December	Defeat of British at Brihuega in Spain

1711

February	Land Property Qualification Act
May	South Sea Company founded; Harley created earl of Oxford
November	Jonathan Swift's *The Conduct of the Allies*, advocating peace
December	Marlborough dismissed as commander-in-chief of the allied armed forces; second session of Anne's fourth parliament (to June 1712): Occasional Conformity Act; support for peace; repeal of Protestant Naturalization Act

1712

January	Robert Walpole expelled from Commons and imprisoned
March	Scottish Toleration Act passed in favour of episcopalianism
June	Henry St John created Viscount Bolingbroke
August	Bolingbroke visited the Pretender in Paris

1713

April   Third session of Anne's fourth parliament (to July): Tory splits
             apparent on the succession; Treaty of Utrecht between Britain, the
             Dutch and France; appointment of Hanoverian Tories, Bromley as
             secretary of state and Hanmer as speaker of Commons

September   General elections resulted in massive Tory victory

1714

February   New session of Anne's fifth parliament (to July)

June   Death of Sophia, electress of Brunswick-Luneberg, heir to the throne;
             succeeded by her son George; Schism Act

July   Harley dismissed as lord treasurer, and replaced by earl of Shrewsbury

August   Death of Queen Anne; accession of George I

Index